T5-AQA-689

Jewish-Christian Encounters over the Centuries

American University Studies

Series IX:
History

Vol. 136

PETER LANG
New York • Washington, DC/Baltimore • San Francisco
Bern • Frankfurt am Main • Berlin • Vienna • Paris

Jewish-Christian Encounters over the Centuries

Symbiosis, Prejudice, Holocaust, Dialogue

Edited by
Marvin Perry
Frederick M. Schweitzer

PETER LANG
New York • Washington, DC/Baltimore • San Francisco
Bern • Frankfurt am Main • Berlin • Vienna • Paris

Library of Congress Cataloging-in-Publication Data

Jewish-Christian encounters over the centuries: symbiosis, prejudice, Holocaust, dialogue / Marvin Perry, Frederick M. Schweitzer, editors.
p. cm. — (American university studies. Series IX, History: vol. 136)
Includes bibliographical references.
1. Judaism—Relations—Christianity. 2. Christianity and other religions—Judaism. 3. Christianity and antisemitism. 4. Holocaust (Christian theology) 5. Judaism (Christian theology) I. Perry, Marvin. II. Schweitzer, Frederick M. III. Series.
BM535.J44 1994 261.2'6'09—dc20 93-31044
ISBN 0-8204-2082-4 CIP
ISSN 0740-0462

Die Deutsche Bibliothek-CIP-Einheitsaufnahme

Jewish-Christian encounters over the centuries: symbiosis, prejudice, holocaust, dialogue / Marvin Perry; Frederick M. Schweitzer. - New York; Washington, D.C./Baltimore; San Francisco; Bern; Frankfurt am Main; Berlin; Vienna; Paris: Lang, 1994
(American university studies. Series 9, History: vol. 136)
ISBN 0-8204-2082-4
NE: Perry, Marvin [Hrsg.]; American university studies / 09

Cover design by George Lallas.

The paper in this book meets the guidelines for permanence and durability of the Committee on Production Guidelines for Book Longevity of the Council on Library Resources.

Printed in the United States of America.

Table of Contents

PREFACE

Two ancient peoples are the source of the Western tradition—the Greeks who originated scientific and philosophical thought, and the Hebrews, who conceived the idea of ethical monotheism. The Hebrews' view of God led in turn to a new view of the individual. The Hebrews believed that God, who possessed total freedom himself, had bestowed moral freedom on human beings. Of all his creations, only men and women had been given the freedom to choose between righteousness and wickedness. The idea that each person is responsible for his or her actions gave new value and dignity to the individual. Inherited by Christianity, these ancient Jewish conceptions of moral autonomy and human dignity are central to the Western tradition.

The links between early Christianity and Judaism were strong. Early Christianity's affirmation of the preciousness of the human being who was created in God's image, its belief that God rules history, its awareness of human sinfulness, its call for repentance, and its appeal to God for forgiveness are rooted in Judaism. The concept of the messiah, respect for the sabbath, congregational worship, and the notion of conversion also stem from Judaism. The Christian invocation of God as a "merciful Father" derives from Jewish prayer. Also rooted in Judaism are the moral norms proclaimed by Jesus in the Sermon on the Mount. Because of these strong connecting links, we speak of the Judaeo-Christian tradition. However, as Christianity distanced and dis-identified itself from Judaism, it also developed an antisemitic tradition, replete with irrational myths, that has had tragic consequences.

Numerous scholars have analyzed the links between modern antisemitism and traditional Christian attitudes towards Jews and Judaism. Nationalist and racist antisemites may have broken with their Christian origins, but they retained a Christian antipathy towards Jews, updating and secularizing venomous myths about Judaism that had roots in the Christian past. Christian myths that demonized Jews generated irrational hatred and fear that nourished modern antisemitism and made the Holocaust possible.

Immediately after Auschwitz, few people would indulge in antisemitic rhetoric, and it seemed that Jew-baiters had forfeited their audiences. Lately, however, antisemitism has undergone a resurgence, particularly in eastern Europe where an extreme nationalism threatens to fill the vacuum left by the collapse of communism. That antisemitic movements have re-emerged in lands which have only a minuscule Jewish population attests to antisemitism's deep-seatedness, virulence, and irrationality. This irrationality is demonstrated further by the popularity of two myths: Jews are conspiring to rule the planet, an old myth; and a new one, the Holocaust is a Jewish fabrication.

A positive development is that in recent decades Christian thinkers, moved by past wrongs and an ecumenical spirit, have striven to examine the religious roots of antisemitism, to interpret the meaning of the Holocaust for Christianity, and to rid Christian teachings and attitudes of a historic anti-Jewish bias that for centuries had contaminated the soul of Westerners. They have also investigated and stressed the numerous connecting bonds between first-century Judaism and early Christianity. Scholars and theologians dedicated to fostering ecumenical sensibilities hope that a common biblical monotheism, commitment to prophetic morality, and a shared belief in the oneness of humanity are powerful enough imperatives to overcome an age-old hatred and dispel pernicious myths.

A fruitful dialogue has arisen among Christian and Jewish scholars and clergy. Supporting the objectives of Christian-Jewish dialogue, Manhattan College, a Catholic institution in Riverdale, New York, and Baruch College, City University of New York, jointly sponsored a conference entitled "Jewish-Christian Relations: Symbiosis, Prejudice, Holocaust, Dialogue," 1 - 3 March 1989. The papers read at this conference form the nucleus of this book. We are grateful to both colleges for supporting the book's publication. The essays here presented are works of synthesis designed for the non-specialist reader. For the interested but non-specialist reader and college students addressing these issues for the first time, we have provided a headnote for each essay placing it in context and a glossary explaining technical terms. Each essay concludes with an annotated list of readings in English selected by the author for those who wish to pursue the subject further. Although we are under no illusion that it will be easy or quick and are aware that James Parkes predicted it will take three hundred years, we remain hopeful that Christian-Jewish understanding and reconciliation will come. Profound changes have occurred since Parkes' observation and, as several of the later essays in this book indicate, the great and good work goes forward, perhaps less dramatically than earlier, but certainly with no loss of momentum. If our efforts help to sustain these endeavors we shall feel amply rewarded.

22 August 1993
New York City

M.P.
F.M.S.

JESUS WAS A JEW

Donald P. Gray

In the quest for the historical Jesus, scholars have focused on both his Jewishness and the religious-political ferment that prevailed in Palestine in the first century C.E. Donald P. Gray treats Jesus within the context of his day.

Jesus—A Christian?

In his study of the Synoptic gospels, published in 1905, the eminent Protestant scripture scholar Julius Wellhausen remarked: "Jesus was not a Christian, he was a Jew."[1] More recently another Christian scholar, Leonard Swidler, has made the same point in elaborate detail:

> The one whom Christians claim is the foundation, the cornerstone of their religion is Jesus or Yeshua, as he was really called, which was just a popular variant of Joshua—meaning 'Yahweh is salvation.' It is interesting to note that Jesus was himself *not* a Christian. He in fact was a Jew. In some twentieth-century circles he would be known as a kyke. He did not go to Mass, or indeed any worship service, on Sunday morning. He went to services on the Sabbath. He did not go to church. He went to synagogue. He did not speak Greek, Latin, Church Slavonic, German, or English. He spoke Hebrew and Aramaic—two Semitic languages. He had a Jewish mother, which means he probably looked a lot like other Jews, i.e., dark hair and complexion, perhaps with a so-called Roman nose, not too large in stature. No one addressed him as Father, Pastor, Reverend, or Minister. But he was addressed as Rabbi. He did not read the New Testament, nor did he think it the inspired word of God. He did read the Hebrew Bible and thought it the Holy Scrip-

tures. He never recited the Rosary, chanted *Hospodi pomilui* (Lord, have mercy) at a litany, nor sang a Wesleyan hymn. Rather, he recited the psalms; he died with one on his lips: '*Eli, Eli, lama sabachtani*?' (My God, my God, why have you abandoned me?) He did not celebrate Christmas and Easter. He celebrated Shavuoth and Passover—not communion, but a Seder. To repeat, Jesus was not a Christian. He was a Jew. He was Rabbi Yeshua.[2]

While the affirmation that Jesus was indeed a Jew, a Jew of his time, represents a clear advance in the direction of concreteness over against the more abstract assertion of Christian tradition that although divine he was nonetheless truly human, it is not unproblematic nor as straightforward in meaning as it might first appear.[3] It assumes, wrongly, that there was one way of being Jewish in Jesus' day. Indeed, Jesus lived in a remarkably pluralistic period of Jewish history, a period marked more by variety than by consensus. In this respect it differed significantly from the period, after the fall of Jerusalem and the destruction of the Temple in 70 C.E., in which the gospels were written.

Recognition of this fact is of no small importance in assessing the complex relationship between the representation of Jesus in the gospels and the Jesus of history himself. The gospel writers, living in the last third of the first century, inevitably and unabashedly mirror the troubled circumstances of their own day as much as they reflect the quite different circumstances of Jesus' time in the first third of the first century before the tragic devastation wrought by the First Jewish Revolt. The gospel writers, and the Christian communities whose *Sitz im Leben* they assume, no longer stood in the same posture as Jesus to the same Jewish world he had known and loved and within which he had ministered.[4] The historical Jesus is not readily available to us on the surface of every page of the gospel texts. Rather, these texts provide an indispensable point of departure for historical investigation of Jesus of Nazareth. Modern critical scholarship typically assumes that the gospels were written only in the third stage of a three-stage development. The historical Jesus is to be found in the first stage of that development.[5]

Rabbi Philip Sigal in his examination of the foundations of Judaism delineates a very diverse range of viewpoints in the first century:

> Samaritans, Apocalyptists, Sadducees, Pharisees, Essenes, Qumranites, Alexandrian Allegorists, Therapeutae, Zealots and perhaps the Sicarii, ten in all. Depending upon the date that serves as point of reference we are able to name more. For example, we will see that after the advent of Jesus and the rise of Christianity new Judaic denominations will form. We are told that at the time of the destruction of Jerusalem in 70 A.D., a year which can serve as our terminal point, there were twenty-four sects in Judaism. And

this does not account for the untranslatable and indefinable mass called *ammei haarez* (the so-called people of the land).[6]

While attempts have been made to associate Jesus with any number of these groups,[7] most widespread today are arguments that would locate Jesus among the Pharisees or the apocalyptists. With regard to the Pharisees, Leonard Swidler provides a helpful survey of the present state of the discussion dealing with "the Pharisee-like Yeshua."[8] He begins with a cautionary statement: "For nearly two thousand years most Christians have thought that Pharisaism, and subsequent Judaism said to be descended from it, were the enemy *par excellence* of Yeshua, and Christianity. However, recent research, mostly Jewish but also Christian, is calling this notion into serious question. Christians have much to learn about themselves from it."

After showing a number of similarities between Yeshua and the rabbinical traditions both prior to and after his time, Swidler cites the views of several contemporary scholars, both Christian and Jewish, who find no significant opposition between Jesus and the Pharisees: "Hence, it is not at all surprising that [John] Pawlikowski, a Catholic, concluded that it would not be wrong 'to consider Jesus as a part of the general Pharisaic movement, even though in many areas he held a distinctive view.' The Protestant scholar E.P. Sanders is somewhat more cautious, but nevertheless moves in the same direction when he states, 'I am one of a growing number of scholars who doubt that there were any substantial points of opposition between Jesus and the Pharisees.' The Jewish scholar Geza Vermes remarks, 'not that there appears to have been any fundamental disagreement between Jesus and the Pharisees on any basic issue...the conflict between Jesus of Galilee and the Pharisees of his time would, in normal circumstances, merely have resembled the in-fighting of factions belonging to the same religious body.'"

Swidler's own conclusions regarding the historical Jesus, decisively influenced by the work of both Philip Sigal and Geza Vermes, are that "perhaps the best way to see Yeshua within the context of the Judaism of his time is as a wandering, wonder-working teacher (rabbi), a sage (*hakham*), from Galilee, a Galilean *hasid*, who was in many ways similar to Hillel (whose teaching eventually came to prevail generally over Shammai's in Rabbinic Judaism), and whom some scholars would also see as having had a close relationship to the Pharisees centered in Jerusalem—whom he nonetheless criticized and who in turn criticized him."

While Jesus' affinities with the rabbinical tradition of his day are becoming at once clearer and more convincing in our day, most Christian scholarship at any rate refuses to locate the Galilean holy man completely and comfortably in that context. Jesus' connections to the baptizing groups, notably and in particular the group inspired by the preaching and activity of John the Baptizer, are perhaps even more significant for interpreting his relationship to the religious pluralism of his time. Jesus' message, as summarized in the earliest of the gospels (Mk 1:14-15), essentially reiterates the preaching of John: "This is the time of fulfillment. The Kingdom of God is at hand. Repent, and believe in the gospel." While Jesus himself did not engage in baptizing as an ingredient in his own independent ministry,[9] he did seek baptism from John, strongly suggesting that he desired to be in solidarity with John's all-consuming preoccupation with the reign of God, either as a disciple or a colleague. It is generally acknowledged in contemporary scholarly discussion that the theme of the approaching reign of God resides at the center of Jesus' concerns as it likewise occupied a central place with John.[10] The notion sinks deep roots into the Jewish past with its insistence that the Creator is rightfully King over all and that the Israelite covenant establishes an even more urgent royal claim from the divine side.

With regard to Jesus and John, however, the theme of God's wondrous reign is best understood within the framework of Jewish eschatology, i.e. within the framework of the Jewish hope for a new age of peace and justice, of divine blessing and therefore human well-being. The announcement of the nearness of this reign on the part of these two correlated figures is at once a protest against the present age of suffering and oppression in which "the powers," both earthly and cosmic, rule by means of a reign of terror, and a statement of confidence in the divine triumph. This gospel requires *metanoia* (repentance with respect to one's overall priorities in life) and a willingness to take sides in the awesome conflict now underway between these vastly different reigns.

Does this mean, then, that the baptizer John and the wonder-worker Jesus are to be situated primarily within the apocalyptic currents of intertestamental Judaism? A case can be made for such a proposition. However, it seems preferable to interpret both of them against the background of classical Jewish prophetism without discounting or minimizing their own sense of living at the close of one age and at the juncture of a new age.[11] In relating these two commanding personalities to earlier prophetical activity, it is essential to avoid a common Christian misunderstanding of the prophet's role. The prophet's principal function is not to make predictions about the future, even if prophets regularly spoke to the issue of the future. The prophet is a divine messenger whose principal preoccupation is with the present interpreted in relation to the divine intent. The prophet, and John and Jesus are no exception, reveals the divine discontent with the existing state of affairs and summons the people, and especially their leaders, to fundamental change, away from the path of destruction and onto the path leading to life (Dt 30:19), in the light of past covenant agreements and future consequences. The prophet binds the dimensions of time together by intensely focusing attention on what God is now doing and therefore what human beings need to be doing now.

If Jesus is appropriately categorized by means of the title prophet, then he stands in continuity not only with his mentor John but also with Amos and Hosea, Isaiah and Jeremiah from the Israelite past as well as with prophetical figures in other religious traditions both before and after him. Does such a category admit of significant discontinuity as well? To say of Jesus that he was the greatest of all the prophets represents a meaningful Christian assessment, but it ultimately raises more questions than it answers. Typically, contemporary Christian scholarship sees Jesus as a very special prophet indeed: the eschatological or final prophet, the prophet of the last days, the Moses-like prophet of Deuteronomy 18:15. While comparable to other prophets in most respects, Jesus is incomparable, according to this view, with respect to his role as the one who both announces and inaugurates the reign of God, thereby concluding one stage of a protracted salvation history while simultaneously opening a new one.

The search for other illuminating categories from the history of religions field to identify Jesus will pose similar problems of continuity and discontinuity for Christian interpretation as those encountered in the use of the prophet typology, let alone the rabbi typology, which ranges Jesus with great rabbinical teachers of the first centuries B.C.E.–C.E. like Hillel or Johannan ben Zakkai. If Jesus was indeed a remarkable Galilean charismatic *hasid*, both holy man and healer, as Geza Vermes[12] argues, how distinguishable is he from others of the same type such as Honi the Circle-Drawer or Hanina ben Dosa to whom he is compared. Was he a sage, as Marcus Borg[13] has suggested, and therefore comparable to Israel's sages as they are available to us in the Writings (or Wisdom Literature)? Perhaps, to stray beyond the frontiers of Jewish history for a moment, he can be validly viewed as a latter-day shaman[14] or an ancient guru.[15] Images of Jesus abound[16]—each seeks to render him intelligible and meaningful and in that sense relevant. Does he fit any (or all!) of these typologies? With what degree of continuity? What then is special (unique, original, definitive, final) about him? Does he simply shatter the various types so that none of them is genuinely clarifying? If he is utterly in a class by himself, do we have any meaningful way of interpreting him and therefore of understanding him? Perhaps some dialectic of continuity (similarity) and discontinuity (dissimilarity) will do justice to this complex and enigmatic figure.

In the last analysis, the Christian in particular is confronted with the question as to how much discontinuity on the part of the historical Jesus is required to ground Christian beliefs as they emerged in the first century, let alone in subsequent centuries. To put it another way, how much continuity on the part of the historical Jesus can Christian faith live with? How open to the conclusions of modern historical investigation is Christian faith prepared to be? In the classical period of christological elaboration Christians spoke eloquently of his being "like us in all things, except sin," but they were at the same time clearly uncomfortable with that degree of continuity in light of their belief that this humanity was none other than the human nature of the divine Son of God from heaven. By multiplying exceptions and exemptions to his true humanity, Christians so stressed discontinuity that they virtually annihilated his connectedness to the human condition as we do in fact experience it. Will discussion of the Jewishness of Jesus, especially as it is carried on by Christian scholars, inevitably tend to heighten Jesus' discontinuity from his Jewish heritage and environment? How much continuity are Christians prepared to live with?

The Distinctiveness of the Historical Jesus

In a recent survey and assessment of the current discussion about the Jewishness of Jesus, Daniel Harrington observed among Jewish scholars a marked tendency to minimize the distinctiveness or originality of the historical Jesus vis-a-vis his heritage and the historical situation in which he ministered:

> Those Jews who do not dismiss Jesus as an apostate but approach him sympathetically as a brother often do so on the assumption that Jesus the Jew remained entirely within the boundaries of Judaism. They employ a criterion of similarity or continuity and assign whatever does not fit into their idea of Judaism in Jesus' time to the early church or to the evangelists. They will argue that Jesus' teaching has been misunderstood or mistranslated, that it was only part of an inner-Jewish conflict, and that it has been distorted by the early church's mission to the Gentiles. The picture that emerges from such arguments is that of a basically loyal and observant Jew, with perhaps a few odd ideas. Whatever differs from Judaism is dismissed as uninteresting or unimportant or simply mistaken.... Modern Jewish proponents of the quest leave Jesus in the confines of Judaism as they understand them and thus echo the famous statement made by Claude G. Montefiore: 'His teaching where good, was not original, and where original was not Jewish or good.'[17]

Harrington further notes, at an opposite extreme, that "modern Christian proponents of the quest of the historical Jesus take Jesus out of his Jewish context and focus mainly on his 'un-Jewish' teachings," appealing to a criterion of dissimilarity or discontinuity.

Beyond such extreme attitudes it is possible to locate Jesus solidly within his Jewish environment while at the same time noting various aspects of distinctiveness. Donald Senior's attractive and popular study of the mid-nineteen seventies, *Jesus: A Gospel Portrait*, provides a useful case in point.[18] While acknowledging connections between Jesus' discipleship group and the rabbinical academies of his time, Senior distinguishes Jesus' relationship to his disciples from those typical of a rabbinical master in several ways: (1) Jesus took the initiative in calling disciples to follow him; (2) Jesus apparently intended his disciples to remain permanently associated with him—they were not to anticipate any sort of "graduation" which would enable them to act independently of Jesus on their own; (3) Jesus expected his disciples to share actively and generously in the ministry of preaching and healing in which he himself was engaged; (4) in a highly unusual move, Jesus incorporated women into his discipleship group, indeed he showed an extraordinary concern for women—so much so that some Christian commentators have gone so far as to refer to him as a first-century feminist.[19]

According to the same analysis, Jesus also stood out from the rabbis of his day in the manner of his teaching for he never appealed, in any explicit fashion at least, for support of his teaching to the authority of the great rabbinical tradition in general or some renowned rabbinical master in particular. He taught from a unique sense of personal authority, not like the scribes and the Pharisees (Mt 7:28-29 and parallels). At times, on the basis of this special sense of authority, Jesus even resorted to the use of the formula "amen, amen, I say to you,"[20] to contrast his teaching with what were taken to be conventional interpretations of the law. Indeed, Senior argues that Jesus came at the question of the observance of the law from a different angle altogether:

> Jesus' teaching views the relationship between men and God from a fundamentally different perspective. It was not a case of his rejecting the Law as useless or harmful. Nor did he hold in contempt the Pharisees' efforts to make the Law applicable to everyday life. But, as the famous British scholar C.H. Dodd says, the angle at which Jesus' teaching touches life is different. True fidelity to God, genuine religion, can be nothing less than a full, loving response to God and to neighbor. Here is the center that judges all else, prescriptions of the Law included. True fidelity can never be measured by how many laws we have kept. Its only test is the quality of our love.[21]

While the question of Jesus' relationship to the Pharisees remains controversial, current trends in scholarship point to a more positive connection than traditional views which relied uncritically on the stereotype provided by the gospels, a stereotype which was itself the product of polemics between Christians and Jews of the post-70 C.E. era.[22] Even Senior and Dodd seem to overplay a contrast between Jesus and the Pharisees at this point.

It is in Jesus' prayer life, however, that Senior and many others have found what they believe to be an exceptionally significant indication of his distinctiveness vis-a-vis his heritage as well as his contemporary religious environment. In this regard an enormous amount of scholarship has been devoted to Jesus' use of the Aramaic term *abba* in prayer. Senior underlines the importance of this issue in this way:

> The use of *Abba* could have entered the Gospel tradition only because Jesus used it. The ordinary word for 'father' in Aramaic

> and Hebrew is *ab*. *Abba* is an intimate diminutive, almost like 'Dad' or 'Daddy' in English. A rabbinic text says that 'when a child experiences the taste of wheat, it learns to say *abba* and *imma* (mommy).' But the word was not used only by small children. Texts have been found where adults use the term *abba* as an expression of intimacy and affection for their father. But there is no parallel in Judaism for its use as an address in prayer to God. No text, either in the Old Testament or in rabbinic writings, ever dared to address Yahweh in such familiar terms. The first example of it ever found in Jewish circles is from a medieval prayer from southern Italy.[23]

After emphasizing "Judaism's reverence for its God," Senior goes on to say that "Jesus' prayer stands as unique against this background of strict reverence." He concludes that "it cannot be doubted that Jesus' reference to God as Father reveals his intimate relationship to God."

Senior's approach to the issue clearly reflects the influence of the pioneering research done by Joachim Jeremias on the prayer of Jesus.[24] More recently, however, Jeremias' sweeping conclusions have been challenged. James Dunn, in his study of *Jesus and the Spirit*,[25] concludes that "It would appear that Jeremias has pressed his argument too far." He adds, nonetheless, that "much of value remains from his researches. In particular, we are not being over bold if we conclude that Jesus' use of *abba* enables us to see into the heart of his relationship with God as he understood it. The divine reality he experienced in those moments of naked aloneness was God as Father." In a later publication Dunn concludes that although it is not possible to maintain that Jesus' use of *abba* in prayer was absolutely unique, "*the evidence points consistently and clearly to the conclusion that Jesus' regular use of 'abba' in addressing God distinguished Jesus in a significant degree from his contemporaries.*"[26]

Acknowledging that "Abba probably really was Jesus' own special way of addressing God, and it is certainly an address suggesting a relationship of mutual love," Peter von der Osten-Sacken[27] goes on to caution that "it would certainly be mistaken to play off this form of address against the understanding of God held by other teachers of Jesus' time, or against 'Judaism' in general." Indeed the Our Father, or Lord's Prayer, is a markedly Jewish prayer, as Franz Mussner,[28] among others, has stressed: "It is the prayer of the *Jew* Jesus with which every Jew without inner reservation can pray, as fortunately happens today in joint Jewish-Christian worship services. The Our Father is the great 'bridge prayer' between the Jewish and Christian communities. And in the Our Father 'the Jewish categories' live on to this very day."

The point of this extended survey is simply that Christian scholarship in particular needs to adopt a cautious attitude with regard to what may turn out to be exaggerated claims of distinctiveness and discontinuity on Jesus' part vis-a-vis his Jewish environment. In this regard Jewish scholarship can play a vitally important, indeed indispensable, role in the continuing quest of the historical Jesus. The examination of Jesus' "originality" or "specialness" must, of necessity, continue to be pursued,[29] but it needs to proceed with the modesty and circumspection appropriate to the realization that our sources for first-century reconstruction are at every point quite restricted and the recognition that even the best intentioned scholarly exploration can readily turn tendentious by inflating the significance of the available evidence.

Jesus Crucified

Why did Jesus' ministry in the service of God's approaching reign end catastrophically in a cruel crucifixion at the hands of the Roman oppression in Palestine? Who indeed was ultimately responsible for such a terrible public execution? Was it the Jewish or the Roman authorities who played the decisive role in the proceedings which culminated in Jesus' downfall? Were the charges lodged against him religious or political in nature? Did the people concur in the machinations of the powerful or were they merely helpless bystanders?

When the four gospels are consulted, the answers to these questions seem readily apparent, even if there are differences of emphasis to be noted among the four writers.[30] Jesus died because his gospel was rejected by his people; because he made outlandish, indeed blasphemous, claims about his own person; because in the end he seemed more like an enemy than a friend of his nation and their most sacred traditions and institutions. He died, therefore, because of the religious controversy he inspired. He died because of the unfavorable judgment of his own people and their religious leaders. The Roman prefect in Judaea, one Pontius Pilate, is, by contrast, virtually exonerated of any guilt for the execution since he clearly recognized from the start that the political allegations proffered against Jesus by the Jewish authorities were utterly groundless; in fact, he energetically attempted to secure Jesus' freedom in the face of the stubborn determination of his accusers whose fanatical hostility finally carried the day. The political charges were simply and solely a subterfuge designed to camouflage the underlying religious issues and to persuade the unwilling prefect to cooperate in their murderous intentions.

However regrettable and indeed shameful, it is perhaps not surprising that Christians of later centuries, who read their gospels uncritically as straightforward, unvarnished historical chronicles, concluded that "the Jews" were the "Christ-killers," a deicide and perfidious people, deserving of the severest retribution which Christians often enthusiastically attended to themselves. So entrenched in Christian tradition did the view become that not only the Jews of Jesus' day but the Jews of all time were liable for Jesus' death that the Second Vatican Council recognized an urgent need, especially in light of the Holocaust, to address and explicitly repudiate such erroneous assumptions.[31] Unfortunately, the Council fathers did not see fit to explore in any detail the historical circumstances surrounding the actual death itself. Both Christian and Jewish scholarship have, however, been noticeably preoccupied with the historical questions since the end of the Second World War.[32]

Daniel Harrington helpfully summarizes the major accomplishments of what has been an intense and controversial debate:

> Jesus was a victim of oppression. The trial and death of Jesus have been lively topics of discussion over the past thirty years. What has emerged from this discussion has been almost a consensus on the following matters: The final legal responsibility for Jesus' death lay with Pontius Pilate, the Roman governor. Jesus was executed as a perceived political threat (the 'King of the Jews') according to a Roman mode of punishment. The evangelists deliberately played down Roman responsibility and played up Jewish involvement. The precise degree of Jewish involvement in the events leading up to Jesus' death is still disputed. Were the chief priests and elders the initiators of the procedure, merely active collaborators, passive spectators, or unwilling agents? At any rate, it is recognized that when the Passion Narratives begin, the Pharisees almost entirely drop out of sight.
>
> Jesus was another Jewish victim of oppression. Like John the Baptist, Jesus the son of Ananias, Theudas, the Egyptian prophet, and other prophetic figures of his day, Jesus was perceived as a threat to the political stability of Judea. In the light of Hitler's Holocaust, there has developed among Jews and Christians an attractive approach to Jesus of Nazareth as a symbol of Jewish victimization throughout the ages. Not only does such an approach bring Jesus back into his Jewish context, but it also brings into that same context the many Christians in our world today who suffer with Jesus and for his name. It is a beautiful thought and deserves even more reflection by Christians and Jews together.[33]

The developing consensus which Harrington identifies does not turn the historical Jesus into a political activist or a politically ambitious messiah anxious to attain power, but it does underline precisely what the gospel narratives deliberately seek to obscure: the political implications of the preaching and activity of the prophet Jesus. Paula Fredriksen calls attention to this point:

> Jesus' crucifixion, taken together with his proclamation of the Kingdom, indicates his status as a political figure. This is not to say that Jesus was an insurgent, like Judah the Galilean. Nor is it to say

> that Rome mistakenly thought he was: otherwise, Pilate would have arrested and crucified Jesus' followers too. But *Jesus was an apocalyptic preacher, and the nature of apocalyptic is political.* Its message of an impending new order at least implies a condemnation of the present one; it is in religious idiom the expression of a political critique. The distinction between Jesus or John the Baptist, on the one hand, and Judah or his sons, on the other, is thus not that the former are religious while the latter are political. The one is pacifist (i.e. communicating his message, or expecting to see it realized, without recourse to arms), the other military; both are religious, and both are political.[34]

In light of these observations Jesus' death suddenly takes on a different coloration altogether. Whatever the nature or extent of Jesus' controversies with the Pharisees of his day (and these are almost certainly exaggerated in the gospel accounts owing to the altered circumstances of Christians vis-a-vis Pharisaical Judaism in the post-70 C.E. era)[35] or for that matter any other religious party of the period, it seems increasingly probable that Jesus confronted, in a typically prophetic manner, the powerful in Jerusalem in the name of the absolute primacy of the reign of God and was crushed by those same powerful forces as they reached out to protect vested interests.

In that sense it is not an especially new or unfamiliar story, nor are such stories by any means limited to the ancient world. It was certainly not the first, nor the last, time that the religiously inspired have been struck down by the politically minded. While it is undoubtedly true that there is a certain type of religious outlook which has and still does function as an "opium of the people" and is therefore politically innocuous and consequently warmly endorsed by those in control of the political order, there is just as certainly another type of religious vision which leads to the sort of prophetical activity which genuinely threatens the blatantly unjust and brutal arrangements of the social world. The image of an apolitical Jesus may well be little more than an ideological construct well suited to maintaining the status quo. No one in power has anything to fear from such a Jesus; curiously, those who enjoyed power and privilege in Jerusalem in 30 C.E., the year in which Jesus was crucified, *were* alarmed by his seeming fearlessness in the face of obvious violence.[36] Jesus was free as they were not.[37]

It will likely take Christians a long time, a very long time, to understand and appreciate the fact that it was not the Jews, nor the Jewish people, nor even the Jewish authorities who were responsible for the death of Jesus, not only because these are distorting generalizations which can only serve to encourage prejudice and hostility, but also because the evidence, historically speaking, points in a quite different direction. Some Jews likely did play some role or other in Jesus' death and it is likely that these Jews, specifically Sadducees, not only possessed power but acted against Jesus not so much on the basis of religious concerns but rather owing to politically grounded concerns, having to do with the welfare of the nation as well as their own welfare within the framework of a collaborative relationship with the Roman occupation in the person of the prefect in Judaea.[38] Nonetheless, it is difficult to avoid the conclusion that it is ultimately due to the massive presence of the Roman occupation in Judaea and the alarm of the Roman overlord that Jesus died a Roman death at the hands of Roman troops on the basis of a political charge of insurrection after a trial and verdict in a Roman court presided over by a Roman judge.

It would be far too little to say that Christians need no longer blame the Jews for the death of Jesus; they need clearly and forthrightly to set the historical record straight so that future relations between Christians and Jews will no longer be troubled and muddied by this ancient accusation. Nonetheless, whatever the consensus Jewish and Christian scholarship may achieve with regard to the historical question of responsibility for Jesus' death, and such a consensus is unquestionably of enormous ecumenical significance, there remains and presumably always will remain an unbridgeable gulf between the two traditions in the area of theological evaluation of Jesus' crucifixion. Harrington makes the point in this way: "The Gospels and other NT writings go beyond this common Christian-Jewish theology of martyrdom. They portray Jesus as Savior of the world. They see his death as carried out according to God's will and a divine plan. They use such terms as redemption, reconciliation, justification, and atonement to express what has happened as a result of Jesus' death."[39] The death of Jesus, however, represents only one area among many of divergent theological assessment, albeit a very important one. While it is tempting to confine the Jewish-Christian dialogue about the place of Jesus within Judaism to matters pertaining to the historical Jesus, inevitably dialogue can hardly avoid the seemingly intractable difficulties associated with the Christ of faith, that is with Jesus as he was understood within a theological frame of reference by his followers, not only in the first century but also during the period when the classical christology of the Christian Church developed.

Jesus: An Unconventional Messiah

Christianity is the only Jewish messianic movement that ultimately survived and in that sense succeeded.[40] Needless to say, however, it was not able to survive and therefore did not finally succeed within the Jewish world in which it originated. Early on Christian missionaries penetrated the gentile world and it was in that cultural setting that they eventually made a home for themselves. In the process Christianity underwent a profound transformation which had wide-ranging repercussions on its relationship with its own Jewish heritage, a heritage which derived from Jesus himself and his first disciples, all of whom were themselves Jews. By the time of the rupture between rabbinical Judaism and Christianity, which occurred in a more or less definitive fashion towards the end of the first century, significant discontinuity between the two traditions was already apparent even if a not insignificant continuity remained. The discontinuity was to deepen in subsequent centuries as ties of continuity were further weakened even if never completely severed, largely because of the scriptural inheritance which acted as something of a brake on Hellenization and other later cultural influences.

From the beginning Jesus was a rather improbable messiah and it is uncertain, and indeed unlikely, that he referred to himself, explicitly at least,[41] as the messiah. Gerard Sloyan speaks of Jesus as "The Reluctant Messiah." He offers the judgment that "clearly what has happened is that after Jesus' death there has been bestowed on him a role and a title that in his lifetime he strongly resisted." Earlier he remarks: "The easiest question raised in connection with Jesus' self-awareness is: Did he think he was Israel's messiah? The answer seems to be an unequivocal no."[42]

Monika Hellwig addresses the issue in this way:

> Actually, it appears that Jesus himself did not claim the role of the Messiah during his lifetime, though his disciples later gave him that title, so that we know him as Christ (which means Messiah) almost as though that had been his surname, and it seems to us that he must always have been so named. If Jesus did not claim the title of Messiah, that seems to be for several reasons. First of all, because of the popular military connotations it could be misleading to his followers. Second, he was not concerned with claiming any titles, because his focus was not on himself but on the coming reign of God among human persons. Third, the mission and the person of Jesus in history were unique and there was no pre-existing category into which he could be slotted. Besides this, it is quite clear that when his followers gave him this title after his death and resurrection, they changed the meaning of the title by making it more explicit and also more universal in application than it was in Jewish usage.[43]

By way of contrast, Marinus de Jonge, in a recent study, concludes that, "In view of the central position of the designation (i.e. Messiah) in early Christian Christology, however, it remains likely that the term was not chosen by over-enthusiastic admirers or by his opponents, but was regarded as suitable by Jesus himself," even if it must be added immediately that, "Needless to say, if Jesus did not in fact avoid the designation Messiah, he used it creatively, in his own way, and did not widely advertise it."[44]

It is somewhat startling that the very fact of Jesus' terrible and very public execution did not undermine whatever messianic anticipations had been associated with him—an issue to which attention is called even by Luke 24:13-27. It can only have been owing to their belief in the vindicating resurrection of Jesus that they felt sufficiently confident to find in a crucified prophet Israel's messiah as well as to preach that unusual view of things in the Jewish world and to attempt to ground it authoritatively in a creative rereading of the scriptural tradition. Christians all too easily and uncritically assume that the Old Testament literature, especially the prophetical literature, provides abundant support by way of prophecies or predictions for the sort of crucified and resurrected messiah Christians believe Jesus was. The issue is in fact far more complicated than that.[45]

The difficulties attached to the proclamation of an untraditional crucified and resurrected messiah were further and seemingly fatally compounded by unavoidable questions regarding the messianic age and the reign of God. If Jesus was the messiah, where in fact was the new age of peace and justice, the age of *shalom* in this world, which the messiah was expected to bring? The world seemed, at least to the Jewish objector, quite unaffected and unaltered by the appearance of the messiah Jesus. There was no empirically obvious evidence that any messiah had made his appearance, let alone that Jesus of Nazareth might be such a messiah.

A contemporary illustration will perhaps provide some insight into this issue. The story is told of an ecumenical meeting of Christian and Jewish scholars in Paris at which a rabbi, in the course of a protracted discussion about the messiah, got up from the table and went to the window. His comment went to the heart of the differences under debate: "I look out over the city of Paris and I know that the messiah has not come."[46] The messianic age entails the transformation of every aspect of human life in the setting of earthly realities, and therefore the "spiritualization" of this hope in Christian history represents a marked and indeed questionable reinterpretation and departure from the very notion itself of the messiah's work. Jesus himself points to signs associated with his activity that indicate the nearness of the reign of God, the new age, because they involve the transformation of the lives of the people around him. The theme of the approaching reign of God in Jesus' preaching is not a cryptic code language for life in heaven after death. The contrast between views which emphasize salvation in this world and those which emphasize salvation in an otherworldly context may not exhaust all the possible ways of thinking about the issue of human well-being, but it does focus on two significantly different orientations.

Jesus was after all a Jew who thought about salvation in characteristically Jewish ways. Monika Hellwig underlines the point: "The teaching that Jesus took over and continued was not about an other-worldly hope but about a this-worldly one, or perhaps more accurately about a future-worldly one."[47] Jesus' earliest Jewish disciples recognized that if Jesus of Nazareth was to be interpreted within the framework of messianic traditions, it would have to be acknowledged that his messianic work was as yet unfinished, since it was obvious that the longed for transformation of the world still lay ahead. Consequently, they spoke of his impending *parousia* or second coming, which they clearly expected to occur shortly, as the climactic moment when the messianic promises would be fulfilled and the messiah's work would be completed. Therefore, not only were these messianic Jews (only later to be called Christians) preaching an innovative gospel about the resurrection/vindication of a recently crucified messianic pretender (derisively charged with being "the King of the Jews" and outfitted with a crown of thorns on the "throne" of the cross) whose very death was the centerpiece of his earthly messianic activity since it provided a ransom for sinners, but they were also claiming in a further innovative reinterpretation of messianic traditions that this messiah enacts his role in two stages, one earthly (beginning with his baptism and temptation and ending in his crucifixion) and the other heavenly (beginning with his resurrection/ascension and ending with his *parousia* in the guise of the apocalyptic Son of Man, the judge of the living and the dead).

The so-called "delay of the *parousia*," of course, forced first-century Christians to rethink their convictions about the imminence of the second coming and they seem to have done so without notable turmoil or tribulation. Such a postponement (not a cancellation, to be sure) was necessarily, in their minds, according to the will of God and therefore served a distinct purpose: to provide a vastly enlarged opportunity to preach the gospel of salvation not only to Israel but indeed to all the nations of the earth. It was also becoming clearer (to the eyes of faith) that various blessings typically associated with the new age, such as newness of life, the gift of God's Spirit, reconciliation and vibrant community, were already in part available in the present and therefore need not simply be awaited from the future when the risen one would return. Indeed the Christian eucharistic meal, which anticipates the banquet symbolic of the age to come, afforded a regular opportunity to celebrate his saving presence (or return) in the here and now. In this sense, futuristic eschatology was gradually modified, although never entirely eliminated, by a growing emphasis on a kind of realized eschatology or eschatology-in-process, the *not yet* needing to be balanced by a sense of the *already accomplished.*

This relatively uncomplicated two-stage christology would eventually give way, notably in the Gospel of John,[48] to a three-stage christology which features a pre-existent figure who descends to earth in an incarnation as a prelude to his revelational and redemptive activity and subsequently reascends to the heavenly sphere from whence he originally came.[49] As Raymond Brown remarks: "Johannine christology is very familiar to traditional Christians because it became the dominant christology of the church."[50] He adds that "it is startling to realize that such a portrayal of Jesus is quite foreign to the Synoptic Gospels," which developed within the framework of the earlier two-stage pattern. Paula Fredriksen offers the judgment that "The Johannine Christ is not heralded in Jewish history: he is an utterly untraditional messiah."[51] Perhaps it could also be said that the Johannine version of the Christ represents the final stage of a lengthy and complex process of reinterpreting Jewish messianism, which leads to increasing discontinuity between Christianity and the Jewish world in which it originated, both with regard to the role and identity of the messiah as well as the nature of the salvation he brings. Because the Johannine portrait of the Christ Jesus inspired a more determined emphasis on the divinity of the Messiah/Son of God and ultimately forced a trinitarian reassessment of monotheism, it only served to exacerbate further and possibly definitively the difficulties of achieving any rapprochement between the mother religion and her daughter or, better, these two sister religions of a common mother.[52] Inevitably, Christians and Jews approach the enigmatic Jesus of Nazareth from the perspective of very different christological presuppositions even if, as is often said, they are both awaiting the messiah from the future.

Jesus, A Jewish Brother to Both Christians and Jews

Many years ago Martin Buber, the great Jewish thinker, spoke warmly of his affection for Jesus:

> For nearly fifty years the New Testament has been a main concern in my studies, and I think I am a good reader who listens impartially to what is said.
>
> From my youth onwards I have found in Jesus my great brother. That Christianity has regarded and does regard him as God and Savior has always appeared to me a fact of the highest importance which, for his sake and my own, I must endeavor to understand.... My own fraternally open relationship to him has grown ever stronger and clearer, and today I see him more strongly and clearly than ever before.
>
> I am more than ever certain that a great place belongs to him in Israel's history of faith and that this place cannot be described by any of the usual categories.[53]

Can Jesus become once again a brother to his people as a whole? There is obviously no way at present of answering that question with any certainty. Nonetheless an historic opportunity presents itself, an opportunity opened up by the efforts of both Jewish and Christian scholars, to see and to appreciate the historical Jesus within the Judaism of his day as a brother to his compatriots in their sufferings and longings. While it is unlikely in the extreme that Jesus will ever be meaningful to Jews in the terms dictated by Christian tradition, it is quite likely that a new chapter in his history among his people has already opened up. Indeed a Jewish reclamation of Jesus[54] seems well underway. What role, if any, this Jesus might play in contemporary Judaism is unpredictable.

For Christians Jesus has, of course, been recognized and affectionately followed as a brother,[55] especially when a strong sense of his genuine humanity has prevailed. Today Christians are being invited by the changing currents in scholarship to find in Jesus not only a truly human brother but also a truly Jewish brother. Indeed along with the recovery of Jesus' humanity, inevitably there must come a recovery of his Jewishness. Matching the Jewish reclamation of Jesus as a fellow Jew, there is a Christian reclamation of Jesus as a Jewish brother and their own Jewish heritage. Perhaps the Jesus who has for so long functioned as a barrier to amicable relations between Christians and Jews may now provide a bridge between them, a role undoubtedly far better suited to his aims and to the sort of brother he was and, as Christians believe, still is.

Endnotes

1. Julius Wellhausen, *Einleitung in die drei ersten Evangelien* (Berlin: Reimer, 1905), 113, as cited by Leonard Swidler, *Yeshua: A Model for Moderns* (Kansas City, MO: Sheed and Ward, 1988), 68 n. 7. The second chapter of Swidler's book is entitled "Yeshua and His Followers Were Not Christians—They Were Jews: Implications for Christians Today." On the Jewish side, see Stuart E. Rosenberg, "Jesus Was Not a Christian," *The Christian Problem: A Jewish View* (New York: Hippocrene Books, 1986), ch. 1. Recently, Hans Dieter Betz has subjected Wellhausen's oft quoted formula to a penetrating analysis in his essay, "Wellhausen's Dictum 'Jesus was not a Christian, but a Jew' in Light of Present Scholarship," *Studia Theologica* 45 (1991): 83–110.

2. Leonard Swidler, "The Jewishness of Jesus: Some Religious Implications for Christians," *Journal of Ecumenical Studies* 18 (Winter, 1981): 104-105. My purpose in this essay, as will be clear from the notes, has not been to provide any sort of history of specifically Jewish interest in the figure of Jesus as a Jew, although some Jewish authors have obviously been utilized along the way. For discussion of such largely liberal Jewish interest, the reader may usefully consult Donald Hagner's *The Jewish Reclamation of Jesus: An Analysis of the Modern Jewish Study of Jesus* (Grand Rapids, MI: Zondervan, 1984). See n. 54 below, however, for some critical Jewish cautions with regard to this evangelical Christian study. Also of assistance, from the Jewish side, are Shalom Ben-Chorin, "The Image of Jesus in Modern Judaism," *Journal of Ecumenical Studies* 2 (1974): 401–430, and David Novak, "The Quest of the Jewish Jesus," *Modern Judaism* 8 (1988): 119-138, which has been incorporated into his *Jewish-Christian Dialogue: A Jewish Justification* (New York: Oxford University Press, 1989), ch. 4. My focus is rather on recent Christian attention to this issue which arises from (1) the widespread emphasis on the full humanity of Jesus, (2) the still significant "quest for the historical Jesus" which has gone through many metamorphoses over the last two centuries, (3) a renewed interest in the Jewish matrix of the Christian community and its traditions, and (4) a desire to build bridges to contemporary Judaism after centuries of shameful anti-Jewish defamation and persecution leading to the *Shoah*.

3. Daniel Harrington, S.J., in his presidential address to the forty-ninth general meeting of the Catholic Biblical Association, August 6, 1986, has called attention to this fact in a notably clarifying fashion. I am indebted to his reflections for the basic approach of this essay. His address was subsequently published under the title "The Jewishness of Jesus: Facing Some Problems," *The Catholic Biblical Quarterly* 49 (1987): 1-13. It was republished in a somewhat altered form in *Bible Review* 3 (1989): 32-41. James Charlesworth has now included the original in his collection, *Jesus' Jewishness: Exploring the Place of Jesus in Early Judaism* (Crossroad, 1991), 123-152. Clark Williamson's stimulating essay, "Jesus, A Jew," *Impact* (Claremont) 16 (1984): 1-14, emphatically underlines lines of continuity between Jesus and the world of his day.

4. On the issue of antisemitism in the New Testament, see Norman A. Beck, *Mature Christianity, The Recognition and Repudiation of the Anti-Jewish Polemic of the New Testament* (Cranbury, NJ: Associated University Presses, 1985). Professor Beck provides a more than ample bibliography on the issue, 292-305.

5. See the helpful analysis of this developmental theory in Donald Senior, *Jesus: A Gospel Portrait* (Cincinnati: Pflaum Standard, 1975), ch. 1.

6. Philip Sigal, *The Emergence of Contemporary Judaism*, vol. 1, *The Foundations of Judaism from Biblical Origins to the Sixth Century, A.D., Part One: From the Origins to the Separation of Christianity* (Pittsburgh: The Pickwick Press, 1980), 284. Rabbi Sigal has also authored a study of Jesus' teaching: *The Halakhah of Jesus of Nazareth according to the Gospel of Matthew* (Lanham, MD: University Press of America, 1987).

7. Gerd Theissen, *The Shadow of the Galilean* (Philadelphia: Fortress Press, 1987) offers an attractive approach to the issue in the form of an historical novel (replete with foot notes!), which both connects and distinguishes Jesus from the religious groups of his time. See also Theissen's *Sociology of Early Palestinian Christianity* (Philadelphia: Fortress Press, 1977).

8. Swidler (n. 1), 59-60. He cites in this quotation the work of John Pawlikowski, *Christ in the Light of the Jewish-Christian Dialogue* (New York: Paulist Press, 1982), 92; E.P. Sanders, *Jesus and Judaism* (Philadelphia: Fortress Press, 1985), 264; and Geza Vermes, *Jesus and the World of Judaism* (Philadelphia: Fortress Press, 1983), 11. See also Vermes' important contribution: *Jesus the Jew* (Philadelphia: Fortress Press, 1973); as well as his essay, "Jesus the Jew: Christian and Jewish Reactions," *Toronto Journal of Theology* 4 (1988): 112-123.

9. While baptism is not at all characteristic of Jesus' ministry, the Gospel of John indicates that "Jesus and his disciples went into the region of Judea, where he spent some time with them baptizing" (Jn 3:22). An editorial comment at John 4:2, however, suggests that there was some problem about this assertion among disciples of a later day.

10. Literature on the issue is vast. Helpful orientation can be found in G.R. Beasley-Murray, *Jesus and the Kingdom of God* (Grand Rapids, MI: William B. Eerdmans, 1986).

11. The issues involved are discussed at some length by Donald Goergen, *The Mission and Ministry of Jesus* (Wilmington, DE: Michael Glazier, 1986), chs. 5-6, which deal respectively with "A Prophet from Nazareth" and "Jesus and Apocalypticism."

12. Geza Vermes, *Jesus the Jew: A Historian's Reading of the Gospels* (Philadelphia: Fortress Press, 1973).

13. Marcus Borg, *Jesus: A New Vision: Spirit, Culture, and the Life of Discipleship* (New York: Harper & Row, 1987), ch. 6. Borg also identifies Jesus as founder of a revitalization movement (ch. 7) and as a prophet (ch. 8).

14. Morton Kelsey, *Healing and Christianity* (New York: Harper & Row, 1973), 51, remarks that "an important stúdy might be made comparing the ministry of Jesus with that of Shamanism."

15. Harvey Cox, *Many Mansions* (Boston: Beacon Press, 1988), 89-94, has scrutinized such a possible comparison only to find it ultimately problematic. On "Rabbi Yeshua ben Joseph," see ch. 5.

16. See on this point Jaroslav Pelikan, *Jesus Through the Centuries* (New Haven: Yale University Press, 1985) and Gerard Sloyan, *The Jesus Tradition* (Mystic, CT: Twenty-Third Publications, 1986).

17. Harrington (n. 3), 10-11.

18. See n. 5. The following discussion of Senior's presentation refers specifically to chs. 3–4.

19. On Jesus' relations with women, see Joseph Grassi, *The Hidden Heroes of the Gospels: Female Counterparts of Jesus* (Collegeville, MN: The Liturgical Press, 1989) and also, with Carolyn Grassi, *Mary Magdalene and the Women in Jesus' Life* (Kansas City, MO: Sheed and Ward, 1986); Kathleen Fischer, "Jesus and Women," *Women at the Well: Feminist Perspectives on Spiritual Direction* (New York: Paulist Press, 1988), 75-92; Elizabeth Moltmann-Wendel, *The Women Around Jesus* (New York: Crossroad, 1986); Donald Senior, "Was Jesus a Feminist?" *U.S. Catholic* 50 (October 1985): 41-44; Leonard Swidler, *Biblical Affirmations of Woman* (Philadelphia: Westminster, 1978) and "Yeshua, Feminist and Androgynous: An Integrated Human," *Yeshua: A Model for Moderns* (Kansas City, MO: Sheed and Ward, 1988), 75-110; Rachel Wahlberg, *Jesus According to a Woman* (New York: Paulist Press, 1975); and Ben Witherington III, *Women in the Ministry of Jesus* (New York: Cambridge University Press, 1984). In reaction to a strong tendency among Christian scholars to contrast Jesus' attitudes with those of other Jews of his time, a Roman Catholic scholar has recently observed that "The view that Jesus' positive attitude toward women was a major departure from current Jewish attitudes is challenged in current scholarship." Frederick Cwiekowski, *The Beginnings of the Church* (New York: Paulist Press, 1988), 49. Earlier, an important Jewish feminist, Judith Plaskow, had issued a warning against this practice in "Christian Feminism and Anti-Judaism," *Cross Currents* 28 (1978): 306-309; a rejoinder to Plaskow was offered by Virginia Mollenkott, "Christian Feminism and Anti-Judaism: A Response," *Cross Currents* 28 (1978-1979): 470-471. See also Elisabeth Schüssler-Fiorenza, *In Memory of Her: A Feminist Theological Reconstruction of Christian Origins* (New York: Crossroad, 1983), ch. 4.

20. Matthew's "Sermon on the Mount," chs. 5-7, for example, contains numerous examples of the use of such a contrast formula in Jesus' teaching.

21. Senior (n. 5), 108. See also Gerard Sloyan, *Is Christ the End of the Law?* (Philadelphia: Westminster Press, 1978).

22. Helpful on this whole question is Michael J. Cook's "Jesus and the Pharisees: The Problem As it Stands Today," *Journal of Ecumenical Studies* 15 (1978): 441-466. Also, more recently, D. Goodblatt, "The Place of the Pharisees in First Century Judaism: The State of the Debate," *Journal for the Study of Judaism* 20 (1989): 12-30.

23. His discussion of Jesus' prayer experience and teaching on prayer can be found in Senior (n. 5), 87-98.

24. See especially his *The Prayers of Jesus* (London: SCM Press, 1967) and *New Testament Theology I: The Proclamation of Jesus* (London: SCM Press, 1971).

25. James Dunn, *Jesus and the Spirit: A Study of the Religious and Charismatic Experience of Jesus and the First Christians as Reflected in the New Testament* (London: SCM Press, 1975), 21-26.

26. James Dunn, *Christology in the Making: A New Testament Inquiry into the Origins of the Doctrine of the Incarnation* (Philadelphia: The Westminster Press, 1980), 27. R.H. Fuller endorses Dunn's conclusion in *Who Is This Christ? Gospel Christology and Contemporary Faith* (Philadelphia: Fortress Press, 1983), 51 n. 11. A Jewish reaction to Jeremias can be

found in Geza Vermes, *Jesus the Jew: A Historian's Reading of the Gospels* (Philadelphia: Fortress Press, 1973), 210-211; and *Jesus and the World of Judaism* (Philadelphia: Fortress Press, 1984), 30-43.

27. Peter von der Osten-Sacken, *Christian-Jewish Dialogue: Theological Foundations* (Philadelphia: Fortress Press, 1986), 46-47. Attention is called also to the note on p. 185 n. 17.

28. Franz Mussner, *Tractate on the Jews* (Philadelphia: Fortress Press, 1984), 130. Mussner's entire discussion, pp. 123-130, is well worth reading.

29. Attention, albeit critical attention, needs, for example, to be given to Donald Senior's observation that "the 'love your enemy' text has been described as the most characteristic saying of Jesus, one without direct parallel in Judaism." *The Biblical Foundations for Mission*, ed. Donald Senior and Carroll Stuhlmueller (Maryknoll, NY: Orbis Books, 1983), 159 n. 14. Cf. Senior's *Jesus: A Gospel Portrait* (n. 5), 100-104, and also his essay "Jesus' Most Scandalous Teaching," *Biblical and Theological Reflections on The Challenge of Peace*, ed. John Pawlikowski and Donald Senior (Wilmington, DE: Michael Glazier, 1984), 55-69. It is often said that Jesus' activity of forgiving sins sets him apart from others. Geza Vermes, *Jesus the Jew*, 65-69, however, takes exception to this claim. Jesus' emphasis on the presence of the Kingdom is sometimes singled out as a mark of distinctiveness. Paula Fredriksen, *From Jesus to Christ: The Origins of the New Testament Images of Jesus* (New Haven: Yale University Press, 1988), 101, however, counters with the contention that "those scholars who want to argue that Jesus really did announce a present rather than a future Kingdom somewhat compromise their case by relying, necessarily, on the later strata of the gospel tradition. A Jesus preaching such a Kingdom would have been an excellent Christian theologian but a baffling early first-century Jew." Peter von der Osten-Sacken (n. 27), 44-59, asserts that "the center of Jesus' ministry was his search for the lost in Israel, so that he might lead them back into the 'total self' of the nation, as God's people," (p. 50). This affinity for the rejected and marginated brought him into conflict with the righteous, provoked criticism, and therefore may represent an area of differentiation. Finally, Sean Freyne has suggested that "by claiming that the divine presence, defined both as God's kingly rule and as Father, was accessible to people in his own life and person, Jesus undercut the various systems that had been devised within Judaism to control that presence and people's access to it." *The World of the New Testament* (Wilmington, DE: Michael Glazier, 1980), 140. In this claim Jesus asserts his distinctiveness, Freyne believes.

30. On this point, see Joseph Fitzmyer, *A Christological Catechism: New Testament Answers* (New York: Paulist Press, 1982), 58-62.

31. The text of "Nostra Aetate" can conveniently be found in Walter Abbott and Joseph Gallagher, eds., *The Documents of Vatican II* (New York: America Press, 1966), 660-668. See especially pp. 664-666 for the responsibility issue.

32. The literature on the "passion narratives," especially emphasizing historical matters, is prodigious. What follows is a sampling of the most substantial contributions to the debate: J. Blinzler, *The Trial of Jesus* (Westminster, MD: Newman, 1959); S.G.F. Brandon, *The Trial of Jesus of Nazareth* (New York: Stein & Day, 1968); the various articles in R. Gordis, ed., *The Trial of Jesus in the Light of History*, a special issue of *Judaism* 20 (1971): 6–74; E. Rivkin, *What Crucified Jesus?* (Nashville: Abingdon, 1984); G.S. Sloyan, *Jesus on Trial* (Philadelphia: Fortress, 1973); W.R. Wilson, *The Execution of Jesus* (New York: Scribner's, 1970); Paul

Winter, *On The Trial of Jesus* (Studia Judaica 1; 2d ed., rev. by T.A. Burkill and G. Vermes; Berlin/New York: de Gruyter, 1974); F. Matera, *Passion Narratives and Gospel Theologies* (New York: Paulist Press, 1986); D. Goergen, *The Death and Resurrection of Jesus* (Wilmington, DE: Michael Glazier, 1988). Donald Senior has written a very useful four-volume series on the passion stories which provides a commentary on each of the gospel accounts. It is published by Michael Glazier, Wilmington, DE, 1985-1990. Each volume is entitled: The Passion of Jesus in the Gospel of...

33. Harrington (n. 3), 12.

34. Fredriksen (n. 29), 124-125.

35. On this point, see E.P. Sanders, *Jesus and Judaism* (Philadelphia: Fortress Press, 1985), ch. 10. Also Fredriksen (n. 29), 98-106.

36. Monika Hellwig, *Understanding Catholicism* (New York: Paulist Press, 1981), 83-90, in her discussion of responsibility for the death, emphasizes how the fearlessness of Jesus would have proven provocative to an oppressive military rule which required fear among the oppressed to maintain its power.

37. On the theme of Jesus, the free man, see Ernst Käsemann, *Jesus Means Freedom* (Philadelphia: Fortress Press, 1970) and Donald P. Gray, *Jesus: The Way to Freedom* (Winona, MN: St. Mary's Press, 1979).

38. Richard McBrien, *Catholicism* (Minneapolis: Winston Press, 1981), 419, by contrast, cautions against recent attempts to highlight Roman responsibility for Jesus' execution, observing that "His problem was with the Jews, not with the Romans. That is how the Gospels present it, and that is how early Jewish antagonists of Christianity recalled it as well."

39. Harrington (n. 3), 12.

40. Hendrikus Boers, *Who Was Jesus? The Historical Jesus and the Synoptic Gospels* (New York: Harper & Row, 1989), XV, remarks in this regard: "Whereas the death of other messianic pretenders meant the end of their movements, the movement that had gathered around Jesus grew into one of the greatest religions of the world." See, also, p. 93.

41. It is commonly argued today by Christian scholars that while an explicit christology (i.e. involving explicit use of christological titles) on the part of the historical Jesus is problematic, a convincing case can be made for an implicit christology on his part. A christological self-understanding, according to this view, is implied by a number of unusual and disconcerting aspects of both Jesus' teaching and his activity. A clarifying treatment of the whole issue can be found in Raymond Brown, "'Who Do Men Say that I Am'—A Survey of Modern Scholarship on Gospel Christology," *Biblical Reflections on Crises Facing the Church* (New York: Paulist Press, 1975), 20-37.

42. Gerard Sloyan, *Jesus in Focus* (Mystic, CT: Twenty-Third Publications, 1983), 66-71.

43. Monika Hellwig (n. 36), 86-87.

44. Marinus de Jonge, *Christology in Context: The Earliest Christian Response to Jesus* (Philadelphia: Westminster Press, 1988), 211.

45. As can be seen in Donald Juel's recent study, *Messianic Exegesis: Christological Interpretation of the Old Testament in Early Christianity* (Philadelphia: Fortress Press, 1988).

46. See, for further clarifications, Gershom Scholem, "Toward an Understanding of the Messianic Idea in Judaism," *The Messianic Idea in Judaism and Other Essays on Jewish Spirituality* (New York: Schocken Books, 1971), 1-36.

47. Monika Hellwig (n. 36), 177.

48. That Paul, the earliest New Testament author, already exhibits a preexistence/incarnational type of three-stage christology, most obvious in the Philippian hymn (Phil 2:6-11), is increasingly questioned today. See Raymond Brown, *The Community of the Beloved Disciple* (New York: Paulist Press, 1979), 45-46.

49. On the distinction between two-stage and three-stage christology, see William Thompson, *The Jesus Debate. Survey and Synthesis* (New York: Paulist Press, 1985), 248 ff.

50. Raymond Brown (n. 48), 45.

51. Paula Fredriksen (n. 29), 25.

52. Alan Segal, *Rebecca's Children* (Cambridge, MA: Harvard University Press, 1986) argues for this more felicitous understanding of the relationship of the two traditions to the Jewish heritage.

53. Martin Buber, *Two Types of Faith: A Study of the Interpenetration of Judaism and Christianity* (New York: Harper Torchbooks, 1961), 12-13. See also the helpful study by Donald Berry, "Buber's View of Jesus as Brother," *Journal of Ecumenical Studies* 14 (1977): 203-218, as well as the insightful analysis of this theme in Buber's writing by David Novak (n. 2), 80 ff. Novak notes (pp. 80-81) that so untypical of Jewish thinkers generally was Buber in this regard that he was sometimes accused by critics of having more to say to Christians than to Jews. Novak considers the accusation unfair. Shalom Ben-Chorin, it might be noted, devoted a book to Jesus under the title *Bruder Jesus* (Munich, 1967).

54. Donald Hagner, *The Jewish Reclamation: An Analysis and Critique of the Modern Jewish Study of Jesus* (Grand Rapids, MI: Zondervan, 1984) details just such a reclamation from an evangelical Christian point of view. See, however, the critical assessments of Hagner from the Jewish side by G. David Schwartz, "Is There A Jewish Reclamation of Jesus?" *Journal of Ecumenical Studies* 24 (1987): 104-109, and also by Brad Young, "Jewish Scholarship and Jesus," *Immanuel* 19 (1984-1985): 102-106.

55. Karl Adam's *Christ Our Brother* (New York: Collier Books, 1961; German original, 1930) called attention to the issue some sixty years ago.

Suggestions For Further Reading

Charlesworth, James. *Jesus Within Judaism, New Light from Existing Archeological Discoveries*. New York: Doubleday, 1988. A fascinating account of the state of current "Jesus Research" which itself represents an impressive renewal of interest in careful historical study of the Jew Jesus. An especially useful annotated bibliography of the pertinent literature is also included.

____, ed. *Jesus' Jewishness. Exploring the Place of Jesus in Early Judaism*. New York: Crossroad, 1991. A very useful collection of essays, written by both Jewish and Christian contributors, which explores the Jewishness of Jesus from a wide range of viewpoints.

Crossan, John Dominic. *The Historical Jesus: The Life of a Mediterranean Jewish Peasant*. San Francisco: Harper San Francisco, 1991. A difficult but rewarding interdisciplinary investigation of Jesus of Nazareth within the cultural context of the first century.

Fredriksen, Paula. *From Jesus to Christ. The Origins of the New Testament Images of Jesus*. New Haven: Yale University Press, 1988. An unusually well written and lucid introduction to the literature of the New Testament, focusing on the relation of the christological concerns and imagery of the early Christian movement to what is known today about the Jesus of history.

Lee, Bernard. *The Galilean Jewishness of Jesus. Retrieving the Jewish Origins of Christianity*. New York: Paulist Press, 1988. This is the first of a projected three-volume study entitled "Conversation on the Road Not Taken" which muses in a highly intelligent fashion about the "might have beens" of Christian history as the Jewish matrix was left behind in favor of another road. This volume attempts to make contact with the Jew Jesus in his Galilean homeland before the two roads of Christianity and rabbinical Judaism later diverged.

Meier, John. *A Marginal Jew: Rethinking the Historical Jesus*. Vol. 1, *The Roots of the Problem and the Person*. New York: Doubleday, 1991. This is the first installment of a projected two-volume study. This volume assesses the value of the various sources available for study of the historical Jesus and provides a picture of the pre-ministry period of Jesus' life. For the present, this volume can be helpfully supplemented by a reading of Meier's more comprehensive essay, "Jesus," in *The New Jerome Biblical Commentary*, ed. Raymond Brown, Joseph Fitzmyer, Roland Murphy, 1316–1328. Englewood Cliffs, NJ: Prentice-Hall, 1990.

Pawlikowski, John. *Jesus and the Theology of Israel*. Wilmington, DE: Michael Glazier, 1989. A review of recent Christian efforts to develop a more positive position regarding Jewish-Christian relations around the theme of divine covenant-making. Helpful suggestions are also made in the direction of a renewed christology emphasizing Jesus' links to the Pharisees as well as the possibilities for rapprochement inherent in incarnational christologies.

Sanders, E.P. *Jesus and Judaism*. Philadelphia: Fortress Press, 1985. A landmark study of Jesus within his Palestinian Jewish environment which minimizes Jesus' conflicts with the Pharisees over questions of Torah interpretation. Sanders identifies Jesus as an exponent of what he terms restorationist eschatology.

Swidler, Leonard. *Yeshua. A Model for Moderns*. Kansas City, MO: Sheed and Ward, 1988. A small collection of essays which ties Jesus closely to the Pharisees and stresses his feminist preoccupations. Popularly written.

Theissen, Gerd. *The Shadow of the Galilean*. Philadelphia: Fortress Press, 1987. An historical novel by an eminent New Testament scholar which seeks to make more readily available the results of contemporary scholarship. It particularly seeks to situate Jesus in relation to the religious groups of his time, on the one hand, and the Roman occupation of Palestine, on the other. It comes replete with notes indicating the author's sources of information from the period or nearby it.

Vermes, Geza. *Jesus the Jew: A Historian's Reading of the Gospels*. 1973. Reprint. Philadelphia: Fortress, 1981. A ground-breaking and influential study by a renowned Jewish scholar which seeks to locate Jesus meaningfully in the Palestinian Judaism of his day. This should be read in conjunction with his somewhat later collection of essays entitled *Jesus and the World of Judaism*. Philadelphia: Fortress Press, 1983.

JUDAISM AND EARLY CHRISTIANITY IN THE LIGHT OF THE DEAD SEA SCROLLS

Lawrence H. Schiffman

The discovery of the Dead Sea Scrolls, beginning in 1947, is the most dramatic and the most significant archaeological find of the century. The manuscripts are the only sources we have that are contemporary with the beginnings of Christianity and the formation of rabbinic Judaism. While the documents are difficult to interpret, because they are allusive and anonymous, and because many have not been published, deciphered, or pieced together from myriad fragments, they are compelling a revolution in our understanding of the age. Lawrence H. Schiffman explores the vistas opened by these discoveries and suggests some of the conclusions to which they are leading researchers.

The history of Judaism in the Second Temple period (520 B.C.E.–73 C.E.) is unquestionably the key to understanding the subsequent development of both early Christianity and Rabbinic Judaism. From our vantage point today, and I may add that in my lifetime this is the only vantage point I have known, it is impossible to imagine the study of this period without the benefit of the ancient scrolls from the Judean Desert and the light they have shed on this important era.

The Dead Sea Scrolls, discovered at Qumran at the shore of the Dead Sea, south of Jericho, by bedouin in 1947 and afterwards, constitute the only primary Hebrew and Aramaic sources for the period between the Hebrew Bible on the one side, and the Rabbinic corpus and the New Testament on the other. These manuscripts date from the third century B.C.E. through the first century C.E. Although they were left in the caves by the Qumran or Dead Sea sect, identified by most scholars with the Essenes, these scrolls include not only literature composed by the sect itself, but a vast sampling of biblical texts and of other books known among the Jewish people in this period. Cave 4 clearly served as a library for the community. The other scrolls were most probably hidden in the caves in the last years of the sectarian settlement at Qumran which was destroyed by the Romans in 68 C.E.

In this paper, I choose to address myself to what seem to me to be some of the seminal issues in regard to the history of Judaism in this period, and to ask how the scrolls have contributed and continue to contribute to our knowledge. We shall then ask how these conclusions make possible a more balanced understanding of the way in which Rabbinic Judaism and Christianity emerged from the crucible of the Second Temple period.

We will discuss the following issues to which the scrolls can contribute: (1) the constellation of groups in Second Temple times, (2) the centrality of Jewish law, (3) the "theology" of law, (4) biblical exegesis, (5) sacrifice and liturgy, (6) the role of purity, and (7) messianism. In each case we will seek to understand how the particular aspects were manifested in both Rabbinic Judaism and early Christianity, and, therefore, in what ways the Qumran manuscripts may be profitably used for the understanding of the New Testament and early Christianity, on the one hand, and Talmudic literature and Rabbinic Judaism, on the other.

At the outset I must emphasize that this paper represents a radical departure from the method usually followed in such presentations. It is usual to begin with the basic characteristics of Rabbinic Judaism and early Christianity and then to reach backwards into the Qumran corpus to find parallels of content and language. This method does not allow the scrolls to speak for themselves. We must begin by evaluating the evidence of these important finds. This is especially true after the events of the last few years which have led to the full release of the entire corpus of manuscripts from the Judaean Desert and the reorganization of the publication process. Only then can we ask how they relate to the later developments with which we are concerned.

1. The Constellation of Groups in Second Temple Times

One of the central assumptions of the study of our period before the discovery of the Qumran scrolls was that there were three major sects (or parties), the Pharisees, Sadducees and Essenes. The Pharisees and Sadducees were known from Rabbinic literature, which itself was generally treated uncritically, and from the New Testament. The Essenes were known from Josephus, Philo, Pliny and the Church Fathers. In addition, it was assumed that various minor sects, like the early *hasidim*, were in some way to be related to the Essenes. The Essenes were generally regarded as a Hellenized sect.[1]

Virtually all scholars accepted the fundamental assumption of later Rabbinic Judaism that the Pharisaic approach was, indeed, normative, historical Judaism, and that all other forms were offshoots, indeed corruptions.[2] Only with the rise of knowledge about apocryphal and pseudepigraphal compositions, and, of course, after the discovery of the Cairo *genizah* copies of the *Zadokite Fragments*, did this view begin to change. Scholars began to realize that the claims of Rabbinic Judaism for Pharisaic continuity had to be subjected to more critical inquiry. Indeed, I have been rightly criticized for using the word "sect" in reference to the different groups of Second Temple Jews since this term implies the existence of a recognized "church" from which the sect in some way diverges. Nevertheless, for want of a better word, I will continue to use the term.

In this area, the discovery of the Dead Sea Scrolls radically reopened the question. Beginning with the publication of the medieval copies of the *Zadokite Fragments*,[3] it became clear that the constellation would have to be widened somewhat. Even though the initial discovery of the scrolls soon led to the Essene consensus, which might have allowed the assumption that now at last we had the literature of this group, the matter quickly became more complex. It was not long before some scholars realized that "Essene" was actually a wide term for a variety of groups as used by Josephus, the late first-century Jewish historian, and those who followed his account, and that, in fact, at least two types of Essenes existed.[4] Some of us have maintained that even so, the Essene identification is too facile, and have called for a recognition that we have here what Louis Ginzberg called *An Unknown Jewish Sect*.[5]

In any case, the recent publication of new texts, as well as information now available from those entrusted with the publication of the remaining texts, have caused us to propose new ways of looking at the material. It is now virtually certain that the *Ancient Library of Qumran*, as it was so aptly termed by Frank Moore Cross,[6] preserves material from groups other than the Qumran sect, however we wish to identify those who collected this library. At the center of this collection is certainly the literature of the main group who followed the teacher of righteousness or correct teacher. Cross has convincingly placed the founding of this group in the early Hasmonean period, after 152 B.C.E.[7]

Yet among the scrolls and scraps from the caves are also compositions of other groups. After the publication of the *Temple Scroll* I maintained that this text should be taken as the composition of some group related but not identical to the Qumran sect.[8] The laws of this scroll are based on a different principle of theological authority and the text is devoid of the sectarian animus of the other documents representative of the Qumran group. It now appears that the differences between this text and the Qumran sectarian corpus result from the fact that it was redacted of pre-sectarian sources, most of which probably derived from the Sadducean tradition.

It is now clear that much of the Aramaic apocrypha found at Qumran comes from predecessors of the sect, and that Enochic and other texts seem to have been produced by certain circles or groups which cannot be identified with the main "sect." Some of these compositions are also pre-Maccabean. Liturgical texts have been discovered based on a luni-solar calendar which seems to be represented side by side with the "sectarian" soli-solar calendar.[9] Interestingly, the Talmud indirectly identifies the soli-solar calendar as that in use by the Boethusians.[10] Future research may reveal still more of these inconsistencies between the sectarian library and the other materials found in the caves. Thus our scrolls are not the product of one monolithic group. They are a treasury representing the works of various groups which were either predecessors of or closely related to the main "sect."[11]

Recently, there has come to light the so-called "halakhic letter," 4Q *Miqsat Ma'seh Ha-Torah*, abbreviated as "MMT."[12] This text has opened up a valuable window on the sectarian constellation of the period immediately following the Maccabean revolt.[13] The text is essentially a letter, either actual or "apocryphal," which purports to be from the leaders of the sect to the leaders of the priestly establishment in Jerusalem. The author lists some twenty-two laws in which the writers disagreed with the Temple priesthood.

In a number of cases we can identify the very same controversies which are presented in Rabbinic literature as Pharisee-Sadducee debates. In these, the writers of the letter take the position attributed to the Sadducees in Rabbinic sources and attribute to the Temple priests the position of the Pharisees.[14]

Once we realize that this text takes the "Sadducean" position, we must reopen the question of the relationship of the Sadducees to our sect. It would not be unreasonable to postulate that the sect was founded by disaffected priests who left the Jerusalem Temple after the Maccabean revolt when the Zadokite High Priests were displaced. If so, Qumran may provide us with some Sadducean documents. This possibility is especially heightened in light of some parallels J.M. Baumgarten has already cited.[15] The Sadducean connection may also be a clue to the provenance of the *Temple Scroll.*

All in all, it would seem that in the corpus from Qumran we have the literature of an entire variety of groups, plus some "secondary" literature regarding others. We can pinpoint some representation in this corpus for the Pharisees, who are certainly not dominant at Qumran, the sect themselves, various apocalyptic circles still not clearly identified, and perhaps, the Sadducees or related groups like the still unidentified Baytusim or Boethusians.

This wide perspective on the differing approaches to Judaism which were current in the Second Temple period already points us toward the issue at hand. While the origins of Rabbinic Judaism can be placed among the Pharisees, even this is an over-simplification. Aspects of the Judaism of other groups certainly influenced the Rabbis as well. In the case of Christianity, the Jewish background against which it came to the fore must be sought not in the Pharisaic-Rabbinic approach to Judaism, but in the apocalyptic and sectarian forms of Judaism now so generously illustrated, or better typified, in the Dead Sea corpus. We must understand the manner in which the sorting out of these various trends by the end of this period led to the rise of Rabbinic Judaism and early Christianity.

2. Centrality of Jewish Law

From some of the materials that have been mentioned before, it should be obvious that a large amount of the Qumran material deals with issues of Jewish law, what later Rabbinic tradition called *halakhah*. It must be stated at the outset that in investigating Jewish law in the Qumran scrolls, we should not expect to find what is found in Rabbinic literature. Two reasons may be cited. First, Rabbinic tradition is the product of a long process of development and, by Hasmonean times, it was only a forerunner of the later Mishnaic system. Second, since we have mostly non-Pharisaic material in the Qumran corpus, to expect congruency with post-destruction *halakhah* is unreasonable. I have devoted many studies to the actual details of the laws found in the various Qumran texts, including those dealing with conduct of sectarian affairs.[16] But here I wish instead to point up two basic features, centrality of the law, what Isidore Twersky calls halakho-centrism, and the issue of the sources of authority for extra-biblical Jewish law.

On the issue of centrality of the law, it must be realized that Qumran literature is itself evidence that legal procedures and regulations were a major vehicle for inculcating the theology and meaning of the Jewish way of life. This should be clear from the sheer quantity of the material. Further, we do not find here a dry legalism of the type so often represented in caricatures of Rabbinic Judaism. The laws appear here as a means to come close to God and to one's fellow man, as a binding force for Israel, calling for ethical as well as spiritual and ritual purity. Indeed, this is the concern of all the groups whose writings are represented or who are alluded to at Qumran.

Yet I wish to go even further. I have always maintained that the basic issues which led to the formation of the sect were matters of Jewish law. Priests displaced in the aftermath of the Hasmonean revolt found the rituals and the rulings of the new Jerusalem establishment unacceptable. Shemaryahu Talmon and other scholars have insisted that the underlying issues related to messianism.[17] Yet the new halakhic letter, 4Q MMT, shows beyond a doubt that matters of religious practice were at the very heart of things.

The scrolls show unequivocally that in this respect Rabbinic Judaism represents a continuation of all trends of Second Temple Judaism. The scrolls present no evidence of antinomianism or of a trend toward moving away from the observance of Jewish Law as the path to sanctity, holiness and the fulfillment of the word of God. Therefore, the gradual trend in early Christianity which culminated in the abrogation of the Law cannot be even remotely detected in the writings of the Qumran sect or of the other groups whose views are documented in the Qumran collection.

3. "Theology" of Law

One of the fundamental issues in Second Temple Judaism was that of how to incorporate extra-biblical traditions and teachings into the legal system, and how to justify them theologically. Despite the fact that in antiquity and late antiquity there was little theoretical theological inquiry in Judaism (except in the Hellenistic Diaspora), issues of theology were of central importance and often lie behind other more clearly expressed disputes.

All Jewish groups in the Second Temple period endeavored to assimilate extra-biblical teachings into their way of life. My detailed examination of the writings of the Dead Sea sect has led me to determine that they did so through the concept of the *nigleh* ("revealed") and *nistar* ("hidden"). That which was revealed was the simple meaning of scripture and the commandments which were readily apparent from it. These were known to all Jews. Only the sect possessed the hidden knowledge, discovered by it through what it saw as inspired biblical exegesis, regularly conducted by members of the sect. Tradition was regarded as having no authority, since all Israel had gone astray and the true way had only been rediscovered by the sect's teacher. The laws which emerged from this interpretation were eventually composed in *serakhim*, lists of sectarian laws.[18] These were then redacted into such collections as the *Zadokite Fragments* (*Damascus Document*) or the less organized "Ordinances" (4Q 159, 513, 514). These rules and the interpretations upon which they were based served to make clear the application of the Law of the Torah to the life of the sect, and to make possible life in accord with the "revealed" Torah in the present, pre-messianic age.

Although we do not have Pharisaic texts from this period, we can suggest the general lines of the approach of this group based on later accounts in the New Testament, the writings of Josephus, and on the reports in the even later Rabbinic corpus. Apparently, the Pharisees possessed traditions "handed down by the fathers" and "unwritten laws." These included various legal traditions of great antiquity as well as interpretations of the biblical texts. Indeed, the Pharisees were known as expounders of the Torah and seem to have excelled in the application of the laws of the Pentateuch to their own circumstances and times. Somewhat later, the successors to the Pharisees, the tannaim (teachers of the Mishnah) would enunciate the notion that these traditions had been revealed by God to Moses on Sinai as a second Torah. The Rabbis asserted that God had given two Torahs to Israel, the written and the oral. For the Rabbis, this view essentially elevated the oral Torah to a sanctity and authority equal to that of the written. Yet evidence does not point to such an assertion on the part of the Pharisees themselves, although our sources do not allow us to be certain.

The Sadducean approach has yet to be properly investigated. The general claim that the Sadducees were strict literalists represents a misunderstanding of their approach often predicated on late Rabbinic sources and on a parallel misunderstanding of the medieval Karaite movement. In any case, we should note that the Sadducees apparently saw only the written law as authoritative, although they admitted the need to interpret it. Their interpretations attempted to adhere as closely as possible to the plain meaning of scripture (what the Rabbis later called *peshat*). It may be that we will be able to refine our view of the Sadducees, and perhaps Boethusians, with the help of the Qumran corpus, most notably from 4Q MMT and the *Temple Scroll.*

The author of the *Temple Scroll* seeks to assimilate extra-biblical traditions by the contention that his new, rewritten Torah properly expresses the will of God as revealed in the original document. He asserts that the correct meaning of the divine revelation at Sinai, apparently left vague in the canonical Torah, is to be found in the *Temple Scroll.* Thus, like the sectarians of Qumran, he has no dual Torah concept. Unlike this group, he does not accept the notion of a continuous, inspired revelation through biblical exegesis. He maintains only a one-time revelation, at Sinai. In this respect he agrees with the later tannaim, except that for them the one-time revelation is of two Torahs, yet for him it is of a single Torah, the true contents of which are expressed in the scroll he authored and redacted.

All Jewish groups of the Second Commonwealth had some form of supplement to the Hebrew Bible. It is in this light that we can also understand the development in Christianity of a set of scriptures, eventually redacted into the New Testament. These writings functioned in the early church as fulfilling the purpose of adapting the laws and traditions of the Torah to the beliefs and principles of the sect. In this area, we can say that both Rabbinic Judaism and early Christianity continue trends well established in the Second Temple period.

4. Biblical Exegesis

We have already noted the sect's approach to halakhic (legal) interpretation. It should be added that this form of *midrash* was based on the harmonizing of various apparently contradictory biblical commands into uniform laws, such as those found in the *Zadokite Fragments.* Similar in method, although quite different in theoretical basis, is the legal interpretation found in the *Temple Scroll.* Here the various biblical injunctions on the topics of Temple, sacrifice and related matters are woven together into laws which in biblical language state the results of the exegesis behind them. But the *Temple Scroll* material is radically different in literary form from the *serakhim* of the *Zadokite Fragments* and the *Manual of Discipline.* Like the Mishnah, the *serakhim* were organized by subject. Yet the laws of the *Temple Scroll,* like the later Rabbinic *midrashim,* are organized in biblical order. While legal exegesis is reflected in the New Testament, it is rare. The few passages involved share more in common with the style of later Rabbinic exegetical texts than with the earlier Qumran forms of interpretation.

The situation in regard to non-legal materials, what the Rabbis called *aggadah,* is very different. Two forms are represented in the scrolls. The Qumran sect itself utilized the method of *pesher.* This is a form of contemporizing biblical exegesis in which the Bible, usually Prophets, is quoted phrase by phrase or verse by verse, and an interpretation is then given. Yet this interpretation sees the words of scripture as referring to the very time of the author of the *pesher*, rather than to that of the original author. Accordingly, the contemporary events of the Second Temple period, both internal Jewish affairs and matters of international relations, all are said to be prophesied already by the biblical prophets.[19]

A second type of non-legal interpretation is also found in the scrolls, although it comes primarily from groups whose writings are preserved at Qumran but whose history is not known. Such books as Enoch, Jubilees, and the *Genesis Apocryphon* constitute the genre of rewritten Bible. Here the authors recapitulate biblical history and even law from their own perspective, presenting their views as if they were actually biblical.[20]

Neither of the two forms of non-legal exegesis preserved at Qumran survived into the Rabbinic tradition, except that some traditions represented in the rewritten Bible genre did enter in amoraic Babylonia. Instead the Rabbis chose to use the midrashic method—the same one used for *halakhah*—to interpret the non-legal aspects of the biblical tradition. This led to the development of the aggadic *midrash*.

On the other hand, early Christianity preserved both of these approaches, although at different stages. As regards the method of *pesher*, it was this notion of contemporizing exegesis that made possible the Christian claims that the career and even death of Jesus were the fulfillment of biblical prophecy. Here the prophets of the Hebrew Bible were read as speaking directly of Second Temple times. The genre of rewritten Bible, while not part of the official canon of western Christianity, clearly attracted certain Church Fathers and developing eastern churches. It was in their hands that these early Jewish works were preserved, since they venerated these texts as part of their holy scriptures.

5. Sacrifice and Liturgy

The Qumran corpus provides a rather contradictory picture regarding sacrifice. This is a perfect example of why we cannot assume that all of the scrolls are part of a uniform corpus. The main body of sectarian texts condemns the Jerusalem Temple and excoriates its priesthood for a long list of offenses against the Torah's laws of sacrifices and purity. Indeed, the texts argue that the sect was to serve as a substitute for the Temple and its worship. Sanctity and holiness are now to be attained through participation in the life of the sect. The *Temple Scroll*, however, a document clearly drawing on Sadducean sources, prescribes the details of the Temple and its ritual. This system is intended to bring about the ultimate sanctity of people and land, to allow the divine presence to dwell among Israel. This text seeks to set out the ideal Temple and worship, state and government, for the period up to the messianic age, at which time a new Temple would be built.[21] This scroll certainly assumes that the way to God is through the portals of the Temple and in the courtyards of the House of the Lord.

When we examine the material composed by the Qumran sect, we find a very different situation. Our texts speak of a group which has left the Temple due to disagreement with its practices. Atonement and sanctity are now to be achieved elsewhere, through the sect. The sect itself is seen as a virtual temple, bringing sanctity and closeness to God to its members. The eternal plantation has replaced the eternal house. It is not that the sect rejects sacrifice, but rather that it must be foregone in the present age, until the end of days when the sect will be able to control the Temple and reinstate the proper ritual.[22] The 4Q MMT makes clear that it was such disputes regarding sacrificial law which led to the founding of the sect.

Recently we have seen the publication of many liturgical texts from the Qumran corpus. Still more devotional poetry is found in the recently released photographs of the entire corpus. We can now speak of morning and late afternoon prayers, on the analogy of the daily sacrifices in the Temple. Evidence shows that certain of the later Rabbinic usages are already prefigured here, and certain almost shocking correspondences in prayer language exist. Yet since this daily prayer text seems to follow the luni-solar calendar, it is impossible to know to which group these prayers belonged.[23] Further, the festival prayers appear to speak of a calendar expanded with various additional festivals, similar to that of the *Temple Scroll*.[24]

Yet someone collected these texts, and it seems most likely that they were recited daily by the members of the Qumran sect. If so, we can see prayer already replacing Temple worship, even before the Roman destruction of the Temple in 70 C.E. To put it another way, sectarian groups may have experienced the destruction of the Temple before the rest of Israel. To them an illegitimate shrine was the same as a non-existent shrine. Their solution, the replacement of sacrifice with prayer, would become that of all Israel in the aftermath of the Great Revolt (66–73 C.E.) when Rabbinic Judaism made synagogue liturgy and individual prayer the norm for a growing number of Jews who followed the teachings of the Rabbis.

The Pharisaic-Rabbinic tradition consistently claims that the Pharisees enjoyed halakhic hegemony in the Temple, even though the priests who ministered there were Sadducean. This hegemony is at least claimed for the latter half of the Hasmonean period (from the rule of Salome Alexandra on) and for the Herodian period. This view has been challenged by Jacob Neusner in a number of his works. He sees this as an historical retrojection resulting from the self-image of the Pharisaic-Rabbinic tradition as the carriers of the authentic tradition of Jewish law.

The 4Q MMT requires that we reevaluate this conclusion. As noted above, in a number of cases it is possible to identify in the MMT disagreements recorded in Rabbinic sources as Pharisee-Sadducee debates. The writers of the letter take the very same positions attributed in Rabbinic sources to the Sadducees. The views they impute to their opponents in the Jerusalem establishment are those attributed in Rabbinic sources to the Pharisees. In other words, if this "halakhic letter" does indeed date from a period close to the founding of the sect, and all evidence points to such a dating for this composition, it proves that the views attributed to the Pharisees in Rabbinic sources were indeed being practiced in the Temple in Hasmonean times. This conclusion requires us to give much greater credence to the claims of Pharisaic authority in the Temple, at least for certain periods. This thesis fits well with the prominence given to the Pharisees in the early strata of the New Testament. There they constitute the dominant Jewish group with which Jesus and his followers dispute.

One of the prominent trends in early Christianity is the attempt to see the act of sacrifice as realized through the life of the community and its leaders. In this way, the suffering servant of Isaiah is grafted upon the sacrificial system of the Hebrew Bible. The Qumran sect saw its liturgy as a substitute for Temple worship even while the Temple still stood. The sect considered itself as the realization of the sanctity of sanctuary and sacrifice through its way of life and very existence as a group. While the notion of prayer as a substitute for sacrifice certainly became a dominant idea in Rabbinic Judaism, it is only in early Christianity that we can document the religious community as fulfilling the role of the Temple.[25] No notion of the atoning role of an individual appears in the scrolls.

6. Role of Purity

When we come to discuss the role of ritual purity in the various texts found at Qumran, we find a common thread that runs throughout. Put simply, ritual purity is a pillar on which Judaism rests. All groups represented in the Qumran texts sought to extend ritual purity from the realm of Temple cult to that of everyday life. All these groups constructed boundaries among themselves dependent on the purity regulations they observed.

Some scholars have viewed the mass of minute regulations on ritual purity in Rabbinic texts as part of a theoretical framework invented by the Rabbis when there no longer was a Temple. This theory is similar to the assumption that the laws of Leviticus were all invented after the destruction of the First Temple, when priests had nothing to do but to expand their cultic regulations. In our case, the mass of purity regulations from Qumran, including newly published purification ritual texts, show that this is far from the case. Matters of ritual purity were central issues at this time. Further, it is impossible to maintain that purity was devoid of true religious significance. The Qumran texts, in material deriving from or pertaining to all the groups of Second Temple Jews, make clear that purity is not just a ritual. Rather, it is a spiritual state of mind, an ethic and a way of life.

It is only on this basis that one can understand the institution of baptism in Christianity. While there is no question to my mind that Christian baptism is dependent on Jewish proselyte immersion,[26] it is also to be compared with the role played by immersion in the Dead Sea sect. There we find that immersion is connected intimately with the initiation process. Only upon achieving specific levels in the novitiate were entrants permitted to partake of purification rituals. In this manner, baptism served the early Christian community as a rite of initiation from paganism into the new community.

7. Messianism

Central to the two Jewish revolts against Rome on the one hand, and to the rise of Christianity on the other hand, is the issue of messianism. Here again, the discovery and publication of the scrolls have caused a new understanding of the history of the messianic idea in early, post-biblical Judaism. My remarks here will be limited to the eschatology of the Qumran sect, for the documents from Qumran do not allow us to speak definitively about other groups.

Elsewhere, I have surveyed the references to messianic figures, periods of history, and the end of days in the texts of the Qumran sect.[27] It emerges from that study that a variety of motifs and beliefs are distributed in what may even appear to be a random fashion through different types of texts. Either we are dealing with an example of the historical development of ideas, or of parallel approaches, or, most likely, of a combination of these factors.[28]

I would propose to augment the quest for a historical explanation by recognizing the various messianic trends which existed in Second Temple Judaism. Shemaryahu Talmon is guided by the programmatic essay of Gershom Scholem entitled "Toward an Understanding of the Messianic Idea in Judaism."[29] Scholem set out to understand the dominant trends in Jewish messianism and the tension between them. He identified two poles—restorative and utopian messianism. The restorative seeks to bring back the ancient glories whereas the utopian constructs a view of an even better future, one which surpasses all that ever came before. The restorative can be described as a much more rational messianism, expecting only the improvement and perfection of the present world. The utopian is much more apocalyptic in character, looking forward to vast catastrophic changes in the world with the coming of the messianic age. Neither of these approaches exists independently of the other; rather, both are found in the messianic aspirations of the various Jewish groups. But the balance or creative tension between these tendencies is what determines the character of the messianism in question.

I have traced the roots of this distinction through biblical and early Second Temple literature in a previous study.[30] What is important for our purposes is that these two approaches, the restorative and the utopian, ultimately are based on different biblical traditions. The utopian is influenced by the Day of the Lord motif and the apocalyptic visions of Daniel. Such a perfect world can only be built supposing the destruction of this world with its widespread evil and transgression. The restorative is based on the prophetic vision of a reconstituted Davidic monarchy as well as on hopes for the reestablishment of Israel's power and prosperity.

With this background, we can return to the Qumran corpus. Those texts which espouse the Davidic messiah tend toward the restorative. They therefore emphasize much more the prophecies of peace and prosperity and do not expect the cataclysmic destruction of all evil. The more catastrophic, utopian, or even apocalyptic tendencies usually do not envisage a Davidic messiah. They seek instead to invest authority in a dominant priestly, religious leader and a temporal prince who is to be subservient to him. In this case, where there are two messiahs, there is no requirement of Davidic descent, and the prominent role of the priesthood in the life of the sect is transposed onto the end of days. Some of the utopians sought to limit the leadership to one messianic figure, yet he is not said to be Davidic. Sometimes we may encounter both trends side by side in the same text, influencing its author equally. The appearance of these two trends testifies to the beginning of the long process of their fusion into what later became the messianic ideal of Rabbinic Judaism.

For the Qumran sectarians, it was in the end of days that their aspirations for perfection and holiness in regard to the observance of Jewish law were to be realized. After the eschatological battle in which the wicked were to be destroyed, the sect would assemble for a communal banquet under the leadership of the two messianic figures.[31]

While I do not wish to ignore the historical factor, it is highly doubtful that we will ever be able to construct an exact historical sequence of the messianic ideas and texts found at Qumran. Yet a matrix of history on the one axis and the restorative-utopian dichotomy on the other is the only framework within which to explain the rich and variegated eschatological ideas and approaches which are represented in the literature of the Dead Sea sect. The study of the eschatological materials in the Qumran sectarian texts should again caution us against seeing the materials found in the Qumran caves as a monolithic corpus, the elements of which may be harmonized with one another at will.

The strong tendencies of the Qumran sect and other apocalyptic groups in the Second Temple period towards immediate messianism are manifested in both the rise of Christianity and in the two Jewish revolts against Rome in 66–73 and 132–35 C.E. Investigation of the sources describing the various groups of rebels shows that a number of them were motivated by the messianic pretensions of their leaders or by apocalyptic hopes. This was certainly true for the Bar Kokhba revolt.

In Christianity, the twin motifs of restorative and utopian messianism are both seen to be realized in Jesus. He is carefully tied by the New Testament writers to the Davidic house. At the same time he is cast in the role of the eschatological priest. In both roles, he presides over the eschatological banquet. The immediacy of the Christian messianic claims, as well as the apocalyptic language with which these claims are described, can only be understood against this background. Pharisaism would not, as far as we know, have developed this kind of messianism.

The messianism of Rabbinic Judaism can be traced historically. Initially, in the Mishnaic period, messianism is of a restorative character in which the Davidic king and the Temple and its high priest are expected to be revived. Yet the apocalyptic tendencies observable at Qumran and elsewhere in Second Temple times begin to receive stress in the Rabbinic tradition in amoraic times, especially in Babylonia.[32] These two tendencies, then, coexist throughout the subsequent history of Judaism, being manifested in differing degrees in various periods.

The recent release of the entire Qumran corpus has ignited a controversy regarding two specific texts which have been considered by some to relate to Christian messianism. The first of these, the Aramaic text which seems to refer to a messianic figure and may say that he will be called "son of God," among other titles, has been claimed in some quarters to be the hidden, secret text which led to the delay in publication of the Dead Sea Scrolls. In view of the publication of this text in 1974 this claim is without any foundation.[33] If this interpretation is correct, this fragmentary text would show that we have only begun to appreciate the extent to which Christian messianism draws on the approaches to Judaism that existed in the Land of Israel in the Second Temple period. On the other hand, this text can also be taken as referring to the boasting of some Selucid ruler and would then have no relevance at all to the background of Christianity.

The second document has been claimed in the press to be a description of the piercing of the messiah. While the text in question does draw on Isaiah 10:33–11:4, it is in reality connected to the tradition of the eschatological war, and it describes the death of the Romans at the hands of the sect and its leader, not the death of the leader of the sect or of a messianic figure. Hence, it is totally irrelevant to the issue of Christian messianism.[34]

Conclusions

The discovery of the Dead Sea Scrolls has presented us with the opportunity to learn a great deal not only about the group which collected the "ancient library," but about the entire constellation of sects which existed in the Second Temple period. As texts from the Qumran caves continue to be published, our knowledge about the background against which early Christianity came into existence and Rabbinic Judaism developed will become clearer. We will see that ideas and practices which we could date no earlier than the destruction of the Temple can now be shown to be considerably earlier. The Rabbis will be increasingly seen as inheritors of tradition, who expanded, developed and adapted that tradition to a new time which brought with it new circumstances, most notably the destruction of the Temple and the cessation of sacrificial worship. The early Christians will be increasingly understood to have inherited a variety of apocalyptic and sectarian traditions from Second Temple times which they molded and reshaped into the immediate messianism and realized eschatology of early Christianity.

The scrolls have opened up for us a new method of looking at the development of these two movements which emerged from Greco-Roman Palestine. As the common origins and shared prehistory of Rabbinic Judaism and early Christianity become clearer and more detailed, the differences between the two faiths are better highlighted as well. It can therefore be hoped that the two millennia of strife can be replaced by a new era in which common interests and shared commitments can be the basis for our relationships, even while recognizing the deep differences which divide us.

Endnotes

1. The classic statement of this approach is E. Schürer, *A History of the Jewish People in the Time of Jesus Christ* (New York: Charles Scribner's Sons, 1891), 2 (pt. ii): 10–43, 190–218. Contrast the revised edition, *The History of the Jewish People in the Age of Jesus Christ*, ed. G. Vermes, F. Millar, M. Black (Edinburgh: T.& T. Clark, 1979), 2:388–414, 558–590.

2. This view is typified by G.F. Moore, *Judaism* (Cambridge: Harvard University Press, 1927), 1:3.

3. S. Schechter, *Fragments of a Zadokite Work*, *Documents of Jewish Sectaries*, vol. 1 (Cambridge, UK: Cambridge University Press, 1910).

4. Schürer (n. 1, 1979 ed.), 2:570.

5. L. Ginzberg, *Eine unbekannte jüdische Sekte* (New York, 1922), trans. with additional chapters as *An Unknown Jewish Sect* (New York: Jewish Theological Seminary, 1976).

6. F. M. Cross, *The Ancient Library of Qumran and Modern Biblical Studies*, rev. ed., (Garden City, NY: Doubleday, 1961).

7. "The Early History of the Qumran Community," *New Directions in Biblical Archaeology*, ed. D.N. Freedman, J.C. Greenfield (Garden City, NY: Doubleday, 1971), 70–89.

8. L.H. Schiffman, *Sectarian Law in the Dead Sea Scrolls*, *Courts*, *Testimony and the Penal Code* (Chico, CA: Scholars Press, 1983), 13f.; H. Stegemann, "The Origins of the Temple Scroll," *Suppl. to VT* 40 (1988): 235–246.

9. L.H. Schiffman, "The Dead Sea Scrolls and the Early History of Jewish Liturgy," *The Synagogue in Late Antiquity*, ed. L.I. Levine (Philadelphia: American Schools of Oriental Research, 1987), 38f.; J.M. Baumgarten, "4 Q 503 (Daily Prayers) and the Lunar Calendar," *RQ* 12 (1986): 399–407.

10. B. Menahot 65a.

11. N. Golb, "Who Wrote the Dead Sea Scrolls," *The Sciences* 27 (May/June 1987): 40–49, maintains that the scrolls are the library of the Jerusalem Temple which was deposited in the caves during the Great Revolt against Rome in 66–73 C.E. The fact that this collection of documents leans heavily toward the sectarian tendencies of Essene-like groups, and castigates the Jerusalem establishment and Temple practice at every turn, makes impossible this claim. The materials were certainly collected by a dissident group. Yet Golb is correct that the scrolls represent much more than the compositions of the Dead Sea sect, as observed above.

12. See E. Qimron, J. Strugnell, "An Unpublished Halakhic Letter from Qumran," *Biblical Archaeology Today*, ed. J. Amitai (Jerusalem: Israel Exploration Society, 1985), 400–407.

13. I thank Professor John Strugnell for allowing me the opportunity to read this text and the draft of the commentary he and Prof. Elisha Qimron are preparing.

14. See my study, "*The Temple Scroll* and the Systems of Jewish Law of the Second Temple Period," *Temple Scroll Studies*, ed. G.J. Brooke, (Sheffield: JSOT Press, 1989), 245-251, and Y. Sussmann, "The History of *Halakha* and the Dead Sea Scrolls—Preliminary Observations on *Miqsat Ma'ase Ha-Torah* (4QMMT)" (Hebrew), *Tarbiz* 59 (1989-90): 11-76.

15. "The Pharisaic-Sadducean Controversies about Purity and the Qumran Texts," *JJS* 31 (1980): 157-170. Cf. M. Lehmann, "The Temple Scroll as a Source of Sectarian Halakha," *RQ* 9 (1978): 579-587.

16. See L.H. Schiffman, *The Halakhah at Qumran* (Leiden: E.J. Brill, 1975); idem, *Sectarian Law in the Dead Sea Scrolls, Courts, Testimony and the Penal Code* (Chico, CA: Scholars Press, 1983).

17. S. Talmon, "The New Covenanters of Qumran," *Scientific American* 225, no. 5 (1971): 76-78; cf. his "Types of Messianic Expectation at the Turn of the Era," *King Cult and Calendar in Ancient Israel* (Jerusalem: Magnes Press, 1986), 202-224.

18. Schiffman, *Halakhah at Qumran* (n. 16), 22-76.

19. See W. H. Brownlee, *The Midrash Pesher of Habakkuk*, Society of Biblical Literature Monograph Series, no. 24 (Missoula, MT: Scholars Press, 1979), 23-36; M.P. Horgan, *Pesharim: Qumran Interpretations of Biblical Books*, Catholic Biblical Quarterly Monograph Series, no. 8 (Washington, DC: Catholic Biblical Association of America, 1979), 229-259.

20. The *Temple Scroll* shares some characteristics of this genre, except that it concerns only biblical law.

21. L.H. Schiffman, "The King, his Guard, and the Royal Council in the *Temple Scroll*," *PAAJR* 54 (1987): 257-259.

22. However we explain the animal bones buried around the buildings at Qumran, we cannot see them as the remains of sacrifices, since the texts foreclose this option. See Schiffman, *Sectarian Law (n. 16)*, 200-201.

23. B.Z. Wacholder, M.G. Abegg, *A Preliminary Edition of the Unpublished Dead Sea Scrolls, The Hebrew and Aramaic Texts from Cave Four*, Fascicle One (Washington, DC: Biblical Archaeological Society, 1991), 60-101 have published calendrical texts which include methods for harmonizing the lunar and solar calendars. See pp. x and 68.

24. Schiffman and Baumgarten (n. 9).

25. See B. Gärtner, *The Temple and the Community in Qumran and the New Testament* (Cambridge, UK: Cambridge University Press, 1965).

26. See L.H. Schiffman, *Who Was a Jew? Rabbinic and Halakhic Perspectives on the Jewish-Christian Schism* (Hoboken, NJ: Ktav, 1985), 25-29.

27. "Messianic Figures and Ideas in the Qumran Scrolls," *The Messiah: Developments in Earliest Judaism and Christianity*, ed. J.H. Charlesworth, Anchor Bible Reference Library (New York: Doubleday, 1992), 116-129.

28. J. Starcky ("Les quatres étapes du messianisme à Qumran," *RB* 70 [1963]: 481–505) sought to construct a history of the messianic idea at Qumran which went hand in hand with the stages in the archaeologically attested occupation of the site. In the Maccabean period the teacher authored the *Thanksgiving Scroll* and the *Rule of the Community*. Messianic expectations do not appear in the hymns, and the earliest manuscript of the *Rule of the Community* does not contain the messianic allusion. Hence, Starcky concluded that messianic speculation was absent in this period. In the Hasmonean period, Pharisaic influence led to the presence of messianism in the *Rule* (1QS), as well as in its appendices. Here we find the notion of two messiahs. In the Pompeian period, he identifies the references in the *Zadokite Fragments* where the two messiahs have become one priestly figure. The teacher was the eschatological prophet, the interpreter of the law. In the last period, the Herodian, the anti-Roman feeling exemplified in the *War Scroll* developed. It seems to me, however, that as already noted by J.A. Fitzmyer ("The Aramaic 'Elect of God' Text from Qumran," *Essays on the Semitic Background of the New Testament* [Missoula, MT: Scholars Press, 1974], 129–140) there are numerous problems with this theory. In my view, chief among them is the presumption that the *Zadokite Fragments* should be dated much later than the *Rule of the Community* and the assumption that the omission of material in the still unpublished MS. E can indeed be taken as evidence for the history of the text. Furthermore, the claim that the messianic idea only entered through Pharisaic influence is a gross over-simplification. Finally, the theory in no way accounts for Davidic vs. non-Davidic lay messiahs.

29. *The Messianic Idea in Judaism* (New York: Schocken Books, 1971), 1–36; cf. Talmon, *King* (n. 17), 202–224.

30. L.H. Schiffman, "The Concept of the Messiah in Second Temple and Rabbinic Literature," *Review and Expositor* 84 (1987): 235–246.

31. See L.H. Schiffman, *The Eschatological Community of the Dead Sea Scrolls, A Study of the Rule of the Congregation*, Society of Biblical Literature Monograph Series, no. 38 (Atlanta: Scholars Press, 1989), 53-67.

32. Schiffman, "The Concept of the Messiah in Second Temple and Rabbinic Literature" (n. 30), 243–245; cf. J. Neusner, *Messiah in Context* (Philadelphia: Fortress, 1984), 167–212.

33. J.A. Fitzmyer, "The Contribution of Qumran Aramaic to the Study of the New Testament," *NTS* 20 (1974): 391–394. The text is fully published in É. Puech, "Fragment d'une apocalypse en Araméen (4Q246=pseudo-Dan^{d}) et le 'royaume de Dieu'," *RB* 99 (1992): 98–131.

34. See G. Vermes, "The Oxford Forum for Qumran Research: Seminar on the Rule of War from Cave 4 (4Q285)," *JJS* 43 (1992): 85–90; idem., "The 'Pierced Messiah Text'—An Interpretation Evaporates," *BAR* 18, no. 4 (1992): 80–82; see, however, the reopening of the discussion by J.D. Tabor, "A Pierced or Piercing Messiah?—The Verdict is Still Out," and Vermes' reply, *BAR* 18, no. 6 (1992): 58–59. In this matter, the view of Vermes is to be accepted, as the reading of the others violates Hebrew grammar, ignores context, and fails to take into account the final line of the fragment.

Suggestions For Further Reading

An excellent but dated introduction to the Dead Sea Scrolls is Yigael Yadin, *The Message of the Scrolls* (New York: Simon and Schuster, 1957). The archaeological aspect is discussed thoroughly in Roland de Vaux, *Archaeology and the Dead Sea Scrolls* (London: Oxford, 1973). Important scholarly studies are Frank Moore Cross, Jr., *The Ancient Library of Qumran and Modern Biblical Studies*, rev. ed., (Garden City, NY: Doubleday, 1961) and Geza Vermes, *The Dead Sea Scrolls: Qumran in Perspective* (Philadelphia: Fortress, 1978). The theology of the sect is studied in Helmer Ringgren, *The Faith of Qumran* (Philadelphia: Fortress, 1963). On the relationship of Christianity, see Matthew Black, *The Scrolls and Christian Origins* (London: SCM Press, 1961) and William Sanford LaSor, *The Dead Sea Scrolls and the New Testament* (Grand Rapids, MI: Eerdmans, 1972). Two studies of the importance of the scrolls for the history of Jewish law are Lawrence H. Schiffman, *The Halakhah at Qumran* (Leiden: E.J. Brill, 1975), and *Sectarian Law in the Dead Sea Scrolls* (Chico, CA: Scholars Press, 1983). On messianism at Qumran, see L.H. Schiffman, *The Eschatological Community of the Dead Sea Scrolls, A Study of the Rule of the Congregation*, Society of Biblical Literature Monograph Series, no. 38 (Atlanta: Scholars Press, 1989). For a general survey of the period, see L.H. Schiffman, *From Text to Tradition, A History of Second Temple and Rabbinic Judaism* (Hoboken, NJ: Ktav, 1991). A sampling of recent scholarship is available in Herschel Shanks, ed., *Understanding the Dead Sea Scrolls, A Reader from the Biblical Archaeology Review* (New York: Random House, 1992). A convenient way to keep abreast of developments in Dead Sea Scrolls research is by reading the magazines *Biblical Archaeology Review* and *Bible Review.*

PAUL THE PHARISEE

Lawrence E. Frizzell

St. Paul came from the Greek city of Tarsus in Asia Minor. Called Saul in Hebrew, Paul was probably his Greek name from childhood. He belonged to the Diaspora, or the Dispersion—the millions of Jews dwelling outside Palestine. Trained in the outlook of the Pharisees, the young Saul studied in Jerusalem with Rabban Gamaliel, an outstanding Pharisee teacher. After the crucifixion, Saul participated in the persecution of Jesus' Jewish followers, but then underwent a spiritual transformation and became a convert to Christ and a zealous missionary to both Jews and Gentiles. Lawrence E. Frizzell treats Paul's teachings, particularly his ethical outlook, in relationship to Judaism and Paul's acceptance of Jesus as redeemer.

St. Paul would never have dreamed that his words and work would be the basis for a literature of enormous proportions.[1] Even the simple question about the background of Saul of Tarsus, also known as Paul (Acts 13:9), can be the basis for investigating everything that he wrote, as well as the narratives from the Acts of the Apostles and other early Christian texts.[2] This paper will be divided into four major sections, reviewing the statements by and about Paul concerning his origins, evidence of his attitude toward prayer, his interpretation of the Hebrew Bible, and the thrust of his teaching concerning the moral order.

1. "A Hebrew of Hebrews..." (Phil 3:5)

At several points in the major epistles St. Paul alludes to his Jewish origins. The most detailed list is found in Philippians. "Circumcised on the eighth day, of the people (race) of Israel, of the tribe of Benjamin, a Hebrew of Hebrews, in observance of the Law a Pharisee, in zeal I persecuted the church, in righteousness based on the Law I was blameless" (3:5–6).

Paul indicates first that he was not a proselyte, but was circumcised in infancy according to the law (Gn 17:12; Lv 12:3). This means that he belonged to the people of Israel (a title of honor often used in the liturgy). One recalls that only three tribes survived after the vicissitudes of the First Temple period (the ten tribes of the North Kingdom disappeared in exile after 721 B.C.E.), each with its particular dignity: the Levites (with various privileges and functions relating to the Temple and Torah), the Judaeans (from whom the Messiah, Son of David, would come), and Benjaminites (whose ancestor was the only patriarch born in Israel, the tribe of the first king over Israel).[3] "Hebrew of Hebrews" probably means that his parents maintained the custom of speaking Aramaic (and perhaps Hebrew) in their home, even when they lived in the dispersion.[4] Only in Acts is there explicit reference to Paul's facility with "Hebrew," which may mean Aramaic (Acts 21:40; 22:2; 26:14), but letters written in Greek offered little occasion to demonstrate such knowledge.

During the late Second Temple period (after 100 B.C.E.), there were several approaches to the interpretation of the Torah or "instruction" preserved in the five books of Moses. Under priestly leadership, the Sadducees (who claimed to descend from Zadok, high priest in King Solomon's time), maintained that teaching was their prerogative. The Pharisees were educated laymen who believed that God gave Moses an oral Torah to complement the written Pentateuch. They considered themselves to be heirs of the prophetic tradition. The Pharisee Paul, like Jesus and the early disciples, recognized the legitimacy of Sadducean priestly leadership in the Temple; he held that earnest study under proper guidance would provide insights showing how to live according to the commandments. The priests were respected as mediators of cult but were not recognized to have an exclusive right to interpret the written Torah.

Although Paul does not give details about his education, Luke credits him with a statement that he was a Jew born in Tarsus in Cilicia but brought up in Jerusalem.[5] "At the feet of Gamaliel I was educated strictly in our ancestral law and was zealous for God, just as all of you are today" (Acts 22:3). Although exegetes a generation ago were often skeptical about the historicity of material in Acts,[6] this point about Paul's education is taken seriously by several noted scholars.[7] Gamaliel I was a great teacher who flourished in Jerusalem from approximately 20–50 C.E. The wonderfully irenic plea to let the early Christians practice their faith because "if this activity is of human origin it will destroy itself" is attributed to him (Acts 5:38–39). Some have objected that the intolerant young man named Saul could not have studied under such a tolerant master.[8] However, anyone in higher education during the past three decades knows that such inconsistencies can happen!

"In zeal I persecuted the church..." (Phil 3:6). This brief statement reminds us of an earlier description of Paul's young adult life. "You have heard of my former life in Judaism, how I persecuted the church of God violently and tried to destroy it; and I advanced in Judaism beyond many of my own age among my people, so extremely zealous was I for the traditions of my fathers" (Gal 1:13–14).[9] Although Paul was not a "Zealot" (i.e. a member of the group committed to expulsion of the Roman presence from Judaea) he did belong to a long tradition of total adherence to the God of Israel. "Zeal was more than just a fervent commitment to the Torah; it denoted a willingness to use violence against any—Jews, Gentiles, or the wicked in general—who were contravening, opposing, or subverting the Torah. Further, a zealot was willing to suffer and die for the sake of the Torah..."[10] The description in Acts 8:3; 9:1, 14; and 26:9–12 implies that Saul was very active and commissioned by the chief priests to persecute followers of Jesus far and wide. One has the impression that this covered a considerable period of time. Most scholars consider the statement that Saul cast his vote for the death penalty (Acts 26:10) to mean that he was a judge in the tribunal but construe this to be Luke's literary creation. There are two opinions among those who accept its historicity. Jerome Murphy-O'Connor calls Saul a junior colleague of Gamaliel in the Sanhedrin; however, Simon Legasse thinks that the "vote" may have been only his personal consent to a decision of higher authority. The death of Stephen, the first Christian martyr, was approved by Saul in this way (Acts 8:11; 22:20).[11]

As a Christian, Paul on occasion manifested a fiery temper, leading him to write some things that embarrass his readers in our age when people value tolerance (at least in theory). Reacting against other Christian teachers, possibly converts from gentile background, who call Gentiles to full observance of the Torah, Paul calls them dogs (Phil 3:2) and wishes that they mutilate themselves (Gal 5:12). The invective against "the Jews" (perhaps to be rendered "Judaeans" in the geographical sense of dwellers in Judaea) in the first letter to the Thessalonians (2:14–16) is not only extremely violent but includes a gentile accusation that the "Jews oppose all men," an unjustified general statement that Jews were obnoxious and intolerant. Some have argued that this is an interpolation by a scribe of gentile origin, but every manuscript contains the passage.[12] It is common in many cultures for an angry person to use labels and "racist" statements against one of his own group. However, no weight would be given to those phrases when calm has been restored. Paul exhibited a Mediterranean temper on occasion and perhaps is to be credited with the sage advice: "Do not let the sun go down on your anger!" (Eph 4:26). In any case, since passages like 1 Thessalonians 2:13–16 are part of the canon of the New Testament, Christians must grapple with them. In no case should they be a basis for anti-Jewish sentiments of theological judgment;[13] there are other more detailed texts (such as Rom 9–11) which provide elements for a balanced synthesis.

In ancient as well as modern times, religious (and political) groups use titles descriptive of their ideals and role in society. As the Qumran Scrolls indicate, such names were often contrasted with descriptions of others. "Sons of light" evokes the title "sons of darkness" for Qumran's enemies; "sons of righteousness" are contrasted with "sons of iniquity." In his letter to the Romans, Paul purports to address "a Jew" about the danger of complacency regarding his knowledge of God's will. He seems to turn some of the titles (such as "guide for the blind") used by Pharisees and other Jews against them. "If you are sure that you are a guide to the blind, a light to those who are in darkness, a corrector of the foolish, a teacher of children...you who teach others, will you not teach yourself?" (Rom 2:19–21). While the people of Qumran had little hope even for their fellow Jews, let alone the Gentiles, the Pharisees and Jews in the Diaspora actively sought out and encouraged those searching for enlightenment. Several scholars ask: Was Saul a Jewish missionary? Ernest Best writes: "If before his conversion Paul had been a Jewish missionary seeking to win converts to Judaism, his conversion would have made it reasonably easy for him to understand the need to win them to Christ."[14] If we take seriously the statements in Acts about Saul's education followed by his service of the high priest in attempting to subdue Jewish Christians and then add years as Jewish missionary, we portray an extremely active young man! Why not suggest that he learned about such proselytizing efforts from Jewish visitors to Jerusalem?

Should one take remuneration for teaching about God and the Torah? This question is answered in the gospels and Paul's letters. Because Levites had no share in the land, the ancient tradition sanctioned tithes for their maintenance, and Jesus taught that spiritual blessings could be best appreciated when a mutual sharing taught people to be responsible for each other. The best way to understand Jesus' "mission sermon" (Mt 10:5–42 and Lukan parallels) is from the background of pilgrimage within the Judaism of his time.[15] The apostles sent on mission by Jesus were focused on the kingdom of God like pilgrims on the way to Jerusalem. This dedication precluded working for a livelihood.

As laymen, however, the Pharisees may have sensed the danger inherent in linking spiritual and economic orders. "Excellent is the study of Torah together with a secular occupation" (Mishnah Abot 2:2). This statement is attributed to Rabban Gamaliel, son of Rabbi Judah the Prince; therefore it is dated to the early third century C.E. The idea could well have its roots in the Second Temple period, when priestly privileges and the tithing system were still in place. Paul acknowledged the right to receive his livelihood from the community but did not take advantage of it (1 Cor 9:1–5).

Although some scholars debate whether young Saul would have learned a trade while studying with Gamaliel, he could well have acquired his skill as a tentmaker from his father. "Whoever does not teach his son a trade teaches him to be a robber" (Tosefta Qiddushin 1, 11).[16] Where he learned his craft is of little importance. The reason he practiced it was to avoid being a burden on the communities where he taught (1 Thes 2:9; 2 Thes 3:6; 1 Cor 9:1–5). Of course, the workshop would be a place for Paul to meet a wide range of people and an appropriate setting for discussion.[17]

2. The Man of Prayer

As a pious Jew, Saul would have cultivated the habit of praying at certain times of the day. He would have recited the *Shema'* (Dt 6:4–9, etc.) in the evening and morning; no doubt he linked his prayer with the offering of sacrifices in the Temple at the appropriate hours. He would have developed a deep appreciation for the sabbath and the annual cycle of feasts and fast days. Both in daily prayers and on the feasts he would have sensed a union with Temple worship. The history of Israel's movement from Egyptian servitude to the covenant at Mount Sinai and the gift of the land would have been experienced in the three great pilgrimage feasts (Dt 16).

In the synagogue and probably in daily life the psalms would have been an inspiration to the young Pharisee; he would have blessed God in gratitude and praise, both in formal benedictions and spontaneous acts of praise. A century later Rabbi Meir would declare that each person should utter a hundred spontaneous blessings each day. No doubt the practice of expressing gratitude to God, not only at meals but on many other occasions, would have been taught already in Saul's time. He would have fasted on Mondays and Thursdays (the days half way between the previous and coming sabbath) and so prepared for the celebration of God's gift of sabbath peace.

The mature missionary, dictating letters required because of absence from communities he had founded, manifests both his Jewish heritage and his commitment to Jesus as the Christ. He must have instructed his communities in the use of the Jewish Scriptures, in their Greek garb known as the Septuagint, especially the Psalms. He would have taught them that all prayers of petition must be in the plural and placed within the framework of the blessing (eucharist) for gifts already received. Everything in life must be submitted to the divine will.

Paul's style of writing is saturated by prayerful language, shaped and formed by his awareness of divine presence and activity in the world.[18] His greetings in the introduction to a letter include both Greek and Hebrew elements (grace and peace), both imbued with the spiritual meaning of the biblical heritage.[19] Each letter (even the one to the Galatians, which does not have an initial greeting) has a prayer-filled petition or doxology (Rom 16:25–27) as its conclusion. The mention of a divine title is completed with a blessing (Rom 1:25; 9:5; 2 Cor 11:31). A doxology will complete a major reflection (Rom 11:33–36; 16:27; Phil 1:11).

Like other early Christian teachers, Paul explained aspects of Jesus' life and work, especially his death and resurrection, with reference to the Temple, the sacrificial worship, and the feasts.[20]

3. Teacher of the Jewish Scriptures

Early in this century it was suggested that "a scholarly Christian Jew raked through the Old Testament in order to write a handbook for Paul to carry around on his journeys. In fact Paul did not need one. With his own thorough training as a Pharisee, he had his own vast store of knowledge both of the Old Testament itself and of contemporary exegesis, which he drew on constantly in the course of his missionary labours. He made use of texts already well established in Christian discourse, and also added to this much further biblical material, as the need arose."[21]

Where did Paul stand in relation to the other apostles in education? Would he have been the equivalent of a graduate student under Gamaliel, while the others were in high school? One should not underestimate their exposure to the Jewish heritage, biblical and liturgical, in the synagogue service and *beth-midrash* or classroom. Moreover, they were in the company of Jesus for a considerable length of time. The gospel traditions show that he used the Bible in its liturgical context as the foundation for many of his teachings and debates. He is presented as having precise methods for interpreting the scriptures.[22] Already the House of Hillel in the Pharisee tradition is credited with having hermeneutical principles for grappling with problems in the biblical text.[23] If one accepts the statement of Acts 22:3 that Saul studied under Gamaliel, even for a brief period, and if the master was the grandson of the famous Hillel the Elder, then one may look for examples of the seven *middot* (rules) of Hillel in the epistles of the mature Paul. The great scholar Joachim Jeremias, who delved more into the Jewish tradition than most New Testament scholars of the period between 1920 and 1960, did just that.[24]

Jeremias began his study with a general reflection, the substance of which reads as follows:

> The Pauline letters show that their author not only lived his Bible but also possessed the contemporary tools for its interpretation. He knew *midrashim* (developments of the text to apply it to current needs of the community—Gal 3:19; 4:29; 1 Cor 10:1–4; 2 Cor 11: 3).... He linked key words of different passages and joined a Torah passage with a text from the prophets or writings (Rom 4:1f; 9:12f; 10:6f, 19, 21; 11:8; 12:19f; 15:9–12; 2 Cor 6:16–18).... While he is indebted to Hellenistic allegory in 1 Corinthians 9:9f, Paul's spiritual home is Palestinian exegesis, as shown by his preference for typology which sees the events of salvation history as portrayals of the end-time (1 Cor 10:1f; Gal 4:21–31; Rom 9:13).

Any Jew who frequented the synagogue during the Second Temple period could develop a certain facility with linking passages from different parts of the Hebrew Bible, as this was probably the practice of at least some homilists. In the texts of the Aramaic translation (*targum*) the Torah passages are sometimes expanded, and Paul seems to have drawn upon the amplification of Deuteronomy 30:11–14 in Romans 10:6–8.

The Aramaic translation of Deuteronomy 30:12–13 reads as follows, with additions to the Hebrew text in italics:

> The Instruction [Torah] is not in heaven that one might say: would that we had one *like the prophet Moses* who would ascend to heaven and bring it back for us and make us hear the commandments that we might do them. Neither is the Instruction beyond the Great Sea that one might say: Would that we had one *like Jonah the prophet* who would descend into the depths of the Great Sea and bring it up for us and make us hear the commandments that we might do them (Targum Neofiti at Dt 30:12–13).

After quoting Leviticus 18:5 (Rom 10:5; see Gal 3:12) to show that Moses taught that Jews practice the righteousness that is based on the Torah, Paul makes use of this passage in Deuteronomy. "But the righteousness based on faith says, Do not say in your heart: 'Who will descend into the abyss?' (that is, to bring Christ up from the dead). But what does it say? The word is near you, on your lips and in your heart (that is, the word of faith which we preach)..." (Rom 10:5–8).[25]

Paul refers the ascent to Christ, the one like unto Moses (Dt 18:15, 18) who brought the Torah from heaven. The descent of Jonah into the sea (exaggerated as "the abyss") is a sign of Jesus' descent into the grave and the underworld (see Mt 12:39–40; 14:4; Lk 11:29). So Paul points to the death and resurrection of Jesus, already accomplished, as the basis for righteousness rooted in faith as fulfillment of the work begun by Moses and Jonah.

Jeremias also tried to show that in his letters Paul used five of the seven rules of Hillel. The apostle argued from a minor premise to a conclusion, because a restriction regarding a small matter would certainly apply as well to something important (Rom 5:12–17; 11:12; 2 Cor 3:7–8; 9:11). On the other hand, if a permission is granted for something very important then the same should apply to a minor matter (Rom 5:6–10; 8:32; 11:24; 1 Cor 6:2–3). Analogy was used to show that a decision in a certain case would apply to a similar one. Thus, Paul uses Psalm 32:2–3 in Romans 4:1–12 to argue that forgiveness of sin applies to Gentiles because Abram was righteous before his circumcision, when his name was changed to Abraham (Gn 17:5). The relation between the general and the particular allowed Paul to teach that the detailed commandments of the Decalogue develop from the principle "Love you neighbor as yourself" (Lv 19:18 in Rom 13:9; Gal 5:14).

Rabbi Cohn-Sherbok concludes his study on Paul and rabbinic exegesis by remarking that "certain aspects of rabbinic exegesis, such as the expansion of Scriptural law, are absent from the Epistles. Yet like the Rabbis, Paul attempted to show that Scripture is sacred, that it is susceptible of interpretation, and that properly understood, it guides the life of the worthy. In proclaiming his Christian message, he employed standard techniques of Scripture exegesis, occasionally even using some of the rules of rabbinic hermeneutics. In this sense Paul's teaching and preaching are rooted in Pharisaic Judaism."[26]

These hermeneutical norms do have points in common with Greek approaches to logic and discourse.[27] It is possible that Paul acquired them from the heritage of Greek learning to which he was exposed. However, the Qumran Scrolls bear witness to the penetration of Greek ideas into the Jewish culture long before the time of Paul. Perhaps earlier Jewish teachers integrated these norms into their teaching, the tradition crediting Hillel the Elder with expressing them in a list of seven. Since Paul's use of the rules do not seem as refined as that of the rabbis, he has at times been called an amateur. On that point it might be noted that he was dictating letters destined for his congregation, not his peers. Moreover, the rabbinic examples were honed during a long period of oral transmission, wherein it is likely that only the most polished gems survived.

Shortly after Jeremias published his essay, Klaus Haacker objected that the points enumerated above need not indicate Paul's dependence on Hillel. Paul may have learned the argumentation from the early Christian community, not only for content but also the form. The love commandment is the nucleus of the early Christian interpretation of the law, just as it was stressed in Judaism, so the comprehensive commandment embracing the particular is not *Paul's* application of a Jewish principle. Use of such principles to develop an argument is not unique to Hillel and his school. Perhaps the young Saul belonged to the House of Shammai, which was strict and conservative on most issues where it differed from Hillel.[28]

About the same time Jacob Neusner questioned whether Gamaliel even belonged to the school of Hillel. "If Gamaliel was a member of the House of Hillel, the traditions never reflected it. The references to the members of the House of Gamaliel may mean that he himself conducted his own 'House'. All we know for sure is that Gamaliel traditions are curiously silent on the House of Hillel, but both make Gamaliel an authority for a member of the opposition, and have him rule like a Shammaite."[29]

Hans Hübner follows Haacker in linking Saul's background with the Shammaites.[30] However, it seems that the evidence he adduces, "the all-or-nothing" stance of Galatians 3:10 and 5:3, is too slight to allow such precision. The statement "Every man who receives circumcision is bound to keep the whole Law" (Gal 5:3) would surely be held by Hillel as well as Shammai, by the Sadducee as well as the Pharisee, and it would be stressed by the Qumran community as well. Differences would come when one asks how a particular commandment is to be observed. Those who acknowledge that Paul was Gamaliel's disciple can say that both were Pharisees. Evidence is scanty for giving greater precision to this affirmation.[31] Even if one is skeptical about Paul's dependence on Hillel and his school, the apostle's use of the same principles for interpreting scripture as did the rabbis should be maintained.

Recently two scholars have used the Psalms of Solomon to provide background for appreciating Paul's heritage as a Pharisee. Investigation of this possibility would require another study.[32]

4. The Torah and its Precepts

For many Christians and Christian scholars, the letters of Paul have constituted the center of the New Testament. An unfortunate aspect of the Lutheran tendency to pit law against grace, works against faith, was a reading of Paul that was often antinomian. Since 1977 a veritable revolution has taken place, provoked by the work of E.P. Sanders.[33] He studied the wide range of Jewish literature from the Second Temple period and also the traditions preserved in the Mishnah. Rather than dry "legalism" and a stultified religious experience, he found that George F. Moore (1851–1931) and Travers Herford (1860–1950) were right in their nuanced and positive presentations of the Pharisees.

Sanders calls the Jewish way of life "covenantal nomism." This pattern attributes salvation to God's gracious election of Israel, to its covenant status, and upholds obedience to the law as necessary not to *gain* but to *maintain* this covenantal status. "Paul used the term *nomos* in at least two quite distinct contexts, one discussing how one gets 'in' (not by works of the law) and the other in discussing how one who is 'in' behaves (keeping the law)."[34] This last rather colloquial statement means that entry into the covenant with God is a divine gift, whereas obedience to the commandments is the response upon which each person will be judged.

Sanders considers that Paul's thinking begins from a coherent center, which is the position that sharing in life through Christ is the only way to salvation. A generation ago some scholars sketched a psychological portrait of Paul in order to expose his quirks; others asked whether as a Diaspora Jew he was frustrated because of distance from the Temple. Now scholars are again reflecting primarily on the conversion-call that Paul designated as "a revelation of Jesus Christ" (Gal 1:12).[35]

We emphasize that the thrust of Paul's moral teaching bears the imprint of the gospel message, and that Jesus became his model as he continued to aspire for fulfillment of the great commandment to imitate God (Lv 19:2). However, just as Jesus built on the millennial heritage of the Jewish people, so did Paul.

The work of the English anthropologist, Mary Douglas, is very helpful in trying to enter the world-view of the Jewish people in the Second Temple period, and especially to recognize that the interpretation and application of the commandments constitute a cohesive whole.[36] Whether everyone in the tradition saw this picture clearly need not concern us, because they were *living* it.

The center of focus for Jewish life during this Second Temple period was the Temple, the place of God's dwelling with Israel and the unique place for sacrificial worship. The community's leaders were very concerned about the worthiness of all its members in relation to God. Ritual purity law prepared people for worship and for application of God's will to their daily lives. As devout lay people, the Pharisees held that the entire community constituted "a kingdom of priests, a holy nation" (Ex 19:6).

As much as possible, the Pharisees extended the ideals of priestly holiness and worship into the synagogues and homes of their communities. Of special importance were the laws regarding diet and marital life.

The pattern might be presented as follows:

place:	Temple	field-kitchen	home
agents:	priest-people	farmer-homemaker	husband-wife
focus:	altar	table	bed

The commandments governing service at the altar have their parallels for the Pharisees in those governing preparation of food (so that every meal can reflect God's presence) and sexual activities (so that the partners in marriage reflect the covenant bond between God and Israel). In the same way, the farmer and the person purchasing food as well as the husband and wife in marriage have particular responsibilities and roles, so that laws of tithing and cleanness of food and the commandments governing the menstrual cycle be respected. One might see all aspects of daily life as pointing to the Temple in Jerusalem, and this may have been the vision of many who united spiritually with the hours of sacrifice. "It is equally plausible that the Temple stands for the pure consecrated body of the worshipper and that the rules which protect sanctuary from defilement repeat by analogy the rules which protect the purity of the human body from wrong food and wrong sex, and the people of Israel from false gods."[37]

Although Paul fought to exempt the Gentiles who accepted Christianity from the detailed way in which eating was governed, he did wish to foster a sensitivity to the presence of God in all creation and especially in the Christian community. So he used Temple imagery to describe both the community and the individual Christian (1 Cor 3:9–17; 6:12–20). Each Christian is consecrated to God by baptism, plunging symbolically into the mystery of Christ's death-and-resurrection (Rom 6:1–4). This consecration must be lived out in the pilgrimage of human life, whether one is married or single (1 Cor 7:1–40). Paul continued to live according to the principles of the Pharisee tradition; even though he set aside the precepts of the Torah in certain areas of daily life, he instilled in his communities the insight rooted in the Bible and Jewish tradition that all human beings are created in the divine image and therefore are equal in God's sight and should be united in divine service. He deduced that the work of Jesus and the gift of union with God through baptism caused all political, social, and gender divisions to give way to a new situation willed by God. "There is neither Jew nor Greek, slave nor free, male nor female, for you are all one in Christ Jesus" (Gal 3:28).[38] Through faith all believers are united as children of one God (3:26); the union with Christ in baptism also makes them children of Abraham (3:29), heirs of him whose name means "Father of many nations" (Gen 17:5). This should lead Christians to appreciate their spiritual union with God's great olive tree, the people of Israel (Rom 11:17–24).

Endnotes

1. For surveys of recent work, see Hans Hübner, "Paulusforschung seit 1945," *Aufstieg und Niedergang der römischen Welt* (Berlin: Walter de Gruyter, 1987) II, 25.4, pp. 2649–2840 and O. Merk, "Paulus-Forschung," *Theologische Rundschau* 53 (1988): 1–81. On the general questions, see J. Plevnick, *What Are They Saying About Paul?* (Ramsey, NJ: Paulist Press, 1986).

2. Just as scholars evaluate Paul's own writings with care, early documents written about him must be assessed for bias for or against this provocative personality. The basic flaw of Hyam Maccoby's reconstruction of Paul's life (*The Mythmaker*) is the uncritical acceptance of second-century Ebionite writings (preserved only in fragments) as more accurate than any of Paul's own statements. Because the Jewish-Christian Ebionites were Torah-observant and enemies of Paul, their story that he was a proselyte should not be taken at face value. See reviews of *The Mythmaker: Paul and the Invention of Christianity* (San Francisco: Harper and Row, 1986) in the *Times Literary Supplement* of March 28, 1986, p. 336, by J.L. Houlden; and in *Theology* 90 (1987): 227–229 and 469–470, by M. Goulder; and the review article "Paul's Jewish Odyssey," *Judaism* 38 (1989): 225–234 by Ellis Rivkin. On this period, see Simon Legasse, "La polémique antipaulinienne dans le Judéo-Christianisme hétérodoxe," *Bulletin de Littérature Ecclésiastique* 90 (1989): 5–22, 85–100.

3. In Romans 11:1 Paul identifies himself as an Israelite, a descendant of Abraham, of the tribe of Benjamin; he has already strongly stressed his affiliation with the Jewish people (9:3). A similar text is found in 2 Cor 11:22.

4. In *Paulus der Apostel der Völker* (Tübingen: Mohr, 1989), Jürgen Becker comments that Paul's self-designation "Hebrew of Hebrews" emphasizes true observance of Jewish customs in his family. This would include knowledge of Aramaic. Because of his Pharisee upbringing he would have been able to read and understand the Hebrew Bible, even though in his letters to Greek-speaking Christians he naturally used the Septuagint (the first Greek translation of the Hebrew Bible), known widely in the Mediterranean world (p. 37). For the polemical context of Phil 3:5, see A.T. Hanson, "Who are the dogs?" *The Paradox of the Cross in the Thought of Paul* (Sheffield: Academic Press, 1987), 79–98.

5. See W.C. Van Unnik, *Tarsus or Jerusalem: The City of St. Paul's Youth* (London: Epworth, 1962)) for an extended argument in favor of Paul spending his childhood in Jerusalem, on the basis of the vocabulary in Acts 22:3. Acts 23:16 suggests that Paul's sister lived in Jerusalem. Jerome knew a story that Paul's family came from Gischala in Judaea (*De viris illustribus* 5 and *Commentary to Philemon* 23).

6. See F.F. Bruce, "Commentaries on Acts," *Bible Translator* 40 (1989): 315–321. On Luke's description of Paul, see Jakob Jervell, *The Unknown Paul: Essays on Luke-Acts and Early Christian History* (Minneapolis: Augsburg, 1984); Leander Keck, "Images of Paul in the New Testament," *Interpretation* 43 (1989): 341–351; David Moessner, "Paul in Acts: Preacher of eschatological repentance to Israel," *New Testament Studies* 34 (1988): 96–104.

7. Hübner (n. 1), 2658–2667. On Pharisaism, see D. Goodblatt, "The place of the Pharisee in first-century Judaism: The state of the debate," *Journal for Study of Judaism* 20 (1989): 12–30.

On the New Testament, see Klaus Berger, "Jesus als Pharisaer und frühe Christen als Pharisaer," *Novum Testamentum* (1988): 231–262.

8. For example, Ronald Hock, *The Social Context of Paul's Ministry: Tentmaking and Apostleship* (Philadelphia: Fortress Press, 1980), 22.

9. The deutero-Pauline tradition has Paul acknowledge that he had "formerly blasphemed and persecuted and insulted [Christ] but I received mercy because I had acted ignorantly in unbelief..." (1 Tm 1:13). See Michael Wolter, "Paulus der bekehrte Gottesfeind. Zur Verständnis von 1 Tim 1:13," *Novum Testamentum* 31 (1989): 48–66.

10. Terence L. Donaldson, "Zealot and convert: the origin of Paul's Christ-Torah antithesis," *Catholic Biblical Quarterly* 51 (1989): 655–682 at p. 673.

11. J. Murphy-O'Connor, *Becoming Human Together: The Pastoral Anthropology of St. Paul* (Wilmington, DE: Michael Glazier, 1982), 21–23; Simon Legasse disagrees in "Paul sanhédrite? A Propos d'Act. 26,10," *A Cause de l'Évangile: Études sur les Synoptiques et les Actes: pour Jacques Dupont* (Paris: Editions du Cerf, 1985), 2:799–807.

12. See F. Gilliard, "The problem of the antisemitic comma between 1 Thess. 2:14 and 15," *New Testament Studies* 35 (1989): 481–502; R. Penna, "L'évolution de l'attitude de Paul envers les juifs," *L'Apôtre Paul*, ed. A. Vanhoye (Louvain: Leuven University Press, 1986), 391–397.

13. Those who suggest an expurgated New Testament to simplify the challenge of Christian education should beware of the danger that we might neglect to struggle directly against the varied dimensions of anti-Jewish attitudes. The best way to deal with problem texts is to interpret them in the light of their time. Of course, such passages need not be proclaimed in the liturgy, where study is not always feasible. On the problems raised by 1 Thessalonians and ways to deal with them, see the essay in this volume by Norman A. Beck, no. 5.

14. E. Best, "The revelation to evangelize the Gentiles," *Journal of Theological Studies* 35 (1984): 21. The picture of such itinerant missionaries put forth by D. Georgi, *Die Gegner des Paulus in 2 Korintherbrief* (Neukirchen-Vluyn, 1964) has been questioned. See J. Collins, "Georgi's 'envoys' in 2 Cor. 11:23," *Journal of Biblical Literature* 93 (1974): 88–96 and Bowers, "Paul and religious propaganda in the first century," *Novum Testamentum* 22 (1980): 316–323.

15. L. Frizzell, "Pilgrimage: A study of the biblical experience," *Jeevadhara* 71 (1982): 358–367.

16. Here I argue against Ronald Hock, cited above (n. 8). He places Paul in a tradition of working Cynic philosophers but the examples he gives seem to offer sparse evidence when one considers the few earlier than Nero's time that he can cite. On tentmaking in general, especially in Tarsus, see Peter Lampe, "Paulus-Zeltmacher," *Biblische Zeitschrift* 31 (1987): 256–261. On 1 Thessalonians 4:9–11, see C.J. Roetzel, "Theodidaktoi and handwork in Philo and 1 Thessalonians," *L'Apôtre Paul*, ed. A. Vanhoye (Louvain: Leuven University Press, 1986), 324–331.

17. A point well made by Hock in "The workshop as a social setting for Paul's missionary preaching," *Catholic Biblical Quarterly* 41 (1979): 438–450.

18. Krister Stendahl, "Paul at prayer," *Interpretation* 34 (1980): 240. See Louis Monloubou, *Saint Paul et la Prière* (Paris: Editions du Cerf, 1982), and Roland Gebauer, *Das Gebet bei Paulus* (Basel: Brunnen Verlag, 1989).

19. See T.Y. Mullins, "Greetings as a New Testament form," *Journal of Biblical Literature* 87 (1968): 418–426; Gordon Wiles, *St. Paul's Intercessory Prayers* (Cambridge, UK: Cambridge University Press, 1974.

20. See H.J. Klauck, "Kultische Symbolsprache bei Paulus" in *Gemeinde Amt Sakramente: Neutestamentliche Perspektiven* (Würzburg: Echter, 1989); J. Ponthout, "L'expression cultuelle du ministère paulinien selon Rom. 15:16," *L'Apôtre Paul*, ed. A. Vanhoye (Louvain: Leuven University Press, 1986), 254–262.

21. B. Lindars, "The place of the Old Testament in the formation of New Testament theology," *New Testament Studies* 23 (1976): 63. See Richard B. Hays, *Echoes of Scripture in the Letters of Paul* (New Haven: Yale University Press, 1989).

22. See L. Frizzell, "Religious experience and interpretation: a Christian perspective," *Journal of Dharma* 5 (1980): 80–93; A. Finkel, "Comparative exegesis: a study of Hillel and Kerygma," ibid., pp. 109–122.

23. P.S. Alexander, "The rabbinic hermeneutical rules and the problem of the definition of midrash," *Proceedings of the Irish Biblical Association* 8 (1974): 97–120.

24. Joachim Jeremias, "Paul als Hillelit," *Neotestamentica et Semitica: Studies in Honor of Matthew Black*, ed. E.E. Ellis and M. Wilcox (Edinburgh: T & T Clark, 1969): 88–94. See H. Mueller, "Der rabbinische qal wa-chomer Schluss in paulinischer Typologie," *Zeitschrift für die neutestamentliche Wissenschaft* 58 (1967): 73–92 (on Rom 5:12–21); Dan Cohn-Sherbok, "Paul and rabbinic exegesis," *Scottish Journal of Theology* 35 (1982): 117–132; A.T. Hanson, *Studies in Paul's Techniques and Theology* (London: SPCK, 1974).

25. See S. Lyonnet, "Saint Paul et l'exégèse juive de son temps. À propos de Rom. 10, 6–8," *Mélanges Bibliques en honneur d'André Robert* (Paris: Bloud et Gay, 1957), 494–506; Martin McNamara, *The New Testament and the Palestinian Targum to the Pentateuch* (Rome: Pontifical Biblical Institute, 1966), 72–78.

26. Cohn-Sherbok (n. 24), 132. Concerning Paul's use of Jewish Scripture, see D. Moody Smith, "The Pauline Literature," *As It Is Written: Scripture Citing Scripture*, ed. D.A. Carson and H.G.M. Williamson (Cambridge, UK: Cambridge University Press, 1988), 265–291. For Luke's portrait of Paul, see F.F. Bruce, "Paul's use of the Old Testament in Acts," *Tradition and Interpretation in the New Testament: Essays for E.E. Ellis*, ed. G. Hawthorne (Grand Rapids: Eerdmans, 1987), 71–79.

27. See David Daube, "Rabbinic methods of interpretation and Hellenistic rhetoric," *Hebrew Union College Annual* (1949): 239–264.

28. K. Haacker, "War Paulus Hillelit?" *Institutum Judaicum der Universität Tübingen* (1971–1972), 106–120.

29. J. Neusner, *The Rabbinic Traditions about the Pharisees before 70*, pt. I, The Masters (Leiden: E.J. Brill, 1971), 376.

30. Hübner (n. 1), 2661.

31. See William Lane, "Paul's legacy from Pharisaism: Light from the Psalms of Solomon," *Concordia Journal* 8 (1982): 130–138; Dieter Lührmann, "Paul and the Pharisaic Tradition," *Journal for Study of the New Testament* 36 (1989): 75–94.

32. Joshua Efron, *Studies on the Hasmonean Period* (Leiden: E.J. Brill, 1987), 215–286, argues that these eighteen prayers are Christian texts.

33. E.P. Sanders, *Paul and Palestinian Judaism: A Comparison of Patterns of Religion* (Philadelphia: Fortress Press, 1977).

34. E.P. Sanders, *Paul, the Law and the Jewish People* (Philadelphia: Fortress Press, 1983), 10. On these and other recent studies, see Douglas Moo, "Paul and the Law in the last ten years," *Scottish Journal of Theology* 40 (1987): 287–307; Stephen Westerholm, *Israel's Law and the Church's Faith: Paul and his Recent Interpreters* (Grand Rapids: Eerdmans, 1988); Dieter Zeller, "Zur neueren Diskussion über das Gesetz bei Paulus," *Theologie und Philosophie* 62 (1987): 481–499; and Joseph Plevnick, "The center of Pauline theology," *Catholic Biblical Quarterly* 51 (1989): 461–478.

35. Donaldson (n. 10), 680–682.

36. A summary of her work as an appendix to Jacob Neusner, *The Idea of Purity in Judaism* (Leiden: E.J. Brill, 1973), 137–142, is very useful.

37. Douglas in Neusner (n. 36), 140.

38. Probably Paul lists these three groups as a reflection on the morning prayer of the Jewish man. This prayer reads: "Blessed are you, Lord our God, king of the universe, who have not made me a Gentile" (*goy*; *nokri* or stranger is found in some versions). "Blessed are you... who have not made me a slave. Blessed are you...who have not made me a woman." The rabbis interpreted this text in a non-chauvinist way, pointing to the fact that only the Jewish man had the privilege of keeping certain positive commandments. A Gentile was obligated only to the seven Noahide laws. A slave could not observe some commandments unless a benign master gave permission. A woman was exempt from all positive commandments linked to a specific time or place. Paul accepted Jesus as the Messiah; one of the results of his work was the transformation of the baptized into a new creation (Gal 6:15; 2 Cor 5:17), the first-fruits of the resurrection in the realm of faith. The great challenge for Christians is to live according to this teaching of what the unity of God implies! See John 17:1–24 and my article, "A Catholic Theological Reflection on Mission," *Journal of Dharma* 6 (1981): 141–150.

Suggestions For Further Reading

Bassler, Jouette M., ed. *Pauline Theology*. Vol. 1. *Thessalonians, Phillipians, Galatians, Philemon*. Minneapolis: Fortress Press, 1991. Several American specialists propose a methodology for understanding Paul's thought and interact with essays on five letters.

Dunn, James D.G. *Jesus, Paul, and the Law: Studies in Mark and Galatians*. Louisville: Westminster/John Knox, 1990. Journal essays from 1983–88 by a British scholar concerning "attitudes toward the Jewish law within earliest Christianity" are gathered in book form.

Harrington, Daniel. *Paul on the Mystery of Israel*. Collegeville: Liturgical Press, 1992. Popular level synthesis of recent scholarship on Paul's relation to Judaism and the Jewish people.

Hays, Richard B. *Echoes of Scripture in the Letters of Paul*. New Haven: Yale University Press, 1989. An evocative investigation of the way in which the biblical heritage has permeated the Pauline epistles.

Kaylor, R. David. *Paul's Covenant Community: Jew and Gentile in Romans*. Atlanta: John Knox, 1988. A study of the letter to the Romans to show "that God acted in Christ to unite Jew and Gentile in one covenant community."

Segal, Alan F. *Paul the Convert: The Apostolate and the Apostasy of Saul the Pharisee*. New Haven: Yale University Press, 1990. A Jewish scholar places Paul's mystical experience and conversion in their Jewish background and studies their effects in his exegesis and attitude toward the Torah.

Stockhausen, Carol Kern. *Moses' Veil and the Glory of the New Covenant*. Rome: Pontifical Biblical Institute, 1989. The exegetical substructure of 2 Corinthians 3:1–4:6. This is a doctoral dissertation showing the biblical background and interpretation of an important text in Paul for Jewish-Christian relations.

Tomson, Peter J. *Paul and the Jewish Law: Halakha in the Letters of the Apostle to the Gentiles*. Philadelphia: Fortress Press, 1992. Interpretation of the commandments for application to daily life (*halakha*) in Paul's epistles.

Westerholm, Stephen. *Israel's Law and the Church's Faith: Paul and His Recent Interpreters*. Grand Rapids: Eerdmans, 1988. A review and evaluation of innovative studies of Paul's thought on the law.

BIBLICAL, RABBINIC, AND EARLY CHRISTIAN ETHICS

Asher Finkel

What are the core principles of biblical ethics? How did the Pharisees, the Essenes, Jesus and the gospel writers, and Rabbinic Judaism interpret biblical ethics? What are the continuities and discontinuities between early Christian and Rabbinic ethics? These are the fundamental questions dealt with by Asher Finkel.

1. "*Imago Dei*" and the Polarity of Good and Evil

The ethical system of biblically oriented tradition, which gave rise to the Rabbinic and early Christian teachings, was grounded in a particular view of human nature and of the divine will. Ethical perfection was exemplified by the "Way of God." Such a life will result in the ideal state of human existence. Thus the eschatological reality of the biblical tradition, which describes the end-time, also presents a long history of inner and outer conflict of good and evil which will finally come to an end. Accordingly, human life before the end-time is to be transformed by the ethical imperative to love. This determines the "Way of God" and the very aim of his revelation is to lead humanity to *shalom*, wholesome peacefulness.

The Jewish Bible opens with two significant archetypal stories of creation that focus on human existence. In contradistinction to ancient theogonies or creation myths that ascribe a personalistic view to nature, full of wills, feelings and thoughts, the Torah offers a revolutionary religious orientation. There is only one transcendental God who creates all, both nature and human beings. The latter, however, enjoy a particular relationship to the creator,[1] in that both genders are endowed with the divine image. "*Imago Dei*" defines the special characteristics of humanity. Beyond its physical existence, it possesses a spirit, a mind, and speech. These divine gifts enable the person to enjoy freedom to decide, to choose, to evaluate and to aspire, to create and to control. Thus, the human being shares a partnership with God the creator in the maintenance and mastery of nature. For this reason, the person is held responsible for his/her actions before the God of creation.

The second biblical story of creation focuses on the human predicament and destiny, in view of the person's ability to choose what is good and what is bad. In choosing, a person displays his free will and self-control in the face of human drives and value judgments. God himself chose to create the world as an act of his love and goodness. The person, who is endowed with the "image of God," can aspire, by emulating God, "to walk in the way" of love and goodness. This understanding governs the historical narrative of the Bible and it is central to the biblical view of morality. In the mythopoeic outlook of the ancient Near East, the person is subject to the whims of the gods and of demons in nature, to their clashing wills and conflicting feelings. The person is not free to choose by his/her own will. In contrast the Bible frees the person to seek for him/herself the very way of God.

The second story of creation presents the first encounter between God and humanity as an archetypal event.[2] It relates to God's intent to create a person (Adam) in his image. "You shall multiply and increase upon the earth" (Gen 1: 28). This is a primary obligation of humanity to perpetuate itself through mating.[3] The prophet Isaiah explains (45:18), "God did not create the world to be chaos but He formed it to have it populated."

The paradigmatic account of Adam and Eve illustrates the basic human act of choosing to love, "becoming one flesh." Marriage is endowed with God's presence;[4] for God himself brings Adam his mate. Choosing a mate is described as good in Proverbs 18:22, and even God mourns when marriage fails, according to rabbinic thought.[5] Yet it becomes obligatory to issue a divorce when the marital relationship lacks love. For one should not live in a situation in which the principal commandment to "love thy neighbor" is violated. To be good in a relationship is determined by altruistic love, and God's attributes of goodness[6] describe his compassion and love.

The relationship of love between husband and wife is the model for all human relationships. Proper human relationships require altruistic love, for God is loving and compassionate. This understanding was revealed to Moses, when he sought and was granted divine forgiveness for the heinous sin of the Golden Calf. All the Prophets of Israel understood that the covenantal relationship between God and Israel is rooted in love. Human marriage that is rooted in mutual love becomes the metaphor for the way God relates to Israel. The covenant is depicted nuptially, as in the prophetic tradition (Hos 2:18–22; Ez 16; Is 61:10–62:5) and not from a model of suzerainty,[7] the relationship of a feudal overlord to his dependent subjects. Early Rabbinic exegesis[8] accordingly interprets the Canticles as a parable of the sacred experience of Israel's love for God.

Adam in paradise has the capacity to enjoy wholesome love as he relates to God and to his mate. However, being human, his physical drives toward what is pleasurable affect his choice between good and evil. Thus, the second story of creation continues with the paradigmatic event of Adam and Eve driven from Paradise. This depicts the human predicament in the world: For enticement and desire induce human beings to choose the forbidden and the harmful. In this way, man and woman display independence from God and even estrangement (biblically "hiding") from God. Human beings remain controlled by physical drives, feelings, and will that affect their behavior and moral decisions. Biblical anthropology depicts a polarity of forces which are rabbinically described[9] as a constant struggle between the *"yeser hatov"* (good inclination) and the *"yeser hara'"* (evil inclination).

2. Torah and the Ethical Decalogue

In light of the human predicament, God in his expression of love, offers the Torah to humanity as a guide to the ethical way of life. "See I place before you life and good, death and evil.... Love God and walk in His way and keep His commandments...so you may live.... Therefore, choose life!" (Dt 30:15, 16, 19). God offered the Torah to all nations but it was only accepted by Israel at Mount Sinai.[10] It directs human behavior through a system of "*miswoth*" (commandments), positive and negative. As a system of living, it guides all relationships, whether between person and God (the transpersonal), between persons (interpersonal), between person and non-person (subpersonal), and between person and self (intrapersonal).

The primary form of biblical legislation is presented apodictically in the Ten Commandments at Mount Sinai. The first four commandments determine a transpersonal relationship.[11] "I am the Lord, thy God" (Ex 20:2) binds Israel to God's kingship, as it is experienced through the expression of divine love. He "took them out of Egypt, a land of bondage," a historical restoration to humanity of physical and spiritual freedom.

"Thou shalt not have other gods" (20:3), defines the human response in free will to a transpersonal reality. It requires a total rejection of the polytheistic orientation that was rooted in the personalistic view of the ancient mythology common to Egypt and Near Eastern civilizations.[12] One is not to ascribe divinity to any part of the universe: "not in heaven above, not in the earth below, and not in the nether world." This is the essential thrust of the biblical injunction, a complete denial of the nature worship that subjected humanity to its bondage.[13]

"Do not utter God's name in vain" (20:7). The world view of primitive society was rooted in imitative and contagious magic,[14] which in practice supported the idolatrous myths of polytheism. Magic and myth are absent from the biblical tradition,[15] and they are totally rejected by the prophets and in biblical legislation. The Bible advanced a new human consciousness of reality. God transcends the cosmos which he creates and maintains. He remains eternal even after the world comes to an end.

The commandment to "Remember/Keep the Sabbath to sanctify it" (20:8) offers an effective dramatic occasion enabling the person to experience a transpersonal relationship. It deepens consciousness of God who created the human person and nature, the non-personal. For "in six days God created heaven and earth and all therein" (20:11). The transpersonal relationship is separated from the subpersonal. One cannot attribute to nature a personalistic divine reality. The person relates to the cosmos as a created, inanimate reality that depends on God. Nature itself is subject to human will and work, for the person is made in the image of God. Therefore, on the sabbath, the person frees himself from all work as related to nature[16] in order to enjoy a relationship with God only. Accordingly, the subpersonal relationship must conform to the experience of rest on the sabbath.

The sabbath offers the opportunity for the individual to attain peaceful wholesomeness through separation from the work and anxiety that come with the secular week. A subpersonal law is placed under a transpersonal law of the sabbath: "Let your animals rest." This human concern for animals gives rise to subpersonal laws in biblical legislation.[17] The person is to be guided by care and compassion towards the creation, which is placed under his stewardship during the secular week. On the sabbath, the way of peacefulness and love governs interpersonal relationships, when all acts of violence, forced labor, and war are forbidden. So too, one abstains on the sabbath from hunting animals or destroying nature, even the killing of an insect or plucking out of a plant.

The last six commandments (20:12–14) deal with interpersonal relationships that end with a specific law governing the intrapersonal. "Honor thy father and mother.... Thou shalt not murder, nor commit adultery, nor kidnap, nor commit perjury." These apodictic laws stand unqualified. They promulgate uncompromising principles that guide interpersonal relationships. Their adoption in human behavior engenders a social order in which parent, life, family, human freedom, and truth are inviolable values.

The final commandment governs the human impulse to covet, the very failing of Adam and Eve. "Do not desire [the reading in Dt 5:18]...anything that belongs to your neighbor." It deals with the evil inclination (*yeser hara'*), while the corresponding law[18] in the "Holiness" Code's Decalogue (Lv 19:18) prescribes "love thy neighbor," which guides the good inclination (*yeser hatov*). This intrapersonal principle promotes altruistic love and restrains egoistic desire. It dominates prophetic teachings and became a cornerstone of Torah legislation in rabbinic thought.[19]

Torah guides Israel in its covenantal relationship to God. The covenant is rooted in love, which affects both the transpersonal and the interpersonal. Its "way" aspires to realize what God intends as good and it seeks to arrest the destructive evil inclination in human nature. Thus the prophetic vision of the desired end-purpose of human perfection in history describes a person who is free from the evil inclination. In messianic times, harmonious peace will reign among persons and non-persons, in the spirit of love and compassion. Such peace gives rise to a transformation of humanity, a return to paradisal life.[20]

The prophet Ezekiel (36:26) of the Exilic period promises a new spirit will be given to a humanity that will be free of a stony heart, i.e. the evil inclination. At that time the Torah legislation will become unnecessary, when human nature is motivated only by love and doing good.[21] Thus a messianic ideal emerges that is rooted in a dual commandment of love, love of God and love of fellow humans.

3. Beyond the Measure of the Law and "*Imitatio Dei*"

The ethical condition of humanity after the expulsion from paradise is determined by the conflict of the two inclinations, historical circumstances, and the individual's freedom to choose. The first situation gives rise to values that are good or bad, relative to human pleasure and pain. The second offers the opportunity to translate values into action, and the third entails human accountability to God. In facing the three predicaments, the person can voluntarily invite the awe of God into his life, i.e. to be first moved by inner creature-feelings[22] in the face of the Wholly Other. For "All the Lord seeks from you is only to attain the awe of God" (Dt 10:12). In the Rabbinic view[23] this attainment is the true expression of human freedom; it becomes crucial to transformational choices. The awe of God impels the person to fulfill the divine commandments, which ultimately results in the pursuit of the good and in abstention from evil.

The experience of awe produces a new consciousness. Proverbs 1:7 (cf. Ps 111:10) defines it this way: "the beginning of [experiential] wisdom is the awe of God." Thus the aim of the Torah is to cultivate the numinous feeling for the Wholly Other, rejecting thereby the worship of nature and of self. Israel was delivered from idolatry by this new consciousness, which came precisely at their redemption following the Exodus. "The people were awed by God and they believed in the Lord and Moses His servant" (Ex 14:31).

Imbued with the awe of God, the individual accepts a higher authority that ushers him/her into God's kingdom. The person lives consciously in God's presence, which moves him/her towards a higher spiritual experience, the love of God.[24] The individual is led to the way of righteousness and loving kindness, emulating God's way with the divine creation. This is how the Psalmist describes God's way: "The Lord is good to all and His love is bestowed on all His creatures.... For God is righteous (*saddiq*) in all his ways and is loving-kind (*hasid*) to all his creatures" (Ps 145:9, 17). Thus a person who attains to a life emulating God is called righteous (*saddiq*) and loving-kind (*hasid*). The way of the *hasid* goes beyond the measure of what is good and what is bad, the normative way of the Torah.[25]

Two determinants affect the human response to God's presence, the experience of awe and the experience of love. The first liberates the person from idol worship, either that of nature, of a human creation, or of the human being. The second elevates the person to enjoy spiritual intimacy with God's presence. Thus Rabbi Pinchas ben Yair, a "*hasid*" of the tannaitic (the Tannaim were the rabbis whose views appear in the Mishnah) second century states:

> Torah life brings about cautious living; cautious living brings about affective application; applicative affection brings about to be cleansed [from evil]; to be cleansed brings to set-apartness [the Pharisaic life]; set-apartness brings to purity and purity brings to holiness, which leads to *hasid* life that brings about the Holy Spirit.[26]

This journey follows along a road to holiness: "to be holy (*qadoš*) as I am holy" (Lv 19:2). On the one hand, *qadoš* signifies "set-apartness" (the Pharisaic life). In the Torah, it refers to separation from the ways of all nations who are idolatrous, specifying "from the ways of Egypt and Canaan" (Lv 18:2), from their ethics and religious life. In the days of the Pharisees and the Tannaim, the first two centuries C.E., it meant to separate from the ways of Greece and Rome. Their Torah way was antithetical to those who denied a transcendental reality and an ethics of compassion. On the other hand, *qadoš* means to elevate oneself in a spiritual way beyond the measure of the Torah's norms and, by intimacy with God, to emulate his way of love and compassion.

What Rabbi Pinchas teaches is that there are two successive paths to holiness: the first is the way of the Torah, the second goes beyond its bounds. The way of the Torah promotes, on the one hand, cautious living, heeding the negative commandments and, on the other hand, diligent application of the positive commandments. Thus a person is cleansed from wrong doing. This leads to the Pharisaic form of life, which adopts an even stricter discipline of Levitical purity and sanctity. Since the commandments-system of the Torah is tailored to different persons,[27] the male and the female, the Israelite and the priest, the full proselyte and the semi-proselyte, all embrace a biblically-oriented consciousness of God, although each pursues a different regimen. The Pharisees accepted the highest discipline of the Torah: to became a "kingdom of priests and a holy people" (Ex 19:6). They intended this approach for the entire nation, to democratize the priestly practice, and to adopt for themselves a discipline of purity and sanctity.[28]

However, the way beyond the measures, beyond the Torah-prescribed purity and sanctity, is the way of the *hasid* (of loving kindness). This way leads to a life endowed with the Holy Spirit. Such a way was pursued, for example, by the Essenes who, however, radicalized it. The Essenes[29] (whose name designates *hasidim*) physically removed themselves from the people. They sought a life of purity and sanctity in the desert. They lived in camps facing a holy enclosure surrounded by pools of water for purification. They wished to live life in God's presence as in the days of Moses. They claimed that they enjoyed a holy spirit and the fellowship of angels. Their way of *hesed* remained exclusive, to be shared only with initiates in secret. They are the "children of light," who separated themselves from the "children of darkness." Their way gave rise to a strict monastic discipline,[30] governed by the ethics of communal sharing, Levitical purity, and abstinence. They awaited a final confrontation with the forces of evil.[31]

In contrast to the radical way of the Essenes, the Pharisees remained with the people. They became their preachers and teachers. They promoted the way of the Torah for Jews and non-Jews. However, the way beyond the measure of the Torah they reserved for themselves in private circles. This gave rise to closed associations, setting them apart from the rest of the population in the preparation of meals and in their adherence to the purity laws in a priestly manner. Thus the Pharisees were both inclusive and exclusive, eager to teach the way of Torah to others but also to remain separate from non-strict observers. Their way of behavior was perceived as contradictory by the people, who accused them of hypocrisy and division.[32] Yet within Pharisaism, the way of *the hasid*, or *hesed*, emerged with a special focus on emulation of God's way in human relationships.

God's way is revealed through his acts in human history. These acts serve as a paradigm for human conduct. The Torah opens with God bringing a mate to Adam in marriage and closes with God burying Moses. It also portrays God visiting the sick, namely Abraham after his circumcision, as well as comforting mourners, namely Jacob after the death of his mother and her nurse. He brings comfort to the prisoner, Joseph, and he releases an entire nation from bondage. He restores peace between man and wife, namely Abraham and Sarah. He provides food and clothing to the needy in the desert. He demonstrates a way of forgiveness of sinners, after Israel built the Golden Calf.

These are acts of loving kindness, which are rabbinically defined as "beyond the measure of Torah Law." These acts are not specifically prescribed but are simply described through epiphanic events that demonstrate God's love and compassion. They are not part of the *halakhah* (the norms) rather of the *haggadah* (the narrative). The early interpreters of these revelatory acts ("*dorshe reshumoth*," Midrash Tannaim Dt 11:22) say: "If you seek to know the One Who Spoke and the World came into Being, study the narrative. From such a reflection you will come to know the One Who Spoke and the World came into Being, and you will emulate His ways."

An early account of Rabbinic preaching in the synagogue is preserved in the Aramaic Targum (Pseudo-Jonathan to Dt 34:6 and Yerushalmi, codex Neofiti, to Gn 35:9). It is preserved with its doxological opening and poetic structure of repeated forms:

> Blessed is the name of the Master of the World. May His name be blessed for ever and ever. For he taught us His proper way. He taught us to clothe the naked, from (the way) he clothed Adam and Eve (Gn 3:21). He taught us to bring a groom and bride into marriage, from (the way) he brought Eve to Adam in marriage (2:22). He taught us to visit the sick, from (the way) he appeared to Abraham, in a vision of His word, when he was ill from circumcision (18:1). He taught us to comfort the mourner, from (the way) he appeared to Jacob again when he arrived from Padan Aram at the place where his mother died (35:9). He taught us to feed the poor, from (the way) he brought down heavenly bread to the children of Israel (Ex 16:4). He taught us to bury the dead, from (the way) he appeared to Moses with His Word in the company of angels (Dt 34:6).

This early understanding of the biblical narrative is echoed in the prophetic teaching of Deutero-Isaiah (58:6–7) on corporal acts of loving kindness. "Then will your light burst out like the dawn and your righteousness will go forward and God's presence will embrace you." For these corporal acts translate the way of God's love to humanity, and their performance seeks to imitate him. In the tannaitic tradition,[33] "to walk in God's ways" (Dt 11:22) is to imitate his divine attribute of love (Ex 34:6). It teaches humanity spiritual aesthetics. "This is the Lord, whom I beautify" (15:2), explains Abba Saul:[34] "Imitate Him; as he is merciful and compassionate so you shall be merciful and compassionate."

4. "*Gemiluth Hesed*" and the Love Imperative

To live by God's love and to emulate his way of loving others guides and determines the way of *hasid*, which Pharisaic Judaism elevated, thus transcending the discipline of commandments (*miswoth*). The acts of loving kindness are called "*gemiluth hesed*," and they relate to the interpersonal realm. They represent non-reciprocal acts of altruistic love, involving the whole person in the act of giving.[35] Their pursuit transforms the person who, in his emulation of God's way, is embraced by God's love and spirit.

Simeon the Righteous of the early Hasmonean period (second century B.C.E.) taught that a biblically oriented society is based on three principles. These are Torah (system of *miswoth*), priestly and liturgical service (*'avodah*), and acts of loving kindness (*gemiluth hesed*) (Mishnah Aboth 1:2). These three principles governed the Pharisaic system during the last two centuries before the

Romans' destruction of the Second Temple in 70 C.E.[36] After the destruction, the Temple service was eliminated and the emphasis was shifted to prayer service. Acts of loving kindness were placed on a par with the study of the Torah. Following the destruction, which was viewed as resulting from enmity and conflict between Jewish parties, the way of *hesed* was especially stressed. Moreover, the side of Pharisaic teaching inspired by Hillel became paramount in the determination of *halakhah*, thus confirming the way of humility and love. The shift after the Temple's destruction does not, however, constitute a revolution in the ethical teaching of the Tannaim. For the stress on the life of prayer had long been known as the way of earlier *hasidim*,[37] and the shift to "*gemiluth hesed*" was guided by the Hillelite teaching. Thus what occurred in Judaism after 70 did not emerge as a radical departure from a particular stream of Pharisaism, which was then in the minority. At Yavneh, Rabbi Yochanan ben Zakkai's celebrated academy was now guided by the spirit of Hillelite Pharisaism and the way of the *hasidim*.[38]

The scribe in Mark 12:32–33, in a work published before 70, preserved the pre-destruction understanding of Hillelite Pharisaism. The scribe comments on Jesus' teaching of the dual commandment to love. "Loving thy neighbor as thyself is greater than all the sacrifices," which echoes the prophetic teaching of Hosea 6:6, that God desires love (*hesed)* rather than sacrifice. This is also the approach Rabbi Yochanan ben Zakkai took after the Temple's destruction. It is not, however, a revolutionary approach that breaks with the Pharisaic tradition of the past.[39] A Jewish-Christian scribe of the Matthean school after 70 was guided by the same text of Hosea in explaining the ethical approach of Jesus that parallels Hillel (Mt 9:13, 12:5). For before 70, Jesus was supported only by the minority opinion of his older contemporary Hillel, who taught that the principle "love thy neighbor" governs the Torah way.

Hillel taught[40] that the love imperative determines the commandments-system of the Torah. He added that "the rest of the Torah [i.e. the narrative] offers but a commentary" and explained the measure of altruistic love by the biblical criterion, "as thyself." "Whatever is detestable to you, do not do unto your fellow person." When a person lives by the commandments of the Torah, he attains a way to know what is detestable to his being. He will use this measure to show his love to the other. For the way of Torah arrests the evil inclination (*yeser hara'*) and activates the good inclination (*yeser hatov*).

Hillel also taught (Aboth 1:12), "love peace and pursue peace, love all [human] creatures and you bring them closer to the Torah." To love peace (*shalom*) is to adhere to the way of Torah, which leads to *shalom* (Prv 3:17). Thus, the ways of peace (*darke shalom*) guide the Hillelite legislation.[41] *Shalom* is the goal, for it designates God's name.[42] Loving peace emulates God's way, and in pursuing peace it is motivated by the love imperative towards all persons.

The love imperative is also related in the "Scroll of Hasidim,"[43] an early first-century Rabbinic collection on the way of *hesed* or the *hasid*. "If you seek to attain an altruistic love in a relationship, seek and present the good side of the person." Love is generated in the pursuit of a wholesome relationship, one that is anchored in goodness, and this is the way to *shalom*.[44] What will guide humanity to *shalom*, Hillel taught, is the universal realization of God's kingship. This can be achieved through proselytization. To acquaint people with God's love they have to be led to the way of the Torah. The Rabbis interpreted[45] the transpersonal commandment of "*ve'ahavta*" (you shall love God) as also to be understood as "*ve'ehavta*" (cause God to be loved). For there are two vocalized meanings to the consonantal teaching of God's intent. (The Hebrew text writes only *V'HVT* with no vowels.) Similarly the Hebrew text of Leviticus 19:18 is unvocalized. It appears "*V'HVT LR^cKH KMKH*," to be read Masoretically as "*ve'ahavta lere^cakha kamokha*" (Love thy neighbor as thyself).

Jesus taught[46] that the principle of altruistic love governs the life of the biblically oriented people. He expanded the meaning of "thy neighbor" to include "thy enemy," by reading "*lero'akha*" instead of "*lere'akha*." He vocalized the consonantal text of God's intent in the scriptures differently from the early Rabbinic public reading. He argued that this was God's intent in the commandment. For "the heavenly Father causes the sun to shine on the good and bad, and He brings rain on the righteous and the wicked" (Mt 5:45). The "*imitatio Dei*" governs the love imperative which leads to wholesomeness (*shalom*). He concluded, therefore, "to be wholesome/perfect (*teleos*) as your heavenly Father is *shalem*/perfect" (5:48). This conclusion is preserved in Matthew only, but in Luke (6:36) the conclusion is based on emulating God by loving kindness (*oiktirmon* in view of Lk 10:37 doing *eleos*). For God's love leads to the way of the righteous (the Hebrew *saddiq*; Greek *o dikaios*). Jesus taught that by these two love commandments one attains eternal life (10:25–28). Matthew, however, considers the authentic experience of seeking God's love in prayer to be reflected in the way one relates interpersonally with love. "Pray for your enemy" illustrates the way "you show love to your enemies" (5:44). This affective association between the transpersonal and the interpersonal, in the manifestation of love, defines the intent of Jesus. Thus Matthew (6:14–15) juxtaposes the lesson of "forgiving one another and the heavenly Father will forgive you" with the prayer, "Our Father," in the Sermon on the Mount. Matthew further develops the teachings of Jesus, in contrast to those of the Pharisaic Shammaites, as a way beyond the measure of the law. He calls it the way of righteousness (3:15), by which wholesomeness is achieved (5:48) through emulating God. Furthermore, the same affective association that exists between the transpersonal and the interpersonal in the love commandment, should also affect the intrapersonal. Pure good intention must govern action, achieving "wholesomeness" in human conduct (15:19). For this reason hypocrisy is condemned, particularly in Matthew.

Luke focuses on another aspect of Jesus' teaching of love. For only the Gospel of Luke illustrates the particular reading of "enemy" in lieu of "neighbor" by Jesus. He offers the parable of the Good Samaritan to illustrate "Who is my neighbor?" (10:29–37). For the Jewish classification of neighbors in the days of Jesus consisted of the priest (*kohen*), Levite, Israelite and proselyte (*ger*). The last group includes two types, (1) a full proselyte, who actually was viewed as part of the Israelite category and (2) a semi-proselyte or "Fearer of God" who remained at the periphery. He enjoys biblical rights and recognition but he is not a part of covenantal Israel. Thus an uncircumcised Gentile can become a "Fearer of God" and in rabbinic view he is a Noahide. Noahides are biblically oriented people who, in the awe of God, accept the seven basic criteria (often cited as the Seven Commandments) of the covenant of Noah, but are not obligated to live by the law of Moses.

In Jesus' days "neighbors" also included Samaritans, who accepted the Mosaic law but neither the rest of the scriptures nor the oral tradition (or oral Torah), as these had developed from the days of Ezra. The Samaritans, who worshipped in Shekhem, remained on the periphery. They were also perceived in the last centuries B.C.E. as historical antagonists of Israel.[47] The "enemy" of Jesus' parable is the Samaritan. He also acts by the love commandment that is stipulated in the Mosaic law. Jesus skipped over the Israelite in the parable, as he was addressing an Israelite scribe. He knew that an Israelite is also bound by the rule of "love thy neighbor" to help a victim on the road. As an Israelite, he is not bound by the strict code of the priests and Levites in "moving to the other side" as he faces a seemingly dead body. For a corpse causes Levitical pollution. Thus Jesus widens the meaning of "neighbor" to include the "enemy," namely the Samaritan, in the performance of acts of love (*eleos*). Since this category of neighbor includes the semi-proselytes, whether the Samaritan or the "Fearer of God," it is the principle that eventually guided the apostolic mission to the Gentiles in the early church. Luke reports in Acts (1:8; 6:5; 10:2) that the apostles first directed their attention to the proselytes, Samaritans, and the fearers of God. In the early church the issue was raised whether to accept the uncircumcised in the way of Jesus (15:20–29, cf. Gal 2:12–16). For the way of Jesus was the way of table fellowship; to accept the uncircumcised at the eucharist was permitted, in the view of the church, as long as they had renounced paganism. They were invited to share in the holy (Didache 9:5 on Mt 7:6).

In the Lukan view, Jesus stressed the way of love (*eleos*) and therefore he details how such acts are performed by the Samaritan. Not only does the Samaritan bind the wounds but also nurses and provides for the rehabilitation of the person. To show love is measured by "thyself": "Whatever you want others to do to you." To show love with dignity and worth to the other is the expression of "*eleos*," the highest degree of righteousness. A millennium later Maimonides,[48] in relating his view of Rabbinic righteousness, describes ten degrees of charity, a sequence that culminates with the rehabilitation of the poor person to economic independence. This is clearly a line of development that adheres to the Hillelite tradition of the Rabbis and reflects the way of *hesed* that transforms the person gradually.

Matthew's view of Jesus' way of righteousness centers on the emulation of God (*imitatio Dei*). Accordingly, he alone describes acts of corporal love in the parable of the "Son of Man at the Last Judgment" (25:31–46). "I was hungry and you gave me food, I was thirsty and you gave me drink, I was a stranger and you welcomed me, I was naked and you clothed me, I was sick and you visited me, and I was in prison and you came to me." This teaching, at the end of the Matthean apocalypse, lays bare the transformational ethics of the realized eschatology which brings the person into God's Kingdom. In Matthew it is "a kingdom prepared for you from the foundation of the world." For the end-time corresponds to the paradisal beginning. Matthew perceives that Jesus' ethical teachings address human life in the end-time, to be realized now by his followers. Matthew alone defines "seek first His Kingdom" in the teachings of Jesus (6:33) by the way you seek "His righteousness."

John's Gospel understands Jesus' teaching of the love commandment in the light of Jesus' own ministry, which guides the way of Christians. Thus the ultimate measure of ethics is "*imitatio Christi*." John's Gospel expatiates: "to love one another *as Jesus loved them*; there is no greater love than to give oneself for one's friends" (15:12–13). Jesus' act of love was directed only towards the other, as John in the beginning of the Gospel maintains: "He is the lamb of God, who takes away the sins of the world" (1:29). Thus the example of Jesus governs Christian ethics.

These three views in the gospels of Jesus' teaching of the dual commandment of love reflect the early Christian understanding of ethics. Their inclusion of particular actions or teachings of Jesus indicates his way. The love imperative sets forth a way beyond the measure of the commandments. Therefore, it requires one "to turn the other cheek" (Mt 5:39; Lk 6:29). This agapic (altruistic love) expression even comes to characterize the marital relationship as a divine gift. Christian marriage can not be severed by the human writ of divorce and, if one takes another wife, he commits adultery (Mt 5:32, 19:9; Mk 10:11–12; Lk 6:18). God's intent, at the beginning of creation, was for the marital union to be "one flesh." This points again to the realized eschatology that defined the Christian relationship between husband and wife as following from God's bringing Eve to Adam. Finally, Jesus' own ministry had focused on "table fellowship." It is illustrated in different anecdotes and by Jesus' reference to the contrast between the way of John the Baptist and his own way (Mt 11:18–19; Lk 7:33–34). The purpose of conducting a "table fellowship" was to invite people to repentance and to seek God's love. This is depicted metaphorically by Jesus as a wedding feast. "As long as the Bridegroom is with them, they shall not fast" (Mk 2:19 parallels). This response, too, contrasts Jesus' way with the ascetic way of John, which also calls to repentance. John spoke of the wrath and the awe of God. Jesus's teaching of love also reflects his self-understanding as a "groom." Metaphorically he expresses covenantal love to his bride, the community (see Is 61:10). Jesus' table fellowship was depicted in the early church as an agapic meal representing a messianic banquet. The groom signifies the messiah[49] and the wedding feast is the agapic event. This way of Jesus impacts on the practice of the early church in the celebration of the eucharist that is central to its worship. Through the eucharist, the worshippers are guided by the Christian ethics of emulating Jesus, and through partaking, "in remembrance of him," the Christian participants are evoked to his presence. For "remembrance" connotes affective experience, to be moved by his example.

5. Conclusion: Historical Development of Both Traditions

Rabbinic Judaism after 70 C.E. incorporated as normative the way of loving kindness (*hesed*) in its ethical teachings, in conformity with the Hillelite position of the Pharisaic schools. Prior to the destruction of the Temple in 70, the Pharisaic school of Shammai was paramount and its pursuit of a strict discipline prevailed. Elsewhere I have demonstrated that Jesus' teachings against the Pharisees were antithetical to the Shammaite practice,[50] one strand only of Pharisaism. The Shammaites adopted a priestly way of holiness and purity that was beyond the measure of the law for the Israelite, the average Jew. For they sought ethical transformation in the transpersonal realm of ritual observance. Their members belonged to a religious association (*havurah*), which was governed by this strict rule of separation.

In contrast the Hillelites stressed the way of *hesed*, the affective application of the love imperative in the interpersonal realm. They advocated transformational ethics that went beyond the measure of the law in human relations. Hillel himself is said to have practiced this way of loving kindness (*hesed*) interpersonally and intrapersonally. "They say about Hillel the elder[51] that he acquired a horse to ride on and a servant to escort a poor person of a well-to-do family. Once he did not find a servant to escort [the poor person] and he ran before him for three miles." His way demonstrates how he practiced charity, "extending to the poor any need that he may lack" (Dt 15:8). "To love thy neighbor as thyself" requires to show love to the neighbor to the extent of the need to which he was accustomed, not merely what the norm of charity requires. For the poor only receive a given amount, as fixed by the law of charity.

Similarly, Hillel applied the principle of *hesed* intrapersonally. Biblical Wisdom teaching stipulates that "one who shows kindness to himself is a man of *hesed*" (Prv 11:17). The story is told of Hillel[52] that he performed a good deed, "*miswah,*" by washing himself in the bathhouse. For he taught, "I who was created in the image of God, surely must take great care of the [physical] icon," i.e. the human body. Inner purity parallels cleanliness in the manifestation of *hesed*, as it was later to be presented by Rabbi Pinchas ben Yair. Hillel's practice of *hesed*, interpersonally and intrapersonally, is grounded in humility (*'aniwuth*). This is to be realized by the transformational ethics of *hesed*.[53]

Prior to the Temple's destruction, the contrast was so extreme between the Hillelite way and that of the Shammaites, that Hillel and his followers were persecuted. The third-century Amora, Rabbi Yochanan of Tiberias, presents an early Rabbinic view of the history of these matters. He relates[54] that the unethical behavior of the Pharisaic teachers before 70, in their display of insensitivity to human abuse in the affair of Kamsa and Bar Kamsa, contributed to the destruction. Their behavior paralleled the way of a Zealotic Pharisee, the priest Zecharia of the Shammaites,[55] who insisted on strict observance of the priestly code of sacrifices. Rabbi Yochanan lamented that the Temple's destruction resulted from fraternal enmity and strict judgment. He observed[56] that Jerusalem was destroyed because the teachers judged by the way of Torah and that they did not act "beyond the measure of the law."

Mishnah Pe'ah 1:1 presents the halakhic categories that are beyond the measure of the law as those by which one achieves transformation in order to attain eternal reward. These include the *gemiluth hesed* and the pursuit of *shalom* interpersonally. For this way dominates the legal and ethical tradition of the Mishnah that was edited, c. 200 C.E., by Rabbi Judah, the Hillelitic Patriarch. The great thirteenth-century commentator on the Torah, Nahmanides,[57] finds this way to be grounded in the principle of *imitatio Dei*. The Hillelite approach appears to suggest this understanding.

"Ye shall be holy as I am holy" (Lv 19:1) means that we are to adopt a way beyond the limits of the Torah law. Holiness means moral elevation through emulation of God, who is the Holy One. Otherwise, writes Nahmanides, a person can live like a "scoundrel with Torah license." For such a one's personality was not transformed by the ethics of obligation. A person must strive to set himself apart (Hebrew: to sanctify) by transformational ethics. What is beyond the measure of the law constitutes *imitatio Dei*, the emulation of a god who is holy. This distinction between the ethics of obligation and the ethics of transformation determines the way of *hesed*, that is to say, beyond the measure of the law. Indeed, to follow "the way of the upright" (Prv 2:20) became the norm in amoraic times[58] and it guided the practice of the rabbis over the centuries. Thus, in the medieval period, the Tosaphist Rabbi Isaac of Corbeil in his compilation of the *Miswoth*, includes the "way beyond the measure of the law" within the system of Torah norms. The way of transformational ethics became the key principle.[59]

Both Rabbinic Judaism after 70 and early Christianity espoused the way of *hesed* but from two different historical perspectives. Judaism recognized that the community is living in an unredeemed world and in a period devoid of God's presence in the Temple. This historical awareness necessitated the espousal of the transformational ethics of *hesed*. For it was the failure of the Jewish people to pursue this course prior to the destruction of the Temple that wrought immense interpersonal conflict. Only diligent pursuit of the way of *hesed*, alongside a total commitment to Torah study and the performance of its *miswoth*, can lead to future redemption. At the end-time, Israel itself will be restored to dignity and worth among all nations, when the evil inclination will have been removed from the heart of humanity. Universally, at the end-time, people will love only by a transformed God-awareness which will inaugurate the cessation of human conflict, violence, and war.

Early Christianity espoused the way of *hesed* through *imitatio Christi* and a total commitment to him as the soteric source of their transformation. Paul explains (Col 2; Gal 3; Rom 4) that transformation through faith and *hesed* makes the way of Torah through *miswoth* unnecessary. For one experiences life in Jesus as the Christ (messiah) and *hesed* through elimination of the sinful drive to do evil. This understanding of the ethical way of Jesus was rooted in a realized eschatology. In the view of Maimonides,[60] the Christian way has promoted a biblical awareness that possesses an eschatological significance for humanity. For both traditions have pursued the way of *hesed* and have recognized that the transformational ethics will result in redemption for all humanity.

Differences between the Rabbinic and early Christian ethics can be located in the redemptive awareness of realized eschatology in the life of the believer. The historical events of Israel at birth (Passover and Sinai) and those of Jesus at death (the Crucifixion and Resurrection) sharpened their respective foci on how to follow the "way of God." For God's way was, after all, revealed in redemptive events of history that prefigure the final redemption. This is crucial to biblically oriented peoples who seek closeness to God in their life. Their emulation of God's way determines the ideal good. The rabbis placed their emphasis on the imitation of God, who delivered the Jewish people from bondage. The Torah commandments are rooted in the Exodus experience, recalling God's demonstration of love for the persecuted and needy people as the standard for loving-kindness emulation. The early Christians preserved their ethical teachings in the "Doctrine of the Two Ways" (*Didache* 1:1). This prefaces their presentation of the ecclesiastic life of worship, which was to mark their life between the first and last coming of Jesus. For their eucharistic service ended with a dual cry of "*Maran atha*" (the Lord came) or "*Marana tha*" (Our Lord come), the two possible vocalizations of "*MRN'TH*'" (*Didache* 10:6). Jesus' example offered the standard, since worship guides ethics.

In no way should one locate the differences between Rabbinic Judaism and early Christianity in the literal or blind obedience to the biblical commandments, as supposedly advocated by the Pharisees. For Rabbinic Judaism itself emerged out of the Hillelite understanding of God's way, a particular strand of Pharisaism in the days of Jesus. Hillel's way determined the Rabbinic ethical standard of emulating God in the pursuit of loving kindness, leading to harmonious, wholesome living in all areas of human relationships. Rabbinic Judaism and Christianity alike are religions rooted in the dual commandment of love.

Endnotes

1. *Babylonian Talmud, Sabbath* 119b.

2. On archetypal stories, see H. Gunkel, *Legends of Genesis* (New York: Schocken Books, 1966). On their significance see, A.J. Heschel, *God in Search of Man* (New York: Farrar, Straus & Giroux, 1955), ch. 3.

3. See G. Appel, *A Philosophy of Mizvot* (New York: Ktav, 1975), 110, and refer to *Mishnah Yebamoth* 6, 6.

4. *Genesis Rabba*, 22 and *Babylonian Talmud Sotah* 17a.

5. *Babylonian Talmud Gittin* 90b. On the significance of marriage in the classical rabbinic tradition, see the opening statement of Yaakov ben Asher, *Tur, Even Haezer.*

6. Refer to Exodus 34:6, 7, and the discussion in G.F. Moore, *Judaism*, vol. 2, pt. 5 (1927; reprint, Cambridge: Harvard University Press, 1950). See E.E. Urbach, *Hazal* (Jerusalem: Magnes Press, 1969), ch. 15,4.

7. G.E. Mendenhal, *Law and Covenant in Israel and the Ancient Near East* (New York, 1955); see also his article, "Covenant" in *The Interpreter's Dictionary of the Bible* (Nashville: Abingdon, 1962). He presents the suzerain model. However, see A. Neher, *Prophetic Existence* (London: Thomas Yoseloff, 1969), pt. 3, ch. 2: he demonstrates the matrimonial model from the prophetic writings.

8. See M.H. Pope's commentary to the *Song of Songs*, Introduction, Anchor Bible (Garden City, NY: Doubleday 1982).

9. See S. Schechter, *Aspects of Rabbinic Theology* (New York: Schocken Books, 1961), ch. 15; Urbach (n. 6), ch. 15,6.

10. *Babylonian Talmud, Aboda Zarah* 2b.

11. See *Mekhilta,* ad loc.

12. See Henri Frankfort, *Before Philosophy* (Baltimore: Penguin Books, 1951).

13. Contrast the account of "Enuma Elish" on the creation of the human being with the biblical account. See further Y. Kaufmann, *The Religion of Israel*, trans. M. Greenberg (Chicago: University of Chicago Press, 1960).

14. See J.G. Frazer, *Golden Bough* (1922; reprint, New York: Macmillan, 1964), Introduction.

15. See Y. Kaufmann (n. 13), chs. 2–3, and H. Frankfort (n. 12), concluding chapter; Kaufmann addresses such issues as Moses' rod turning into a serpent, Samson's hair, etc.

16. See A.J. Heschel, *The Sabbath: Its Meaning* (New York: Meridian Books, 1951).

17. See Elijah J. Schochet, *Animal Life in the Jewish Tradition* (New York: Ktav, 1984) and Andrew Linzey, *Christianity and the Rights of Animals* (New York: Crossroad, 1989).

18. See *Leviticus Rabba* 19,2.

19. See L. Jacobs, *The Book of Jewish Values* (Hartford, CT: Hartmore House, 1969), ch. 9, and S. Belkin, *In His Image* (London: Abelard-Schuman, 1960).

20. See D.S. Russell, *The Method and Message of Jewish Apocalyptic* (Philadelphia: Westminster, 1964), ch. 10.

21. Contra W.D. Davies, *Torah in the Messianic Age* (Philadelphia: Fortress, 1952).

22. See Rudolf Otto, *The Idea of the Holy* (New York: Oxford University Press, 1958).

23. *Babylonian Talmud, Berahkot* 33b.

24. Refer to L. Jacob (n. 19), E.E. Urbach (n. 6), G.F. Moore (n. 6), and S. Schechter (n. 9) on the difference between love and awe of God.

25. See Geza Vermes, *Jesus the Jew* (Philadelphia: Fortress, 1973) and his study of Hanina ben Dosa and Hasidim in *Post-Biblical Jewish Studies* (Leiden: E.J. Brill, 1975).

26. *Mishnah Sota* 9, 15 (appendix). Compare *Babylonian Talmud Abodah Zarah* 20b and *Palestinian Talmud Shekalim* 3, 4 (47c). See M. Luzzatto, *Mesillath Yesharim*, Introduction.

27. See the analysis of G. Appel (n. 3), on the *miswoth* system and refer to the accounts of *Saadiah, Hahinukh* and *Sepher Miswoth* on the various categories of commandments.

28. See L. Finkelstein, *The Pharisees* (Philadelphia: Jewish Publication Society, 1962) and A. Finkel, *The Pharisees and the Teacher of Nazareth* (Leiden: E.J. Brill, 1974).

29. Refer to Christian Ginsburg, *The Essenes* (London: Routledge, Kegan, Paul, 1955) and Geza Vermes, *The Dead Sea Scrolls* (London: Penguin Books, 1977).

30. Refer to Eusebius, *Ecclesiastical History* in view of Josephus and Philo on the Essenes.

31. Refer to Y. Yadin, *The Scroll of the War of the Sons of Light against the Sons of Darkness* (Oxford: Oxford University Press, 1962).

32. Refer to the study of E. Rivkin, "Defining the Pharisees," *Hebrew Union College Annual* 40–41 and article "Pharisees" in *The Interpreter's Dictionary of the Bible* (New York: Abingdon Press, 1962–82), Supplementary Volume.

33. *Sifre Deuteronomy* 11:22.

34. *Mekhilta Exodus* 15:2.

35. *Palestinian Talmud Peah* 1, 1 (15b, c).

36. See A. Finkel (n. 28), 17, on Simeon's statement and its parallel in Sirach's work.

37. See *Mishnah Berakhoth* 5, 1.

38. Contra J. Neusner's views in the *Life of R. Yochanan ben Zakkai* (Leiden: E.J. Brill, 1970); see also his *First-Century Judaism in Crisis* (Nashville: Abingdon Press, 1975).

39. *From Politics to Piety* (Engelwood Cliffs, NJ: Prentice-Hall, 1973); R. Yochanan did not implement a revolution of Pharisaic Judaism, as J. Neusner claims; see my study, "The Departures of the Essenes, Christians and R. Yochanan ben Zakkai from Jerusalem" in *R. Mayer's Festschrift "Wie gut sind Deine Zelte, Jaakow"* (Gerlingen: Bleicher, 1986), 29–40.

40. *Babylonian Talmud Sabbath* 31a. See Rashi's commentary.

41. See "Darke Shalom," *Encyclopedia Talmudith*, ed. Zevin, vol. 7 (Jerusalem, 1956) and refer to *Mishnah Gittin* 4.

42. See "Pereq Hashalom, the Treatise of Peace," trans. E. Levine, *Augustinanum* 14 (1974) and refer to Judges 6:24.

43. See S. Belkin (n. 19), last chapter; refer to *Sifra Leviticus* 19:17.

44. A. Finkel, "Sabbath as the Way to Shalom in the Biblical Tradition," *Journal of Dharma* 11 (April–June 1986).

45. See *Sifra Deuteronomy* 6:6.

46. Refer to J. Jeremias, *The Proclamation of Jesus* (Philadelphia: Fortress, 1972).

47. See Sirach 50:26.

48. *Sepher Zera'im, Hilkhoth Matnot 'aniyyim,* ch. 10.

49. See R. Gordon Gruenler, *New Approaches to Jesus and the Gospels* (Grand Rapids, MI: Baker House, 1982), 42.

50. Refer to my book, *The Pharisees and the Teacher of Nazareth* (Leiden: E.J. Brill, 1974).

51. *Tosefta Peah* 4, 10; *Palestinian Talmud Peah* 8, 7; and *Babylonian Talmud Kethuboth* 67b.

52. *Leviticus Rabba* 34, 3.

53. Refer to the teaching of the *hasid* Pinchas ben Yair, quoted above, (cited n. 26).

54. *Babylonian Talmud Gittin* 55b, 56a.

55. R. Yochanan describes his act euphemistically as an act of "meekness," i.e. an act of arrogance.

56. *Babylonian Talmud baba Mesi'a* 30b.

57. See his commentary to Leviticus 19:2 and refer to A. Lichtenstein, "Does Jewish Tradition Recognize an Ethic Independent of Halakhah?" in *Modern Jewish Ethics,* Marvin Fox, ed., (Columbus, OH: Ohio State University Press, 1975).

58. Refer to I. Epstein, *Judaism* (London: Cox & Wyman, 1959).

59. See the criticism of Eugene B. Borowitz, *Exploring Jewish Ethics* (Detroit: Wayne University Press, 1990), ch. 15, who fails to understand this point.

60. *Sepher Shoftim, Hilkhoth Melakhim*, ch. 11, uncensored text. See I. Twersky's *Introduction to the Code of Maimonides* (New Haven: Yale University Press, 1980), 452.

Suggestions For Further Readings

Rabbinic Works:

Bahya ibn Pakuda. *Hobhath Halevavoth* (Duties of the Heart). A classic account of the ethical philosophy of the Rabbinic tradition that blends *halakhah* and *haggadah.*

Kordevero, Moses. *Tomer Devorah* (Palm of Deborah). A study of Jewish ethics from the perspective of mysticism and the Rabbinic tradition.

Luzzatto, Moshe H. *Mesillath Yesharim* (Path of the Upright); *Derek Hashem* (The Way of God). A manual of ethical religious discipline from the vantage point of Pinchas ben Yair's way to spiritual experience.

Maimonides. *Hilkhoth De'oth* (Laws on Human Dispositions) of *Mishneh Torah, Shemonah Perakim* (Eight Chapters of Introduction to *Mishnah Avoth*). Halakhic and philosophical account of ethics by the great master of the rabbinic tradition of the Middle Ages.

Nahmanides. *Commentary to the Torah*, Leviticus, ch. 19. Halakhic and mystical account of the ethical way by the Spanish master of rabbinic tradition of the Middle Ages.

Scholarly Works:

Agus, Jacob B. *The Vision and the Way*, New York: Frederick Ungar, 1966. A systematic interpretation of Jewish ethics in their philosophical development.

Belkin, Samuel. *In His Image*. London: Abelard-Schuman, 1960. The philosophy and practices of traditional Judaism as expressed in rabbinic law.

Borowitz, E.B. *Exploring Jewish Ethics*. Detroit: Wayne State University Press, 1990. Reform Judaism's critical account of ethics as the autonomous Jewish self—living in covenant.

Finkel, Asher. *The Pharisees and the Teacher of Nazareth*. Leiden: E.J. Brill, 1974. A study of Pharisaic teachings of both the Hillelite and Shammaite schools, before the Roman destruction of the Temple, and the teachings of Jesus within the context of variegated Judaism at that time.

Fox, Marvin, ed. *Modern Jewish Ethics*: *Theory and Practice*. Columbus, OH: Ohio State University Press, 1975. A collection of essays on practical problems of the modern Jew in the State of Israel or in the Diaspora.

Jacobs, Louis. *The Book of Jewish Values*. Hartford, CT: Hartmore House, 1969. An account of eleven principal values in Judaism that shape Jewish thought and practice.

Lamm, Norman. *The Good Society: Jewish Ethics in Action*. New York: Viking Press, 1974. Selected accounts and explanations from classical and modern Jewish writings on the individual, family, and society.

Lichtenstein, A. "Does Jewish Tradition Recognize an Ethic Independent of Halakhah?" In *Modern Jewish Ethics*. Ed. Marvin Fox and cited above. An especially valuable study of medieval rabbinic sources on the ethical and the halakhic (legal) aspects of Jewish practice.

Neher, Andre. "Ethics." In the *Encyclopaedia Judaica*. Jerusalem: Keter, 1965. A brief review of the historical development of Jewish ethics, from biblical to modern times.

Urbach, Efraim E. *Hazal*. Jerusalem: Magnes Press, 1969. Translated under the title *The Sages*. Cambridge, MA: Harvard University Press, 1987. A classic study of the principal teachings of early Rabbinic Judaism in their historico-theological development.

THE NEW TESTAMENT AND THE TEACHING OF CONTEMPT: RECONSIDERATIONS

Norman A. Beck

Since the Holocaust many scholars have treated the theme of antisemitism in the New Testament. Norman A. Beck analyzes the anti-Jewish polemics of the New Testament and their impact on Christians and Jews, and suggests ways of combating this teaching of contempt. The acute problem of what to do with a sacred text that excoriates a people, he addresses by offering his own redaction and translation of 1 Thessalonians, a part of the re-translation he is engaged upon of the entire New Testament, and designed to alleviate the religious antipathy and sexist bias.

I shall begin these "reconsiderations" with a brief description of the teaching of contempt for Jews within the specifically Christian Scriptures that we who are Christians commonly call the "New Testament."* I shall include within this description a listing of the three categories of anti-Jewish polemic that I have identified in my book on this subject, *Mature Christianity: The Recognition and Repudiation of the Anti-Jewish Polemic of the New Testament*.[1] I shall continue with seven factors that have contributed to the development of this anti-Jewish polemic and to its continuance through the centuries. Third, I shall refer briefly to results

---

* This article is offered in appreciation for James Parkes and Jules Isaac, who first identified in detail the Christian teaching of contempt for Jews, and for many others who have followed them in these efforts, to name just a few: Richard Rubenstein, A. Roy Eckardt, Alice Eckardt, Edward Flannery, Samuel Sandmel, Krister Stendahl, Franklin Littell, Emil Fackenheim, Rosemary Radford Ruether, Eugene Fisher, A. James Rudin, John T. Pawlikowski, Robert A. Everett, Alan Davies, Solomon S. Bernards, Harold Ditmanson, Trudy Rogness Jensen, Franklin Sherman, Marc Tanenbaum, Clemens Thoma, Jack Sanders, Daniel Harrington, and Paul M. van Buren. To all of these, and to many others, I am indebted for what I say in these "reconsiderations."

of this teaching of contempt in the lives of Jews and of Christians. I shall conclude with a call for the maturing of Christians and of Christianity to which in many ways my professional life is dedicated, suggesting actions that are necessary for maturing Christians and for mature Jews now and in the future in order that we may overcome this teaching of contempt, this "religious racism."[2]

The anti-Jewish polemic in the New Testament that has resulted in so much indescribably horrendous suffering for Jews is basically the work of exclusivistic Christians. These exclusivistic Christians of my own religious tradition have believed and taught, beginning in portions of the specifically Christian Scriptures and continuing even today, that Jews who do not accept the beliefs and the life-style proclaimed and practiced by exclusivistic Christians are to be treated with contempt by God and by exclusivistic Christians. These Christians have believed and taught that Jews who do not accept these Christian beliefs and practices are no longer the "Israel of God" because they have forfeited their right to that designation by their rejection of Jesus, their "Savior" whom God has sent to them, and that they are responsible for the suffering and death of Jesus because they have rejected him. Actually, more specifically, they have believed and taught that Jews are responsible for the suffering and death of "God the Son"; hence, that they are guilty of the crime of deicide, for which they are eternally damned unless they accept Jesus Christ as their only Lord. They have believed and have taught that Jews fully deserve the suffering that they have experienced, since their suffering is punishment from God for their "sin" of the rejection of Jesus as their only Savior. Finally, they have believed and taught that exclusivistic Christians are doing the will of God when they try to force Jews to accept exclusivistic Christian teachings and practices, and when they drive Jews from their land, desecrate their synagogues, sacred writings, homes, businesses, and people—especially their rabbis, their children, and their old people—all out of the "love" these exclusivistic Christians have for the Jews' "eternal souls."

This Christian teaching of contempt for Jews was not the belief nor the practice of the Jesus of history, nor of the Paul of history; neither has it been the belief and practice of those who have followed Jesus and Paul most closely since their time. This Christian teaching of contempt for Jews is not essential to Christianity. Actually, it is in every way detrimental to Christianity. Nevertheless, it is embedded securely within the specifically Christian Scriptures.

I shall quote here only a few of the most blatant examples of this teaching of contempt that is embedded within our Christian Scriptures. One of the most vicious is 1 Thessalonians 2:13–16, a segment that almost certainly was inserted into Paul's letter approximately thirty years after Paul himself had been killed by zealous advocates of Roman civil religion.[3] This interpolation includes several themes that are contrary to what Paul wrote elsewhere. It also includes a reference to the suffering of Jews at the time of the destruction of the Second Temple, an event that occurred after Paul had been killed. I quote here as elsewhere from my own translation from the Greek.

> And because of this also we thank God constantly because when you received the message of God from us you accepted it not as a message of human origin but, just as it truly is, as a message of divine origin that is active in you who believe. For you became imitators, fellow believers, of the churches of God that are in Judaea in Christ Jesus, because you suffered the same things because of what was done by the people who live in your own area as they because of what was done by the Jews, who killed both the Lord Jesus and the prophets and have driven us out, who are not pleasing to God and are against all people, since they prevent us from speaking to people in other ethnic groups so that they may be saved. They have done all of these things in order to fill to the brim the measure of their sins. But the wrath of God has come upon them and will remain on them until the end of time![4]

These four verses were placed into Paul's letter, possibly by the writer of Acts of Apostles, who more consistently than any other writer whose work was brought into the canon of Christian Scriptures proclaimed contempt for all Jews who do not accept the beliefs and the lifestyle of exclusivistic Christians. It was the writer of Acts of Apostles who more than any other person distorted a vital segment of history by making more explicit the transferal of responsibility for the death of Jesus from the Romans to the Jews in order to try to save Christian lives from Roman oppression.[5]

The teaching of contempt for Jews that is embedded within our specifically Christian Scriptures provides the basis for the refusal of the Christians of the German village of Oberammergau to remove all elements of the vilification of Jews from their world-renowned passion play. The defense given for retaining portions of the teaching of contempt in the Oberammergau passion play and in the movies of the passion of Jesus that are shown on prime time television just prior to "Good Friday" each year is always the same, that "These words are in the Bible!" "We base our play on the Bible!" They are correct, of course. The teaching of contempt *is* in the specifically Christian portions of the Bible, especially in the two most dramatic and confrontational of the biblical passion plays, in the Gospel According to Matthew and the Gospel According to John, the two of the four biblical passion plays (the gospels) that are most heavily used at Oberammergau and in the passion of Jesus movies. I shall cite here only a few examples. (For a thorough analysis of this teaching of contempt for Jews in the New Testament, together with a detailed program for the repudiation of the most vicious and defamatory elements of this teaching of contempt, see my book, *Mature Christianity*.)

In the passion play according to Matthew, the character who plays the role of Jesus is made to say to the Pharisees and to all of the Jewish people with him, "You little snakes!" (in our vernacular "You sons-of-bitches!") "You are not able to speak good things because you are evil" (Mt 12:34a), and "Woe to you, scribes and Pharisees! You hypocrites! You remind me of whitewashed tombs that look good on the outside but inside are packed full of dead bones and of rotting flesh" (Mt 23:27). In Matthew 27:25, the writers of the passion play according to Matthew gave to all of the Jewish people, who in this passion play are made to insist to the reluctant Roman government official Pilate that Jesus must be crucified, the infamous lines that no real-life Jews would ever speak, "May his blood be on us and on our children!" In the eighth chapter of the passion play according to John, the character who plays the role of Jesus is made to say to the Jews who are conveniently gathered before him for that purpose in the play, "You are the offspring of your father the devil" (Jn 8:44). "You have never known God! I know God. If I were to say that I do not know God, I would become a liar just as you are liars" (Jn 8:55).

As I promised earlier, I shall include here the three categories of anti-Jewish polemic that I have identified in *Mature Christianity*. Only the second and third of these categories contain what we generally call the teaching of contempt. Nevertheless, I am including the first category, the christological, because the christological polemic led to the supersessionistic, and the supersessionistic polemic led to the vicious, name-calling, defamatory polemic.

Let us look, therefore, at the christological polemic. According to this polemic, Jesus the Messiah (Christ) now raised from the dead—more than *Adonai*—is LORD. This christological polemic, expressed in virtually every segment of the New Testament, is essential to the particularity of Christianity. It is not inherently an expression of the teaching of contempt, and it should not in any way be repudiated by Christians. It is our expression of faith. It is our expression of our most significant perception of God as Active in History. We have the right to perceive Jesus as the Christ raised from the dead and to perceive anyone else whom we wish to perceive as God Active in History for us, just as Jews and people in every other religion have the right to develop their own particular perceptions of God Active in History. It is primarily their perceptions of God as Active in History (rather than of God as Transcendent and of God as Pervasive) that distinguish people in one theistic religion from people in another.

It was the perception of ancient Israelites that *Adonai* more than someone else is LORD (God Active in History) that distinguished the ancient Israelites from other Semites. The various Semites of antiquity shared somewhat similar perceptions of God as Transcendent, using words such as *El*, *El Elyon*, *El Shaddai*, and *Elohim*. They also had somewhat similar perceptions of God as Pervasive, using terms such as the Spirit of Elohim, the Wisdom of Elohim, the Word of Elohim, and the Wrath of Elohim. God as Transcendent and God as Pervasive perceptions are somewhat general in all theistic religions. Our primary differences lie in our perceptions of God as Active in History. Our perceptions of God as Active in History differ because we each have our own unique, particular history.

For us as Christians, God has been Active in History most decisively and definitively (though certainly not exclusively) in the life, death, and resurrection of Jesus, whom we as Christians believe lives now as Jesus the Christ our LORD. We also believe that God has been Active in History and remains Active in History as Adonai, who is also LORD for us. These two primary perceptions of LORD come together for us, with the perception of Jesus the Risen Christ as LORD having prominence as our own peculiar perception, and as closer in time and space for us than is our perception of Adonai as LORD, because of our own peculiar history. This distinguishes us as Christians from Jews, for whom the most decisive and definitive manifestation of God as Active in History has been and remains Adonai. This distinguishes us as Christians also from Muslims, Hindus, and other theists, and in that sense is also anti-Muslim polemic, anti-Hindu polemic, etc. Our christological statements are much more anti-Jewish, however, than they are anti-Muslim or anti-Hindu simply because we use so much Jewish terminology and because Christianity had its primary origin within a Jewish context rather than within a Muslim or Hindu context.

As stated above, unfortunately the christological anti-Jewish polemic of the New Testament and of early Christianity, which is not in itself a teaching of contempt for Jews, led to the second category of anti-Jewish polemic, the supersessionistic anti-Jewish polemic, which is a teaching of contempt. I am less tolerant of the supersessionistic anti-Jewish polemic of the New Testament today than I was when I wrote *Mature Christianity*. I still can say that supersessionistic polemic is to be expected within religious literature, particularly within religious literature that is developed during the formative period of a religious community when the leaders of the community are establishing their identity over against parent religious groups and in competition with them. We are not surprised by the supersessionistic polemic that is present in many places within the New Testament, though it is much less frequent than is the christological polemic. We find similar supersessionistic polemic, for example, directed against both Judaism and Christianity in the Qur'an of Islam, and directed against Christianity (or more precisely against other forms of Christianity) in the sacred scriptures that are peculiar to the members of the Church of Jesus Christ of Latter-day Saints and of the Unification Church.[6] I can still say that mature sensitivity is needed in our translation and usage of New Testament material that includes anti-Jewish supersessionistic polemic. Since, however, this supersessionistic anti-Jewish polemic within the New Testament has induced most Christians to refuse to acknowledge that Jewish faith is a valid and living form of spirituality, that Jewish people are inspired by God, and that the Jewish Rabbinical Writings are "Word of God," and because the supersessionistic anti-Jewish polemic of the New Testament contributed directly to the development of the third type, the vicious name-calling, defamatory polemic, I am much more critical of the supersessionistic anti-Jewish polemic today than I was when I was writing *Mature Christianity*.

It is the third type of anti-Jewish polemic in the New Testament, the vicious, name-calling, defamatory polemic, that we usually associate with the terminology "the teaching of contempt." This is the type of anti-Jewish polemic that I referred to above in the examples that I cited from 1 Thessalonians 2:13–16, from Matthew 12:34a, Matthew 23:27, Matthew 27:25, and from John 8:44 and 8:55. This is the type of anti-Jewish polemic that is present consistently throughout Acts of Apostles and in many places in the four gospels in which responsibility for the arrest, torture, and crucifixion of Jesus was transferred from the oppressive Roman occupation forces in Galilee and Judaea and from the few among Jesus' own people who cooperated fully with them to "the leaders of the Jews" and in some instances to "all of the Jews." It is this cruel, crucial distortion of a vital segment of history, precipitated by the factors that I shall identify later in this essay and accompanied by the vicious, defamatory, damaging epithets, that constitutes the most virulent form of the teaching of contempt in the New Testament.

This most virulent form of the teaching of contempt is firmly embedded within our specifically Christian Scriptures, the New Testament, the foundation documents of our Christian Church. If it remains within the texts used in our public and private worship and devotional life, all of our church statements in which we have repudiated the charge of deicide and the vicious denunciations of the Pharisees and of all the Jews will not eradicate this teaching of contempt. This teaching of contempt will continue to appear in our Christian educational materials, in our Christian liturgies and sermons, and in our Christian passion plays. We can try to sensitize all of our fellow-Christians, we can watchdog all of our educational materials and liturgies, and we can object to negative portrayals of Jews in our Christian passion plays, but the source of this teaching of contempt for Jews in our Christian foundation documents will remain.

At the conclusion of this essay I shall suggest various actions that are necessary now and in the future in order that we may reverse the cruel distortion of a vital segment of history in which responsibility for the arrest, torture, and crucifixion of Jesus was transferred from the oppressive Roman occupation forces in Jerusalem, and from the few among Jesus' own people who cooperated fully with them, to "the leaders of the Jews" and in some instances to "all of the Jews." I shall provide specific examples of what can be done with specific texts.

Before we do this, however, let us look briefly at some of the factors that have contributed to the development of this teaching of contempt and to its continuance through the centuries. We shall also examine briefly results of this teaching of contempt in the lives of Jews and of Christians. Without going into great detail, I shall suggest seven somewhat interrelated factors, allusions to a few of which I have already made.

First, I suggest that this teaching of contempt was caused by human perversity, to human but animal-like rapacity that can be compared to chickens picking at the wounds of one of their own number until it is dead. This teaching is a result of human beings, even of inspired human beings, yielding to the evil impulse. I am saying that the teaching of contempt is sinful, the work of sinful people. The teaching of contempt is morally repulsive, even though it is firmly embedded in our Christian Scriptures and has been accepted by millions of Christians as "Word of God" for more than one thousand eight hundred years.

Second, as indicated earlier, the Christian teaching of contempt for Jews was caused by the arrogance of exclusivistic religionists who, having deluded themselves into thinking that they alone have possession of the "truth" and access to God, are the most rapacious of all people. A careful application of various historical-critical methodologies to the foundational biblical documents of the Christian Church reveals that the Jesus of history, the Paul of history, and the majority of the earliest followers of Jesus and of Paul were not arrogant exclusivists. Arrogant exclusivists were a minority among the writers of the specifically Christian Scriptures, being confined largely to the writers of the Gospel According to John and Acts of Apostles. The minority position quickly became, however, the majority position within the Christian Church and remains the majority position within the Christian Church today, although it is losing some ground during this twentieth century. The majority of our fellow-Christians today think that only Christians will be "saved." Many think that only those who live "correct" lives within their particular denomination of Christians will be "saved." Most think that Christians must be exclusivists, and most incorrectly think that all Jews, Muslims, and Hindus are also exclusivists just as they are. The Christian teaching of contempt for Jews is inextricably connected with arrogant Christian exclusivism, to which has been added in recent centuries Christian biblical literalism, or what is commonly called Christian fundamentalism. The Christian teaching of contempt for Jews that is embedded in the Christian Scriptures will not be rejected and relinquished unless arrogant Christian exclusivism and Christian biblical literalism are also rejected and relinquished.

Third, the Christian teaching of contempt for Jews was caused in part by the frustrations of exclusivistic Christians over their failure to "convert" Jews to their exclusivistic beliefs and lifestyle. Instead of sharing the good news that there is "salvation" in Jesus perceived as the Risen Christ, they insisted that there is "salvation" *only* in Jesus perceived as the Risen Christ, transforming thereby the "good news" for Christians into "bad news" for all who are not Christians. Frustrations led to anger and anger to the vicious, defamatory expressions of the teaching of contempt.[7]

Fourth, the Christian teaching of contempt for Jews was caused in part by the failure of most exclusivistic Christians to understand and to articulate the essence of all theistic perceptions, their similarities and their ambiguities. Most of them have failed to understand that virtually all theists have perceptions of God as Transcendent, of God as Active in History, and of God as Pervasive. Although the perceptions of God by theists are dynamic and constantly changing as a result of dynamic and changing human experiences, as we can easily see in a careful study of Jewish, Christian, and Hindu sacred scriptures in their original settings over a considerable period of time, the perceptions of God as Transcendent (Creator, Progenitor, Omniscient, Omnipotent, etc.) differ little from one theistic religion to another, as we have seen above. Also, the perceptions of God as Pervasive (as the ever-present Spirit of God Transcendent) differ relatively little from one theistic religion to another. The greatest differences from one theistic religion to another occur in the perceptions of God as Active in History (as "The Lord" present as Adonai [*HaShem*] in the Garden of Eden, with Moses and the prophets for Jews, as Jesus the Christ raised from the dead for Christians, as Rama, Krishna, and other avatars of Vishnu for Hindus, etc.). Most exclusivistic Christians have not understood this. When they understand this, it becomes easier for them to diminish their teaching of contempt for Jews.

Fifth, and closely related to reasons three and four above, is the reason articulated by Dennis Prager and Joseph Telushkin in *Why the Jews? The Reason for Antisemitism*;[8] it is associated with jealousy by non-Jews over the Jews' mature ethical monotheism and over their tenacity in maintaining their traditions. Prager and Telushkin suggest that the universal and indeed ultimate reason for antisemitism is the Jewish challenge to the values of non-Jews that is inherent in the Jewish perception of God, in the Torah and how it is perceived by Jews, and in the Jewish perception of themselves as chosen by God with a mission of perfecting the world. Productive interreligious dialogue can reduce this jealousy factor.

Sixth, the Christian teaching of contempt for Jews was caused in part by the desire of persons such as the writer of Acts of Apostles to protect Christian lives during periods of persecution by the Romans at the expense of Jewish lives. Such writers would not write openly about how the Romans had tortured and killed Jesus, Paul, Peter, James, and other leaders revered by Christians, owing to the danger of increased retaliation by the Romans if they were to do this. Instead, these early Christian writers resorted to scapegoating. They transferred blame for the death of Jesus, and to a lesser extent for the death of others whom they revered, to "all of the Jews." They were able to do this—even though it was a distortion of a vital segment of history—because of the reasons cited above and because there had been a few of Jesus' own people (most notably priests such as Annas and Caiaphas and those who had been hired by them) who had cooperated with the oppressive Roman occupation forces in Jerusalem and had not objected to the arrest, torture, and crucifixion of Jesus. I am personally greatly interested in the study of this subject.

Finally, the Christian teaching of contempt for Jews was caused in part by the immaturity of some of the most arrogant and most exclusivistic followers of Jesus within the early Christian Church, and it has been maintained by generation after generation of our arrogant and exclusivistic fellow-Christians from the mid-first century of the common era through to this present day. The foundational documents of the Christian Church were developed during the adolescence of the

Christian religion, when resentment against the principal parent religion of Christianity was at its height. Recognition of this reason for the Christian teaching of contempt for Jews—a basic thesis of my *Mature Christianity* book—provides the hope that with the maturity of Christianity as a religion, to be accomplished through the maturation of individual Christians and groups of Christians, the Christian teaching of contempt for Jews can be overcome. We are contributing to this process in this book.

We move on now from causes of this Christian teaching of contempt for Jews to results of this teaching in the lives of Christians and of Jews. I shall summarize these results in two brief statements.

One result of this Christian teaching of contempt for Jews is that a pernicious mindset was established within generation after generation of our fellow-Christians that numbed and even destroyed their sensitivities, dehumanized them, and made many of them largely impervious to the suffering of others. We see this most clearly from the time of the first of the Christian crusades in the Middle Ages until the end of World War II, although this pernicious mindset was obviously established prior to the last decade of the eleventh century and continues beyond the middle of the twentieth.[9]

The other result of this Christian teaching of contempt—closely related of course to the first—is that Jews have suffered horrendously simply because they were and are Jews. Jews have suffered through being systematically deprived of most or all civil rights in lands controlled by Christians, through scapegoating by our fellow-Christians, through deprivation of economic opportunity, and through direct physical violence against them by Christian crusaders in Europe and continuing in countless pogroms, slanders, inquisitions, indecencies, and, within the lifetimes of some of us, the *Shoah.*[10] They continue to suffer through the resurgence of neo-Nazi groups and of other even more insidious forms of antisemitism, including the denial of the right of the nation of Israel to exist, except perhaps as a "sign" for some Christians of the imminent end of this evil age.

I shall conclude now with a call for the maturing of Christians and of Christianity that will involve the total rejection of Christian exclusivism, manifested in a sustained open proclamation of the validity of Jewish religion and of other theistic religions, of Jewish spirituality and of other theistic spiritualities, of Jewish inspired individuals and of other inspired individuals, and of Jewish sacred writings and of the sacred writings of other theistic religions. Although this will involve relinquishing a claim that has been cherished by millions of Christians for many centuries, the benefits not only in overcoming the Christian teaching of contempt for Jews but also in striving for the goal of "peace on earth, good will toward all" are immeasurable.

With specific reference to the teaching of contempt for Jews within the New Testament texts, I suggest for consideration and discussion the following three ways in which we ought, as the title of this essay stipulates, to reconsider the teaching of contempt for Jews in the New Testament.

First, we should revise or replace the three-year lectionaries currently being used in most liturgical churches in the United States so that biblical texts that express this Christian teaching of contempt for Jews will not be read and used as the biblical basis for sermons and homilies within these churches. For example, more use should be made of Markan texts that have less fully developed anti-Jewish supersessionistic and name-calling statements than their redactions in Matthew, and the extensive readings from Acts of Apostles during the Easter Season each year should be reduced and realigned to avoid the vicious indictment of the "Men of Israel" for responsibility for the arrest, torture, and crucifixion of Jesus.[11]

Second, we should accelerate the tremendous task of educating Christian leaders, pastors, teachers, and lay people regarding the nature of this teaching of contempt, factors that have contributed to its origin and development, results of this teaching of contempt in the lives of Christians and of Jews, and what must be done in order that we may overcome this teaching. Many Christians have begun this task. Much more must be done.

Finally, we should engage vigorously in ongoing, sensitive revisions of the major translations of the Greek New Testament into modern languages and in producing redactions that employ circumlocutions,[12] that relegate the most vicious, defamatory texts to small-print type status, and that involve refusing to translate cruel, name-calling epithets.[13] My own specific program for doing this is provided in *Mature Christianity*, and an implementation of this process is in progress in my sensitive new translation and redaction of the New Testament from Greek to English in a form that will be usable in the future.[14] A sample of my translation and redaction concludes this article. If we fail during this generation to provide sensitive translations and redactions of the Greek New Testament that repudiate and remove the most vicious elements of the Christian teaching of contempt for Jews, and that also repudiate and remove the sexist segments that prescribe for all women a second class status within the church,[15] we shall find that many of our own children and grandchildren will reject our religious tradition entirely. We cannot expect the next few generations of Christians to be as tolerant of religious racism and of sexism within the church as this present generation has been.

The First Letter to the Thessalonians

A new translation and redaction that dares to be sensitive,
Sensitive to anti-Jewish polemic and to sexism,
And dares to be innovative for our time
By moving back into the past of early church development
And forward into the future of the church
That is still to come.

Prepared by Norman A. Beck
With encouragement and suggestions from many others.

Translator's Preface

Many of the concerns of Paul as a pastor of predominantly gentile-background followers of Jesus are apparent in this brief letter. The document indicates that it was important to Paul that close, positive relationships be maintained and that the Thessalonian community of faith provide a model lifestyle for other gentile-background followers of Jesus in Macedonia and Achaia. This relatively early letter of Paul reveals also what Paul thought at that time about the nature and purpose of the anticipated visible return of Jesus to his followers.

Ever since the last decade of the first century of the common era, the beauty of this pastoral letter has been marred by what was almost certainly an addition that was, still later, numbered as 2:13–16. This interpolation by someone who imitated Paul's literary style put into this letter the only viciously defamatory anti-Jewish polemic within the entire Pauline corpus. The interpolation disrupted the symmetry of the letter, contradicted what Paul himself had written elsewhere about the Jews, and reflects later conditions, a period some time after zealous advocates of Roman civil religion had killed Paul and after the cruel suppression by the Romans of the Jewish revolt in Galilee and Judaea from 66 to 73 C.E.

This letter that Paul wrote to the Thessalonians must have been used as a primary resource by the Lukan writer during the composition of Acts of Apostles. It is probable that the Lukan writer condensed a rather extensive ministry of Paul in Thessalonica into a single brief scene in the Acts of Apostles' literary drama. It was possibly the Lukan writer of Acts who composed the 1 Thessalonians 2:13–16 addition to Paul's letter and interpolated it into the original letter, since the viciously defamatory anti-Jewish polemic of the interpolation corresponds closely to major motifs within Acts of Apostles and contradicts Paul's own writings.

In this translation, the viciously anti-Jewish interpolation is reduced to small-print type status as a statement against the interpolation and as an encouragement to those who use this translation to read the letter as Paul composed it, without the addition.

Translation

1:1 Paul, Silvanus, and Timothy, to the congregation of the Thessalonians in God the Father and the Lord Jesus Christ. Grace and peace to you.

2 We give thanks to God our Father constantly concerning all of you,

remembering you in our prayers, 3 recalling your faithful work, your loving labor, and your steadfast hope regarding our Lord Jesus Christ, 4 knowing, fellow believers, loved by God, that you are set apart 5 because the good news that we brought to you did not come to you in word only but also in power and in the Holy Spirit and in full assurance, just as you know what sort of persons we were while we were among you on your behalf. 6 And you became imitators of us and of the Lord, receiving the message with much tribulation, but with joy provided by the Holy Spirit, 7 so that you became an example for all who believe in all of the regions of Macedonia and Achaia. 8 For the word of the Lord has been made known from you not only in Macedonia and Achaia, but in every place your faith that is now turned to God has come to be known, so that we have no need to add anything. 9 For they show clearly what kind of access we had to you, and how you turned from your earlier idolatrous practices to serve the one true living God 10 and to wait for God's Son, whom God raised from the dead, to come from the heavens, Jesus who rescues us from the wrath that is coming.

2:1 For you are well aware, fellow believers, that our coming to you was not in vain, 2 but that, as you know, even though we had endured ridicule and insult in Philippi, we had the courage in our faith in God to speak to you the good news of God under adverse conditions. 3 For our appeal was not from deceit nor from impure motives nor self-interest, 4 but just as we have been approved by God to be trusted with the gospel, thus we speak, not as people-pleasers but as ones who seek to please God, who examines our hearts. 5 For never at any time did we resort to flattery, as you know, nor greedy motive, as God is our witness. 6 Neither were we seeking glory from any people, neither from you nor from any others, 7 even though we could have asserted our authority as apostles of Christ. But we were tender among you, like a nursing mother providing milk for her own children. 8 Therefore, having such feelings as these for you, we were willing to share with you not only the gospel of God, but also our own lives, because you have become so loved by us. 9 For you remember, fellow believers, our hard work and toil, how night and day as we worked to earn our living in order that we would not burden any of you we proclaimed to you the gospel of God. 10 You are witnesses and God is our witness of how appropriately and justly and blamelessly we conducted ourselves among you who believe. 11 As you know, we treated each one of you just as a father treats his own dear children, 12 guiding you and encouraging you and speaking well of you, so that you would live your lives in a manner worthy of God, who calls you into God's own kingdom and glory.

13 And because of this also we thank God constantly because when you received the message of God from us you accepted it not as a message of human origin but, just as it truly is, as a message of divine origin that is active in you who believe. 14 For you became imitators, fellow believers, of the churches of God that are in Judaea in Christ Jesus, because you suffered the same things because

of what was done by the people who live in your area as they because of what was done by the Jews, 15 who killed both the Lord Jesus and the prophets and have driven us out, who are not pleasing to God and are against all people, 16 since they prevent us from speaking to people in other ethnic groups so that they may be saved. They have done all of these things in order to fill to the top the measure of their sins. But the wrath of God has come upon them and will remain on them until the end of time!

17 But since we have been separated from you, fellow believers, for this brief time, by face but not by heart, we have been most eager, we have wanted so much, to see you again. 18 We desired to come to you, especially I, Paul, again and again, but Satan[16] has prevented us. 19 For who is our hope, our crown of happiness in the presence of our Lord Jesus when he shall visibly return to us? Is it not you? 20 For you are our glory and our joy.

Endnotes

1. Norman A. Beck, *Mature Christianity: The Recognition and Repudiation of the Anti-Jewish Polemic of the New Testament* (Selinsgrove, PA: Susquehanna University Press, 1985).

2. I use the term "religious racism" in the broad sense of the word "racism," fully aware that the Jews are a "people," not a "race," just as the Christians are a "people," not a "race."

3. In addition to my detailed discussion of these four verses in *Mature Christianity*, 40–46, see Birger Pearson, "1 Thessalonians 2:13–16: A Deutero-Pauline Interpolation," *HTR* 64 (1971): 79–94, and Daryl Schmidt, "1 Thess 2:13–16: Linguistic Evidence for an Interpolation," *JBL* 102 (1983): 269–279.

4. This spurious charge in 1 Thessalonians 2:13–16 that the Jews killed the Christ and its arrogant claim that the Jews will always suffer because the wrath of God is upon them until the end of time provided theological justification for the persecution of Jews by Christians in countless pogroms and for the murder of millions of Jews in the *Shoah*, especially in Eastern Europe.

5. As Christians, we are beginning to recognize the distortion of a vital segment of history that occurred when early Christian writers transferred the responsibility for the death of Jesus from the Romans to the Jews. This recognition occasionally now appears in scholarly journals, e.g., Helmut Koester, "Jesus the Victim," *JBL* 111 (Spring 1992): 10, "[Jesus'] death was a political execution by Roman authorities—it must be remembered that only at a later time did the Christians assign the responsibility for Jesus' death to the Jewish authorities." When what Koester wrote here and expressed verbally in his presidential address at the annual meeting of the Society of Biblical Literature in Kansas City, Missouri, on November 23, 1991 becomes common knowledge within our churches and among Christians generally, the results will be profound.

6. For examples of these, see my *Mature Christianity*, 25–30.

7. For a more detailed description of this, see Eric Gritsch, "The Jews in Reformation Theology," below, essay 9.

8. (New York: Simon and Schuster, 1983).

9. This has been well documented during the past four decades. Within this present volume, see essays 6,7,8,9, and 10.

10. For one of the most noted expositions of this, see Rosemary Radford Ruether, *Faith and Fratricide: The Theological Roots of Anti-Semitism* (New York: Seabury, 1974).

11. For specific suggestions for revisions of the currently used Roman Catholic, Lutheran, and Common Three-Year Lectionaries, see my three small books of exegetical comments and practical guidelines for pastors and worship leaders, *Scripture Notes B*, *Scripture Notes C*, and *Scripture Notes (Series A)*, (Lima, OH: C.S.S. Publishing Company, 1984, 1985, 1986).

12. For example, in certain instances we should translate *οἱ Ἰουδαῖοι* ("the Jews") as "some

of Jesus' own people," συναγωγαί ("synagogues") as "religious gathering places," and φυλακτήρια ("phylacteries") as "devotional aides."

13. In Matthew 23:25 and 23:33, for example, we should appropriately redirect what has become external criticism of Jews by Christians into internal self-criticism of Christians by reducing "Woe to you, scribes and Pharisees, hypocrites! For you cleanse the outside of the cup...." to "Woe to you who cleanse the outside of the cup...." and "You serpents, you brood of poisonous snakes! How will you escape from the judgment of hell?" to "How will you escape from the judgment of hell?"

14. What we need for the future is more than supine translation. We need also some significant and sensitive redaction if the "Word of God" of our Christian Scriptures is to remain in the words of Hebrews 4:12 "living and active, sharper than a two-edged sword." There is ample precedent for redaction in our biblical tradition itself. We see radical redaction of the narratives of Exodus, Leviticus, and Numbers into the sermon genre of Deuteronomy in the Torah itself. It is readily apparent that 1-2 Samuel and 1-2 Kings were redacted to produce 1-2 Chronicles, with entire chapters eliminated or condensed into a few sentences. We are fully aware that the Gospel According to Mark was redacted into the Gospel According to Matthew and into the Gospel According to Luke, and that there was modest but significant redaction of all of the New Testament texts over a period of more than one thousand years after they had been accepted as canonical. This modest but significant redaction was halted only by the use of movable print in 1516 C.E. The time has come to resume the process of redaction. If our biblical tradition is to remain "living and active, sharper than a two-edged sword," it must be permitted to grow again, and it must be "pruned" and shaped where needed, just as inspired transmitters permitted it to grow and pruned and shaped it where needed until 1516. The alternative is to retain the "same Bible" that we have had for the past five hundred years and to witness the escalating erosion of its authority. Actually, of course, we have not had the "same Bible" for the past five hundred years, thanks to the arduous labors of those engaged in the discipline of textual criticism. Children's Bibles and the Bible on videotape provide the Bible in radically new and different configurations, and that process is rapidly accelerating.

15. My translation and redaction also repudiates the most blatantly sexist statements in 1 Timothy 2:11-15, 1 Corinthians 14:33b-35, and elsewhere by reducing them to small-print type status.

16. It is possible that Paul used the word "Satan" here and elsewhere as an anti-Roman cryptogram, a coded reference to zealous advocates of the Roman imperial religion who hounded Paul and eventually killed him.

Suggestions For Further Reading

Beck, Norman A. *Mature Christianity: The Recognition and Repudiation of the Anti-Jewish Polemic of the New Testament.* Selinsgrove, PA: Susquehanna University Press, 1985. In addition to a thorough analysis of the nature of the anti-Jewish polemic and reasons for the anti-Jewish polemic in each of the New Testament documents, this book provides a specific program for the repudiation of the most vicious, defamatory polemic through sensitive translation and redaction that relegates the most defamatory segments to footnote status.

_____. "Reflections on the Statement of the Presbyterian Church (USA), 'A Theological Understanding of the Relationship Between Christians and Jews' (1987)." *Texas Lutheran College Theology/Philosophy Review*, 6 (1989): 19–31. This article is a theological and practical critique of the Presbyterian statement. The critique is designed to be a basis for the statement on the relationship between Christians and Jews that will be developed during the next few years within the Evangelical Lutheran Church in America.

_____. "Teaching the 'New Testament' in the Light of Jewish-Christian Dialogue." *Shofar*, 6:4 (Summer, 1988): 44–54. Included in this article are the author's guidelines for productive interreligious dialogue, a listing of benefits to Christian theology from the Jewish-Christian dialogue, and insights from the dialogue into the life and work of the Jesus of history and of the Paul of history applied to teaching the New Testament.

Davies, Alan T., ed. *Antisemitism and the Foundations of Christianity*. New York: Paulist Press, 1979. Twelve Christian theologians (John C. Meagher, Douglas R.A. Hare, Lloyd Gaston, John T. Townsend, David Efroymson, Monika K. Hellwig, Gregory Baum, John T. Pawlikowski, Douglas J. Hall, Alan T. Davies, Terence R. Anderson, and Rosemary Radford Ruether) explore the development and the dynamics of the roots of Christian antisemitism in this important collection. The volume is a response to Rosemary Radford Ruether's *Faith and Fratricide*, and is dedicated to James Parkes, who provided the preface.

Eckardt, A. Roy. *Elder and Younger Brothers: The Encounter of Jews and Christians*. New York: Scribner's, 1967. This book is designed to remove barriers between Christians and Jews and to promote brotherly thinking and action by Christians in their relationships with Jews. Eckardt rejects the traditional Christian missionary attitude with regard to Jews in a manner that testifies to the uniqueness and integrity of Christian faith.

Fisher, Eugene J. *Faith Without Prejudice*. New York: Paulist Press, 1977. As its title indicates, this book offers ways of overcoming Christian misconceptions about Jews by providing for Christian readers, catechists, and homilists strategies for implementing Christian faith without its traditional prejudice against Jews.

Isaac, Jules. *The Teaching of Contempt: Christian Roots of Anti-Semitism*. New York: Holt, Rinehart and Winston, 1964. In this book, the title of which has become a standard phrase to depict Christian antisemitism, Isaac identifies and refutes the three principal doctrines of the traditional Christian teaching of contempt: that Jewish religion was degenerate at the time of Jesus, that the Jews are a "deicide race," and that the Jewish dispersion has been a divine punishment for their complicity in the crucifixion of Jesus.

Parkes, James. *The Conflict of the Church and the Synagogue: A Study of the Origins of Antisemitism*. 1934. Reprint. New York: Atheneum, 1969. This book, completed by the pioneer Christian advocate of Jewish-Christian dialogue in 1934, sketches the history of Jewish intellectual and religious interaction with the Roman world, with nascent Christianity, and with Byzantium and Visigothic Spain, exploring the legal, social, political, and theological underpinnings of Christian antisemitism and the Jewish response.

Ruether, Rosemary Radford. *Faith and Fratricide: The Theological Roots of Anti-Semitism*. New York: Seabury, 1974. In this hard-hitting theological critique of Christian anti-Judaism, Rosemary Radford Ruether asserts that, given the realized eschatology of the church, the pro-Christ "right hand of Christology" that Jesus is the Messiah invariably is accompanied by its dualistic counterpart, the anti-Jewish "left hand of Christology" that the Jews be damned. Ruether suggests that the deadly fratricidal side of Christian faith can be overcome only through genuine encounter with Jewish identity on a massive scale.

Sandmel, Samuel. *Anti-Semitism in the New Testament?* Philadelphia: Fortress Press, 1978. Sandmel is optimistic in this book that, even though antisemitism is deeply embedded within the New Testament, concerned Christians will find ways of rising above it.

ANTISEMITISM AND THE CHURCH FATHERS

Robert Michael

Between Early Christianity and Judaism there are numerous positive connecting links. However, as the new religion evolved, many thinkers began to show hostility to Judaism. Several factors led to this anti-Judaism: the role in Jesus' death ascribed to the Jews by the New Testament; the refusal by Jews to convert; resentment against those Jewish converts who continued to observe Jewish rituals; and reaction to anti-Christian polemics delivered by the Jewish establishment. What made Christian anti-Judaism particularly ominous was the effort of several theologians to demonize the Jewish people—to make Jews a cursed nation, children of the devil, whose suffering was intended by God. Robert Michael analyzes the anti-Jewish theology in the writings of the Church Fathers and suggests its relationship to the antisemitism of the modern centuries.

Introduction

The degree of historical antagonism to Jews among average Christians and among even the greatest of Christian thinkers brings to the researcher's mind a sharp sense of the monumental tragedy that had taken place over the last two millennia. The exalted concept of the "Judeo-Christian" tradition has often been simply a mockery of the cruel realities that lay beneath. Yet, there are, and have always been, righteous Christians who have regarded the Jews with friendship, respect, and good neighborliness. And, even though they have generally chosen not to write about it, in times of crisis these Christians have risked their very lives to continue to treat Jews with decency and kindness. At the same time, tragically, many of the brightest and best Christian minds have often been guilty of advocating the most offensive and shocking ideas and behaviors.

It is unarguable that moral perception and behavior are shaped by the society into which we have been socialized and acknowledge as our own. For Christians, the dominant moral community is the church.[1] It was, in fact, what the church thought about Christ and its identity as an institution that have determined what most Christians believed about Judaism and Jews.[2] Anti-Jewish theological defamations, communicated and empowered by the church, provided much of the Christian populace with justification for their antisemitic[3] ideas. Moreover, this ideological repugnance has often boiled over into contemptuous feelings and behaviors. The Church Fathers (the outstanding Christian theologians writing before the eighth century) refused to allow Jews to shake off their image as minions of Satan and the Antichrist. These negative perceptions have existed independent of what Jews themselves have actually done, or, indeed, of a Jewish presence at all.[4] In this *adversus judaeos* tradition, God was always pictured as "in there punching"[5] on the side of Christianity and Christians against Judaism and Jews.

Christianity's normative theological position in regard to Judaism and Jews has been called *theologia gloriae*, the theology of glory, or triumphalism. It holds that:

- The Christian Church, the new Israel—"ordained and sanctioned by God himself"—has succeeded the cursed and rejected old Israel morally, historically,and metaphysically.
- The Jews denied the true messiah, the Christ, and murdered him, for which all Jews are forever collectively guilty and must forever suffer.
- The Jews were evil-doers even before their atrocious act of deicide.

The major source of this anti-Jewish theology is the writings of the Church Fathers, who in turn exploited and elaborated the negative themes contained in scripture.

Pagan Attitudes

Although there is evidence that the word "Jew" was sometimes used as a term of derision before it was influenced by the Latin Church, the Greeks and Romans regarded the Jews little differently from other peoples.[6] There was no intense emotional or ideological hostility. When the Jews of Judaea revolted against the Romans, for example, they were treated no more savagely than any other seditious people within the Empire. When Greeks and Romans wrote about the Jews, we find that roughly half of these authors were neutral toward the Jews, one-quarter hostile,[7] and one-quarter friendly. In all, out of 161 Greek and Roman authors who discussed the Jews, only twenty-eight were negative toward them.[8] The pagans respected the Jews' long antiquity, their well-documented history, and their great literature; the Jewish emphasis on family and community; Jewish monotheism, rejection of images, and elevated moral code. The Jews were regarded as a *gens*, a people, an "*insignissima religio, certe licita,*" a notable religion, certainly lawful.[9]

Those pagans who were hostile sniped at the Jews because they were different or annoying. Their antagonism, in contrast to Christian polemic, was social rather than religious, detached rather than emotional, querulous rather than eschatological, literary and aristocratic rather than "propagandistic" (brought down to the level of the common person, and introduced even into the sermons, art, liturgy, and the sacred calendar of the church), petulant and superficial rather than emotional and dramatic. There was among the pagans no belief or feeling that eternal salvation depended on hating Jews. There was no array of theological ideas supporting, justifying, legitimizing, or sanctifying anti-Jewish hostilities. It is true that charges of sacrilege and ritual murder were found in a few pagan authors (Manethon, Democritus, Apion), but most of their readers appear to have been incredulous. This was evidenced by the fact that these stories caused no pagan pogroms against the Jews. It is true that we have to await the Middle Ages before the mass murder of Jews results from such charges within Christendom, but it was not till then that Europe was fundamentally Christianized.[10]

Although the pagans did provide some material that Christians directly exploited against the Jews,[11] universal pagan antisemitism is a myth that has served to allow many Christians to exculpate themselves from responsibility for theological antisemitism. Nowhere among the pre-Christian Greeks or Romans do we find the elemental hatred of the Jews that we find first and foremost among Christian writers and Christianized Roman officials beginning with the fourth century, when the conversion of the Empire to Christianity took hold. Christianity brought a completely new factor into the relationship between Roman society and the Jews, and this was *the theological interpretation of Judaism.* Only with Christianity came the idea and sentiment that there was between Christians and Jews a theological war to the death.

Antisemitism in the Christian Scriptures

The profound antisemitism that we know of today began not with the pagans but with the Christian Scriptures. The foundation of the Christian faith was the New Testament, whose writers and later interpreters chose to express an anti-Jewish invective not in their own name but *as if* antagonism to the Jews was part of the mission of Jesus of Nazareth. It was this anti-Jewish "message" that the Church Fathers seized upon, elaborated, and communicated to future generations of Christians. To love Christ came to mean eternal hatred of his alleged murderers and their kin. The Jews had lost their place, their chosenness, to the believers in Christ. The "historical" proof of this theology was evidenced by the fall of Israel: the overthrow of the Jewish king, the fall of Jerusalem, the destruction of the Temple, and the Diaspora of the Jewish people. How could any Christian have ever learned to love the Jewish people, asked Pierre Pierrard, when favorable religious ideas about Jews "were lost in the blood of Calvary"?[12] It is a sad fact that those Christians most immersed in their own scriptures have often become the most thoroughly bigoted against the Jews.[13]

It is here, first in the Christian Scriptures, and later, in the patristic exegesis of these writings and of the Jewish Scriptures themselves, that Christian anti-Jewish defamation began.[14] For the Christian Scriptures served as great storehouses that the Church Fathers exploited for material to defame the Jewish people. The scriptural passages damning the Jews as rapacious hypocrites, children of hell and the devil, haters of and rejected by God, and deicides were the focus of nearly all Christian writers of the first seven centuries of the Common Era. Christ-killers was *the* essential Christian accusation against contemporary Jews throughout the patristic period. Tertullian accused the Jews of deicide in twenty passages in ten of his works. Origen, the third-century exegete, regarded the tragic fate of the Jews as due to punishment for their deicide, the culmination of a history of crime, rebellion against God, blindness, hard-heartedness, carnality.[15] In this metaphysical clash of religious identities, "we are now dealing," as Robert Wilken has stated it, "with...a conflict devoid of reason and logic, a bitter war, the spoils to be nothing less than life itself."[16]

The anti-Jewish portions of the Christian Scriptures that have been seared into the Christian psyche have been these: *Acts:* "Men of Israel...this Jesus, delivered up according to the definite plan and foreknowledge of God, you crucified and killed by the hands of lawless men" (2:22-3). "You [Jews] denied the Holy and Righteous One,...and killed the Author of life..." (3:13-15). "You stiff-necked people, uncircumcised in heart and ears, you always resist the Holy Spirit. As your fathers did, so do you.... And they killed those who announced beforehand the coming of the Righteous One, whom you have now betrayed and murdered..." (7:51-2). *Matthew:* "The Kingdom of God will be taken away from you [Jews] and given to a nation producing the fruits of it [the Christians]" (21: 43). "Let him be crucified.... His blood be on us and on our children" (27:23, 25). Perhaps the most anti-Jewish assertion attributed to Jesus in all Christian Scripture is reported in the *Gospel of John:* "Your father is the devil and you choose to carry out your father's desires. He was a murderer from the beginning, and is not rooted in the truth..." (8:44-5).

Although Paul wrote his epistles before the gospels were set down, the letters attributed to him seem to encapsulate the New Testament perspective on the Jews. Paul recognized that he was a Jew by birth and background (Phil 3:5). As to his fellow Jews, Paul sometimes argued that God had "certainly not" rejected them, "God's people" (Rom 11:1-5). For the Jews possessed "the sonship, the glory, the covenants, the giving of the Torah, the worship, and the promises. The fathers are theirs, and of them is the Christ, as a human person" (Rom 9:1-5). John Gager, Clark Williamson, and Norman Beck, among others, have argued that despite his ambivalent feelings toward Judaism, Paul saw that the "old" Law was valid for the Jews, but the "new Law" of Christ was legitimate for Christians. Jews and Christians are regarded each as a people chosen by God in its own way (Rom 11:16). Gager concludes that Paul's gospel "did not entail repudiation of the legitimacy of Israel or the Torah."[17]

But many of the writings attributed to Paul discounted much that was essential in Judaism and introjected a high level of emotional polemic into the controversy between Jews and Christians. Paul's words often expressed a hatred for Judaism in general and for the very Torah that made Jews Jews. As David Flusser has recently written, "Opposition among Christians against 'legalism' demonizes the Jewish law and makes the Jewish religious way of life monstrously hostile to God."[18]

- In Romans ll:25, Paul posited that Judaism was not as "valid" as Christianity, for in the last days the Jews would reject the religion of their fathers and allow themselves to be converted to Christianity.
- Romans argued that in Judaism faith and law are separate, i.e., it is a "legalistic" religion. Paul took the supersessionist position that "What once had splendor has come to have no splendor at all, because of the splendor that surpasses it" (3:4-16).
- Of the Torah, which Jews considered indispensable to their Jewishness, Corinthians stated that "the written code kills," it is "the dispensation of death," "whenever Moses is read a veil lies over their minds" (2 Cor 3:4-15).
- It was implied that the Torah was the essential basis for Jewish conduct (Rom 2), yet its physical sign, circumcision, was a "mutilation" (Phil 3:2) and the whole Torah "a curse" (Gal 3:13).
- In Philippians 3:8, Judaism was referred to as "refuse" or "dung."
- In the same letter (3:2-8), the Jews, or Judaizing Christians, i.e., Christians who were backsliding into Jewish customs, rituals, etc., were called "dogs" and "evil-workers."
- Paul argued that "as regards the gospel [the Jews] are enemies of God" (Rom 11:28-9).
- In 1 Thessalonians (2:13-16) the whole Jewish people were defamed as murderers of Christ.
- 2 Thessalonians 2:3 noted that the great theological enemies of Christ were not the gentile Greeks or Romans, but the Jews. The Antichrist was the false Jewish messiah who worked through Satan. He was sent to the Jews by God specifically because they have refused to believe in the true messiah, Jesus Christ.[19]

In some of these passages Paul may in fact be polemicizing only against Judaizing Christians, but in the exegesis of the patristic theologians and of later Christians no such distinction was made. The key to understanding the fourth-century Cyril of Alexandria, for example, is to realize that he adopted Paul's interpretations of Moses and the Law as death; Christ as life. Cyril wrote that Paul "considered [the Law] rubbish," and gained Christ. Paul's testamental antagonism to Jews and Judaism, like the gospels and Acts, as well as the references in Revelation to the Jewish Jews as a "synagogue of Satan" (2:9, 3:9), have provided a justification for the antisemitism of most Church Fathers and later Christian theologians.[20] These are the basic myths that have dominated the Christian West's perception of the Jews for two millennia. Even when we factor in the competition between Christianity and a thriving Jewish community that denied the validity of the new religion, it is still obvious that the antisemitic interpretation of the New Testament by the Church Fathers is the main root of antisemitism.

Functions of the Jews for the Fathers

Judaism and Jews served five functions for the Church Fathers. ***First***, the Judaism of the past was utilized by the Church Fathers to supply Christianity with an unimpeachable history and with a prestige the new church otherwise would not have possessed. In order to establish that Christ was not a Greek or Roman god, the early Christians argued that Christian history was even older than Jewish history, having begun not with Abraham or Moses, but at the beginning of time, as recorded in the Jewish Scriptures. The Church Fathers claimed all the Jewish Scriptures as their own birthright. The Old Testament patriarchs were treated as the first Christians. The church co-opted all the Jewish saints and true believers in God all the way back to Adam as Christians; Abraham was "father of the faithful"; Abel was progenitor of the church.[21]

A ***second*** goal of Christian theologians was to render the persistent Jews hateful in order to keep the faithful from being attracted to Judaism. The Fathers believed, as did Augustine, that "The one and true God, creator of goodness...is the author of both Testaments; but what is New is predicted in the Old Testament, and what is Old is revealed in the New."[22] In light of this exegesis of the Jewish Scriptures, the Fathers falsified the whole of Jewish moral history. They announced that the Jews are, have always been, and will always be evil. No evil was too great for the Jews not to have reveled in; no crime too appalling for the Jews not to have rejoiced in. Whatever good the ancient Jews apparently did was in reality Christian; their evil deeds quintessentially Jewish. The Jews were evil-doers even before their atrocious act of deicide. The Jews were collectively guilty of all the sins of their fathers, including deicide, which they repeated over and over again each year by ritually murdering an innocent Christian child during Holy Week, and each day in their synagogue prayers when they allegedly insulted Christ and the Holy Virgin. The Jews were pictured no longer as the Chosen People, heros of holiness and moral living; they were instead the very model of radical evil, "the earthly representatives of the power of Darkness."[23] For these crimes, Jews had to suffer continual punishment on earth, and eternal damnation, unless they sought salvation through the one true faith, Christianity. The patristic writers thus employed not only the words of the Christian Scriptures against the Jews, but also the texts of the Jewish Prophets themselves. According-ing to Irenaeus, had the Jews realized to what use their Law and Prophets would be put by Christians, "they would never have hesitated themselves to burn their own Scriptures."[24]

Third, antisemitism in the form of a powerful, pervasive anti-Jewish theology has supplied virtually all the churches and denominations with a crucial aspect of Christian self-identity. For in order for Christianity to establish its own sense of self, its legitimacy, its sanctity, it had to overthrow the theological dominance of Judaism. Jews therefore served as "an indispensable reference group, enabling Christians to know themselves as Christians and to incarnate good by contrast with [Jewish] evil."[25] When Jews persisted as authentic Jews proudly asserting their Judaism, they had to be ghettoized, expelled, converted, or sometimes killed; for their loyalty to their own beliefs was seen as an insult and a danger to the Christian image of itself. Anti-Judaism and antisemitism, therefore, both derived from the need for Christianity to define itself in opposition to Judaism. As the patristic John Chrysostom had so bluntly put it, "Don't you realize, if the Jewish rites are holy and venerable, our way of life must be false."[26] The Christian dilemma was that without Judaism, Christianity had no independent meaning. Judaism therefore had to be preserved, but in a condition where it could do no "harm" to Christianity, as a corpse in suspended animation.

Fourth, by focusing on the Jewish scapegoat and villain as the cause of all the specific historical ills of Europe, the church could explain away the evidence that contravened its claim that the Kingdom of God had truly arrived with Christ, and account for the continued existence of evil in the world. The Jewish people served as a "magic betrayer" to help Christians explain the plagues, wars, and revolutions of history.[27]

Fifth, it should also be noted at this point that despite these patristic attacks, Jews were often subjects of Christian good will. Christian goodness and righteousness toward the Jewish people are difficult to discern among the documentary evidence. But there are indications that in every generation there were Christians friendly toward Jews. Every time we read of prohibitions against Christian-Jewish fraternization, we must assume that worthwhile relationships existed. Christian theologians continually complained about Christians who grew close to Jews or treated them as human beings rather than as theological types. During the Carolingian era, for example, Jews were respected as the heirs and descendants of the Patriarchs and Prophets of testamentary times. This pro-Jewish, indeed, pro-human stance required the faithful to follow the moral teachings of the Jewish Scriptures as interpreted by Jesus of Nazareth in the Christian Scriptures even in regard to the Jews. This perspective underscores the solidarity of suffering among all human beings. Moreover, alongside the emotional *adversus judaeos* tradition Wolfgang Seiferth has identified an intellectual tradition called *Concordia Veteris et Novi Testamenti* ("The Harmony of the Old and New Testaments"). This spirit of *Concordia* held that there was an inner harmony between the two testaments, the gospels being rooted in the Jewish Scriptures.

Fully to be understood and appreciated, Christianity needed the ethical, monotheistic, and prophetic aspects of Judaism. This motif can also be discerned in some of the art and literature of the Middle Ages.[28]

Value-Inversion as a Technique of Patristic Exegesis

The Church Fathers selected scriptural texts and elaborated on them. But first, they resorted to a process called value-inversion to destroy Judaism's credibility. In the sixteenth century, Martin Luther wrote of a theology of glory (*theologia gloriae*) that "calls evil good and good evil...everything has been completely turned up-side-down."[29] In a like manner, Christian theologians have turned the values of Judaism on their head. Value-inversion was first employed by Christians in response to the crucifixion itself. Most ancient peoples, Jews and Gentiles, regarded crucifixion as demeaning. But the followers of Christ converted the "scandal of the Cross" into an act of metaphysical and eschatological importance. A meaningless execution in the political life of the Roman Empire and Judaean politics became, for Christians, the most meaningful act in history. Jesus' death would lead to his life (resurrection) and potentially to eternal life for all the faithful.[30]

This same principle of value-inversion was exploited by the Church Fathers to attack the traits and ideas most identified as Jewish (covenant, monotheism, synagogue, kosher rules, circumcision, chosenness, Promised Land, Jerusalem, and Temple). They reinterpreted, modified, and adopted these Jewish identities to fit the requirements of the Christian self-image. Christian value-inversion took several forms: The Jews claimed to have discovered a spiritual God, who they believed created all humanity, and with whom they had entered into a covenant. In it, they agreed to fulfill moral and ritual obligations in return for which God would make them the chosen people, the males marked by the holy ritual of circumcision. Their covenant with God carried with it the obligation to act as a kingdom of priests and a holy nation (Ex 19:6), whose purpose was to set an example to help human beings toward righteousness. Jews saw themselves as living witnesses to God's moral purpose for mankind, even if as God's servants they had to suffer and die for it. All this was recorded in the Jewish Scriptures, which the Jews considered sacred, besides being the historical record of their covenant with God and their history as a people.

But in the patristic mind, the Jews were treated instead as God-murderers—people who first rejected and then slew God who came to them incarnated in the form of Jesus Christ. Replaced as the true Israel by the "newly and truly chosen" Christians, Jews thus became hated by God the Father. According to Augustine's doctrine of the "Witness People," the Jews were no longer witnesses to their positive relationship to God's existence and goodness. Instead, God intended for Jews to suffer throughout history, like Cain, so that all human beings would realize the penalty for deicide and other religious crimes. Augustine's dogma became the predominant position of the church.

The Jewish circumcision no longer marked the covenant with God, instead, it was treated as the mark of the devil, or the mark of Cain the murderer. It was believed that the Jews were taught circumcision by God to soften their hardness of heart, or to identify the Jews so that the Romans would not allow them to return to Jerusalem. The fourth-century theologian Ephraem of Syria called the Jews circumcised dogs; for John Chrysostom they were marked by circumcision like beasts.[31]

Vilification

When the Fathers confronted the pagans *outside* the Christian community, they argued that Christianity fulfilled the prophecies of the Jewish holy books, especially concerning the messiah. It was, therefore, incumbent upon Christians to establish the validity of this "very distinguished religion"—Tertullian's phrase applying to Judaism.[32] Origen's anti-pagan critique, *Contra Celsum*, praised the Torah as inspired by the holy spirit of God and as the moral-legal principles upon which most Christian thinking was based. Yet this praise of the Jewish foundations of Christianity was of *past* Jewish achievement and made for external, pagan consumption.[33]

But the existence of an independently thriving Jewish community, which persisted in denying the validity of Christianity by its refusal to convert, gave pagan anti-Christians ammunition for their attacks on Christianity and justified pagan rejection of Christian missionizing. As a result, Christian theological writers increasingly came to write of the Jews as paragons of evil and satanic adversaries. The intensity of their language clearly crossed the boundary between a reasoned debate and an emotional polemic. It seemed to be a *theological* necessity that *all* Jews, whether biblical or contemporary, be implicated in mythic religious crimes. "The phrase 'a Jew,' or 'some Jews,' is almost unknown in patristic literature."[34] The Fathers argued that God had damned the Jewish people because of their continuous history of crime, which climaxed in the gravest crime and sin of all, deicide, God-murder. Here is how three of the Church Fathers summarized the church's predominant theological position on the Jews, Judaism, and Jewish history.

- Gregory, the fourth-century bishop of Nyssa, a Church Father of the golden age: "Murderers of the Lord, killers of the prophets, enemies and slanderers of God; violators of the law, adversaries of grace, aliens to the faith of their fathers, advocates of the devil, progeny of poison snakes,...whose minds are held in darkness, filled with the anger of the Pharisees, a sanhedrin of satans. Criminals, degenerates,...enemies of all that is decent and beautiful. They are guilty of shouting: Away with him, away with him. Crucify him. He who was God in the flesh!"[35]

- In the words of Hilary of Poitiers, Judaism was "ever...mighty in wickedness; ...when it cursed Moses; when it hated God; when it vowed its sons to demons; when it killed the prophets, and finally when it betrayed to the Praetor and crucified our God Himself and Lord.... And so glorying through all its existence in iniquity...."
- Pseudo-Cyprian summarized the church's interpretation of Jewish history: "Moses they [the Jews] cursed because he proclaimed Christ,...David they hated because he sang of Christ,...Isaiah they sawed asunder shouting [Christ's] glories,...John they slew revealing Christ,...Judas they loved betraying [Christ]."[36]

Thus, in the *internal* communication only among Christians, where their authentic attitudes were expressed, most Christian writers of the first seven centuries wrote against the Jews.[37] This was the so-called *adversus judaeos* tradition, with which the church impregnated the Christian mind, at both the conscious and unconscious levels. In the Byzantine East as well as in the Latin West, the theology of the Church Fathers distorted whatever neighborly relations had existed between Christians and Jews. The patristic Christians at bottom said to the Jews that their God, holy books, messiah, and a portion of their law belonged to the New Israel, the church; whereas the Jews were to be disinherited and to survive only as a warning of the consequences of obdurate wickedness.[38] Patristic theologians regarded the habits and institutions of the Jews as hateful indications of the sinfulness and criminality of a Judaism that was so deaf and so blind to Christian truth and goodness that it dared not to have died—as it should have done—upon the coming of Christ. The effect of these patristic ideas was devastating for the future status of Jews in Christendom, where Jews would be considered stateless beings long before the Nazi Nuremberg Laws of 1935, and where they would be murdered in their hundreds of thousands if not millions long before the Holocaust.

We can find nearly all the elements of *theologia gloriae* already in the Christian theologians of the first three centuries of the Common Era. To them, as to the Fathers of the Eastern Church, Jews were devilish Cains and antichrists. Eusebius of Alexandria coupled the devil and the Jews. He began *every* paragraph in the first half of his sermon on the resurrection thus: "Woe to you wretches,...you were called sons and became dogs. Woe to you, stiff-necked and uncircumcised, from being the Elect of God you became wolves, and sharpened your teeth upon the Lamb of God. You are estranged from His Glory; woe to you, ungrateful wretches, who have loved Hell and its eternal fires.... Hell...shall imprison you with your father the devil."[39]

For Tertullian, the outstanding North African theologian of the second and third century, antisemitism was as crucial to his religious beliefs as it was essential to his rhetoric. Anti-Jewish diatribes, for instance, are contained in twenty-seven of his thirty-two extant works. He regarded the Jews' fierce loyalty to Judaism as tantamount to a public denial that Jesus Christ was the true messiah. In Jewish belief the messiah had not come, and it was the theological ramifications of this Jewish challenge that Tertullian seemed to perceive as a danger to the emerging Christian identity. Like the other Fathers of the Church, Tertullian "needed Jews and Judaism as a kind of antitype to define nearly everything he was and stood for.... He uses [anti-Judaism] rhetorically to win arguments against his opponents and he uses it theologically...to construct a Christianity, a Christian social identity, which is centrally, crucially, un-Jewish, anti-Jewish...."[40] Theological antisemitism thus seemed to define for him what it meant to be a Christian, and to be a Christian was to denigrate Jews, Judaism, and Jewishness.

Like the other Fathers of the Church, Tertullian's writings were replete with attacks on the Jewish people for a whole panoply of "crimes"—for him there were twenty-three categories of Jewish sin—from deicide and prophet-bashing to "bad habits" like clinging to the past. He held that the Jews were "the very anti-type of true virtue."[41] His major charge against Jews was that they murdered Jesus Christ. In *De Oratione*, he wrote that "though Israel may wash all its members every day, it is never clean. Its hands...are always stained, covered forever with the blood of the prophets and of our Lord himself."[42] Tertullian identified Jews with heresy, implying that it was the Jews who most inspired heretics. In *Against Marcion*, he explained that "from the Jew the heretic has accepted guidance in this discussion [that Jesus was not the Christ]. Let the heretic now give up borrowing poison from the Jew...the asp, as they say, from the adder."[43] Deviations from orthodox Christianity were seen not merely as Christian splinter groups but as heresies that were essentially Jewish in spirit. Like many theologians of the Latin Church, those of the East also identified most heresies with Judaism. The Iconoclasts, who opposed the worship of religious images, were referred to as having "Jewish minds" by Peter of Antioch. When the Byzantine theologians debated Latin theologians on the issue of the Latin use of *azymes*, unleavened bread for the Eucharist, the Eastern Church condemned their opponents as "sharing in fellowship with the Jews."[44]

In *De Spectaculis*, Tertullian gloated and exulted when he imagined how Christ would punish the Jews for having "thrown God, i.e., Christ, out." Israel was not merely *extra ecclesiam* (outside the church); it was *extra Deum* (outside of God). "I...would prefer to turn an insatiable gaze on those who vented their rage on the Lord. 'This is he,' I will say, 'the son of the carpenter and the harlot.... This is he whom you [Jews] purchased from Judas, this is he who was struck with the reed and fist, defiled with spittle.'"[45]

What was new in Jerome—one of the greatest minds of the later golden age of the Church Fathers—was the identification of all Jews with Judas and with the immoral use of money, two themes that would bedevil Christian-Jewish relations for two millennia. Judas' sin and punishment was, and would continue to be, that of all Jews. In his bitter, anti-historical, and anti-Jewish theology, Jerome sermonized that

> Christ is saying: 'Judas betrayed Me, the Jews persecuted and crucified Me'.... In particular, this is the story of Judas; in general it is that of the Jews [*Specialiter intelligitur de Juda: generaliter autem de Judaeis*].... Judas, in particular, was torn asunder by demons—and the [Jewish] people as well.... Judas is cursed, that in Judas the Jews may be accursed. [Even] the repentance of Judas became worse than his sins. [Just as] you see the Jew praying;...nevertheless, their prayer turns into sin.... Whom do you suppose are the sons of Judas? The Jews. The Jews take their name, not from Juda who was a holy man, but from the betrayer.... From this Iscariot, they are called Judaeans.... Iscariot means *money and price*.... Synagogue was divorced by the Savior and became the wife of Judas, the betrayer.[46]

In another emotional passage that could have served as the basis of the later anti-Jewish Good Friday liturgy called the Reproaches, Jerome contrasted the gifts God had given the Jews with the "evil" with which the Jews repaid them. This homiletic assault went on for four thousand words like these:

> My enemies are the Jews;
> they have conspired in hatred against Me,
> crucified Me,
> heaped evils of all kinds upon Me,
> blasphemed Me.

Curiously, Jerome ended his sermon by asking his parishioners to forgive the Jews. Reminiscent of Paul, he argued that this should be done since God "has not altogether uprooted them.... We have been grafted upon their root; we are the branches, they the root. We must not curse our roots; rather we ought to pray for them."[47] Yet one must wonder about the effect of this sermon on a Christian audience when after thousands of words of bitter attack, Jerome changed course to remind the faithful to pray for the Jews as an act of moral conviction. Because his positive recommendation was positioned at the end of his tirade, almost as an afterthought, it may simply have been a sop to his moral sensibilities. Its actual effect must have been nil. Instead, the words of Jerome that ring down through history are not a plea for forgiveness, but the complaint that "the ceremonies of the Jews are harmful and deadly to Christians, and...whoever keeps them, whether Jew or Gentile, is doomed to the abyss of the Devil."[48]

Perhaps the most influential Father of the Church was Augustine. The fourth- and fifth-century bishop of Hippo was a prolific and inventive theologian.

Like Paul, although he was ambivalent toward the Jews, in the end he came down hard on them. He did mention the need to "love" the Jews, although it was in the context of trying to convince them to leave their Judaism and convert to Christianity—which in itself demonstrated a kind of disrespect for Jews as Jews, and for Judaism. Christians, he argued, "should preach to the Jews whenever possible, with a spirit of love...without exulting over them."[49] Like Jerome, he sometimes identified all Jews with Judas. He and Cyprian developed the idea that "there is no salvation outside the church," a notion that dominated the triumphant church until at least 1965. Like his teacher, the virulently anti-Jewish Ambrose, famed bishop of Milan, he made the Jews a special subset of those damned to hell.

His theological construct in regard to the Jews, repeated at least twenty times in his work, was the "Witness People."[50] This proposition—that Jews are to exist as suffering Cains in collective punishment for their deicide until their conversion to Christ—has served to legitimize, even to sanctify, the suffering enslavement of Jews to Christians. Yet, at the same time, by establishing a limit to such suffering, i. e., the Jews were not to be murdered, this principle served to protect Jewish people from mass murder for the next eight hundred years, although many Christian theologians questioned the Jews' right to exist at all.[51] The stigmatic mark of Cain was, for the Jews, Augustine believed, Judaism itself. "Not by bodily death," he wrote,

> shall the ungodly race of carnal Jews perish.... To the end of the seven days of time, the continued preservation of the Jews will be a proof to believing Christians of the subjection merited by those who, in the pride of their kingdom, put the Lord to death.... 'And the Lord God set a mark upon Cain, lest any one finding him should slay him.'... Only when a Jew comes over to Christ, he is no longer Cain.[52]

Moreover, in his Commentary on Psalm 58–59, Augustine wrote:

> The Jews have been scattered throughout all nations as witnesses to their own sin and to our truth. They themselves hold the writings that have prophesied Christ. If a pagan doubts Christ, we can prove his Messiahship because he was predicted in the writings of the Jews themselves a long time ago. And so by means of one enemy [the Jews] we confound another enemy [the pagans]. 'Scatter them abroad, take away their strength. And bring them down O Lord' (Ver. 12).[53]

The most bitter of the Church Fathers in regard to the Jews was John Chrysostom. It is a positive sign of changing times that in the most recent edition of his works, his Catholic editor, Paul Harkins, wrote that Chrysostom's anti-Jewish theological position "is no longer tenable. Even if he was motivated by an overzealous pastoral spirit, many of his remarks are patently antisemitic. For these objectively unchristian acts he cannot be excused, even if he is the product of his times."[54] Although the church has come to realize the antisemitism inherent in his theology, there has been much more resistance to the admission that Chrysostom's ideology was nearly identical with the predominant theological position of the church on the Jews.

We find in John Chrysostom as in most of the Church Fathers, and later Christian theologians, a kind of *presentism* in his assault on the Jews. All Jewish sins whenever they were committed were associated with the Jews of the contemporary generation. The sins of the Jews were endless, committed by the Jewish people both before the advent of Christ, during his lifetime, and into the present day. Chrysostom saw in his Jewish neighbors the alleged crimes of all preexisting Jews. If, for example, a scriptural passage referred to Jews as having worshipped idols, Chrysostom applied this prophetic self-criticism to the Jews of his own day.[55] In his exegesis on Psalm 106:37, he wrote that the Jews had "slaughtered their progeny with their own hands to serve the accursed demons, who *are* the enemies of our life."[56] And, like the other Fathers, he applied the New Testament passages concerning the Jewish involvement in the crucifixion to the Jews of his own day. He even quoted a Jew of Antioch as saying to him proudly, 350 years after the event, "*I* crucified him."[57]

Although John Chrysostom was critical of many groups, for him as for so many other of the Fathers, the Jews were the ultimate evil. In expounding on his program of hostility, Chrysostom sought to alienate any Christian feelings of affinity with, or of common humanity toward, the Jews. The goal of "the Church's greatest preacher" was to locate the Jews nowhere on this earth; instead, as Rosemary Ruether has concluded, he situated them in "the realm of the demonic."[58] Here are some examples of his assessment of the synagogue, the Jews' relationship with God and the devil, and their punishment for crucifying Christ:

- "Here [in the synagogue] the slayers of Christ gather together, here the cross is driven out, here God is blasphemed, here the Father is ignored, here the Son is outraged, here the grace of the Spirit is rejected. Does not greater harm come from this place [than from pagan temples] since the Jews themselves are demons?"[59]
- "[Jews] fought against the commands of God and danced with the Devil."[60]
- "It was not by their own power that the Caesars did what they did to you [Jews]; it was done by the wrath of God, and his absolute rejection of you."[61]
- In a stunning passage, John Chrysostom went so far as to assert that because Jews rejected Christ, they therefore deserved to be killed.[62] Like other obsti-

nate animals, the Jews "are *fit for killing*. And this is what happened to the Jews: while they were making themselves unfit for work, they grew *fit for slaughter*."[63]

- Chrysostom made the same argument about murdering Jews elsewhere. Quoting Luke 19:27, he claimed that Jesus was referring to the Jews when he said, "As for these enemies of mine who did not want me to reign over them, bring them here and *slay them* before me."[64]

John Chrysostom contributed a profound sense of rage to the anti-Jewish polemic, which resulted in violence against the Jews and their communities. Even though his diatribes against the Jews of Antioch seemed to have had no immediate effect, there were riots twenty-eight years later against the synagogues there. Can there be any doubt that his verbal and written assaults on the Jews helped form the attitudes of many Christians toward their Jewish neighbors? The attack on the synagogues was sparked by a rumor that a Christian boy in a nearby town had been murdered by Jews. Would Christians not be more likely to believe such rumors having been exposed to Chrysostom's hatred? Moreover, was it only a historical coincidence that Eastern Emperor Arcadius, who had confirmed the Jews in certain privileges in 396 and 397, with the arrival of Chrysostom as the bishop of Constantinople issued anti-Jewish edicts? To confirm the probability that Chrysostom, or his reputation, was a factor in Arcadius' changed Jewish policy, we must note that in 404, when Chrysostom was expelled from Constantinople, Arcadius re-established a policy favorable to the Jews.[65]

From the eighth until the twentieth century, the great preacher's homilies against the Jews, considered among the greatest examples of rhetoric ever uttered, were used in Christian schools and seminaries where priests were taught to preach and to hate Jews.[66]

The Church Fathers and the Issue of Race

Ironically, a case can be made for racism as one of the elements in the church's antisemitism, although certainly not a dominant strain. It is axiomatic that baptism and conversion re-create a person as an authentic Christian. Yet several Church Fathers approached racist thinking in regard to the Jews, doubting that Jews could authentically be converted. Citing Jeremiah 13:23, "Can the Ethiopian change his color or the leopard his spots?"[67] Isidore of Seville had declared that the Jew's evil character never changes. Augustine had argued that no Jew could ever lose the stigma of his forebears having disbelieved in and murdered Christ.[68] The evil of the Jews, "in their *parents*, led to death." ("*Occidistis Christum in parentibus vestris.*"[69]) Chrysostom called Jews "inveterate murderers, destroyers, men possessed by the devil...."[70]

The Church Fathers and Roman Law

With its prestige and authority, the church had the greatest impact of any institution on the secular laws of the late Roman Empire. On the basis of their reading of the scriptures, their interpretation of the Christian creeds, their adherence to patristic exegesis, and their vulnerability to the suasion of the Church Fathers, Christian emperors enacted laws that governed all men in general and the Jews in particular.

It was only after the Empire had become thoroughly Christianized that the secular government turned essentially anti-Jewish. In holy vindictiveness, the Church Fathers, all of whom apparently were Gentiles,[71] continually preached and wrote against the Jews, persuading emperors and ordinary people that contact with Jews was pollution. From the fourth century on, what Christian theologians believed about the Jews not only dominated catechetical instruction, sermons, and liturgy, but it also took concrete form in anti-Jewish laws and imperial policies.

Before the co-option of the late Roman Empire by the church, Jews had done rather well. Under pre-Christian Greek and Roman law, Judaism had usually been referred to neutrally. It was defined simply as the body of laws and customs unique to the Jewish people—its national habits, its rites, its belief. Drawing upon Christian theology, the Theodosian (II) and Justinian law codes of the fifth and sixth centuries contained the seeds of all future church and church-generated secular legislation. They concluded that Judaism was "a sad and hateful sect," "a perversity" whose meetings were "sacrileges," and contact with which resulted in "pollution." The religiously indoctrinated imperial lawmakers regarded the Jews as "enemies of Roman law," "insulters of the Christian faith," "the worst of men," whose very name, Jew, was "frightful and hideous."[72] Judaism was considered a "hopeless disease" for which there was "no cure."[73] The "notable [Jewish] religion" had become through Christian influence the "filthy [Jewish] cult."[74] The Jew as he is encountered in the pages of fourth-century theologians and incorporated into Roman law is hardly human. In the words of James Parkes, "[The Jew] is a 'monster,' a theological abstraction, of superhuman cunning and malice, and more than superhuman blindness."[75]

The pagan emperors had previously taken a few legal measures against the Jews. But it was the Christian Roman emperors who, under the powerful influence of their faith and of the church, were the first whose Jewish policy was based on discrimination, that is, that Jews deserved less protection under the law than Christians. Thus if a Jew violated a Christian's rights, he was punished more severely than the Christian would have been had he oppressed a Jew, and the rationale for such legal discrimination was theological. Although some discriminatory laws also affected pagans or heretics, the enormous number of anti-Jewish laws and the theological rhetoric they expressed indicated that it was the Jews who were the essential targets. Although Jews were equally subject to the same laws as non-Jews up through the first years of the reign of Constantine at the beginning of the fourth century, in the Christianized Empire later in the century, the law saw to it that the perfidious Jews could never occupy a status of equality with the faithful, who recognized in Jesus Christ the true Son of God. At this point, the emperor was under the influence of Christian bishops at his court.[76] By keeping Jews from any position of authority over Christians, excluding them from all public offices, proclaiming that neither their goods nor their lives were as well protected as those of Christians, and by awarding the clerical orders the same privileges as the Roman civil service, the theologically-inspired imperial legislation insured that the Jews would be recognized as the cursed subjects of Christianity.

Guided by Christian theology and often delegating authority over Jewish religious practices to the church itself, whose priests were legally empowered to act like state officials, the Theodosian and Justinian law codes anticipated canon law of the future and set precedents for church-generated secular legislation.[77] The hostility of Latin Christian law to Jews and Judaism was expressed not only in the explicit meaning of the laws themselves but also in the tone implicit in the language. Constantine referred to the synagogue, for example, as *conciliabulum*, literally, "a place of assembly," a term neither he nor later emperors applied to other places of worship, and meaning, in Latin slang, a brothel[78] (*Codex Theodosianus* 16:8:1).[79]

The fifth-century *Codex Theodosianus* was a compilation of all the legislation in regard to the Jews that was in force at the time. Its legal language demonstrates how the rights, privileges, and security of the Jewish communities of the empire had declined, and its rhetoric provides evidence that the primary reason for this deterioration was the triumph of Christianity. Although neither the church nor the empire ever outlawed Judaism itself, included in the *Codex* after it had become Christian was a series of laws that clearly discriminated against Jews and Judaism. Indeed, one of the first laws of the Christianized Empire was the law of Constantine of 18 October 329 that made it a criminal offense to become a Jew, with exile or death assumably the penalties set for Jews who tried to prevent their coreligionists from apostatizing to Christianity or who encouraged Christians to convert to Judaism.[80]

> The Jews must be informed that if they...dare attack anyone escaping from their deadly sect and choosing to join the cult of God [Christianity]...they shall be delivered immediately to the flames and burnt with all his associates. But if one of the people [lay Christians] shall approach their sacrilegious sect and join himself to their *conciliabulum*, he shall suffer with them the punishment he deserves (*CT* 16: 8:1).

Two laws of 383-384 on the same subject punished conversion to Judaism by exile, expropriation, or death. "Those Christians who have insulted the dignity of their own religion and name and have contaminated themselves with the Jewish disease will be punished for these shameful acts" (*CT* 16:7:3). "To convert a Christian to Judaism meant contaminating him with Jewish sacraments." A punishment would result "commensurate with and appropriate to the crime" (*CT* 3:1:5). Moreover, a law of 14 March 388 prohibited marriage between Christians and Jews. If such liaisons took place, they were to be treated like adultery, punished by exile, expropriation, or death. "No Jew shall take a Christian woman in marriage, nor shall a Christian marry a Jewish woman. Should anyone commit such a crime, it will be considered an adultery" (*CT* 3:7:2). Appropriately, one of the last laws of the *Codex*, a decree of Emperors Honorius and Theodosius II of 1 April 409, elaborated the same Christian position. "[It is prohibited to] cease being a Christian and adopt the abominable and disgusting name of the Jews [that is,] to adopt the Jewish perversity, which is alien to the Roman Empire which has now become Christianized.... For it is an issue of life and death when someone rejects the Christian faith and replaces it with the disgusting Jewish form of perverse belief" (*CT* 16:8:19). The reasons for these anti-Jewish laws were patently religious. Several laws repeated that "Whatever differs from the faith of the Christians, is contrary to Christian [Roman] law." The third appendix of the *Codex Theodosianus* insulted the Jews again and subjected them to the death penalty should they corrupt the faith of a Christian. "The blind and senseless Jews...heretics...abominable." Typically, the law makes clear that any Jewish tampering with the Christian faith would result in the most terrible of punishments. "Whoever coerces or persuades any Roman, slave or free, to leave the cult of the Christian religion and join instead that abominable sect and rite [Judaism] shall be sentenced to death and expropriation." Finally, the law clearly stated the traditional principle of *theologia gloriae* that Jews should never be put in a position of authority over a Christian.

> No Jew...may receive any honors and dignities of office. For it is abominable that an enemy of God and of the Roman laws shall be empowered to execute these laws...and have the power to judge and pronounce sentence against Christians, many of whom are priests of that sacred religion, thereby insulting our faith (*CT*, *Novella* 3).

Another office that the church wanted to exclude Jews from was that of military rank, which was accompanied by a number of privileges. Moreover, the church naturally opposed this kind of authority of Jews over Christians because it violated the theological precept that Jews must never have such power. Throughout the Roman Empire, with the possible exception of Italy, the Jews had served widely in the Roman army. In fact, there were so many Jewish soldiers that by the end of the fourth century, the Church Fathers became alarmed. And so, they succeeded in having a law passed excluding Jews from the army, although they still could serve in the defense of the towns in which they lived. For a Jew to serve in the military, he had to have himself baptized as a Christian (*CT* 16:8:24, published on 10 March 418).

Justinian's laws concerning the Jews were also motivated primarily by religion. Among the first promulgated, in 527, were those that cancelled Jewish rights and classified Jews along with heretics (*Codex Justinianus* 1:5:12-13, 21; 1:3:54; 1:10:2; and *Novella* 45). Another law, published "in the name of our Lord and God Jesus Christ," punished Jewish marriages as "abominable" and forbade the construction of synagogues (*Novellae* 139, 131). As in the Theodosian Code, the laws of Justinian treated Jewish citizens with a double standard as compared to Christians. An early law of 213, for example, collected much later by Justinian, disallowed the Jewish community of Antioch from receiving a legacy (*Codex Justinianus* 1:9:1).

Furthermore, Justinian invited the ecclesiastical authorities to oversee laws affecting the Jews' status and rights. Indeed, the Justinian Code attempted to determine the very tenets of Judaism as well as the way in which the Jews could celebrate their divine service. The Code implied that the whole Talmud and Midrash should be forbidden to the Jews. *Novella* 146 of the Code, published on 8 February 553, stated that Jews should interpret their holy books only as "announcing the Great God and the Savior of the human race, Jesus Christ," not for their "literal" meaning. Jewish exegesis was "malignant," "extraneous and unwritten nonsense." Jews who denied the resurrection or the last judgment shall suffer "the harshest punishments."

In the end, by means of these theologically oriented law codes, the Jews were classified as strangers and unbelievers, deprived of civil rights, and subjected to special discrimination. Jewish religious, economic, legal, and ultimately political privileges fundamentally depended on Christian theological premises. For the Christian-imperial laws embodied in the Theodosian and Justinian codes determined what the Jews could or could not do. The laws were issued by the emperors; the emperors conditioned by the church; and the church's Jewish policy depended on its theology of triumph. The way was therefore open to the legal destruction of synagogues, forced baptisms (in the next century, the Eastern Emperor Heraclius ordered all Jews to be baptized),[81] the medieval trials and burnings of the Talmud, as well as the defamations and massacres of the High and Late Middle Ages.

The attack on the synagogue as a symbol of Judaism makes a striking case study in the relationship between the theology of glory, the church, the law, and the secular authorities. Among the pagans, there had been almost no synagogue attacks.[82] But to Christian theologians, the synagogue represented Judaism, the hated rival of Christianity. And so the destruction of synagogues was the most obvious external sign of the antagonism toward Judaism of a politically empowered and theologically motivated Christianity.[83] To destroy or damage the synagogue building, to transform it into a church, or to prevent the construction of a new synagogue were means of persecuting the Jews, lowering their prestige, and destroying their attraction for the Christian faithful. Indeed, several synagogues were transformed into churches. When this happened a special mass using the Gelasian Sacrament was required to consecrate the building. In this mass, Judaism was referred to as a "deception that had been driven out," a "filthy superstition," "degenerate," and "disloyal."[84]

Synagogue attacks would not have been possible merely by ecclesiastical fiat. Christian prelates realized that they had to mold the minds of the faithful so that their policies in regard to the Jews would be effectuated. Let us recall Jerome's judgment on the synagogue: "if you call it a brothel, a den of vice, the devil's refuge, satan's fortress, a place to deprave the soul, an abyss of every conceivable disaster or whatever else you will, you are still saying less than it deserves."[85] Although Jewish attacks against churches occurred rarely, and then apparently in response to Christian destruction of synagogues, in both East and West synagogues were confiscated or destroyed in great numbers with the tacit or open approval, and sometimes even at the instigation, of local ecclesiastical authorities.[86]

Perhaps the most famous incident of synagogue destruction and its political ramifications occurred in 388, when a synagogue in Callinicum in Mesopotamia was burned by a Christian crowd led by the local bishop himself. We do not know precisely why it was attacked. But the Roman governor, in a decision based on Roman law,[87] punished the arsonists and ordered the bishop to pay to rebuild the synagogue from his own funds—the decision was confirmed by the Emperor Theodosius I himself. It is clear that Theodosius had no legal right to deny the Jews compensation for their loss, since they were at this time still a legally recognized religion in the empire. At this point, however, Ambrose, the very influential bishop of Milan and a mentor of Augustine, wrote to the emperor defending the incendiaries and indicating that he would have loved to have done the burning himself. Like Hilary of Poitiers, Ambrose saw any contact with Jews as a defilement. He took a radical position on the Jews. "Wasn't it the Jews," he asked elsewhere, "who in the synagogue were possessed by the unclean spirit of demons, the Jews who were encompassed by serpents' coils and caught in the devil's snare, and the Jews who polluted their pretended physical purity with the inner filth of their soul?"[88] His argument in defense of the attack on the synagogue at Callinicum was that God himself had already destroyed the synagogue both as symbolic of Judaism in general and as a physical manifestation of local Jewish communities.

During one Sunday's mass, Ambrose preached a sermon on the church and synagogue attended by Emperor Theodosius, who had recently been excommunicated by Ambrose, and was now penitent and very much under his influence.[89] Ambrose reproached Theodosius for his action in support of the Jewish claims, arguing that it was a moral act to burn synagogues and if the laws forbade it, then the laws were wrong. For Christians to destroy a synagogue was, according to Ambrose, a glorious act, so that "there might be no place where Christ is denied. [Because the synagogue is a] place of unbelief, a home of impiety, a refuge of insanity, damned by God himself."[90] Ambrose threatened that the emperor and his sons would be excommunicated again unless he rescinded his penalties against the incendiary bishop. In the end, Theodosius promised to do what was demanded.

This event was of great importance, for here we have an example of how an assertive prelate could bully even an emperor into an illegal action when it came to oppressing Jews. It demonstrated what control the church could wield over the secular authorities and their legislation on the Jews. In Ambrose's mind, even fairness for the Jews was inconsistent with his faith as a Christian. And he made his opinion stick in the political world outside the church. This was how a theologically conditioned Christian emperor, Constantine, expressed his opinion on the Jews:

> [The Jews are] a people who, having imbrued their hands in a most heinous outrage, have thus polluted their souls and are deservedly blind.... Therefore we have nothing in common with that most hostile of people the Jews. We have received from the Savior another way...our holy religion.... That detestable association[,] on what subject will they be competent to form a correct judgment, who after that murder of their Lord...are led...by...their innate fury?[91]

Creeds and Liturgy

In the patristic age the church also carried out its theological attack on the Jews in great part by means of anti-Jewish creeds and liturgy. The church hoped to use liturgy to impress on Christians that they should shun the Jews. Even the slightest positive liturgical reference to or action for the Jews, such as the faithful's genuflection and saying *Amen* after the Good Friday prayer for the Jews, the *Oremus*, was to be suppressed. This prayer singled out the "perfidious" Jews for special treatment: they are "unfaithful"; their hearts are "veiled"; they are "faithless"; and they are "blind" and in "darkness." It was in the ninth-century Amulo of Metz, successor to Agobard as bishop of Lyon, that we first read an explanation for the wording and instructions for the *Oremus*. Amulo wrote:

> When we pray we must genuflect in order to symbolize our spiritual humility through this bodily expression. But when we pray for the perfidious Jews, we do not genuflect. For they had genuflected in mockery [of Christ in His Passion]. Let us demonstrate our revulsion at this act by not genuflecting when we pray for the Jews. In like manner, let us abstain from the kiss of peace...so as not to duplicate the evil Judas kiss, which led to Christ's suffering.... We

> should abstain from doing things that associate us with the Jews. As Augustine has said, Easter should be commemorated on a Sunday so that it will be distinguished from the Jewish holiday.[92]

The very initiation process whereby pagans became Christians was full of anti-Jewish invective. The early Apostle's Creed that served as the basic instructional tool for training new Christians emphasized that the true messiah was Jesus Christ, whom the Jews had rejected and murdered. As Cyril of Jerusalem explained, the Creed was directed not at pagans, who did not believe in the coming of any messiah, but at the Jews.[93] Typical of sermons based on the Creed was one attributed to Augustine that was delivered to Christian catechumens (neophytes or novices). The homilist began his sermon emphasizing the importance of the catechism itself: "Receive, my Children, the Rule of Faith.... Write it in your heart, and say it to yourselves daily; even before you go to sleep, before you go out, arm yourself in your Creed."[94] But then he went on to describe Christ's passion in a dramatically anti-Jewish fashion: "The end of the Lord has come. It was the Jews who held him; the Jews who insulted him; the Jews who bound him; the Jews who crowned him with thorns; who soiled him with their spit; who whipped him; who ridiculed him; who hung him on the cross; who stabbed his body with their spears."[95] As Jules Isaac commented, "What a text! What an exegesis! It is a vivid model for the Christian literature, art, and teaching to come."[96]

In a homily, Jerome had established a basis for the Good Friday liturgy called the *Reproaches*:

> 'I had come to protect My people...as the hen to shelter them, but they received Me with hatred and malice. I had come as a mother, and they, as it were their own slaughterer, slaughtered Me.... They treated me just as if I were a swarm of locusts! What did I do? Was I angered? Did I defend Myself? Did I curse them? Did I abandon them? No, not any of that did I do. What did I do? I prayed for them.' [All the Jews shouted] Crucify him! Crucify him!... 'In return for the kindness that I had lavished upon them, they slandered me....' 'They repaid me evil for good. When I was hung on the cross, I pleaded for those who were crucifying Me, and they jeered at Me....' 'Hatred for my love.'[97]

By the eighth century, this portion of the Easter Week liturgy, also called the *Improperia*, was delivered in emotional and devastatingly anti-Jewish language, which continued until 1965. It pictured Christ crucified, hanging upon the cross, and addressing the Jewish people:

My people, what have I done to you?... Because I led you out of Egypt, you have prepared a cross [for] your savior....
Because I led you through the desert for forty years and fed you with manna, and introduced you into a very good land: you have prepared a cross [for] your savior....
I have planted you as my most precious vine: but...with vinegar you have quenched my thirst, and with a lance you have pierced the body of your savior....
Because of You I have slain the Egyptian through his first-born sons: and you have delivered me flogged....
I have opened the sea before you; and you have opened my body with a lance.... I went before you in the column of the fiery cloud: and you have led me to the tribunal of Pilate....
I fed you with Manna in the desert: and you fell on me with slaps and whips....
I have led you to drink the waters of grace from the rock: and you gave me gall and vinegar to drink....
I have hit, for your sake, the kings of Canaan: and you have hit my head with a stick....
I granted you the royal sceptre: and you granted me a crown of thorns....
I have exalted you with great strength: and you have hanged me at the gallows of the cross.[98]

The Jewish roots of the Christian service were disguised and the faithful were conditioned to believe that only the Christian religion was valid, only Christianity was capable of providing eternal life. As Jean Juster noted, the Christian religious service was employed to demonstrate "that Judaism as a religion was dead, that its benefits had passed on to the Christians, and that its flaws belonged to the Jews who still adhered to their faith."[99] As a result, the religious service was often followed by attacks on Jews, foreshadowing the mass murders of Jews in the Middle Ages.

Conclusion

The predominant patristic position on the Jews was the antagonistic *theologia gloriae*. Augustine's theological doctrine of the "Witness People," enunciated by most medieval theologians,[100] provided medieval Jews only the flimsiest of shields.[101] As a result, during the eleventh through fourteenth centuries, and into the twentieth, Christians murdered hundreds of thousands of Jews with only occasional interference from papal or princely authorities.

Endnotes

1. Terrence Anderson, "An Ethical Critique: Antisemitism and the Shape of Christian Repentance," in Alan Davies, ed., *Antisemitism and the Foundations of Christianity* (New York: Paulist Press, 1979), 213.

2. Robert Wilken, *Judaism and the Early Christian Mind: A Study of Cyril of Alexandria's Exegesis and Theology* (New Haven: Yale University Press, 1971), x, 229.

3. The term today applied to all negative ideas about, feelings and behavior toward, Jews. It can be expressed as avoidance, antilocution, discrimination, assault, expropriation, expulsion, physical attack, torture, murder, and mass murder. The *Great Brockhaus* dictionary of 1882 clearly defined antisemite as "Hater of Jews. Opponent of Judaism." See also Moshe Zimmermann, *Wilhelm Marr: The Patriarch of Antisemitism* (New York: Oxford University Press, 1986), 113; Gavin Langmuir, "Toward a Definition of Antisemitism," in Helen Fein, ed., *The Persisting Question: Sociological Perspectives and Social Contexts of Modern Antisemitism* (Berlin: Walter de Gruyter, 1987), 86–127.

4. See "Réflexions sur la genèse du discours antisemite," in Valentin Nikiprowetzky, ed., *De l'antijudaïsme antique à l'antisémitisme contemporaine* (Lille, 1979), 281; Bernard Glassman, *Anti-Semitic Stereotypes Without Jews: Images of the Jews in England, 1290–1700* (Detroit: Wayne University Press, 1975).

5. Rosemary Ruether, *Faith and Fratricide* (New York: Seabury 1974), 147.

6. Moshe Herr, "The Sages' Reaction to Antisemitism in the Hellenistic World," in Shmuel Almog, ed., *Antisemitism Through the Ages* (Oxford: Pergamon Press, 1988), 27.

7. A minority criticized Judaism along with Christianity in the same manner. Molly Whittaker, *Jews and Christians: Graeco-Roman Views* (New York: Cambridge University Press, 1984), 190, 148; Robert Wilken, "The Christians as the Romans (and Greeks) Saw Them," in E.P. Sanders, ed., *Jewish and Christian Self-Definition* (Philadelphia: Fortress Press, 1980), 1:105, 120.

8. Menachem Stern, *Greek and Latin Authors on Jews and Judaism*, 2 vols., (Jerusalem: Israel Academy of Sciences, 1980).

9. Wilken, "The Christians as the Romans (and Greeks) Saw Them" (n. 7), 1:62–64.

10. H.H. Ben-Sasson, "Effects of Religious Animosity on the Jews," in H.H. Ben-Sasson, ed., *A History of the Jewish People* (London: Weidenfeld & Nicolson, 1976), 411; Gavin Langmuir, "Anti-Judaism as the Necessary Preparation for Antisemitism," *Viator: Medieval and Renaissance Studies* 2 (1971): 385.

11. See Marcel Simon, *Verus Israel: Étude sur les relations entre chrétiens et juifs dans l'empire romain* (Paris: Boccard, 1964) 135–425; Jules Isaac, *Jesus and Israel* (New York: Holt, Rinehart & Winston, 1971); Jean Juster, *Les Juifs dans l'Empire romain* (1914; reprint, New York: Burt Franklin, 1965), 1:45–48 n. 1.

12. Pierre Pierrard, *Juifs et Catholiques Français* (Paris: Fayard, 1970), 298.

13. Norman Beck, *Mature Christianity* (Selingrove, PA: Susquehanna University Press, 1985), 223.

14. Rosemary Ruether, "Christology and Jewish-Christian Relations," in Abraham Peck, ed., *Jews and Christians After the Holocaust* (Philadelphia: Fortress, 1982), 27, 34–35.

15. David Efroymson, "Tertullian's Anti-Judaism and Its Role in His Theology" (Ph.D. diss., Temple University, 1975), 1, 4, 14, 22, 82, 85, 109; Nicholas De Lange, *Origen and the Jews* (New York: Cambridge University Press, 1976), 78–83.

16. Robert Wilken, "Insignissima Religio, Certe Licita? Christianity and Judaism in the Fourth and Fifth Centuries," in Jerald Brauer, ed., *The Impact of the Church Upon Its Culture* (Chicago: Chicago University Press, 1968), 49. Or, as it has recently been put, "it was a matter of life and death." John Gager, *The Origins of Anti-Semitism* (New York: Oxford University Press, 1983), 157.

17. Gager (n. 16), 260.

18. David Flusser, "Foreword," to Clemens Thoma, *A Christian Theology of Judaism* (New York: Oxford University Press, 1980), 7.

19. Wilhelm Bousset, *The Antichrist Legend: A Chapter in Christian and Jewish Folklore* (London: Hutchinson, 1896), 158, 166–170.

20. Wilken (n. 2), 174, 226–228. See also Peter Richardson, ed., *Anti-Judaism in Early Christianity: Paul and the Gospels* (Waterloo, Ontario: Wilfrid Laurier University Press, 1986).

21. Eusebius, *Ecclesiastical History*, 1.4.6; Augustine, *City of God*, 15.1, and *Against Two Epistles of the Pelagians*, 3.4.11.

22. Augustine, "Contra Adversarium Legis et Prophetarum," in J.-P. Migne, ed., *Patrologiae, Cursus Completus, Series Latina* (Paris 1844–), 42:623 (Hereafter cited as *PL*).

23. Hyam Maccoby, "Christianity's Break with Judaism," *Commentary* (August 1984).

24. Irenaeus, *Contra Haereses*, III, 21.

25. Léon Poliakov, *The History of Antisemitism* (New York: Vanguard, 1975), 3:28.

26. *Adversus Judaeos*, 1.6.

27. Richard Rubenstein, *After Auschwitz* (Indianapolis: Bobbs-Merrill, 1966), 72–73.

28. Wolfgang Seiferth, *Synagogue and Church in the Middle Ages* (New York: Ungar, 1970).

29. Martin Luther, "Explanations of the 95 Theses," in Harold Grimm and Helmut Lehmann, eds., *Luther's Works* (Philadelphia: Fortress Press, 1959), Thesis 58, 31:225–227, and "Heidelberg Disputation," Article 21, in Grimm and Lehmann, ibid., 31:40.

30. Clemens Thoma, *A Christian Theology of Judaism* (New York: Paulist Press 1980), 131.

31. Juster (n. 11), 1:264 n. 11.

32. *Apology*, 18:2, 5–6.

33. David Rokeah, "The Church Fathers and the Jews," in Shmuel Almog, ed., *Antisemitism Through the Ages* (Oxford: Pergamon Press, 1988), 61; and David Rokeah, *Jews, Pagans, and Christians in Conflict* (Jerusalem: Magnes Press, 1982).

34. James Parkes, *The Conflict of Church and Synagogue* (1934; reprint, New York: Atheneum 1969), 160.

35. Gregory of Nyssa, *In Christi Resurrectionem*, in J.-P. Migne, *Patrologiae, Cursus Completus, Graeca* (Paris 1863), 46:685–686.

36. Parkes (n. 34), 105–106, 160–161.

37. Jaroslav Pelikan, *The Emergence of the Catholic Tradition, 100–600* (Chicago: University of Chicago Press, 1971), 15.

38. Stephen G. Wilson, "Marcion and the Jews," in Stephen G. Wilson, ed., *Anti-Judaism in Early Christianity* (Waterloo, Ontario: Wilfrid Laurier University Press, 1986), 2:58.

39. Parkes (n. 34), 300.

40. Wilken (n. 2), x.

41. Robert Wilde, *The Treatment of the Jews in the Greek Christian Writers of the First Three Centuries* (Washington, DC: Catholic University Press, 1949), 149.

42. Efroymson (n. 15), 15.

43. Even Tertullian's heretical opponent, Marcion, attacked the Jews as more wicked than any other people.

44. Jaroslav Pelikan, *The Spirit of Eastern Christendom* (Chicago: University of Chicago Press, 1974), 201.

45. Efroymson (n. 15), 125.

46. Jerome, *The Homilies of Saint Jerome* (Washington, DC, 1964), 1:255, 258–262 (my italics).

47. Jerome (n. 46), 1:263–264, 255–257, 267.

48. Letter 112 to Augustine, in Terrance Callan, *Forgetting the Root* (New York: Paulist Press, 1986), 88.

49. Augustine, *Treatise Against the Jews*, in Migne, *PL*, 42:63.

50. Augustine, in Migne, *PL*, 36–37:705.

51. See Joshua Trachtenberg, *The Devil and the Jews* (New Haven: Yale University Press, 1943); Werner Keller, *Diaspora* (New York: Harcourt, Brace & World, 1969); Yitzhak Baer, *A History of the Jews in Christian Spain*, 2 vols., (Philadelphia: Jewish Publication Society, 1978); Paul Grosser and Edwin Halperin, *Antisemitism* (Secaucus, NJ: Citadel, 1976); Heinrich Graetz, *History of the Jews*, 6 vols., (1891–8; reprint, Philadelphia: Jewish Publication Society, 1940), vol. 4.

52. Augustine, "Reply to Faustus, the Manichaean," in F.E. Talmage, ed., *Disputation and Dialogue* (New York: Ktav and the Anti-Defamation League, 1975), 31.

53. Migne, *PL*, 36–37:705.

54. John Chrysostom, *Saint John Chrysostom: Discourses Against Judaizing Christians*, trans. with Introduction by Paul Harkins (Washington, DC: Catholic University of America Press, 1979), x.

55. Fred Grissom, "Chrysostom and the Jews: Studies in Jewish-Christian Relations in 4th Century Antioch" (Ph.D. diss., Southern Baptist Theological Seminary, 1978), 166.

56. *8 Orations Against the Jews*, I.6 (my italics).

57. *8 Orations Against the Jews*, V.1 (my italics), see also I.4.

58. Ruether (n. 5), 180. His "intention [was] to expel the Jews once and for all from humanity." Manes Sperber, *The Achilles Heel* (Garden City, NY: Doubleday, 1960), 122.

59. *8 Orations Against the Jews*, VI.3.

60. *8 Orations Against the Jews*, VI.7.

61. *8 Orations Against the Jews*, VI.3.

62. *8 Orations Against the Jews*, I.

63. *8 Orations Against the Jews*, I.1 (my italics).

64. John Chrysostom, *Demonstration to the Jews and Gentiles That Christ Is God*, 4 (my italics).

65. Juster (n. 11), 1:231 n. 7.

66. Malcolm Hay, *Thy Brother's Blood* (New York: Hart, 1975), 27.

67. Quoted by Ruether (n. 5), 130.

68. Gerhart Ladner, "Aspects of Patristic Anti-Judaism," *Viator: Medieval and Renaissance Studies*, 2 (1971): 362.

69. Augustine, *Adversus Judaeos* 7.10. See also 8.11.

70. *8 Orations Against the Jews*, I.4.

71. Jaroslav Pelikan, *The Emergence of the Catholic Tradition* (n. 37), 12.

72. Juster (n. 11), 1:48 n. 22+, 252–253.

73. Clyde Pharr, trans., *The Theodosian Code and Novels and the Sirmondian Constitutions* (Princeton: Princeton University Press, 1952), 489.

74. Graetz (n. 51), 2:563–564.

75. Parkes (n. 34), 174–175, 160, 158, see also 323.

76. Amnon Linder, "The Roman Imperial Government and the Jews Under Constantine," *Tarbiz*, 44:109–110.

77. See Edward Peters, *Inquisition* (Berkeley: University of California Press, 1989), 27.

78. The term was used before Constantine as a synonym for *ecclesia*. Amnon Linder, ed., *The Jews in Roman Imperial Legislation* (Detroit: Wayne State University Press, 1987), 131 n. 17.

79. Hereafter referred to as *CT*.

80. At this time, circumcision was treated legally like castration. See Linder, ed. (n. 78), 82.

81. Pelikan, *The Spirit of Eastern Christendom* (n. 44), 200.

82. "The Church was always jealous of especial beauty in a synagogue." Parkes (n. 34), 182. Only in Alexandria under Caligula is there sure evidence that Jewish places of worship were destroyed. But once the empire was Christianized, attacks against synagogues dramatically increased.

83. The Eastern Empire's Christian Emperor Zeno in 489 had asked at the burning of Jewish corpses in the Antioch synagogue, "Why did they not burn the living Jews along with the dead? And then the affair would be over." Juster (n. 11), 1:469 n. 1; Robert Grant, *Augustine to Constantine: The Rise and Triumph of Christianity in the Roman World* (New York: Harper & Row, 1970), 287; Parkes (n.34), 244.

84. Juster (n. 11), 1:468 n. 1.

85. Quoted by Friedrich Heer, *God's First Love* (New York: Weybright & Talley, 1970), 37.

86. See Marcel Simon (n. 11), 265.

87. See Carol H. Krinsky, *Synagogues of Europe: Architecture, History, Meaning* (Cambridge, MA: MIT Press, 1985), 36.

88. Ambrose, "In Expositionem Evangelii Secundum Lucam," in J.-P. Migne, *PL*, 15:1630.

89. Ramsay MacMullen, *Christianizing the Roman Empire* (New Haven: Yale University Press, 1984), 100.

90. Wilken, "Insignissima Religio, Certe Licita?" (n. 16), 63.

91. Wilken, "Insignissima Religio, Certe Licita?" (n. 16), 58.

92. Migne, *PL*, 105:1027.

93. Juster (n. 11), 1:299–301.

94. Augustine, "On the Creed: A Sermon to the Catechumens," *Seventeen Short Treatises* (Oxford, 1847), 563.

95. Augustine, "De Symbolo: Sermo ad Catechumenos, Tractatus IV," in Migne, *PL*, 40:634.

96. Jules Isaac, *Genèse de l'Antisémitisme* (Paris: Calmann-Lévy, 1956), 167.

97. Jerome, *The Homilies* (n. 46), 1:263–264, 255–257, 267.

98. Eric Werner, "Melito of Sardis, the First Poet of Deicide," *Hebrew Union College Annual*, 37 (1966): 192–193. See also K.W. Noakes, "Melito of Sardis and the Jews," *Studia Patristica*, 13 (1975): 244–249.

99. Juster (n. 11), 1:336.

100. Among them, Peter the Chanter, Cassiodorus, Peter Damien, Peter Lombard, Pseudo-Bede. See Gilbert Dahan, "L'article *Iudei* de la *Summa Abel* de Pierre le Chantre," *Revue des études Augustiniennes* 27 (1981): 110–111.

101. See Gavin Langmuir, *Toward a Definition of Antisemitism* (Berkeley: University of California Press, 1990), 139; Salo W. Baron, "Ghetto and Emancipation: Shall We Revise the Traditional View?" in *The Menorah Journal* 26 (June 1928): 518–519. Yosef Yerushalmi suggests the existence of a "subliminal" awareness the church had of "its Jewish matrix," but he discounts the power of this theological recognition to have saved the Jews from destruction, "Response to Rosemary Ruether," in Eva Fleischner, ed., *Auschwitz: Beginning of a New Era?* (New York: Ktav, 1977), 98–101.

Suggestions For Further Reading

Flannery, Edward H. *The Anguish of the Jews*. 1965. Rev. and expanded. New York: Paulist Press, 1985. A ground-breaking work on the history of Christian, especially Catholic, anti-Jewishness; Flannery has both the advantages and disadvantages of writing as a priest.

Gager, John. *The Origins of Anti-Semitism*. New York: Oxford University Press, 1983. A recent and reasoned discussion.

Isaac, Jules. *Jesus and Israel*. New York: Holt, Rinehart & Winston, 1971. A passionate discussion of Christian antisemitism by the Jewish historian and Holocaust survivor who convinced Pope John XXIII to call Vatican Council II.

John Chrysostom. *Saint John Chrysostom: Discourses Against Judaizing Christians*. Trans. with Intro. by Paul Harkins. Washington, DC: Catholic University of America Press, 1979. A series of anti-Jewish sermons by the most vituperative of the Church Fathers.

Linder, Amnon, ed. *The Jews in Imperial Legislation*. Detroit: Wayne State University Press, 1987. A complete collection of all Roman laws pertaining to Jews; this book demonstrates the anti-Jewish influence of the church on secular law.

Parkes, James. *The Conflict of Church and Synagogue*. 1934. Reprint. New York: Atheneum, 1979. A classic work of enormous scholarship and detail.

Ruether, Rosemary Radford. *Faith and Fratricide*. New York: Seabury, 1974. An early work on Christian antisemitism; very strongly written but lacks good annotation.

Simon, Marcel. *Versus Israel*. New York: Oxford University Press, 1986. An extended discussion of the conflict between early Christians and their Jewish contemporaries; Simon argues that the church inherited pagan anti-Jewishness.

Stern, Menachem. *Greek and Latin Authors on Jews and Judaism*. Jerusalem: Israel Academy of Sciences and Humanities, 1980. Two volumes that collect all the references to Jews among the Greeks and Romans, and demonstrate that most non-Christian authors were neutral or favorable toward the Jews.

Trachtenberg, Joshua. *The Devil and the Jews*. New Haven: Yale University Press, 1943. This volume, a pioneer study of the demonization of the Jews, shows how the Church Fathers' antisemitism was carried out in the Middle Ages; it can now be supplemented by the recent work of Joel Carmichael, *The Satanizing of the Jews: The Origin and Development of Mystical Antisemitism*. New York: Fromm International, 1992.

MEDIEVAL PERCEPTIONS OF JEWS AND JUDAISM

Frederick M. Schweitzer

Beginning with the First Crusade in 1096 the position of the Jews in Europe deteriorated sharply. Their expulsion from England in 1290 inaugurated the series of massacres, forced conversions, expropriations, and expulsions that, by 1500, left Western Europe barren of Jews. The flames of hatred were fanned by several myths, including the blood libel—that Jews, made bloodthirsty by the spilling of Christ's blood, tortured and murdered Christians, particularly children. Christian art, literature, and religious instruction depicted the Jews in a derogatory manner. Deeply etched into the minds and hearts of Christians, the distorted image of the Jews as contemptible, but dangerous creatures persisted in the European mentality into the twentieth century. Frederick M. Schweitzer discusses these distorted perceptions of Jews and Judaism during the Middle Ages.

Among historians of the Middle Ages, Jewish or non-Jewish, whether religious or secular in outlook, a consensus has emerged that the twelfth and thirteenth centuries marked the decisive stage in the formation of antisemitism as a lethal mode of hatred which, though it ebbed and flowed in intensity, had a continuous existence until its genocidal climax in the Nazi *Shoah* of European Jewry. This extreme form of Judaeophobia Gavin Langmuir has appropriately designated "chimeria," a term derived from *chimera* (unreal monsters, fantasies, etc.) and intended to distinguish the types of antisemitism that are irrational and anti-empirical from anti-Judaism, which is no more than a dislike of Judaism or of Jews and comparable to anti-Catholicism or anti-Buddhism. Chimeria, a lapse into the irrational and "illicit reification," requires a mentality that defies common sense, that flouts empirical evidence, tangible factors, or genuine witnesses, but, enveloped in subjectivity, is susceptible in literal extreme to allegory, myth, and symbol. In the Christian imagination, Jews, abetted by demonic powers, engaged in vile acts, including—as we shall see—ritual crucifixion, ritual murder-cannibalism, host desecration, poisoning of wells, and much else of the same tenor leading on to Christendom's destruction and Jewish domination of the world. These superhuman crimes also hinged on the Jews being identified as animals, the other side of a double dehumanization—supermen and subhumans. Thus the era that opened with the crusades and the invention of the crucifixion libel did not end until Auschwitz ceased functioning in 1945.[1]

Foundations of Church Policy Towards the Jews

By the end of the patristic period we have a conception of the Jews that was equivocal and ambivalent. On the one hand, there is philosemitism, for the Jews—with whom Christians are "co-heirs" according to St. Paul (Eph 3:2–6)—are the people of the patriarchs, the prophets, and the promises, from whom the savior came, and who will be gathered into the fold at the end of days. On the other hand, there is Judaeophobia, stemming principally from the arch-crime of deicide, for which, said St. John Chrysostom, "no expiation is possible, no indulgence, no pardon," only "woe and degradation." The most authoritative and influential exposition of what became the medieval paradigm was St. Augustine's "witness theory," by which the Jews, punished in dispersion and degradation for the crucifixion, testified to the authenticity of Hebrew Scripture and the truth of Christianity. Thus Jewish existence was providential to the great in-gathering at the end of time. In the interim, till the end-time and the resolution of all things, Jews must not be coerced into conversion but approached lovingly by the Christian missionary with his proof-texts.[2] The codification of these ideas as the basis of medieval papal policy and church tradition came with Pope St. Gregory I the Great (590–604), who declared: "Just as license must not be granted to the Jews to presume to do in their synagogues more than the law permits them, so they should not suffer curtailment in that which has been conceded to them."[3]

The law invoked by Gregory was Christian Roman law, the *Codex Theodosianus*, which, on Jewish rights and status, remained essentially the same as pagan Roman law: Judaism, which had been unique in its exemption from the imperial cult, continued to be recognized as a lawful religion; Christianity, earlier outlawed and persecuted, became the established religion; the pagan cults, once established, were outlawed. Although Jews continued to be tolerated with rights other outsiders did not have, Christianization of Roman law tended to affect Jewish status adversely, e.g., the right to build and maintain synagogues, proselytizing and conversion, slave ownership and slave trading, and access to honorable careers in the army, civil service, agriculture, etc., were abolished. These limitations were carried over into the church's canon law, where the negative aspect was intensified and extended. Here then, in Christian Roman law and in patristic theology, is the origin of the medieval church's dual policy toward the Jews, by which, on the one hand, they were reduced to pariahs hedged in with much abuse and contempt, and rendered vulnerable to forced conversion and persecution, but on the other, guaranteed minimal rights that allowed them to practice Judaism and to enjoy extensive local self-government.

One can see the difficulty clearly in Gregory's time. As a theologian he castigated Jews and Judaism in a flow of invective and vituperation in the Chrysostian vein, and as an ecclesiastic he was constantly on his guard to curb what he called their "insolence" in exceeding legal right. Yet his letters also ring with injunctions to bishops and others to correct abuses or make restitution to Jews who had been molested, attacked, and robbed, or whose synagogues had been destroyed or commandeered. Obedient to the law, Gregory permitted forcibly baptized Jews to revert to Judaism—"like a dog to its vomit," he said.[4] As were many popes after him, Gregory was not infrequently astonished and angered when he found that priests and monks, bishops and abbots took him at his polemical word—papal language was often harsh—and inflicted injury or humiliation on Jews. If it were frequently the case that churchmen could not split theological hairs with sufficient subtlety in adhering to the dual policy, what then of the masses whose religiosity was fired up by the inflamed preaching of crusade, the dramatic rhetoric of the antichrist and passion plays, or even the simple narrative of the gospels which themselves are passion plays?

The Age of the Crusades

The first crusade, 1095–99, has been traditionally interpreted as a milestone in Jewish history. In previous centuries, Jews had suffered sporadic violence, as had Christians in a turbulent and anarchical age, and the persecution of Jews in 1007–12, facing them with conversion or death, was exceptional and limited in scope. But the Rhineland region in 1096 saw the massacre of Jews on a large scale for the first time. The authors of that carnage were not animated primarily by economic motives, but were the footloose humanity fired up for these death-dealing rampages by preachers of crusade like Peter the Hermit, exalted by a sense of messianic longing and fulfillment. For the wandering pilgrims and common folk—in contrast to almost all the leaders and feudal warriors—the crusades were bathed in an atmosphere of eschatological mirage: the spiritual Jerusalem would descend from the heavens, God would divide the waters for this new exodus, and a purified Christianity would ensue. "God exalt Christianity," cried out many of these swarming hives of humanity, displaced peasants, lower class ruffians, and a few knights animated, in Norman Cohn's apt phrase, by "the messianism of the poor." They were led by a few rabble-rousers like the "very unstable," "unbalanced" Count Emicho of Leiningen, who, according to the chronicler Ekkehard, was "long infamous in the extreme" for his brutal conduct until, abruptly, "so the story went, [he was] called to religion...by divine revelations [and] usurped the leadership of nearly 12,000 who had taken the Sign [of the Cross]." It was not a coincidence that Emicho was hailed by his followers as "Emperor of the Last Days," who, as apocalyptic prophecy foretold, would be followed by the reign of antichrist and the second coming.[5] But the millennium would not dawn until the way had been cleared by the obliteration of the Jews and Moslems and the shattering of all unbelief. Their tormentors called them "God's worst enemies" and offered them the choice of baptism or death. As reported by a contemporary, Guibert of Nogent, the crusaders pondered: "After traversing great distances, we desire to attack the enemies of God in the East, although the Jews, of all races the worst foes of God, are before our eyes. That's doing our work backwards."[6] Marginal people, displaced by changing socio-economic conditions, filled to the brim with disaffection and millenary expectations, inflamed by Pope Urban II's preaching at Clermont on Moslem atrocities and Christ's suffering and death—such is the profile of the attackers.

"Because they were Christians," says Langmuir, Emicho and his followers "killed Jews because they were Jews."[7] They were, in 1096, the lunatic fringe whose massacres were an aberration, violating the prevailing Augustinian-Gregorian paradigm that Jews were to be preserved in a life of ignominy. It should be noted that while greed and booty—traditionally emphasized as the crusaders' motives—were not absent, the primary motive was the annihilation of the Jews as "God's worst enemies," whether by sword or baptism, born of a desire for revenge for the crucifixion. "Let us, therefore...extirpate them among the nations, so that the name of Israel will no longer be mentioned; [or] else they must ...profess our faith."[8] Hence the ferocity of the attackers, their "cruel thoroughness" in murdering pregnant women, children, the infirm, etc., as well as their exceptional rejoicing over converts.[9] And while bribery dissuaded some attackers, with Emicho and his zealot followers, as a Jewish chronicler lamented, "It was of no avail."[10]

The immediate response of the threatened Jews was defiance. Few accepted conversion voluntarily; many were killed, and many with the *Shema* on their lips killed their wives, children, and themselves in mass suicide rather than apostatize (although there were more converts than martyrs). It is to be noted, however, that only three Jewish communities—Mainz, Cologne, Worms—were actually wiped out in 1096; that Emperor Henry IV and many of the bishops endeavored to protect the Jews; that while some villagers and townsmen (presumably economic rivals of the Jews) joined the raging marauders, other Christians rallied to the Jews' assistance; that Jews placed valuables for safe keeping with their Christian neighbors; and much else of a similar nature that suggests a high degree of interaction of Jews and Christian society. This helps to explain why the Jewish community as a whole quickly recovered, the devastated sites soon being resettled. In fact, the Jews of northern Europe went on to their medieval zenith in numbers, prosperity, and cultural life. Nevertheless, for Christian perception of the Jews, 1096 was a milestone: the unprecedented and aberrant view of Emicho and his followers was to become prevalent over the next two centuries as the typical if not official attitude. By Emicho's generation the hierarchical structure of the church and the enforcement throughout Christendom of its teachings and dogmas, biblical and patristic, were far advanced. While the age of the crusades added little to the Christian theology of the Jews and Judaism, by then the views of the Church Fathers on the "damned" and "sacred" Jew had trickled down to permeate the masses.[11] Such developments augured ill for all minorities, but particularly for the Jews, the most salient and vulnerable.

Pope Urban was taken aback by the widespread, tumultuous response to his appeal at Clermont and the massacres that ensued. While he did not intend any attack on the Jews and made no specific reference to them in his famous sermon, he remained silent on Jewish suffering as his predecessors since Gregory I had done.[12] Other churchmen seem to have had a clear sense that the mayhem of 1096 was unacceptable, and they bent every effort to avoid such outbreaks in the future. Part of the church's response was the famous *Constitutio pro Judeis* (Constitution for the Jews) issued by Pope Calixtus II in 1120, building on a 1061 version of Nicholas II, a re-statement of Gregory I's position and an extension of it in the direction of leniency rather than rigor. It was re-issued at least fifteen times by 1450 and constituted a kind of negative *Magna Carta* condemning forced baptisms, assaults on Jews and their property, and desecration of synagogues and cemeteries; it also acknowledged their right to local self-government and to practice Judaism—to keep "the good customs which they have had until now in whatever region they inhabit."[13]

By the second and third crusades, 1145–49, 1185–92, churchmen and, spurred by them, lay rulers had matters under much closer rein: while there were many attacks on Jews, the incidence of successful attacks and the number of casualties were significantly lower, although, as a chronicler of the second crusade, Rabbi Ephraim of Bonn, reported, "the Jews did lose a great deal of money. For the king of France [pursuant to Pope Eugenius III's decree freeing crusaders of all obligation to pay interest on loans] commanded, 'Anyone who has volunteered to journey to Jerusalem shall have his debts forgiven, if he is obligated to the Jews'."[14] The masses continued to be stirred up to murderous fever pitch by popular preachers, and every crusade was punctuated, especially in Germany, by anti-Jewish violence. Many Christians now viewed the murder of a Jew as a meritorious act, a way to secure remission of sins and reduced time in purgatory. Many a crusader vowed that he would not depart for the Levant till he had dispatched a Jew: an appropriate way to avenge the blood of Christ was to begin by spilling the blood of Jews.

Against such preaching and threats to Jews, St. Bernard of Clairvaux reacted, even in the face of threats to his life by fanatic crusaders, although less out of human kindliness for suffering than out of allegiance to the church's dual policy. He praised some rabid clergy, who were inciting mobs to attack Jews, for "the zeal of God [that] renders you fervent," but he also maintained that the

> Jews must not be persecuted.... Ask those who know the Sacred Scriptures.... [They] are for us living words, for they remind us always of the divine passion. They are dispersed into all areas so that, while they suffer the appropriate punishment for such a crime [deicide], they are everywhere the witnesses of our redemption.... Under Christian princes they have endured a hard captivity. However.... when the time is ripe all Israel will be saved.... If the Jews are utterly wiped out, what will become of their promised salvation,

> their eventual conversion?... It is an act of Christian piety to...those from whom we have a law and a promise, from whom we have our forefathers, and from whom we have Christ of the flesh.[15]

These are the accents of Vatican II's *Nostra Aetate*, for both statements utilize St. Paul in speaking in behalf of the Jews but do so without valuing them for their own sake. And despite St. Bernard's courageous efforts, as a contemporary reported, "a large number of Jews were killed in this stormy uprising" perpetrated by crusaders.[16]

Peter the Venerable was a pivotal figure in the transition from anti-Judaism to chimerical antisemitism. A redoubtable combatter of heretics, Moslems, and Jews, Peter became abbot of Cluny c.1125. He was exalted by the glory of the church triumphant and was acutely Satan-conscious. In the 1140s Peter visited Spain and returned from that land of three religions with Moslem writings, including the Koran which was translated, the better to refute it. By 1147 he had written a diatribe *Against the Inveterate Stubbornness of the Jews*, one of seven major and many minor treatises *adversus Judaeos* that appeared between 1070 and 1150 (there had been practically none since the patristic age). Verging on "chimeria," Peter discloses a lethal antisemitism, accusing Jews of what they did not do—though never on the testimony of witnesses—and of being what they obviously were not—animals and demons. An impassioned preacher of crusade, he was grieved by the bleak results of the second crusade. His remedy for reanimating crusading efforts was, "Let their lives be spared and their money be taken away, so that the audacity of the infidel Saracens may be conquered by the right hands of the Christians, aided by the money of the blaspheming Jews."[17]

Cluny's financial problems got Peter into the toils of every description of "usurer," but it was pawning church items to Jews that roused his ire, which was "as if crucifying [Christ] again, [since the Jews] had despoiled [him] of his clothes." Peter believed, as he wrote to King Louis VII, that Jews rob Christians by their usuries, receive stolen goods, especially chalices and ritual objects stolen from churches which they use to finance Moslem wars against Christians in Spain, thwart crusading efforts, and engage in much else of a criminal nature. Peter's fears and phobias generated an implacable hatred for heretics, Moslems, usurers, but most of all for the Jews:

> It seems to me, Jew, that I.... dare not declare that you are human lest perchance I lie, because I recognize that reason, that which distinguishes human beings from...beasts, is extinct in you or in any case buried.... Truly, why are you not called brute animals? Why not beasts? Why not beasts of burden?... The ass hears but does not understand; the Jew hears but does not understand.

Peter launched into a pioneering attack on the Talmud:

> I extend to you before the whole world, O beastly Jew, that book of yours—yes, your book, that Talmud of yours, which is to be preferred to prophetic books and all authentic teachings.... Who besides Satan can teach such absurd things, and who besides the Jew can listen to, if not believe, them—that the reading of the Talmud can prejudice the power of God, that the incredible recitation of an infernal book can impede the will and mandate of God? For is that book of yours, O Jew, holier than the five books of Moses, holier than the books of the prophets, better or more worthy?... You have fought for so long against divine books with diabolical ones, and you have striven to tinge and obscure heavenly doctrine with the smoke of the eternal pit.[18]

Perforce, the Jews must "be punished in a way suitable to their wickedness," meaning not murder but that they "be execrated and hated," be "preserved in a life worse than death, like Cain the fratricide, for greater torment and greater ignominy."[19] We are on the verge of the chimerical stuff of which genocide is made. Peter's aspersions effected a double dehumanization, demoting Jews from humanity to animaldom and equating them with Satan's superhuman demons.[20]

One of the dilemmas raised as early as the crusades was large numbers of sword-point conversions. Since at least Pope Gregory I's time and consonant with Christian Roman law, the church had opposed and condemned forcible baptism. "A novelty, indeed a thing unheard of, is this doctrine that extorts faith through blows," was Gregory's denunciation.[21] For centuries there had been no widespread disposition to convert Jews by compulsion *en masse*. With the increase in forced conversions that came in the wake of the crusades, a distinction was drawn between "absolute" and "conditional" force whereby, under the first, reversion to Judaism was sanctioned following Christian Roman law, but under the second such backtracking was deemed apostasy, with the consequence that "they cannot now evade the penalties of heretics" and the inquisition. The distinction soon became meaningless, since it was rare indeed in the High Middle Ages for victims of sword-point conversions to be allowed, by ecclesiastical authorities, to return to Judaism; ordinarily it was lay rulers, like Emperor Henry IV in the aftermath of the first crusade and for which he was denounced by clerical opponents, who enabled Jews to return to their ancestral faith. It was no less than Pope Innocent III who pronounced, in 1201, that even if torture and intimidation had been employed in administering the sacrament, nevertheless one:

> does receive the impress of Christianity and may be forced to observe the Christian Faith as one who expressed a conditional willingness though, absolutely speaking, he was unwilling.... [For] the grace of Baptism had been received, and they had been anointed with the sacred oil, and had participated in the body of the Lord,

> they might properly be forced to hold to the faith which they had accepted perforce, lest the name of the Lord be blasphemed, and lest they hold in contempt and consider vile the faith they had joined.[22]

In practice papal condemnation of forced baptism was similar to papal guarantee of the existence of synagogues and the practice of Judaism in them: after the fact of a synagogue being seized and consecrated by a bishop as a church, all the king's horses and all the king's men could not restore it to its Jewish congregation. Coerced baptism entailed further impediments, whether the victims returned to Judaism or not, i.e., whether they did so openly and freely or secretly and surreptitiously, or became steadfast and sincere Christians, they or their descendants: this was the pervasive suspicion and incessant accusation that Jewish converts—all of them—remained secret Jews.[23] The ancient notion was thus strengthened of the Jew as a "perfidious" conspirator. This phenomenon is familiar with the *marranos* or *conversos* in Spain after 1391, but it is traceable two centuries earlier and was prevalent in much of Christendom.

The Talmud Attacked

Christian Roman law condemned the Talmud as the *Second Publication* (second to the Bible): "We forbid it," the Emperor Justinian ordained, "since it is not connected with the Sacred Books, nor handed down from the Prophets; rather it is an invention contrived by men, who speak from earth, for they possess within themselves nothing of the divine."[24] Here too church policy followed in the wake of Roman law and the emperors. Pope Innocent IV (1243–54), concluded that their use of the Talmud exceeded Jewish rights specified by the dual policy:

> An immense book it is, exceeding the text of the Bible in size, and in it are blasphemies against God and his Christ, and against the blessed Virgin, fables that are manifestly beyond all explanation, erroneous abuses, and unheard-of stupidities—yet this is what they teach and feed their children...and render them totally alien to the teachings of the law and the prophets, fearing lest the truth, which is understood in the same law and prophets, bearing patent testimony to the only-begotten son of God, who was to come in the flesh, they be converted to the faith, and return humbly to their redeemer.[25]

From c.1070 through the twelfth century nearly twenty *adversus Judaeos* treatises appeared, a great upsurge, to which Jews replied in kind or had even partly provoked. "There had always been a polemical literature by Jews against Christians and by Christians against Jews," writes John Mundy, and it "had always been crude."[26] The scurrilous *Toldoth Jeshu* (*Jesus' Story*), which made him the illegitimate son of a Roman soldier, a magician, a sarcastic parody of the gospels boasting that Jews had killed him, and so on, dates from the third century or earlier, and was a piece of popular polemic and folklore; it was known to Christians throughout the Middle Ages and was utilized polemically (printed for that reason in 1681). A mine for antisemites, it served their purposes much better than the Talmud which makes few and veiled references to Christianity, and was never the official or rabbinic view of Christianity. For that one should turn to Maimonides who held that Christianity was not pagan or idolatrous, but a vehicle bearing Judaism's historical monotheism and ethics to the Gentiles.

A clearer indication of the dimensions and vitality of the Jewish response to the Christian missionary campaign is found in the sprawling miscellany of polemic, debate, and analysis, the *Milhemet Mizvah* (*The Obligatory War*) written in the mid-thirteenth century by Rabbi Meir ben Simon of Narbonne. One segment is a penetrating historical study of the origins of Christianity, a remarkably sophisticated quest for the historical Jesus; an anonymous work, anticipating Morton Smith, interpreted Jesus' miracles simply as magic.[27] Well into the thirteenth century, however, there were friendly contacts between Jews and Christians who debated each other in dialogue rather than disputation, for it was a time when it was possible to "learn Hebrew from the Jew next door [who was] a kind of telephone to the Old Testament."[28] Christians thus gained direct access to post-biblical texts, e.g., the Mishnah, Talmud, various midrashim and commentaries, and the *Mishneh Torah* and *Guide to the Perplexed* of Maimonides.

The Talmud had become an integral part and formative influence in the life of European Jewry in the course of the eleventh century, owing largely to the great scholar Rashi (Rabbi Shlomo ben Isaac of Troy, 1040–1105) whose commentary and exposition have remained a key part of the Talmud ever since.[29] Christian discovery of the Talmud was a product of the Bible study and growing knowledge of Hebrew of twelfth-century scholars such as Hugh of St. Victor, Andrew of St. Victor, and Herbert of Bosham, whose biblical exegesis made extensive use of Rashi and other Jewish sages.[30]

Paradoxically, Maimonides provided one of the main portals for Christians to the world of Jewish learning. After the great sage's death in 1204, some Jews tried to prohibit the study of his works, which they denounced as rationalistic and heretical. In the course of the controversy the anti-Maimonidists invoked Christian authorities, and were obliged by inquisitors who gladly burnt the offending works in 1232. Thereafter Christian attacks on the Talmud and post-biblical Judaism multiplied. Polemicists condemned the Talmud as heretical, accusing the rabbis of fashioning a "new" law and religion, of manufacturing fables (the *Aggadah*), and of being led astray by Aristotelian rationalism. Pope Gregory IX (1227–41), directed the monarchs and bishops of France, England, Spain, and Portugal to confiscate the books of the Jews and have them inspected by the friars in order that those tainted by doctrinal error and theological delusion be destroyed. In France, the first step was to pit the apostate Nicholas Donin in disputation—a kind of ordeal by verbal combat—against Rabbi Yehiel of Paris, with the Queen Regent Blanche of Castile presiding (the first of many such contests). Donin had earlier been censored by the rabbis for his iconoclasm in attacking the Talmud and all the post-biblical commentary and interpretation in favor of the pure text of the Bible. Perhaps in revenge, he presented a long list of accusations and denunciations against the Jews and Judaism to the pope. A second step was to put the Talmud itself on trial before the clerical professors of the university of Paris; a third was to convict the Talmud and sentence it to be burnt at the stake. For the better part of two days in 1242 a crowd of mourning Jews witnessed some twenty wagon loads of the Talmud—estimated as 10–12,000 volumes—being burnt as a criminal might have been. More papalist than the pope, Blanche's son St. Louis IX, the quintessential medieval king and much enamored of the friars, confided to his biographer and fellow crusader, Joinville, that "only a very learned cleric should dispute with the Jews, but a layman, when he hears the Christian law mis-said by a Jew, should not defend the Christian law, unless it be with his sword, and with that he should pierce the mis-sayer in the stomach, so far as the sword will enter."[31]

Church officials compiled a large compendium of passages that were supposedly malignant and anti-Christian. These *Extractiones de Talmut,* together with excerpts from Jewish liturgical and other Hebrew material, were used as weapons of inquisitional attack. As Gregory IX expounded to the monarchs and prelates in ordering the Talmud's burning:

> If what is said about the Jews...is true, no punishment would be sufficiently great or sufficiently worthy of their crime. For they, so we have heard, are not content with the Old Law which God gave to Moses in writing: they even ignore it completely, and affirm that God gave another Law which is called 'Talmud,' that is 'Teaching,' handed down to Moses orally.[32]

"The Jewish teachers of France had uttered a falsehood," the university chancellor of Paris reported to Gregory, "when they said that without these books, which in Hebrew are called 'Talmud,' they cannot understand the Bible and the other precepts of their laws, in accordance with their faith."[33] To churchmen, Talmudic Judaism was simply a heresy replete with "innumerable errors, abuses, blasphemies and wickedness," which threatened dire "injury to the Christian faith."[34] In an outrageous defamation, they accused the rabbis of utilizing the Talmud's precepts to demand that Jews kill, injure, cheat, and deceive Christians at every opportunity. Thus as Langmuir comments, "a new stereotype was born, that of the mysterious Talmudic Jew,"[35] to be reborn with Johannes Eisenmenger's flagrantly distorted *Entdecktes Judentum (Judaism Unveiled)* of 1700, and the even more notorious, plagiarized calumnies of August Röhling's *Talmudjude (The Talmud Jew)* of 1871, and still troubling Jewish-Christian dialogue.

The contention that the Talmud was heretical vis-a-vis biblical Judaism, blasphemous vis-a-vis Christianity, could be countered by the argument that it is a *midrash* on the Hebrew Bible as the New Testament is on the Old Testament—which a delegation of Jews seems to have made to Gregory IX. This proposition appears to have been accepted in time, since condemnation of the Talmud as heresy faded from later papal decrees, and the popes—presumably reverting to the dual policy—were content to have the Talmud censored by snipping out the presumed repugnant passages.[36] Nevertheless, the Talmud long remained in danger of annihilation and was subject to inquisitorial proceedings and *autos-da-fé*. The accusation of heresy continued to be leveled at it, as by a fourteenth-century Dominican who opined, "The entire text is heretical."[37]

Christian Appropriation of the Talmud

By the 1260s the second stage in the attack on the Talmud and post-biblical Judaism was underway. This time the Jews' own books were taken over as proof-texts testifying to the truth of Christian dogma, thus buttressing the view that Jews were proper game for forcible missionizing and conversion: missionary zeal had by then taken the place of crusade in the emotions of many Christians. In 1278 Pope Nicholas III enjoined the Franciscans and Dominicans to:

> summon them [the Jews] to sermons in the places where they live, in large and small groups, repeatedly, as many times as you may think beneficial. Inform them of evangelical doctrines with salutary warnings and discreet reasonings, so that after the clouds of darkness have gone, they may shine in the light of Christ's countenance, having been reborn at the baptismal font.[38]

It followed that Jews were rounded up and preached to in synagogues by friars, who were often Jewish apostates, and/or forced to participate in unequal disputations (as at Paris in the 1240s). Sometimes the friars were wildly enthusiastic and excessive, even in the eyes of churchmen and monarchs, who issued decrees for restraint and moderation. The friars burned, edited, and censored Jewish books; invaded synagogues, terrorized worshippers, fomented mob action in order to intimidate Jews to the baptismal font; accused Jews of ritual murder, "usury," and much else. Such excesses induced King James I of Aragon, who had himself sponsored the well-known Barcelona disputation of 1263 and even preached a conversionist sermon in the synagogue, to moderate his own decrees. Jews, he ordered, were not to be forced to leave their districts to be exposed to proselytizing; although he empowered a commission of friars to censor Jewish books by expurgating offending passages or burning the entire work, the volumes were to remain with the Jews until they had the opportunity to appeal to the commission to defend or explain the portions under attack. At the same time James enthusiastically encouraged the missionary activity of Paul Christiani. A defector from Judaism, Paul became a Dominican, was a principal in the 1263 disputation, and pursued a vendetta against his former coreligionists and the Talmud over much of western Europe until his death in 1274.[39]

The Jewish spokesman in the 1263 disputation at Barcelona was Ramban, also called Nahmanides (Rabbi Moses ben Nahman of Gerona), one of the great scholars of his generation, who wrote an account of the proceedings intended to fortify his fellow Jews, shaken by "the Dominicans, who cast terror everywhere." He also penned a powerful and original messianic treatise, asserting that the messiah "will come and will issue commands to the pope" to be converted or to restore Jewish freedom. Ramban's vigorous defense of Judaism (reportedly James awarded him a prize or commended his good defense of a bad cause) and the possible annoyance with the paucity of converts from the missionary blitz led religious authorities to call for his arrest; Ramban fled to the Holy Land.[40]

One of the leading figures in the second stage of this assault on the Jews of Latin Europe was the Spanish Dominican, St. Raymond de Peñaforte (c.1175–1275), the confident of Gregory IX who made him the Dominican master-general in 1238. St. Raymond played a role in initiating the 1263 Barcelona disputation, established the papal inquisition in Aragon, and persuaded St. Thomas Aquinas to write the *Summa contra gentiles* to attract converts. He and his two protégés, Raymond Martini and the apostate Paul Christiani, were proponents of a grand missionary effort directed toward Jews and Moslems. To equip missionaries with their tools, the friar founded several schools to teach Hebrew and to confer licenses to teach, debate, and dispute.

The masterwork of the Peñaforte school was Martini's *Pugio fidei* (*Dagger of Faith against Moors and Jews*, 1278) an enormous volume of great erudition, addressed to missionaries and inquisitors. Martini was determined to confront the Jews' "impiety and perfidy" so as to extinguish "their pertinacity and their impudent insanity."[41] In his exposition, he characteristically quoted the original Hebrew or Aramaic, which he translated into Latin. He was closely familiar with the Talmud, works of commentary, and particularly the writings of Rashi and Maimonides. This made the *Pugio fidei* an encyclopedic treatise that served Catholic polemical and missionary purposes well into the seventeenth century.[42] That the messiah had come he demonstrates by citations from Bible and Talmud. To establish the truth of the trinity he uses the same tactics (a favorite device of the time was to note that *Elohim*, one of the Hebrew words for God, is plural and demonstrates that Jews knew and believed in the trinity). Such arguments were used to buttress his central point—that Jewish books prove the Christian case, that Jewish reasoning against Christianity can be turned about to confirm Christian truth. In his zealotry, Martini forged passages the better to convince.

Another element in the friars' strategy was to re-write Jewish history. Martini's was a typical specimen of Christian historiography: owing to their criminal past, he said, the Jews were denied a legitimate existence in the present and condemned to a future of retribution—degradation, madness, illness, poverty, and humiliation. Their only hope was conversion. To Martini, Jewish history was tripartite. The first age was that of the Old Testament, when the Mosaic law curbed the evil disposition of fallen man, an ethos from which Jews had never been freed. The second period ran from Jesus' revelation of an antinomian religion of love down to the Romans' destruction of the temple, city, and kingdom, which was caused by "the reprobation, reproaching, and repulsion of our messiah," the acceptance of Bar Kochba as messiah, and other "villainies" such as awaiting "a third messiah." For Martini (and St. Thomas Aquinas, who probably got the idea from him), the Jews in Jesus' time knew he was the divine messiah, but, driven "by the most impudent folly, go out of their minds" and persist in their "demonic" insanity. "The devil undoubtedly...misled them and deprived them of a sense of understanding the truth." The present third stage finds the Jews sunk in "impudence" and "evil." The rabbis and sages, "infatuated by the devil," spun the insane tangle of cobwebs that comprise the Mishnah and Talmud, obscuring the Old Testament's christological passages. Hence the Talmud was "not the law of God but the artifice of the devil," and this third period of Jewish history is not one of "the service or worship of God, but the cult of the devil." God had inflicted "madness" on the Jews, because they abandoned him for the rule of the devil, their "insanities and wiles" making them a danger to Christians; for they are "prone to kill Christians, to hurl their children in pits and wells, and even to cut them to pieces when they can secretly." The idea of Jewish madness—linked to disease, plague, indeed a pervasive pathology, including criminality—has a long history from St. Paul to the present and is a major strand of antisemitism; such ideas had papal imprimaturs, e.g. Honorius IV's, when, in 1286, he pronounced Judaism to be a "pernicious and dangerous disease."[43]

Martini's polemic signifies that the Jews no longer served a providential role: they were not Augustinian "witnesses" but a mortal danger to Christendom. Such was the fruit of the new knowledge of Hebrew and rabbinics that the Christian world boasted. We "like to believe that intolerance originates in ignorance," says Amos Funkenstein, but the friars' endeavor "confirms the opposite," for the new knowledge was used to replace the Augustinian paradigm with one of destruction by mass conversion and expulsion—yet, given the nature of medieval religiosity, it could not have been different.[44] Mass conversion did not, in fact, occur, and in that sense the friars' war on the Jews failed. Yet, beginning in 1290 in England, Jews were progressively expelled from one domain after another until expulsion from Portugal in 1497 rendered Western Europe *Judenrein*.

The friars' campaign went on relentlessly in the High Middle Ages, as some examples will show. Duns Scotus (1266–1308), celebrated as "the subtle doctor" of theology, fell in with the great missionary effort directed at Jews (and Moslems). Arguing that divine law (in this case, extension of the faith) transcended natural law (in this case, integrity of the family and parents' rights), he urged Christian rulers to kidnap Jewish children and do so without the parents' foreknowledge, lest they kill the children to prevent their baptism:

> Moreover, I believe that it would be a pious deed to coerce the parents themselves with threats and terror to receive baptism and to cling to it thereafter. For even though they would not be true believers in their hearts, it would be still less harmful for them to be unable to keep safely their illicit religion than to be able to keep it freely. Their descendants, if properly brought up, would become true believers by the third or fourth generation.

Duns Scotus complied with the Augustinian theology of Jews as witness in that he would settle a few on an island somewhere, what has been appropriately called a "medieval 'Madagascar Plan'."[45]

The tireless inquisitor and prolific author Bernard Gui (c.1261–1331), was much concerned with relapsed Jewish converts and with Jewish books, especially the Talmud, which he wanted destroyed since it is "expedient and necessary for the purity of the orthodox faith that doctrinal errors be eradicated not only from the hearts of the errant but also from books."[46] Raymond Lull (c.1231–1315), urged energetic, high-pressure sermons and disputations as well as forced tuition of Jews in "colleges" where they would learn Latin and a host of Christian subjects, whereupon if they did not convert, "let them be ejected from Christendom." Either conversion or banishment for these "outlaws" who refused to recognize the doctrine of the trinity in their own scripture.[47] Lull's mysticism may have been shaped by the massive corpus of Jewish mystical lore, the Kabbalah; its history parallels the Talmud's—for it too was attacked by churchmen as a source of danger to Christians and was also appropriated as a grand proof-text of Christian doctrine. Later Christian humanists were ardent students of Kabbalah, finding in it the secrets of biblical exegesis and magic as well as a kind of talisman to effect the conversion of the Jews.[48]

Barnstorming mendicant preachers, of whom there were a great many, reached the uneducated and illiterate in the vernacular. The harsh, aggressively anti-Jewish prototype of these preachers was the German, Berthold of Regensburg (c.1205–72). His long, eventful career took him through the Holy Roman Empire and France, preaching that Jews were allies of the devil and awaited the antichrist.[49] St. Bernardino da Siena (1380–1444), was a redoubtable fulminator against Jews in northern Italy, declaiming ardently that through their usurers and physicians Jews schemed the destruction of Christianity by poverty and poison.

The Dominican St. Vincent Ferrer (c.1350–1419), that "scourge" who set off anti-Jewish riots wherever he went, was also a widely emulated, inspiring example of Jew-baiting. He did much to ignite the massacres and forcible conversions of Jews in Aragon in 1391, "the year of persecutions and oppression" in Jewish chronicles. A similar wildfire of massacre and sword-point conversions swept over Castile the same year. The Dominican was the prime mover in the most sensational of all the conversionist disputations, that held at Tortosa, presided over by the anti-Pope Benedict XIII and lasting nearly two years, 1413–14, "the year of apostasy." It was a characteristic theme of St. Vincent's preaching that "Jesus Christ was a Jew, and the Blessed Virgin was a Jewess.... This circumcised God is our God." Yet the inference the flaming preacher drew from such facts was that damnation awaited anyone "who dies a Jew," that "Christians should not kill the Jews with knives, but with their [own] words,"[50] i.e. utilizing post-biblical Jewish writings as proof-texts of Christian doctrine. The conversions 1391–c.1425 were unique in the Middle Ages in number—as many as 200,000—but also because a kind of malaise or hysteria came over the Jewish communities of Spain, inducing many to be baptized even apart from external pressures. Often it seems they rushed off to baptism on the terrorizing report that St. Vincent was on his way to preach to them. These same years saw a battery of laws in Aragon and Castile intended to degrade and segregate the Jews.

Despite their fulminations and cruel actions against Jews, it should not be concluded that the friars had taken it upon themselves to solve the Jewish question by a combined strategy of systematic conversion and expulsion punctuated now and then by massacre.[51] Many friars had nothing to do with this war on the Jews, and some opposed it, adhering to the traditional dual policy. Nor did the papacy call for the expulsion or persecution of Jews. Medieval popes repeatedly reissued the *Constitutio pro Judeis*. It is significant that the Jewish community of Rome is the only one in Europe, until World War II, to have a history uninterrupted by massacre or expulsion. A striking indication of the papal stance can be seen in the pages of the chronicler of the Hundred Years' War, Froissart, who reports for the year 1349: "At that time the Jews were taken and burnt everywhere in Christendom, and their possessions seized by the rulers under whom they lived, except [at] Avignon [then the papal residence] and the domains of the church beneath the protection of the pope." The church's position, says Froissart, was that the Jews "should not be put to death because they would be saved if they returned to our faith"[52]—a succinct restatement of the dual policy.

Demonization of the Jews

Much reference is made above to the Jews as agents of Satan doing his will by plundering, enslaving, and killing Christians. In Martini's *Pugio fidei* we have a primer of this demonization of the Jews, which is, I think, the most lethal element in antisemitism, the quintessence of chimeria. It originates in the gospels where Jesus rebukes the Jews as children not of God but of the devil; dedicated to the devil's desires, they do not hear Jesus' word (Jn 8:43–7; cf. Mt 25:41). While there is much metaphorical play on the equation of Satan and the Jews in patristics and in later writings, it is not until the pivotal thirteenth century that these generally rhetorical flourishes became a formidable ideological conception transmuting the Jews into "the Counter-Incarnation."[53] The image of the Jew as a standing menace, as kin and ally of the devil, armed with his superhuman powers, was equated by Christians with everything they feared and hated. This image—given expression in art, literature, and folklore—became omnipresent in a world in which Satan was a real presence and fearful antagonist of God's rule and providence rather than a mere abstraction or vague symbol of evil.[54]

The ritual crucifixion libel was invented c.1150 by the monk Thomas of Monmouth, his maleficent gift to our civilization and the warrant for the murder of many Jews in the centuries since. "St. William the Martyr of Norwich" was an apprentice boy of twelve when he was murdered in 1144. Thomas arrived at least four and probably six years after the event, and between c.1150 and 1173 composed *The Life and Miracles* of that "most precious treasure" to relate how each year in the Easter-Passover season the Jews, as was their "custom," re-enacted their role in the crucifixion of Jesus by a facsimile crucifixion of a Christian child "in mockery and scorn of the Lord's passion." Initially, Thomas was not much believed, especially by a group of his fellow monks and the prior who had been present at the time. Their skepticism he condemns rather than rebuts, urging that only the "Christianicide Jews" could have "wrought such a deed, especially at such a time"; they "ought to be utterly destroyed as constant enemies of the Christian...religion," Thomas reports, and would indeed have been except for "their one and only protector," the sheriff, the king's agent. As proof our credulous monk offers many "miracles" but evidence only in the form of seven "arguments." The most cogent of these was, to Thomas, the purported testimony of one Theobold, ex-Jew become a fellow monk, who asserted that Jews required the annual "sacrifice [of] a Christian" if they were ever to "obtain their freedom" and "regain their homeland." Hence Jewish leaders worldwide met each year in Narbonne to decide by lot which country was to re-enact the crime that year, whereupon the leading Jews of that country decided by lot in which city it was to be. In 1144, it fell to Norwich, where many Jews assembled "that so they might avenge their sufferings on Him [Christ]." Despite the lack of evidence or eyewitnesses Thomas prevailed, and Norwich became a famous as well as profitable shrine for pilgrims, who found confirmation for their beliefs and, as Langmuir wryly puts it, "turn[ed] murder into a miraculous cure for disease."[55]

The gospel text that inspired this and other blood-dripping chimeras was Matthew 27:25, where the Jews are made to admit their guilt for the crucifixion, "His blood be upon us and upon our children," which—Christians believed—caused Jews to suffer endless hemorrhages and bloody sores, male and female alike to menstruate, and contributed mightily to the Jew-as-disease strand of antisemitism. The remedy for these many "Jewish maladies," and also an aphrodisiac—so we learn in a 1494 report on ritual murder in Hungary—was "to offer yearly sacrifice with Christian blood." Such malignant fantasizing echoes the bizarre medieval proverb, "Jews cannot exist or live without Christian blood."[56]

Thomas's new mode of defamation radiated contagiously to several sites elsewhere in England and northern France, climaxing at Lincoln in 1255. There the pattern repeated itself, except that the king, the pious Henry III, drove the proceedings along, although under the spur of one Sir John Lexington, a learned royal councilor and brother of the bishop of Lincoln. Sir John contrived to get a written confession that Jews had kidnapped little Hugh, carried out a ritual crucifixion—after first having "fattened [Hugh] for ten days with white bread and milk," said the contemporary Matthew Paris—and then had miraculous difficulty in disposing of the lacerated body. Matthew also relates how Lincoln's Jewish leaders were massacred and how ninety-one other Jews were hauled off to the Tower of London; in subsequent trials all but two were convicted, eighteen executed and seventy-one released, either because royal doubts had set in or because Henry, who had already "skinned" his Jews, found it more profitable to turn the remnant over to his brother Richard earl of Cornwall to "skewer" them. The Jews as religious issue were not yet to undermine the Jews as financial asset. "Little St. Hugh of Lincoln" is memorable as the first case of Jews being executed for ritual murder by a secular ruler. Henry's action and Chaucer's Prioress' Tale (the poet's usual mockery deserts him for seriousness in telling of Hugh and in describing the Jews as "Satan's waspish nest") together "gave support for irrational beliefs about Jews from 1255 to Auschwitz," Langmuir remarks.[57] In 1955 Anglican authorities dismantled the shrine at Lincoln cathedral and incised the confession that such "fictions cost many innocent Jews their lives."[58]

A parallel but distinct accusation stems from Fulda, Germany, where on Christmas 1235, while the miller and his wife were at mass, their five sons died in a fire at home. The Jews of Fulda were accused of murdering the sons and siphoning off their blood into waxed bags for religious, medicinal, magical purposes. An enraged mob murdered thirty-four Jews of the town. Emperor Frederick II intervened, appointing an international commission that included converted Jews; on the basis of its report, and probably also his own native skepticism, he issued in 1236 a resounding condemnation of the myth of Jewish ritual cannibalism, and prohibited clergy and laity from making such accusations. It reads pithily, and one would think unanswerably:

> Neither the Old nor the New Testament states that the Jews lust for human blood; on the contrary, it is expressly stated in the Bible, in the law of Moses, and in...the Talmud, that they should not defile themselves with blood. Those to whom even the tasting of animal blood is prohibited surely cannot thirst for that of human beings, because of the horror of the thing; because it is forbidden by nature; because of the human tie that also binds the Jews to the Christians; because they would not willingly imperil their lives and property.[59]

Nonetheless, Frederick's action did not nip this chimerical mode of accusation in the bud. In 1247 at Valréas, just across the German-French border, Jews were tortured into confessing that a missing child had been crucified (Norwich style) to acquire its blood for ritual cannibalism (Fulda style). When surviving Jews appealed to Innocent IV, the pope issued a forceful denunciation and prohibition along the lines of Frederick II's. Yet despite bans on these accusations, promulgated century after century by popes, kings and others, the chimera persists into the present, eventually making its way to the United States. Evidence was always irrelevant. If the issue was addressed the will to believe evil of the Jews nullified the rules of evidence. A contemporary account from Gloucester in 1168 illustrates chimerical antisemitism: "The boy Harold," found dead in the Severn,

> is said to have been carried away secretly by Jews, in the opinion of many [they held him for three weeks until] the Jews of all England coming together...they tortured the lad placed before them with immense tortures. It is true that no Christian was present, or saw or heard the deed, nor have we found that anything was betrayed by any Jew [under interrogation. Nevertheless the boy's wounds having been examined] those tortures were believed or guessed to have been inflicted on him in that manner [of ritual crucifixion]. It was clear that they had made him a glorious martyr to Christ.[60]

In 1475 the Lenten sermons of St. Bernardino da Feltre had the effect of instigating the Trent libel. In inveighing against the Jews, demanding their displacement from the money trade by Christian pawn shops, he foretold that Jewish evil would soon be manifest. A few days later the body of Simon, age three, was found in the home of a local Jewish community leader; accusations of ritual murder burst forth. The whole community was arrested, tortured, seventeen confessed, executions followed until halted by papal intervention. Sixtus IV's legate, however, withdrew, intimidated by the wily prince-bishop of Trent Johannes Hinderbach, and the "trial" and executions resumed. Wire-pulled by Hinderbach, a papal commission approved the trial, and in 1478 Sixtus formally endorsed the proceedings (attesting that the Jews martyred Simon "in hatred of the faith of Christ," not ritual murder—an over-subtle distinction lost on the simple pious). The source of 129 "miracles" by mid-1476, "Blessed Simon of Trent" became the object of a pilgrimage cult and a fountain of profit, joining his counterparts of Norwich and Lincoln as the most notorious, in the words of a famous hagiographer, "victim[s] of the implacable rage of the Jews against our holy religion."[61] Forever barred, Jews were not allowed even to pass through Trent as travelers.

An oddly related parallel was that of "Blessed Andrew of Rinn," age two, found by his mother hanged on a tree in 1462 after being "sold" by his uncle to merchants only later identified as Jews. There was neither agitation nor judicial inquiry at the time, and veneration began "spontaneously" only after 1475 in imitation of Simon at nearby Trent. Though neither Andrew nor Simon was ever formally beatified or canonized, both "martyrs"—having been murdered *in odium fidei*—were popular local cults with papal blessing. In 1912 a Catholic scholar, Abbé Elphège Vacandard, concluded that "not a single case [of ritual murder] has ever been historically established." Finally acknowledging error, the church suppressed Simon's cult in 1965 and the garish shrine was dismantled. In 1961 Pope John XXIII had ordered an end to Andrew's cult, but owing to local episcopal reluctance and popular defiance, could only erect, by "secret order," a plaque stating that the cycle of events centering on Andrew had "nothing to do with the Jewish people." Pious fraud and profits also appear to win out over history in Spain, where an accusation against Jews of La Guardia came to trial in 1490–91 for ritual murder supposedly committed c.1488, although unremarked at the time. Indeed, the evidence and the lack of evidence indicate there was *no* "child of La Guardia," although the trial and "confessions" fueled Ferdinand and Isabella's propaganda to expel the Jews in 1492. And it was left to Lope de Vega, the Spanish Shakespeare, to propagate the myth in the Spanish-speaking world through his drama, *El Niño inocente [innocent child] de la Guardia*, c.1606.[62]

The related accusation that Jews stole the communion wafer of the sacrament of the eucharist, either for magical and curative purposes or to mock Christian belief and ritual, dated from the 1290s and followed from a long tradition that Jews and the devil together defiled all the sacraments, as they did holy water, blessed oils, crucifixes, biblical texts, indeed anything consecrated or sacred. This "body of Christ" the Jews beat and stabbed, crucified, cast into the fire, trampled underfoot, stoned, and so on. Host desecration was more problematic for the medieval church than ritual murder and was less resolutely combatted. The annual feast of Corpus Christi (body of Christ) was instituted by Urban IV in 1264 in the aftermath of a host that "bled." Purloined and tortured hosts were said to cry out and to "bleed," probably the result of a scarlet microbe that forms on stale bread kept in dark, damp places, and many Jews were killed and communities expelled over what for them was no more than a piece of unleavened bread. By 1500 there had been over a hundred accusations of host desecration, with many shrines dedicated to such miracles, most in Germany and Austria where the delusion flourished in contrast to other areas in Europe which still had Jewish communities. The brutal massacres in Germany led by Rindfleisch and extending over a period of six months in 1298 were borne on such accusations; this "abortive genocide" cost between 20,000 and 100,000 lives. The Armleder brothers, 1336–38, led a ferocious *Judenschläcther* (Jew-slayers) band of pogromists across south Germany in a swathe of murder and pillage, justifying it—but only after the savagery was well underway—by invocations of mystical summonses to punish the Jews for deicide and host profanation.

One offshoot of such suggestibility was the accusation of host desecration in the Bavarian village of Deggendorf, which became from c.1360 (when the church was dedicated) the scene of an annual antisemitic festival until 1992, when Bishop Manfred Müller of Regensburg corrected its history and erected a plaque acknowledging that the events of 1338 were murder and robbery of Jews, not vengeance for the sacrileges alleged against the local Jews. Occasionally popes intervened to suppress such monstrosities, as Benedict XII did twice in 1338, exposing the fraud of Austrian priests who sprinkled blood on wafers; he was successful in one instance but overruled sixty years later when Boniface IX sanctioned a chapel memorializing "the body of our Lord."[63]

King St. Louis IX's habitual reference to the Jews' "poison" and "filth" highlights another motif of demonization. That Jews were bent on poisoning Christians—church councils warned against or forbade the faithful to buy foodstuffs from Jews, the "enemies who might perfidiously poison it"—was a long-standing charge, which came into its own in the fourteenth and fifteenth centuries. It was an apocalyptic age rich in disasters—famine, the Hundred Years' War, the Black Plague which carried off one-third of the entire population, economic dislocation, corruption and schism in the church, and numerous heresies. All this radical change and turmoil required explanation, scapegoats, and resolution. These were not far to seek, in Satan and the Jews principally, the whole complex of fears and hopes being compounded into a new Christian messianism and apocalyptic eschatology. The trajectory of Christian messianism spans the later Middle Ages from Abbot Joachim of Fiore's eschatological system ("the most influential one known to Europe until that of Marxism") to "the Revolutionary of the Upper Rhine's" *Book of a Hundred Chapters* (in means and ends "almost uncannily similar to the phantasies which are the core of [Nazi] 'ideology'"). A felt need to slaughter misbelievers was the common denominator to most of the messianic movements of secular redemption. By fire and sword the way would be made straight for the rule of the saints, eliminating sin and usury, and ending antichrist's reign. This meant, primarily but not solely, the annihilation of the Jews—by mass death or mass conversion. Anything was possible once Joachim's "age of the spirit" dawned or "the Revolutionary" took over.[64]

The years 1315–17 saw a calamitous famine, which gave rise to the Shepherds' Crusade of starving, pauperized, crazed peasants roving the French countryside and, in a blaze of messianic fervor and sanctity, massacring Jews as the authors of their sufferings. After the event, the accusation took firm shape that Jews together with lepers (just then a feared group) and Moslems, had, by Satan's command, conspired to poison the water supply to the utter destruction of Christendom. The poison used included pulverized hosts, thus linking this new chimera to the host desecration phobia. The cycle was one of massacres of Jews, fear of revenge for those massacres, and the consequent manufacture of new accusations, followed by renewed massacres, the most harrowing example occurring during the Black Plague, 1348–49.

The first reaction in 1348 was "spontaneous" attacks on Jews for causing the plague. These petered out after a few months, possibly—as Pope Clement VI urged in trying to stop the butchery—because it was seen that Jews also suffered grievously from the plague, or that Christian communities continued to be ravished even where there had never been Jews or they had been annihilated or expelled. Owing to ritual hygiene and purity law requirements, Jews may have suffered less from the disease; that is unlikely (records are eloquent with Jewish acquisition of additional cemetery land). But if so, it was taken as further proof of their guilt and of the need to "punish" these avatars of infection and disease.[65]

Renewed attacks on Jews blazed forth in the summer of 1349 at the instigation of flagellant bands, abetted by crowds of poor followers—the same type of footloose humanity seen in the first crusade—and townsmen. The pattern had been set by accusations in Chillon (a town now in Switzerland) where Jews "confessed" to being part of a plot "to kill and destroy the entire Christian faith": "for seven years back," the town's prosecutors avowed, "no Jew could plead innocence for all had known of it [the conspiracy] and are culpable of the fact," i.e., poisoning food, wine, water, the air, and taking precautions to avoid infection among themselves. This alert went round to city after city, and they acted accordingly, until some three hundred German communities disappeared.[66]

Though reminiscent of the Shepherds and even the crusades, the vogue of flagellation by roving bands seems to have been an outgrowth of the Black Plague, which enkindled the greatest mass slaughter of Jews until the *Shoah*: self-scourging in imitation of Christ's passion, flagellants beat themselves in unison with barbed leather whips, singing hymns and punctuating their redemptive sacrifice with much groaning and cries of "Arise by honor of pure martyrdom and henceforth guard yourself against sin." Having crushed all sin out of themselves, the flagellants felt themselves to be a holy elite infallibly doing God's will: they proceeded to attack God's enemies—the church, clergy, and worst of all, the Jews, massacring them in much of Germany and the Lowlands, as some of them explained, "because they thought to please God in that way."[67]

In general, established authority sought to check the violence, but with little effect against what was a mass movement driven by hate and greed. Particularly did the rulers fail in Germany, where the emperor's authority was so fragmented and chaotic as to render him powerless. Some, such as Charles IV, seemingly capitalized on disaster by ceding rights and claims over "his Jews" and their property to towns or princes for a profitable fee, thus inviting the municipality or magnate to massacre or expel the Jews, and also to profit. Jewish policy was thus a matter purely of expediency, since the church's traditional dual policy meant little to secular lords and townsmen in a society saturated with fear and hatred of the Jews. By the early sixteenth century, a great many Jewish communities were extinguished, more often by expulsion than massacre, until few were left. And to judge by his correspondence, even those remnants were a source of exasperation to Martin Luther, who indefatigably wrote to princes to have them expunged. The cycle of massacre, expulsion, re-admission (out of financial calculation) and expulsion several times over, was cynically employed, as at Mainz in 1420, 1438, 1462, 1471. Another expedient was to fine communities enormous sums for poisoning, arson, etc., and, once bled white, to fleece and expel them. The casualties included the Jews of Austria, eliminated in the 1420s by a combination of executions, conversions, and expulsions. The venerable Jewish community of Vienna was memorialized by an inscription marking "the expiation of the terrible crimes committed by the Jewish dogs who paid the penalty upon the stake."[68] Rather is it a monument to chimeria. So also in the 1490s when the Jews were blamed for spreading syphilis, supposedly bringing it from America to Europe in revenge for their expulsion from Spain in 1492.[69]

We remain in the realm of phantasy and phobia when we come to that singularly culpable poisoner, the Jewish doctor, who was at once feared, envied, and depended upon—as in other areas of medieval life, here too the Jew was condemned but necessary. The 1246 council of Béziers had pronounced excommunication on Christians resorting to Jewish physicians, "for it is better to die than owe one's life to a Jew," although the popes thought differently and almost all of them from the twelfth to the sixteenth century utilized Jewish doctors, as did bishops and princes. By the Jewish physician's "fiendish arts" many a Christian patient was allegedly poisoned, as one can see in Luther's diatribe: If the Jews

> could kill us all, they would gladly do so, aye, and often do it, especially those who profess to be physicians. They know all that is known about medicine in Germany; they can give poison to a man of which he will die in an hour, or in ten or twenty years.

"The devil can do much," he avers in explaining Jewish medical capacity. As Luther indicates, all Jews were implicated, and the Jew as poisoner long served dramatists as a stock character, as in Marlowe's *Jew of Malta*, c.1589, indeed until the new day of Lessing's *Nathan the Wise*, 1779. In 1610, we find the medical faculty of Vienna going on formal record that Jewish doctors are required by their religious law to kill every tenth Christian patient by dealing out the wrong drugs. That it was the devil's work we have confirmed in 1657, when a German cleric urged the ancient prohibition as vehemently as ever, "Rather die in Christ than be cured by a Jewish doctor and Satan."[70]

A corollary of the Jew as the devil's agent was the phantasmagoria of the antichrist, an emanation of Satan characteristically equated with the messiah whom Jews awaited, since, as a Christian commonplace had it, "if Jesus was the messiah, the only person for whom the Jews could be waiting...is the antichrist." Variously, the antichrist was said to be a Jew, the Wandering Jew,[71] Satan, or the son of a Jewish prostitute: he would rule Christendom for three and a half years of tribulation and be followed by the parousia. He had a mighty army: his "soldiers" were "the Jews," the Jews were "cannibals." The antichrist was often a figure of great, demonic erudition in that the source of his omniscience was Satan. Strikingly, early versions of the Faust legend fashion him into a Jew who signs the pact with Satan in blood in order to gain power, omniscience, virility, etc. The alliance with antichrist would "raise up Judaism again," making the

Jews powerful enough to destroy Christendom. The Viennese professor and theologian Heinrich von Langenstein (c.1325–97), avouched that antichrist, "with the help of Jewish money, would conquer the world in two and a half years."[72]

Still another ramification of the demonization of the Jews was the role assigned to them as magicians or sorcerers and the many diabolic enterprises they were supposedly engaged in (necromancy, witchcraft, alchemy, astrology, etc.). Sorcery was felt as an awesome and frightening phenomenon, perfectly real to the haunted-house temperament of the Middle Ages. In 1189, at the coronation of Richard the Lion-Heart, an attack on the Jews, lasting for several months and costing many casualties throughout England, was ignited by the charge that the Jews present were sorcerers bent upon casting a spell over the king. Sorcery was the quintessential explanation for the prowess of the Jewish physician, and indeed a large part of his activity—as in all medieval medicine—was magic and superstition as well as science. It was as magicians that Jews were arraigned for stealing the communion host. The blood accusation was woven into these fantasies in that Jews required innocent Christian blood for diabolic purposes, a common one being to offer sacrifice to Satan on Passover. An earlier accusation, that Jews fashioned a wax image of Jesus, torturing and mutilating it to inflict harm on him and his followers, may have been a precursor of the ritual murder myth. Poisoning was indubitably a skill of sorcerers. One reason to burn the Talmud was the belief that it was a massive book of magic, an arsenal of weapons to the eternally plotting Jews and a source of danger to Christians. The same fate befell the mystical Kabbalah, taken equally to be a great corpus of the magic arts. Books of magic, of which there were libraries, were understood to have been written by Jews, Moses and Solomon among others. For Hebrew was presumed to be *the* language of magic, and those who spoke Hebrew were feared as sorcerers and as having supernatural powers. Thus, to the Christian world the Jew was the magician par excellence, the supreme sorcerer.

There was indeed a distinct body of medieval Jewish magic, derived from antiquity. Yet the Jewish magician performed all his hocus pocus by invoking the "Ineffable Name of God," his angels, the spirits or demons, and the biblical "Word of God," but not Satan. Magic, or thaumaturgy, in the Middle Ages was acceptable to a degree, and was not beneath the dignity of some churchmen who used it to trap heretics. Nonetheless, the church declared war on what it designated sorcery, as it did on usury, following the Bible's proscriptions, and equating both with the Jews. The 1240 council of Worcester forbade Christians to practice sorcery and condemned Christian resort to Jewish sorcerers, and the 1255 council of Béziers pronounced that "Jews should desist from usury, blasphemy and sorcery."[73] Since Christian sorcery *was* Satan-centered, Christians assumed—how could it have been otherwise?—that Jewish magic was based on the same dark forces. The source of power and success in all occult doings was seen by Christians, literally, as the devil. It was the Renaissance age before the Christian world discovered that Jewish magic was God-centered and thus a legitimate object of study and action. Such was the perception of two notable humanists, the Florentine Pico della Mirandola and the German Johannes Reuchlin, who took up kabbalistic studies with great zest and earnestness. Both men ran into stout resistance and condemnation as judaizers and satanists, although Reuchlin was vindicated by Pope Leo X after a protracted battle of the books.

It was left to the Counter-Reformation popes to resume the war on sorcery, to forbid the Kabbalah to Christians, have it censored and burnt, because, as Pope St. Pius V said in 1569, the Jews "seduce [innocent Christians] with their satanic illusions, their fortune-telling, their charms and magic tricks and witcheries, and make them believe that the future can be foretold." Hence he expelled these "sorcerers" from the Papal States, except for Rome and Ancona.[74]

Hate and fear of the Jew as Satan's factotum pre-date the image of the Jew as the ogre of usury, and did much to form it and to render it so tenacious, long after the decisive importance of Jews in Europe's economic life had past. For the Jewish financier, the "usurer," was also seen as partner and abettor of Satan. Usury was the devil's invention, according to popular wisdom and ecclesiastical pronouncement. By the twelfth century, theologians and canonists had classified usury as a crime in the same heinous category as arson, sorcery, homicide, and sacrilege. In the thirteenth century, *Jew* was as automatically equated with *sorcerer* or *magician* as with *usurer* or *merchant*, a usage echoed in King St. Louis IX's decree of 1254: "Let the Jews abstain from usury, blasphemies, sorcery, and magic arts." In the same decade Pope Alexander IV declared usury to be the worst of crimes, heresy, which by theological definition had its origin in Satan and was subject to the inquisition. In 1311, Clement V and the council of Vienne rendered the definition more solemnly binding under canon law: "[Those who] practice usury...[will] be punished as a heretic...and the inquisitors [are] to proceed against [them] as they would against those accused publicly or suspected of heresy."[75] The prominence of Jews as jewel merchants contributed to the myth in that gems were not merely beautiful adornments or investments, but potent talismans to ward off evil spells. Shakespeare's Shylock, "the fiend who is...the devil himself" pursuing the pound of flesh in a variant of ritual murder, is quintessentially medieval: "Certainly the Jew is the very devil incarnation."

Jews as a fifth column conspiring with every possible enemy of Christendom litter the annals of medieval Europe. It was held that Jews had betrayed Christian Spain to its Moslem conquerors in the eighth century and Barcelona and Bordeaux to their Viking looters in the ninth, and that the profits of Jewish usury went to finance Moslem wars and thwart the crusades. In the eleventh century, the Egyptian ruler Al-Hakim, who persecuted both Christians and Jews, had demolished the Church of the Holy Sepulcher in Jerusalem, but the real author of this atrocity, a contemporary recounts in this early attribution of an international conspiracy of Jews, was "the devil...using his accustomed instruments, the Jews."[76] As noted, the Norwich crucifixion libel was borne on wings of a Jewish cabal annually assembling from far and wide at Narbonne.

Innocent III qualified his 1199 re-issue of the *Constitutio pro Judeis* with the proviso, "We wish...to place under the protection of this decree only those [Jews] who have not presumed to plot against the Christian faith."[77] In the thirteenth century the Mongols constituted a mortal danger to Christendom; to Christians the khan was both the herald of antichrist and the hell-hound acknowledged by Jews to be "the son of David." They accused Jews of plotting to aid the Mongols with weapons and as spies, a tale told by the historian Matthew Paris, reporting vividly but chimerically on events for the year 1241.[78] The Black Plague was attributed to a far-flung network of relentlessly conspiring Jews.

It has been cogently argued that the Nazi-Hitlerite fixation with the Jews as a menace and highly organized race of negative supermen is a modern, secular version of the medieval demonized Jew.[79] Hitler certainly spoke in medieval accents when he asserted, "The struggle for world domination will be fought between...Germans and Jews. We are God's people.... Two worlds face one another—the men of God and the men of Satan!"; equally when he stated that "The Jews...invented capitalism.... an invention of genius, of the devil's own ingenuity," and much else in that vein.[80] Irrational obsessions with mythical supermen is the most unexpected continuity between medieval phobias and the *Shoah*.

Dehumanization

The counterpart to demonization, effecting a unique double dehumanization, was the depiction of Jews in medieval iconography and polemic as animals, as not really human, a distinction later employed by German genocidists who gassed millions of Jews with a poison, Zyklon-B, developed for rodents. Livestock metaphors abound in Christian polemic, such as St. John Chrysostom's use of goat, pig, horse, etc.: Jews, like a decrepit plough horse, are "marked for slaughter." Peter the Venerable testifies to all the chimerical categories: you Jews are "a monstrous animal...brute beast.... You hatch the eggs of basilisks [chimeras whose glance or smell could kill] which infect you with the mortal poison of ungodliness.... They will be so evilly hatched by you as at last to produce antichrist, the king of all the ungodly." Beginning in the pivotal thirteenth century, German church sculpture portrayed Jews as pigs and pigs as Jews.

This icon of the *Judensau* (Jewish swine) was probably drawn from the early medieval writers, Isidore of Seville and Hrabanus Maurus, for whom it symbolized the deadly sins of sloth, greed, luxury, etc., rather than having a specifically anti-Jewish purpose. But by the end of the Middle Ages the *Judensau* emblem had been transformed into a vile and aggressive antisemitic stereotype. It was widely used in German-speaking lands (to which it was essentially confined and persisted to the 1820s), where it had spread from application to ecclesiastical structures to municipal buildings and even private homes. This prurient imago was widely disseminated—much aided by the invention of printing—in woodcuts, prints, broadsheets, pamphlets, books, popular drama, and so forth; such lewd media did not stop short of picturing the sow as defecating on Jews who consume its feces and urine, use the sow ludicrously as a mount the way normal humans ride horseback, and proclaim the "porcine paternity" of the Jewish people. A monstrous inference from the *Judensau* idea was the requirement in Germany that Jews engaged in litigation must stand, usually barefoot, on a sow's hide in swearing the oath to tell the truth. But it was left to Luther to impart an especially obscene and influential interpretation to the *Judensau* motif:

> There is here in Wittenberg, on our parish church, a sow carved in stone, young piglets and Jews lie under it and suck teats. Behind the sow stands a rabbi who lifts the sow's right leg up, and with his left hand pulls the tail over himself, bows and stares with great attentiveness under the tail of the sow into the Talmud, as if he wanted to read and understand something intricate and extraordinary.

That view was taken up alike by Lutheran and Catholic writers over the next century. Popular prints and broadsheets continued to embellish the Wittenberg *Judensau.* Ever more prominence was given to Satan who "tricks" and "makes fun of the Jews, his prisoners," etc. Full play was made in the lubricous dissemination of the *Judensau* icon on the Jews' animal stench as well as on the equation of the sow or its rectum with Judaism, the Talmud, or whatever. Although neither the racial antisemites after 1870, nor the Nazis employed the motif (their equation of Jews with cholera bacilli and the whole range of parasitology is closely parallel, however), *Judensau* as a form of verbal assault persisted until 1945. Although the opprobrious iconography fell out of use by 1850, its significance in dehumanizing the Jews lingered on as a poisonous miasma: thereby the Jews were reduced to an "abominable category of beings; they are the sow's offspring.... implicitly but clearly, labelled as not being human 'like us'.... [This linkage displaces Jews] to a distinctly different and loathsome category—by implication sanctioning aggression, and then in itself expressing an aggressive attitude." We are in that world of chimeria, where predatory Jews devour children—as in the *Kinderfressenbrunnen* (child-devourers' well) commemorating "martyrs" of the 1294 ritual murder performed by the Jews of Berne in Switzerland, the realm of Peter the Venerable's "beastly Jews" and basilisks, and of the Nazi anthropologists' subhuman Jewish specimens.[81]

Royal Protector and Nemesis

A pivotal development for the fate of medieval Jewry was the growth, institutional and territorial, of national monarchies in England, France, Spain, and elsewhere from the twelfth century on. There was a progressive strengthening of national consciousness among the peoples of Europe, as they were differentiated from each other by growing royal centralization and sovereignty ("the king is emperor in his realm," the jurists said), separate economic structures, distinct languages and cultures, and, well before the Reformation, religious and ecclesiastical differentiation. That meant that the Jews, "a people that dwells apart, that has not made itself one with the nations" (Nm 23:9), stood out more visibly and anomalously, more vulnerably. National consciousness was a decisive factor in the sense that it was superadded to religious antipathy and economic rivalry. The expulsions from 1290 on were the work of national monarchies with apparatus (not available previously) to rally public opinion against the Jews (or the papacy, foreigners, anyone not part of the national community) and injure or expel them from the kingdom. In England, France, Spain, and Portugal some degree of national unity had been attained and the Jews were expelled; in Germany and Italy lack of such unity explains why expulsions there were piecemeal and never total.

The Jews had long been protected by the church for theological reasons and by lay rulers for economic reasons, "and their status depended on an uneasy equilibrium between those conflicting interests and authorities," notes Langmuir.[82] Royal documents characteristically refer to Jews as "serfs" and "serfs of the royal chamber," but their status was quite different from serfs. The king could arbitrarily fleece and expel "his Jews" from the land of their birth; but serfs, proverbially tied to the land, could be proceeded against only by law. In that sense the status of the Jews was akin to slavery. St. Augustine, following St. Paul, had said that Jews are slaves, and in 1205 Innocent III defined their place in Christian society as "perpetual servitude."[83] In preempting authority over Jews, kings began to translate these airy theological hypotheses into daily practice. However, their Jewish servants—as financial agents or masters of the mint—were almost royal "officials."[84] King St. Louis IX, who saw in Jews only perils for the soul and no profits for the realm, resolved matters: "Concerning the Christians and their usuries, that pertains to the prelates.... To me pertains those of the Jews, because they are under the yoke of my servitude." Yet Louis was unusual in demanding that "the Jews give up usury or leave my land," since kings normally strenuously resisted the church's war on usury as infringing upon their prerogative of sole jurisdiction over Jews and their property.[85]

In England royal authority was fullest and less challenged by ecclesiastical or baronial claims: to King John they were "our Jews," or in the words of the famed jurist Bracton, "A Jew, indeed, can have nothing of his own because whatever he acquires he acquires not for himself but for the king, because they live not for themselves but for others, and so they acquire for others and not for themselves."[86] The royal monopoly was resisted by the feudal magnates, who claimed the right to plunder Jews for themselves; in *Magna Carta* they curtailed Jewish financial rights significantly, and over the ensuing half century baronial turbulence was cruelly directed at Jews as minions of the crown. The insurgent barons were typical of medieval oppositional movements, whether by nobles against kings, townsmen against the local bishop or feudal magnate, plebs against patricians, or peasants against their lords: medieval revolutionism—whether actual and political or messianic and apocalyptic—saw the Jew as enemy.[87]

The wave of the future was, accordingly, that national monarchs more, popes and councils less, were the arbiters of the Jewish people's fortunes, and realpolitik calculations of wealth and power, unleavened by the Augustinian necessity to preserve the Jews, was the stance taken increasingly by the kings. In many respects, however, the national monarchs, as the secular arm, simply implemented church policy toward the Jews. As we have seen, the starting point for Christian legislation on the Jews was Roman law, which had defined the Jew as free and conferred citizenship upon him. This conception was carried over under the papal dual policy, augmented by the protections set forth in the *Constitutio pro Judeis*, but weakened by a long line of edicts and canons designed to keep the Jew in his degraded place. These stipulations included being barred from holding office that enabled Jews to exercise authority over Christians and from owning land, not to build new synagogues, employ Christian servants, nor eat with Christians, have intercourse or intermarry with them (since "those cohabiting with Jews and Jewesses, [like] those engaged in bestiality, and sodomites are to be buried alive," according to the English law book *Fleta)*, wear distinctive clothing and the badge, restore usuries on pain of boycott or exhumation, be segregated in ghettos, and so on. The import of all this legislation—implemented in varying degrees by monarchs—was that the Jews were dangerous, and so had to be quarantined and publicly branded, the irony being that this web of enactments created an ethos and served as the means to support and confirm the chimerical fantasies about Jews, although often the church either opposed or did not officially subscribe to and formally proclaim the fantasies. Such were the perils of the papal dual policy. A medieval annalist, referring to Pope Gregory IX, stated—more pertinently than he could have imagined—the church's dilemma in simultaneously preserving and persecuting the Jews: Gregory, he said, "wished their [the Jews'] crimes to be repressed in such a way that no crime would be committed in their prosecution."[88] That was impossible for church or state.

The sharp decline in Jewish status, in life as in law, in Germany as elsewhere, registers dramatically after 1250: the Bavarian *Schwabenspiegel*, a secular law code (c.1275), which was drawn up by a Franciscan in the monastery of Augsburg, is a translation *in extenso* of the theological teaching of perpetual Jewish servitude; on the grounds that they were guilty of deicide and had forfeited all right upon their conquest and enslavement by Emperor Titus in 70, the code denied many rights to Jews, including most significantly the right to bear arms. That right, the badge of free men, was replaced by the badge of shame. In distant Castile King Alfonso X's law code, *Las Siete Partidas* (1263), was remarkably intolerant of Jews, sanctioning the crucifixion libel among other things that mark a sharp break with Iberian traditions. By the High Middle Ages was completed, in R.I. Moore's title, *The Formation of a Persecuting Society*: all along the line from the later twelfth century mounting, organized, institutionalized hatred and intolerance were directed against Jews, Moslems, heretics, schismatic Greeks, homosexuals, lepers, and, later, witches and Gypsies.[89]

Conclusion

To students of Jewish history the Middle Ages do not end until the American and French revolutions. The traditional marker of 1500 has little significance. Advances made in the Renaissance were lost in the Reformation (although Calvinism became an exception). Martin Luther, rebel against medieval church and theology though he was, gathered up and gave a new lease on life to medieval antisemitism: on the axis of the demonization of the Jews, he replicated every feature of the chimerical delusions that arose in the twelfth-thirteenth centuries but shorn of the restraints and protections inspired by the dual policy. Aside from his vile language, Luther's theology of the Jews and Judaism was shared by most of his contemporaries. Thus Erasmus, prince of humanists: "If it is Christian to hate Jews, then we are all good Christians." "But if the Reformation did not benefit Jews," notes Joel Carmichael, "the Counter-Reformation...was even worse."[90]

By 1500 European Jewry had been either expelled, forcibly converted, or immured in ghettos; refuge was limited to little more than Christian Poland and the Moslem Ottoman Empire, where, indeed, the exiles built up large new communities that flourished for centuries. In Russia, where the same socio-economic conditions prevailed that made Jewish settlement attractive to the Polish kings, we have Judaeophobia without Jews: until the eighteenth century, when the partitions of Poland brought millions of Jews under the scepter of the tsars, Russia remained *Judenrein*, fearful of the evil, destructive "enemies of Christ."[91]

However, under neither prelates nor monarchs was it all persecution and "the lachrymose conception of Jewish history": "the widespread belief that Jewish life in medieval Europe consisted in an uninterrupted series of migrations and sufferings, of disabilities and degradation," Salo Baron urged nearly sixty years ago, "is to be relegated to the realm of popular misconceptions." There is much else to tell. The long list of massacres is paralleled by a long list of scholars, poets, philosophers of the highest attainments, from Rashi in the eleventh century to Rabbi Meir of Rothenburg in the thirteenth. Among many extraordinary figures, one may note the *Minnesinger* Süskind of Trimberg and the poet Immanuel of Rome who gained entry to Christian society, Immanuel perhaps as a member of Dante's circle. He definitely wrote a parody in Hebrew of the *Divina Commedia, Mahberet ha-Tofet ve-ha-Eden* (*Journey from Hell to Paradise*): led by "Daniel" (possibly Dante), his journey brings him at last to paradise, where he sees enthroned the righteous Gentiles who were merciful to Jews and tolerant of Judaism. The conversion of the Khazars and the existence for several centuries of Jewish Khazaria indicated that the scepter had not departed from Israel.

More familiar is the Golden Age of Spanish Jewry. Jewish venturing in commerce and finance is also a story of creative achievement. Until late in the Middle Ages, Baron argued, Jews were "a privileged group, in most countries [where they still resided] belonging to the privileged minority."[92]

Indisputably, however, the great achievement of medieval Jews was that they survived: they did so because neither the coercive bureaucratic apparatus nor the technical means of annihilation that were utilized in the twentieth century by the Germans were available to Christian society. Jewish survival was owing more specifically to the continuation, or resumption, of the dual policy, which lasted, though much attenuated, through the end of the Middle Ages: while it persecuted with one hand, the church protected with the other.[93] It was in the High Middle Ages that the idea of the Jewish world conspiracy—which would be updated and secularized in the notorious *Protocols of the Elders of Zion*—took shape, and Judaism, talmudic rather than biblical, was defined as a "satanic law" in obedience to which Jews sought to inflict injury and destruction on Christian society in manifold ways—ritual crucifixion and cannibalism, poisoning everything and everyone, draining away the kingdom's wealth and debasing its currency as they did its blood and health. This whole evil heritage was secularized and reinforced by the racial phobias and pseudo-science conjoined to the hyper nationalism of the nineteenth and twentieth centuries: it was surely no accident that chimerical racial antipathy fastened on the same people as had the chimerical theological variety.[94] The continuities that connect Count Emicho or Peter the Venerable with Hitler and Auschwitz are suggested by Amos Funkenstein's pithy insight that in Nazi ideology "Jews were the hypostatized negation of sanity, creativity, health, and order, a secularized antichrist."[95]

Undoubtedly there came down to us from the High Middle Ages an irrational "fear of the Jews."[96] Fear generates hatred and aggression, a sequence most notably seen by an Italian war correspondent who knew the Nazi death machine first hand: "That which drives the Germans to cruelty, to deeds most coldly, methodically and scientifically cruel, is fear. Fear of the oppressed, the defenseless...fear of the Jews."[97] The burden of Christian responsibility for Jewish suffering over the centuries is very great, indeed scandalous. The churches were transmitters rather than combatters of medieval myths, which endured and were modernized, and profoundly affected the thinking and feelings of the elites and the masses. When the test came, the churches were true to their religious traditions—they failed to resist, and fell among the bystanders who were indifferent to the victims or supportive of the perpetrators. Historians estimate that seven to ten million Jews were killed *before* the Holocaust, most under Christian auspices; in the reckoning of Irvin Borowsky, "in the past thousand years one out of every two Jews born into the world has been murdered."[98] Such was what Léon Poliakov called "the harvest of hate." We may take heart from Pope St. Gregory the Great, with whom this essay began: "Though scandal be taken at truth, it is better to permit the scandal than to abandon the truth."

Endnotes

1. Gavin I. Langmuir, *Toward a Definition of Antisemitism* (Berkeley: University of California Press, 1990), 334; he explores, ibid., 76–77, 302 and in his *History, Religion, and Antisemitism*, (Berkeley: University of California Press, 1990), 289 the circumstances in which patristic Judaeophobia might have been transmuted into irrational antisemitism and persecution, possibly leading to annihilation of the Jews in Christendom; certainly Visigothic Spain, 587–711 and its twenty church councils at Toledo went far to translate what patristics seemed to require into law and action: a dress rehearsal for all of Christian Europe 1095 on. Langmuir's books are hereafter cited as *TDA* and *HRA* respectively.

2. Jeremy Cohen, *The Friars and the Jews*, (Ithaca: Cornell University Press, 1982), 19–22; idem., "The Jews as Killers of Christ in the Latin Tradition: From Augustine to the Friars," *Traditio*, 39 (1983): 1–27; St. Augustine is not so sunny as my brief statement might imply: he refers to the Jews as fratricides (Cain), parricides (deicide), "the slave of the Christian," poisonous snakes, carnal and materialistic, and other assertions that justified forced conversion, degradation, badges and ghettos, expulsion, or, as he prayed, "Bring them down O Lord"; nevertheless, his witness theology did set limits to Jewish suffering in a Christian world.

3. Salo W. Baron, *A Social and Religious History of the Jews*, 2d ed., 18 vols., (New York: Columbia University Press, 1952–83), 3:32; hereafter cited as SWB.

4. Jacob R. Marcus, *The Jew in the Medieval World* (New York: Harper & Row, 1965), 112.

5. Edward A. Synan, *The Popes and the Jews in the Middle Ages* (New York: Macmillan, 1965), 71; Norman Cohn, *The Pursuit of the Millennium*, 3rd ed., (New York: Oxford University Press, 1970), 61, 73, 285; *TDA*, 96–99.

6. *Memoirs: Self and Society in Medieval France*, ed. & intro. by John F. Benton, (Toronto: Toronto University Press, 1984), 134–135; Jewish chroniclers of the crusade confirm this attitude almost verbatim.

7. *TDA*, 97; *HRA*, 293.

8. Synan (n. 5), 71.

9. Robert Chazan, *European Jewry and the First Crusade* (Berkeley: University of California Press, 1987), 71–73; Jonathan Riley-Smith, "The First Crusade and the Persecution of the Jews," *Studies in Church History*, 21 (1984): 66.

10. Chazan (n. 9), 86.

11. Joel Carmichael, *The Satanizing of the Jews* (New York: Fromm, 1992), 44, 51–54, 63.

12. James Parkes, *The Jew in the Medieval Community*, 2d ed., (New York: Hermon, 1976), 211; exceptional was Alexander II's 1063 protest of crusaders' assaults on Jews in Spain.

13. Synan (n. 5), 231; the first edition of the *Constitutio* does not survive.

14. Chazan (n. 9), 182.

15. Synan (n. 5), 75; Chazan (n. 9), 175–176.

16. Otto of Freising, *The Deeds of Frederick Barbarossa*, trans. & ed. Charles C. Mierow with Richard Emery (New York: Norton, 1966), 74.

17. *TDA*, 201.

18. Jeremy Cohen, "Scholarship and Intolerance," *American Historical Review*, 91 (1986): 603; in an important essay, "Changes in the Pattern of Twelfth-Century Anti-Jewish Polemics" (in Hebrew), *Zion*, 23 (1968): 126–145, Amos Funkenstein argued that Peter's treatise effected the decisive shift in Christian perception of Judaism as satanic; the fact, however, that only few copies of that vicious manuscript circulated suggests that Peter was more symptomatic than influential, that the decisive change came in the thirteenth century.

19. *TDA*, 201; for this topic see Langmuir's essay, "Peter the Venerable," ibid., and his part in the "AHR Forum," *American Historical Review*, 91 (1986): 576–624; he notes that Peter was a beneficiary of the twelfth-century Renaissance and Renewal's knowledge of Aristotelian thought and ancient science, and so found empirical evidence contradicting his belief desperately hard to contend with, his aggressive fear and anger being directed especially against the Jews as proverbial disbelievers impervious to the logic and truth of conversion; he notes, *TDA*, 202, how modern scholars who find Peter an important and engaging figure view him through "stained glass" to defend or exculpate him from a towering Jew-hatred—that he attacked only dishonest Jews, that he was moderate in not advocating murdering them, that his antipathy was religious rather than racial, and so on, which are either simply wrong or irrelevant but typical of scholars who are ignorant of the Jewish segment of their field of study.

20. *TDA*, 208, arguing that reduction to animal status was far more significant and fatal than demonization, the one significant point on which I disagree with him and will pursue below.

21. Synan (n. 5), 49.

22. Solomon Grayzel, *The Church and the Jews in the Thirteenth Century*, rev. ed. (New York: Hermon, 1966), 103.

23. See Joachim Prinz, *Popes from the Ghetto* (New York: Schocken, 1968), 45–48 for long-term suspicions of converts.

24. Synan (n. 5), 29.

25. Synan (n. 5), 112; size itself was often a fatal fact in indictments of the Talmud.

26. *Europe in the High Middle Ages, 1150–1309* (London: Longman, 1973), 96, 102; David Berger, *The Jewish-Christian Debate in the High Middle Ages* (Philadelphia: J. P. S., 1979).

27. On Meir's "quasi-historical attack" on Christ's historicity, Robert Chazan, *Daggers of Faith* (Berkeley: University of California Press, 1989), 54–57; SWB, 11:354 n. 22.

28. Beryl Smalley, *The Study of the Bible in the Middle Ages,* 2d ed., (Oxford: Blackwell, 1952), 362.

29. That momentous transformation is noted in *TDA*, 301 and *HRA*, 295 n. 21.

30. Smalley (n. 28) testifies to the stimulating impact the study of Hebrew and rabbinics had on Christian scholarship; there was, she notes pp. 360–361, a strong disposition to prefer the study of Hebrew to the neglect of Greek. The birth of Hebrew studies was part of *The Renaissance of the Twelfth Century,* the title of a famous book of 1927 by Charles H. Haskins, which acknowledges significant contributions by Jews to that Renaissance; the fiftieth-anniversary conference, 1977, made no such acknowledgement, for not one paper on the Jewish strand of twelfth-century Europe was presented, nor are Jews so much as referred to in its proceedings, *Renaissance and Renewal in the Twelfth Century,* ed. Robert L. Benson & Giles Constable, (Cambridge: Harvard University Press, 1982); such compartmentalized historiography is common: see Langmuir's observations on how historians of medieval Jewry and those of the growth of royal administration suffer from ignorance of each other's work, *TDA,* 137–138.

31. *Memoirs of the Crusades by Villehardouin and Joinville* (New York: Dutton, 1958), 148.

32. Cohen (n. 2), 66.

33. Cohen (n. 19), 609.

34. Cohen (n. 2), 68; for the slight degree of validity these wild accusations might have had, see Edward H. Flannery, *The Anguish of the Jews*, rev. and updated (New York: Paulist Press, 1985), 105–106; a number of conversions to Judaism angered churchmen.

35. *HRA*, 297; that the Protestant Eisenmenger's work was barred from publication for a time and Röhling, a Catholic priest, forfeited his professorship for his fraudulence did nothing to extinguish the irrational bogey they had unleashed on the world; like their medieval forebear Martini, they freely forged passages.

36. Chazan (n. 27), 33.

37. Cohen (n. 2), 79.

38. Cohen (n. 2), 83; Nicholas sanctioned a practice—vividly seen in Robert Browning's 1855 poem "Holy-Cross Day"—lasting centuries, longest in Rome itself until abolished after 1830.

39. Jeremy Cohen, "The Mentality of the Medieval Apostate," *Jewish Apostasy in the Modern World*, ed. Todd M. Endelman (New York: Holmes & Meier, 1987), 35–40.

40. Robert Chazan, *Barcelona and Beyond* (Berkeley: University of California Press, 1992), chs. 2, 7, esp. pp. 75, 193; messianic "hopes that redemption was at hand" certainly sustained Jews in the medieval veil of tears: see SWB, 1937, 1:80.

41. Cohen (n. 2), 132.

42. There are striking parallels with Catholic action against the Jews in the sixteenth century, making the Counter-Reformation popes' policies appear to be a re-run of the friars' offensive against talmudic Judaism. See Kenneth R. Stow, *Catholic Thought and Papal Jewry Policy, 1555–1593,* (New York: Jewish Theological Seminary, 1976).

43. Cohen (n. 2), 136–156; for Honorius IV, Shlomo Simonsohn, *The Apostolic See and the Jews: Documents: 492–1404* (Toronto: Pontifical Institute of Medieval Studies, 1988), document 255; among many examples, St. John Chrysostom referred memorably to the "madness"

that blocks Jews from being led to Christ by their own scriptures; the theme of Jewish pathology is dealt with ironically by Heinrich Heine in an 1842 poem about the dedication of a hospital for "poor sick Jews": they suffer from the three diseases of "poverty, physical pain, and Jewishness." See Sander L. Gilman, "The Madness of the Jews," *Difference and Pathology* (Ithaca: Cornell University Press, 1985), 150–151.

44. "Basic Types of Christian Anti-Judaism in the Later Middle Ages," *Viator,* 2 (1971): 382; this important historiographical essay concludes that the "anti-Judaism" arising in the twelfth century represented a radically different and dangerous hatred from the attitude which had prevailed since St. Augustine, particularly the accusation that the Talmud was anti-biblical and heretical, therefore subject to extreme sanctions; as such the new Christian stance is, I think, better designated *antisemitism* than *anti-Judaism*.

45. Quoted in Benjamin Z. Kedar, *Crusade and Mission,* (Princeton: Princeton University Press, 1984), 187; Yosef H. Yerushalmi, "Reply to Rosemary Ruether," *Auschwitz: Beginning of a New Era?* ed. Eva Fleischner (N.p.: Ktav, 1977), 100.

46. Cohen (n. 2), 93.

47. Cohen (n. 2), 204, 217, 223; in 1311 the council of Vienne ordered Oxford, Paris, Bologna, Salamanca universities to teach Greek, Hebrew, Arabic, Syrian for missionary purposes.

48. Moshe Idel, *Kabbalah: New Perspectives* (New Haven: Yale University Press, 1988), 1–6, 256–257, 263.

49. Cohen (n. 2), 232, 234.

50. Flannery (n. 34), 134; Léon Poliakov, *The History of Anti-Semitism*, 4 vols., (New York: Vanguard, 1965–86), 1:144–146; 2:166. Articles on these notable churchmen and saints in the *Catholic Encyclopedia*, 1967, make quaint reading now and suggest how far we have come since Vatican II in that there is no mention of their antisemitism at all or it is glossed over, e.g. St. Vincent Ferrer "protecting" the Jews.

51. I have made much use of Jeremy Cohen's *The Friars and the Jews* (n. 2), an original work that appears to propound such a thesis but has been criticized as exaggerated, e.g., by Chazan (n. 27), 170–181; see Cohen's reply to some of his critics (n. 19), 609 and n. 46.

52. *Chronicles*, ed. Geoffrey Brereton, (Baltimore: Penguin, 1968), 111–112; Froissart is referring to massacres kindled by the black plague; he adds, the pope and the kings of Aragon, Castile, and Navarre gave them refuge but "laid them under tribute."

53. Carmichael (n. 11), 31.

54. Medieval art rendered this image visible and palpable, depicting the Jew with the physical features that identify him with the devil. He is provided graphically with horns, as still seen in Michelangelo's famous statue of Moses, (since Satan was modeled on the great goat-god Pan, he is equipped with horns, goat's beard or goatee, tail, cleft foot, etc., hence also the "lustful" and "carnal" Jews, their "satanic lechery," *foetor Judaicus* or animal stench, and much else of the same tenor). Often the devil disguised himself as a goat or *Judensau* (pig) and was used by Jews as a means of conveyance the way witches would later use brooms. The devil-Jew equation appears also in the red wig of stage dramas worn by the devil and Jewish characters,

an echo of which is found in the red hair of Dickens' Fagin, the gangster version of Shylock. His Satanic Majesty assembled his Jews in parliamentary conclave or council of war, where they pledged their allegiance and engaged in such evils as debasing the currency or ritual murder. The Christian theological image of the Jew also permeated sermons, songs and ditties, and fairy tales, *none* of which last speak in friendly terms of Jews and are often brutally antisemitic in the way of the Grimms' blood-curdling "Jew in the Thistles."

55. Thomas of Monmouth, *The Life and Miracles of St. William of Norwich*, ed. and trans. Augustus Jessopp and Montague R. James (Cambridge, UK: Cambridge University Press, 1896), bks. 1–2, passim; Langmuir's superb essays, "Thomas of Monmouth: Detector of Ritual Murder" and "Historiographic Crucifixion" in *TDA*.

56. Poliakov (n. 50), 1:143 n. 13; the proverb quoted in SWB, 11:153–154.

57. Langmuir's splendid essay, "The Knight's Tale of Young Hugh of Lincoln" in *TDA*; how the fearful image reverberates down the centuries one may judge by Charles Lamb's "Imperfect Sympathies," c.1820, "I confess that I have not the nerves to enter their synagogues.... I cannot shake off the story of Hugh of Lincoln. Centuries of injury, contempt, and hate, on the one side—of cloaked revenge, dissimulation, and hate on the other.... Why [do they] keep up a form of separation, when the life of it [Judaism] is fled?" *The Works of Charles Lamb*, 12 vols., ed. William MacDonald (New York: Dutton, 1914), 1:120–121.

58. Quoted in F.M. Schweitzer, *A History of the Jews since the First Century A.D.* (New York: Macmillan, 1971), 117 n. 7.

59. Quoted in Joshua Trachtenberg, *The Devil and the Jews: The Medieval Conception of the Jew and its Relation to Modern Anti-Semitism* (New Haven: Yale University Press, 1943), 132–133.

60. Trachtenberg (n. 59), 130; for this topic, see Langmuir's scintillating essay, "Ritual Cannibalism" in *TDA*; he notes, *TDA*, 287, the same credulity in the seventeenth-century Bollandists who suspected that medieval Jews "vented their rage in the blood of innocent Christians more frequently than it would please historians to report in chronicles or than God would permit to become known publicly."

61. Langmuir quoting Alban Butler's immensely popular *Lives of the Saints*, 1750s, *TDA*, 287; on Trent, Poliakov (n. 50), 1:62–63, 272; Flannery (n. 34), 100, 116; the monograph of R. Po-Chia Hsia, *Trent 1475* (New Haven: Yale University Press, 1992) tells the story in the round.

62. Vacandard quoted in SWB, 11:155; for John XXIII see *The Blood Libel Legend*, ed Alan Dundes (Madison: University of Wisconsin Press, 1991), 342–343; on Spain, ibid., 167–170.

63. SWB, 11:164–177; *TDA*, 122–127, 308; *HRA*, 259, 300–301.

64. Norman Cohn (n. 5), 108–126; Joachim's division of history parallels Martini's.

65. Poliakov (n. 50), 1:112–113, and in general 99–122; *HRA*, 301–302; Trachtenberg (n. 59), 97–108; on Clement VI, Synan (n. 5), 131–134.

66. SWB, 11:162, 270.

67. On the flagellants, Cohn (n. 5), 127–141.

68. SWB, 11:276.

69. SWB, 17:283; and also to North America, the Middle East, India, China, Japan.

70. Poliakov (n. 50), 1:149, 152; Luther quoted in SWB, 11:159, 143.

71. The archetype—theological, literary, and folkloric—of a Jew present at the crucifixion and condemned by Jesus for injury and insult (cf. Jn 18:20–22) to wander the earth in anguish and misery until judgment day dates from early in church history in the east, but took root only in the later Middle Ages in the west. At first the tale had little Jewish content but eventually centered on Ahasuerus (the Persian king's name, Est 1:1ff; the connection may be the surmised "crucifixion" of Haman in Purim plays and liturgies) whose tribulations made him the emblem of the Jewish people in a way that parallels the Christian depiction of Cain; by their afflictions both bear out the truth of Christianity, St. Augustine's witness theory in miniature as it were; in the same Christian vein, some versions make him a convert. Ahasuerus became a stock figure in passion plays and was equated with antichrist or his disciple; in German lands he was more usually called the *Eternal*, in France and England the *Wandering* Jew. Some 2000 writings and numerous works of art and music (some portray him as heroic, Promethean, sympathetic, etc.) testify to the myth's hold on human imagination, including Goethe, Shelley and Hans Christian Andersen, all of which disseminated the image of the Jews as cosmic fugitives who determine Christendom's destiny. See George K. Anderson, *The Legend of the Wandering Jew* (Providence: Brown University Press, 1965); SWB, 11:177–182; Edgar Rosenberg, *From Shylock to Svengali* (Stanford: Stanford University Press, 1970), 187–205.

72. SWB, 11:133; on antichrist, see Trachtenberg (n. 59), ch. 2.

73. Grayzel (n. 22), 331, 337; on sorcery, Joshua Trachtenberg, *Jewish Magic and Superstition* (1939; reprint, New York: Atheneum, 1977), 1–24; SWB, 11:139–146; Lynn Thorndike's magnum opus interprets medieval experimental science and magic interacting creatively.

74. Trachtenberg (n. 59), 76.

75. St. Louis is quoted SWB, 10:61; the Vienne decree in Joseph Schatzmiller, *Shylock Reconsidered* (Berkeley: University of California Press, 1990), 46.

76. Rodolphus Glaber, *The Five Books of the Histories*, ed. John France (Oxford: Clarendon, 1989), 133–137; Rodolphus, a monk-historian of Burgundy (c.980–c.1046), explains that those who survived did so per the Augustinian paradigm "to serve as witnesses...or testimony."

77. Grayzel (n. 22), 95.

78. SWB, 18:302; in the 1240s Pope Innocent IV sent out Franciscan friars to convert the much-feared Mongols and/or ascertain whether they intended to invade Europe.

79. Norman Cohn, *Warrant for Genocide: The Myth of the Jewish World Conspiracy and the Protocols of the Elders of Zion*, (New York: Harper & Row, 1967), which he connects to Joshua Trachtenberg's *The Devil and the Jews* (n. 59).

80. Herman Rauschning, *Hitler Speaks* (New York: Putnam's, 1940), 237–238, 241.

81. Peter the Venerable, *P.L.* 189:648–650, a reference I owe to Robert Michael; for the rest of these two paragraphs see Isaiah Shachar, *The Judensau: A Medieval Anti-Jewish Motif and its History* (London: Warburg Institute, 1974), passim; Luther quoted, pp. 45, 86 n. 236.

82. *TDA*, 165.

83. *HRA*, 294; Grayzel (n. 22), 115.

84. H.H. Ben-Sasson's insightful suggestion, *A History of the Jewish People*, (London: Weidenfeld & Nicolson, 1976), 472; cf. *TDA*, 184; Yerushalmi (n. 45), 99–100.

85. Mundy (n. 26), 96 quoting the contemporary biographer William of Chartres.

86. *TDA*, 177, although this dictum may be wrongly attributed to Bracton.

87. Mundy (n. 26), 91.

88. *Fleta* quoted in Mundy (n. 26), 101; Gregory IX in Synan (n. 5), 109.

89. Moore, *The Formation of a Persecuting Society: Power and Deviance in Western Europe, 950–1250* (Oxford, UK: Blackwell, 1987); also Mundy (n. 26), ch. 3; John Boswell, *Christianity, Social Tolerance, and Homosexuality* (Chicago: University of Chicago Press, 1981), 15, that "the fate of Jews and gay people has been almost identical throughout European history, from early Christian hostility to extermination in concentration camps"; Guido Kisch, *The Jews in Medieval Germany* (Chicago: University of Chicago Press, 1949), 108, 185, 205.

90. Erasmus quoted in Flannery (n. 34), 151; Carmichael (n. 11), 86.

91. Poliakov (n. 50), 1:281.

92. SWB, 1937, 2:31–32, 86.

93. For this line of thought, see Yerushalmi (n. 45), 97–107.

94. *TDA*, 309-310; Carmichael (n. 11), 131.

95. "History, Counterhistory, and Narrative" in *Probing the Limits of Representation: Nazism and the "Final Solution,"* ed. Saul Friedlander (Cambridge, MA: Harvard University Press, 1992), 76.

96. Nicolas Berdyaev, *Christianity and Anti-Semitism* (New York: Philosophical Library, 1954), 7; in this remarkable lecture of 1940, he deplored a "mystical fear of the Jews" on the part of Christians, a perception I think rendered better as *irrational* than *mystical*.

97. Curzio Malaparte, *Kaputt* (New York: Dutton, 1946), 91. On reflection, I am conscious of a close parallel between my use of *fear* and Langmuir's use of Christian *doubt* in the Middle Ages and the aggression against Jews it gave rise to; see *inter alia HRA* and *TDA*, esp. ch. 12 in *HRA*, "Doubt in Christendom" and "Peter the Venerable: Defense against Doubts" in *TDA*.

98. Flannery (n. 34), 349 n. 1; Borowsky, Foreword, *Overcoming Fear between Jews and Christians*, American Interfaith Institute, xii.

Suggestions For Further Reading

Baron, Salo Wittmayer. *A Social and Religious History of the Jews*. 2nd ed. Expanded and Enlarged. 18 vols. New York: Columbia University Press, 1952–1983. History on the grand scale by the master of those who would know Jewish history.

Carmichael, Joel. *The Satanizing of the Jews: Origin and Development of Mystical Anti-Semitism*. New York: Fromm, 1992. A stimulating essay on demonization with new insights on the Middle Ages and a brilliant chapter on Soviet use of the idea.

Chazan, Robert. *Daggers of Faith: Thirteenth-Century Christian Missionizing and Jewish Response*. Berkeley: University of California Press, 1989. Important for its critical analysis of Jeremy Cohen's thesis in the book cited below.

Cohen, Jeremy. *The Friars and the Jews: The Evolution of Medieval Anti-Judaism*. Ithaca: Cornell University Press, 1982. An original work arguing that the friars overturned the Augustinian theology of tolerance with one that interpreted talmudic Judaism as "heretical" and thus established a basis for forced conversion, expulsion, and demonization.

Cohn, Norman. *The Pursuit of the Millennium: Revolutionary Millenarians and Mystical Anarchists of the Middle Ages*. 3rd ed. New York: Oxford University Press, 1970. Study of the bloody-messianic underside of popular religiosity; whether these movements were condemned by or influenced churchmen, they were fateful for Jewry; ironically Jews had to endure Christian messianism based on Jewish apocalyptic and eschatology.

Langmuir, Gavin I. *History, Religion, and Antisemitism*. Berkeley: University of California Press, 1990. Drawing on the social sciences, this immensely suggestive study distinguishes among realistic, xenophobic, and chimerical hostility towards Jews and Judaism.

____. *Toward A Definition of Antisemitism*. Berkeley: University of California Press, 1990. A collection of penetrating essays written 1960–90; these two books constitute a decisive breakthrough in our understanding of antisemitism and should serve long as the organizing principle for all histories of the Jews, Jewish-Christian relations, and antisemitism.

Parkes, James. *The Jew in the Medieval Community: A Study of his Political and Economic Situation*. 2nd ed. New York: Hermon, 1976. A classic work of keen insight and remarkable empathy by this author's intellectual hero.

Poliakov, Léon. *The History of Anti-Semitism*. 4 vols. Trans. from the French. New York: Vanguard, 1965–86. A profound and very readable study: lucid, detailed and analytical, keen insights, the full sweep of antisemitic thought and action over two millennia.

Synan, Edward A. *The Popes and the Jews in the Middle Ages*. New York: Macmillan, 1965. A work of solid scholarship, making many documents available in Latin and translation, by a Catholic priest reflecting the new perspectives that came in with Vatican II.

Trachtenberg, Joshua. *The Devil and the Jews: The Medieval Conception of the Jew and its Relation to Modern Anti-Semitism*. New Haven: Yale University Press, 1943. Pioneering work on demonization, vivid, eloquent, a triumph of research, still indispensable.

JEWS, *CONVERSOS*, AND THE INQUISITION IN SPAIN, 1391–1492: THE AMBIGUITIES OF HISTORY

Scarlett Freund & Teofilo F. Ruiz*

Growing violence against Jews, particularly the pogroms of 1391, led many Spanish Jews to convert to Christianity. Since the conversion of a good number of these New Christians or conversos *was feigned—they continued to practice Judaism in secret—the authorities were incensed. Anti-Jewish sentiment culminated in 1492 with the expulsion of those Jews who refused to accept baptism. Between 40,000 and 150,000 Jews, depending on the different interpretations, went into exile. The Inquisition carefully scrutinized the behavior of the* conversos *and their descendants to make sure there was no relapse. Scarlett Freund and Teofilo F. Ruiz discuss the tenor of Jewish life in late medieval Spain and the attitude of Christian authorities, including the Inquisition, toward the* conversos.

The expulsion decree of 1492, with its hard choice of conversion or exile from *Sefarad* (the Hebrew for Spain), brought to an abrupt end more than a millennium and a half of Jewish life in what we know today as Spain. The earliest records attesting to the settlement of Jews in Iberia date back to Roman Imperial times. These references, however, are too few to provide any reliable information. The acts of the church council of Elvira (early fourth century of the C.E.) are one of the starting points for this history; its proceedings already reveal the

---

* The responsibility for this article has been divided as follows: T.F. Ruiz prepared a preliminary draft of this paper and undertook research and writing for the period before 1391. S. Freund researched and wrote sections dealing with the 1391 pogroms, the coming of the Inquisition, and the nature of the present historiographical debate; in addition she is responsible for stylistic changes and editing throughout the entire paper.

church's suspicions of Jewish activities and a concern with the issue of Jewish-Christian relations. The coming of the Visigoths and the demise of Roman rule in the mid-fifth century brought little change to the status of the Jews.

The early Visigothic rulers practiced Arianism, a heretical version of Christianity, and thus did not support the anti-Jewish sentiments of the Iberian Church. Yet, once they converted to Roman Catholicism in 589, the Visigothic kings and the influential Visigothic church councils initiated a policy of persecution against Jews and the practice of Judaism. Much of the anti-Jewish legislation of the seventh-century acquired a normative character and was reenacted almost verbatim in the Christian kingdoms of the late Middle Ages. This persistence of anti-Jewish attitudes explains why the Jews may have played a role in support of the Muslim invasion of 711; in many respects, the overthrow of Visigothic rule prevented the eventual eradication of Jews from Hispania.

We do not know enough about the course of Jewish life in the first two centuries of Muslim rule, but, as Suárez Fernández has pointed out, it must have been vigorous and significant. Otherwise it would be difficult to explain the achievements and vitality of Jewish communities in the tenth and eleventh centuries. In that "garden protected by our [Muslim] spears," to use Peter Brown's felicitous description of the Muslim Mediterranean, Jewish life prospered and developed to dazzling heights. Equally at home in Arabic, Hebrew, Syrian and Latin, Spanish-Jewish merchants traveled freely across the Mediterranean to the rich trading depots of the East, playing an important role in Western commerce. Under the tolerant and protective gaze of the Caliphs of Córdoba, their communities grew in numbers and wealth throughout the lands of al-Andalus.

Culturally, socially, and politically, the tenth century and most of the eleventh were, despite sporadic confrontations and persecutions, the true Golden Age of medieval Spanish Jewry. As influential political advisors and ambassadors (Abu Joseph ibn Hasday ibn Shaprut, c. 915–970), and as scholars, poets and teachers (Dunas ibn Labrat, c. 920–80; Judah ibn Daid Hayyuy, c. 940–1010), Jews greatly enriched the complex web of Spanish-Muslim culture. But the fall of the Caliphate and the Berber invasions from North Africa in the eleventh and the late twelfth centuries (the Almoravids and the Almohads), most of them followers of ascetic and fundamentalist forms of Islam, brought to an end the prosperity and security of the Jews. Civil wars, political fragmentation and religious persecution in al-Andalus led to a significant migration of Jews to the newly-formed Christian kingdoms in the north. Nevertheless, it was during this turbulent period that Solomon ibn Gabirol (c. 1020–58), writing in Arabic in Muslim Zaragoza, composed philosophical and religious poetry, particularly his *Fons vitae (Fountain of Life)* and *Keter Malkhut (The Crown of the Kingdom)*, which deeply influenced the course of Western thought.

Jewish life in Christian lands during the central Middle Ages was marked by official acceptance and economic opportunities but also by latent popular hostility. In spite of occasional outbursts of violence, usually coinciding with downturns in the economy, the Jews prospered in Christian cities, above all in Toledo, where they continued their intellectual pursuits and religious life. Below we will examine in closer detail aspects of Jewish life in late medieval Castile. Here, in this brief introduction to the subject, it suffices to say that periods of relative peace were interrupted by outbursts of anti-Jewish violence and restrictive legislation. This growing antagonism rose to unprecedented levels in the pogroms of 1391, culminating in the establishment of the Inquisition (see below) in the 1480s and the Edict of Expulsion in 1492. The latter drove the Jews into exile, first into Portugal, North Africa, southern France and Italy, and, gradually (as these countries became the new sites of anti-Jewish persecution), to the settlement of the Sephardim throughout the Mediterranean world, northern Europe, and the New World.[1]

This complex history is not easy to relate. Despite a plethora of recent works on Jewish life, on the relations of Jews to the predominant Christian majority and on the persecution of *conversos*[**] by the Inquisition, long-held beliefs and inaccurate historical generalizations still grip the popular imagination. This in part results from historians' disagreement over many of these issues.

Our aim in this article is as follows: First, we wish to present a brief outline of the history of the Jews in late medieval Spain, with special emphasis on the following topics: a) the tenor of Jewish life in the fourteenth century and the impact of the massive conversions from Judaism to Christianity in 1391 and afterwards; b) the peculiar nature of conversion and of *converso* society between 1391 and 1492; c) the changing and often ambivalent Christian attitude towards Jews and *conversos*, culminating in the establishment of the Inquisition in Castile in the early 1480s, and in the subsequent decree of expulsion in 1492; d) the activities of the Inquisition against the *conversos* in the years before and after 1492.

Second, within our chronological narrative, we will examine the current scholarly debate on—and the ambivalence of historians towards—the Jews and *conversos* of this period. What are the diverse and, often, contradictory interpretations? To what extent are clear-cut answers prevented by the ambiguities surrounding this historical problem? Finally, in our discussions, we will provide tables summarizing the relevant primary data for the crucial years 1484–1520.

1. Jewish Life in Late Medieval Iberia

The first commonplace we must abandon is that Jewish life in late medieval

---

[**] We have chosen the more inclusive term *converso* over *marrano* (which refers solely to Jews who outwardly converted to Christianity but continued to practice Judaism in hiding and to retain a secret Jewish identity), because one of the contentions of this paper is that it is very difficult to assess the true religious affiliation of most *conversos*.

Iberia can be placed into well-defined categories. Although there were important Jewish communities in the kingdoms of the Crown of Aragon, neither the number of Jews nor their wealth matched those of Castile. Each kingdom had a distinct Jewish history, shaped by the institutional, economic, and social structures of their respective realms. Thus the history of the Jews in Castile was quite different from that of the Jews in Valencia or Catalonia. Within Castile itself, Jewish life varied from town to town, each having its own peculiar characteristics.

As we have already argued in a forthcoming article, Christian attitudes towards the Jews depended to a large extent on social identification. Members of the aristocracy and the ruling groups were on the whole more tolerant than the lower classes. Similarly, the economic and social structure of specific Jewish communities was often predicated on the economic pursuits of the Christian oligarchies in each town. For example, in Ávila, where the Christian urban patriciate derived its income from land rents and ranching, the Jews played an important role in artisanal and commercial activities; so too did the Moors. Moreover, the Jews of Ávila, although numerically predominant in certain areas of the city, could also be found in other neighborhoods, living alongside Christians.

There was little or no violence there against the Jews in 1391, and, if the tax records are any guide, the Jewish community seemed to have remained fairly stable and undisturbed until 1492. As can be seen in Table I, the case of Ávila contrasts sharply with those communities that experienced violent pogroms against the Jews in 1391. It is only in the latter that we find a drastic drop in the income of the *servicio*, a head tax based on the number of Jewish inhabitants.

TABLE I

DECLINE OF JEWISH COMMUNITIES IN CASTILE
A COMPARISON BETWEEN THE *SERVICIO* PAID BY JEWS
IN 1291 AND 1474 (SELECTED CITIES)

CITY	1291	1474	POGROM
Valencia	8,607 *mrs.*	2,000 *mrs.*	Yes
Burgos	22,161 *mrs.*	700 *mrs.*	Yes
Calahorra	2,898 *mrs.*	3,000 *mrs.*	No
Ávila	14,550 *mrs.*	12,000 *mrs.*	No

Source: J. Amador de los Ríos, *Historia social, política y religiosa de los judíos de España y Portugal*

In Burgos, on the other hand, where Christians controlled foreign and short-distance trade as well as artisanal occupations, Jews were not active in these pursuits; moreover, they were confined to the *judería*, the Jewish neighborhood.

Burgos witnessed repeated violence against its Jewish population, and if the Burgalese *conversos* escaped some of the atrocities perpetrated against their counterparts in Andalusia and elsewhere, it may have been due in part to the influence the *converso* family of Santa María exercised in the city.[2] Thus Jews in Castile and in most of Iberia performed a wide range of economic activities (as farmers, doctors, tailors, tax farmers, tax collectors, shoemakers, soldiers) and occupied diverse social situations. The vision of Jews concentrating exclusively on usury and finance, enjoying high positions in the royal court, or leading uniform lives throughout the peninsula, is misleading and incorrect.[3]

Jewish communities in Castile were adversely affected by the crisis of the late thirteenth and fourteenth centuries. Deteriorating economic conditions led to social conflict and endemic violence throughout the peninsula.[4] Jewish claims to exemption from municipal taxes and obligations and their competition with Christian merchants and tax collectors for ever-decreasing tax revenues produced growing animosity against them among the Castilian and Aragonese bourgeoisies. The extant ordinances of the Cortes (the Castilian parliament) cast light on the history of this conflict from the mid-thirteenth century to just before the expulsion in 1492. These urban petitions to the crown show the continuous antagonism against Jews because of their economic activities and their interaction with Christian society. Jews were forbidden to marry or cohabit with Christians or to use Christian names. Moreover, their financial activities and service in the royal bureaucracy were severely limited by successive legislation of the Cortes. The repetitive nature of these complaints, however, reveal the failure of Christians in limiting the roles of Jews in Castilian life.[5]

In spite of the success of the Jews in fending off Christian attacks in the Cortes, the economic and social changes sweeping through Castile and, to a lesser extent, Aragon were mostly catastrophic in nature and gravely affected the Jews. This was evident not only in the legislation of the Cortes, but also in the widespread millenarian agitation which swept Jewish communities in the late thirteenth century. Spurred by an ever-increasing financial burden, these apocalyptic visions led to a turning inward for mystical escape. Note, for example, Moses of Leon's *Zohar*[***] or *Book of Splendor*, the fundamental Kabbalistic text, dated by Gershom Scholem to around 1285. They also produced some important conversions, such as that of Abner of Burgos, who under the Christian name of Alfonso of Valladolid wrote a bitter polemical work, *The Wars of the Lord*, against his former coreligionists. Moreover, a growing interest in secular philosophy, or Averroism,[6] fostered religious skepticism.[7]

The fourteenth century, with its long periods of royal minorities, civil wars, the plague, and excessive violence by nobles and outlaws, did little to improve

---

[***] The *Zohar* or *Book of Splendor* is the most important text in Kabbala mysticism. A commentary on the Pentateuch, with magical and astrological accretions, it had great impact on Renaissance thought and on the spread of Kabbalistic doctrines among Christians.

the conditions of the Jews.[8] The melancholy state of the Jews in Castile, albeit the prosperity of some, is partly reflected in the beautiful but somber poetry of Rabbi Don Sem-Tob of Carrión. He addressed and dedicated his work to Peter I (1350–65)—a king as sympathetic to the Jews as could be expected, given the regal proclivity to oppress Jews financially and to discard or execute Jewish financial advisers who were no longer useful. In the chronicles of his reign he is called by his enemies Peter the Cruel, and one of the most frequent accusations hurled against Peter I by his opponents was that he favored the Jews, and that he was himself the illegitimate son of a Jew—yet another case in which anti-Jewish feelings served political ends. In the bitter civil war which was fought against Peter I's half-brother, the bastard Henry of Trastámara, the Jews supported the king with money and arms. In backing Peter I, however, the Jews chose the wrong side.[9]

When Henry murdered his brother on the field of Montiel in 1369, the Jewish communities in Castile found themselves besieged. Fanned by longstanding popular anti-Jewish feelings and by the indifference of city officials, attacks against the Jews were launched in several towns. Crushing fines were imposed, 1,000,000 *maravedises* on the *aljama* (community or quarter) of Burgos alone, and equally oppressive financial measures were foisted on the *judería* of Toledo. Yet, even while denouncing Peter I's support of the Jews and attacking their *aljamas*, once he had secured the throne, Henry II also continued to rely on their services. These contradictory policies indicate the crown's ambivalence towards the Jews, an ambivalence which remained unresolved throughout the next two centuries; they also reveal the precariousness of the Jews' position in Castile.[10]

As the fourteenth century drew to a close, the Jewish communities in Castile and the Crown of Aragon were impoverished, embattled, and vulnerable to further attacks. Society as a whole had not fared well under the blows of economic decline, depopulation, and civil war; but the Jews also had to face the exacerbation of anti-Jewish feelings—that strange mixture of religious bigotry, greed, envy, and unspoken fears—which always flourish in times of economic and social crisis.[11] It is within this framework that the events of 1391 must be understood.

2. Jewish Life After 1391

Like a raging fire, violence against the Jews spread throughout the peninsula. Some localities—such as Ávila, Madrid, and Valladolid—were spared, but in Seville, Córdoba, Jaén, and several other Andalusian towns (all of them with large *aljamas*), angry mobs exacted a frightening toll. Violence against the Jews was, of course, not unknown in the peninsula, and it continued, both against Jews and *conversos* (although mostly against the latter), into the fifteenth century. None of the previous violence, however, reached the virulent level of 1391.

TABLE II

ATTACKS AGAINST JEWS AND CONVERSOS (1250–1492) Partial

YEAR	PLACE
1277	Pamplona (Navarre)
1285	Gerona (Catalonia)
1295	Tierra de Campos (Castile)
1321	Tudela (Navarre)
1328	Tudela, Estella, Viana, Funes, etc. (Navarre)
1348	Murviedro (Valencia)
1355	Toledo (Castile) Civil War in Castile
1360	Nájera, Miranda del Ebro (Castile) Civil War
1385	Ribadavia (Galicia) English Invasion
1391	Pogroms throughout the peninsula: Seville, Córdoba, Montoro, Andújar, Ubeda, Baeza, Jaén, Huete, Villareal, Cuenca, Burgos, Toledo, Palencia (Castile), Valencia, Barcelona, Lérida, Teruel, Palma de Mallorca, Gerona (Crown of Aragon)
1406	Córdoba (Castile)
1449	Attacks against *conversos* in Toledo and León
1459–64	Unrest in Burgos against *conversos*
1461	Against Jews and French merchants in Medina del Campo (Castile)
1465	Racial conflicts, Toledo and Seville
1467	Riots against *conversos*: Toledo, Seville and Burgos
1468	Massacre of Jews in Sepúlveda (Castile)
1469	Attacks on Jewish tax collectors in Tolosa
1473	Massacres of *conversos* in Córdoba, Montoro, Bujalance, Adamar, La Rambla, Santaella, Ecija, Andújar, Ubeda, Baeza, Almodóvar del Campo, Jaén
1474	Attacks on *conversos* in Segovia and Valladolid

Source: Amador de los Ríos, *Historia social, política y religiosa de los judíos*; A. MacKay, "Popular Movements and Pogroms in Fifteenth Century Castile," *Past & Present*, 55 (1972)

The pogroms of 1391 cannot be easily explained, and no single hypothesis is fully satisfying. The death of John I in 1390 and the upheaval which followed the minority of Henry III probably triggered some popular unrest. Other elements served as catalysts for the violence. Among them, we must note the following: a) the inflammatory preaching of some of the mendicant friars, above all Ferrán Martínez de Ecija in Seville and, less vitriolic, Vincent Ferrer; b) social unrest, i.e., the factionalism of power elites in urban Castile and the conflict between nobility and bourgeoisie which led to popular violence and strife; c) longstanding popular anti-Jewish sentiment; d) an undefined fear and pessimism, important aspects of late medieval life, which were fed in Spain by the circulation of mythical stories about Jewish deeds, such as blood libels and sacrileges. Furthermore, the traditional relationship between the Jews and the crown, which often prevented the Jews from siding with the urban patriciate in their resistance to royal taxation and centralization, also increased the urban oligarchies' antagonism against the Jews.[12]

In towns such as Valencia violence was directed against the Jews by persons of diverse social backgrounds; in others, as in Barcelona, antisemitism predominated among the lower classes, while the bourgeoisie attempted to suppress the violence. In some cases, as Philippe Wolff has pointed out, the riots turned into a general attack on property regardless of religion, moving from blind antisemitism to social and fiscal insurrection.[13]

What these contrasts reveal, aside from uneven economic developments and contrasting social structures, is a country in which popular unrest could be expressed and vented only through religious antagonism. Moreover, noble factions often used mob violence against the Jews as an added weapon in their struggle to control town resources, or to confront royal authority (since the Jews were legally the property of the king). The intervention of crown officials and high church dignitaries on behalf of the Jews, and legislation in the following years aimed at restoring Jewish property and punishing the rioters, did little to alter the nefarious effects of 1391. Hundreds, perhaps thousands, had been slain, and many more had been forced to convert to save their lives and fortunes. Some Jewish communities disappeared entirely, as happened in Jaén and Ciudad Real, where their members were killed or converted.[14]

This last consequence provides the key to much of subsequent Iberian history. The uniqueness of 1391 resided precisely in the large number of forced and voluntary conversions which took place. For apart from human and material losses, 1391 marked an unprecedented psychological break from the cherished tradition of *convivencia* (coexistence with and acceptance of Jewish life), which even if idealized in the best of conditions, could never be returned to.[15] The outburst of 1391 was a prelude to the escalation of violence and anti-Jewish measures which followed in the fifteenth century and which culminated in the establishment of the Inquisition.

Not all conversions, however, were forced. Some important conversions to Christianity took place before the pogroms, the most notable by Selomoh Ha-Levi, the pious and learned rabbi of Burgos who, after studying theology in Paris, became bishop of Burgos and Patriarch of Aquilea under the name of Pablo de Santa María.[16] As Benjamin Gampel and others have pointed out, many more conversions occurred in the two decades following 1391, and, especially, after the disputation of Tortosa in 1413–14.[17] The inconclusive outcome of that debate, which church officials nonetheless touted as a victory, and the troubling vehemence of prominent former Jews, especially Jerónimo de Santa Fé (formerly Joshua Halorqui), succeeded in swaying those of wavering faith, mostly members of the intellectual and mercantile elites.[18]

After 1391, the once prosperous Jewish communities of *Sefarad* split off into separate tributaries. On the one hand, a thinned out, economically and socially weakened group, remained faithful to the religion of their fathers but lived on the edge of doom. The political upheavals of the mid-fifteenth century and the absence of strong royal power in the reigns of Juan II (1407–54), and Henry IV (1454–74), led many Jews to abandon their dwellings and businesses and to resettle in the lands of the great lords and the powerful Military Orders, where they found the protection which was no longer provided by the crown.

On the other hand, the *converso* communities, mostly urban, staked out an important place in Castilian and Aragonese societies. Their intellectual, economic, religious, and social success varied greatly. Many of these New Christians retained the economic roles they had filled as Jews. Petty-merchants, artisans, tax farmers, they remained in the same communities, practiced endogamy, and lived in the same houses and settings as they had as Jews. Other *conversos* entered the church with astonishing success or joined the ranks of the urban oligarchies and of the growing *letrado* groups (university-trained lawyers and bureaucrats). In Toledo, half of the rich benefices in the cathedral chapter were held by New Christians or their descendants. A number of important bishops, royal advisers, and chroniclers were members of the great *converso* families of Santa María, de la Caballería, Santa Fé, and others.[19]

Even King Ferdinand the Catholic had *converso* ancestors through his mother's family, and New Christians appeared prominently in the Jesuits' ranks and, ironically, in the early tribunals of the Inquisition. The Jesuits, nevertheless shunned the consequent racial policies of *limpieza de sangre* (purity of blood) and refused to discriminate against *conversos*, "advising them to join the Company in Italy rather than in Spain."[20] These *conversos* made the transition to Christianity and into the Christian world quite easily, sometimes marrying into prominent Old Christian families. St. Theresa of Ávila (1515–82), the revered mystic, writer, and religious reformer, traced her roots to *conversos* from Toledo.

During the first half of the fifteenth century, *converso* life developed with relative calm. Yet, after mid-century, another confluence of economic crises, antisemitic propaganda, and popular uprisings occurred. Owing to their success and visibility, and because popular anti-Jewish feelings had now been transferred to the *conversos*, violence began to mount against the New Christians. This antagonism manifested itself in two forms: legal actions sought to draw distinctions between recent converts and Old Christians, and competition developed for important posts within the church.

In Toledo, Old Christians, fighting a rear guard action, attempted to exclude or limit the numbers of New Christians in the chapter through appeals to Rome, bribes, and violence.[21] More significantly, after the 1440s numerous popular riots against *conversos* erupted in many cities throughout Castile. Their main object was the removal of *conversos* from public office. Ignited by alleged offenses against Christianity, by the perceived practice of Jewish customs and rituals on the part of *conversos*, and by deep underlying social causes—i.e., the enduring economic and political antagonism of the lower classes against the Jews, aimed now, after the massive conversions of 1391, at some segments of the *converso* population—the level of violence against New Christians escalated.[22]

The chronicle of Diego de Valera, a contemporary witness to the events, describes the assaults in Córdoba and Jaén in laconic, yet angry, words: Since "Old Christians had conceived this hatred of the *conversos*, they went together to burn their houses.... The attacks were characterized by theft and murder in city and countryside [against] *conversos* who without any cause died."[23] And on this ambivalence—on the uncertainty about the place of most *conversos* in society, and on the failure of Castilians to accept New Christians—the story turns. The refusal to allow a majority of the *conversos* to integrate into Spanish society made the coming of the Inquisition unavoidable.

Here we pause to examine in some depth the historiographical controversy surrounding the *conversos*. If Christians were ambivalent as to the identity, allegiances, and social standing of *conversos*, it was because these characteristics varied greatly. Some Jews converted out of a genuine religious conviction, and then went on to become clergymen, theologians, and leaders whose Christian zeal was unquestioned. Others, religious skeptics, adopted the new religion out of necessity or convenience. Versed in the humanistic disciplines then popular at noble and royal courts, they simply resembled the members of the Christian upper-classes and haute-bourgeoisie without changing their mental outlook in any significant way. Many converted simply to retain or gain social and economic advantages.

A far greater number, however, converted under duress and continued to believe in and to practice the precepts—or at least some of the precepts—of Judaism in hiding and in defiance of the consequences. With the passage of time and in the absence of religious instruction in Judaism, crypto-Judaism gradually acquired a syncretistic character, consisting of a mixture of both Jewish and Christian practices. Many third- and fourth-generation *conversos* adhered to elements of both religions without fully understanding either.[24]

Historians differ about the social and religious identification of the *conversos*, and no single hypothesis suffices to explain the *converso* phenomenon. Clearly, the *conversos* did not constitute a socially united group. Their divergent religious attitudes resulted not only in clashes with Christian society but also in "intracommunal and intrafamilial" disputes. The diversity of their religious practices was further underscored by an ambivalence towards their former brethren and an uncertainty as to their own identity. Often they did not know who they were, or where they belonged in society. This ambivalence was often shaped by social class: the *converso* elite alternated between those who attacked their former coreligionists and denied their ancestral faith, and those who used their position in Christian society as a means to mitigate the plight of the Jews and to protest against the Inquisition. On the other end of the social ladder, the artisan groups, who tended to remain faithful to Jewish traditions, formed a more cohesive and mutually supportive community.

In the latter half of the fifteenth century, the quick assimilation of some *conversos* into Christian society and their advance to important positions in the royal, urban, and ecclesiastical administrations re-ignited popular antisemitism. Before 1391, legal impediments could be imposed on the Jews, limiting the extent of their influence and social status, whereas conversion legally removed all these restrictions. Hatred of the *conversos* and envy of their success thus grew into racial hatred. For in the eyes of lower-class Christians, and of their zealous counterparts in the upper echelons, the *conversos* remained Jews despite their conversion and had, therefore, to be removed from positions of authority. Thus Jews and *conversos* alike suffered from the rise of antisemitism: the former, via harassment and expulsion; the latter, via punishment for vestiges of their ancestral religion.[25]

3. The Coming of the Inquisition

The medieval Inquisition was instituted by the papacy in Languedoc in the 1230s as a weapon against the widespread Cathar heresy. Although the diocesan and papal inquisitions had been active in the Crown of Aragon in the thirteenth and fourteenth centuries, the kings of Castile had jealously forbidden their operation within the realm.[26] In the 1460s, the inflammatory writings of Alfonso de Espina added further impetus to the movement against *conversos*. In *Fortalitium Fidei* (*Fortress of Faith*), he presented a methodical program for dealing with false *conversos*; he accused them of treason, homosexuality, child-murder, poisoning, and usury, and he called for the expulsion of the Jews. Thus Espina provided a formula that would serve both as a model for the Inquisition and as a justification for the formal repression of *conversos* by the crown.[27] When the Inquisition was instituted in the early years of the 1480s (officially in 1484), it did so under conditions hitherto unknown in the medieval West. Under direct royal control, it was indeed the only institution in Spain which could be called truly national.

Hernando del Pulgar, chronicler of the Catholic Kings—Ferdinand and Isabella—and himself of *converso* origin, described the first Inquisition trials in Seville and Córdoba. The targets were New Christians "practicing Judaism in secret, not believing in the Christian faith, and not performing those pious acts associated with Christianity."[28] This is important: the Inquisition could not claim jurisdiction over the Jews and rarely persecuted them except for blasphemy or proselytizing. Yet Jews remained under attack; for the Inquisition constantly intervened and greatly affected the lives and fate of Jews. One particular form of intimidation and intrusion into Jewish life was the demand that rabbis excommunicate from their congregations those Jews who refused to testify on the judaizing activities of *conversos* which they might have witnessed or aided. The final blow was given by the Inquisition when it pressed Ferdinand and Isabella to expel the Jews from Andalusia in 1483 and from Spain in 1492. That these edicts were officially promulgated by the Catholic Kings does not conceal the fact that they were conceived by the Inquisition.[29]

During the first phase, 1480–92, the victims of the Inquisition were almost exclusively *conversos*, whose families had practiced Christianity for more than three generations, and who, regardless of sincere or feigned orthodoxy, were suspected of practicing Judaism. Henry Kamen cites figures that unequivocally illustrate who were the targets of the Inquisition: "99.3% of those tried by the Barcelona tribunal between 1488 and 1505, and 91.6% of those tried by that of Valencia between 1484 and 1530 were *conversos* of Jewish origin." Moreover, "over 3/4 of all those who perished under the Inquisition in the three centuries of its existence did so in the first twenty years."[30] Table III provides some indication of the number of people executed by order of the Inquisition in the early years.

TABLE III

Tribunal	Period	Relaxations (Executions)		Other Victims
		In Person	Effigy	
Ciudad Real	1483–1485	52	220	183
Toledo	1485–1501	250	500	5,400
Zaragoza	1485–1502	11	15	904
Valencia	1484–1530	754	155	1,076
Barcelona	1488–1498	23	455	421

Source: H. Kamen, *Inquisition and Society*, p. 42.

Nevertheless, the Inquisition was not established without protest. Opposition came from municipal councils in Aragon, such as those of Teruel and Zaragoza, which saw its establishment as an infringement of their liberties, since the Inquisition was a Castilian creature. It also came from the *conversos* themselves, especially those of the elite capable of mounting protests, who soon identified the Inquisition for what it was: a serious threat to their social status, wealth, and lives. Opposition was equally forthcoming from members of Christian aristocratic and intellectual circles, who denounced its harsh measures and unjust procedures—such as the procurement of secret denunciations and secret witnesses (i.e., neither the full content of the accusations, nor the identities of the accusers were revealed to the *converso* accused of judaizing)—but did not question the Inquisition's legitimacy. Instead of coercion and terror, they proposed education and moderation as the proper enticements to conversion.

These protests, however, were never effective. As Kamen shows, public concerns about the justice and methods of the Holy Office gained prominence only after 1500, when the Inquisition—having decimated the *conversos* or forced them into exile—turned its attention from judaizers to other kinds of heretics, most of them of Old Christian lineage. The letup in the persecution of converted Jews, however, proved to be only temporary, for it was reactivated in the mid-seventeenth century. When Portuguese New Christians arrived in Spain, seeking refuge from the Portuguese Inquisition, they too were charged with crypto-Judaism.[31] Tables IV, V, and VI illustrate select aspects of inquisitorial activity in these early years.

TABLE IV

NUMBER AND PERCENT OF PERSONS CHARGED WITH JUDAIZING BY THE INQUISITION IN TOLEDO TO 1530, BY SEX, TIME PERIOD, AND DISPOSITION OF CASE

Sex and Disposition	Time Period									
	Up to 1494		1495–1500		1501–15		1516–30		Total	
Females										
Absolved	15	(5.5)	4	(7.84)	15	(12.82)	6	(12.24)	40	(8.31)
Condemned	96	(35.69)	18	(35.29)	36	(30.77)	17	(34.69)	167	(34.36)
Sentence Incomplete	7	(2.60)	5	(9.80)	3	(2.56)	0		15	(3.08)
Sentence Suspended	0		0		1	(0.85)	0		1	(0.20)
Total	118	(43.86)	27	(52.94)	55	(47.01)	23	(46.94)	223	(45.88)
Males										
Absolved	10	(3.71)	1	(1.96)	16	(13.67)	5	(10.20)	32	(6.58)
Condemned	131	(48.69)	21	(41.17)	44	(37.60)	19	(38.77)	215	(44.24)
Sentence Incomplete	8	(2.97)	1	(1.96)	2	(1.71)	2	(4.08)	13	(2.67)
Sentence Suspended	2	(0.7)	0		0		0		2	(0.41)
Reprimanded	0		1	(1.96)	0		0		1	(0.20)
Total	151	(56.14)	24	(47.06)	62	(52.99)	26	(53.06)	263	(54.10)
Grand Total	269		51		117		49		486	

Notes to Table IV: The chronological division here is designed to emphasize the distinction between those accused before the expulsions of 1492–94, who in theory had been Christian for almost a century, and those who converted in 1492–94 as a way of avoiding expulsion. The percentages condemned or absolved in relation to the totals by sex are as follows: 85.55 percent of all males condemned, 12.17 percent absolved; 74.89 percent of all females condemned, 17.93 percent absolved. Of the 195 persons identified by trade, 16 belonged to the urban elites or the clergy. The rest belonged to the petty bourgeoisie, ranging from weavers and hat makers to a seller of spices. There were 26 shoemakers or relatives of shoemakers, 13 tailors and 14 merchants. Of the condemned, 114 were already dead or had fled; 26 were tortured.

Source: T.F. Ruiz, "The Holy Office in Medieval France and in Late Medieval Castile," in Angel Alcalá, ed., *The Spanish Inquisition and the Inquisitorial Mind*

TABLE V

INQUISITION TRIALS IN ZARAGOZA, 1484–87
PERSONS CHARGED WITH JUDAIZING (PARTIAL LISTING)

SEX AND DISPOSITION	1484	1485	1486	1487	TOTAL
Females					
Penitence & Confiscation	3				3
Penitence			12	17	29
Burned		1	12	5	18
Burned in effigy	1		1	3	5
Total	4	1	25	25	55
Males					
Penitence & Confiscation	1		1	1	3
Penitence			17	5	22
Burned (Executed)	1(1)	1	26(2)	4(2)	37
Burned in effigy			9	21	21
Prison			1		1
Total	3	1	56	24	84
Grand Total	7	2	81	49	139

Notes to Table V: Professions or trades of those condemned or their relatives, as mentioned in the *Memorias* of the Inquisition of Zaragoza as follows:

Merchants, shopkeepers, financial activities	22
Liberal professions (notary, etc.) and clergy	8 (2 clergy)
Artisans (tailors, shoemakers, dyemakers. etc.	24
People described as knights (*caballeros*)	2

One Christian and one Jew were charged with blasphemy. Two Old Christians were condemned for converting to Judaism. Four of those brought to trial were also charged with bigamy and sexual crimes, three with witchcraft, one with practicing Judaism and Islam at the same time. Most of those burned in effigy (who had escaped) belonged to the clergy or professional groups.

Source: Henry C. Lea, *A History of the Inquisition in Spain*, vol. 1

TABLE VI

THE INQUISITION OF VALENCIA, 1478–1530

Number of individuals processed:	2,354
Males:	1,197
Females:	1,157
Charges:	
Judaizing:	91.6% of all the accused
Muslim practices:	3.3%
Lutheranism, sorcery, blasphemy, etc.:	5.1%

Breakdown by social and professional categories (736 individuals):

- Nobility: 4 (charges of judaizing, all received light penalties)
- Clergy: 27
- Bourgeoisie: 245 (34%)
  a) 124 merchants; b) *corredores* (money changers, etc.); in addition, 96 of the women brought before the Valencian tribunal had husbands who can be described as members of the bourgeoisie
- Municipal officials et al.: 6 (includes 4 functionaries of the Inquisition itself)
- Liberal professions: 74
  a) 40 notaries; b) 5 lawyers; c) 10 medical doctors; d) 2 barbers or surgeons; e) 1 pharmacist; f) 1 teacher; g) 8 book sellers; h) 1 musician; i) 6 scribes
- *Rentistas* (those living from their rents): 6
- Artisans: 317 (43% of the total)
- Peasants: 7
- Servants: 21

Source: Ricardo García Cárcel, *Orígenes de la Inquisición española: El tribunal de Valencia, 1478-1530*, pp. 171–173

If only in passing in this general overview, we must note again the social class of most of the victims. One of the issues most hotly debated at present is whether the Inquisition functioned as an agent for the enforcement of religious orthodoxy, or whether it sought to preserve specific social and economic structures—thus bringing pressure to bear upon the members of certain professions or trades. For what we encounter throughout the long history of the Inquisition in Spain is the persecution of those social and economic ranks—we may identify them as classes—which threatened, by their economic pursuits and expectations, the existing structures of Castile and Spain.

This was a society in which the hegemonic groups—crown, landed aristocracy, and church—derived their income and privileges from land rents and taxes on transhumance (the movement of livestock from winter to summer grazing lands). In fact, the records of the Inquisition clearly show that some *conversos* were more suspect than others, while many were not suspect at all. Prevailingly, it was their location in the established order which determined how much attention they drew from the Inquisition.[32] Thus most of those brought before the Inquisition, whether male or female, belonged to mercantile and artisanal groups—the bourgeoisie and petty-bourgeoisie of Spain. The merchants' economic activity and mentality posed a challenge (above all, in Castile with its traditions of crusading and military ideals) to the traditional social and economic order. Shopkeepers and artisans (the masters of trade, butchers, silk-workers, pharmacists, shoemakers, and others) were a volatile social group in frequent and at times violent conflict with the aristocratized urban oligarchies. Politically disenfranchised and overburdened by taxes, artisans and shopkeepers also appeared as a menace to those who ruled.

Yet such a strict social and economic interpretation is not entirely satisfactory. Even we, co-authors of this article, are not of one mind on this issue: Freund emphasizes, in her interpretation, religious intolerance and longstanding racial and popular antisemitism as the main propellers of inquisitorial activities against the *conversos*; Ruiz, although agreeing on the importance of these aspects, maintains that economic and social factors played an equally important role. Whatever the choice of emphasis, it is illuminating to place the rise and activities of the Inquisition in Spain within the context of a Weberian construct: the monopoly of legalized violence by the nascent modern state. By the end of the fifteenth-century in Spain and elsewhere in the West, the turmoil and conflicts of the century, private violence, war, and usurpation of regal power gave way to new and more forceful ways of exercising authority. The centralized monarchies of the early modern period differed from their medieval ancestors in their centralizing tendencies, in the fostering of coercive institutions which repressed and tamed the enemies of the crown, and in the methodical identification, targeting, confinement, or eradication of scapegoats (Jews, women in northern Europe, heretics, and the poor).

The Inquisition in Spain proved to be an unholy alliance between church and state; aimed at stamping out political and religious subversion, it served the overlapping ends of both institutions. Trials and sentencings were carried out by the Inquisition, whereas punishment—such as burning at the stake and confiscation of property—was executed by the secular arm of government. And yet, it hardly mattered whether the Inquisition burned its victims or whether it reconciled them to the church. Any notice by the Inquisition cast a pall of uncertainty and fear over one's life. This is the point made by Bartolomé Benassar and others: that all *conversos*—whether crypto-Jews or devout Christians—were targets of persecution by guilt of association. The Inquisition was an effective tool of repression because it fostered a permanent state of fear. Its best weapon was not torture, but secrecy, random denunciation, arbitrary sentencing, and the threat of misery and shame.[33]

One should particularly keep in mind the inconsistent and arbitrary nature of Inquisitorial procedures, given the limited means of verifying the truth of confessions elicited from victims. What emerges from the evidence is a tendency of leniency towards the wealthy and influential *converso*, and of prosecution and execution towards the simple artisan. The Inquisition, notably in Toledo, found most of its victims among the latter; while humble Jewish women were burned in Ciudad Real, rich, acculturated women were acquitted in Toledo.[34]

The question, however, remains: were the *conversos* crypto-Jews or not? The traditional view of such historians as Baer, Kamen, Beinart, and Yerushalmi has been that the aim of every *converso* was to live as a Jew and that most *conversos* adhered to the Jewish traditions consciously and by conviction: "*Conversos* and Jews were one people united by one destiny and one religion." The "religion of the *marranos*" (as the *conversos* were pejoratively called) "ran the entire gamut, from the most attenuated awareness of Jewish roots, to a readiness to endure martyrdom for the 'Law of Moses'.... Every New Christian was a potential *Marrano*, whom any of a variety of circumstances could transform into an active *Marrano*."[35] Ironically, the view of these historians coincides with the position taken by the Inquisition itself: that the majority of *conversos* practiced Judaism in secret, refrained from participation in Christian rituals, and endangered the integrity of the Christian faith.

Not everyone, however, agrees with this interpretation. Historians such as Netanyahu and Rivkin have gone so far as to deny the Jewishness of most of the New Christians. Most *conversos*, they argue, were really devout Christians, of whom only a minority were judaizers. The Inquisition used this dwindling minority as a pretext for attacking the entire *converso* population, and for carrying out a policy based on racial hatred and socio-political considerations rather than religious zeal. The object of the Inquisition, the argument continues, was not to weed out the "bad Christians" or to re-educate the wayward ones, since the Inquisition simply made wild use of the epithets of heresy. Rather, it was to "defame, degrade, segregate and ruin the whole group economically and socially." For despite their Christian belief, they had retained their *de facto* status of social aliens; moreover, their success in all fields was intolerable. The only way to remove the advantages obtained by New Christians was, therefore, to de-Christianize them.[36] Rivkin and Netanyahu are emphatic:

> The Jewishness of the New Christians is a myth spawned by the Inquisition and nurtured throughout the centuries by the Church and the Synagogue. From the Jewish point of view it is a myth so inspirational that it is not likely to dissolve.... How could a class of wealthy and powerful Christians [Rivkin asks] be toppled legitimately [and made] to give way to Old Christians?... By charging them with Judaizing, and by parading self-confessed *conversos* in dramatic *autos de fé*...thereby justifying the scourging, burning and expropriating in which the Inquisition engaged.[37]

As Angus MacKay and Henry Kamen have observed, the Inquisition was simply the institutionalization of undying popular prejudices and attitudes, and the turning of popular insurrection into state policy to consolidate political and spiritual power.[38]

Rivkin dismisses all confessions of judaizing as elicited under duress, and thus false; according to him, *conversos* died as Christian, not Jewish, martyrs. Baer, on the other hand, maintains that *conversos* voluntarily sought reconciliation with the church only because they were thus enabled to continue their heroic and secret practice of the Judaic laws. Beinart, too, based on Inquisitorial records, presents a portrait of the painstaking zeal with which the *conversos* of Ciudad Real sought to retain, and succeeded in perpetuating, their undercover Jewish identities and practices until the coming of the Inquisition.[39]

For Netanyahu, however, it was precisely the Inquisition that gave marranism a new lease on life. Crypto-Judaism would have ceased to exist had not the process of assimilation been tampered with. In this, however, both Baer's and, more recently, Yerushalmi's interpretations concur with Netanyahu's: second- and third-generation *conversos* often sought refuge in Judaism out of disgust with the unjust practices of the Inquisition. The Inquisition and *limpieza de sangre* (purity of blood) played an important role in activating the *marrano* potential of New Christians.[40]

Which is the correct interpretation? How Jewish were the New Christians? The evidence is inconclusive. Many went to their deaths protesting their Christianity, and many died as Jews; others, whether secret Jews or Christians, fled and continued to flee throughout the following decades. The complex and elusive nature of the evidence encourages divergent interpretations. Of those who died as official Christians, for example, many may in fact have been crypto-Jews who converted at the stake, moments before their deaths, in return for the clemency of having their throats slit prior to being engulfed by the flames of the *auto da fé*. The attempt to determine the religious affiliation of those seeking refuge in other countries is equally troublesome: for although a great number of migrating *conversos* resettled in Jewish communities and reclaimed their Jewish identities, many others sought to preserve their Christianity.[41]

How successful was the Spanish Inquisition? Very successful, according to John Elliott. For Elliott, the Inquisition was masterminded by zealous *conversos* practicing a particularly strident form of Christianity and committed to the persecution of their former co-religionists; the Edict of Expulsion—its logical end-product, entailing the complete eradication of Jews and Judaism from Spain—thus represented the ultimate victory of this powerful group.[42]

This, however, is only one answer to the question. The crown's official reason for the Edict of Expulsion of 31 March 1492, as worded by the Catholic Monarchs, was "the great harm suffered by Christians [i.e., *conversos*] from the contact, intercourse and communication which they had with the Jews, who always attempted in various ways to seduce faithful Christians from our Holy Catholic Faith."[43] Yet in Kamen's view and that of other historians, the decision to expel the Jews did not come from Ferdinand and Isabella, but from the Holy Office, as an extension of regional expulsions (such as the Andalusian one, mentioned above), which failed to eradicate the judaizing tendencies of the *conversos*.[44] In the end, what the Edict of Expulsion attests to is the ultimate failure of the Inquisition to uproot crypto-Judaism from the peninsula, an objective which was to remain unattainable throughout the four centuries of its existence in Spain.[45]

The reasons why the Catholic Monarchs expelled the Jews, the effects of the expulsion on the Spanish economy and society, the number of Jews who actually left—all these are questions for which there are no easy or certain answers. Some historians have argued that the Decree of Expulsion was aimed at converting—not expelling—the Jews, and that it sought to remove them from Spain only after conversion of the entire Jewish population proved impossible. The Edict of Expulsion was certainly a departure from the age-old royal policy of protecting the Jews from the abuses of the more powerful elements in society: it contradicted the policies of Ferdinand and Isabella, who continued to protect and welcome Jews at court even while sponsoring the persecution of *conversos*.[46]

On the other hand, and contrary to popular myth, the expulsion of the Jews did not seriously weaken the economic foundations of the Spanish monarchy. The Jews, their numbers already heavily drained by conversion, were a small and industrious but marginal and by no means rich minority. Moreover, many had transferred their assets to *conversos* prior to their departure, so that the loss was even further minimized. Much more detrimental to the economy was the substantial *converso* emigration which, provoked by unrelenting persecution, continued for many years.[47]

What did Spain attain, finally, with the Edict of Expulsion? For one, the order of expulsion aggravated the *converso* problem it had set out to resolve. The number of forced—and presumably false—converts doubled, since a great number of Jews could not afford, or did not have the strength, to leave Spain. These mass conversions, once again, proved no solution. *Conversos*, for the most part, and in the eyes of the Christian populace, remained an unintegrated group for whom baptism served primarily as a legitimizing facade. Instead of integrating the *converso* into Spanish society, the Inquisition and the Edict of Expulsion provoked the inception of the statutes of *limpieza de sangre* (purity of blood). The latter represented an attempt to find new means of imposing legal restrictions on New Christians and of retaliating against their intrusion into Spanish society, despite the fact that their conversion had been actively sought. Mere conversion no longer sufficed; henceforth racial purity, not faith, was to be the determining standard.[48]

The Expulsion also resulted in the irrevocable loss of a pluralistic society of *convivencia*, in which Jews had played an important role for centuries. Although the concept of *convivencia* had often been a tenuous and idealized one, it had nonetheless fostered diversity and tolerance; it had enriched the culture and life of Spain.[49] Yet from this moment on, because they continued to remind *conversos* of their ancestral faith, the Jews were banished from *Sefarad* into bitter exile, after having dwelled many generations in Iberia, extending back to the very beginnings of the Christian era and to the age of Imperial Rome. What pride and elegance there had been in these collective lives can be seen to this very day by those visiting the Synagogue of the Transito in Toledo. Built in the mid-fourteenth century, when all hope, especially in Toledo, was beginning to vanish, its serene and austere beauty speaks to us across time of the enduring sense of self and community.

Endnotes

1. For a summary of the history of Jews in Spain, see Luis Suárez Fernández, *Judíos españoles en la edad media* (Madrid: D.L. Rialp, 1980); Abraham Neuman, *The Jews in Spain: Their Social, Political and Cultural Life During the Middle Ages*, 2 vols., (Philadelphia: Jewish Publication Society, 1944). See also note 3.

2. For a general survey of Iberian history in the period discussed in this article see Angus MacKay, *Spain in the Middle Ages: From Frontier to Empire* (London: St. Martin's Press, 1977), 121–210; also Joseph F. O'Callaghan, *A History of Medieval Spain* (Ithaca: Cornell University Press, 1975), 549–676. For the contrast in the social and economic position of Jews according to localities see Teofilo F. Ruiz, "Jewish-Christian Relations in Urban Northern Castile, 1200–1350," forthcoming in *Congreso Internacional. Judíos y Conversos en la Historia*, Ribadavia, Galicia, 1994. For a more detailed discussion of Jewish life in the late Middle Ages see Y. Fritz Baer, *A History of the Jews in Christian Spain*, 2 vols., (Philadelphia: Jewish Publication Society, 1961–66), 2:95–444; the relevant documentation is found in Baer, *Die Jüden im Christlichen Spanien*, 2 vols., (Berlin, 1929–36; new printing, Westmead, UK: Gregg, 1970); see, above all, vol. 2 and bibliography accompanying new printing, collected by H. Beinart. Also the old but still valuable work by J. Amador de los Ríos, *Historia social, política y religiosa de los judíos de España y Portugal* (Madrid: Aguilar, 1973). For the life of Jews in specific localities see the valuable articles found in the journal *Sefarad*. For the Jews of Burgos and the influence of the Santa María family see Carlos Estepa, Teofilo F. Ruiz et al., *Burgos en la Edad Media* (Valladolid: Junta de Castilla y Leon, 1984), 50–52, 149–153, 371–386; F. Cantera Burgos, *Alvar García de Santa María. Historia de la judería de Burgos y de sus conversos más egregios* (Madrid: C.S.I.C., 1952).

3. See, for example, the findings of Miguel Angel Ladero Quesada, who points out in his book, *El siglo XV en Castilla. Fuentes de renta y política fiscal* (Barcelona: Ariel, 1982), 143–167, the presence of many Christian tax farmers and collectors. For examples of Jewish activities elsewhere, see Angel Barrios García, *Documentación medieval de la catedral de Ávila* (Salamanca: Universidad de Salamanca, 1981), 211–481; for Calahorra see F. Cantera Burgos, "La judería de Calahorra," *Sefarad*, 15 (1955): 355–358; and his "Documentos de compraventas hebraícos de la catedral de Calahorra," *Sefarad*, 6 (1946): 37–62. Also note 1. For Jewish life in other parts of Europe see Maurice Kriegel, *Les juifs à la fin du Moyen Age dans l'Europe mediterranéen* (Paris: Hachette, 1979); Brian Pullan, *The Jews of Europe and the Inquisition of Venice, 1550–1670* (Totowa, NJ: Barnes & Noble, 1983).

4. For the crises of the late fourteenth century in both kingdoms see Julio Valdeón Baruque, "Aspectos de la crisis castellana en la primera mitad del siglo XIV," *Hispania*, 111 (1969): 5–24; T.F. Ruiz, "Expansion et changement: La conquête de Séville et la société castillane (1248–1350)," *Annales E.S.C.*, (mai-juin 1979): 548–565; Thomas N. Bisson, *The Medieval Crown of Aragon. A Short History* (New York: Oxford University Press, 1986), 162–173.

5. *Cortes de los antiguos reinos de León y Castilla*, 5 vols., (Madrid: Real Academia de la Historia, 1861–63), 1:59, 68, 77, 99, 104, 111 et passim. See also Joseph F. O'Callaghan, *The Cortes of Castile-León, 1188–1350* (Philadelphia: University of Pennsylvania Press, 1988), 180–183.

6. Averroism is the name given to the philosophical ideas of Ibn Rushd (Avërroes), 1126–96, Islamic Spain's most renowned philosopher, as interpreted by later medieval thinkers. Defending philosophical inquiry, his works, among them the *Fasl* and *Tahāfut*, embraced Aristotelian philosophy and influenced Spanish Jews into adopting a more critical view of religion and a secular outlook. See Rushd Ibn (Avërroes) in *Dictionary of the Middle Ages* (New York, 1988), 10:571–575.

7. For the dating of the Zohar and apocalyptic agitation in Castile see Gershom Scholem, *Major Trends in Jewish Mysticism* (New York: Schocken, 1973), 156–204; on Abner of Burgos see Baer, *A History of the Jews* (n. 2), 1:327-331.

8. On the problems after 1350, see Julio Valdeón Baruque, *Enrique II: La guerra civil y la consolidación del régimen, 1366–1371*(Valladolid: Universidad de Valladolid, 1966); also MacKay (n. 2), 165–187.

9. The poetry of Rabbi Don Sem Tob of Carrión, his *Proverbios morales*, can be found in *Poetas castellanos anteriores al siglo XV*, Biblioteca de autores españoles, 57 (Madrid, 1966): 331–372; For Peter I's relations with the Jews, Jewish support, and accusations of his Jewish origins see *Crónica del rey don Pedro* in *Crónicas de los reyes de Castilla* I, Biblioteca de autores españoles, 66 (Madrid, 1953): 510, 580–583 et passim.

10. Baer, *A History of the Jews* (n. 2), 1:354. Those unable to pay were to be sold into slavery. For punitive measures against the Jews of Toledo in 1369 and Henry II's use of the Jews after the civil war was over see Valdeón Baruque, *Enrique II de Castilla* (n. 7), 326–334. For the relation of the Trastámaras with the Jews in the late fourteenth century see Julio Valdeón Baruque, *Los judíos de Castilla y la revolución Trastámara* (Valladolid: Universidad de Valladolid, 1968).

11. See the connection between economic decline and anti-Jewish violence in Antonio Ubieto Arteta, *Ciclos económicos en la Edad Media española* (Valencia, 1969); for the fear underlying late medieval and early modern life see Jean Delumeau, *La peur en Occident, XIVe–XVIIIe siècles* (Paris: Fayard, 1978), 49–50 et passim. For antisemitism in Spain see the excellent book by José María Monsalvo Antón, *Teoría y evolución de un conflicto social. El antisemitismo en la corona de Castilla en la baja edad media* (Madrid: Siglo Veintiuno Editores, 1985), see bibliography, 337–342.

12. See above n. 10. Also Johan Huizinga, *The Waning of the Middle Ages* (Garden City, NY: Doubleday, 1954) for the pessimism of late medieval life and H.R. Trevor-Roper, *The European Witch-Craze of the Sixteenth and Seventeenth Centuries and Other Essays* (New York: Harper & Row, 1967), 90–192. For the pogrom of 1391 and the agitation by the friars see Baer, *A History of the Jews* (n. 2), 2:166–169; and Philippe Wolff, "The 1391 Pogrom in Spain: Social Crisis or Not?" *Past & Present*, 50 (1971): 4–18. See below for the effect of the pogroms on Ciudad Real and Jaén. Stephen Haliczer, "The Expulsion of the Jews and the Economic Development of Castile," *Hispania judaica. Studies on the History, Language and Literature of the Jews in the Hispanic World*, ed. J. Solá-Solé et al., (Barcelona: Puvil, 1980), 1:39–47.

13. Wolff (n. 11), 11, 16. On general social unrest in late medieval Castile see Julio Valdeón Baruque, *Los conflictos sociales en el reino de Castilla en los siglos XIV y XV* (Madrid: Siglo Veintiuno, 1975) and for anti-Judaism, ibid., 28–37, 125–139, 174–183.

14. Wolff (n.11), 4, 14–16; Angus MacKay, "Popular Movements and Pogroms in Fifteenth-Century Castile," *Past & Present*, 55 (1972): 33, 58–60, 63–64; T.F. Ruiz, "The Holy Office in Medieval France and in Late Medieval Castile: Origins and Contrasts," in Angel Alcalá, ed., *The Spanish Inquisition and the Inquisitorial Mind* (Highland Lakes, NJ: Brooklyn College Press, 1987), 41; Baer, *A History of the Jews* (n. 2), 2:336. For Ciudad Real see Haim Beinart, *Conversos on Trial. The Inquisition in Ciudad Real* (Jerusalem, 1981), chs. 1–2. See also his *Trujillo. A Jewish Community in Extremadura on the Eve of the Expulsion From Spain* (Jerusalem: Magnes Press, 1980), 4–19. On Jaén see Luis Coronas Tejada, *Conversos and Inquisition in Jaen* (Jerusalem: Magnes Press, 1988).

15. On *convivencia* see the polemical work by Américo Castro, *The Structure of Spanish History* (Princeton: Princeton University Press, 1954); and the reply by Claudio Sánchez Albornoz, *España: Un enigma histórico*, 2 vols., (Buenos Aires: Editorial Sudamericana, 1956). The best example of *convivencia* has always been the court of Alfonso X, where Muslim, Jewish, and Christian scholars worked together in the royal *scriptoria*. Also Henry Kamen, *Inquisition and Society in Spain in the Sixteenth and Seventeenth Centuries* (Bloomington: Indiana University Press, 1985), 1, 17, 263; Wolff (n. 11), 17.

16. On the Santa María family see F. Cantera Burgos, *Alvar García de Santa María y su familia de conversos*. Also Baer, *A History of the Jews* (n. 2), 2:141; Kamen, *Inquisition and Society* (n. 15), 19.

17. B. Gampel, "Gazing on the Face of Gentile Women." Paper read at conference on Marginality, held at Princeton University, 1988.

18. For the disputation of Tortosa and the writings and polemics of Jerónimo de Santa Fé and other prominent *conversos* see Kamen, *Inquisition and Society* (n. 15), 11, 24; Baer, *A History of the Jews* (n. 2), 1:171–242.

19. Antonio Domínguez Ortiz, *La clase social de los conversos en Castilla en la edad moderna*, Monografías histórico-sociales, 3 (Madrid: Instituto Balmes de Sociologia, 1955): 7–69.

20. Kamen, *Inquisition and Society* (n. 15), 124–125; for Ferdinand's Jewish ties John H. Elliott, *Imperial Spain, 1469–1716* (Harmondsworth, UK: Penguin, 1975), 21. The concept of *limpieza de sangre* or purity of blood, the requirement to show a blood line going back several generations without the presence of Jewish blood, for election to one of the profitable benefices of the Military Orders, dates from this period, but its impact was not felt until the sixteenth century. For *limpieza de sangre* see Albert A. Sicroff, *Los estatutos de limpieza de sangre. Controversias entre los siglos XV y XVII* (Madrid: Taurus, 1985).

21. Kamen, *Inquisition and Society* (n. 15), 24–29.

22. Kamen, *Inquisition and Society* (n. 15), 28–29; Mackay, "Popular Movements and Pogroms" (n. 14), 47, 52–62.

23. *Crónicas de los reyes de Castilla*, III, Biblioteca de autores españoles, 70 (Madrid, 1953): 77–79.

24. Baer, *A History of the Jews* (n. 2), 2:395–937; Yosef H. Yerushalmi, *From Spanish Court to Italian Ghetto. Issac Cardoso: A Study in Seventeenth-Century Marranism and Jewish Apologetics* (New York: Columbia University Press, 1971), 35. On the other hand, John

Edwards in a suggestive article, "Religious Faith and Doubt in Late Medieval Spain: Soria *circa* 1450–1500," *Past & Present*, 120 (1988): 3–25, argues that anti-religious remarks were not traceable to either Judaism or Christianity, but to a religious skepticism pervading both elite and popular elements of society.

25. MacKay, "Popular Movements and Pogroms" (n. 14), 45–52; Kamen, *Inquisition and Society* (n. 15), 19, 20, 40–41; Yerushalmi (n. 23), 2, 11–14; Baer, *A History of the Jews* (n. 2), 2:272–275.

26. On the origins of the Inquisition see T.F. Ruiz, "The Holy Office in Medieval France and in Late Medieval Castile: Origins and Contrasts," 33–42 and bibliography included in notes. For the eastern kingdoms see Ricardo García Cárcel, *Orígenes de la inquisición española. El tribunal de Valencia, 1478–1530* (Barcelona: Editores Peninsula, 1976), 37–67.

27. On Alfonso de Espina see Baer, *A History of the Jews* (n. 2), 2:283–287; Kamen, *Inquisition and Society* (n. 15), 24, 29, 116. An edition of the *Fortalitium fidei contra fidei Christianae hostes* (Strassburg, c. 1471) is very much in order.

28. Hernando del Pulgar, *Crónicas de los reyes católicos*, 3:331–332: He describes events in Seville and Córdoba and gives the figures of 15,000 judaizers reconciled and 2,000 burned.

29. Henry C. Lea, *A History of the Inquisition in Spain*, 4 vols., (New York: Harper, 1906–7), 1:45; Baer, *A History of the Jews*, 2:339. For the Inquisition going into synagogues and asking rabbis to cooperate with its work: Kamen, *Inquisition and Society* (n. 15), 13, 40–41. Also Haim Beinart, "La Inquisición española y la expulsión de los judíos de Andalucía" in *Jews and Conversos. Studies in Society and the Inquisition* (Jerusalem: Magnes Press, 1981), 104–105, 121.

30. Kamen, *Inquisition and Society* (n. 15), 42.

31. Kamen, *Inquisition and Society* (n. 15), 35; Baer, *A History of the Jews* (n. 2), 2:363–364. J. Angel Sesma Muñoz, *El establecimiento de la Inquisición en Aragón (1484–1486). Documentos para su estudio* (Zaragoza: C.S.I.C., 1988) includes the relevant documentation illustrating the resistance of the city councils of Teruel and Zaragoza and the violent reprisals by the king; see also his valuable introduction, pp. 1–11. For the actions against Portuguese Jews see Stephen Haliczer, "The First Holocaust: The Inquisition and the Converted Jews of Spain and Portugal," *Inquisition and Society in Early Modern Europe*, ed. S. Haliczer (Totowa, NJ: Barnes & Noble, 1987), 11.

32. See Ruiz, "The Holy Office" (n. 26), 42–46; Martin Cohen, "Towards a New Comprehension of the Marranos," *Hispania judaica*, 1:30–32; Stephen Haliczer, "The First Holocaust" (n. 31), 7–18.

33. Bartolomé Benassar, "Patterns of the Inquisitorial Mind as the Basis for a Pedagogy of Fear," in Alcalá, ed., *The Spanish Inquisition and the Inquisitorial Mind* (n. 14), 177–184. Yet, even Benassar's forceful paradigm of fear must be qualified. As Richard Kagan has pointed out, the incompetence of the Inquisition, the corruption and venality of many of its officials and familiars often rendered the institution far less effective and terrifying than the menacing portrayal of recent historiography: Kagan "*El teatro del tribunal*: The Trial of Lucretia de León," paper given at the Annual Meeting of the Society for Spanish and Portuguese Historical Studies, April 20–23, 1989.

34. Baer, *A History of the Jews* (n. 2), 2:344–354; Kamen, *Inquisition and Society* (n. 15), 146; Yerushalmi (n. 23), 2.

35. Baer, *A History of the Jews (n. 2)*, 2:278, 424; Kamen, *Inquisition and Society* (n. 15), 27; Beinart, *Conversos on Trial (n. 14)*, 5–6. See also Yerushalmi (n. 23), 39–40.

36. Benzion Netanyahu, "The Primary Cause of the Inquisition," in Alcalá, ed., *The Spanish Inquisition and the Inquisitorial Mind* (n. 14), 26.

37. Ellis Rivkin, "How Jewish Were the New Christians?" *Hispania Judaica*, 1:114.

38. MacKay, "Popular Movements and Pogroms" (n. 14), 64; Kamen, *Inquisition and Society* (n. 15), 264.

39. Rivkin (n. 36), 111–112; Baer, *A History of the Jews* (n. 2), 2:327; Beinart, *Conversos on Trial* (n. 14), 237–299.

40. Benzion Netanyahu, *The Marranos of Spain. From the Late Fourteenth to the Early Sixteenth Century* (New York: American Academy for Jewish Research, 1966), 3; Yerushalmi (n. 23), 41; Baer, *A History of the Jews* (n. 2), 2:272.

41. Yerushalmi (n. 23), 31–32; Rivkin (n. 36), 112; on fleeing, see Henry Kamen, "The Mediterranean and the Expulsion of the Jews in 1492," *Past & Present*, 119 (1988): 30–55. Also the excellent book by Benjamin Gampel, *The Last Jews on Iberian Soil. Navarrese Jewry 1479–1498* (Berkeley: University of California Press, 1989), 120–134 which complements Kamen's findings.

42. Elliott (n. 19), 109.

43. Kamen, *Inquisition and Society* (n. 15), 14. See also Stephen H. Haliczer, "The Castilian Urban Patriciate and the Jewish Expulsion of 1480-92," *American Historical Review*, 78 (1973): 35–62; and T.F. Ruiz's comments, ibid., 1164–1165.

44. Kamen, *Inquisition and Society* (n. 15), 14–15; Baer, *A History of the Jews* (n. 2), 2:433–434; Beinart, "La Inquisición española y la expulsión de los judíos de Andalucía" (n. 28), 104, 121.

45. Crypto-Judaic practices survive to this day in rural enclaves of Spain. See José Jiménez Lozano, "The Persistence of Judaic and Islamic Cultemas in Spanish Society, or The Failure of the Inquisition," in *The Spanish Inquisition and the Inquisitorial Mind* (n. 14), 408–412.

46. Kamen, *Inquisition and Society*, 14, 43; see also his "The Mediterranean and the Expulsion of Spanish Jews in 1492" (n. 41), 30–55; Baer, *A History of the Jews* (n. 2), 2:320–322.

47. Kamen, "The Mediterranean and the Expulsion of Spanish Jews in 1492" (n. 41), 51; Kamen, *Inquisition and Society* (n. 15), 10–17, 43; Stephen Haliczer, "The Expulsion of the Jews and the Economic Development of Castile," *Hispania judaica*, 1:43, 46–47.

48. Yerushalmi (n. 23), 13–14; Kamen, *Inquisition and Society* (n. 15), 115–133.

49. Kamen, *Inquisition and Society* (n. 15), 17, 263.

Suggestions For Further Reading

Alcalá, Angel, ed. *The Spanish Inquisition and the Inquisitorial Mind.* Highland Lakes, NJ: Brooklyn College Press, 1987. This volume includes essays given at a conference on the Inquisition, held in New York in 1987. It collects the most recent research and interpretations on the origins, nature and work of the Inquisition. A large number of the articles deal with the history of *conversos.*

Baer, Yitzhak. *A History of the Jews in Christian Spain.* 2 vols. Philadelphia: Jewish Publication Society, 1961–66. This is the standard history of Jewish life in the Iberian peninsula. Although some of Baer's interpretations have been challenged in recent years, his narrative of events remains a most useful guide to the topic.

Beinart, Haim. *Conversos on Trial. The Inquisition in Ciudad Real.* Jerusalem: Magnes Press, 1981. Although a study of Jewish and *converso* life in the Castilian city of Ciudad Real and of the impact of the Inquisition on both communities, Beinart's work has opened new avenues of research. His study provides an entry into the *converso* life of an Iberian city at the end of the fifteenth century.

Gampel, Benjamin. *The Last Jews on Iberian Soil. Navarrese Jewry 1479–1498.* Berkeley: University of California Press, 1989. A sober and intelligent book, Gampel, based upon a masterful command of the archival evidence, offers a vivid portrait of Jewish life in Navarre before the expulsion. His findings corroborate those of Kamen as to the smaller number of Jews leaving the peninsula after the Expulsion.

Kamen, Henry. *Inquisition and Society in Spain in the Sixteenth and Seventeenth Centuries.* Bloomington: Indiana University Press, 1985. A revised edition of his *The Spanish Inquisition*, the book provides a thorough narrative and an insightful interpretation of the role of the Inquisition in Spanish life and of its relation to Jews and *conversos.*

____. "The Mediterranean and the Expulsion of Spanish Jews in 1492." *Past & Present*, 119 (1988): 30–55. The latest entry into the bitter controversy as to the number of Jews expelled from Spain in 1492, and as to the impact of the expulsions on Spanish society, Kamen's article drastically revises downward the estimated number of those exiled from Spain.

Lea, Henry C. *A History of the Inquisition in Spain.* 4 vols. New York: Harper, 1906–1907. Lea's work, although almost a century old, remains the most thorough treatment of the Inquisition in Spain. Moreover, the volumes include documents which illustrate the history of Jews and *conversos* in late fifteenth-century Spain.

MacKay, Angus. "Popular Movements and Pogroms in Fifteenth-Century Castile." *Past & Present*, 55 (1972): 33–67. A lively and sound narrative and interpretation of the violence against *conversos* and Jews in mid-fifteenth-century Castile.

Netanyahu, Benzion. *The Marranos of Spain from the Late Fourteenth to the Early Sixteenth Century*. New York: American Academy for Jewish Research, 1966. In this scholarly and impassionate description of the *Marranos*, Netanyahu advanced his thesis that the *conversos* were mostly Christians and not, as had been argued, crypto-Jews.

Yerushalmi, Yosef H. *From Spanish Court to Italian Ghetto. Issac Cardoso: A Study in Seventeenth-Century Marranism and Jewish Apologetics*. New York: Columbia University Press, 1971. Yerushalmi's excellent book offers a lucid discussion of Jewish and *Marrano* life as an introduction to his study of Issac Cardoso.

THE JEWS IN REFORMATION THEOLOGY

Eric W. Gritsch

What was the attitude of Reformation reformers, particularly Luther, toward the Jews? How did post-Reformation theologians respond to Luther's diatribes? What is the relationship between Luther's anti-Judaism and the racial antisemitism of the nineteenth and twentieth centuries? These questions are treated by Eric W. Gritsch.

The sixteenth-century Reformation was a movement led by Martin Luther and other reformers who appealed to Scripture as the norm of Christian faith and life. With the Reformation, therefore, came a keen interest in the Hebrew Scriptures, the Old Testament, and in Judaism. When confronting Jews, most reformers adhered to the early but enduring and decisive notion that God's Old Testament covenant with Israel had been abrogated, or superseded, by a new covenant grounded in Jesus which thus created the Christian Church, a "new Israel."

It is well known that this "theology of supersession" was intimately linked to a rampant medieval anti-Judaism propagated by official ecclesiastical policies and disseminated in a flood of pamphlets, most notably the infamous *Hammer Against the Jews* which appeared in Germany in 1513 as a companion to the popular *Hammer Against Witches* of 1487.[1]

By the eve of the Reformation, Jews had been thoroughly demonized. It was suggested that they were to be no longer tolerated as members of humankind unless they converted to Christianity. Otherwise tolerant intellectuals like Erasmus of Rotterdam sided with bishops in condemning Jews. "If hate of the Jews is the proof of genuine Christians, then we are all excellent Christians" he wrote in 1519.[2] When the bishop of Speyer ordered a complete quarantine of the Jews in that same year, the bishop justified his action by declaring that Jews were "not humans but dogs."[3] Not even the Anabaptists (the "rebaptizers" from Switzerland and elsewhere, who were being persecuted by both Protestants and Catholics) tolerated the Jews. In the words of Balthasar Hubmaier, the Anabaptist leader in Regensburg, Jews must by driven out because they are "idle, lecherous, and greedy."[4] Much more of the same tenor could be cited.

This paper sketches Reformation formulations of the theology of supersession, the avoidance of it by some reformers, and the critique of it by the heirs of Reformation theology.

Martin Luther

Reformation theologians—Luther, John Calvin, Ulrich Zwingli, and others—are, in some respects, closely linked to the Renaissance and to Humanism. The Humanists, in particular, provided these reformers with sources, such as the Greek text of the New Testament edited by Erasmus or the records announcing the dogmatic decisions of the ancient Christian councils (Nicaea in 325, Chalcedon in 451, and others), on which to base their own theology.

In the early years of the sixteenth century, Reformation theologians joined the Humanists in opposing Catholics who advocated the burning of ancient Jewish literature—a commonplace occurrence in the general climate of hostility during the Middle Ages. In the famous feud (1510–1514) between Humanists and the Dominican faculty of Cologne over the value of the Talmud, Luther and the German Humanist John Reuchlin defended the use of the Talmud in Hebrew to interpret the Bible, whereas the Dominican faculty prohibited it on the basis that Jewish sources were blasphemous. The Dominicans' argument was that Jews had killed Jesus the Messiah, and indeed God Himself, thus committing deicide. Reuchlin and other Humanists contended that scholarly dialogue with Jews, based on authentic literary sources such as the cabala, would open the way for Jews to accept Jesus as the Messiah. Although the Humanists did not exhibit the traditional hatred of the Jews, they nevertheless agreed with their Christian contemporaries that Jews must recant their own faith and convert to Christianity. According to Reuchlin, Jews know the truth about Christ, but are too perverted to see it.[5] The Humanists' argumentation did not alter the basic Christian medieval attitude toward the Jews as the people of God's wrath. The long tradition of hatred prevailed.

As a biblical theologian, Luther intensified the medieval Christian interpretation of the Old Testament: it is not only the "prefiguration" of the New Testament but also a witness to a legalistic self-righteousness that becomes more obvious at the end of days. Luther, using increasingly apocalyptic language from 1513 to the end of his life in 1546, called for the immediate conversion of all enemies of Christendom—Jews, pagans, Turks, as well as false Christians. This tone is particularly dominant in his biblical commentaries. Only when the Dominicans called his opposition of Rome a Jewish abomination and labeled him and "enemy of the cross of Christ" did Luther speak more favorably of Jews.

In 1521, he pleaded for more toleration of Jews because Jesus Himself had been born a Jew and Jews might, in time, convert. "There are future Christians among them," he said; after all, they are blood-relatives of Jesus. And he expressed the hope that Christians might still be able to work and trade with them.[6] He was also in touch with several rabbis and with Josel of Rosheim, the most famous leader of German Jews, who had good relations with the imperial court.

But when, during a visit to his home in 1526, three of these rabbis refused to apply a prophetic passage to Jesus, Luther dismissed the encounter with the comment, "They did not stick to the text but tried to escape from it." He did hope that an agreement might be reached at a later date.[7] By 1537, he was so frustrated and annoyed by his lack of success in persuading Jews to accept Christianity that he refused to support Josel of Rosheim's request for safe-conduct through Saxony, declaring that good will would only strengthen Jews in their error.

Rumors spread that Jews had begun to convert Christians. In response, Luther drew a theological conclusion from what he considered to be solid historical evidence: since Jews had for 1500 years been without a temple, without a land of their own, and had not converted to Christianity, God had deserted them—proof that Christians were indeed the "new Israel." As he put in 1538, "It is impossible that God would leave His people, if they were truly His people, without comfort and prophecy for so long."[8] Luther here linked the traditional theology of supersession (Christians have inherited the covenant) to a statement about the "hidden God," the God who is not revealed in Jesus. This statement, however, violates his own theological method, which was to make no statements about what God does when He is not revealed in Jesus. Luther was otherwise quite consistent: a student once asked "What did God do before He created the world?" and his answer was "God was making hell for those who are inquisitive."[9] In other words, Luther insisted that one cannot be speculative in one's theology; one must instead adhere only to what God has revealed in Christ. All else is metaphysical theology, which he called "theology of glory"; and which must give way to a "theology of the cross." Yet in his frustration over the unsuccessful Christian mission to the Jews, he violated the basic mandate of his own theology, namely to reflect only about the God revealed in Jesus and to avoid any speculation about the God who is hidden. Luther should have confined himself to the notion that God, in His revelation in Christ, offers the promised Messiah to all people, and not go on to conclude that those who, like the Jews, refuse to accept Jesus as the Messiah are condemned by God.

Luther vented this wrath against the Jews in his 1543 treatise entitled "On the Jews and Their Lies," in which he proposed something of a final solution for the Jews, a "sharp mercy" as he called it: synagogues and schools must be eliminated, burned if need be; Jews should be moved into communal settlements; Jewish literature should be confiscated, because it is blasphemous; Jews should not be allowed to migrate; Jewish money should be used to support converts; Jews should be allowed to do only manual labor.

Luther strongly advised the political authorities to enforce these recommendations.[10] They did not do so, perhaps because there were few Jews left in Germany by 1543. Other Reformation theologians like Philip Melanchthon and Henry Bullinger (1504–1575) criticized Luther for being too harsh, and the Zurich city council issued a declaration in 1545 chastising Luther as a crude scholar below the dignity of a swineherd.[11] None of these critics, however, went so far as to call for the toleration of Jews.

Other Voices

Reformed theologians, like Ulrich Zwingli (1484–1531) in Zurich and John Calvin (1509–1564) in Geneva, advocated the theology of supersession and urged the conversion of Jews to bring them into the new covenant. Zwinglians, Calvinists, Presbyterians, and Puritans in general read the Old Testament as the Prophecy announcing the realization of the old covenant and its laws in the person and teachings of Jesus. Zwingli accused his opposition, the Roman Catholic Church, of "judaizing ceremonies" by legalistic liturgies and papal laws, which he considered tyrannical. On the other hand, Henry Bullinger (1504–1575), Zwingli's successor in Zurich, opposed any alterations in the Hebrew text of the Bible, and also objected to Luther's violent attacks on the Jews. John Calvin, (1509–1564), the most influential reformer of the sixteenth century, maintained that the divine promise of salvation still belonged to the Jews, the "children of Abraham," but that they must convert to Christianity since only in Christ is the promise fulfilled.[12] It is the Christian claim to possess absolute truth that prevails in this view of history, perceived as a "history of salvation" which progresses from Abraham to Jesus. But unlike Luther, Calvin viewed Judaism and its holy writings, the Old Testament, as part of the history of salvation which extends beyond Holy Scripture into the church as the "new" people of God. That is why he did not advocate using violence against Jews; he did not publish tracts against them; and he favored using Jewish laws as spiritual pillars of the Genevan theocracy. Thus Calvin displayed an "incipient modernity"—a spirit of toleration that characterized later Calvinism.[13]

Some theologians, who tried on other matters to mediate between Luther and the Reformers in Switzerland, sided with Luther completely when he called for strong measures against the Jewish population remaining in Germany (Jews were not allowed to settle in Switzerland). The prominent Strasbourg theologian Martin Bucer (1491–1551), for example, demanded that Jews be confined to hard manual labor. Ambrosius Blarer (1492–1564), one of Bucer's friends and the leading reformer of Württemberg, advocated the enslavement of Jews. But Protestant princes like Philip of Hesse did not heed such advice. Most Jews had already been expelled from these territories, and those who remained were relegated to ghettos.

Other Lutheran theologians did not always follow Luther's lead. Antonius Corvinus (1510–1553), who was the bishop of Calenberg-Göttingen and an advisor to Philip of Hesse, stressed the solidarity of guilt that links Jews and

Christians: both share the sin of rebellion against God, a sin redeemed by faith in Christ. Andreas Osiander (1498–1552), the leading reformer of Nuremberg, rejected the medieval propaganda that Jews practiced ritual murder by killing babies as sacrifice. Instead, he linked the persecution of Jews to debts incurred by Christians, explaining that persecution had become a substitute for payment of debts to Jewish creditors. Like most Protestants, Osiander wanted Jews to become Christians so that the divine promise of Scripture might be fulfilled. Sebastian Münster (1489–1552), a well known Reformed theologian and scholar in Basel, became the principal advocate of conversion, and was dubbed "the father of the Protestant mission to the Jews."[14] Urbanus Rhegius (1489–1541), the Lutheran bishop of Lüneburg, tried to attract Jews to the Lutheran faith instead of persecuting them.[15]

Some non-mainline reformers, later labeled "radical" or "left wing," offered somewhat different views with regard to the Jews. Often persecuted by both Catholics and Protestants, they were concerned with the question of religious liberty. Some of these reformers envisaged an invisible, mystical community of believers in which everyone would be tolerated for moral reasons and no one would be judged on the ground of theological differences. Thomas Müntzer (1489–1525), the most radical mind of the Lutheran Reformation, held the view that spiritual and physical suffering is a sign of divine election and encompasses people from all nations, especially the Jews. Jews would join with other groups of the "elect" and constitute a suffering company—an apocalyptic spearhead, as it were, of a new world to come, in which all divisions have disappeared.[16] Mystical reformers like the German Sebastian Franck (1499–1542) rejected the externals of religion, particularly the cult and structures of authority. They contended that these externals prevent the unity of humankind.[17]

Other non-mainline reformers were less Utopian or apocalyptic in their search for unity. They thought that it was the Christian dogma of the Trinity that separated Jews from Christians, and therefore opted for a "unitarian" Christianity. The Spaniard Michael Servetus (1511–1533), the father of Protestant unitarianism, contended that the dogma of the Trinity looked blasphemous to the Jews, who viewed it as a betrayal of monotheism that led to tri-theism. He therefore denounced the Trinity as unbiblical, since it had not been taught explicitly in the New Testament but had instead been introduced later at the Council of Nicaea in 325. Servetus was condemned by Calvin and executed by the Inquisition. Yet unitarian views endured, especially in Poland under the leadership of Faustus Socini (1539–1604) who founded a unitarian group known as "Socinians."[18]

The Lithuanian unitarian reformer Jacob Palaeologus in 1572 developed a theology that called for the integration of Christians, Muslims and Jews. He contended that to be "saved," or "blessed" meant to belong to a community rooted in the Jewish one; Jews are the original people of God, although Christ is still their Messiah. Palaeologus believed that all three communions would in time be able to accept the Messiah; meanwhile, as people of God, they should tolerate each other, maintain contact with each other, and join in mutual acts of mercy. Rome hunted this former Dominican and executed him in Rome in 1585.[19] Religious liberty had to await the age of Enlightenment, more than a century later.

A Historical Trajectory

Only two editions of Luther's 1543 treatise "On the Jews and Their Lies" were published in German during his lifetime; a Latin translation was distributed in France and Italy. After Luther's death, one Lutheran Pastor, Georg Nigrinus of Giessen, published a book entitled *Enemy Jew* in 1570 in which he tried to persuade governments to banish Jews as blasphemers of Christ. Nicholas Selnecker, co-author of the 1577 *Formula of Concord* (the document that tried to resolve intra-Lutheran theological controversies), published an anthology of Luther's writings on the Jews which included Luther's "suggestions" in the 1543 treatise to segregate Jews from Christian society. Selnecker was addressing the business community, hoping that they would persuade the political authorities to banish Jews; his goal was the establishment of pure Lutheran territories cleansed of "sacramentalists, Calvinists, enthusiasts, Epicureans, and Jews." Luther's 1543 treatise was published in Dortmund in 1595, and it was reissued, along with other treatises, in Frankfurt am Main in 1613 and 1617. The Frankfurt editions may have encouraged the authorities to banish Jews from the city, since they did so at about that time, but the Dortmund publication was confiscated by the government in reaction to pressure from Jews.

The theology of supersession, though widely accepted during the Reformation, had its critics then and has been increasingly criticized since. Luther's most anti-Jewish writings embarrassed most Lutherans. Sixteenth-century Lutheran confessional documents, hymns, and devotional literature contain no polemics against Jews, only against Muslims and the pope.

In the early years of the seventeenth century, Lutheran theologians in general appealed to the younger Luther and to the tolerant attitude towards the Jews he expressed in his 1523 treatise. When the city fathers of Hamburg asked theological experts on the faculties of Jena and Frankfurt an der Oder to deliver opinions on whether or not Jewish refugees should be allowed to stay in their Lutheran City, both faculties responded affirmatively. These Lutherans theologians declared in 1611 that Jews should be granted the right to stay, albeit under the condition that they not build synagogues and could not enjoy all the rights of citizenship. They agreed with Luther "that Jews can very well be tolerated and permitted in Christian states and towns."[20] John Gerhard, the most important Lutheran theologian of the seventeenth century, did start a lively debate by demanding that Luther's advice to segregate Jews from Christians be heeded, but the compromise of limited toleration prevailed.

Eighteenth-century churchmen and theologians preferred to quote only Luther's pro-Jewish writings. This attitude is well summarized by Count Nicholas of Zinzendorf (1700–1760), famous for his "pietist" community and his hymns: "Jesus was a Jew, and for that reason one should love all Jews, as Luther writes to the Jew Josel of Rosheim."[21] Gottfried Arnold (1666–1714), the most prominent Lutheran church historian of the period, criticized Luther for having revoked his tolerant attitude towards the Jews in later years; and in 1747, John G. Walch, the editor of Luther's works, charged that Luther, in his zeal, "did not keep within fair bounds, and went too far in this matter."[22]

The age of Enlightenment only strengthened Protestant tolerance towards Jews. Sigmund J. Baumgarten (1706–1756), one of the most influential theologians at the University of Halle, set out to show that Protestant toleration of the Jews was not confined to the "philosemites," an elitist group of intellectuals. He attested to a deep Christian conviction that Jews had a right to their own public worship. In his opinion about Jews in 1745, he wrote that Protestants should be able to understand this, since they too had been persecuted and deprived of that right.[23] Baumgarten's disciple and colleague, John S. Semler (1725–1791), regretted Christian antisemitism openly. "The Jews were much better off under the Romans, Greeks and Muslims," he declared, "than was usually the case under the Christians."[24]

Thus Luther's anti-Judaism received little, if any, hearing until the late nineteenth century when antisemitism was propagated by racists and German nationalist, undergirded by Arthur de Gobineau's "Aryan-Semite" dichotomy of the 1850s.[25] Luther's influence was limited to Germany, mainly because there were no substantial Jewish communities in Scandinavia, France and England. Moreover, Western European attitudes were shaped by Calvin rather than Luther.

Although polemics against Jews did prevail in some quarters, the radical views of the old Luther were not shared by Lutheran theologians who succeeded him; they either criticized or ignored him.[26] Typical is the Lutheran theologian Frederick Lezius, who taught at Königsberg and summarized the reception of Luther's anti-Jewish polemics in 1892: Luther's "suggestions" to the princes were "scandalous measures, clearly contrary to the spirit of the Gospel...the errors of an aging reformer...not binding on the church."[27] Lutherans generally accepted the interpretation of the Jewish scholar Reinhold Lewin who viewed Luther in 1911 as the father neither of Lutheran nor of German antisemitism, maintaining that Luther's early attitude of friendliness towards Jews—expressed in the 1523 treatise "That Jesus Christ Was Born a Jew"—had been the accepted one, rather than his later violent polemics against them.[28] This interpretation is also accepted by other contemporary Jewish historians.[29]

It was the German nationalist ideologues who revived the anti-Jewish Luther, although antisemitism had been kept alive by a few Protestant pastors and theologians who had continued the tradition of crude polemics based on the works of sixteenth-century Jewish converts. Antonius Margeritha was a favorite source. He wrote *The Whole Jewish Faith (Der ganze jüdische Glaube)* which repeated the medieval slander against Jews. In 1700, the German Calvinist theologian, Andreas Eisenmenger, had summarized the traditional Christian polemics with the publication of a 2000 page work, *Judaism Unmasked (Entdecktes Judentum)*, a truly monomaniacal effort.

Theodor Fritsch, the founder of "practical antisemitism," reissued Luther's 1543 advice to the princes in 1931, as part of a catechism of antisemitism. Some of his cohorts complained that it had taken several centuries to revive the antisemitic Luther. As Alfred Falb, a prominent nationalist agitator, put it in 1921: "What have they [Protestant theologians] made of our German prophet! They have suppressed his assessment of the dangers of Judaism and withheld it from the German people."[30] Falb seemed aware of the fact that theologians showed little, if any, interest in lifting up Luther as an antisemitic "German Prophet," as did ideologists in Hitler's camp. Thus Nazi propaganda tried to exploit Luther's views on the Jews, and many German Lutherans fell prey to this propaganda. The rest is the history of terror launched against Jews during the reign of Adolf Hitler which resulted in the holocaust.

During the Nazi period, most Protestant theologians in Germany remained silent about Judaism. Some, like Dietrich Bonhoeffer (1906–1945), opposed the Nazi government's "Aryan clause" which abrogated all civil rights for Jews in 1933 and practically enslaved them.[31] Those Protestants who did support Hitler, "German Christians," declared in their 1932 "platform" that they opposed racially mixed marriages and any mission to the Jews.[32] The Lutheran bishop of Thuringia, Martin Sasse, used Luther's hatred of the Jews to support the Nazi program of November 9, 1938, known as "Crystal Night" (*Kristallnacht*).[33] In the "Barmen Declaration" of 1934, those who opposed Hitler, the "Confessing Christians," refused to cooperate with the new regime but did not mention the Jews.[34] Only in Scandinavia, and particularly in Norway, did Protestant church leaders and theologians with great unanimity oppose Nazism; they saved the majority of their Jewish citizens from the holocaust.[35]

Critical Considerations

There is a difference between the sixteenth-century anti-Jewish theology of supersession and the antisemitic racism of the late nineteenth and twentieth centuries. The theology of supersession called for the conversion of the Jews and, in the face of Jewish resistance to conversion, for their banishment. Racist antisemitism classified Jews as sub-human and therefore subject to annihilation.

In 1962, in his book on the Christian roots of antisemitism entitled *The Teaching of Contempt*, the French Jewish scholar Jules Isaac listed three main themes in the teaching of contempt for Jews: 1) the view that the dispersion of the Jews is a provisional punishment for crucifying Jesus; 2) the notion that because of the degenerate state of Judaism at the time of Jesus, Christianity inherited the divine promise originally given to the Jews to be the people of God; 3) the crime of deicide.[36]

Although some heirs of the Reformation have clung to the theology of supersession, various Christian groups and churches, both Catholic and Protestant, have begun to refute these "teachings of contempt." The German churches of Reformation, in particular, have tried to overcome Christian antisemitism in their ranks by undertaking solid historical studies and theological reflection. These attempts need to be viewed in the light of the abysmal record of German Protestants with regard to the antisemitic program of Hitler's "Third Reich."[37]

The Critical considerations in Christian-Jewish relations need to lead to a refutation of what Jules Isaac called "the teaching of contempt": the theme of dispersion, the crime of deicide, and the theology of supersession.

1. Concerning the theme of dispersion, it must be noted that the dispersions of the Jews predated the Christian era, beginning with the successive destruction of the Jewish kingdoms—Israel by the Assyrians in 722 B.C., and Judah by the Babylonians in 586 B.C. In the face of such historical data, the notion of a divine punishment by dispersion because of Jesus' crucifixion is at best theological speculation. Moreover, the destruction of the temple by the Romans in 70 A.D. does not warrant the conjecture that Jews were dispersed among the nations of the world at that time. Sixty years later, in the 130s A.D., the second Judean war took place under the emperor Hadrian, and it was just as bloody as the first one of 70 A.D. At the time of the first crusade in 1099, crusaders reported they had trapped Jews in the synagogue of Jerusalem after setting fire to it.[38] In the face of such data, "it is not history that must come to terms with theology; on the contrary, it is theology that must come to terms with history."[39]

In addition to such historical evidence on Jewish dispersion, it must be noted that the early Christian tradition, as well as Christian theology in general, has always affirmed the world-wide dispersion of Christians. Unlike the Jews, they are not intended to have a land; instead, they are to wait as dispersed pilgrims among all nations for the "promised land" at the end of time. The true differences between Christians and Jews is the experience of *Christian*, not Jewish dispersion, and Zionist insistence on a Jewish state in Israel. Thus the notion of dispersion identifies Christians better than Jews.

2. Concerning the connection between dispersions and the crime of deicide, it must be noted that the very idea of deicide is unintelligible to both Christians and Jews who respect history and common sense. The conditions for such a charge simply did not exist. Jesus was only known to a minority of Jews; thus the charge can be made only against such a minority, provided that they knew that Jesus was God. The apostles themselves accused the Jews of having killed Jesus "in ignorance" (Peter in Acts 3:17—"You acted in ignorance as did also your rulers"). It was homicide through ignorance, rather than premeditated deicide. The charge of deicide did not become a popular notion until well into

the second century, and was based on a theological concept projected back in history through uncritical, indeed polemical, hindsight. Finally, even speculative Christian theology must admit that deicide, like the betrayal of Jesus, was a necessary condition for salvation, if salvation exists through the "death of God" in Jesus. The church of the third century was highly critical of such syllogistic speculations and insisted that God's incarnation in Christ is a doxological rather than logical matter, that is, God is to be praised rather than explained. One can only conclude that, on the basis of historical evidence and normative ecumenical Christian tradition, the crime of deicide and its link to the dispersion of the Jews makes no sense at all. Such assertions are the product of a hermeneutics of suspicion that ignores historical reality and violates common sense.

3. Concerning the theology of supersession or replacement, it must be noted that the New Testament portrays Jesus as the fulfiller of Jewish law (Mt 5:17—"Think not that I have come to abolish the law and the prophets...but to fulfill them"). Paul interpreted such sayings of Jesus as evidence of an opposition between Jewish law and salvation in Christ. Paul and the early church believed that as a way of salvation the law was surpassed by the atoning death of Christ. Otherwise, Christ would have died to no purpose (Gal 2:21—"For if righteousness were through the law, then Christ died to no purpose"). Jesus was "put to death for our trespasses and raised for our justification" (Rom 4:25). To Paul, therefore, it was Abraham who was the model of "father" of faith rather than the exemplary "Torah Jew" (Rom 4; Gal 3). Since Israel rejected Jesus as the Messiah, Paul contended, "their minds were hardened" and their view of the Old Testament was veiled (1 Cor 3:14—"For to this day, when they read the old covenant, that same veil [that Moses put over his face when faced with divine splendor] remains unlifted because only through Christ is it taken away").

Yet Paul never stated any reasons *why* God did harden their hearts; he only spoke of God's unsearchable and inscrutable ways (Rom 11:33) through which the Gentiles are led to salvation. To be sure, Paul denied the salvific character of Jewish law after the Christ event (one is "justified" before God by faith rather than by "the works of the law"—Rom.3:28). But he also continued to hold that the law is "holy, just and good" (Rom 7:12); that the law is not just for the Jews but also for the Gentiles who have it written in their hearts (Rom 2:15). Accordingly, both Jews and Gentiles live in sin when they violate the law, and "*all* fall short of the glory of God" (Rom 3:23). When he attacked Jewish legalism, he did so on the basis of his experience with Jewish Christians. But he was certainly no antisemite.

Paul, therefore, cannot be used to support a theology of supersession or replacement. He viewed the relationship between the church and Israel in an eschatological context. God, according to Paul, "hardened the hearts" of the Jews toward the Christian gospel to make them a negative witness, as it were, to God's unsearchable ways that will be revealed at the end of time. Just as God once hardened the heart of Pharaoh, who refused to let God's people go (Ex

9:16), so God hardened Israel to reveal His power in the world. This is God's "eschatological reservation": He reserves His final judgement regarding the relationship between Jews and Christians. Both church and synagogue are called to tell the world that God—not anyone else—will finish the work of salvation. That is why Christians cannot claim to be the "new Israel" in the sense of having received all the blessings of the "old Israel." The Jews are and remain the people of God, even though they do not accept Jesus Christ as their messiah. Why this is so only God knows.

Rosemary Ruether and Franklin H. Littell have spearheaded the work of Christian reparation in the United States.[40] They enlisted Christian theologians and produced "A Statement to our Fellow Christians" with the assistance of the Commission on Faith and Order of the National Council of Churches in collaboration with the Secretariat for Catholic-Jewish Relations of the National Conference of Bishops. The Group recommended fourteen propositions for study and discussion in Christian communities: 1. The church is rooted in the life of the people of Israel. 2. Christians and Jews depend on each other for mutual enrichment in the light of a far-reaching value crisis in the Western world. 3. Faith in Christ does not abrogate the covenant relationship of God with Israel. 4. The quest for Christian unity and the tragic reality of the Holocaust, together with the conflict in the Middle East, make urgent a reconsideration of the relationship between Christians and Jews. 5. The rampant antisemitism of the past must be faced with penance in the present. 6. Christian churches must confront the problems associated with the state of Israel, the question of Palestinians, and the problem of Arabs, especially the problem of refugees in the Middle East, both Jewish and Arab. 7–9. Christians must support the state of Israel as a nation that has a moral and legal right to exist as an alternative to dispersion. 10–14. The lessons of history must be used for a ministry of reconciliation and a guard against the infectious virus of antisemitism.[41]

It is better for Christians to concentrate on those who are not yet a part of the people of God, if any mission is to be undertaken at all, than to try to convert Jews who are already among the people of God. Moreover, the long history of Christian antisemitism requires a Christian witness guided by penance rather than by triumphalist claims of spiritual superiority. Neither a special mission to the Jews, nor a theology of supersession have a place in Christian tradition. What is called for is an honest dialogue between Christians and Jews.[42]

Dialogue is always burdened by the differences existing within each religious community, ranging from divergences on the authority of the Bible to ways in which the community interprets its tradition. Nevertheless, in the light of the Holocaust, there is a common task that might unite Christians and Jews: sharing the watch against evil.

The Hebrew Scriptures define evil as idolatry, that is, as the most serious violation of the First Commandment of the Decalogue ("I am the Lord your God.... You shall have no other gods besides me"). This definition appears in the account of the Fall (Gn 3) when the serpent tempts Eve to "be like God" (Gn 3:5) Although Christians and Jews may disagree radically on what their faiths affirm, they can unite on what constitutes evil according to the biblical story of the Fall—the desire to be like God. Christians and Jews who share a faith in the one God, the Lord of history, could find convergence in the common task of standing guard against the evil of idolatry—be it in the realm of politics, of morals, or even of religion. Hitler was not the first and not the last to view himself as a god who could challenge the Judeo-Christian Lord of history. Hitler and his followers created the Holocaust, which has become part of a common history. That is why Christians and Jews must now, more than ever before, share sentry duty against evil even though they remain divided in their religious affirmations.

Endnotes

1. *Malleus maleficarum* appeared in 29 editions between 1487 and 1669. The *Hammer Against the Jews* (literally "quiver of arrows of the Catholic faith—*pharetra catholice fidei—Köcher wider die Juden*") appeared in Nuremberg in an edition by Hans Folz. See Heiko A. Oberman, *The Roots of Anti-Semitism in the Age of Renaissance and Reformation*, trans. James I. Porter (Philadelphia: Fortress, 1984), 84.

2. Quoted in Oberman (n. 1), 40. Letter to Hochstraten, 11 August 1519, *Opus Epistolarum Des. Erasmi Roterodami*, ed. P.S. Allen et al., 12 vols., (New York: Oxford University Press, 1906–1947), 4:46, 142–143.

3. Quoted in Oberman (n. 1), 96. *Mandat gegen die Juden*, Hagenau, 4 April 1519, University Library, Tübingen.

4. Quoted in Oberman (n. 1), 77. *De Ratisbona metropoli boiorariae et subita ibidem iudaeorum proscriptione* (Regensburg, 1519), fol. CIIV.

5. Reuchlin's position is well summarized by Oberman (n. 1), 24–31. The anti-Jewish views of John Pfefferkorn, a converted Jew, were more popular; he proposed the burning of the Talmud in his 1507 book *Mirror of the Jews (Judenspiegel)*; for a summary of his activities, see Oberman, 32–37.

6. "That Jesus Christ was Born a Jew," 1523. *Luther's Works*, American Edition, ed. Jaroslav Pelikan and Helmut T. Lehmann, 55 vols., (Philadelphia: Fortress; St. Louis: Concordia, 1955–1986), 45:210, 229. Hereafter cited as *LW*.

7. The passage was Jeremiah 23:6 ("This is the name by which he will be called: 'The Lord is our righteousness'"). See sermon of 25 November 1526, *Luthers Werke. Kritische Gesamtausgabe* (Weimar: Böhlau, 1833–), 20:569.36–37. Hereafter cited as *WA*. Table Talk, 21 May–11 June 1540, no. 5026, *WA, Tischreden* (Weimar: Böhlaus Nachfolger, 1912–1921), 4:620.5–8. Hereafter cited as *WA.TR*.

8. "Against the Sabbatarians," 1538. *LW*, 47:96.

9. *Table Talk*, 1540, no. 5010, *LW*, 54:377.

10. *LW*, 47:268–272.

11. Quoted in *WA* 53:574. The massive literature focusing on Luther's 1543 polemical tracts against the Jews deals with the development and historical context of Luther's polemics. See especially Reinhold Lewin, *Luthers Stellung zu den Juden* (Berlin: Trowitsch & Son, 1911); and Salo W. Baron, *A Social and Religious History of the Jews*, vol. 13, *Inquisition, Renaissance, and Reformation*, 2nd. ed., rev., (New York and London: Columbia University Press, 1969), 216–229. Critical summaries of the literature, as well as differing views on historical context and theology, are offered in Mark U. Edwards, Jr., *Luther's Last Battles. Politics and Polemics, 1531–1546* (Ithaca and London: Cornell University Press, 1983), 115–142; and Eric W. Gritsch, *Martin—God's Court Jester. Luther in Retrospect* (Philadelphia: Fortress, 1983), 130–145. But Luther research has not sufficiently highlighted the theological error in Luther's own thought. See Eric W. Gritsch, "Luther and Israel: Trial and Error" in Walter Homolka

and Otto Ziegelmeier, eds., *Von Wittenberg nach Memphis. Festschrift für Reinhard Schwarz* (Göttingen: Vandenhöck & Ruprecht, 1989), 38–46.

12. *Institutes of the Christian Religion*, IV, 16:14, trans. Henry Beveridge, 2 vols., (London: Clark, 1957), 2:538.

13. Persuasively argued by Baron (n. 11), 291–296.

14. See Gerhard Müller, "Antisemitismus VI" in *Theologische Realenzyklopädie*, ed. Gerhard Krause and Gerhard Müller (Berlin and New York: De Gruyter, 1976–), 3:149. Hereafter cited as *TRE*.

15. *TRE* 3:148–149.

16. For a summary of Müntzer's life and work, see Eric W. Gritsch, *Thomas Müntzer—A Tragedy of Errors* (Minneapolis: Fortress, 1989).

17. See "The Lonely Individualist: Sebastian Franck" in Hans J. Hillerbrand, *A Fellowship of Discontent* (New York, Evanston, London: Harper & Row, 1967), 31–64.

18. Socinians flourished in Poland. See George H. Williams, *The Radical Reformation* (Philadelphia: Westminster, 1962), 749–763.

19. Williams (n. 18), 741–743.

20. Quoted in Johannes Wallmann, "The Reception of Luther's Writings on the Jews from the Reformation to the End of the 19th Century," *Lutheran Quarterly* 1 (1987): 82.

21. Quoted in Wallmann (n. 20), 83.

22. See Johann G. Walch, ed., *D. Martin Luther sämtliche Schriften*, 23 vols. in 25 (1747; reprint, St. Louis: J.J. Gebauer, 1880–1910), 20:91.

23. Wallmann (n. 20), 84.

24. Quoted in Wallmann (n. 20), 85.

25. This is the matrix of modern racism. See Arthur de Gobineau, *Essai sur l'inégalité des races humaines*, 1853–1855. Although he was not an antisemite and placed Jews among the white races, Gobineau gave wide currency to the term "Aryan," to designate people representing a superior Nordic race over against the inferior "Semites." German racists quickly identified "Aryan" with "German," thus establishing the ideological foundation for their antisemitism. Wilhelm Marr (1818–1904) was the first organizer, and in 1878 founded the League of Antisemites (*Antisemitenliga*). See Léon Poliakov, *The Aryan Myth: A History of Racist and National Ideas in Europe*, trans. Edmund Howard (New York: Basic Books, 1971).

26. This is the well documented and widely accepted conclusion of Johannes Wallmann (n. 20). Much of this section of the paper is based on his work.

27. Quoted in Wallmann (n.20), 88.

28. Reinhold Lewin, *Luther Stellung zu den Juden: Ein Beitrag zur Geschichte der Juden während des Reformationszeitalters* (Berlin: Trowitsch & Son, 1911), 97ff. The work was published by the Protestant editors of "Neue Studien zur Geschichte der Theologie und der Kirche" as no. 10 in the series, and received the annual prize in 1911 from the Protestant Faculty at the University of Breslau.

29. See, e.g. Haim Hillel Ben-Sasson and J. Ettinger, eds., *Jewish Society Through the Ages* (New York: Schocken Books, 1972).

30. Quoted in Wallmann (n. 20), 97; on Fritsch, ibid., 89.

31. See Eberhard Bethge, *Dietrich Bonhoeffer, Man of Vision, Man of Courage*, trans. from the German edition of 1967 by Eric Mosbacher et al., ed. Edwin Robertson (New York, San Francisco, London: Harper & Row, 1977), 235, 241. Bonhoeffer made the public announcement that the exclusion of Jews from German citizenship, as the "Aryan clause" required, must be opposed in the same manner as the separation of Christians from the church of Christ. He was eventually martyred as a participant in the assassination plot against Hitler.

32. See the English text of the platform of the "German Christians" (*Deutsche Christen*) in Franklin H. Littell, *The German Phoenix, Men and Movements in the Church in Germany* (Garden City, NY: Doubleday, 1960), 182.

33. He entitled it "Away With Them!" (*Weg mit ihnen!*). See Wallmann (n. 20), 96, n. 93.

34. English text of the Barman Declaration of the "Confessing Church" (*Bekennende Kirche*), in Littell (n. 32), 184–188.

35. See, for example, Bjarne Hoye and Trygve M. Ager, *The Fight of the Norwegian Church Against Nazism* (New York: Macmillan, 1943), esp. 146–148. Bishops, clergy, theologians and lawyers banded together to create an effective resistance movement.

36. Jules Isaac, *The Teaching of Contempt. Christian Roots of Anti-Semitism*, trans. Helen Weaver (New York, Chicago, San Francisco: Holt, Rinehart & Winston, 1964), 39, 74, 109.

37. Pertinent documents are printed in Helga Croner, *Stepping Stones to Further Jewish-Christian Relations: An Unabridged Collection of Christian Documents* (London and New York: Stimulus Books, 1977). On the attitude of German Protestants in the "Third Reich," see Kurt Meier, *Kirche und Judentum. Die Haltung der evangelischen Kirche zur Judenpolitik des dritten Reiches* (Göttingen: Vandenhöck & Ruprecht, 1968), esp. 46. Particularly helpful is the revisionist history of the relationship between church and synagogue by Wilhelm Maurer, *Kirche und Synagoge. Motive und Formen der Auseinandersetzung der Kirche mit dem Judentum im Laufe der Geschichte*, Franz Delitzsch-Vorlesungen 1951 (Stuttgart: Kohlhammer, 1953), esp. chs. 3–4 on the Reformation and subsequent periods.

38. Isaac (n. 36), 70

39. Isaac (n. 36), 71.

40. Rosemary R. Ruether, *Faith and Fratricide, The Theological Roots of Antisemitism* (New York: Seabury, 1974); Franklin H. Littell, *The Crucifixion of the Jews* (New York: Harper & Row, 1975).

41. Littell (n. 40), Appendix A, pp. 134–138.

42. There are some good primers for such a dialogue. See, for example, Lily Edelman, *Face to Face*, Jewish Heritage Book Series (New York: Anti-Defamation League of B'nai B'rith, 1967). On the dialogue between Lutherans and Jews, see *Christian Witness and the Jewish People*, A Report of the Consultation Held Under the Auspices of the Lutheran World Federation, Department of Studies, Oslo, August, 1975, ed. Arne Sovik (Geneva: LWF, 1976).

Suggestions For Further Reading*

Baron, Salo W. *A Social and Religious History of the Jews*. Vol. 13, *Inquisition, Renaissance, and Reformation*. 2nd ed., rev. New York and London: Columbia University Press, 1969). Chapter 58 is a comprehensive survey of the reformers' attitude to the Jews, with special attention to John Calvin.

Edwards, Mark U., Jr. *Luther's Last Battles. Politics and Polemics, 1531-1546.* Ithaca and London: Cornell University Press, 1983. Chapter 6 is a detailed analysis of Luther's final tracts against the Jews, and a critical interpretation of Luther research on this topic.

Gritsch, Eric W. "The Gospel and Israel." In *Martin—God's Court Jester. Luther in Retrospect*, 130–145. Philadelphia: Fortress, 1983. A summary of Luther's attitude to the Jews, labeled a "neuralgic heritage" of Luther.

Littell, Franklin H. *The Crucifixion of the Jews*. New York: Harper & Row, 1975. A persua sive attempt by a Protestant theologian to overcome antisemitism.

Luther, Martin. *That Jesus Christ was Born a Jew. Luther's Works*, 45:197–229. American Edition. Ed. Jaroslav Pelikan and Helmut T. Lehmann. 55 vols. Philadelphia: Fortress; St. Louis: Concordia, 1962. Luther's early (1523) and quite tolerant view that shaped later Reformation theology.

____. *On the Jews and Their Lies. Luther's Works*, 47:123–306. American Edition. Ed. Jaroslav Pelikan and Helmut T. Lehmann. 55 vols. Philadelphia: Fortress; St. Louis: Concordia, 1962. Luther's vitriolic outburst, written in his last years (1543), that repeated and surpassed medieval anti-Jewish slander.

Matheson, Peter C. "Luther and Hitler: A Controversy Reviewed." *Journal of Ecumenical Studies* 17 (1980): 445-453. A good summary of evidence to refute the claim that Luther was the spiritual father of Hitler's antisemitism.

Oberman, Heiko, A. *The Roots of Anti-Semitism in the Age of Renaissance and Reformation.* Trans. James I. Porter. Philadelphia: Fortress, 1984. The best book on the topic, with a critical assessment of Reformation theology as a source of modern antisemitism.

Wallmann, Johannes. "The Reception of Luther's Writings on the Jews From the Reformation to the End of the 19th Century." *Lutheran Quarterly* 1 (1987): 72-97. A convincing demonstration that Luther's anti-Jewish writings were not well received by his Protestant heirs.

* This subject is not well covered by English-language writings.

THE IMAGE OF JUDAISM IN NINETEENTH-CENTURY CHRISTIAN NEW TESTAMENT SCHOLARSHIP IN GERMANY

Susannah Heschel

The historical study of Jesus and his times is one of the most persistent intellectual pursuits of the modern age. It is handicapped by the lack of contemporary evidence and eye-witness accounts. The principal sources, the gospels, date from a generation and longer after Jesus' lifetime, from c.65 to c.120 C.E. or later. This has meant—and continues to mean—that even the most objective scholar tends to be governed more by his/her controlling assumptions and biases than would be the case in other fields; or, as an aphorism sardonically expressed it: the Higher Criticism turned out to be the Higher Antisemitism. Susannah Heschel examines one of the most influential traditions of New Testament history, scholarship, and interpretation; it profoundly vitiated Christian-Jewish understanding, and continues to hamper Jewish-Christian dialogue.

During the long history of Christian writings concerning Judaism, some friendly, some nasty, the continued existence of Judaism after the advent of Christianity has been a chronic theological headache. Within the modern period that headache grew sharper with the emergence of a liberal Protestant theology based not on the Christ of dogma, but on the Jesus of history. With the emphasis on the historical Jesus, the historical reality of Jesus' Jewish context was brought to the fore. The interaction between Jesus and the Judaism of his day led to a new dimension in Christian consideration of Judaism. No longer was Judaism the rejected religion against which Christianity polemicized; the core of Christianity—the religious teachings of Jesus—now had to be viewed within the context of his own religion, Judaism.

Liberal Protestants, seeking the faith *of* Jesus, rather than the faith *about* Jesus, brought Judaism into the center of Christianity; the faith of Jesus *was*

Judaism. Judaism and Christianity could no longer be conceived as independent antagonists but as standing in a relationship whose configuration became crucial to the definition of Christianity's origins and telos. The historical study of Christian origins, a field of scholarship undertaken by both Jews and Christians, led inevitably to questions concerning Jewish influence on early Christianity, the Jewishness of Jesus, and the reasons for the split between believers in Jesus and those who followed more traditional and conventional Jewish teachings.

Liberal Protestants began their study of the historical Jesus in the late eighteenth century with Gotthold Lessing's publication between 1774 and 1778 of the seven anonymous *Fragments*, written by Hermann Samuel Reimarus (1694–1768).[1] The *Fragments* provoked a storm of controversy, costing Lessing his freedom from official censorship as the ducal librarian at Wolfenbüttel. It is the final, seventh *Fragment*, entitled, "On the Intention of Jesus and His Apostles," which became the most significant, raising many of the issues central to New Testament scholarship throughout the nineteenth century. What has not been remarked upon by scholars is that the *Fragments* also formulate the problem of Judaism as it subsequently took shape in modern New Testament studies.

According to Reimarus, Christianity is the formulation of the apostles, not of Jesus. He argues that it was not Jesus' intention to establish a new religion. The argument rests upon two assertions: that Jesus himself proposed no new mysteries or articles of faith; and that Jesus had no intention of abrogating the Levitical ceremonial law. Rather, the teachings which characterize Christianity were introduced, Reimarus argues, by Paul and the apostles in a deliberate and duplicitous distortion of Jesus' message.[2]

In order to prove his argument, Reimarus claimed that not only Jesus' teachings, but more importantly his actions, fell within the normative framework of the Judaism of his day. At this point, an accurate depiction of first-century Judaism becomes the key factor to the success of Reimarus' argument. All of Jesus' actions and teachings, Reimarus argues, were in accord with Jewish practice; his goal was simply to strengthen the religiosity of the Jewish community and to reawaken the Jews to the eschatological promise of a worldly redeemer.

Jesus' intentions were deliberately distorted by his apostles after his death, Reimarus claims. The apostles devised the doctrines which came to constitute classical normative Christianity in order to attain greater personal power for themselves at a time when Jesus' followers, disillusioned by his death, would have otherwise disbanded. Christianity's break with Judaism came not with Jesus, but with the apostles, and did not constitute a divinely ordained mission, but a striving for personal political gain. Reimarus writes,

> ...the apostles taught and acted exactly the reverse of what their master had intended, taught, and commanded, since they released not only the heathen from this law but also those who had converted from Judaism—released them from a burden such as neither they nor

> their fathers had been able to bear.... Soon, therefore, circumcision, sacrifice, purification, Sabbath, the new moon, feast days, and the like were abolished completely and Judaism was laid in its grave. This cannot possibly agree with Jesus' intention and design.[3]

The *Fragments* unleashed a host of theological controversies. The most important of the attacks on Reimarus' position came from Johann Salomo Semler (1725–91), a prominent liberal theologian of the period who made significant contributions to early New Testament studies.[4] Semler's objective was to refute the conclusions of the *Fragments*, and Judaism retained a central position in his argument. Whereas Reimarus had argued that Jesus' messianism must have been worldly, because that was the Jewish understanding of messianism in his day, Semler claimed that Jesus' messianism was spiritual, because Jewish messianism was spiritual. In contrast to Reimarus, however, Semler distinguished between the message of Jesus and that of Judaism, developing a new hermeneutic that was adopted by subsequent generations of New Testament scholars.

Following the work of Reimarus and Semler, New Testament studies during the first half of the nineteenth century took several different courses. On the popular level, a genre of "lives of Jesus" emerged, in which fictionalized accounts of gospel events were presented with great elaboration and no effort at historical verification. On the scholarly level, the important Tübingen School of research emerged which investigated developments in the post-apostolic period, leading up to the establishment of the church at the end of the second century. Finally, the tedious scholarly work of determining the dating and ordering of the gospels and Pauline corpus began. Defining the nature of early Judaism was a central issue in the publications of both popular and scholarly literature on the New Testament.

Jesus as an Essene

The literature of the popular "lives of Jesus" of the late eighteenth and early nineteenth centuries betrays a general uniformity; indeed, Albert Schweitzer suggests, tongue in cheek, that Karl Heinrich Venturini's multi-volume version was simply reprinted annually under different authors' names.[5] Whatever the impact of a particular life of Jesus, an overview of the corpus reveals a nearly identical plot. Jesus is presented as a member of the order of the Essenes, which is, in turn, depicted as a secretive, mysterious sect with both political ambitions and the secret knowledge of magical, medicinal healing techniques. Rather than dying on the cross, Jesus was rescued and lived on in the Essene community. The genre combines two central motifs: an overall story of mystery and intrigue, together with a naturalist explanation of the miracle accounts of the gospels.

Franz Volkmar Reinhard depicts Jesus as a great man of history, a powerful teacher who stressed a self-evident morality, in his *Attempt at the Plan which the Founder of Christianity Outlined for the Betterment of Humanity*, published in 1781.[6] Jesus' teachings appealed to the enlightened moral sensibilities of his listeners. By contrast, Karl Friedrich Bahrdt, in his eleven-volume *Exposition of the Plan and Goals of Jesus: Letters to a Truth-Seeking Reader* (1784–92), presents Jesus as emerging from an Essene community which had a plot to transform Jewish society.[7] The Essenes maintained a secret organization run by Nicodemas and Joseph of Arimathea, with the object of diverting the Jews from a hopeless political revolt to a more peaceful transformation through a messianic figure. Jesus grew up among them, was instructed in medicinal secrets, indoctrinated against temple worship, and finally forced by them to declare himself the messiah. The crucifixion is faked, according to this account, and rather than dying on the cross, Jesus is rescued, only to reappear among his followers (and later Paul) in order to convince them that he had risen from the dead. His teachings were actually communications to the initiated about the secret organization, although some were also for public consumption. Together with the emphasis on the mysterious, Bahrdt gives a rationalist explanation for the miracles—secret stores of bread, for instance, fed the five thousand.

The idea of a secret, powerful organization of Essenes continued in Venturini's *Natural History of the Great Prophet of Nazareth* (4 volumes, 1800–1802, totalling 2700 pages), which is similar to Bahrdt's account on many points.[8] Venturini continued the rationalist explanation of the miracles, along with the idea of an Essene plot for control of Israel. While the crucifixion actually did take place in this account, Jesus was nonetheless rescued by Joseph of Arimathea, according to Venturini, and subsequently revived.

August Friedrich Gfrörer, himself a student of Jewish literature, wrote a two-volume *Critical History of Christian Origins* (1835–38), which traces the rise of Jewish theology, culminating with Philo whose "Therapeutae," he alleges, were identical with the Essenes.[9] The second volume traces the life of Jesus, whom Gfrörer portrays as a spiritual messiah influenced by Philonic ideas. Like the others, Gfrörer writes that Jesus was resuscitated after a faked crucifixion. Rescued by the Essenes, Jesus essentially began Christianity within their framework. Yet Gfrörer's conclusions are particularly significant because of the weight of research behind them. Gfrörer inaugurated the modern period in Christian studies in Judaism through his publication of *Philo and Alexandrian Theosophy, or, On the Influence of the Jewish-Egyptian School on the Teachings of the New Testament* (2 volumes, published in 1831); and *The Century of Salvation* (2 volumes, published in 1838).[10] Gfrörer's argument is that Christianity was decisively influenced by the Judaism that flourished in Alexandria, which entered Palestine through the Essenes and other sects. He distinguishes between the Judaisms of the two sites, but ultimately makes Alexandria the origin of the more important Jewish ideas and movements. Gfrörer's work is especially significant because he attempts to distinguish among different strains within Judaism, particularly in relation to messianic ideas, rather than present a single, monolithic tradition. His presentation of Jewish thought draws extensively on the collections of rabbinic, midrashic, and kabbalistic texts prepared by earlier Christian scholars, from Raymund Martini (thirteenth century) onward, as well as on his own readings of Talmudic texts, and he cites the new critical work of Leopold Zunz. The underlying thrust of his work, however, is of primary significance: that early Christianity must be understood through knowledge of the history of the contemporaneous Judaism. George Foot Moore offers the following evaluation of Gfrörer's work: "It was the first time that the attempt had been made to portray Judaism as it was, from its own literature, without apologetic, polemic, or dogmatic prepossessions or intentions.... this fact alone is enough to make the work memorable."[11]

However memorable an achievement his work appears from hindsight, Gfrörer's contemporaries seem not to have been particularly impressed. His work is cited infrequently, whether by Jews or Christians, and his impact cannot be compared to later Christian historians of Judaism, such as Emil Schürer. Although the study of rabbinic Judaism came to be accepted in the late nineteenth century as necessary to an understanding of the New Testament, it was not due to Gfrörer's efforts.

Finally, Friedrich Wilhelm Ghillany introduces a new element into his version: gnosticism. His three large volumes of *Theological Letters to the Educated of the German Nation* (1863) and his *Judgment of Pagan and Jewish Writers of the First Four Christian Centuries Concerning Jesus* (1864) were published under the pseudonym Richard von der Alm.[12] He argues that early Christian belief was a compound of Judaism, Mithraism, and oriental religions generally, and he defines Christianity as a form of gnosticism. Jesus himself grew out of the Essene order and held himself to be the messiah. His own ideas, however, all have their source in contemporary Judaism.

The shadowy, mysterious quality of a secret society—the Essenes—which nonetheless was able to produce a figure of truth and leadership—Jesus—who would overcome the political oppression of the villain—the Romans—presents a picture typical of the two-sided nature of the German Enlightenment as described by Karl Barth. As Barth pointed out, the Enlightenment is not only to be characterized by rationalism, but also by "a peculiar and widespread and various knowledge and pursuit of the mysterious."[13] Similarly, in the lives of Jesus, Jesus appears, on the one hand, as the model of rationalism and morality, while on the other hand, the entire story is filled throughout with mysterious, secret societies, shadowy figures, and intrigues. The scenario is repeated in different contexts—for example, Mozart's *Magic Flute*—and is clearly not without political implications. The most striking parallel to the depiction of the Essenes in the lives of Jesus is the order of Freemasons, founded in 1717. Dedicated to Deism, the Freemasons nonetheless required an initiation ceremony as if it were a mystery religion, and, indeed, claimed its rituals were derived from the ceremonies of the First Temple in Jerusalem. While the connection between the secret order of Freemasons and the Jews was not made explicit until the mid-nineteenth century, the rapidity with which the association developed might suggest an earlier association in the popular imagination. By the end of the century, the association of Jews with Freemasons in a sinister plot came to play an important role in the Dreyfus Affair, as well as in the *Protocols of the Elders of Zion*, as Jacob Katz and others have demonstrated.[14]

The function of a Christian life of Jesus which emphasizes his involvement in a secret society preserves sensibilities central to the Enlightenment. On the one hand, the story seems to "explain" rationally the miracles without denying their reality by attributing the miracles to secret knowledge Jesus acquired from the Essenes. On the other hand, the secretive Essene society preserves the sense of religious mystery in the face of the threat to faith posed by rationalism. The metaphysical figure of Christ was thereby contained within the historical figure of Jesus.

Judaism as a Negative Criterion

During the decades of the first half of the nineteenth century, several more "biographies" of Jesus were published, similar to the model established by Venturini. The distinguished New Testament professor H.E.G. Paulus lent new dignity to the genre in his study, *The Life of Jesus as the Foundation for a Pure History of Christian Origins*, a work which is taken by both Schweitzer and Colin Brown to initiate a new era in the genre,[15] but which in fact continues the basic lines of argument already established in the earlier, popular lives of Jesus. Paulus' work is significant, however, since he was the first prominent professor of theology to publish a life of Jesus. Paulus accepted the gospel reports concerning the miracles performed by Jesus, but he developed explanations for each of them based on rational principles and the natural sciences, although for him God remained the ultimate cause of all phenomena. In claiming to follow historical method, Paulus used historical explanation as a form of theological rationalism. Like the Enlightenment writers, Paulus "explained" Jesus' healing "miracles" as secret medicinal cures learned from the Essenes. Historical explanation was thus a form of rationalizing miracles through Jesus' alleged association with other historical groups.

Regardless of his claims to rationalism, the major criterion in Paulus' work for evaluating what is to be rejected within the gospel accounts is represented by what Paulus termed "the Jewish popular mind." According to Paulus, the earliest gospel can be recognized by its affinity to Judaism, represented, in his opinion, by the Gospel of Matthew. Later gospels may contain some Jewish influence, but that influence is modified by other factors. Paulus thus made Judaism a central criterion for dating and evaluating New Testament texts: the more Judaism, the earlier the text; the less Judaism, the more advanced the Christianity. Jesus and his followers may have emerged from Judaism, but they devoted themselves to its repudiation. It might be noted that Paulus was active in the contemporary discussions in Germany concerning Jewish emancipation and that he wrote several antisemitic tracts in opposition to the emancipation of the Jews in Europe.[16]

From the 1830s to the 1860s the dominant voice in Christian New Testament studies was that of the Tübingen School, founded by Ferdinand Christian Baur (1792–1860). Baur reshaped both the methods and topics of New Testament scholars and his School served as a rallying-point for those rejecting conservative Protestantism as well as the radicalism of David Friedrich Strauss and the other left-wing Hegelians. Horton Harris notes "...the Tübingen School became the focal point of all avant-garde Biblical investigations. It initiated and established the historical-critical investigations of the Bible, which made it possible for others to branch out on their own lines of thought and pursue the more specialized aspects of Biblical research."[17]

The significance of the Tübingen School lies in Baur's three methodological innovations. First was his assertion of the independence of the historical study of Christianity from theological considerations. Second, Baur and his followers evaluated texts as expressing a *tendenz*, a political and religious undercurrent which must be brought to light in order to assess the period and setting in which the text was developed. Third, the School asserted that conflicts between Jewish Christians and gentile Christians dominated the post-apostolic period until the formation of the church in about 200 C.E., and that New Testament texts have to be dated and evaluated in light of those conflicts.

It is the third point which is the best-known aspect of the Tübingen School and which is most relevant to the question of Judaism's image in the historiography of the School. The idea that conflict between Jewish and Pauline Christianity dominated early Christianity was not original to Baur but had already been suggested by Semler. Semler suggested two types of early Christianity, a law-obedient, particularistic Jewish-Christian community led by Peter and a law-free, universalistic gentile Christian community led by Paul. Prior to Baur, however, biblical scholars had seen the disputes between the two groups as marginal events within early Christianity.[18] For Baur, however, these disputes were central to the shaping of Christianity during the first two centuries. Baur led a revisionist interpretation of 2 Corinthians, arguing that the text represented the climax of disputes concerning the law between Paul and his Jewish-Christian opponents. That dispute, Baur argued, was not marginal to the development of the post-apostolic period, but was, in fact, its central concern.[19] Only with the establishment of the church at the end of the second century, Baur argued, was the conflict resolved with the dominance of the gentile Christians.

Baur was the first historian to see Jewish Christianity as a key to understanding developments in the post-apostolic period, and his interpretation of the nature of Jewish Christianity, as well as of its role in the formation of later Catholic Christianity, reveals the image of Judaism he promoted. For Baur, Jewish Christianity represented the conservative, aristocratic tendencies among early Christians, while gentile Christianity represented the democratic, reformist influence. Ultimately, it was gentile Christianity which triumphed and shaped the later course of Christianity. Jewish Christianity was an outgrowth of Judaism, and Judaism, for Baur, stood as the opposite pole of gentile Christianity, whose major spokesperson was the apostle Paul.

Baur's understanding of Jewish Christianity and of early Judaism was drawn entirely from his study of Christian and Pauline documents. That the Jewish Christians remained strong during both the apostolic and post-apostolic periods was claimed by Baur on two grounds. First, he used the reports of the Church Fathers, particularly Eusebius, Epiphanius and Irenaeus, who mention a variety of Jewish-Christian sects and claim that Jewish Christians continued to flourish as late as the end of the second century. Second, Baur based his studies on polemics he claimed to identify within those writings that he considers authentically Pauline. The second point, however, tends to be a circular argument. Baur identified a text as Pauline if it polemicized against Jewish Christianity, but his evidence for the existence of the Pauline polemic is based on the text. After describing what he considered to be the characteristics of Jewish and Pauline Christianity, Baur classified the gospels and other New Testament texts by reference to their expression of one or the other side of the polemic.

Pauline Christianity, which ultimately triumphed and emerged as normative Catholic Christianity, had to struggle, according to Baur's schema, against a Jewish Christianity mired in the religious tenets characteristic of Judaism. At the same time that Baur presented a clear break between Pauline and Jewish Christianity, he emphasized the similarities between Christianity and Judaism. Christianity grew out of Judaism, developed within Jewish soil, and wants nothing more than to be a spiritualized Judaism. The difference between Judaism and Christianity lies in the fact that the Old Testament concept of God is stamped with nationalism and particularism, factors from which the concept of God had to be liberated in order to become universal and absolute.

The problem of demonstrating Jewish influence in shaping later Christianity, and describing the Jewish context out of which Christianity developed is that it raises the challenge of originality. If Christianity is nothing more than a refinement of Judaism, a universalization of Jewish concepts, its claim to religious truth is called into question. Baur resolved the problem by locating the originality of Christianity in the Beatitudes of the Sermon on the Mount and asserted that Jesus' teaching is a qualitative revision of Mosaic law because it stresses the inwardness of the law. Baur writes,

> ...in insisting that the absolute moral value of a person depends simply and solely on his disposition, Christianity was essentially

> original. In this way the affirmative relation which Jesus assumed towards the law involves in itself the opposite relation of antithesis to the law.[20]

Jesus remained affirmative not only toward the Old Testament, but even toward the Pharisees themselves, whom he recognized as legitimate successors of Moses, although he declared their requirements to be heavy and intolerable burdens.

Christianity really emerged, in Baur's view, with the resurrection of Jesus, which, regardless of whether it actually occurred, functioned as a solid fact in the faith of the disciples and provided the basis for the further historical development of Christianity. And yet that faith remained sufficiently malleable that it could support both sides of the argument regarding the continuing significance of Jewish law. That argument was the central issue at stake, according to Baur, in the controversies between Paul and the apostles. In the writings of the Tübingen School no further development within Judaism is recognized; Judaism is described in terms of the Old Testament, apocryphal writings, and Jewish Christianity (as described by the Church Fathers). The evaluation of Judaism within early Christianity, however, remained problematic. Indeed, the influence of Jewish Christianity became a theological Trojan horse for the Tübingen School. On the one hand, Western Christianity is said to have overcome Judaism and its Jewish Christian ideas in the Catholic Church; on the other hand, writing from a Lutheran perspective, it is in the interests of Baur, Albrecht Schwegler, and the other adherents of the School, to see continuing influences of Judaism and Jewish Christianity within Catholicism, which were later eliminated in the Protestant Reformation. In any case, the degree of Jewish-Christian influence within Catholicism must be kept in check; while Baur, Schwegler, and even Albrecht Ritschl (whose work, although bringing an end to the Tübingen School, nonetheless shares many of its assumptions) each demonstrate differing definitions of the nature of that Jewish influence, they agree that it had to be subordinated to gentile Christianity by the Catholic Church, just as they agree that the Catholic Church should be subordinated to Lutheran Protestantism. The problem is that if Catholic Christianity is said to be permeated by Jewish Christianity, whereas the Lutheran Reformation represents the triumph of gentile Christianity, the early church is, implicitly, a failure in its goal of overcoming Judaism.

The writings of Baur and the other members of the Tübingen School remained controversial among nineteenth-century New Testament historians, and the School itself began to disintegrate by the end of the 1850s, even prior to Baur's death.[21] Still, the impact of the School on the field of early Christianity was of crucial importance, in terms of methodology, the agenda of research issues, and the relationship it envisioned between Christianity and Judaism.

Throughout the course of the nineteenth century, and well into the twentieth century, the impact of Judaism on the origins of Christianity came to be of increasing importance to scholars. At stake was not only defining the relationship between Jewish and Pauline Christianity, but clarifying the extent to which Christianity itself could be considered original. While Baur simply distinguished between a particularistic Judaism and a universalistic Christianity, stressing in other respects the similarities between the two religions, later scholars saw the problem in more complex terms. For Baur,

> Judaism and Christianity stand in a narrow and unmediated relationship. Christianity itself wants to be only a spiritualized Judaism, and goes back with the deepest roots of its origins in the ground of the Old Testament religion. The specific characteristic of Judaism is its pure monotheistic God idea which was, since the oldest time, the essential foundation of the Old Testament religion. In its God consciousness Christianity knows itself to be above all united with Judaism; the God of the Old Testament is also the God of the New Testament, and all that the Old Testament teaches about the essential distinction of God from the world, the absolute sublimity [*Erhabenheit*] and holiness of his essence, is also an essential part of Christian teaching. But the Old Testament concept of God has, on the other side, also such a genuinely nationalist imprint that the whole stands in its particularism in the most distinct opposition to Christianity.[22]

Rabbinic Literature in New Testament Studies

Equating Judaism in a generalized way with the Old Testament was characteristic of much Christian writing during the first half of the nineteenth century, while two new arguments were introduced during the second half of the century.[23] According to the first, a sharp distinction should be drawn between biblical religion of the period prior to the Babylonian exile (586 B.C.E.) and after the exile. According to the second argument, rabbinic literature not only taught a desiccated religion but also defamation of Christianity. The work of the Old Testament scholar, Wilhelm de Wette (1780–1849), has been credited with inaugurating the first argument in his *Biblical Dogmatics*, published in 1813. De Wette claimed that post-exilic Israelite religion deteriorated into a dry legalism which led into rabbinic Judaism, whereas pre-exilic religion, particularly as represented by the classical prophets, formed the background for Christianity.[24] His argument gained strength later in the nineteenth century, particularly in the writings of Julius Wellhausen (1844–1918), as well as in the theological arguments of liberal Protestants who saw Jesus as renewing the religious message of the eighth-century B.C.E. classical prophets.[25]

Rabbinic literature became a point of political controversy in Germany during the 1830s, in the debates of both liberals and conservatives concerning emancipation of the Jews. Rabbinic texts were cited by both sides of the political spectrum as demonstrating the alleged intolerance of Judaism vis-a-vis other religions, or the alleged immorality and nationalistic particularism of Judaism. While conservatives promoted missions to the Jews, viewing conversion to Christianity as the price for emancipation, liberals demanded radical reform of Judaism, emphasizing, in particular, Jewish renunciation of the Talmud. The debate continued throughout the century, gaining strength during the years before and after German unification in 1871. Conservatives sought to maintain special privileges for the church in the modern German state, while liberals were unable to concede that Judaism was not an inferior religion, theologically, to Christianity.

Both during the pre-1848 period and during the later decades of the century, a central issue for Christian opposition to Jewish emancipation concerned the attitudes of Judaism toward Christianity, often based on the notorious *Judaism Revealed* (1700), by the Heidelberg Orientalist Johann Andreas Eisenmenger.[26] Eisenmenger's book, a polemic against Judaism and the Talmud, was not particularly popular during the eighteenth century, but was revived in the early nineteenth century to support arguments that Jews view Christianity as a form of idolatry and defame Jesus. Eisenmenger was cited during the first decades of the nineteenth century to support claims that the degenerate moral character of the Jews did not permit their emancipation.[27] The only solution, if Jews were to be emancipated, was their renunciation of the Talmud.

Given the highly negative view of rabbinic Judaism promoted in political as well as theological writings of the early nineteenth century, the historical question of parallels between the New Testament and the Talmud took on political overtones. The Talmud had become a bone of contention in the debate over emancipation, but it also became a problem for Reform Jews seeking modification of Jewish religious observance. Jewish calls for reform of Judaism and modification of the Talmud's religious laws had to be combined with efforts to defend the Talmud against Christian charges of its degenerate nature. Thus, even as Jewish reformers called for curtailing Jewish law, *halakhah*, to make Judaism conform to modern values and life-styles, they defended the *halakhah's* religious and moral integrity.

Meeting that conflict, between a progressive reform of Judaism and a defense of rabbinic Judaism's moral integrity and theological significance for Western civilization, was addressed with surprising success by Abraham Geiger (1810–74), one of the most distinguished Jewish theologians of nineteenth-century Germany. Geiger, a leader within the Reform movement, developed an original argument about the origins of Christianity within the context of Judaism that shaped the subsequent course of Jewish understandings of Christian origins, as well as Christian understandings of rabbinic Judaism. With Geiger's publications a turning-point can be identified within the history of Jewish and Christian scholarship on Jesus and early Christianity.

By the mid-nineteenth century Geiger had established himself as a major leader of the left-of-center position within the Reform movement in German

Judaism. His controversial appointment as rabbi in Breslau in the late 1830s, his revised editions of prayer books, and his numerous publications had brought him fame within the Jewish community. Geiger's doctorate had been awarded on the basis of a prize essay on Islam, published in 1833,[28] which was favorably reviewed by prominent German and French Islamicists, but his major work of scholarship, the *Original Text and Translations of the Bible in their Connection to the Inner Development of Judaism*, was not published until 1857.[29] The *Urschrift* is not only Geiger's best-known book; it is the single book by a Jewish author which attracted the greatest amount of attention in the Christian scholarly world in Europe during the nineteenth century. The *Urschrift* examines the variations in ancient translations of the Bible (Hebrew, Greek, and Aramaic versions) and argues that the emendations they contain represent evidence for political and theological disputes among the various parties of Jewish life during the Second Temple and Mishnaic periods (c. 565 B.C.E.–c. 220 C.E.). Geiger's aim was to reconstruct the diversity within Palestinian Jewish life and demonstrate the usefulness of rabbinic literature for historical reconstructions of early Judaism and, by extension, of early Christianity. While the *Urschrift* directly addresses issues of Christian origins only occasionally, its implications for the study of early Christianity abound, and were made explicit by Geiger in a subsequent article, "Sadduzäer und Pharisäer," published in 1863.[30] Those implications reached an even broader audience in Geiger's popularized Jewish history, *Das Judentum und Seine Geschichte*, published in 1864, which devotes a disproportionate amount of attention to the figures of Jesus and Paul and to the rise of Christianity.[31]

The most important challenges to New Testament studies of Geiger's work stem from his original arguments regarding the nature of Pharisaism and Sadduceeism. Throughout the centuries, Christian commentaries on the New Testament had viewed the Sadducees, like the Karaites, the medieval Jewish opponents to Talmudic authority, favorably, as the party within Judaism which tried to keep biblical religion "pure," that is, free from rabbinic influence. At the same time, Christian commentators traditionally presented the Pharisees in a negative light, as the party of dry legalism. In contrast, Geiger presented the Sadducees as the ruling party of the Second Temple period, representing the interests of the influential priestly class and aristocracy. Rather than being innovators in opposition to a stodgy Pharisaic party, the Sadducees were conservative and exclusive, seeking to preserve, rigidly and obstinately, the traditional norms, and, in fact, were, according to Geiger, the defenders of what he calls the old priestly *halakhah*. During the second-century B.C.E. revolt of the Maccabees against the Syrians, however, a new class emerged among the Jews. This new middle class had not been involved in the Maccabees' wars, but now laid claim to their own sphere of influence. Out of this middle class, according to Geiger, emerged the Pharisees.

Geiger attempted to transform the Pharisees from being viewed as the party of tradition, conservatism, and status quo into the party of transformation, reform, and forward-looking movement. The Pharisees, in Geiger's depiction, were arguing for the individualization of religion, its democratization which requires freeing it from priestly—Sadducean—control. What Geiger accomplished was to invert the categories attributed by Baur to Jewish and Pauline Christianity. For Geiger, it is the Sadducees who are the conservative, materialistic, aristocratic party, like Baur's Jewish Christians, while the Pharisees are described by Geiger along the lines of Baur's gentile Christians, namely, as egalitarian, progressive, and democratic. While Baur leaves the figure of Jesus largely undefined relative to the Judaism of his day, focusing instead on the post-apostolic period, Geiger identifies Jesus as a Pharisee. He suggests a clear break between the Pharisaic teachings of Jesus and the Sadducean-like qualities of post-apostolic Christianity, an argument he develops more clearly in his later writings. Since Jesus was himself a Pharisee, Geiger explains that the Jews attracted to the early Jesus movement must have been former Sadducees, distraught after the destruction of the Second Temple. Indeed, Geiger claims to find Sadducean influences in early Christian writings, such as the Epistle to the Hebrews, in the priestly motifs used to depict Jesus.[32]

Jesus, however, was a Pharisee who taught in the traditions of other Pharisees of his day, such as Hillel. In Geiger's *Lectures on Judaism and Its History*, published in 1864, he writes: "Jesus was a Jew, a Pharisaic Jew with Galilean coloring, a man who joined in the hopes of his time and who believed that those hopes were fulfilled in him. He did not utter a new thought, nor did he break down the barriers of [Jewish] nationality.... He did not abolish any part of Judaism; he was a Pharisee who walked in the way of Hillel."[33] But despite the comparison, Geiger subtly indicates Jesus' inferiority to Hillel on two counts: first, he argues that Jesus actually represented a stricter position than Hillel, an early first-century C.E. rabbi, in regard to Jewish law; second, he asserts, with a final punch, that although Jesus' historicity remains problematic, "Hillel was a fully historical man."

While Geiger's discussion of the Sadducees met with widespread acceptance by Christian scholars, his radically new depiction of the Pharisees and his description of Jesus as a Pharisee evoked controversy and condemnation. Christian responses to Geiger's work came swiftly. First, during the 1860s there was a new rise in the publication of lives of Jesus by liberal theologians, including Theodor Keim, Adolf Hausrath, Karl von Hase, Daniel Schenkel, and, of course, Ernest Renan, all of whom cite Geiger extensively. Second, the 1870s saw the rise of historical surveys of the Jewish background to early Christianity by Christian scholars, including Julius Wellhausen, Emil Schürer, and, a little later, Wilhelm Bousset. Geiger's work is credited with having inaugurated the historical study of the Pharisees, Sadducees, Samaritans (a sect in northern Israel with its own version of the Pentateuch), Karaites, and, to a large degree, the general history of Judaism during the Second Temple and rabbinic periods (fourth century B.C.E. to second century C.E.).[34]

Christian Responses to Geiger

Although Geiger's work is cited in nearly all of these studies, his conclusions regarding the progressive nature of Pharisaism and the relationship between Judaism and early Christianity were not accepted. Instead, two trends can be identified in the responses to Geiger. Within the lives of Jesus literature of the 1860s, Geiger's work is used not to reinterpret Jesus, Paul and early Christianity, but to lend a veneer of historical respectability to traditional arguments. For example, the historical background of first-century Judaism was used to explain aspects of the gospels which appeared in conflict with reason; the miracles, for instance, were attributed to medical secrets Jesus learned from the Essenes. In another approach, Hausrath and Schenkel distinguished between Jesus' alleged inner life and his outward behavior.[35] In this way, they argued that although Jesus' messianic position appeared outwardly to be an adaptation from contemporary Judaism, messianism was, in fact, part of his inner consciousness and constituted the starting point, and not the result, of his ministry. If Jesus' messianism was in accord with the Judaism of his day, Hausrath argued, that was no more than accidental, since his messianic awareness was something inborn, not learned. The historical descriptions of first-century Judaism, then, could be used either as tools for rationalizing the apparent miracles, or could be made irrelevant by positing a distinction between Jesus' outer and inner messages. Thus, Geiger's descriptions of the Jewish background to early Christianity could be acknowledged in these lives of Jesus without in any way affecting the traditional presentation of the New Testament. Geiger's work was appropriated in this context in a manner similar to Paulus' use of the Essenes as the source of Jesus' medicinal healings: historical evidence functioned as a veneer to protect, rather than challenge, the integrity of the theological message of the gospels.

The harshest criticism of the *Urschrift* came in a small book by Wellhausen, *The Pharisees and the Sadducees*, published in 1874 and based on a series of lectures Wellhausen delivered in 1871 in the theology faculty of Göttingen with the purpose of refuting the claims in Geiger's *Urschrift*.[36] The book opens with the assertion, "Jesus was certainly no Pharisee," and continues that "the Pharisees are the Jews in superlative, the true Israel." While Wellhausen supports many of Geiger's analyses of the Mishnah, the earliest section of the Talmud (completed about 250 C.E.), in regard to the Pharisees, Wellhausen makes himself clear: the Pharisees are characterized by their "religious materialism.... the Pharisees killed nature through the commandments. 613 written commandments and 1000 other laws and they leave no room for conscience. One forgot God and the way to him in the Torah."[37]

While Wellhausen's influence came primarily in the field of Hebrew Bible, his *History of Israel*, published in 1878,[38] and subsequent studies on the Hexateuch, the first six books of the Hebrew Bible, were followed by publications on the gospels and Acts of the Apostles in the early 1900s, and his conclusions affected scholars both in the fields of Hebrew Bible and Christian origins. Wellhausen was heir to de Wette. De Wette had claimed that during the Babylonian exile the Hebraism of biblical religion was transformed into a new religion, Judaism, whose main characteristic was devotion to the letter of the law and an estrangement from the religious spirit promoted by Moses. Jesus, according to de Wette, had come to give a spiritual rebirth to prophetic religion and stood in total opposition to Pharisaism. Judaism after the Babylonian exile, for de Wette, becomes the dark background against which the light of Jesus and the New Testament might shine. Wellhausen continued de Wette's schema, arguing like him that it is law which dominated post-exilic Judaism: "Religious worship was a natural thing in Hebrew antiquity.... The law...severed this connection."[39] For Wellhausen, Jesus' original contribution was his restoration of prophetic teachings which had been lost to the sterile, legalistic Judaism of his day.

Following Wellhausen, the two most influential studies of Second Temple Judaism were those of Emil Schürer and Wilhelm Bousset. Schürer's work, *Textbook of New Testament History* was first published in 1874,[40] then revised ten years later under the title, *History of the Jewish People in the Time of Jesus Christ*.[41] This multi-volume work came to be the authoritative source for the history of Judaism in the field of New Testament. It is striking that in his discussion of the historiography concerning the Pharisees and Sadducees Schürer acknowledges Geiger as having originated the field, and that he accepts many of Geiger's conclusions, particularly concerning the Sadducees. Yet Schürer remained unwilling to consider Geiger's positive evaluation of Pharisaic and rabbinic Judaism, presenting instead a highly negative overall characterization of the Pharisees and rabbinic Judaism. Apparently, Geiger's scholarship was acceptable only if it did not contravene the conventional sharp contrast between Judaism and Christianity.

A prime example of that contrast is found in Schürer's chapter, "Life Under the Law," which depicts first-century Jewish life as obsessed with legalism and external behavior. He writes, for example, "All free moral action was now completely crushed under the burden of numberless separate statutory requirements."[42] In concluding the chapter, Schürer cites, with approval, two gospel passages critical of the Pharisees, Matthew 23 and Luke 11, and adds, "Life was a continual torment to the earnest man, who felt at every moment that he was in danger of transgressing the law.... On the other hand, pride and conceit were almost inevitable for one who had attained to mastership in the knowledge and treatment of the law."[43]

Schürer's purpose is transparent: he paints a highly negative picture of first-century Judaism, in order to contrast it with a positive picture of early Christianity. Equally troubling is Schürer's judgment concerning sources for first-century Jewish history. While Schürer argues that rabbinic literature is too unreliable and too late to be used for reconstructing political developments within Second Temple Judaism, he nonetheless uses rabbinic texts for his reconstruction of the alleged legalism and religious sterility of first-century Jewish life.

As in the case of other Protestant scholars in Germany, Schürer's depiction of Judaism carries the overtones of contemporary political debates. For example, Schürer emphasizes that the Pharisees, the rabbis, and all Jews in Palestine became apolitical and isolated themselves from Hellenistic (Greek) culture, with the implication that religious Jews in nineteenth-century Germany would be similarly unable to assimilate into contemporary culture.[44]

Similar arguments are found in Bousset's study, *The Religion of Judaism at the Time of the New Testament*, first published in 1903, which also drew heavily on Geiger's work, particularly in characterizing the relationship between the Sadducees and Pharisees.[45] The struggle between the two groups, he writes, was between the old aristocracy (Sadducees) and a new leading class arising out of the populace (Pharisees). But Bousset breaks with Geiger in asserting that, although the Pharisees were originally the representatives of progress in Judaism, "piety in their hands soon became stiff and lifeless," and the Pharisees, once they attained power, "very quickly developed into the conservatives, the representatives of a hard and rigid piety, a new aristocracy which forcibly displaced the old."[46] Ultimately, he concludes, Judaism is a religion of external observance lacking sincerity. On the question of reliable sources for reconstructing the history of Judaism during this period, Bousset argues that Josephus, the first-century Jewish historian, and the New Testament are reliable, while the Mishnah is not. And while Bousset acknowledges that the presentation of Pharisaism in the gospels is intended to be polemical, he nonetheless claims that the gospels give the best illustration of the character of the Pharisees and Sadducees, a contradiction pointed out by Ismar Elbogen.[47] Bousset's work came under sharp critique by contemporary Jewish scholars, provoking further restatements of the positive religious nature of Pharisaic Judaism by German-Jewish theologians such as Leo Baeck.[48]

In evaluating the negative presentations of Judaism in the writings of Wellhausen, Schürer, and Bousset, it should be made clear that their significance lies not so much in the originality of their arguments, but in the widespread credence they imparted, as historians, to traditional Christian theological anti-Jewish motifs. Indeed, it was because such arguments appeared in an historiographical framework that they derived an objective, scholarly overtone, and their polemical quality could be denied. The historiography received an additional dimension of theological influence through the writings of leading German liberal Protestants at the turn of the century, such as Wilhelm Herrmann and, particularly, Adolf von Harnack, in his landmark statement of *Kulturprotestantismus*, *Das Wesen des Christentums*.[49]

The historical setting of the New Testament within the context of first-century Judaism, and, particularly, the comparison of Jesus with the Pharisees, raised a new challenge for liberal Protestants of the originality of Christianity. If the words and teachings of Jesus and the apostles could be shown to be not original, but taken over from Judaism, then Christianity appears to be in some way subservient to Judaism. Harnack made the dilemma clear in his effort to claim a distinction for Jesus. He wrote, in *The Essence of Christianity*, published in 1900:

> It is quite true that what Jesus proclaimed...was also to be found in the prophets, and even in the Jewish tradition.... The Pharisees themselves were in possession of it; but unfortunately they were in possession of much else besides. With them it was weighted, darkened, distorted, rendered ineffective and deprived of its force, by a thousand things which they also held to be religious and every whit as important as mercy and judgment. They reduced everything to one dead level, wove everything into one fabric.... As regards purity, the spring of holiness had, indeed, long been opened; but it was choked with sand and dirt, and its water was polluted.[50]

In this passage, which aroused great furor among Harnack's Jewish theological contemporaries, Geiger's arguments regarding the essential equation of Jesus with the teachings of the Pharisees are accepted. Jesus, Harnack acknowledges, taught nothing new. But that leads to the new theological problem of the originality—or lack thereof—of the Christian message. What was new in the teachings of Jesus? Harnack was unable either to deny or to refute Geiger's historical arguments, but had to accept their essential validity. There was nothing new or original in the gospels, he conceded. Harnack's recourse was to claim the purity of Jesus' teachings in contrast to the Pharisees:

> Now however [with Jesus] the spring broke through afresh, broke a new path through the dirt and rubble, through that dirt that priests and theologians had piled up, in order to choke the earnestness of religion.[51]

Harnack acknowledged that Jesus taught nothing new, but argued nonetheless that he taught in a new way. Whereas Judaism had smothered its religious teachings, Jesus broke through the rubbish of Pharisaism to present Christian teachings in a pristine form. Once again, the historical method showing the influence of Pharisaic Judaism on Jesus can be side-stepped by intensifying the anti-Pharisaic portrayal and maintaining the *difference* of Jesus. With Harnack that difference extends to the scriptures themselves; in his famous study of the second-century Christian heretic, Marcion, Harnack concluded that Marcion had been correct: the wrathful God of the Old Testament was not the same as the loving God of the New Testament. Harnack urged the church to eliminate the Old Testament from the Christian canon as a "heroic action demanded of Protestantism today."[52]

Harnack's *Wesen des Christentums* won an enormous readership; by 1927 it had been through fourteen printings and translated into as many languages. It also provoked a loud and angry response within the Jewish community. While Harnack's arguments were not new, nor particularly sophisticated, his prestige as an historian gave his essentially a-historical polemical writing added weight. In addition, the nature of his argument, which both conceded the correctness of Geiger's claim and yet attempted to undermine it, was an additional frustration for Jewish scholars.

Conclusion

A review of the role of Judaism in nineteenth-century German historiography concerning Christian origins makes clear several points. First, the increasing attention paid to first-century Judaism by Christian historians and theologians during the course of the nineteenth century must be evaluated according to the relationship which they define between Judaism and early Christianity. Simply examining first-century Jewish history did not necessarily alter either the understanding of the origins of Christianity, nor the anti-Judaism of the historian. Second, setting Jesus within the context of the Judaism of his day seems to have become increasingly perilous for historians and theologians following Geiger's inauguration of the field of Second Temple Jewish history and his positive presentation of the Pharisees. The strategies of Christian historians for avoiding the comparison of Jesus with the Pharisees indicate to us the extent to which Geiger's claims were in fact taken seriously and perceived as threatening. Jesus' originality and uniqueness, after all, are theological, not historical categories. Third, what is troubling about the depiction of Judaism in the writings of Wellhausen, Schürer, and Bousset is not so much *what* they say, since their anti--Judaism is not new but repeats older motifs. Instead, what is troubling is first, the credence they lent as supposedly objective historians to Christian theological prejudices and, second, their insistence on such prejudices even after Geiger had introduced a new agenda and new interpretations. As historians today analyzing developments in the nineteenth century, we have to realize that by the 1860s Christians were no longer writing in a closed environment, but in an intellectual atmosphere to which Jewish historians were articulating their own perspectives.

Yosef Yerushalmi contends in his book, *Zakhor*, that with the rise of historicism in the nineteenth century, historical writing and the historical memory of the religious community took two different courses.[53] Christian theologians have been similarly concerned that investigating the events of Christian origins from an historical perspective would clash with the non-temporal claims of Christian religious faith. In the particular dimension under investigation in this paper, however, such fears appear to be unfounded. History and historical memory appear to have persisted along the same course when it came to nineteenth-century Christian treatments of Judaism. One wonders how much difference there really was between the attitudes toward Judaism of a village pastor in nineteenth-century Germany and those of Schürer or Harnack, other than the idiom in which they are expressed. To what degree does historical criticism aid the historian in becoming free from bias? In this case, at least, not enough. These historians apparently did not try to free themselves from traditional Christian biases toward Judaism, even when alternative historical models and interpretive modes had been developed by Jewish historians such as Geiger.

The persistence of discussions by both Christian and Jewish historians of the Jewish background to the origins of Christianity is in itself a matter which deserves interpretation. One way to conceptualize the situation is by viewing nineteenth-century Judaism and Christianity as locked into an "anxiety of influence," to use a term from Harold Bloom.[54] Nineteenth-century Christianity can be understood as harboring the fear that it is not its own creator, but that Judaism and its Old Testament have a historical and moral claim to theological superiority by virtue of having been developed first. If Christian teachings, particularly the words and actions of Jesus himself, can be shown to be not original, but taken over from Judaism, as Jewish historians such as Geiger asserted, Christianity can be shown as in some way subordinate to Judaism. The anxiety of not being original, but rather secondary and derivative, is part of the motivating power behind Christian denial of Judaism's religious legitimacy, as in Wellhausen's depiction of post-exilic Judaism. On the Jewish side, telling the story of Christian origins as a movement within Jewish history makes the claim that Judaism was the original religion precisely at a time when the Jews were reforming their liturgy, synagogue architecture, and religious observances along the lines of Protestantism—hence, claiming Jesus for Judaism is, similarly, an expression of a Jewish anxiety of influence.

More recent trends in the scholarship on Christian origins should be investigated to demonstrate the extent to which continuities and discontinuities with the nineteenth century persist. The theologians involved in the notorious pro-Nazi "German Christian" movement rejected the Old Testament and called for the excision of all Jewish references within the New Testament and hymnal, on the grounds that Jesus came not to fulfill Judaism, but to destroy it.[55] Basing themselves on the historical-critical method of liberal Protestant New Testament scholarship, these German Christian theologians, such as Walter Grundmann and Emmanuel Hirsch, carried the arguments of Wellhausen, Schürer, Bousset, and Harnack to an extreme conclusion.

Less extreme is the persistent undercurrent of anti-Judaism which simply sets Jesus' teachings in opposition to a Pharisaic Judaism depicted in negative terms. However much Jesus might have been influenced by Jewish religious currents of his day, he is depicted as engaged in polemics against those currents. Such "mild" forms of anti-Judaism consist of a presentation of Pharisaic and rabbinic Judaism as legalistic, alienated from God, and particularistic, in contrast to the religion formulated by Jesus. That Jesus himself taught the Judaism of his day is subordinated to the argument that he polemicized against at least the leading forms of Judaism.

While the influence of Baur, Wellhausen, Schürer and others seems to remain strong in much of contemporary German scholarship, counter-trends have also emerged, in the work of, among others, Dieter Georgi and Peter von der Oster-Sacken. In their writings, as in the work of many American scholars, the teachings of Jesus are presented as one of the many voices within the Judaism of his day. By contrast, the so-called New Quest for the historical Jesus, which emerged in the decades following World War II, frequently reproduces anti-Jewish stereotypes. Those stereotypes result both from the strong influence on the New Quest of Rudolf Bultmann, whose depictions of Judaism's legalism are highly negative, and from the effort to support the claim of Jesus' uniqueness and, hence, contrast to Judaism.[56]

In contrast to Germany, twentieth-century American New Testament scholarship was influenced by the picture of the Pharisees found initially in the writings of Kaufmann Kohler, George Foot Moore, Jacob Lauterbach, Louis Finkelstein, among others, and that is essentially the portrait originally drawn by Geiger. Geiger's optimistic claim that rabbinic literature is crucial to a proper understanding of Christian origins has spawned an enormous literature of comparative studies in rabbinics and New Testament. Today, the presentation of Jesus as a Pharisee is common among both Jewish and Christian commentators on the New Testament, and the issue of Jewish influence on early Christianity no longer evokes the anxiety it did less than a century ago. Whatever the various reasons for the change in attitudes—and certainly the American setting and the awareness of the Holocaust have been influential in the post-war years—it is only fair to note that new paradigms have emerged, as any reader of this book will be able to see, and that much in the scholarship on Christian origins today would have pleased Geiger far more than Harnack or Schürer.

Endnotes

1. Hermann Samuel Reimarus, *Fragments*, trans. Ralph S. Fraser (Philadelphia: Fortress Press, 1970).

2. Reimarus, *Fragments*, 101.

3. Reimarus, *Fragments*, 101.

4. Johann Semler, *Beantwortung der Fragmente eines Ungenannten insbesondere vom Zweck Jesu und seiner Jünger. Andere, verbesserte Auflage. Anhang zur Beantwortung der Fragmente des Ungenannten* (Halle, 1780).

5. Albert Schweitzer, *The Quest of the Historical Jesus: A Critical Study of Its Progress from Reimarus to Wrede*, trans. W. Montgomery (New York: Macmillan, 1930; German original, 1906).

6. Franz Volkmar Reinhard, *Versuch über den Plan, welchen der Stifter der christlichen Religion zum Besten der Menschheit entwarf* (1781).

7. Karl Friedrich Bahrdt, *Ausführung des Plans und Zwecks Jesu. In Briefen an Wahrheit suchende Leser*, 11 vols., (Berlin: August Mylius, 1784–92).

8. Karl Heinrich Venturini, *Natürliche Geschichte des grossen Propheten von Nazareth*, 4 vols., (Copenhagen, 1800–1802).

9. August Friedrich Gfrörer, *Kritische Geschichte des Urchristentums*, 2 vols., (1863).

10. August Friedrich Gfrörer, *Philo und die alexandrinische Theosophie, oder vom Einflusse der jüdisch-ägyptischen Schule auf die Lehre des Neuen Testaments*; and idem., *Das Jahrhundert des Heils*, 2 vols., (1831, 1838).

11. George Foot Moore, "Christian Writers on Judaism," *Harvard Theological Review* 14 (1921): 197–254 at p. 225.

12. Friedrich Wilhelm Ghillany [Richard von der Alm, pseud.], *Theologische Briefe an die Gebildeten der deutschen Nation* and *Die Urteile heidnischer und jüdischer Schriftsteller der vier ersten christlichen Jahrhunderte über Jesus* (1863).

13. Karl Barth, *Protestant Thought: From Rousseau to Ritschl*, trans. Brian Cozens (New York: Simon and Schuster, 1969), 13.

14. See Jacob Katz, *Jews and Freemasons in Europe: 1723-1939* (Cambridge, MA: Harvard University Press, 1970).

15. H.E.G. Paulus, *Das Leben Jesu als Grundlage einer reinen Geschichte des Urchristentums*, 2 vols., (1828).

16. Jacob Katz, *From Prejudice to Destruction* (Cambridge, MA: Harvard University Press, 1980).

17. Horton Harris, *The Tübingen School* (Oxford: Oxford University Press, 1975), 250.

18. Dieter Georgi, *The Opponents of Paul in Second Corinthians* (Philadelphia: Fortress Press, 1964, 1986), 2.

19. Ferdinand Christian Baur, "Die Christuspartei in der korinthischen Gemeinde, der Gegensatz des petrinischen und paulinischen Christenthums in der ältesten Kirche, der Apostel Petrus in Rom," *Tübinger Zeitschrift für Theologie* 4 (1831): 61-206. Reprinted in Klaus Scholder, ed., *Ausgewählte Werke in Einzelausgaben* (Stuttgart-Bad Cannstatt: Fromann, 1963–70), 1:1–146.

20. Baur, *The Church History of the First Three Centuries*, trans. A. Menzies (London: Williams and Norgate, 1878–79), 1:30.

21. See Harris, *The Tübingen School* (n.17).

22. Baur, *Die christliche Gnosis oder die christliche Religionsphilosophie in ihrer geschichtlichen Entwicklung* (Tübingen, 1835; new edition, Darmstadt, 1967), 32.

23. For an excellent survey of Protestant anti-Judaism during the period of the Second Reich, see Uriel Tal, *Christians and Jews in Germany*, trans. Noah Jacobs (Ithaca: Cornell University Press, 1975).

24. Hans-Joachim Kraus, *Geschichte der historische-kritischen Erforschung des Alten Testaments von der Reformation bis zur Gegenwart* (Neukirchen-Vlyun: Neukirchner Verlag, 1956).

25. See Lothar Perlitt, *Vatke und Wellhausen: Geschichtephilosophische Voraussetzungen und historigraphische Motive für die Darstellung der Religion und Geschichte Israels durch Wilhelm Vatke und Julius Wellhausen* (Berlin: Tüpelmann, 1965).

26. Johannes Andreas Eisenmenger, *Entdecktes Judentum* (1700).

27. Charles David Smith, "Protestant Attitudes toward Jewish Emancipation in Prussia," Ph. D. diss., Yale University, 1971. See also Johann Maier, "Die religiös motivierte Judenfeindschaft," 22–47, and Karl Thieme, "Aus christlicher und mahammedanischer Sicht," 48–79, in *Judenfeindschaft: Darstellung und Analysen*, ed. Karl Thieme (Frankfurt am Main: Fischer, 1963). See also Horst Fischer, *Judentum, Staat und Heer in Preussen im frühen 19. Jahrhundert* (Tübingen, 1968).

28. Abraham Geiger, *Was hat Mohammed aus dem Judentume aufgenommen? Eine von der Königl. Preussischen Rheinuniversität gekrönte Preisschrift* (Bonn: F. Baaden, 1833; reprint, Leipzig: M. W. Kaufmann, 1902); in English translation, *Judaism and Islam* (Madras, 1898; reprint, New York: Ktav, 1970).

29. Abraham Geiger, *Urschrift und Übersetzungen der Bibel in ihrer Abhängigkeit von der inneren Entwickelung des Judentums* (Breslau: Julius Hainauer, 1857; reprint, Frankfurt am Main: Verlag Madda, 1928); in Hebrew translation, *Ha-Mikra v'Targumav* (Jerusalem: Bialik Foundation, 1972).

30. Abraham Geiger, *Sadducäer und Pharisäer* (Breslau, 1863).

31. Abraham Geiger, *Das Judentum und seine Geschichte. In zwölf Vorlesungen. Nebst einem Anhange: Ein Blick auf die neuesten Bearbeitungen des Lebens Jesu* (Breslau: Schlettersche Buchhandlung, 1864); in English translation, *Judaism and Its History*, trans. Maurice Mayer (New York, 1866).

32. Abraham Geiger, "Apokryphen zweiter Ordnung," *Jüdische Zeitschrift für Wissenschaftliche Literatur* 7 (1869): 116–135; "Noch Ein Wort über die Hebräerbrief," ibid., 8 (1870): 163.

33. Abraham Geiger, *Das Judentum und seine Geschichte von der Zerstörung des zweiten Tempels bis zum Ende des zwölften Jahrhunderts. In zwölf Vorlesungen* (Breslau: Schlettersche Buchhandlung, 1865), 117–118.

34. See, for example, Simeon Lowy, *The Principles of Samaritan Bible Exegesis* (Leiden: E.J. Brill, 1977).

35. Adolf Hausrath, *A History of New Testament Times*, trans. Charles T. Pyonting and Philip Quenzer, 2 vols., (London: Williams and Norgate, 1878); Daniel Schenkel, *The Character of Jesus Portrayed: Biblical Essay with an Appendix*, 2 vols., (Boston, 1866).

36. Julius Wellhausen, *Die Pharisäer und Sadduzäer: Eine Untersuchung zur inneren jüdischen Geschichte* (Göttingen: Vandenhöck und Ruprecht, 1874; reprint, 1967).

37. Wellhausen (n. 36), 10, 17–18, 19.

38. Julius Wellhausen, *Geschichte Israels* (1878).

39. Wellhausen (n. 36).

40. Emil Schürer, *Lehrbuch der neutestamentlichen Zeitgeschichte* (1874).

41. Schürer, *Geschichte des jüdischen Volkes im Zeitalter Jesu Christi* (1884).

42. Schürer, *A History of the Jewish People in the Time of Jesus Christ*, trans. Sophia Taylor and Rev. Peter Christie (New York: Charles Scribner's Sons, 1891), 2:95.

43. Schürer (n. 42), 2:124–125.

44. See Shaye Cohen, "The Political and Social History of the Jews in Greco-Roman Antiquity: The State of the Question," in Robert A. Kraft and George W.E. Nickelsburg, eds., *Early Judaism and Its Modern Interpreters* (Atlanta, GA: Scholars Press, 1986), 33–56.

45. Wilhelm Bousset, *Die Religion des Judentums im neutestamentlichen Zeitalter* (Berlin: Verlag von Reuther und Reichard, 1903; expanded and revised, 1906). See also the sharp critique of the first edition by Felix Perles, *Boussets Religion des Judenthums im neutestamentlichen Zeitalter kritisch untersucht* (Berlin: Wolf Peiser Verlag, 1903). Bousset wrote a response to Perles, *Volksfrömmigkeit und Schriftgelehrtentum: Antwort auf Herrn Perles Kritik meiner 'Religion des Judentums im N.T. Zeitalter'* (Berlin: Verlag von Reuther und Reichard, 1903).

46. Bousset (n. 45), 186, 213.

47. The Jewish historian Ismar Elbogen was particularly critical of Bousset; see his *Die Religionsanschauungen der Pharisäer mit besonderer Berücksichtigung der Begriffe Gott und Mensch* (Berlin: 22nd Bericht über die Lehranstalt für die Wissenschaft des Judentums in Berlin erstattet vom Curatorium, 1904).

48. See Baeck's *Das Wesen des Christentums*, first published in 1905; expanded in 1922.

49. Wilhelm Herrmann, *The Communion of the Christian with God*, trans. J. Sandys Stanyon (New York: G.P. Putnam's Sons, 1906; reprint, Philadelphia: Fortress Press, 1971); Adolf von Harnack, *What Is Christianity?* trans. Thomas Bailey Saunders (New York: Harper & Bros., 1957).

50. Adolf von Harnack, *Das Wesen des Christentums* (Berlin, 1900), 47–48.

51. Harnack (n. 50), 30–31.

52. Adolf von Harnack, *Marcion* (Leipzig, 1924[2]), 222.

53. Yosef Hayim Yerushalmi, *Zakhor: Jewish History and Jewish Memory* (Seattle: University of Washington Press, 1982).

54. Harold Bloom, *The Anxiety of Influence* (New York: Oxford University Press, 1973).

55. See my forthcoming article, "Making Nazism a Christian Movement: The Development of a Christian Theology of Antisemitism during the Third Reich," *Festschrift for Richard Rubenstein*, ed. Michael Berenbaum and Betty Rubenstein.

56. See Dieter Georgi, "The Interest in Life of Jesus Theology as a Paradigm for the Social History of Biblical Criticism," *Harvard Theological Review* 85, no. 1 (1992): 51–83.

Suggestions For Further Reading

Brown, Colin. *Jesus in European Protestant Thought: 1770–1860.* Durham, NC: Labyrinth Press, 1985. A clear and detailed presentation of understandings of Jesus in the work of modern New Testament scholars and philosophers, primarily in Germany but with some attention to England as well.

Herford, R. Travers. *Christianity in Talmud and Midrash.* London: Williams and Norgate, 1903. One of several valuable books by the English scholar whose career as a student of Judaism paralleled that of the American, George Foot Moore.

Klein, Charlotte. *Anti-Judaism in Christian Theology.* Trans. Edward Quinn. Philadelphia: Fortress Press, 1978. A short, powerful book that analyzes German and French New Testament scholarship, and contrasts it with the much more enlightened Anglo-American schools, pointing out the ignorance of Jewish sources among Christian scholars and their consequent uninformed and prejudicial presentations of early Judaism.

Moore, George Foot. "Christian Writers on Judaism." *Harvard Theological Review* 14 (1921): 197–254. A classic essay in the field of Religious Studies, Moore critiques the anti-Jewish bias that entered German New Testament scholarship in the nineteenth century.

____. *Judaism in the First Centuries of the Christian Era: The Age of the Tannaim.* 3 vols. Cambridge, MA: Harvard University Press, 1927–1930. A pioneer work, massive in scale and free of prejudicial distortions, that continues to serve students of rabbinic Judaism.

Kraft, Robert A. and George W.E. Nicklesburg, eds. *Early Judaism and its Modern Interpreters.* Atlanta, GA: Scholars Press, 1986. A collection of articles reviewing historical study of Judaism in the Greco-Roman world and in relation to Christian origins, with information on the latest scholarly discussions.

Osten-Sacken, Peter von der. *Christian-Jewish Dialogue: Theological Foundations.* Trans. Margaret Kohl. Philadelphia: Fortress Press, 1986. One of contemporary Germany's leading New Testament scholars, who directs an institute in Berlin for Christian-Jewish relations, analyzes the current state of theological discussions between Christians and Jews.

Sanders, E.P. *Jesus and Judaism.* Philadelphia: Fortress Press, 1985. With sharp awareness of the problem of anti-Judaism in New Testament scholarship, Sanders formulates a new kind of approach to Judaism. See also his *Paul and Palestinian Judaism: A Comparison of Patterns of Religion.* Philadelphia: Fortress Press, 1977. It has effected a revolution in Pauline studies.

Sandmel, Samuel. *Anti-Semitism in the New Testament?* Philadelphia: Fortress Press, 1978.

____. *A Jewish Understanding of the New Testament.* Cincinnati: Hebrew Union College, 1956. Sandmel presents Jewish perspectives on Christian origins and the New Testament.

Schürer, Emil. *The History of the Jewish People in the Time of Jesus Christ: 175 B.C.–A.D. 135*. Trans. T.A. Burkill et al. Rev. and ed. Geza Vermes, Fergus Millar, and Matthew Black. 3 vols. in 4 books. Edinburgh: T. & T. Clark, 1973–1987. A recent updating and correction of the vastly influential work of nineteenth-century scholarship; purged of its prejudicial interpretations, which Moore castigated, its breath, which Moore commended, and the up to date bibliographical information make it a very serviceable reference work.

Schweitzer, Albert. *The Quest of the Historical Jesus: A Critical Study of Its Progress from Reimarus to Wrede*. Trans. W. Montgomery. New York: Macmillan, 1930; German original, 1906. Still the best critical review of images of Jesus in modern German thought.

RACIAL NATIONALISM AND THE RISE OF MODERN ANTISEMITISM*

Marvin Perry

What made modern antisemitism particularly virulent was its link to nationalist and racist thinking. Nationalists and racists, often using the language of Social Darwinism, characterized Jews as a lower and wicked race that threatened the nation. Marvin Perry discusses the rise of racial nationalism and its relationship to antisemitism.

Modern antisemitism was fueled by religious, socio-economic, and nationalist-racist forces. Religious antisemitism rested essentially on two assumptions which originated in the New Testament and the writings of the Church Fathers: (1) the Jews as a people were collectively guilty for the crucifixion and eternally punished for this "crime of deicide"; (2) and the Jews were agents of Satan, enemies of Christianity, equipped with supernatural powers of evil and destruction. Thus, during the Middle Ages, Jews were accused of torturing and crucifying Christian children in order to use their blood for ritual purposes, of stabbing the communion bread until it ran with Christ's blood, of poisoning wells and planting the plague to kill Christians, and of organizing a secret government that conspired in alliance with the Mongols or other invaders to destroy Christendom. Christian art, literature, and religious instruction depicted the Jews in a derogatory manner. The Jew, "the seed of Satan," appeared in the company of the devil or wore the devil's horns and tail. Deeply etched into the minds and hearts of Christians, this distorted image of the Jew as at once a contemptible creature and a danger-

---

* In preparing this article, I used some material from my previously published works, notably *An Intellectual History of Modern Europe* (Boston: Houghton Mifflin, 1993). I am grateful to my colleague Frederick M. Schweitzer for his critical reading of the manuscript. The final version incorporates his ideas and several quotations to which he referred me.

ous power persisted in the popular mentality into the twentieth century. Medieval Christian antisemitism, which saw the Jew as vile and fearful and Judaism as repulsive—which had stamped the Jew with the mark of Cain—fertilized the soil for modern antisemitism. A mystical fear and hatred of Jews rooted in Christian perceptions underlay modern conceptions of antisemitism and contributed to their lethal quality.

In the modern world, socio-economic factors supplemented the old religious bigotry. In the nineteenth century, under the aegis of the liberal ideals of the Enlightenment and the French Revolution, Jews gained legal equality in most European lands.[1] They could leave the ghetto and participate in many activities that had been closed to them. Traditionally an urban people, the Jews, who were concentrated in the leading cities of Europe, took advantage of this new freedom and opportunity. Motivated by the fierce desire of outsiders to prove their worth, aided by deeply embedded traditions that valued education and family life, and conditioned by many centuries of poverty and surviving by their wits in a hostile environment, Jews were admirably prepared to compete in a society where effort and talent counted more than birth or religion. Jews achieved striking success as entrepreneurs, bankers, lawyers, journalists, doctors, scientists, scholars, and performers, particularly in Germany. By the early twentieth century no area of German life was unquickened by Jewish energy and creativity. By 1930 Jews, although less than one percent of the population, counted for thirty percent of Nobel Prize winners in Germany. Vienna affords much the same picture of Jewish achievement. In 1880 Jews constituted about ten per cent of the city's population but were nearly forty percent of the medical students and nearly twenty-five per cent of the law students. Vienna was home to Sigmund Freud and his circle, and Viennese cultural life before World War I was shaped to a large extent by Jewish writers, musicians, critics, and patrons. All but one of the major banking houses were Jewish.[2] "Future historians are likely to call the first third of the twentieth century the golden age of Ashkenazi [northern] Jewry in Europe,"[3] noted renowned historian Salo W. Baron in his testimony at the Eichmann trial.

The meteoric rise of the Jews aroused resentment, particularly after the worldwide depression of 1873, among Gentiles, who saw Jews as competitors in the professions, the arts, business, and finance. Thus in 1889, as a French Catholic newspaper remarked with more venom than truth:

> The Jews have a right to celebrate the anniversary of the Revolution. They have been here only one hundred year [that is, since emancipation in 1790-1791] and already they own half the land; soon they will own it all. They control our land, our money, our government, and our press. Rothschild and his fellows are more the masters of France than the president and his ministers. They rule the stock exchange, and that is now the real center of action and power.[4]

Antisemites called for reversing Jewish emancipation: they wanted to deprive Jews of their civil rights, bar them from professions, and even to expel them from the country; some even proposed annihilation.

Beginning in the 1830s radical Left thinkers castigated Jews as ruthless exploiters. Russian-born anarchist, Mikhail Bakunin (1814–76), called the Jews "an exploiting sect, a bloodsucking people, a unique devouring parasite, tightly and intimately organized." French anarchist Pierre-Joseph Proudhon (1809–65), who looked back longingly to preindustrial society, wrote in *Caesar and Christianity*, which was published posthumously in 1883:

> The Jew is by temperament an anti-producer, neither a farmer, nor an industrialist, not even a true merchant. He is an intermediary, always fraudulent and parasitic, who operates in trade, as in philosophy, by means of falsification, counterfeiting, horse-trading.... It is the principle of evil, Satan...incarnated in the race of Shem.[5]

Like other antisemites of both the Left and the Right, Proudhon believed intensely in a Jewish conspiracy, arguing that Jews had control over all of France. Proudhon's Jew-hatred fused religious, nationalist, and socioeconomic factors. Thus an entry in his notebooks for 1847 reads:

> Demand their expulsion from France with the exception of individuals married to French women.—Abolish the synagogues; don't admit them to any kind of employment; pursue finally the abolition of this cult. It is not for nothing that the Christians call them deicides. The Jew is the enemy of the human race. One must drive this race back to Asia or exterminate it.... By fire or fusion, or by expulsion the Jew must disappear.[6]

Marx, whose father had converted to Protestantism in order not to lose his livelihood, expressed contempt for Jews and Judaism, both in his formal works and private letters. His interpretation of Judaism as the flesh and blood of bourgeois capitalism goes far to explain why later communist/socialist regimes did not condemn antisemitism or were themselves antisemitic. Some socialists dismissed antisemitism as "the socialism of fools," but matters turned out more as the early Zionist Max Nordau had predicted: "If we should live to see socialist theory become practice, you will be surprised to meet again in the new order that old acquaintance, anti-Semitism."[7]

By the end of the nineteenth century, however, the antisemitism of the Left was eclipsed in virulence and importance by the Jew-hatred of the radical Right, which rested chiefly on national and racial considerations. Whereas Christian antisemites believed that through conversion, Jews could escape the curse of their religion, racial antisemites, who used the language of science to justify their hatred, said that Jews were indelibly stained and eternally condemned by their genes. Their evil and worthlessness derived from inherited racial characteristics, which could not be altered by conversion. In 1862, Moses Hess, a pioneer Zionist, noted insightfully:

> The Germans hate the religion of the Jews less than they hate their race—they hate the peculiar faith of the Jews less than their peculiar noses.... Jewish noses cannot be reformed, and the black, wavy hair of the Jews will not be changed into blond by conversion or straightened out by constant combing.[8]

Thus Hermann Ahlwardt, an antisemitic deputy (and author of *The Desperate Struggle Between Aryan and Jew*, 1890) stated in a speech before the German Reichstag in 1895:

> If one designates the whole of Jewry, one does so in the knowledge that the racial qualities of this people are such that in the long run they cannot harmonize with the racial qualities of the Germanic peoples and that every Jew who at this moment has not done anything bad may nevertheless under the proper conditions do precisely that, because his racial qualities drive him to do it...the Jews...operate like parasites.... You'd better exterminate these beasts of prey.[9]

A xenophobic nationalism, which viewed the Jews as a conspiratorial race with limitless power for evil and an alien race that threatened the nation's very existence, had emerged in full force in the decades before World War I. The extreme racial nationalism of this period, which was the seedbed of Hitler's ideology, is the subject of this paper.

Extreme Nationalism: The Setting for Modern Antisemitism

In the first half of the nineteenth century, nationalism and liberalism went hand in hand. Liberals sought both the rights of the individual and national independence and unification. Liberal nationalists believed that a unified state free of foreign subjugation was in harmony with the principle of natural rights, and they insisted that love of country led to love of humanity. As nationalism grew more extreme, however, its profound difference from liberalism became more apparent. Concerned exclusively with the greatness of the nation, extreme nationalists rejected the liberal emphasis on political liberty. They regarded liberty as an obstacle to national power and maintained that authoritarian leadership was needed to meet national emergencies. The needs of the nation, they said, transcended the rights of the individual. Placing the nation above everything, nationalists became increasingly intolerant of minorities within the nation's borders and hateful of other peoples. In the name of national unity, they persecuted minorities at home and stirred up animus against other nations. In the pursuit of national power, they increasingly embraced imperialistic, racist, and militaristic doctrines that glorified war as a symbol of the nation's resolve and will.

Interpreting politics with the logic of emotions, extreme nationalists created a cult of ancestors and a mystique of blood, soil, and a sacred national past. In these ancestral traditions and attachments, the nationalist found a higher reality akin to religious truth. Loyalty to the nation-state was elevated above all other allegiances. The nation-state became an object of religious reverence; the spiritual energies that formerly had been dedicated to Christianity were now channeled into the worship of the nation-state. In 1902, Friedrich Paulsen, a German philosopher, warned of nationalism's threat to reason and morality:

> A supersensitive nationalism has become a very serious danger for all the peoples of Europe; because of it, they are in danger of losing the feeling for human values. Nationalism, pushed to an extreme, just like sectarianism [religious conflicts], destroys moral and even logical consciousness. Just and unjust, good and bad, true and false, lose their meaning; what men condemn as disgraceful and inhuman when done by others, they recommend in the same breath to their own people as something to be done to a foreign country.[10]

In the late nineteenth century, conservatives became the staunchest advocates of nationalism, and the nationalism preached by conservative extremists was stripped of liberal ideals of liberty, equality, and the fellowship of nations. Landholding aristocrats, generals, and clergy, often joined by business and industrial magnates, saw nationalism as a convenient instrument for gaining a mass following in their struggle against democracy and socialism. A radicalized Right championed popular nationalist myths and dreams and employed Social Darwinist and racist doctrines in order to harness the instinctual energies of the masses.

Social Darwinists, who applied Darwin's biological theories to relations between nations, injected dangerous elements into nationalism. They maintained that nations and races were engaged in a struggle for survival in which only the fittest survive and deserve to survive. In their view, war was nature's stern way of eliminating the unfit. Darwinian biology was used to promote the belief in Anglo-Saxon and Teutonic racial superiority. Social Darwinists attributed the growth of the British Empire, the expansion of the United States to the Pacific, and the extension of German power to racial qualities. The domination of other peoples—American Indians, Africans, Asians, Poles—was regarded as the natural right of the superior race. The Social Darwinist notion of the struggle of races for survival became a core doctrine of Hitler's movement; it provided the "scientific" and "ethical" justification for genocide.

Volkish Thought: The Rejection of Modernity

While extreme nationalism was a general European phenomenon, it proved particularly dangerous in Germany. The unification of Germany in 1870-71 turned the new state into an international power of the first rank, upsetting the balance of power in Europe. To German nationalists, the unification of Germany was both the fulfillment of a national dream and the starting point of an even more ambitious goal—the extension of German power in Europe and the world. Sometimes this goal was expressed in the language of Social Darwinism—nations are engaged in an eternal struggle for survival and domination. Moreover, under Bismarck's authoritarian leadership, liberal ideals and true parliamentary government, which might have served as a countervailing power to an aggressive nationalism, were stifled.

Volkish thought, a clear example of mythical thinking, was an ominous expression of that romantic German nationalism that etherealized everything German and denounced as alien to the German soul everything non-German, particularly the liberal-humanist Enlightenment tradition which was identified with France and the West.[11] (*Volk*, which originally simply meant folk or people, became synonymous with race.) To German Volkish thinkers the Enlightenment and parliamentary democracy were foreign ideas that corrupted the pure German spirit. These thinkers sought to bind the German people together through a deep love of their language, traditions, and fatherland. They felt that the Germans were animated by a higher spirit than that found in other peoples. With fanatical devotion, Volkish thinkers embraced all things German—the medieval past, the German language, the German landscape, the simple peasant, the village.

Volkish thought attracted Germans frightened by all the complexities of the modern age—industrialization, urbanization, materialism, party politics, and class conflicts. They feared an impersonal and excessively rationalized capitalist system that destroyed ancient social forms and traditional virtues, that seemed indifferent to their individual needs and communal traditions, that alienated people from themselves and each other. Seeing their beloved Germany transformed by these forces of modernity—which they often identified with the Jew—Volkish thinkers yearned to restore the sense of community that they attributed to the preindustrial age. Only by identifying with their sacred soil and sacred traditions would Germans escape from the rootlessness and alienation of modern industrial society. A return to roots would restore authenticity to life and stimulate genuine cultural creativity. Only then could the different classes band together in an organic unity.

Volkish thinkers glorified the ancient Germanic tribes that overran the Roman Empire, contrasting their courageous and vigorous German ancestors with the effete and degenerate Romans. They loved to cite the ancient Roman historian Tacitus' *Germania* as proof that they were an *Urfolk*, an original people not stained by race mixture, that they spoke an *Ursprache*, a pure and original language, and that they were morally superior to Latin peoples. A few Volkish writers tried to reconcile ancient heroic Germanic traditions with Christianity; this often meant expunging Jewish elements from Christianity. In this they made much of the quintessential German, Martin Luther, who had burst the bonds of a foreign, Latin Christianity to create a truly German faith. The later Luther's antisemitic tirades also served the cause of Volkish nationalists.

In several ways Richard Wagner (1813–83), the great opera composer, epitomized Volkish thinking. He glorified a pre-Christian Germanic past and called for the spiritual redemption of German society through art that stemmed from the rich soil of German tradition, particularly heroic legends and myths. For Wagner, modern society was lacking in soul. A cultural rebirth inspired by the common heritage of the Volk would unite a fragmented German nation and overcome the mediocrity, materialism, philistinism, and atomization of modern life. Wagner called for a revitalized Christianity. By this he meant a Germanized Christianity, unorthodox, simple, enthusiastic, vaguely mystical, and centering on sacred ancient Germanic myths. In his later years, influenced by Gobineau's racial theories (see below), Wagner warned that race-mixing produced cultural decline. In 1877, he founded the *Bayreuther Blätter*, a monthly review that promoted his cultural, Volkish, and antisemitic views.

After Wagner's death in 1883, his followers, the Bayreuth Circle, led first by his widow Cosima and then by the English Germanophile Houston Stewart Chamberlain, built a cult around the master's person and mission to attain the spiritual renewal of the German soul through his art. Wagnerians helped to popularize Volkish ideas and were active members of several Volkish and racist societies, including the Pan-German League, which demanded imperial expansion and taught the inherent superiority of the German Volk. A generation later, the Nazis praised Wagner's music and treatment of Germanic myths for brilliantly expressing the inner feelings and hopes of the German Volk. "It is very difficult to exaggerate the importance of Wagner in Hitler's life and thought," notes one student of Hitler. "[Wagner was] the primary inspiration for National Socialism."[12] Hitler had nurtured himself since his Vienna years on Wagner's operas, memorizing long passages from the scores, and before attaining power he attended the Bayreuth festivals to symbolize the continuity between the National Socialist movement and Germany's great culture hero. Hitler's Third Reich subsidized the Bayreuth festivals. Down to 1945, Wagner's still active disciples praised Hitler for possessing a "genuine folk soul" and sought to promote a link between the master's world-view and National Socialism.

Volkish thinking led Germans to see themselves as an heroic people fundamentally different from and better than the English, French, Slavs, or any other people. It induced them to regard German culture as unique—innately superior to and in opposition to the liberal-humanist outlook of the Enlightenment. Volkish thinkers held that the German people and culture had a special destiny and a unique mission. They pitted the German soul against the Western intellect, feeling, intuition, and spirit against a drab and dissecting rationalism. They accused liberalism of fostering a vulgar materialism, an anarchic individualism, and a soul-stifling rational-scientific outlook all of which separated people from the true genius, the peculiar character, of the German nation. And behind the corrosive forces of modernity, said Volkish thinkers, was the Jew, the principal corrupter of the German soul. The radical nationalist, racist, antisemitic, irrational, and anti-liberal outlook shaped by these late nineteenth-century Volkish thinkers undermined support for the democratic Weimar Republic established in Germany after World War I and provided Hitler with receptive listeners.

Race: The Key to History

Volkish thinkers were especially attracted to racist doctrines. Racist thinkers held that race was the decisive factor in history, and that not only physical features but moral, aesthetic and intellectual qualities distinguished one race from another. In their view, a race demonstrated its vigor and achieved greatness when it preserved its purity; intermarriage between races—"miscegenation"—was contamination that would result in genetic, cultural, and military decline. While liberals held that anyone who accepted German law was a member of the German nation, Volkish thinkers interjected the notion that a person's nationality was a function of his or her "racial soul" or "blood." On the basis of this new conception of nationality, racists argued that Jews, no matter how many centuries their ancestors had dwelled in Germany, could never think and feel like a German and should be deprived of citizenship.

Like their Nazi successors, Volkish thinkers claimed that the German race was purer than, and therefore superior to, all other races; its superiority was revealed in such physical characteristics as blond hair, blue eyes, and fair skin—all signs of inner qualities lacking in other races. German racists claimed that the Germans were descendants of ancient Aryans. (The Aryans emerged some 4,000 years ago, probably between the Caspian Sea and the Hindu Kush Mountains. Intermingling with others, the Aryans lost whatever identity as a people they might have had.) After discovering similarities between core European languages—Latin, Greek, Germanic, Slavic—and ancient Persian and Sanskrit (the language of the fair-skinned conquerors of India), nineteenth-century scholars contended that these languages all stemmed from a common tongue spoken by the Aryans. From there, some leaped to the unwarranted conclusion that the Aryans constituted a distinct race endowed with superior racial qualities.

The Aryan myth enabled race-thinkers and antisemites to view the Jews as alien in race, language, religion, and civilization and as unabridgeably separate from Europeans. Here was philological and ethnographic evidence—scientific proof, as it were—that Jews must not be emancipated and integrated, but ghettoized, expelled, or even annihilated. Some intellectuals drew a dichotomy between "Asiatic Judaism" and "Aryan Christianity" founded by the "Aryan Jesus" but vitiated by the "Jew Paul." Therefore, it was necessary to de-judaize Christianity "in order that the spirit of the Indo-European race predominate in its bosom," as one famous biblical scholar declared.[13] Axiomatic was the racial superiority of Aryans and inferiority of Jews, who were seen as a danger to racial hygiene as well as to high culture.

A key figure in the shaping of racist thinking was Arthur de Gobineau (1816–82), author of *Essay on the Inequality of Human Races* (1853–55). Gobineau, often referred to as the "Father of Racism," held that three basic races, each with its own distinguishing features, existed in the world—the yellow, the black, and the white. He organized the races in a hierarchy of ability and value with the white race at the apex. The yellow race, he said, was concerned with material prosperity and excelled in commerce, but it had little physical energy, was inclined to apathy, and lacked the imagination for theorizing. The black race had well developed senses, especially taste and smell, but a weak intellect. The white race, in which Gobineau also included Jews, was gifted with an energetic intelligence, possessed noble virtues—honor, spiritedness, a love of liberty—generally lacking in other races, and had a monopoly of beauty and strength. Marx saw class as the key to history; for Gobineau it was race. In the Dedication to *Essay*, he wrote: "I was gradually penetrated by the conviction that the racial question overshadows all other problems of history, that it holds the key to them all."[14] Racial factors accounted for the rise and fall of civilizations. The white race, particularly the Aryans, had created high civilization but miscegenation had caused its civilization to decline and threatened its extinction. "The problem is this," Hitler was later to say: "How can we arrest racial decay? Must what Count Gobineau says come true?"[15]

Gobineau was not well received in his native France, but he gradually gained a following in Germany. Wagner and the Bayreuth Circle befriended Gobineau and employed his theories to support their belief in a superior German race. Ludwig Scheemann, a Wagnerian, founded the Gobineau Society which, like the Pan-German League and other Volkish and nationalist groups, promoted Gobineau's racial outlook. While Gobineau himself was no antisemite, his German disciples made use of his theory of racial decay to justify their hatred of Jews. In their view, the Jews were the racial inferiors who were corrupting the blood of the superior Aryan race and undermining German culture.

Volkish thinkers embraced the ideas of Houston Stewart Chamberlain (1855–1927), an Englishman whose boundless devotion to Germanism led him to adopt German citizenship. An ardent admirer of Wagner's music, Chamberlain became an active member of the Bayreuth Circle. (After divorcing his first wife, he married Wagner's daughter in 1908.) He regarded Wagner as the highest expression of German creativity. Contact with the Wagnerians' antisemitism intensified Chamberlain's own dislike of Jews. In 1888 he wrote in a letter to his aunt that the Germans "are menaced by a complete moral, intellectual, and material ruin if a strong reaction does not set in in time against the supremacy of the Jews, who feed upon [Germans] and suck out—at every grade of society—their very life blood."[16] He came to see Jew and German as dialectical opposites, locked in a struggle of world historical significance, a theme that he developed in his major work, *Foundations of the Nineteenth Century* (1899).

In *Foundations*, Chamberlain asserted in pseudo-scientific fashion that races differed not only physically but also morally, spiritually, and intellectually and that the struggle between races was the driving force of history. He held that the Germans, descendants of the ancient Aryans, were physically superior and bearers of a higher culture. He attributed Rome's decline to the dilution of its racial qualities through miscegenation. The blond, blue-eyed, long-skulled Germans, possessing the strongest strain of Aryan blood and distinguished by an inner spiritual depth, were the true ennoblers of humanity.

Demonstrating the typical irrationality of the antisemite, Chamberlain denied that Christ was a Jew, hinting that he was of Aryan stock, and he held that the goal of the Jew, required by his religion, was "to put his foot upon the neck of all the nations of the world and be Lord and possessor of the whole earth."[17] He pitted Aryan and Jew against each other in a titanic struggle. As agents of a spiritually empty capitalism and divisive liberalism, the Jews, said Chamberlain, were undermining German society. Materialistic, cowardly, and devious, they were the very opposite of the idealistic, heroic, and faithful Germans.

Chamberlain's book was enormously popular in Germany with the nationalist and racist Right. Pan-German and other Volkish-nationalist organizations frequently cited it. Kaiser Wilhelm II called *Foundations* a "Hymn to Germanism" and read it to his children. What greater accolade could be bestowed on Volkish nationalism! "Next to the national liberal historians like Heinrich von Treitschke and Heinrich von Sybel," concludes German historian Fritz Fischer, "Houston Stewart Chamberlain had the greatest influence upon the spiritual life of Wilhelmine Germany."[18]

Chamberlain's loathing of liberalism, parliamentarism, Marxism, and materialism, his obsession with the Jews to whom he imputed a sinister influence, and his belief in Aryan/Teutonic superiority and in blood and soil agrarianism make him a spiritual forerunner of Nazism, and he was praised as such by Alfred Rosenberg, the leading Nazi racial theorist in the early days of Hitler's movement. Joseph Goebbels, the Nazi propagandist, hailed Chamberlain as a "pathbreaker" and "pioneer" after meeting him in 1926. In 1923 Chamberlain, then 68 years old, met Hitler, whose movement was still in its foundation stage. Chamberlain subsequently praised the National Socialist movement as Wagnerism in politics, and exulted "that Germany in its hour of need has given birth to a Hitler," that the führer shares "our conviction about the pernicious, even murderous influence of Jewry on the German *Volk*."[19] Hitler visited Chamberlain on his death bed and attended his funeral. The Third Reich placed Chamberlain in the Nazi pantheon and excerpted his writings in school books and pamphlets.

German racial nationalists and Volkish thinkers singled out Jews as the most wicked of races and a deadly enemy of the German people. To German doctors of race, the Jews were both an inassimilable "anti-national nation" and a *Gegenrasse*, an anti-race.[20] Antisemitic organizations and political parties sought to deprive Jews of their civil rights, and antisemitic publications proliferated. The radical Right viewed Jew-hatred as a popular formula for mobilizing and uniting all social classes, a precondition for strengthening the nation and thwarting liberal democracy and Marxism. Thus there is continuity between Nazism and pre-World War I German racial nationalists who saw race as the key to world history, denounced Jews as an evil race, and insisted that as a superior race Germans had a national right to dominate other peoples, particularly the "racially inferior" Slavs of the East. Hitler, whose thought was an agglomeration of the nineteenth century's ideological detritus, declared in *Mein Kampf*: "All great cultures of the past perished only because the originally creative race died out from blood poisoning.... All who are not of good race in this world are chaff.... A state which in this age of racial poisoning dedicates itself to the care of its best racial elements must some day become lord of the earth."[21] Aryanism was central to his world-view:

> All the human culture, all the results of art, science, and technology that we can see before us today, are almost exclusively the creative product of the Aryan.... He alone was the founder of all higher humanity.... He is the Prometheus of mankind from whose bright forehead the divine spark of genius has sprung at all times.... The first cultures arose in places where the Aryan, in his encounters with lower peoples, subjugated them and bent them to his will.[22]

And the Jew was the Aryan's Manichean antithesis:

> The mightiest counterpart to the Aryan is represented by the Jew.... He is and remains the typical parasite, a sponger who like the noxious bacillus keeps spreading as soon as a favorable medium invites him.... Wherever he appears, the host people dies out after a short or longer period.... He poisons the blood of others, but preserves his own.... The personification of the devil as the symbol of all evil assumes the living shape of the Jew.... With satanic joy in his face, the black-haired Jewish youth lurks in wait for the unsuspecting girl whom he defiles with his blood, thus stealing her from her people. With every means he tries to destroy the racial foundations of the people he has set out to subjugate.[23]

Rejecting the principle of equality, racial antisemites judged a person not by his accomplishments but by his or her "blood" over which the individual had no control. Blood determines the way a person thinks, talks, behaves, and creates—or destroys. While racist thinkers claimed that their ideas were rooted in science, ultimately their theories derived from primordial feelings; they rested on a mythical not a rational foundation.

Modern Antisemitism: The Power, Appeal, and Danger of the Irrational

Antisemitism was a Europe-wide phenomenon by the end of the nineteenth century. All over Europe, a radical Right viewed Jew-hatred as an effective means of uniting the nation and of protecting it from the unsettling forces of modernity—rampant capitalism, liberalism, and Marxism. The popularity of the myth of the wicked Jew demonstrates the truth of Georges Sorel's insight that people are moved and united by myths that give emotionally satisfying explanations of life and history, that simplify and clarify the complexities of the modern world.

Antisemitism was particularly vulgar and vicious in eastern Europe. In several eastern lands, Jews were put on trial for the old libel of ritual murder, a survival of the Middle Ages. Romania officially declared its Jews to be a "menace to the state" and treated them as such. The government barred most Jews from holding office and from voting, imposed various economic restrictions on them, and restricted their admission into secondary schools and universities. The Romanian government even financed an international congress of antisemites that met in Bucharest in 1886. Periodically riots and pogroms, in which the police joined in, resulted in Jewish deaths.

Russia, like Romania, was a land of official antisemitism; it placed a quota on the number of Jewish students admitted to secondary schools and higher educational institutions, confined Jews to certain regions of the country, and "to purify the sacred historic capital" expelled some 20,000 Jews from Moscow. Squeezed into the Pale of Settlement, Jews endured terrible poverty and hardships. Some government officials encouraged and even organized pogroms against Jews. Between 1903 and 1906 pogroms broke out in 690 towns and villages, most of them in Ukraine, traditionally a hotbed of antisemitism. (Ukrainian folk songs and legends glorified centuries-old massacres of Jews.) The attackers looted, burned, raped, murdered, generally with impunity. Sometimes the authorities joined in with the rioters. In response to the Revolution of 1905, defenders of Tsar Nicholas II perpetrated a white terror, one of whose aims was revealed in the slogan: "Save Russia, Kill the Jews." At the time of the Beiliss trial for ritual murder in Kiev in 1911, a leaflet distributed by antisemites read:

> The Yids [a derogatory term for Jews] have tortured [the victim] to death. Every year, before Passover, they torture to death several dozens of Christian children in order to get their blood to mix with

> their *matzos*. They do this in commemoration of our Saviour, whom they tortured to death on the cross. [Therefore] Russians...beat up Yids...until there is not a single Yid left in Russia.[24]

The trinity of poverty, persecution, including antisemitic legislation and pogroms, and a sense that emancipation would never come induced Russian Jews to emigrate by the hundreds of thousands.

The French Right—army, clergy, aristocracy, and nationalists—blended traditional Catholic antisemitism with nationalist, racist, and economic stereotypes. In antisemitism, they found a convenient explanation for France's defeat in the Franco-Prussian War, 1870–71. Charles Maurras, the principal spokesman of the ultranationalist and anti-democratic *Action Française*, was strongly antisemitic, holding that "Jewish capitalism" and "Jewish democracy" were corrupting the French soul. Maurras attributed a destructive individualism to Judaism, for it had conceived the idea of one God who had instilled in everyone a conscience: "it is in the Law and the Prophets...that are to be found the first expressions in antiquity of the individualism, egalitarianism, humanitarianism, and social and political idealism that were to mark 1789."[25] He saw the Jews as agents of revolution and alien conspirators. The *Action Française* waged a fierce campaign against a pardon for Dreyfus, the Jewish army officer who was falsely convicted of treason, at times engaging in organized vandalism and violence against Dreyfus' supporters. Maurras lived long enough to applaud the acts of the Vichy regime relegating Jews to second class citizenship, and was indifferent to the deportation of French Jews to German death camps in World War II.

In 1886, Edouard Drumont, a French journalist published *La France Juive*, which argued that the Jews, racially inferior and believers in a primitive religion, had gained control of France. The book sold over a million copies. Drumont blamed the Jews, "covetous, scheming, subtle and cunning," for introducing capitalism, materialism, and greed into France and for accumulating fortunes at the expense of the exploited French people. The Jew is "your true enemy," Drumont told the French people. The Semitic Jew and the Aryan French, he said,

> represent two distinct races which are irremediably hostile to each other, whose antagonism has filled the world in the past and will disturb it even more in the future.... In fact the Semite has dreamt constantly, obsessively of reducing the Aryan into a state of slavery.... Today the Semites believe their victory is certain. It is no longer the Carthaginian [Hannibal who had gravely threatened Rome in the third-century B.C.] or the Saracen [Muslims defeated by the Christian Franks in southern France in the eighth century A.D.], who is in the vanguard, it is the Jew—he has replaced violence with cunning. Dangerous invasion has given way to silent, progressive

and slow encroachment. The noisy armed hordes have been replaced by single individuals, gradually forming little groups, advancing sporadically, unobtrusively occupying all the jobs, from the lowest to all the highest in the land.[26]

Like medieval Christian antisemites, Drumont accused Jews of deicide and of using the blood of slaughtered Christian children for ritual purposes. (In rural France, the accusation of ritual murder still persisted, at times fomented by the clergy.) During the antisemitic outbursts accompanying the Dreyfus affair, when the French Right was shouting "Death to the Jews," Drumont's newspaper, *La Libre Parole* (founded with Jesuit funds), tried to inflame public opinion with sensational polemics against the Jews; it blamed all the ills of France on the Jews, called for the confiscation of their property and their expulsion from the nation, and predicted that they would be massacred.

There is significant continuity between turn-of-the-century French antisemitism, particularly as expressed by the anti-Dreyfusards, and the Vichy regime set up in France after its defeat in World War II. Several key figures in the regime, including Marshall Pétain, its head, retained an unmodified antisemitism that had been conditioned by the Dreyfus affair. The Vichy government's anti-Jewish legislation and its deportation of French Jews to Nazi death camps had a measure of popular backing.

German Jews rarely suffered physical violence. However, in Germany antisemitism developed into a systematic body of beliefs that had enormous consequences for the future. "Germany became the fatherland of modern anti-Semitism," says Hans Kohn, "there the systems were thought out and the slogans coined. German literature was the richest in anti-Jewish writing."[27]

The Jewish population of Germany was quite small: in 1900 it was only about 497,000, or 0.95 percent, of the total population of 50,626,000. Jews were proud of their many contributions to German economic and intellectual life and considered themselves patriotic Germans. They were bent on becoming "more German than the Germans," as Chaim Weizmann the influential Zionist leader said. In the nineteenth century, German Jews made a spectacular leap from "despised and rejected," in Arnold Zweig's phrase, to *Bildung & Besitz*, cultivation and wealth, so that by the early twentieth century Jews had greatly enriched German commercial, artistic, and intellectual life.[28] Jews regarded Germany as an altogether desirable place to live—a place of refuge in comparison to Russia and Romania, where their kinsmen lived in terrible poverty and suffered violent attacks. German Jews, who felt that they already had a homeland, had little enthusiasm for Zionism. But the German Jews' love affair with German culture, as German-Israeli historian Gershom Scholem wrote, "remained one-sided and unreciprocated."[29]

European Jews who were members of the commercial and professional classes, like other bourgeois, gravitated toward liberalism. Moreover, as victims of persecution, they naturally favored governments that were committed to the liberal ideals of legal equality, toleration, the rule of law, and equality of opportunity. As strong supporters of parliamentary government and the entire system of values associated with the rational-humanist tradition of the Enlightenment, the Jews became targets of conservatives and Volkish thinkers who repudiated the humanist and cosmopolitan outlook of liberalism and professed a militant nationalism. German historian Karl Dietrich Bracher concludes: "Anti-Semitism was a manifestation of a rejection of the 'West' with which Jews were identified,...because the Enlightenment and democracy were essential preconditions for their acceptance and progress."[30] Many conservatives had opposed Jewish emancipation, interpreting it as a victory for the Enlightenment and liberalism which they detested.

Like conservatives in other lands, German conservatives deliberately fanned the flames of antisemitism to win the masses over to conservative causes. The Christian Social Workers' party, founded in 1878 by Adolf Stoecker, a prominent Protestant preacher and court chaplain to Kaiser Wilhelm I, engaged in antisemitic agitation in order to recruit the lower bourgeoisie to the cause of the Protestant church and the Prussian monarchy. The party denounced Jews as capitalists and deicides and blamed them for all of Germany's problems. "Jewry is a drop of alien blood in our people's body,"[31] Stoecker declared, and he hoped that a future "liberator" would take up the fight against Jewry. In German-speaking Austria, Karl Lueger, a leader of the Christian Social People's party, founded by conservative German nationalists, and mayor of Vienna from 1897 to 1910, exploited antisemitism to win elections in the overwhelmingly Catholic city; his ballot-box exploitation of popular antisemitism, which offered striking examples of the ideology's mobilizing power, greatly impressed the young Hitler. Georg von Schoenerer, founder of the German National party in Austria, wanted to eliminate Jews from all areas of public life.

Like their medieval forebears, modern antisemites abhorred and shunned Jews and protested against their social acceptance. German antisemites saw Jews as interlopers, a foreign Asiatic tribe in their midst—even though the Jewish presence in Germany went back to Roman times. In 1847 the playwright Heinrich Laube wrote: "In recent time a foreign element has penetrated everywhere in our midst, and into literature as well. This is the Jewish element. I call it foreign with emphasis; for the Jews are an Oriental nation as totally different from us today as they were two thousand years ago."[32] Driven by such sentiments, antisemitic groups pressed for rescinding emancipation in part or whole.

Antisemitic publications proliferated and some, like Wilhelm Marr's *The Victory of Judaism over Germanism* (1879) and Theodor Fritsch's *The Anti-Semitic Catechism* (1887) went through numerous printings and editions. Antisemitism gained considerable respectability in Germany and Austria, for it was preached by leading university scholars including philologist Paul de Lagarde, economist Eugen Dühring, and historian Heinrich von Treitschke, by the court chaplain,

Adolf Stoecker, by politicians, and by the immensely popular composer Richard Wagner.

These pundits touched off a great debate in Germany and Austria on the status of the Jews. Treitschke fashioned the much-used slogan—"The Jews are our misfortune"—while Marr minted and propagated the Latin-sounding term antisemitism as appropriate to the modern scientific form of Jew-hatred as distinguished from a merely emotional-religious anti-Judaism. In 1865, Dühring had called explicitly for genocide as the solution of the Jewish question, apparently the earliest to demand resolution by "killing and extirpating."[33] Addressing the antisemitic Reform Association in 1882, the agitator Franz Holubek said: "The Jews have not shown themselves worthy of emancipation.... The Jew is no longer a co-citizen. He made himself our master, our oppressor.... Do you know what gives these people the right to put their foot on our neck? The Talmud, in which you Christians are called dogs, donkeys, and pigs."[34] This produced a near riot, which the police halted. Arrested and tried for incitement of religious conflict, Holubek was acquitted when the defense showed that his polemics coincided with "learned judgment." For scholarly support, the defense relied on *The Talmud Jew*, written by August Röhling, a professor of Hebrew literature and fanatical priest, who wildly fabricated quotations from Jewish sources. Extracts from Röhling's and similar works served as evidence and testimony in court proceedings for many years. Although Crown Prince Frederick (he died after a very short reign in 1888) condemned antisemitism as "the shame of the century," all this ferment in high and low places made antisemitism acceptable, indeed, "virtuous" as Fritz Stern notes.[35]

Antisemitism became the subject of international congresses, the first of which met in Dresden in 1882, on the premise that Jews were a danger to every nation and that antisemitism was the universal cure to a universal disease. "More and more does Judaism undermine the Christian religion that turned into a specific race religion of the European-Aryan nations," agreed the delegates from Germany, Austria, Hungary, and Russia in their manifesto.[36] A second congress met in 1883 at Chemnitz, where its German, French, Romanian, and Serbian representatives proclaimed an economic boycott and the social isolation of Jews.

This synthesis of Volkish nationalism, antisemitism, "racial science," and demagoguery was exemplified by Wagner. In *Judaism in Music*, first published in 1850 under a pseudonym and republished in 1869 under his own name, Wagner, who resented the prominence of the Jewish composers Felix Mendelssohn and Giacomo Meyerbeer, asserted that Jews debased German music. They could not possess or express the feelings that animated the German soul; they had their own folk soul, which had been shaped by a degenerate culture. Devoid of a creative imagination and concerned only with self-centered materialist pursuits, said Wagner, Jews were the opposite of German artists, who set aside personal gain in order to pursue the ideal. Wagner insisted that Jews could only have a destructive influence on German culture. He expressed the view of many of the

German elite toward acceptance of Jews. "For with all our speaking and writing in favor of Jewish emancipation, we always felt instinctively repelled by any real, active contact with Jews. [The German people have] the most profound repugnance for the Jewish nature." Wagner protested that "the Jew has gone far beyond emancipation. He *rules* and will continue to rule as long as money means power."[37] And in the concluding passage of the essay, Wagner wrote: "There is only one possible way of redeeming the Jews from the terrible curse that hangs over them—annihilation." In later essays published in the Wagnerian journal, the *Bayreuther Blätter*, Wagner's antisemitism grew even more vitriolic and racist. Holding that artistic creativity was a function of race, he saw Jews as the deadly opponent of the German spirit and rejected their participation in a hoped for cultural regeneration of the Volk.

The thought processes of Volkish antisemites demonstrate the mind's monumental capacity for irrational thinking. Antisemites invented a mythical evil who could be blamed for all the social and economic ills caused by the rapid growth of industries and cities and for all the new ideas that were undermining the old order. Their anxieties and fears concentrated on the Jews, to whom they attributed everything they considered evil in the modern age, all that threatened their traditional way of life and corrupted the German Volk. To these people the great changes occurring in Germany did not stem from impersonal historical forces but was the work of Jews who had uncanny powers.

In the mythical world of Volkish thinkers, Jews were regarded as evil entrepreneurs and financiers who exploited hardworking and decent Germans, manipulated the stock exchange, and caused depressions; as international socialists who were dragging Germany into class war; as democrats who were trying to impose an alien system of parliamentary democracy on Germany; as cold and calculating intellectuals devoid of aesthetic sensibilities who corrupted traditional German culture; as city people who had no ties or love for the German soil; as materialists who were totally without German spiritual qualities; as foreign intruders, "half-Asiatics," who could never be loyal to the fatherland; as racial inferiors whose genes could infect and weaken the German race; and as international conspirators who were plotting to dominate Germany. This last accusation was a secularized and updated version of the medieval demonological myth that Jews, in the service of Satan, were plotting to destroy Christendom. In an extraordinary display of irrationality, antisemites held that Jews throughout the world were gaining control over political parties, the press, and the economy in order to dominate the planet.

The Jew as International Conspirator

The myth of a Jewish conspiracy found its culminating expression in the notorious forgery, *The Protocols of the Elders of Zion*. The *Protocols* was written in

France in the 1890s by an unknown author in the service of the Russian secret police which sought to justify the tsarist regime's antisemitic policies. Drawing upon earlier antisemitic conspiracy works—and one work that had nothing to do with Jews but attributed ambitions of world domination to Napoleon III—the forger described an alleged meeting of Jewish elders in the Jewish cemetery of Prague. In these eerie surroundings the elders plot to take over the world. First published in Russia in 1903, the *Protocols* was widely distributed after World War I and widely believed. During the civil war that followed the Bolshevik seizure of power, the Whites circulated the *Protocols* in order to inflame the antisemitic masses against the Bolsheviks; propagandists described the Communist Revolution as an attempt by Jews to subjugate Christian Russia. No doubt the *Protocols* contributed to the brutal pogroms that took the lives of some 100,000 Russian Jews between 1918 and 1920. Simon Petlyura, leader of the Ukrainian independence movement, gave his wildly antisemitic troops free reign in pillage and rapine of the defenseless Jews.

Defeat in World War I and a revolution that replaced the kaiser's government with an unpopular democratic republic made many Germans receptive to the *Protocols*' message. In their twisted view, the *Protocols* provided convincing evidence that the Jews were responsible for starting the war, for American entry on the side of the Allies, for Germany's defeat—the "stab-in-the-back"—and for the revolution that toppled the monarchy. They saw further proof of Jewish power and machinations in the World Zionist Organization, the Balfour Declaration, the Bolshevik Revolution, the newly established communist regime of Bela Kun in Hungary, the Versailles Treaty, and the League of Nations. In 1924, a Jewish observer described the book's impact in postwar Germany:

> In Berlin I attended several meetings which were entirely devoted to the *Protocols*. The speaker was usually a professor, a teacher, an editor, a lawyer or someone of that kind. The audience consisted of members of the educated class, civil servants, tradesmen, former officers, ladies, above all students.... Passions were whipped up to a boiling point.... [The Jews] caused all ills—those who had made the war and brought about the defeat and engineered the revolution, those who had conjured up all our suffering. This enemy...slunk about in the darkness, one shuddered to think what secret designs he was harboring.... I observed the students.... Now young blood was boiling, eyes flashed, fists clenched, hoarse voices roared applause or vengeance.... German scholarship allowed belief in the genuineness of the *Protocols* and in the existence of a Jewish world-conspiracy to penetrate ever more deeply into all the educated sections of the German population, so that now it is simply ineradicable.[38]

As early as 1921, the *Protocols* was conclusively proven to be a forgery, but the work continued to be translated and distributed. Translated into all the European languages and published in many editions, the *Protocols* was an inter-war best seller. Henry Ford sponsored its circulation in the United States until 1927 when he withdrew support and apologized to the American Jewish community. In 1934 in Berne, Switzerland the distributors of the *Protocols* were put on trial at the behest of the Swiss Jewish community. After hearing expert testimony, the judge emphatically denounced the *Protocols* as "ridiculous nonsense," a blatant forgery. But this decision had little influence on the mind-set of anti-semites, for whom a Jewish world-conspiracy had become an integrating principle that provided answers to the crucial questions of existence.

From the beginning of their movement to the end of the Third Reich, Nazi propagandists exploited the *Protocols* to justify their quest for power (to save Germany from the Jews), their fight against Bolshevism (the tool of the world-Jewish conspiracy), the war against the Allies (started by the Jews), and extermination (ridding the world of evil). Thus at the end of December 1944, with Berlin in ruins, the war nearing its end, and the Jews of Europe only a bleeding remnant of a people, Goebbels' Propaganda Ministry continued to harp on the myth of the world Jewish conspiracy: "The central issue of this war is the breaking of Jewish world-domination. If it were possible to checkmate the three hundred secret Jewish kings who rule the world, the peoples of this earth would at last find their peace."[39]

Regression to Mythical Thinking

German antisemitic organizations and political parties failed to induce the state to pass antisemitic laws, and by the early 1900s these groups had declined in political power and importance. But the mischief had been done. Late nineteenth-century antisemites had constructed an ideological foundation on which Hitler would later build his movement. In words that foreshadowed Hitler's, Paul de Lagarde said of the Jews: "One does not have dealings with pests and parasites: one does not rear them and cherish them; one destroys them as speedily as possible."[40] The theory, language, and justification of extermination were in place.

Racist and antisemitic ideas had become a mobilizing ideology. In varying forms and intensity antisemitic assumptions and vocabulary characterized the political and cultural views of many Germans before 1914, and they were not contested in any systematic way. In the minds of many Germans, even in respectable circles, the image of the Jew as an evil and dangerous creature had been firmly planted. It was perpetuated by the schools, youth groups, the Pan-German League, and an array of racist pamphlets and books. In 1892, the Conservative party, borrowing from the fringe Jew-hating parties, adopted antisemitism as a plank in its national platform: "We combat the manifold upsurging and decomposing Jewish influence on our national life."[41]

It is, of course, absurd to believe that a nation of fifty million was threatened by a half-million citizens of Jewish birth, or that the eleven million Jews of the world (by 1900) had organized to rule the planet. The Jewish birthrate in Germany was low, the rate of intermarriage high, and the desire for complete assimilation into German life great. Within a few generations the Jewish community in Germany might well have disappeared. Moreover, despite the paranoia of the antisemites, the German Jews and the Jews in the rest of Europe were quite powerless. There were scarcely any Jews in the ruling circles of governments, armies, civil services, or heavy industries. As events were to prove, the Jews, with no army or state and dwelling among people many of whom despised them, were the weakest of peoples. But the race mystics, convinced that they were waging a war of self-defense against a satanic foe, were impervious to rational argument. Antisemites, said Theodor Mommsen, the great nineteenth-century German historian, would not listen to

> logical and ethical arguments.... They listen only to their own envy and hatred, to the meanest instincts. Nothing else counts for them. They are deaf to reason, right, morals. One cannot influence them.... [Antisemitism] is a horrible epidemic, like cholera—one can neither explain nor cure it.[42]

A deeply illiberal Volkish nationalism and antisemitism fertilized right wing politics in Germany. It showed that segments of the population could be aroused by irrational ideas and demagogic appeals, and that idealism could be debased and science misused. This witches' brew, heated to boiling point by the humiliation of defeat in World War I, an unpopular revolution, and hard times in the immediate aftermath of the war, was the larva from which Nazism sprung.

The antisemites of the Wilhelmine era did not call for extermination—there were some exceptions but their words were taken as rhetorical flourishes—but for revoking the civil rights of Jews, for barring them from influential positions, and for their emigration or expulsion. However, the racial nationalists' denigration of Jews and glorification of Aryanism, their popularization of irrational but emotionally satisfying racial myths that purported to explain history and life, and their linking of a racial ideology with a noble idealism inspired a large number of racial activists and help to account for the capitulation to National Socialism in a later generation by even the high-minded and the respectable. The Nazis employed the antisemitic myths and stereotypes propagated by their Volkish predecessors. After World War I racists were more radical in thought and deed than their Wilhelmine mentors. They eagerly responded to Hitler's racial nationalism and did not shrink from translating their hatred into state persecution and ultimately mass murder.

Nazi racial antisemitism should have been sufficient warning to decent Germans of the kind of man Hitler was and of the moral nihilism of his movement. But antisemitism had become so commonplace and respectable in Germany that even if it did not attract many voters to Hitler—as recent research seems to indicate—it did not repel Germans either. Decades of racial antisemitism (and a centuries-old Christian antisemitism) had poisoned the German mind, blinding people to the dangerous implications of Jew-hatred when Hitler was building his movement and making them insensitive to the persecution of Jews after he had gained power. No doubt the reflection of Albert Speer, the gifted architect and Hitler's Minister of Armaments and War Production, applied to many of the cultural elite for whom Jew-hatred was either acceptable or a matter of indifference: "Hitler's hatred for the Jews seemed to me so much a matter of course that I gave it no serious thought."[43]

And the Nazis could always rely on German academics to write "learned" treatises, as they had done in the Wilhelmine era, attesting to Jewish inferiority and wickedness. Thus Eugen Fisher, Professor of Anthropology at the University of Berlin, told an audience of French intellectuals in Paris in 1941, shortly after the Nazi invasion of Russia, that the "morals and actions of the Bolshevist Jews bear witness to such a monstrous mentality that we can only speak of inferiority and of beings of another species."[44] When it came to antisemitism, the cultural elite, with some exceptions, set no moral example, as Fritz Stern reminds us: "The anti-Semitism of the upper classes was part of a good form, part of what I have called vulgar idealism, and for many it paved the way either for accepting the radical anti-Semitism of the [Nazi] regime or for shutting one's eyes to the ever-worsening persecutions."[45]

Antisemitism, which was widespread in late-nineteenth-century Europe, provides a striking example of the perennial appeal, power, and danger of mythical thinking. Ancient Christian myths that had demonized the Jews—which liberals believed would disappear in a world pervaded by the Enlightenment's legacy—were secularized by radical nationalists who held the Jews responsible for all the ills afflicting the nation. Nationalist and racist myths and stereotypes provided true believers with a comprehensive world-view, an interpretation of life and history that fulfilled the mind's yearning for coherence and meaning. By defining themselves as the racial and spiritual opposites of the "vile Jew," true believers of all classes derived a feeling of worth and felt joined together in a mystical Volkish union. True believers also felt that they were engaged in a struggle of universal significance—protecting the Aryan race and a higher civilization from a deadly enemy. "There cannot be two Chosen People. We are God's people," Hitler declared. "Two worlds face one another—the men of God and the men of Satan."[46]

By cloaking their hatred in the mantle of science—nature demands that the favored race triumph over the wicked race—racists could view persecution and even liquidation coldly, matter-of-factly, undeterred by human values. The SS, who carried out mass murder with fanatical zeal and bureaucratic efficiency, were motivated by just such an outlook. In exterminating the Jewish people they believed that they were noble souls defending the sacred Volk and civilization itself from fiendish foes, "an all-embracing world power" as Hitler defined the Jews.[47] They saw themselves as idealists charged with a noble mission to rid the world of worthless life—human devils, poisonous bacteria that were infecting the sacred Volk. These race mystics believed that they were engaged in a life-and-death struggle with evil itself, as the following tract issued by SS headquarters during World War II indicates:

> Just as night rises up against the day, just as light and darkness are eternal enemies, so the greatest enemy of world-dominating man is man himself. The sub-man—that creature which looks as though biologically it were of absolutely the same kind, endowed by Nature with hands, feet and a sort of brain, with eyes and mouth—is nevertheless a totally different, a fearful creature, is only an attempt at a human being with a quasi-human face, yet in mind and spirit lower than any animal. Inside this being a cruel chaos of wild, unchecked passions: a nameless will to destruction, the most primitive lusts, the most undisguised vileness. A sub-man—nothing else!... Never has the sub-man granted peace, never has he permitted rest.... To preserve himself he needed mud, he needed hell, but not the sun. And this underworld of sub-men found its leader: the eternal Jew![48]

Many of the SS were ideologues committed to racist doctrines which they believed were supported by the laws of biology, true believers driven by a utopian vision of a new world founded on a Social Darwinian fantasy of racial hierarchy. Awaiting execution in 1947 for war crimes, SS Captain Dieter Wisliceny perceptively analyzed the mythical component of Nazi antisemitism. He described it

> as a mystical and religious view which sees the world as ruled by good and evil powers. According to this view the Jews represented the evil principle.... It is absolutely impossible to make any impression on this outlook by means of logical or rational argument. It is a sort of religiosity.... Against this world of evil the race mystics set the world of good, of light, incarnated in blond, blue-eyed people who were supposed to be the sources of all capacity for creating civilization.... Now these two worlds were alleged to be locked in a perpetual struggle.... The usual view of [Reichführer SS] Himmler is that he was an ice-cold cynical politician.... [In reality] Himmler was a mystic who embraced this world-view with religious fanaticism.[49]

Racial nationalism, a major element in nineteenth-century intellectual life, attacked and undermined the rational tradition of the Enlightenment. Racial nationalists denied equality, scorned toleration, and dismissed the idea of the oneness of humanity. They employed reason and science to demonize and condemn an entire people and to justify humiliation and persecution. They succeeded in presenting a racial ideology fraught with unreason and hate as something virtuous and idealistic, and made myth and superstition vital forces in political life. In 1933, the year Hitler came to power, Felix Goldmann, a German-Jewish writer, commented astutely on the irrational quality of racial antisemitism: "The present-day politicized racial anti-Semitism is the embodiment of myth,...nothing is discussed...only felt,...nothing is pondered critically, logically or reasonably,...only inwardly perceived, surmised.... We are apparently the last...of the age of the Enlightenment."[50] That many people, including intellectuals and members of the elites, believed these racial theories was an ominous sign for Western civilization. It showed how tenuous the rational tradition of the Enlightenment is, how receptive the mind is to dangerous myths, and how speedily human behavior can degenerate into inhumanity. Ending in the Holocaust, racist thinking constitutes a radical counter-ideology to the highest Western values, both Christian and humanist. For this reason, the Holocaust is the central event of the twentieth century, or as a Jewish prayer expresses it: "Auschwitz is the fact and symbol of our era."

Endnotes

1. While it is true that several philosophes, notably Voltaire, expressed antisemitism, nevertheless, the Enlightenment provided the theoretical justification for Jewish emancipation, which the French Revolution enacted. Emancipated Jews generally aspired to integrate into the majority while still retaining their Jewish identity. Many Gentiles, on the other hand, hoped that emancipation would lead Jews to abandon their faith.

2. But most European Jews—peasants, peddlers, laborers—were quite poor. Statistics for the Jews of Paris, 1800–1870, show that over 60 percent died paupers. Perhaps 5,000 to 6000 Jews of Galicia in Austria-Hungary died annually of starvation, and many Russian Jews fled to the United States to escape desperate poverty. The antisemites, however, saw only "Jewish influence," "Jewish manipulation," "Jewish domination," "Rothschild power."

3. "European Jewry Before and After Hitler," *American Jewish Yearbook*, 63 (1962): 34.

4. Quoted in Robert F. Byrnes, *Anti-Semitism in Modern France* (New York: Howard Fertig, 1969), 202.

5. Quoted in Léon Poliakov, *The History of Anti-Semitism* (New York: Vanguard, 1975), 3:374.

6. Poliakov (n. 5), 3:376.

7. Quoted in Walter Laqueur, *A History of Zionism* (New York: Holt, Rinehart & Winston, 1972), 388–389.

8. Excerpted in Arthur Hertzberg, ed., *The Zionist Idea: An Historical Analysis and Reader* (New York: Meridian, 1960), 120–121.

9. Excerpted in Paul W. Massing, *A Study of Political Anti-Semitism* (New York: American Jewish Committee and Harper & Row, 1949), 147.

10. Quoted in Friedrich Meinecke, *The German Catastrophe* (Boston: Beacon, 1963), 23–24. Paulsen also opposed antisemitism, but like many other Germans he believed that it was impossible to "remain a complete Jew and a complete German."

11. This discussion of Volkish thought draws considerably from the works of George L. Mosse, particularly *The Crisis of German Ideology* (New York: Grosset & Dunlap Universal Library, 1964).

12. Robert G.L. Waite, *The Psychopathic God* (New York: Basic Books, 1977), 99, 103.

13. Quoted in Ernst Nolte, *Three Faces of Fascism* (New York: Holt, Rinehart & Winston, 1966), 43.

14. Excerpted in Michael D. Biddiss, ed., *Gobineau: Selected Political Writings* (New York: Harper Torchbooks, 1970), 41.

15. Hermann Rauschning, *Voice of Destruction* (New York: Putnam's, 1940), 229.

16. Quoted in Geoffrey G. Field, *Evangelist of Race: The Germanic Vision of Houston Stewart Chamberlain* (New York: Columbia University Press, 1981), 90.

17. Quoted in Field (n. 16), 189.

18. Quoted in Field (n. 16), 225.

19. Quoted in Field (n. 16), 437, 441.

20. See Patrick Girard, "Historical Foundations of Anti-Semitism," in Joel E. Dimsdale, ed., *Survivors, Victims, and Perpetrators* (Washington, DC: Hemisphere Publishing, 1980), 67; Shmuel Almog, *Nationalism and Antisemitism in Modern Europe, 1815–1945* (Oxford: Pergamon, 1990), 148.

21. Adolf Hitler, *Mein Kampf*, trans. Ralph Mannheim (Boston: Houghton Mifflin, 1962), 289, 296, 688.

22. Hitler (n. 21), 290, 295.

23. Hitler (n. 21), 390, 305, 316, 328.

24. Quoted in Almog (n. 20), 66.

25. Quoted in Michael Sutton, *Nationalism, Positivism and Catholicism: The Politics of Charles Maurras and French Catholics, 1890–1914* (Cambridge, UK: Cambridge University Press, 1982), 38.

26. Excerpted in J.S. McClelland, ed., *The French Right* (New York: Harper Torchbooks, 1971), 88, 91–92.

27. Hans Kohn, *Nationalism: Its Meaning and History* (Princeton, New Jersey: Van Nostrand Anvil Books, 1955), 77.

28. Chaim Weizmann, *Trial and Error* (London: Hamish Hamilton, 1949), 143; Arnold Zweig, *Insulted and Exiled: The Truth about the German Jews* (London: John Miles, 1937), passim.

29. Gershom Scholem, *On Jews and Judaism in Crisis* (New York: Schocken, 1976), 86.

30. Karl Dietrich Bracher, *The German Dictatorship* (New York: Praeger, 1970), 36.

31. Quoted in Gilmer W. Blackburn, *Education in the Third Reich* (Albany: State University of New York Press, 1985), 144.

32. Quoted in Jacob Katz, *The Darker Side of Genius: Richard Wagner's Anti-Semitism* (Hanover, New Hampshire: Brandeis University Press & University Press of New England, 1986), 19; see also Bryan Magee, *Aspects of Wagner* (New York: Stein and Day, 1969).

33. Quoted in Conor Cruise O'Brien, *The Siege* (London: Weidenfeld & Nicolson, 1986), 55.

34. Quoted in Jacob Katz, *From Prejudice to Destruction: Anti-Semitism, 1700–1933* (Cambridge, MA: Harvard University Press, 1980), 285.

35. Fritz Stern, *Gold and Iron: Bismarck, Bleichröder, and the Building of the German Empire* (New York: Knopf, 1977), 512.

36. Quoted in Katz, *From Prejudice to Destruction* (n. 34), 279.

37. Quoted in Katz, *The Darker Side of Genius* (n. 32), 35.

38. Quoted in Norman Cohn, *Warrant for Genocide: The Myth of the Jewish World Conspiracy and the Protocols of the Elders of Zion* (New York: Harper Torchbooks, 1967), 186–187.

39. Quoted in Cohn (n. 38), 209.

40. Quoted in Helmut Krausnick et al., eds., *Anatomy of the SS State* (London: Collins, 1968), 9.

41. Quoted in Richard S. Levy, *The Downfall of the Anti-Semitic Political Parties in Imperial Germany* (New Haven: Yale University Press, 1975), 83.

42. Quoted in Peter G.J. Pulzer, *The Rise of Political Anti-Semitism in Germany and Austria* (New York: Wiley, 1969), 299.

43. Albert Speer, *Inside the Third Reich* (New York: Macmillan, 1970), 112.

44. Quoted in Benno Müller-Hill, *Murderous Science* (Oxford: Oxford University Press, 1985), 46.

45. Fritz Stern, *Dreams and Delusions* (New York: Knopf, 1987), 123.

46. Rauschning (n. 15), 241.

47. Rauschning (n. 15), 147–148.

48. Quoted in Cohn (n. 38), 188.

49. Quoted in Cohn (n. 38), 180.

50. Quoted in Uriel Tal, "Consecration of Politics in the Nazi Era," in Otto Kulka and Paul R. Mendes-Flor, eds., *Judaism and Christianity under the Impact of National Socialism* (Jerusalem: The Historical Society of Israel and the Zalman Shazar Center, 1987), 70.

Suggestions For Further Reading

Cohn, Norman. *Warrant for Genocide: The Myth of the Jewish World Conspiracy and the Protocols of the Elders of Zion*. New York: Harper & Row, 1967. An illuminating discussion of the Protocols, tracing their roots to the Middle Ages.

Field, Geoffrey G. *Evangelist of Race: The Germanic Vision of Houston Stewart Chamberlain*. New York: Columbia University Press, 1981. The evolution and significance of Chamberlain's thought.

Katz, Jacob. *The Darker Side of Genius: Richard Wagner's Anti-Semitism*. Hanover, NH: Brandeis University Press & University Press of New England, 1986. Wagner's antisemitism.

____. *From Prejudice to Destruction*. Cambridge, MA: Harvard University Press, 1980. The close connection between traditional Christian antisemitism and modern racial-nationalist antisemitism.

Mosse, George L. *Toward the Final Solution*. New York: Fertig, 1978. An analysis of European racism.

____. *The Crisis of German Ideology*. New York: Grosset & Dunlap Universal Library, 1964. A valuable study of Volkish thought.

Pulzer, Peter G.J. *The Rise of Political Anti-Semitism in Germany and Austria*. New York: Wiley, 1964. Relationship of antisemitism to changing socioeconomic conditions; impact of antisemitism on politics.

Stern, Fritz. *Dreams and Delusions: The Drama of German History*. New York: Knopf, 1987. Penetrating essays on German and German-Jewish history, of which "The Burden of Success: Reflections on German Jewry" and "National Socialism as Temptation" are particularly relevant to the theme of modern antisemitism.

____. *Gold and Iron: Bismarck, Bleichröder, and the Building of the German Empire*. New York: Knopf, 1977. A magisterial study of Bismarck's thirty-year collaboration with his Jewish banker; Part III, on the "Anguish of Assimilation" and the "New Anti-Semitism" after 1873, is instructive.

Tal, Uriel. *Christians and Jews in Germany: Religion, Politics, and Ideology in the Second Reich, 1870–1914*. Ithaca: Cornell University Press, 1975. A work of great insight on the relations between Jews and Germans in the decades prior to World War I.

PHILOSEMITES COUNTER ANTISEMITISM IN CATHOLIC POLAND DURING THE NINETEENTH AND TWENTIETH CENTURIES

Celia S. Heller*

Jews have often spoken of Polish antisemitism. The depiction of the recurrent and widespread antisemitism often overshadows the fact that some Poles defended Jews against their traducers and persecutors. Celia S. Heller examines the phenomenon of philosemitism in Poland.

The broad theoretical basis of my study derives from the sociological empirical generalization that whenever a persecuted minority exists, there are some members of the majority who are positively disposed towards that minority. And indeed in examining the many centuries-long existence of the Jews in Poland, one finds that side by side with antisemitism there existed a counter current of philosemitism. Although it was far less prominent than antisemitism, it is important that historians and social scientists address themselves to this twin phenomenon in order to rectify the depiction of Poland as entirely antisemitic.

Proverbial among Jews as well as Poles in inter-war Poland was the case of King Casimir the Great (Kazimierz Wielki (1333–70). Although his positive attitude towards Jews was mainly part of his policy to attract foreign settlers whom he considered useful for the development of Poland, he had some personal sympathy for Jews. There is the story of his love for a Jewish woman, Esterke, with whom he supposedly had four children.[1] Less known among Poles but widely circulated among Jews was the story of Count Walentyn Potocki, a scion

---

* This essay is based on research supported by the Littauer Foundation and the Memorial Foundation for Jewish Culture.

of the celebrated Potocki family, who became a Jew and took the name of Abraham ben Abraham. For this he was put on trial and was burned at the stake in 1749 in Vilno (now Vilnius). Some Jews of Vilno marked the anniversary of Potocki's death by reciting the Kaddish and by making pilgrimages to his alleged grave.[2]

Apart from such stories, little if anything has been written about philosemitism in Poland or elsewhere.[3] This being the case, it becomes especially proper to begin with an attempt to conceptualize the term. I am using this word as a referent to a broad sociological concept, similar to the general use by historians of the term antisemitism for the opposite concept. Philosemitism refers to positive beliefs about and positive attitudes or actions towards Jews (*ergo*, philosemites are individuals who manifest these). Furthermore, in this essay I shall approach the phenomenon of philosemitism not from the subjective side but from the objective one. Subjectively, an individual might not think of himself as a lover of Jews (the Greek meaning of the term) and yet be a philosemite in the sociological sense of this term in so far as he treats Jews positively, opposes anti-Jewish stereotypes, and objects to differential (negative) treatment of Jews.

Now this distinction is especially relevant to my subject because the word philosemite has been more widely recognized and used in Poland than in the United States. And it is not uncommon for Poles so designated to object by saying that they are not philosemites. A historical example is that of J. Baudouin de Courtney, one of the founders of modern linguistics, who began a lecture in Warsaw in February of 1913 by emphasizing that he was not a philosemite: all that he wanted was that Jews be treated as individuals. But his presentation was largely a plea for Poles to put aside their negative stereotypes of Jews and to accord them equal rights and equal treatment. As he put it: "All of you who inoculate antisemitism into minds of children (none is born an antisemite), who scare the little ones...and teach them to hold Jews in contempt and to step aside from them, you accustom your children not to see a human being in the Jew."[4] Similarly, I have encountered a few Poles who felt a bit bothered when I implied that they were philosemites, asserting that they are rather believers in ethnic equality.

In writing about the philosemites of Poland, I must confine myself mostly to prominent individuals since few data are available about their existence in the general population. It is important to recall that between 1795 and 1918, the end of World War I, Poland did not exist as an independent state. (It was under the rule of Russia, Prussia/Germany, and Austria.) Philosemitism during that period was tied to the struggle for independence and was part of the quest for equal rights for all the inhabitants of Poland. It manifested itself among those who struggled for these objectives in exile abroad as well as on the territories of former Poland. Still, it should be added in this context that negative attitudes, feelings, and behavior towards Jews predominated among Poles at home and abroad.[5]

In the Nineteenth Century

In September of 1808 in the short-lived Grand Duchy of Warsaw, 1807–12, a decree was issued depriving the Jews of the right to vote for the Sejm (diet, parliament) and the following month, a decree was passed denying the Jews all political and civil rights. The general view of those favoring such decrees stripping Jews of political and civil rights was that Jews, although born in Poland, were in custom and religion foreigners. They first had to become "enlightened" in order to be granted citizenship and equal rights. (Parenthetically, the same argument was used in the nineteenth century on the question of the peasants' emancipation.) The opposite stand was taken by philosemites. They held that Jews had to be given such rights at once because, among other things, it would lead to their general enlightenment. They pointed to the West where Jews were emancipated and, as a result, they said, civilized and assimilated.[6]

The clash of these two approaches persisted throughout the nineteenth century in the Congress Kingdom of Poland, a semi-autonomous entity in the Russian Empire which came into being as a result of the Congress of Vienna in 1815. It also characterized the Polish emigrés abroad. Prior to and during the November uprising, 1830–31, it took the form of a polemic on whether Jews should be allowed to participate in the Polish independence movement.[7] Foremost among those who maintained that they definitely should be was the great and internationally known poet Adam Mickiewicz. He maintained that Israel, as "the older brother," should have the same rights in Poland as a Pole, including the right of his own religion and customs. In his best known work, the celebrated *Pan Tadeusz*, he painted a very sympathetic portrait of the Jew Jankiel, as indigenous to Poland. In the poet's words Jankiel "loved the fatherland like a Pole." Mickiewicz's idea was to create a Jewish legion and he worked hard to realize it. After he died in 1855, his friend, Armand Levy, devoted himself to realizing the Mickiewicz dream of a Jewish legion but he did not succeed.[8]

In the 1850s a vicious campaign against the Jews was conducted in the Polish press. To the old arguments that they were foreign and uncouth, was added the allegation that the tremendous growth of the Jewish population spelled a great danger to the land. But even then there were voices sympathetic to Jews. To them belonged that of Joachim Lelewel, the foremost Polish historian, who from exile in Belgium spoke out firmly for Jewish equality. Also worthy of mention is Antoni Żybicki, editor of the *Polish Democrat*, organ of the Polish Democratic Society, issued abroad, first in France and then in England. He ran a long article in defense of the Jews, calling for their complete emancipation and integration. As he expressed it, "because we place the hope of the independence of the fatherland only in the unity of all social strata, we consider harmful every manifestation of hostility towards Jews."[9]

A pro-Jewish stand characterized the planners of the January 1863 insurrection. In the appeal to their "brothers of Mosaic faith," they promised them equality in the resurrected Poland to come. As they set forth the principle: "You and your children will have all citizenship rights, without any exceptions or limitations. The national government will not inquire about one's religion or descent but only about his place of birth."[10] But the insurrection failed and what followed its defeat was a new era of Polish history. After the dashed hopes of freedom, young Polish patriots turned away from romantic nationalism and towards the idea of positivism, which became the prevalent ideology. They now saw the solution of Poland's weaknesses and ills in the economic development of the country. Many of them viewed the Jews as capable of playing an important role in this development. Polish positivism found its expression in the literary movement of that day whose exponents were mostly writers, poets, and publicists. They called for equal rights and equal treatment of Jews.[11] Among the foremost fighters for Jewish equality were the novelists Bolesław Prus and Eliza Orzeszkowa. Both campaigned tirelessly against the degradation of Jews and for their emancipation, pointing to the commendable characteristics of the Jewish population in Poland.

In contrast to the press which was mostly antisemitic, the novels, short stories, and poems of the positivist period depicted Jews in an affirmative way. As Aleksander Hertz put it, "the Jew figures frequently in Polish *belles lettres*. The attitude towards him is most often friendly and sometimes very warm. In this respect Polish literature is different from Polish folk art and Polish political journalism."[12]

Jewish characters appeared in almost all the major novels of Polish positivism. Religious Jews and their rabbis were painted as noble biblical characters. It was argued that, on the basis of values inherent in both Judaism and Christianity, these Jews identified themselves with Poles in the struggle for freedom. The literature also pointed to the similar historical and spiritual experiences of Poles and Jews: "The fall of insurrectionary Warsaw was compared to that of Jerusalem. Poland was referred to as Zion; the Polish freedom fighters were identified with the Maccabees; the pain and humiliation of defeat found their equivalents in biblical imagery such as the Babylonian exile and destruction of the Temple."[13]

Since the Middle Ages the Talmud had been attacked in Poland as instructing Jews in wickedness and evil. But the prominent positivist writer Józef Ignacy Kraszewski embarked on its unprecedented defense in his novel, *The Jew*. He presented the teachings of the Talmud as compatible with good Polish-Jewish relations, defended it against false accusations, and commended its noble ideals.[14]

Soon a broad reaction set in against positivism: the Polish conservatives accused the positivists of betraying the venerable Polish ideal of nationhood. The Catholic Church condemned it as weakening the religious fibre of the nation. To radicals, influenced by socialist ideas, positivism was the philosophy of economic exploitation. And the populists asserted that under the cloak of economic positivism, foreigners—such as Jews and Germans—became enriched, while the Polish people remained impoverished. The assassination of Czar Alexander II in 1881 was followed by anti-Jewish violence in Congress Poland, as well as in Russia. Anti-Jewish sentiments flourished and the atmosphere of the 1880s in Poland was charged with hate and violence.[15] But there were some Poles who rose in defense of the Jews. The following words of the novelist Eliza Orzeszkowa testify to this:

> In case of outbreaks, which are very probable among us, we have decided to defend and protect with all our might the wronged ones. The stupid and dark masses will probably embark on crimes and madness. But let at least a *handful* of Polish intelligentsia protest before mankind and history not only with words and deeds, but with our lives. I for one and a few more are ready, even if we are to perish, to stand between the raging wave and the doors of the victims [italics supplied].[16]

In Inter-War Poland

In the twentieth century and especially in the inter-war period the figure of Józef Piłsudski, the hero of Polish independence, looms large. Prior to independence, in his socialist period, some of his closest collaborators in the Polish Socialist Party were Jews, like, for example, Feliks Perl. In a party publication, *Walka* (*The Struggle*), Piłsudski appealed in 1903 to workers to set aside their prejudices against Jews and to fight together with them for the end of oppression. He wrote:

> ...the less antisemitism will exist among Christians, the easier it will be to unite the social forces..., and the sooner a workers' solidarity will emerge: a solidarity of all who are exploited and wronged. Jew, Pole, Lithuanian, we are equally exploited...we are all equally wronged by Moscow.... Let us encourage Jewish comrades whenever we meet them.[17]

In independent Poland during Piłsudski's rule Jews held responsible positions in the army, in the government, in the judiciary, and in diplomacy.[18] In the 1920s many Jewish refugees fled to Poland from the Baltic states, Russia, and Ukraine, increasing the large Jewish population. The minister of the interior, General Składkowski, and many others in the administration referred to them as second class citizens. When in the fall of 1926, the general discussed this "problem" with Piłsudski, he received a directive from him to recognize these refugees as full citizens. Piłsudski emphasized that Poland could not afford second class citizens.[19]

Piłsudski abhorred antisemitism, yet in his passionate Polish patriotism showed certain mixed feelings towards Jews: on the one hand, his warm remembrance and approval of those Jews who contributed to Polish independence, and on the other, his hurt resentment of those in the border areas who cooperated with the Bolsheviks.[20] Piłsudski's resentment of those Jews who sided with the Russians dated back to the end of the nineteenth century. As a young socialist, he had published an appeal in 1893 "to the Jewish Socialist comrades in the dislodged Polish provinces." He warned about the rising antisemitism among Poles as a result of the Russification of the Jewish intelligentsia, especially in the former Grand Duchy of Lithuania.[21]

In the inter-war period, the chief bastion of antisemitism was the National Party, commonly referred to as *Endecja,* which Roman Dmowski shaped and whose chief theoretician he remained for a long time. Central to Polish nationalism, as it crystallized before and became dominant during independence, was the idea of the Polish nation-state as the organic entity growing out of the soil, blood ties, Catholic Church, folkways, and memories. Thus, to the National Party the Jews of Poland represented the specter of a state within a state. The *Endecja* was consistent and persistent in its solution to all Poland's ills: freeing the country from Jews.

Antisemitism was not a manifestation of the lunatic fringe only; it was respectable and in the forefront of political affairs. This fact must be grasped in order to understand how pervasive Polish antisemitism really was in the inter-war period. Anti-Jewish feelings, beliefs, attitudes, and activities constituted a strong link among diverse elements of the Polish nation. Still, *political* opposition to antisemitism did exist, primarily the Polish Socialist Party (*PPS*) and the Polish Communist Party. The *PPS* cooperated with the Jewish socialist parties—mostly with the Jewish Bund and sometimes with the Zionist *Poale Zion*—in their fight against concrete anti-Jewish measures. In the last years before World War II, this party vigorously attacked the government's policy of official antisemitism. Among the prominent *PPS* members who stood up for Jews were Adam Ciołkosz (who learned Yiddish and addressed Jewish workers in that language) and Zygmunt Żuławski, Vice-Marshal of the *Sejm.*

Whether as a matter of tactics (to attract Jews to the party) or as a matter of principle, the Communist Party during the inter-war period was consistent in its condemnation of antisemitism as a tool of the ruling class (including Jewish capitalists) which they used to split the natural unity of the working class.[22]

The political opposition to the anti-Jewish campaign became increasingly confined to the Polish Left, which commanded the allegiance of only a small part of the Catholic population. The exception was the Democratic Clubs (founded in 1937) and their successor, the Democratic Party (1938) which fought antisemitism as part of their struggle to rescue Polish democracy from the fatal assault upon it by the forces of extreme nationalism and by the government itself.[23] The Democratic Party attracted outstanding individuals of different ideological shadings, as well as some who had previously been nonpolitical. Among the best known names of members of this organization—popularly known as the "Party of the Progressive Intelligentsia"—who spoke out against antisemitism were Colonel January Grzedzíński, Professor Marcel Handelsman, and the diplomat, Tytus Filipowicz.

Among Poles who courageously continued their association with Jews and who as individuals spoke out against the promoters of brutal methods were not only leftists, but also conservatives, liberals, and some without political identification. In the forefront were the Greek Catholic Bishop Grzegorz Chomyszyn, the writer Maria Dąbrowska and some prominent scholars, such as the sociologist Stefan Czarnowski, the philosopher Tadeusz Kotarbiński, the geophysicist and pioneer of higher public education Atoni Bołesław Dobrowolski, the classicist Tadeusz Ganszyniec, and the linguist Henryk Ułaszyn.[24] Among the people who could not be intimidated was one of the best known novelists in Poland, Maria Kuncewiczowa. In response to an article in the radical nationalist periodical *Prosto z Mostu*, which had attacked her for actively supporting Jews, she wrote:

> Jews today are placed outside the law. In their misery, who will support them?... The blood of my forefathers spilled for Poland in the Dąbrowski Legion, in prisons and in uprisings, as well as my own conscience, give me the right to want an honorable Poland, chivalrous and Christian. In such a Poland I believe and I shall never betray her.[25]

In the inter-war period Polish universities became the stage of the most extreme antisemitic activities. From the very beginning of independence, social antisemitism was dominant: the university dormitories were run by fraternities which excluded Jews. In the 1930's an anti-Jewish political campaign became widespread. Its focus was agitation for a *numerus clausus*, an exclusionary Jewish quota. The university administrators abdicated to sowers of hate: a stringent Jewish exclusionary quota was openly instituted at all the schools of higher learning in order to "bring peace" to the university.

In 1937 classroom seating ghettos, separate seats for Jews, were established. A minority of brave Polish teachers—conservative as well as liberal—opposed the introduction of seating ghettos. They were often insulted and bodily attacked by militants. Among them were such leading professors as the geophysicist Stanisław Kalinowski, the philosopher Tadeusz Kotarbińsky, the sociologist Ludwik Krzywicki, and a professor of medicine, Mieczysław Michałowicz. A devout Catholic, Michałowicz pleaded as "a Senator of the Polish Republic who swore to uphold the Constitution" and as one who in his "conscience wants to remain a faithful Christian": "If God did not hesitate to put the spirit of His Son in a Semite's body, it is not for us humans to decide who is better or worse."[26]

But Catholic organizations and the Catholic press were among the most effective propagandists of the anti-Jewish cause: "In no other country did such a massive 'Catholic' Jew devouring literature exist as in Poland."[27] Among those who encouraged and produced such literature was Father Maksymilian Kolbe, who after the war was crowned with sainthood by Pope John Paul II for his heroic act of sacrificing himself for another Pole at Auschwitz. This Franciscan before the war opened a publishing center at the monastery in Niepokalanów near Warsaw. It propagated clerical antisemitism in many of its publications, among them the *Little Daily* (*Mały Dziennik*), directed at a wide reading public.[28]

Catholic priests figured prominently among the authors of antisemitic literature. One of the most prolific was Józef Kruszyński, the author of the *Talmud, What it Contains and What it Teaches*. It was a compendium of lies and distortions presented as the teachings of the Talmud that supposedly instructed Jews in wickedness. But the prominent Polish orientalist Tadeusz Zaderecki (who knew Hebrew) energetically refuted these fabrications in his book *Talmud w Ogniu Wieków* (*The Talmud in the Fire of the Ages*).[29] Unfortunately the mass-circulation publications ignored it, and therefore it did not reach many Poles who were generally so influenced by the calumny against the Talmud that its very name caused discomfort.

What did reach most Poles was the message against the Jews of Poland by the head of the Polish Church: It was no longer left to the discretion of individual priests and bishops whether to engage in anti-Jewish teaching and preaching. In 1936, the primate of Poland came out openly in support of the anti-Jewish campaign. August Cardinal Hlond, in a pastoral letter read from the pulpits of most churches, gave his spiritual blessing to Polish antisemitism:

> It is a fact that the Jews fight against the Catholic Church, they are free-thinkers, and constitute the vanguard of atheism, of the bolshevik movement and of revolutionary activity. It is a fact that Jewish influence upon morals is fatal, and their publishers spread pornographic literature. It is true that the Jews are committing frauds, practicing usury, and dealing in white slavery. It is true that in schools, the influence of the Jewish youth upon the Catholic youth is generally evil.... One does well to prefer his own kind in commercial dealings and to avoid Jewish stores and Jewish stalls in the markets.... One ought to fence oneself off against the harmful moral influences of Jewry, to separate oneself against its anti-Christian culture, and especially to boycott the Jewish press and the demoralizing Jewish publications.[30]

However, the Cardinal added that "it is not permissible to assault Jews, to hit, maim or blacken them," while Polish young adults and youths—led by high school and university students— were engaging widely in such activities. One should note that this pastoral letter was issued a year before the government formally announced its antisemitic policy through the Ideological Declaration of the Camp of National Unity. Actually, the pastoral letter expressed substantially how far the Polish nation had travelled down the antisemitic road by the beginning of 1936.

In light of this official call by the head of the church to the faithful Catholic nation, it is not surprising to learn that the appeals and supplications of the philosemites turned out to be voices in the wilderness. The writer Aleksander Świętochowski could not be counted among the friends of Jews, but he correctly conveyed the reaction of most Poles to the denunciation of antisemitism by a few prominent Poles:

> The Jews and their defenders...unfold in vivid images the monstrosity of their [the antisemitic terrorists'] acts; they remind the Polish people of a whole catechism of religious commandments and a whole code of civil duties [but]...most people do not care and, if they do, they harbor loud or quiet sympathy and recognition for the antisemitic perpetrators.[31]

Salient from a sociological perspective is the fact even among the Polish philosemites who courageously opposed antisemitism, there were few who in their thinking could go beyond religious pluralism and admit the validity of cultural pluralism. The same could be said about the Polish Socialist Party. While it consistently opposed antisemitism, it refused to recognize the Jews as a separate national group and insisted on their eventual full assimilation into the Polish nation which would take place under democratic socialism.[32] The idea of Jewish cultural distinctiveness, that a separate Jewish nationality could be fostered on Polish soil, was unacceptable to most opponents of antisemitism. They were convinced that full Polonization of the Jewish masses would eventually take place in a democratic and tolerant Poland. Antisemitism, they were sure, was playing a major role in slowing the process of Polonization, especially among the Jewish masses. They thought it natural that in a democratic Poland, enlightened Jews would prefer Polish to Jewish ways.

Among the small number of fighters against antisemitism whose vision extended beyond religious pluralism to cultural pluralism were the publicist Tadeusz Hołówko, the philosopher Count Dunin-Borkowski, the writer Stanisław Vincenz, and the gifted essayist and reporter Ksawery Pruszyński.[33] The last maintained that the Jewish question was above all a moral question: whether people have the right to determine their own destiny. He put forth the advanced idea that the Jews themselves should have the right to decide how much they wished to participate in the larger society. Thus he maintained that assimilation, Zionism, and Orthodoxy were equally valid. Accordingly, he urged the Polish government to refrain from taking sides in the matter and to leave it completely to the individual Jews to decide which road they wanted to follow. Pruszyński perceived with unusual clarity the negative effects of organized antisemitism on the country at large. He pointed out, for example, how much more beneficial it would be if Jews were allowed to develop Poland's industry instead of being squeezed out of it. Warning against the impoverishment of Polish arts and sciences, he emphasized the tremendous contributions that individuals of Jewish background had made to Polish culture.[34]

During the Holocaust

The help that some Poles extended to Jews during the Holocaust period is well documented in a few scholarly books as well as numerous memoirs of survivors.[35] Their help is especially noteworthy because in aiding Jews these Poles risked their own lives and those of their spouses and children. More than a few of them were beaten, tortured, and killed by the Germans. The Jewish people have recognized the debt they owe to these exceptional Poles by planting trees in their memory at Yad Vashem and bestowing upon them the title of honor, "Righteous Among the Nations." By doing so they have not absolved in any measure those Poles who could and did not help, the many who gloated over the misery of the Jews, or the fewer who from naked hate or for private gain reported Jews in hiding to the enemy. The "Righteous Poles" included individuals from all walks of life, from the very humble to proud aristocrats. Among the prominent Poles of this type who survived the war are Władysław Bartoszewski—known abroad for his post-war writings about the Holocaust—and Stanisław W. Dobrowolski—the scion of a distinguished Cracow family—who became a lawyer and diplomat after the war's end.[36] During the war both were leaders in the underground Council of Aid to Jews (*Rada Pomocy Żydom*, commonly referred to during the war years as *Żegota*), headed by Julian Grobelny, a member of *PPS*. The first led the Warsaw branch and the latter the Cracow one. This organization came into being towards the end of 1942 and the beginning of 1943 at the initiative of the Polish Government-in-exile (known as the London Government) to organize help for and rescue Jews from Nazi persecution and annihilation. Invited to participate in its formation were all underground political parties.

It should be pointed out that, to its credit, before the Polish government-in-exile initiated the foundation of this committee, it was informed by the head of the partisan army in Poland (*Armia Krajowa*) of the reigning antisemitism among the conquered Polish population:

> A crushing majority of the country is antisemiticly disposed. The existing differences concern only the practice and procedure: there are almost none who advocate the emulation of German methods. Even the most radical underground organizations, under the in-

> fluence of prewar activists...accept the postulate of emigration as the solution of the Jewish question. This is obvious to all, similar to the necessity of removing the Germans from our country.[37]

Among the first to take up the government's call for forming a committee to aid Jews was the prominent Catholic writer Zofia Kossak Szczucka, whose anti-Jewish views were known in pre-war Poland. Portentously a few months earlier, in August of 1942, she issued an acerbic call concerning the Jews in the name of the underground Catholic organization which she headed, appealing "to the heart and conscience of all Poles who believe in God":

> He who is silent in face of murder becomes a partner in crime. He who does not condemn, approves.... We Catholic Poles therefore raise our voice. *Our feelings towards Jews have not changed. We do not cease to consider them political, economic, and ideological enemies of Poland.* Moreover, we are aware that they hate us more than they do the Germans, that they hold us responsible for their adversities. The awareness of these feelings does not, however, free us from the duty to condemn the crime [italics supplied].[38]

There is ample evidence that such sentiments were not uncommon among those members of the Catholic clergy who helped Jews. *Żegota* placed Jewish children in orphanages run by such clergy as well as the few among them who were not prejudiced against Jews. It also found some individual homes of friendly and courageous Poles who were willing to hide Jewish children, especially infants. In addition, the organization concentrated on producing authentic-looking "Aryan papers" in order to smuggle selected Jews into the "Aryan side." According to Dobrowolski, it took the involvement of up to ten Poles to rescue one Jew.[39]

Under Post-War Communism

These Polish fighters who risked their lives for Jews were not honored in the communist Poland that followed the war. On the contrary, they were excluded from the Veterans Organization, *ZBoWiD*, and individual efforts by former *Żegota* members to join the organization on the grounds of having fought against the Nazi occupiers met with no success. Those of them who did win any decorations received them only from Israel as "Righteous Gentiles"! Commenting on these occurrences in his memoir published towards the end of communist rule in Poland, Dobrowolski asked this rhetorical question: "Is this just? Does a Pole who during four years risked his life to protect Jewish fellow citizens deserve recognition as a fighter against the Hitlerite occupation or does he not?"[40]

The neglect of Polish heroes who aided Jews was part of a larger pattern: the fulfillment of the anti-Jewish communist line, some details of which will emerge in the course of my forthcoming discussion of post-war Poland. It must be stressed that the small numbers of Jews who survived Nazi destruction on Polish soil, (about 50,000) and the larger number who returned from the Soviet Union (about 200,000) faced much hostility. Those who came out of hiding to return to their homes and towns were often threatened and sometime murdered.[41] As for those who came back from the Soviet Union, I interviewed a number of them and learned how they were greeted by some Poles when they disembarked from the trains that brought them to Western Silesia (the German territory ceded to Poland in compensation for the Ukrainian and Lithuanian territories annexed by the Soviets). Such remarks as "the rats have come out from hiding," or "I thought you were dead, what are you doing in Poland?" were not uncommon.

However, again there were other Poles, individuals who were deeply concerned about the gruesome truth that antisemitism did not decrease in Poland, despite the fact that the bulk of its Jewish population had perished in such a monstrous way. Some of these solicitous Poles formed the All-Polish League for the Fight against Racism (*Ogólnopolska Liga do Walki z Rasizmem*). Its first president was the socialist leader Julian Górecki and the next, the writer Zofia Nałkowska, the general secretary was the democrat, Mark Ferdynand Urczyński, and his deputy the above-mentioned Stanisław W. Dobrowolski, the former head of the wartime Cracow Council for Aid to Jews.[42] But their work was "neutralized": the country was run by Stalinists, cynical in their pacification and their manipulation of antisemitism in order to ingratiate themselves with the Polish people and thus gain power over them. To cite perhaps an extreme example, at the head of the Chief Commission to Investigate Hitlerite Crime was put Czesław Pilichowski, a prominent member of the pre-war fascist group *ONR* (National Radical Camp) which, inspired by the Nazis, had proclaimed a program to deprive all Jews of Polish citizenship, expropriate their property, and expel them from Poland.[43]

And so the much rumored pogroms were not prevented: they were organized in a number of towns (Cracow, Chełm, Rzeszów and others), of which the one in Kielce became the best known. About 200 Jews returned to this town and they attempted to reconstruct a community, even if undersized, on the ashes of the pre-war one that consisted of around 18,000 members out of a total population of 60,000. When attacked, they could not defend themselves because the few defensive weapons they possessed were confiscated by the police a day before the pogrom took place on July 4, 1946. As a result, 42 Jews were killed and some wounded. Similar to prewar times, this pogrom—as well as all the others—started with accusations of ritual murder and blood libel. (The "tortured and murdered" boy of Kielce was hidden away by the organizers of the pogrom and found alive afterwards.)[44] Think of it, after rivers of blood of hundreds of thousands of Jews soaked Polish soil (before the gassing of millions began), the medieval blood accusation was raised once again against the Jews!

The pogroms were not officially condemned by the Catholic Church although the *Tygodnik Powszechny*, the intellectual Catholic weekly, did protest and appeal to Poles to stop the carnage of the Jewish remnant.[45] News of the pogroms prompted many of the Jewish survivors to flee *illegally*, risking their lives, for refugee camps in Austria and Germany (former German concentration camps) in the hope of eventually being able to go to Palestine (Israel did not exist yet).[46] But about 85,000 continued to live in Poland, many lured by the promise of a just socialist society. Among them were those who did not leave Poland because they considered it their moral duty to try to reconstruct Jewish life, even on a tiny scale, in the country where a Jewish community had existed for almost a millennium. Then there were the people who did not depart because they were too old, too sick, or too tired to embark on a new journey. More numerous than this last category were those individuals who stayed on because they considered themselves Poles: they were linguistically, culturally, and identificationally Polish. Some were married to Catholic Poles. Many of them had been communists or communist sympathizers before World War II.

But then, nearly a decade after the pogroms, a great new wave of antisemitism surfaced, during the "Polish October" of 1956 when de-Stalinization was launched in Poland. (This was consistent with the pattern of modern Polish history: anti-Jewish manifestations accompany major social changes.) It resulted in many Jewish cooperative enterprises folding up, especially in the former German "Recovered Territories." When Władysław Gomulka, who became the new head of Poland during de-Stalinization, allowed Jews to go to Israel, over half of them departed.

The ones who were left, about 30,000, were confined almost entirely to the category described above: individuals who considered themselves to be Poles. Their self-identity was either *not* Jewish or minimally Jewish. They achieved top or middle positions in the government and its bureaucracy, in the ruling party, in the army, in the intelligentsia, and in the academic and other professions. Nevertheless, ten years after the people who felt Jewish had left Poland, a vicious antisemitic campaign was unleashed against those self-defined "Poles" or "Poles of Jewish descent" under the guise of anti-Zionism. Their tragedy was that, although most of them celebrated their Polishness and tore Jewishness out of their minds and hearts, they were singled out as pariah Jews; although they championed, supported, or accepted communism, they were branded as enemy Zionists. The defeat of the Arabs in the Six-Day War of 1967 marked, among other things, the appearance of an indurated anti-Israel and anti-Zionist drive in the Soviet Union and some of the other eastern European countries. The drive also achieved a measure of prominence in New Left circles in the United States and western Europe.[47] But in Poland it came at the end of the phase of communist liberalization and turned into one of the most extensive witch hunts in the history of that country. It began with an attack on and purge of a few people in top positions in the party, in the army, and in public life but soon it broadened to include individuals of Jewish origin in all walks of life. They were harassed and pressured to provide proofs of loyalty to the state and party, proofs, which when given, failed to exonerate them.[48] Antisemitic insults were hurled at individuals of Jewish or partially Jewish descent. The students protesting peacefully against the end of liberalization and the tightening of controls in Poland were alleged to be misled into insurrection and counter-revolution by clever traitorous Zionist plotters. They were mercilessly suppressed. When students who were "real Poles" were interrogated by the police, they were asked such questions as "why did you tie yourself to these filthy Jews?" (*plugawymi Żydami*) or "why did you allow yourself to be used by these kikes?" (*Mośki*).[49] Their "Zionist" leaders were arrested and put on trial. Their parents—sometimes prominent communists—were removed from their jobs, as were other individuals of Jewish origin. All these were urged to leave Poland, but permission to do so was given only if they renounced Polish citizenship and applied for exit-passes to Israel. (Many who did so changed course in Vienna.)

Of particular interest to social scientists and historians is to learn that the anti-Jewish drive was essentially not the manifestation of an ethnic problem (from the objective rather than subjective approach): in contrast to the pre-war years marked by major ethnic groups, in 1967–68 Poland was ethnically almost homogenous and contained a very small number of people of Jewish descent. The anti-Jewish occurrences were manifestations of the struggle of various factions within the Polish political elite, operating in the context of Poland's position in the Soviet orbit.[50] They also differed from the earlier ones in communist Poland in that they were part of an official policy, openly proclaimed at party and mass meetings, as well as in the mass media (rather than secret machinations of certain powerful communists).

The fact that the campaign was given a different name, that of "anti-Zionism," did not prevent the Polish people from recognizing it as antisemitism. The following saying circulated in Poland:

Question: What is the difference between present-day and pre-war antisemitism?
Answer: Before the was it was not compulsory.

And indeed my content analysis of the Polish communist daily paper, *Trybuna Ludu*, bears out the saying just quoted. The 1968 "anti-Zionist" propaganda contained all the major themes of the organized pre-war antisemitic campaign in Poland.[51] Thus the "anti-Zionist" campaign in Poland demonstrated impressively that the ideology of Marxism-Leninism did not deter the communists from using antisemitism as a political weapon. All that was needed was another name, a euphemism for antisemitism, to avoid transgressing the ideology.

Because it recognized the "anti-Zionist" campaign for what it was, antisemitism by another name, does not mean that the Polish public disapproved of it. On the contrary, there was little sympathy for the "Jews" who despite their small number in the general population constituted a sizable proportion in Poland's communist elite.[52] One of the strongest myths, quite widespread in all strata of the Polish population, even the intelligentsia, was that these "Jews" were responsible for the economic and other difficulties that the Polish nation was facing: the "Jews" in high positions in Warsaw. Therefore, they tended to see the March 1968 campaign as a successful attempt to transform their country into "the Poland of Poles." And this perhaps explains the, apparently unprecedented, lack of any prominent Poles who defended the "so-called" Jews. I say "so-called" because, as I already indicated, with minor exceptions, they had given up their Jewish identity, still more their Jewish religion. What accounted for the oppressive activities of those who were part of the communist elite was not their origin or the religion into which they had been born, but their communist ideology and indoctrination. It will take a long time, if ever, for the Poles to recognize this!

During a large part of communist rule in Poland, the subjects of Jewish history, Jewish culture, and Jewish consciousness were largely taboo. Eradicated was the memory of the Jewish struggle and of Jewish martyrdom during the Nazi period. The Polish government, like the Soviet one to whom it owed its existence, decreed that the Jews could not be cited as *particular* victims of the Nazis in writings and commemorations of that period. For example, the special nature of the Warsaw Ghetto Uprising of 1943 could not be mentioned. The uprising was depicted as part of "the national Polish struggle against forces of racism and fascism."[53]

The silence was broken dramatically by Pope John Paul II when, during his first visit to Poland on June 7, 1979, he made a pilgrimage to what he called the heart of cruelty and hate, to Auschwitz. There in the captions and exhibits, the term Jew hardly appeared. But the Pope found an inscription in Hebrew, paused before it and said to the crowd that followed him:

> In particular I pause...before the inscription in Hebrew. This inscription awakens the memory of the people whose sons and daughters were marked for total destruction. This people draws its origin from Abraham, our father in faith.... *It is not permissible for any one to pass this inscription with indifference* [italics supplied].[54]

Poland's rulers could not even attempt to still the voice of the pope but they did try to silence the poet, Jerzy Ficowski, who did not "neutralize" his memory of the Jewish tragedy that he witnessed as a youth. He was "frequently and generously endowed with bans," to quote Zbigniew Herbert, his friend and fellow poet (the latter of Jewish origin). Ficowski continued to gaze at the "ashes" and to give "artistically convincing shape to what cannot be embraced by words..." His poems project how this Pole misses the Jews who had been so much part of the Polish landscape and Polish life:

> and I wander round cemeteries
> which are not there
> I look for words
> which are not there....
> to rescue after the event.[55]

Perhaps more than Ficowski's poems (mostly published underground in Poland), an article in the esteemed Catholic weekly, *Tygodnik Powszechny*, which appeared towards the end of communist rule in Poland—in January of 1987—became a sort of sensation: it bore the title "The Poor Poles Look at the Ghetto" and was written by Jan Błoński. This prominent Catholic dared to raise the forbidden issue of the role that Poles had played in the destruction of Polish Jewry. To realize how he shook up the Poles by this act, one must bear in mind that they, in general, and their intelligentsia, in particular, wash their hands of this iniquitous crime committed on their soil. Statements that the Poles played a part in the *Shoah* are regarded by them as a part of the anti-Polish plot to discredit Poland abroad. After all there were Poles who saved Jews, thus risking their own and their families' lives, they argue. And the reason why more Poles did not help, they say, is that they feared for their lives. But here was Jan Błoński, a "real Pole"—a distinguished professor of literature at the illustrious Jagiellonian University and a devout Catholic—who asked his countrymen to reclaim their memory:

> To purify after Cain means above all to remember Abel. This particular Abel...his blood has remained in the walls, seeped into the [Polish] soil. It has also entered into ourselves, into our memory in the core of our identity.... We must carry it within us even though it is unpleasant or painful.

He pleaded for Poles to face the question of responsibility "in a totally sincere and honest way." They must, he said, admit their failure during the Nazi period to "fulfill their duties of brotherhood and compassion." And Błoński went on to instruct his fellow Poles how to expiate for this sin:

> We must say first of all.... Yes we are guilty...when we lost our home, and when within that home, the invaders set to murdering Jews, did we show solidarity towards the Jews? How many of us decided that it was none of our business? I repeat, instead of haggling and justifying ourselves, we should consider our own faults

and weaknesses.... It is only this that can gradually cleanse our desecrated soil...[56]

Under Democratization

There was much discussion of Błoński's position: many Polish intellectuals were critical but some expressed their support. His appeal is still referred to today, especially in connection with the discussion of the manifestations of antisemitism that have accompanied the collapse of communism in Poland and the advent of democratization. These manifestations testify to the unbroken continuity of antisemitism in Poland. The surfacing of this malady in the new Poland seems especially curious because so few Jews are left in Poland. It is estimated that there are about six to ten thousand Jews out of Poland's population of thirty-eight million. (There were more than three million Jews in Poland prior to the Holocaust.) Few people of Jewish origin identify themselves as Jews and those who do are mostly old people. The rest gave up their Jewishness or their parents had. Many of them tried to pass as Poles but, if at all, succeeded only in fooling themselves. Their Jewish origin is being unearthed with glee as well as spite. The Jews are being blamed for the post-communist economic problems facing Poland, as well as for the brutal communist past. The advent of the free press and free speech heralded anti-Jewish expressions. Antisemitic graffiti have been staring from Polish buildings: "Jews go to Israel," "Jews to the gas," and the Nazi slogan, *Juden raus*. The concept of the "real Pole of pure blood," as contrasted with the "secret Jew" or the individual in whose veins Jewish blood flows, echoes widely in conversation as well as in the press. Even Lech Wałęsa referred to himself as a "one hundred percent Pole" and demanded that Jews in politics not hide their Jewishness but identify themselves as such. (It must, however, not be overlooked that after having been elected to the presidency, Wałęsa went to Israel and there pleaded for forgiveness. This evoked much criticism in Poland.)

However, exceptional Poles do exist, even if not many, who are ashamed of these developments and denounce them. Among them is the editor of the Catholic weekly *Tygodnik Powszechny*, Jerzy Turowicz, a good friend of the pope. But the best known is the former prime minister, Tadeusz Mazowiecki. It may well be that his speaking up for Jews was not the sole factor that cost him his presidency, but it certainly accounts for the very small vote he received in the presidential election. After he publicly condemned the new antisemitism, the rumor spread that he, who in fact is a devout Catholic and the former editor of a Catholic paper, was secretly a Jew. His supposed Jewishness was proclaimed in signs on walls and condemnatory pamphlets.

Among Poles residing abroad voices were also heard expressing shame that this could happen again in Poland and revealing profound sympathy for Jews.

One of them was Jan Karski who, as a young man during World War II, had been sent to Britain and the United States by the Polish resistance to inform the Allies about the ordeal and suffering of Polish Jewry. Now Karski sorrowfully observed that the 1935 Nuremberg Laws are echoed in Poland in the widely used phrase "a real Pole of pure blood." He went on to plead: "We will be defenseless against those who want to stain the image of Poland abroad if the antisemitic manifestations will not meet with a general and decisive condemnation in our country."[57]

Another who has continuously waged war on antisemitism is Bolesław Wierzbiański, the editor of the New York Polish language newspaper, the *Polish Daily News*. Upon his return from a visit to Poland, he decried in the December 15–16, 1990 issue the fact that antisemitism accompanied the first general election in post-communist Poland. Wierzbiański acknowledged that "for a Pole living in the heterogenous American society or in the liberal Western European countries the phenomenon of antisemitism and the placing of responsibility for Polish tragedies and inefficiency on Jews is incredible, embarrassing and harmful." He concluded that if antisemitism in Poland is "artificially" promoted, then in must be "eradicated," if it is a sickness, then it must be "treated."

Is this the final chapter in the Polish historical drama of sparse philosemitism and widespread antisemitism in a Poland almost void of Jews? We know how risky it is for social scientists or historians to predict the future and yet I would venture to say that the end is not yet here. True, on Sunday, 20 January 1991, an unprecedented event took place in Poland: a pastoral letter from the Polish bishops, echoing Vatican Council II's *Nostra Aetate*, was read out at each mass in all the Roman Catholic churches of the land, informing the Poles of the Jewishness of Jesus and Mary (a fact largely unknown to the Polish masses) and condemning antisemitism as "contrary to the spirit of the Gospel" and "opposed to the Christian vision of human dignity."

However, one reading of a pastoral letter, as commendable as it may be, will not eradicate the poison of antisemitism lodged in the Polish nation. True the church, more than any other institution or organization in Poland, could play a decisive role in erasing the widespread prejudice and hatred of Jews. But to do so, it would have to conduct continuous and concentrated pastoral work and reshape its religious instruction in the schools.

It would be particularly fitting for the church to embark upon such an influential program because it was the initiator of anti-Jewish activities at the beginning of the Jews' presence in Poland. It was also a bastion of hate against Jews throughout their centuries-long existence in Poland.[58] In promoting such an unprecedented drive against antisemitism the church could utilize not only religious sources but also the writings and legacy of the philosemites who left an alternate Polish tradition for Poles to turn to.

Endnotes

1. Chone Shmeruk, *The Esterke Story in Yiddish and Polish Literature: A Case Study of Mutual Relations of Two Cultural Traditions* (Jerusalem: The Zalman Shazar Center, 1985).

2. *Encyclopaedia Judaica* (Jerusalem: Macmillan, 1972), 13:934–935; A. Litvin, *Yiddishe Nshumes* (New York: Folksbildung, 1916).

3. Among the exceptions are Cecil Roth, *Essays and Portraits of Anglo-Jewish History* (Philadelphia: Jewish Publication Society, 1962); Alan Edelstein, *An Unacknowledged Harmony—Philo-Semitism and the Survival of European Jewry* (Westport, CT: Greenwood Press, 1982); Salomon Rappaport, *Jew and Gentile: The Philosemitic Aspect* (New York: Philosophical Library, 1980); Rudolph Glantz, "The Philosemitic Element in American History: A Social and Cultural Approach," YIVO Archives, unpublished notes.

4. J. Baudouin de Courtney, *W Kwestji Żydowskiej* (Warsaw, 1913).

5. Arthur Eisenbach, *Wielka Emigracja Wobec Kwestji Żydowskiej, 1832–49* (Warsaw, 1976), 296–297; Stefan Kieniewicz, "The Jewish Problem in the 19th Century," in Shimon Abramsky et al., *Jews in Poland* (Oxford: B. Blackwell, 1986).

6. Artur Eisenbach, *Kwestia Równouprawienia Żydów w Królestwie Polskim* (Warsaw: Książka i Wiedza, 1972), 26–27.

7. Artur Eisenbach, *Wielka Emigracja Wobec Kwestji Żydowskiej, 1832–49* (Warsaw: Państwowe Wydawnictwo Naukowe, 1976).

8. Roman Brandstaetter, *Legion Żydowski Adama Mickiewicza, Dzieje i Dokumenty* (Warsaw, 1932).

9. Antoni Żybicki, "Żydzi w Polsce," *Demokrata Polski*, July 31, 1858, as quoted in Eisenbach (n. 7), 271–272.

10. "Żydzi a Powstanie Styczniowe," prepared for publication by A. Eisenbach, D. Fajnhaus, and A. Wein (Warsaw, 1963).

11. Henryk Grynberg, "The Jewish Theme in Polish Positivism," *Polish Review*, 1980, no. 3-4; Jan Winczakiewicz, "Uwagi Wstępne," *Izrael w Poezji Polskiej—Antalogia* (Paris: Instytut Literacki, 1958), 15.

12. Aleksander Hertz, *Żydzi w Kulturze Polskiej* (Paris: Instytut Literacki, 1961), 438.

13. Magdelena Opalska, "Polish Jewish Relations and the January Uprising: The Polish Perspective," *Polin*, 1 (1986), 71.

14. Opalska (n. 13), 72.

15. Hilary Nussbaum, *Żydzi w Polsce, Historya Żydow od Mojżesza do Epoki Obecnej*, vol. 5 (Warsaw, 1890).

16. Cited in the introduction by G. Pauszer Kłonowska to Eliza Orzeszkowa, *Z Jednego Strumienia* (Warsaw, 1960), 6.

17. Józef Piłsudski, "Kwestja Żydowska na Litwie," *Walka*, November 1903, reprinted in Józef Piłsudski, *Pisma Zbiorowe*, vol. 2 (Warsaw, 1937).

18. Wacław Jendrzejewicz, *Józef Piłsudski* (New York, 1982).

19. Jendrzejewicz (n. 18), 248.

20. "Wywiad Korespondenta Kuriera Porannego," in Józef Piłsudski, *Pisma Zbiorowe* (Warsaw, 1937), 5:165–167.

21. The appeal appeared in the socialist paper, *Przedwit*, May 1893 and was reprinted in Piłsudski, *Pisma Zbiorowe* (n. 20), 1: 28–33. For more on Piłsudski's relation to Jews, see P. Szwarc, *Yózef Piłsudski, Zayn Batsiung Tsu Der Yidn-Frage Un Zayn Kamf Gegen Bund* (Warsaw, 1936); Józef Piłsudski, *Poprawki Historyczne* (Warsaw, 1931); Józef Zygmuntowicz, ed., *Józef Piłsudski, o Sobie—Z Pism, Rozkazów i Przemówień Komendanta* (Warsaw, 1929); Jan Weiss, "Józef Piłsudski and the Jews," *Program and Abstracts of Papers*, Second Congress of Polish-American Scholars and Scientists (April 1971); Israel Cohen wrote of his audience with the Marshal in "Documents—My Mission to Poland, 1918–19," *Jewish Social Studies* 13 (April 1951): 167–168.

22. *Unter der Fun Fon KPP* (Warsaw, 1959); M.K. Dziewanowski, *The Communist Party of Poland* (Cambridge, MA: Harvard University Press, 1959).

23. For reprints of declarations of Poles who were friendly to Jews, see *Polacy o Żydach* (Warsaw, 1937).

24. For a concise treatment of the emergence of official antisemitism after the death of Piłsudski, see: Edward D. Wynot, Jr., "'A Necessary Cruelty': The Emergence of Official Anti-Semitism in Poland, 1936–39," *American Historical Review* 76, no. 4 (October 1971): 1035–1058.

25. Reprinted as "Ład Serca," *Nasz Przegląd*, Dec. 11, 1938, p. 7.

26. From part of his declaration, reprinted in "Głosy Swiatłych Polaków," *Głos Gminy Żydowskiej* 1, no. 4 (October 1937): 80.

27. Wiesław Mysłek, *Kosciół Katolicki W. Polsce W. Latach 1918–39* (Warsaw: Książka i Wiedza, 1966), 264–265.

28. Jerzy Surdykowski, *Duch Rzeczypospolitej* (New York: Bicentennial Publishing Corporation, 1989), 199.

29. Tadeusz Zaderecki, *Talmud w Ogniu Wieków* (Warsaw: F. Hoesicka, 1936).

30. From the pastoral letter of February 29, 1936: August Cardinal Hlond, *Listy Pasterskie* (Poznań, 1936), 192–193; for a larger portion of the pastoral letter in English translation, see Celia S. Heller, *On the Edge of Destruction* (New York: Columbia University Press, 1977), 113.

31. Aleksander Świętochowski, "Antysemityzm," in "Pisarze Polscy o Kwestji Żydowskiej," *Wiadomosci Literackie* 16 (April 1937): 3.

32. M.K. Dziewanowski, "Social Democrats versus 'Social Patriots': The Origins of the Split in the Marxist Movement in Poland," *American Slavic and East European Review* 10 (February 1951): 14–25.

33. Tadeusz Hołówko, "Przemówienie w Sprawie Kresów Wygłoszone Dnia 9 Lutego, 1931 r.," in *Ostatni Rok* (Warsaw, 1932); Wincenty Rzymowski, *W Walce i Burzy—Tadeusz Hołówko na Tle Epoki* (Warsaw, 1933); Stanisław Vincenz, *On the High Uplands—Sagas, Tales, and Legends of the Carpathians* (New York: Roy, 1955); see also his *Tematy Żydowskie* (London: Oficyna Poetów i Malarzy, 1977).

34. "W Najwiekszym Skrócie," *Wiadomosci Literackie* 21 (May 16, 1937); see also Hertz (n.12), 238–248.

35. See, for example, Władysław Bartoszewski and Zofia Lewin, *The Samaritans—Heroes of the Holocaust* (New York: Twayne Publishers, 1966); Philip Friedman, *Their Brothers Keepers* (New York: Holocaust Library, 1978); Moshe Bejski, "The Righteous among the Nations and their Part in the Rescue of Jews," in Yisrael Gutman and Livia Rothkirchen, eds., *The Catastrophe of European Jews* (Jerusalem: Yad Vashem, 1976), 582–607.

36. Among Bartoszewski's best known works in English translation are: Władysław Bartoszewski and Zofia Lewin, *The Samaritans—Heroes of the Holocaust* (cited in n. 35); Władysław Bartoszewski, *The Convent at Auschwitz* (New York: George Braziller, 1991). His Polish book about the Jews of Warsaw was published as *Los Żydów Warszawy, 1939–43* (London: Puls Publications, 1983).

37. Jerzy Surdykowski, *Duch Rzeczypospolitej* (New York: Bicentennial Publishing Corporation, 1989), 206.

38. The appeal of Zofia Kossak Szczucka is reproduced in Teresa Prekerowa, *Konspiracyjna Rada Pomocy Żydom* (Warsaw: P1W, 1982), 112; Surdykowski (n. 37), 207–208. One might note that Poles generally omit reference to the latter part of the appeal. Even Władysław Bartoszewski used such elliptical quotes in his posthumous article about Kossak Szczucka's underground activities. See his "Zofia Kossak W. Podziemiu," *Tygodnik Powszechny* (June 16, 1968), 1.

39. Stanisław W. Dobrowolski, *Memuary Pacyfisty* (Cracow: Wydawnitwo Literackie, 1989), 194–201; also see the review of this book in English by Celia Stopnicka Heller, *The Polish Review* 37, no. 3 (1992).

40. Dobrowolski (n. 39), 202–203.

41. Lucjan Dobroszycki, "Restoring Jewish Life in Post-War Poland," *Soviet Jewish Affairs* 3, no. 2 (1973): 55, 58, 72.

42. Dobrowolski (n. 39), 238–242.

43. Heller (n. 30), 115, 135, 290.

44. Dobroszycki (n. 41), 58–72.

45. Surdykowski (n. 37), 212.

46. We do not know how many survivors were shot crossing borders illegally. But in the Cracow Jewish cemetery, for example, a grave exists, marked in Hebrew for 17 members of the Jewish youth organization *Gordonia* who were killed by a Polish terrorist *Ogień* band when they tried to cross the "green line." See Artur Sandauer, *Publicystyka, Pisma Zebrane*, vol. 3 (Warsaw: Czytelnik, 1985).

47. See Robert S. Wistrich, ed., *The Left Against Zionism: Communism, Israel and the Middle East* (London: Vallentine Mitchell, 1979).

48. Jerzy Eisler, *Marzec 1968—Geneza, Przebieg, Konsekwencje* (Warsaw: Państwowe Wydawnictwo Naukowe, 1991); Z. Kozik, "O Wydarzeniach Marcowych 1968r," *Nowe Drogi*, no. 2 (1988): 60–75.

49. Gustaw Kerszman, "Książka o Marcu," *Zeszyty Historyczane*, no. 99 (Paris, 1992): 157.

50. Celia S. Heller, "'Anti-Zionism' and the Political Struggle within the Elite of Poland," *The Jewish Journal of Sociology* 2, no. 2 (December 1969): 133–151.

51. For the analysis of these themes, see Heller (n. 50), 143–145.

52. J. Holzer, "Doświadczenia Marca 68," *Kierunki*, May 17, 1981.

53. Heller (n. 30) "Epilogue," 296–298; also see: Irwin Iwona-Zarecka, *Neutralizing Memory* (New Brunswick, NJ: Transaction Press, 1989).

54. "Przemówienia i Wypowiedzenia Jana Pawła II," in *Żydzi i Judaizm w Dokumentach Kościelnych i Nauczaniu Jana Pawła II, 1965–89* (Warsaw: Akademia Teologji Katolickiej, 1991).

55. Jerzy Ficowski, *A Reading of Ashes* (London: The Menard Press, 1981), 2; the Herbert quotes are from his forward to the book, p. 1.

56. Jan Błoński, "The Poor Poles Look at the Ghetto," in Anthony Polonsky, ed., *My Brother's Keeper—Recent Polish Debates on the Holocaust* (London: Routledge, 1990), 35, 42–43.

57. "Wypowiedź," *Odra*, no. 10 (1991): 149–153.

58. Celia S. Heller, "Historical Perspective: Tolerance and Hate," in *On the Edge of Destruction* (n. 30), 13–47. See also Artur Eisenbach, *Kwestia Równouprawnienia Żydow w Królestwie Polskim* (Warsaw: Książka i Wiedza, 1972); Adam Vetulani, "The Jews in Medieval Poland," *Jewish Journal of Sociology* 4 (December 1962); Bernard Dov Weinryb, *The Jews of Poland—A Social and Economic History of the Jewish Community in Poland, 1100–1800* (Philadelphia: Jewish Publication Society, 1973).

Suggestions For Further Reading

Heller, Celia S. "'Anti-Zionism' and the Political Struggle within the Elite of Poland." *The Jewish Journal of Sociology*, 11, no. 2 (December 1969): 133–151. Based on content analysis of the Communist press in Poland, the article demonstrates how a strong antisemitic drive was launched and sustained under the guise of anti-Zionism.

____. *On the Edge of Destruction: Jews of Poland Between the Two World Wars*. 2nd ed. Detroit: Wayne State University Press, 1993. It is based on the extensive literature and archival materials in Polish, Yiddish, English, and Hebrew. Also contains a chapter on the millennial history of the Jews in Poland and a new epilogue on the post-war Jewish remnant in Poland under communism and democratization.

Hertz, Aleksander. *The Jews in Polish Culture*. Evanston, IL: Northwestern University Press, 1988. This is the English translation of the classic work of this Polish sociologist which appeared in Polish in 1961. The reading of the superior original is recommended to those who know Polish.

Iwona-Zarecka, Irwin. *Neutralizing Memory*. New Brunswick, NJ: Transaction Press, 1989. An important work by a Polish sociologist in America who relied on her own experience, as well as other sources, to give us insight into the process of how awareness of Jewish existence was "neutralized" in Poland and the attempts by some young people to recover that awareness.

Mishkinski, Moshe. "Communism in Poland." Vol. 5, *Encyclopaedia Judaica*. Jerusalem: Macmillan, 1971. A concise summary of the role of Jews in the Communist movement of Poland, from its beginning, by a scholar well versed in the subject.

Opalska, Magdelena. "Polish Jewish Relations and the January Uprising: The Polish Perspective." *Polin* 1 (1986). An objective and thorough analysis by a scholar trained in post-war Poland.

Polonsky, Anthony, ed. *My Brother's Keeper—Recent Polish Debates on the Holocaust*. London: Routledge, 1990. An exciting book of essays (in English translation) by Polish intellectuals on the Poles' behavior towards Jews during this tragic period. The leading article is that by Jan Błoński.

Weinryb, Bernard Dov. *The Jews of Poland—A Social and Economic History of the Jewish Community in Poland, 1100–1800*. Philadelphia: Jewish Publication Society, 1973. An important contribution by an outstanding scholar, based on meticulous knowledge of old sources.

Wynot, Edward D., Jr. "'A Necessary Cruelty': The Emergence of Official Anti-Semitism in Poland, 1936–39." *The American Historical Review*. 76, no. 4 (October 1971): 1035–1056. A carefully researched treatment of an important but controversial subject by an American historian.

THE VATICAN AND THE HOLOCAUST:

UNRESOLVED ISSUES

John T. Pawlikowski

The role of the Vatican during the Nazi era is the subject of often partisan and acrimonious debate. Defenders of Pope Pius XII view him as a great humanitarian who did what he could to rescue Jews; some critics of the papacy accuse him of indifference and silence. John T. Pawlikowski assesses the historiography and responds to the charge that traditional Christian antisemitism influenced the Vatican's policy.

1. A Preface

One approaches the question of the Vatican and the Holocaust with some trepidation. It has elicited an emotionally-charged debate for over two decades with exaggerated charges and counterclaims by both Jews and Catholics. Therefore I deem it imperative to set a context for the remarks that follow. For I wish to assume the role neither of antagonist nor of apologist. Strongly partisan stances on this question that tread lightly in the realm of authentic scholarship violate the movement towards reconciliation and enhanced bondedness that have become the clarion call of all the official documents on Catholic-Jewish relations issued since the II Vatican Council.

My interest, and my principal expertise, in the matter at hand come primarily from my background as a social ethicist vitally interested in how the church as an institution has functioned in the public order and what theological/ethical perceptions may have enhanced and/or impeded this functioning. In short, I am not an historian doing original documentary analysis. This in my judgment requires that I sift through the various views of historians regarding the subject, introducing a partially subjective factor as I make a judgment as to which analysis seems to bear greater credibility. On the other hand, as a social ethicist, I can sometimes discern broader patterns and underlying causal factors to which the trained historian may not be as attuned. It is my conviction that the trained historian and the professional social ethicist can genuinely complement each other in the investigation of Vatican activities during the Nazi era.

Since the appearance of Rolf Hochhuth's highly controversial play *The Deputy* in 1963 most of the energy of researchers has concentrated on the person of Pope Pius XII. How much did he actually do to save others? How much could he in fact have been reasonably expected to do, given the isolated situation of the Vatican in the heart of Fascist Italy? Can we judge Pius XII indifferent, callous, or discretely caring with respect to the Jewish community of the day? Such questions and other similar ones certainly remain valid and need to be pursued.

But the entire focus of the discussion should not be placed on the person of Pius XII. We must also examine how churches in other parts of Europe were reacting and whether they were in anyway affected by Vatican pressures. Likewise we must look to issues of ecclesial self-identity at the time to see how these may have conditioned the Vatican's response. For whatever the final evaluation of historians on Pius XII's papal tenure, and much remains to be researched in this regard, his record has been buried with him. There is nothing the church can do to change that record. It can, however, profoundly adjust its ecclesial self-identity in certain areas.

Following historian Michael Marrus' comments at the November 1988 International Jewish-Christian Conference in Vienna a measure of humility must surround any evaluations of individual and/or group responses during this trying period. Marrus persuasively argued at Vienna that the question, "Why didn't they [i.e. the pope, American Jews, Churchill, Roosevelt, etc.] do more" during the Holocaust is dangerously misleading. For behind it lay the automatic presumption that we today would have done better. Marrus labeled such an assumption "narcissistic".

Another caution that must be sounded has to do with the tendency to generalize about the Vatican or overall Catholic responses to the Holocaust. As Bernard Lewis, also at the Vienna Conference, strongly urged, this must be resisted at all costs. Instead we must undertake a painstaking country by country analysis in Europe, taking into account the church's particular social and political position in each nation. Only such an approach can lead to a fair assessment of the Catholic response.

Clearly there are those in the Catholic community who wish to avoid any critical questions regarding the church's behavior and to look upon Christians purely as victims during the Nazi period. Such a position fortunately has been rejected by an increasing number of responsible Catholic leaders. At the May 1992 meeting of the Vatican-Jewish International Dialogue in Baltimore Cardinal Joseph Bernardin of Chicago, in a plenary address, praised the four-hundred page report by a panel of historians commissioned and supported by the Cardinal Archbishop of Lyons (France) regarding the diocese's response to the Nazi challenge. He said that "it is only through candor and willingness to acknowledge mistakes where documentary evidence clearly warrants it that Catholicism can join in the pursuit of contemporary global justice with full moral integrity."[1] He urged the church as a whole to submit its World War II record to a thorough scrutiny by respected scholars.

2. The Vatican Response—What the Historians Say

The strongest defense of the Vatican, Pius XII in particular, during the Holocaust has come from Fr. Robert Graham, S.J., who has worked on documents in its archives for two decades. He especially focuses his energies on the final year and a half of World War II. Based on his analysis of the documents contained in the now published eleven-volume official documentary of Vatican activities he concludes that Pius XII must be judged a "great humanitarian," truly deserving of "that forest in the Judaean hills which kindly people in Israel proposed for him in October 1958."[2]

Graham's argument, to present it succinctly, follows this track. Though Pius XII was disappointed at having failed to prevent the outbreak of World War II, he committed himself from its onset to the mitigation of human suffering to the fullest extent possible. While the pope showed deep concern for all the victims of the Nazis there is ample evidence in the official Vatican *Acts* of an ever increasing predilection for the plight of the Jews. While it is true that the Vatican received many requests from Jewish organizations for assistance (a sign, for Graham, of genuine confidence in the pope and the Catholic Church), many actions on behalf of the Jewish community were launched on the sole initiative of the Vatican. This situation created an unparalleled amount of communication between the Holy See and Jewish leaders. In the early years of the war, when emigration was still a live possibility, diplomatic pressure was placed upon countries with close Vatican ties such as Spain and Portugal to grant exit and transit visas to fleeing Jews. And when the emigration option was gradually closed off between 1940–1942, the Catholic strategy shifted to diplomatic protests over deportations.

Slovakia represents a good illustration, according to Graham, of the latter approach. When it became known in March 1942 that some eighty thousand Slovak Jews were to be forcibly removed from the country the Vatican's response was instantaneous. Protests came from the papal representatives in Bratislava and the papal nuncio in Hungary. And when another round of deportations was scheduled for 1943 the Vatican again raised its voice in denunciation of the proposal. Finally, in 1944 when it appeared that yet more deportations were in the works the Holy See instructed its representative in Slovakia to approach both the foreign ministry and President Tiso (a Catholic priest) in its name. The representative's instructions were to make clear "that the Holy See expects from the Slovak authority an attitude in conformity with the Catholic principles and sentiments of the people of Slovakia."[3] At the same time it suggested that a joint protest by the Slovak bishops might prove extremely helpful in stopping the deportations. In a follow-up action Vatican officials spoke with the Slovak minister to the Vatican, giving him the following formal message: "The Holy See, moved by those sentiments of humanity and Christian charity that always inspire its work in favor of the suffering, without distinction of parties, nationalities or races, cannot remain indifferent to such appeals...."[4]

The Vatican showed special regard for the Jews in its midst, according to Graham, making direct interventions with the Nazi authorities for the safety of the Jewish community of Rome and giving support to the many religious houses that gave shelter to Jews during this difficult period. In October 1943, for example, the Vatican Secretary of State, Cardinal Maglione, in a private meeting with the Reich ambassador Ernst von Weizsäcker, vigorously protested the special SS raid which had seized some one thousand Jews for transfer to Poland. He speaks of the pain experienced by the Holy Father over this act and over the suffering of so many persons solely because of their race. Those who managed to escape the raid were hidden in Roman monasteries and convents for the remaining months of the Nazi occupation.

One of the most noteworthy and successful instances of Vatican activity for the security of Jews is to be found in Hungary. Prior to 1944 this country's Jewish community enjoyed relative freedom despite the passage of severe antisemitic legislation before that time. The Hungarian government had steadfastly refused to turn over its own Jewish citizens, as well as Jewish refugees from Poland and Slovakia, for the greater part of the Nazi era. But all that changed in March of 1944 when German armies advanced into Hungary. The previous leader of Hungary Admiral Horthy was eventually replaced by a local government composed primarily of fanatical antisemites of the Arrow Cross movement. Deportations to Auschwitz and Austria (for forced labor) and outright massacre now became the fate of the Jews.

Volume ten of the official *Acts* of the Vatican relative to World War II contains massive documentation on the Holy See's central role in the international effort to save Hungarian Jews. While Admiral Horthy was still in charge after the Nazi invasion the papal nuncio Angelo Rotta engaged in ongoing communication with governmental officials, and with the Vatican, trying to find ways to bring the Jewish deportations to a halt.

This furious activity by Rotta during the first part of the period of Nazi occupation culminated with the release of an "open" telegram to Admiral Horthy from Pius XII which read in part:

> We are being beseeched in various quarters to do everything in our power in order that, in this noble and chivalrous nation, the sufferings, already so heavy, endured by a large number of unfortunate

people, because of their nationality or race, may not be extended and aggravated. As our Father's heart cannot remain insensitive to these pressing supplications by virtue of our ministry of charity which embraces all men, we address Your Highness personally, appealing to your noble sentiments in full confidence that so many unfortunate people may be spared other afflictions and other sorrows.[5]

This papal appeal was followed in quick succession by other international interventions, including a press campaign in Switzerland and a warning from British Foreign Secretary Sir Anthony Eden. The bombing of Budapest was also ordered. These joint efforts resulted in a suspension of Jewish deportations by Horthy for which Jewish organizations and the War Refugee Board, according to Graham, expressed special gratitude to the Vatican.

After Horthy was finally deposed, Rotta found his work in behalf of Jews far more difficult. With the help of the neutral Swedish ambassador he arranged for a meeting with the new Arrow Cross leadership. But, as he himself confessed, his plea to spare the Jews fell on totally deaf ears. He found these leaders full of "fanatical hatred" towards the Jewish community.

But, despite the severe setback at the governmental level, Rotta was not to be completely deterred. He turned to a new scheme. He began to issue "Letters of Protection" which seemed to stall at least the deportation process for Jews, especially baptized Jews, who received them. It appears that these letters, along with similar ones granted by other neutral foreign embassies, served as a sort of *habeas corpus* for those who received them. Rotta's report to the Vatican on the matter claims the issuance of some 13,000 of them.

It is certainly clear from Graham's extensive treatment of the Hungarian situation that he considers this country one of the very best examples of Vatican activity in behalf of the Jewish community. The collaboration of the papal nuncio and the Vatican was as intense as could have been possibly hoped for under very trying political conditions.

Looking at Graham's presentation as a whole, it shows some definite limitations. Because most of Graham's writings have appeared in what may be termed a "polemical context," i.e. they are aimed at fending off the charge that Pius XII and his Vatican administration were *silent* on the Jewish issue, they simply are bereft of the kind of overall critical analysis that one may legitimately expect of an historian. In one sense Graham has ably performed his task. He has clearly demonstrated that simplistic claims about papal silence at this time are grossly overstated. There is absolutely no question that Pius and members of his administration in Rome undertook important initiatives in behalf of *all* Jews and not merely Jewish converts to Christianity. In fact, on the basis of Graham's evidence alone (which can easily be substantiated from other Christian and Jewish sources) we should permanently strike the word "silence" from all Christian-Jewish conversations about the role of institutional Catholicism during the Holocaust. There is a perfectly legitimate discussion to be pursued about the adequacy and the suppositions of Pius' and the Vatican's approach. But this is an altogether different issue from the charge of basic "silence". Those in the Jewish community who continue to allow this charge to go unchallenged are failing in their leadership responsibilities.

What has Graham not done? First of all, he never questions whether the interventions he describes were pursued over a long course rather than a single attempt. Was there really official Catholic persistence in pursuing this question or did the Jewish organizations continually have to remind Rome of the seriousness of the Jewish plight? Only the former in my mind would indicate a deep, primary policy-commitment to the issue. Nor does Graham ever ask whether Pius should have reconsidered his position on some matters (i.e. his unwillingness to criticize the Nazis by name or to single out the Jews by name as victims) in light of the gravity of the situation? In each and every insistence Pius is accorded the benefit of the doubt and those (including certain representatives of the Jewish and Polish communities where the hostility towards Vatican policy was the strongest) who sustain Pius' judgment are always placed on a level above those who maintained a critical stance.

Graham's chief focus is also on Vatican activities during the final year of World War II. He does assert that the Vatican *Acts* show interventions prior to that and in fact he makes mention of some of them in his narrative. But the inclusion of some examples prior to 1944 when coupled with the acknowledged increase in interventions during this final year of Nazi terror serves to blunt serious discussion of the question whether Vatican response to Jewish annihilation was far too slow in coming. Such a linkage creates the subtle impression, intentionally or not, that the number of interventions in the earlier years of the war is more or less on a par with 1944. This is clearly not the case. Hence, Gerhart Riegner's far more careful delineation of various stages of Jewish-Vatican collaboration during the Nazi period (which will be discussed shortly) is a welcome corrective to Graham's approach.

Another drawback in Graham's perspective is the impression he creates of rather harmonious collaboration between Jewish organizations and the Vatican throughout the war years. The subtle message seems to be that criticism is only coming from Jewish scholars and organizational representatives in the post-war era who are overlooking the testimonies of Jewish leaders at the time. This again is a case of oversimplification on Graham's part.

Finally, Graham's materials show little inclination on his part to raise questions about the controlling ecclesiology in the Vatican at the time. The same is true about the fairly evident commitment of Pius XII and his circle to the defense of a traditional social order which many other historians see as a factor muting *direct* papal condemnation of Nazism, which was considered by some Catholic leaders as a bulwark against destruction of this social order, especially by the Bolsheviks. While it might be argued that it is legitimate for Graham as an historian to refrain from discussion of such broader theological/ethical issues, he should at the very least insure that his limited research is not used solely for polemical purposes by groups such as the Catholic League for Religious and Civil Rights.

For a perspective on the Nazi period considerably different from that of Graham we turn to Dr. Gerhart Riegner of the World Jewish Congress, who was an active participant in the effort to save European Jewry while Hitler was in power. What he offers us by way of analysis of the Catholic response to Nazism clearly raises some questions about several of Fr. Graham's claims and shows that considerable research remains to be undertaken in a number of areas.

In his Stephen S. Wise lecture at the Hebrew Union College-Jewish Institute of Religion in Cincinnati in 1983, Riegner devoted considerable time to his recollection of Vatican-Jewish relations during World War II.[6] In the first years of the war Jewish organizations, he maintained, were very apprehensive about soliciting help from Rome, much more so than from the Protestant religious establishment. This reluctance was in large measure the result of favorable inclinations towards the Third Reich on the part of many German Catholic bishops as well as the perceived appeasement policy that dominated pre-Concordat Nazi-Vatican relations. Other factors contributing to this Jewish inhibition included antisemitism in many sectors of Polish Catholicism in the interwar period as well as the seeming ineffectiveness of Catholic protests on those occasions when they were forthcoming. Jewish leaders were also conscious of the Vatican's enclave position within a Fascist state.

It was not until 1942 that the Jewish policy on dealings with institutional Catholicism began to change, in large measure because of a growing feeling of desperation over the ever-worsening condition of European Jewry. Pius XII now became a special target of Jewish organizational appeals in the light of his acknowledged moral authority. These appeals were coordinated through contacts with papal representatives in Switzerland, New York, and London. Some responses resulted, according to Riegner, particularly with regard to the situation in Slovakia where President Tiso relaxed pressure on the Jews for a time after Vatican intervention. But in Riegner's judgment little of substance was done with respect to other countries. What steps occurred in Romania seemed more the product of local initiative rather than Vatican directive. And Rome's reaction to the condition of Jews in the unoccupied sectors of France was much weaker in Riegner's estimation than that of several leading French bishops, particularly Bishop Saliege and Bishop Theas, who in response to Jewish appeals strongly criticized Vichy's anti-Jewish legislation and the deportations in the summer of 1942.

Riegner then raises an important question which seems to go unanswered in Graham's analysis. In March 1942 Riegner helped prepare a joint World Jewish Congress/Jewish Agency memorandum at the request of the papal nuncio in Bern. This document detailed the condition of Jews in those countries where the

Vatican was deemed to have particular influence because of a substantial Catholic population. Included on the list were Slovakia, Croatia, Hungary, Romania and Vichy France. "Strangely," says Riegner, "the detailed memorandum is not reproduced in the collection of documents published by the Vatican on its action during World War II. The collection contains only the letter of transmittal."[7] This is a very critical omission in his mind. The memorandum demonstrates that the Vatican was privy to extensive information about Nazi attacks on the Jews throughout Europe at a relatively early moment. When the Vatican first acquired detailed knowledge of the gravity of the Jewish situation certainly is a vital element in any assessment today regarding the tardiness of its response to Hitler.

Another central moment in Vatican-Jewish relations came in autumn 1942 when the Vatican was asked by the U.S. Under-secretary of State Summer Welles to confirm Allied reports about massive extermination of Jews. After some delay and follow-up requests by the U.S., the Vatican Secretary of State Cardinal Maglione responded that the Vatican could not confirm the accuracy of these reports. Again, Riegner sees this reply as "strange," given the reports the Vatican had received from its nuncios about the deportations of Jews from Bucovina and Bessarabia in December 1941, from Bratislava in March 1942, and in July 1942 from both Paris and Zagreb.

The year 1942 also witnessed a concerted effort by several nations to induce Pius XII to condemn the Nazis by name for their treatment of the Jews. Among them were Britain, the Polish Government-in-Exile, Brazil, the United States, and Uruguay. This effort was the result of new revelations about the extent of Jewish suffering made public in London by the World Jewish Congress and the Polish Government-in-Exile. The pope eventually did respond to these appeals in his Christmas radio message of that year. But in typical fashion the Jews were not specifically named.

Riegner acknowledges that a first reading of the papal statement leaves the impression of significant courage on Pius' part. But when one places it against the moving appeals of Polish President Raczkiewicz and others to the pope, as well as the blunt statement of Cardinal Hinsley of London at a mass protest meeting in New York in early 1943 in which he explicitly named Jews as the primary victims and the Nazis as the oppressors, the fundamental weakness of Pius' stance shines through for Riegner. It is obvious he does not fully accept the position of Graham and others that diplomatic reserve on the part of the pope helped rather than hindered the safety of European Jewry at the time.

The one region where Riegner clearly acknowledges positive Vatican/Jewish collaboration is in Hungary. His narrative in this regard is not all that dissimilar from that given by Graham. He concludes:

> On the whole, one can probably say that the Vatican action in Hungary stands out as effective and energetic; it certainly contributed to the saving of many Jewish lives.[8]

Riegner also says that certain papal nuncios, especially those in Slovakia and Romania, appear to have undertaken numerous efforts to save Jews. But the same level of activity is not apparent in other capitals. In this analysis Riegner is confirming a position held by Fr. John Morley about Vatican diplomacy that we shall examine shortly.

Riegner argues as well that in the first years of Nazi rule the Catholic Church was primarily interested in baptized Jews. This was particularly true in Germany itself. Ernst Christian Helmreich, a scholar fundamentally sympathetic to the church's difficulties in responding to the Nazi regime, and recent research on internal Nazi documents which monitored church activities in Germany, tend to support Riegner's assertion on this point.[9]

Overall, Riegner is forced to the conclusion that Vatican comprehension of the full extent of the Jewish catastrophe was very late in coming, if it was ever understood at all. Certainly the matter never assumed high priority within the upper echelons of the Vatican. Riegner offers the following personal example to undergird his contention regarding Vatican misperceptions of the Jewish situation:

> In a long conversation with Msgr. Montini, subsequently to become Pope Paul VI, in October, 1945 in Rome, during which I pleaded with him to help us obtain the return of Jewish children who had seen saved by Catholics or Catholic institutions, I was shocked when the Catholic prelate contested the accuracy of my statement that at least 1,500,000 Jewish children had perished in the Holocaust. It took me more than half an hour to explain and justify my statement and for him to accept it. If one of the senior personalities of the Church...could take such an attitude in good faith...it seems to me fair to say that high Vatican diplomacy never really understood the extent of the tragedy that had befallen the Jewish people.[10]

Riegner has certainly raised some critical points that demand further research and reflection by scholars. His recollections definitely reveal important weaknesses in the Graham narrative that need addressing before Catholics today can rest content. If there is a questionable assumption in Riegner's analysis, it would be the unstated conviction that if the Vatican had spoken more candidly in the public realm a greater number of Jewish lives would have been spared. We now know from recent publications such as the memoirs of Cardinal Henri de Lubac[11] that even the indirect language of Pius XII in condemning the Nazi attack on the Jewish people played a central role in molding Catholic resistance in such countries as France. And Gunther Lewy, hardly a Vatican apologist relative to the Third Reich, has insisted that a "flaming protest" by Pius XII would almost certainly have made no appreciable dent in the final Jewish death figures and might well have made matters worse for both Jews and Catholics.[12] Thus the question may in fact be far more open-ended than Riegner would seem to allow.

Having examined two perspectives on Vatican activities during the Nazi era in some detail, we can conclude this section with a brief overview of several other scholarly viewpoints. Fr. John Morley has argued, rather convincingly despite Graham's one-line rejection of his thesis, that the Vatican could have done far more through its papal nuncios than in fact was the case. In concert with most other historians who have analyzed the period, Morley sees the problem as centered not in crass papal indifference to Jews but in the tone of Vatican diplomacy which Pius XII himself set during this era. Prudence and reserve were its prevailing characteristics. It studiously tried to avoid "offending" any nation, the Third Reich included. This approach had a straitjacket effect on Vatican diplomacy and in no way differentiated it from the posture of the civil states. In fact, on occasion, representatives of the Allied camp spoke more candidly and specifically about the Jewish question than the Vatican.[13]

As was indicated above, Gerhart Riegner's recollections would seem to lend support to Morley's basic argument. Even Graham's own research, when read carefully, shows that most of the initiatives began with a particular papal nuncio, not the Vatican. The possibilities for direct Catholic institutional action differed from country to country. Therefore, it is misleading to generalize from the success of a situation such as Hungary. Nonetheless, there seem to be enough instances of important successes in alleviating the Jewish plight in those countries where nuncios did act, and sometimes secured Vatican intervention as well, to warrant Morley's more general argument. Michael Marrus of the University of Toronto, whose work has attracted considerable attention of late,[14] has joined those critically assessing the overall Vatican response. He too locates the problem fundamentally in the style of diplomacy that Pius XII had helped to shape during the political storms of the Depression era as Pius XI's Secretary of State.

He acknowledges Vatican arguments with both Hitler and Mussolini on race, but insists that the opposition had more to do with the Christian theology of baptism than it did with concern about Jews. Even after the release of *Mit Brennender Sorge*, the papal encyclical against Nazism in 1937, the Vatican strove to prevent an open breach. The primary goal remained, in Marrus' words, "political neutrality and the safeguarding of the institutional interests of the Church in a perilous political world."[15]

The first few years of the war saw little Vatican protest against growing Nazi hostility towards the Jewish community, no more in fact than in the 1930s. Catholic representatives spoke generally about justice, but remained largely unconcerned about the new antisemitic campaigns being developed by the Third Reich and collaborationist governments. When the murder of Jews began in earnest, says Marrus, the Vatican refused to issue more than the most general of condemnations despite its excellent information on the seriousness of the Jewish condition. It is obvious that Marrus is not persuaded by Graham's argument that, though the Vatican's language was most often general in nature, referring explicitly neither to Jews nor to Nazis, everyone understood the specific intent of the Holy See's statements.

Marrus joins many other historians in arguing that the root cause of the limited Vatican response was diplomatic style. Vatican documents, he insists, do not show any guarded pro-Nazism or a supreme priority of opposition to the Soviet Union. Clearly they reveal that neither simple hostility nor indifference explains Rome's posture during this time. What they establish beyond all doubt is the dominance of a policy of "reserve and conciliation" under Pius XII, which not only shaped his approach but served on the whole as a model for the church's diplomatic corps as well:

> The goal was to limit the global conflict where possible, and above all to protect the influence and standing of the Church as an independent voice. Continually apprehensive of schisms within the Church, Pius strove to maintain the allegiance of Catholics in Germany, in Poland, and elsewhere. Fearful too of threats from the outside, the Pope dared not confront the Nazis or the Italian Fascists directly.[16]

Thus for Marrus the controlling reality under Pius was preservation of the church. All else took second place.

This same perspective, it might be noted, is shared by another Jewish historian of the Holocaust Nora Levin, though she attributes somewhat more direct influence to the Bolshevik factor as a principal threat to Catholic survival than Marrus. This priority of church survival led Pius XII, in Levin's words, to view the Jews as "unfortunate expendables."[17] In the terms of Helen Fein they fell outside the "universe of moral obligation."[18]

To further underscore the predominance of the survival factor over pure antisemitism in the Vatican response to the Jewish question, Marrus introduces the issue of the Holy See's reaction to other groups targeted by the Nazis. Here too, he says, the Holy See basically followed a policy of reserve even when it involved strong appeals from Polish bishops to denounce Nazi atrocities against Polish Catholics as well as in the case of the Third Reich's "euthanasia campaign" and the Italian attack against Greece.

The relations between the Vatican and Poland, as Marrus has indicated, provide a useful parallel study to the question of the Holy See and the Jewish community during World War II. For here there was a staunchly Catholic community which, as historians are increasingly bringing to light, became nearly as critical as the Jews regarding the reserve posture assumed by papal diplomacy.

Polish-American historian Richard Lukas has surfaced this issue in his writings on the Nazi attack against Poland. He recognizes the practical difficulties the Vatican faced with respect to Poland, in part due to the flight of Cardinal Hlond, the primate, from the country which caused great disruption in the Polish church. Pius XII's cold reception of Hlond in Rome is considered one saving feature of the pope's overall approach to Poland. Yet the balance sheet for Lukas does not read well. And he supports his evaluation with references to concrete reactions by Poles during the period.

"In the face of the persecution of the church of Poland," says Lukas, "the Vatican pursued a timid, reserved attitude."[19] This was likely the result of a constellation of forces—a sentimentality about Poland on Pius' part, a tinge of Germanophilism, and fears that public denunciations would make matters worse for the Poles. It was not until 2 June 1943 that the pope finally issued the long awaited statement. And here again, just as in the case of the Jews, Pius shied away from directly condemning the Nazis.

The 1943 statement, which admittedly did ease Polish-Vatican tensions to some degree, was an effort to counteract the widespread criticism that had grown up within clerical ranks because of the Vatican's seeming hesitancy on the Polish question. There were even Polish voices calling for the severing of ties with the Vatican. Some Poles, according to Lukas, were so upset at Rome that they left church at the mention of Pius' name. The Jesuits of Warsaw were so concerned about the situation that they published a defense of the Vatican's activities in behalf of Poland. And John Morley, who also raises the Polish question and sees Vatican inaction there as a result of the primacy in Vatican eyes of the relationship with Germany, relates that Rome explicitly instructed its nuncios on how to counter the mounting dissatisfaction with its approach to Poland.[20]

Graham does attempt in his analysis to respond to the charges against Pius XII relative to Poland. But he concentrates almost exclusively on the 1943 speech and thereafter. And even in this regard his defense depends on the favorable comments of a few representatives of the Polish Government-in-Exile. It is obvious that a contemporary historian of Poland such as Lukas has not been fully persuaded by this defense.

The example of Vatican policy in Poland serves to undercut the claims of Catholic defense agencies that the criticism of Pius XII is merely Jewish anti-Catholicism. No one can accuse the people of Poland of anti-Catholicism. They were abandoned by their cardinal and for several years received only lukewarm assistance from the Holy See because, somewhat like the Jews, they were classed, it would seem, as "unfortunate expendables" in the diplomatic calculations of the Vatican aimed at maintaining ties with Germany as a bulwark against Bolshevism.

To round off this survey of the approach of historians to the Vatican-Nazi relationship question, we shall look very briefly at an English Catholic historian, J. Derek Holmes, and an Anglican historian from Canada, John Conway. Holmes is among the staunchest defenders of the regime of Pius XII outside of Graham. But his views are presented in a less polemical setting. In general, he contends that Pius' quiet diplomacy worked far better than many are willing to acknowledge. He appeals in fact to an unnamed Israeli consul in Italy who claimed that the Holy See, the papal nuncios, and regional Catholic leaders helped to save some

400,000 Jews from certain death.[21]

Yet even Holmes, unlike Graham, seems prepared to grant that some major flaws existed in Vatican policy. Overall he is convinced that Vatican officials did not show sufficient resolve in resisting racist attitudes throughout the Nazi period and Pius XII did not exhibit an aggressive enough style of leadership relative to initiatives by local churches. A case in point, says Holmes, is Vichy France. When the Vichy government's ambassador in Rome made inquiry at the Vatican whether proposed new legislation on the Jews would create problems for the Vatican Marshall Pétain, head of the Vichy government, was able to claim, says Holmes, "unfairly but not without some justification that the Vatican had adopted a careless or even an 'inhuman' attitude."[22]

John Conway shares some of the same cautions as does Holmes in his consideration of Vatican policy.[23] He recognizes that Catholic protest was not so strong as might have been anticipated. He attributes this largely to a twofold conclusion on the part of the Catholic leadership elite, both in Germany and in Rome. This conclusion, he argues, was common to the leadership of much of the Protestant Evangelical Church as well, resulting in the growth of an anti-establishment Confessing Church that did publicly challenge the Nazis. Both the Catholic and Protestant leadership were convinced that the Christian faithful would abandon the hierarchy if they protested too strongly against the Nazis, and they feared such opposition might open the doors for the emergence in Germany of a liberal, pluralistic society that would threaten their fundamentally conservative social outlook. In their minds the church's well-being was inescapably tied to the preservation of the old social order in Germany and elsewhere in Europe.

3. Some Tentative Conclusions

With the above survey of the attitudes of a select number of Christian and Jewish scholars towards Vatican activities during the period of the Third Reich, we are now in a position to formulate several tentative conclusions. The first, to repeat a point made above, is that accusations of "silence" against Pius XII and the Vatican are simply unfounded. We must move beyond this code term to a much more nuanced discussion of the issues if we are to gain any insights from our analysis. On the other hand, no other historian, Christian or Jewish, has been convinced that Fr. Graham's work, however valuable on the restricted "silence" issue, has resolved all the serious questions at hand.

What clearly emerges from the research of nearly all the scholars who have examined the question is the conclusion that Pius' commitment to a "diplomatic" church model at the level of the Vatican, flowing in large measure from his desire not only to preserve the church as institution, but also to ensure continuation of the conservative social order he and his circle deemed essential for Catholicism's well-being, played an absolutely critical role in conditioning his response to the plight of the Jews, Poles, and other Nazi victim groups. Behind his "diplomatic" model in practical affairs there seemed to lay a fundamental theological understanding of the church as a "holy and spotless" reality whose true meaning was beyond this world. It is only in some of the Christmas addresses towards the end of his papacy that we have hints that Pius may have concluded that a totally new social order was now necessary, even from the perspective of the church. While it would be difficult to prove decisively, it can at least be suggested that this general shifting of posture on the social order in Europe may have been responsible in part for his heightened commitment to Jewish and Polish security in the final years of the Third Reich.

Giving priority to an examination of the ecclesial context of the Vatican's response during the Nazi period provides us with a perspective rooted in historical experience that can prove extremely valuable as the church confronts other difficult social situations in the present and the future. In fact, it is my conviction that consciously or not Catholicism is beginning to learn from the failings of its policy of reserve in the face of the Nazi challenge, though not without some struggle. I can point to several examples, such as the resolve of the Catholic bishops to encourage active resistance to the Marcos regime when the papal representative was urging caution upon the Vatican, the strong reaction of the Catholic hierarchy in South Africa to the local Vatican legate's appeal for similar public reserve towards apartheid, the unified stand of the Catholic hierarchy of Malawi against human rights abuses by the government, and the forthright manner in which the February 1989 Pontifical Justice & Peace Commission document on racism condemned apartheid, antisemitism, and anti-Zionism by name. While the diplomatic model of the church is surely not totally dead in Catholic circles, there are clear signs the church is putting it aside as it speaks in a manner that unquestionably carries some measure of risk for its institutional well-being. The tendency to view certain groups as "unfortunate expendables" in the process of Catholic preservation is slowly disappearing. No doubt this change is due at least in part to the basic theological change in understanding the church-world relationship which emerged from Vatican II's document on the Church in the Modern World, where there is a sense of a far greater integration between the events of human history and the ultimate purposes of the kingdom of God than was true in Pius XII's fundamental ecclesiology.

Returning to the question of continuing post-Holocaust developments in Catholicism, we note a second trend which involves abandonment of a principle that appeared to curtail the Vatican's response to the "Final Solution" of the Jewish question. I speak of the strong desire to preserve the aristocratic social system in Europe and the consequent fears of both Western liberalism and Bolshevism so evident in the pre-Vatican II social encyclicals. Since Vatican II the Catholic Church has increasingly let go of these fears in their extreme sense as well as of the concomitant commitment to defense of Europe's old social order. The seeds of change were in fact already seen in some of Pius XII's comments about a totally new social order after World War II in his last several Christmas radio messages. Social ethicist David Hollenbach has laid great stress on the significance of this change of ecclesiological perspective:

> ...In following John XXIII, the council did not propose a single model of society or nostalgically seek the elimination of pluralism. It adopted a normative framework for a pluralistic world.
>
> This move amounts to a shift from a social ethic that proposed a concrete model of the structure of society as a necessary exigency of natural law to a social ethic in which all social models and structures are held accountable to the standards of human rights.[24]

Under this new ecclesiology designation of any group as "unfortunate expendables" or outside the "universe of moral obligation" becomes infinitely more difficult. As was pointed out previously, examples of church leaders willing to risk institutional security are becoming frequent enough to warrant the claim that the "reserve" model of ecclesial response, so strongly dominant during the World War II period, is gradually being relegated to the pages of history.

Two final considerations are in order before concluding this analysis. The first has to do with the question of how great a part traditional Catholic antisemitism played in determining the Vatican stance towards the Jews during the Nazi era. There is ample evidence to suggest it had a significant impact, at least in several countries, including France, Germany and Poland.[25] At the level of the Vatican the picture is much harder to determine with great precision. There was little or no public antisemitism at this level, as Jewish commentators such as Riegner have noted. But what subtle impact regional Catholic antisemitism may have had on policy formulation towards the Jews by the Holy See is an issue that awaits further research. This also obtains with respect to more private letters and discussions at the Vatican level which have not been thoroughly examined. At this point, however, despite the remaining ambiguity regarding these areas, we are on safe scholarly grounds in asserting that traditional Christian antisemitism was not a principal determinant of the Vatican's approach.

The second consideration allows for somewhat more definite statement. It is related to the point made previously about the centrality for Pius XII of the preservation of Europe's traditional social order. Several of the papers in the published volume from the Historical Society of Israel's 1982 Conference on "Judaism and Christianity under the Impact of National Socialism"[26] clearly show that many Catholics in Germany especially (but elsewhere as well) perceived the Jews as a threat to their own security and, in some cases, as agents of liberalism and Bolshevism. This seemed to be a far more burning issue relative to Jews than charges connected with traditional antisemitism. While often there was genuine dismay about what was happening to the Jews on the human level, there was also relief that the Jewish community's "subversive" influence on the traditional social order was being removed. Though the case has not been documented and remains one of those unresolved issues, there is reason to suspect that, given Pius XII's deep connection with the German church where this attitude was particularly strong, concern about this Jewish "erosion" factor likely played a role in the shaping of Vatican policy.

This concludes our examination of issues related to the Vatican's response to National Socialism. To repeat, some conclusions are beginning to emerge but much research remains to be done. We serve the well-being neither of contemporary Judaism nor contemporary Catholicism by exaggerated charges or by attempts to suppress parts of the actual record. A carefully nuanced approach is definitely the need of the present hour.

Endnotes

1. Cf. Cardinal Joseph Bernardin, "Tikun Olam, 'Healing the World'," *Catholic International*, 3:13 (1–14 July 1992): 610–617.

2. Robert Graham, S.J., *Pius XII's Defense of Jews and Others: 1944–45* (Milwaukee: Catholic League for Religious and Civil Rights, 1982), 34.

3. As quoted in Graham (n. 2), 21.

4. Graham (n. 2), 21.

5. As quoted in Graham (n. 2), 29–30.

6. "A Warning to the World. The Efforts of the World Jewish Congress to Mobilize the Christian Churches Against the Final Solution," *The Inaugural Stephen S. Wise Lecture* (Cincinnati: Hebrew Union College-Jewish Institute of Religion, November 17, 1983).

7. Riegner, "A Warning" (n. 6), 7.

8. Riegner, "A Warning" (n. 6), 10.

9. Ernst Christian Helmreich, *The German Churches under Hitler: Background, Struggle, and Epilogue* (Detroit: Wayne State University Press, 1979), 364; Otto Dov Kulka, "Popular Christian Attitudes in the Third Reich to National Socialist Policies towards the Jews," in Otto Dov Kulka and Paul R. Mendes-Flohr, eds., *Judaism and Christianity under the Impact of National Socialism* (Jerusalem: The Historical Society of Israel and the Zalman Shazar Center for Jewish History, 1987), 251–267.

10. Riegner, "A Warning" (n. 6), 11.

11. Cf. Henri de Lubac, *Christian Resistance to Anti-Semitism: Memories from 1940–1944* (San Francisco: Ignatius Press, 1990).

12. Cited in Michael R. Marrus, "The Vatican and the Holocaust," *Congress Monthly*, January 1988, 7.

13. John Morley, *Vatican Diplomacy and the Jews during the Holocaust: 1939–1943* (New York: Ktav, 1980), 209.

14. "The Vatican and the Holocaust" (n. 12), and *The Holocaust in History* (Hanover, NH: University Press of New England, 1987).

15. Marrus (n.12), 6.

16. Marrus (n.12), 7.

17. Nora Levin, *The Holocaust* (New York: Schocken, 1973), 693.

18. Helen Fein, *Accounting for Genocide: National Responses and Jewish Victimization during the Holocaust* (Chicago: University of Chicago Press, 1984), 33.

19. Richard Lukas, *Forgotten Holocaust: The Poles under German Occupation 1939–1944* (Lexington, KY: University Press of Kentucky, 1986), 16.

20. Morley (n. 13), 140, 146.

21. J. Derek Holmes, *The Papacy in the Modern World* (New York: Crossroad, 1981), 158.

22. Holmes (n. 21), 164.

23. John Conway, "The Churches" in Henry Friedlander and Sybil Milton, eds., *The Holocaust: Ideology, Bureaucracy, and Genocide* (Millwood, NY: Kraus International Publications, 1980), 199–206.

24. David Hollenbach, *Justice, Peace & Human Rights: American Catholic Social Ethics in a Pluralistic Context* (New York: Crossroad, 1988), 29, 90.

25. Cf. Kulka and Mendes-Flohr, eds., (n. 9).

26. See Kulka and Mendes-Flohr, eds., (n. 9).

Suggestions For Further Reading

General:

Fein, Helen. *Accounting for Genocide. National Responses and Jewish Victimization during the Holocaust*. Chicago: University of Chicago Press, 1984. An historical analysis of how various countries responded to the plight of the Jews. The author develops some useful categories for understanding why Jewish victimization took place.

Friedlander, Henry and Sybil Milton, eds. *The Holocaust: Ideology, Bureaucracy, and Genocide*. Millwood, NY: Kraus International Publications, 1980. A study of the social, cultural and historical roots of the Holocaust by a group of leading Christian and Jewish scholars. Also includes a section on the ethical implications of the event.

Hilberg, Raul. *The Destruction of the European Jews*. 1961. Reprint. New York: Harper and Row, 1979. Revised. 3 vols. New York: Holmes & Meier, 1985. A pioneering study on the Holocaust based on the entire unindexed collection of Nuremberg documents and materials in the Federal Records Center in Virginia. It contains valuable information and references found nowhere else. Hilberg focuses largely on the Nazi machinery of destruction about which he writes comprehensively. His treatment of Jewish responses to the Holocaust and to the direct links between Christian antisemitism and the Nazi annihilation of Jews are open to question.

Levin, Nora. *The Holocaust*. New York: Schocken, 1973. One of the leading interpretative accounts of the Holocaust. Her judgments about church complicity may require refinement but her position should be considered in any overall assessment.

Marrus, Michael. *The Holocaust in History*. Hanover, NH: University Press of New England, 1987. A critical, comprehensive analysis of the significance of the Holocaust as a central event in Western history. The author takes up the question of church responsibility with a candor combined with a sympathetic appreciation for the dilemmas any institution faces in such a situation.

Pawlikowski, John T. *The Challenge of the Holocaust for Christian Theology*. Revised Edition. New York: Anti-Defamation League, 1982. A brief synthesis of important issues for Christian theology in the light of the Holocaust experience. Also briefly considers the role of Pius XII.

Specific:

Graham, Robert A., S.J. *Pius XII's Defense of Jews and Others: 1944–45*. Milwaukee: Catholic League for Religious and Civil Rights, 1982. A strong defense of Pius' record is offered by the author. While his argument may be challenged, he has at least demonstrated that the question is not whether Pius acted at all but whether he could have done more and sooner.

Helmreich, Ernst Christian. *The German Churches under Hitler: Background, Struggle, and Epilogue*. Detroit: Wayne State University Press, 1979. An in-depth analysis of how the churches reacted to Jewish victimization. A solid peace of research.

Kulka, Otto Dov and Paul R. Mendes-Flohr, eds. *Judaism and Christianity under the Impact of National Socialism*. Jerusalem: The Historical Society of Israel and the Zalman Shazar Center for Jewish History, 1987. The most comprehensive country-by-country analysis of church reactions to Jewish victimization yet produced. An indispensable volume that includes many of the leading figures in Holocaust interpretation, both Christian and Jewish.

Littell, Franklin H. and Hubert G. Locke, eds. *The German Church Struggle and the Holocaust*. Detroit: Wayne State University Press, 1974. An excellent examination by a variety of Jewish and Christian scholars of aspects of German church resistance. An important early contribution to Holocaust research.

Lukas, Richard. *Forgotten Holocaust. The Poles under German Occupation, 1939–1944*. Lexington, KY: University Press of Kentucky, 1986. This volume is excellent in its account of the Nazi effort to subjugate the Polish nation and the Polish Catholic concern that the Vatican had abandoned Poland during this critical period. It shows serious flaws in its treatment of Polish antisemitism and in its attempt to equate Polish and Jewish suffering under the Nazis.

Morley, John. *Vatican Diplomacy and the Jews During the Holocaust: 1939–1943*. New York: Ktav, 1980. The author argues that the Catholic Church could have done more to save Jews by making this a priority for its papal nuncios. The volume's biggest drawback is that it fails to cover the final, critical years of World War II.

ALLIED FOREIGN POLICY AND THE HOLOCAUST: THE ROLE OF ANTISEMITISM

Henry L. Feingold

That the Allies were indifferent to the fate of European Jews during World War II is an undisputed fact. But was this indifference due to antisemitism? Henry L. Feingold explores this question.

Imagine this. The millennial scourge of antisemitism, which heretofore has nested in the cultural and political crevices of Western civilization, is miraculously dissipated so that when the National Socialists come to power in Germany in January 1933, Germans are neutral about Jews, even philosemitic. I call it a miracle because that is what the suspension of such a persistent historical phenomenon comes to. Few readers would give credence to such a happening. Yet it is necessary to imagine such a miracle in order to conclude, as some do, that antisemitism bears little relation to Allied indifference to the fate of the Jews during the fateful years of the Holocaust.[1]

Paradoxically, the reverse assumption, that the Holocaust is the ultimate and logical expression of European antisemitism, and lies behind the callous indifference of the witnessing nations, is equally untenable. In the case of the Nazi "final solution," we know today that the mass murder of the Jews was not only discontinuous with prior German and Austrian antisemitism, but actually became public policy without popular consensus. The position of prominent Germans like Karl Goerdeler, the mayor of Leipzig, may have been more representative of German public opinion at large. He wished the Reich to be *Judenrein* but opposed the genocide being committed in the name of the German people. The implementation of the "final solution" required some all-powerful enabler which was the "führer." There is good reason to believe that the Holocaust would not have happened without the demonic presence of Hitler on the world stage.[2] He acted as the trigger and through a totalitarian dominance, which rendered the German people as subjects rather than as "citoyens," was able to impose his personal pathological hatred of Jews on a people whom history and circumstance had made ready to accept, or at least not resist, what was being done in their name in the East.

But what of the witnessing nations, what of the Allies? Surely their indifference to the saving of life cannot be considered apart form the prevailing antisemitism which was especially virulent during these years. London circumvented its own rules of blockade to feed the occupied Greeks throughout the war, but refused even to consider a change in designation to Prisoner of War for the Jews in concentration camps, much less to allow the sending of food packages. That marked a considerable change from World War I when the Jewish question did earn considerable attention from the Allies. It was, in fact, partly British concern about Jewish influence in Washington which led to the issuance of the Balfour Declaration in 1917. But despite incessant antisemitic rhetoric about Jewish power no such influence was at play during World War II. There had been a pronounced diminution in the effectiveness of Jewish power and influence during the interwar period.[3]

Can one then conclude that Allied indifference to the fate of the Jews was caused by antisemitism? In order to respond to that query the historian needs first to probe certain assumptions regarding the making of public policy: can we assume that the prevalence of an antisemitic mind-set among policy makers and bureaucrats willy-nilly translated itself into policy? Is there a way we can differentiate antisemitism from other motivations which influence a particular policy? There is no certain answer to these questions. In the end we are left with millions of Jewish dead and the destruction of a dynamic Jewish civilization, and no reasonable way to determine what role antisemitism in the minds of Allied decision-makers might have played in it.

This discussion limits itself to some observations regarding the policies of the United States, Britain, and the Soviet Union during those fateful years. It does not deal with certain major policies such as appeasement and isolationism, which indirectly impinged on the Jewish fate by allowing National Socialism to secure and extend its power. Such policies were imagined at the time to serve the national interest. There was no consideration of how they affected European Jewry.

In the case of American policy, it is the immigration laws of 1921 and 1924, passed well before the crisis, which offer the most relevant example of the link of antisemitism to public policy. The link is indirect before 1933 and direct after that year. The quota system which favored immigrants whose national origin was northern and western European depended on the theory of "nordicism," also known as "nordic supremacy." In the Germany of National Socialism it would be known as "aryanism." The ideological anchorage on which the "final solution" depended found prior expression in American immigration law.

That law, which allowed for no distinction between refugees in dire need of haven and normal immigrants, would ultimately contribute much to the destruction of European Jewry. That was especially true during the thirties when a directive of the Hoover administration calling for strict enforcement of the "likely to become a public charge" (LPC) provision of the law, cut off even those who might have found refuge. Only in 1939 were the relevant quotas filled. The linkage seems clear. Jews were extruded from Germany and later exterminated, for the same reason that they were unacceptable immigrants to the United States—they had the wrong blood. That connection has a special relevance for our examination. There is little question today that had Germany succeeded in making the Reich *Judenrein* through immigration, the decision for a final, more drastic solution, might never have been made, or at the least, might have been postponed. Karl Schleunes reminds us that the road to Auschwitz was twisted, and that there was nothing pre-ordained about the Holocaust.[4] We cannot assume that Hitler knew in 1939 precisely how he would solve the "Jewish problem." But the failure to find alternate solutions like emigration, as remote as the possibility of implementation was, certainly contributed to the nexus of circumstances in which the decision for mass murder was made. In a sense the struggle to save European Jewry was lost in the first round, partly as a result of our restrictive racialist immigration law.

But having noted the racialist origins of the law and the drastic impact of its implementation, we are beset by problems concerning the role of antisemitism. Serious questions can be raised whether the intent of the original law was to specifically restrict Jews. From the Congressional hearings in 1921 and 1924 we learn that the lawmakers were heavily influenced by rumors that Polish Jewry, which had been utterly devastated by the war, stood poised to "flood" America. In 1920, 119,000 had entered the country, so over-burdening reception facilities in New York that ships were rerouted to Boston. But notwithstanding the impassioned voices of the Yiddish press, only one case of antisemitism by a State Department official was uncovered. It concerned a memorandum which used well-known pejoratives to describe the potential Jewish immigrants and a vastly exaggerated estimate of the number of those who wanted to enter the United States.[5] The memorandum embarrassed Charles E. Hughes, then Secretary of State, who was reminded of its questionable legality by Louis Marshall. He issued corrective directives so that it could not recur. But in the text of the immigration law itself, Jews are not mentioned and, of course, there was no Jewish quota. Paradoxically, Italian-Americans can make a far better claim than Jews that the laws were aimed at them. Senator "Cotton Ed" Smith, who was one of the sponsors of restrictive legislation, would have exempted the Jews from the quota system, as they were from the Literacy Test Act of 1917. But he was adamant about keeping Italians out. When a Jewish journalist and activist, Gedaliah Bublick, openly accused the committee members of antisemitism at the hearings, it was "coolly" denied by the chairman who insisted that it was all fortuitous. Had the Jews had the foresight to settle in Scotland, they would have been under the more generous English quota.[6]

Antisemitic intent is difficult to prove and it is even more difficult to demonstrate that the law did what it was intended to do. For example, the "national origins" system was designed to restore the ethnic composition of the nation to what it was in 1890. But we know today that it did no such thing. By the twenties the pioneering types, Scandinavians, Germans, and English stock, so extolled by the "nordomaniacs," preferred to remain at home and enjoy the benefits of the developing welfare state. Their quotas went unfilled while those for Italy and Poland were over-subscribed. Those who needed to come were unwanted, and those who were wanted, would not come. So much for social engineering through public policy.

Finding a direct link between public policy and antisemitism becomes even more elusive during the crucial period between 1933 and 1945. The highly restrictive implementation of the law, initiated by Hoover's LPC directive, exacerbated the refugee crisis which was a harbinger of the Holocaust. But ostensibly it was issued, not because of a distaste for Jews, but because the Depression had created a virtually unanimous consensus that America must concern herself first with her own unemployed. That was also the opinion of most American Jews. Even so, as the crisis grew in intensity, some exceptions to the directive were allowed for prominent refugee scholars and political leaders and culture carriers.

Yet every son of a Jewish mother knew that to prepare oneself for a career in the foreign service of the State Department was an exercise in futility. The evidence we have in the memoirs of State Department officials substantiates that they did not misperceive.[7] Jews were not wanted. There was also some antisemitism among the consuls who, under the law, made the final decision about the issuance of visas. Yet recently a suggestion that the antisemitism of State Department officials like Wilbur J. Carr, William Phillips, and Breckinridge Long has to be factored in to explain the inhuman implementation of policy in such cases as the *St. Louis* and the SS *Quanza*, two ships blocked from landing refugees by the Department, was questioned by younger historians. They doubt "that anti-Semitism was the primary instruction behind the State Department's policies affecting Jewish refugees" and see no evidence of it in the grand policy design. State Department officials were more concerned, and legitimately so they insist, with the fear that spies had infiltrated the refugee stream. I am admonished that "the recognition of anti-Semitism must not become a substitute for the intricate and difficult work of analyzing the political and bureaucratic processes of government during the Holocaust and the preceding decade."[8] Nor can we assume that antisemitic officials necessarily implement antisemitic policies. There were, for example, many such Endec xenophobic types in the Polish Government-in-Exile, yet in 1940 that government entered into negotiations with Jews to find some *modus vivendi* during the crisis. It was the London Poles who requested retributive bombing in December 1942. From a contemporary perspective, the idea of bombing German cities in 1942–43 in retaliation for what the SS was doing in the East seems far more realizable than the later proposal to bomb the rail lines and the gas chambers, which only became possible in the spring of 1944 when most of the Jews were already in ashes.[9]

If the restrictive immigration laws and their implementation can serve as a prism to view the question of American policy in relation to the Holocaust, then the White Paper of 1939 serves the same purpose for British policy. Is it conceivable that a policy which severely curtailed Jewish immigration and land sales in Palestine, in the teeth of the crisis, was not at least partly motivated by antisemitism? Palestine was such a logical haven for at least a portion of the refugees, that to deny it meant that death was almost certainly the alternative. That much was clear by the early months of 1943. Yet the first shots fired in World War II were by British soldiers at Jews trying to enter Palestine, and there is the incredibly heartless case of the *Struma* and the *Patria*, illegal refugee ships which went down with heavy loss of Jewish life because of the difficulty of access to Palestine. Yet historians like Michael Cohen and others, while not denying that antisemitism was rampant in British ruling circles, give far greater emphasis to national interest as the source of this ruthless policy. There was a conviction that the impending crisis required strong ties to the Arab world whose oil and loyalty were requisite for British security.[10]

Yet antisemitism there was and it was sometimes put to perverse use. British and American officials were wont to cite fear of arousing antisemitism as the reason for not offering Jews haven. Herbert Morrison, the British Home Secretary, counseled rejection of a 1940 Vichy offer to release Jewish children, because it would "stir up an unpleasant degree of anti-Semitism (of which there is a fair amount just below the surface) and that would be bad for the country and the Jewish community."[11] Breckinridge Long, an Assistant Secretary of State, used much the same argument to thwart Jewish pressure for the admission of more refugees to the United States. When the Archbishop of Canterbury warned the House of Lords that the use of the fear of arousing antisemitism as a strategy to avoid the rescue of threatened lives was cynical and unchristian, his voice was not heard. When the same argument was used to thwart the policy of retributive bombing, suggested by the Polish Government-in-Exile in 1942, the results were lethal for Jews. Retributive bombing would have required no change in wartime priorities, which had become the chief stumbling block to rescue. By 1943 German cities were already being savaged from the air and all that was required was that the German people be informed through leafletting and other means, that the bombing was retribution for what was being done in their name in the East. Had it been used, it would undoubtedly have created a serious morale problem for Berlin, much the way *Kristallnacht* had. More important, it would have opened up the question of the fate of the Jews who had been deported and lifted the curtain of silence surrounding the "final solution." Indeed, Goebbels and Himmler fully expected that the Allies would play this card and had prepared a counter-atrocity campaign. They were convinced that bombing was a Jewish plot.

But the card was never played. It was rejected by middle-echelon officials in the British and American government bureaucracy because they believed that retributive bombing was illegal. They continued to insist upon that while they knew the extermination of the Jews was occurring, because they feared that it would turn the war into one to save the Jews, a linkage German propaganda exploited endlessly. As stated by Chief of the Air Staff, Sir Charles Portal on January 2, 1943: "[Hitler] has so often stressed that this is a war by the Jews to exterminate Germany that it might as well be, therefore, that a raid, avowedly conducted on account of the Jews, would be an asset to enemy propaganda."[12] Instead the bombing of Dresden was carried out in February 1945, but was never announced as a response to the "final solution," which might have given it some justification. Ironically, that failure allows it to be considered a separate and equivalent atrocity in contemporary Germany.

The amalgamation of ideology and policy makes the case of the Soviet Union more difficult to judge. In the antisemitic cosmology of National Socialism, Communism and Judaism were inexorably intertwined. It was a linkage reflected in policy and propaganda. Thus the Commissar Order, the only written evidence of an order for extermination, which was given to German commanders in 1941, ordered the execution of *Politrunkniks* (political officers which began at the battalion level in the Soviet Army) and Jews. The order was carried out by the *Einsatzgruppen,* the murder squads that followed behind the invading *Wehrmacht* in June 1941. The mass killing by starvation of thousands of Soviet POWs served as a model for the operation of the death camps. The first inmates of Auschwitz wore the uniforms of these murdered Soviet POWs. Clearly, the Soviets had much more direct evidence of the murderous Nazi intent and were faced with a direct link to the fate of the Jews. It was to be their fate too. But that did not lay the groundwork for common cause.

About 2,000,000 Jews found a momentary precarious haven in Russia during the war. About 300,000 of these were able to flee eastward from German occupied Poland and additional thousands came from the Baltic states and the reoccupied areas of Romania. They were not rescued as part of a Soviet policy towards threatened Jews, but rather fled or were evacuated together with the general population. Only in the Crimea were Jews evacuated collectively. Since the twenties, when a trickle of Jewish communists had been welcomed to join resettlement projects in the Crimea and later in Birobidzhan, Soviet policy rejected Jewish refugees, not for religious reasons, to be sure, but because they often stemmed from the despised bourgeoisie. Afterwards the Soviet Union was invited to join the League of Nations' Refugee Commission. Both agencies strove vainly to bring order into the refugee chaos. A disproportionate number of Jewish artists and intellectuals were victims of the purges during the thirties. Soviet foreign policy remained adamantly opposed to Zionism and its settlements in Palestine. During the interwar period thousands of Zionists vanished into the Gulag.

But after the German invasion of the Soviet Union in June 1941, as many as 1.5 million Jews made their way into the interior of the Soviet Union where, together with other fleeing Russians, they sometimes found a precarious safety. The number rescued might have been much higher had the Holocaust not been preceded in the Soviet Union by a Sovietization policy which deprived Jewish communities of their leadership, and destroyed all communal and cultural organizations. The *Einsatzgruppen* thus found their Jewish victims to be an unorganized leaderless mass, amazingly uninformed about what fate had in store for them. For the preceding decade they had lived virtually in an informational vacuum. Some even greeted German troops as saviors.[13] Of those who were evacuated to the interior, thousands were interned in camps, and many died of malnutrition. When the tide of war turned, the Soviets again proved to be indifferent regarding the fate of Jews in death camps. They too rejected suggestions to bomb the death chambers, although by 1944 they were in a far better position to do so. Dov Levin's conclusion might just as easily have been written about the United States and Britain. "The humanitarian component and the desire to save Jews," he concludes about Soviet policy, "were insignificant."[14] The meaning of the destruction of European Jewry, which should have been especially clear to Soviet leaders, since their fate was linked to that of the Jews, was deliberately underplayed. Even today Moscow does not acknowledge the anti-Jewish thrust of the Holocaust in its war memorials. As in Poland, the Jewish victims are granted in death what was never given in life. They are considered honored martyrs of the nation.

Yet as in the United States and Britain, there are extenuating circumstances. The treatment of the Russian people by the occupying Germans was harsh. Soviet losses were extremely heavy. It took a long time to recover from the shock of the invasion and for almost two years it seemed as if the Soviet Union would not survive. Such a government was hardly in a position to concern itself much about the fate of the Jews or to contemplate the meaning of the death camps. They were probably more concerned that they would be compelled to join the assembly line of death. Moreover, having themselves produced a "world of camps" and their own version of mass murder of Kulaks and of Polish prisoners at Katyn, they were hardly fitting subjects for moral suasion concerning Jews. When former Soviet officials are broached on the question of their indifference to the fate of their Jewish subjects, they inevitably cite the Constitution of 1936 which outlawed antisemitism. Yet only the timely death of Stalin in 1953 prevented the deportation of Soviet Jewry to the Gulag where, undoubtedly, an unhappy fate would have awaited them.

* * * * *

What then might one reasonably conclude regarding the relationship between

Allied wartime policy and the Holocaust? That the Jews of Europe were ground to dust between the twin millstones of a murderous Nazi intent and a callous Allied indifference, seems evident. But whether that indifference to the saving of life was caused by the fact that it was primarily Jewish life is far less apparent. We have research which indicates that the Catholic Church was equally passive regarding the murder of its own adherents, Poles, Gypsies, and even its priests who died in Dachau and Auschwitz. The Vatican's rescue program for Catholic refugees was underfinanced and poorly organized.[15] The same is true of Soviet inaction regarding the liquidation of its soldiers who had been taken prisoner. It may be that we assume that the nation-state has more power to influence events than it possesses in reality and then assign it a responsibility which it cannot fulfill, at least not during wartime, with an enemy state particularly immune to moral suasion.

Clearly much of Allied indifference to the fate of the Jews during the Holocaust can be rationalized under the general rubric, "reasons of state." Until the spring of 1943, shortly after the battle of Stalingrad, the Allies thought of themselves as likely potential victims of the Nazi juggernaut. But that leaves unexplained the inaction of the period before the war, the refugee phase of the thirties, and the two years following the spring of 1943, when the light of victory could be seen at the end of the tunnel. Something more substantial is required to explain Allied inaction during these periods. Antisemitism was prevalent among Allied decision-makers as it was in the general population. But oddly enough, it is difficult to link it to a specific policy step. That is so because antisemitism rarely existed in a vacuum. The historian cannot overlook the fact that the Depression conditioned the "hard" implementation of the immigration laws and that national security considerations played a major role in Britain's decision to limit Jewish immigration into Palestine at a critical juncture. Consideration of the Jewish plight did not take precedence over consideration of national interests.

In the case of the Jews, it was not so much that they were hated, but that they were not important or powerful enough to be of concern. Ironically, the reality was precisely the reverse of what antisemitic propaganda imagined the Jews to be. Beyond the exigencies of war, European Jewry was not considered to be within the "universe of obligation" of Western civilization. They were not citizens of a state in the western sphere which could make their case. They had become so much excess baggage on a crowded lifeboat, itself in danger of sinking. But even had they been part of that "universe," there is still no guarantee that the outcome might have been otherwise. The Armenians can attest to that. It may be that the very assumption of assigning states a humanitarian mission, which is an integral part of Jewish political culture, is misplaced. Jews, together with other vulnerable peoples, assume automatically that the state ought to seek justice and that there exists a moral spirit in the world which will protect them. The weak always cry for justice and morality, while the powerful call for order. It is in their interest to have such a caring world. But not everyone makes such assumptions. Japanese-Americans, who certainly have a more direct claim against the Roosevelt administration, did not file that claim until very recently, and Armenians do not write books about the inaction of the Wilson administration. The question "Did Roosevelt do enough?" is quintessentially a Jewish one. It is based on the assumption that one ought to care. It is the same principle which lies behind their overwhelming support of welfare state legislation in the domestic arena.

Finally, there seems little doubt that, especially in the case of the implementation of immigration policy during the refugee phase of the crisis, there was an inurement. Much more might have been done during the thirties to grant haven to those in need. That initial failure spilled over into the war. Of course, there were ample reasons for not opening the gates to Jewish refugees. Few Allied leaders were able to imagine that the alternative would be genocide.

But beyond that there is something that becomes startlingly apparent to the historian. Policy makers in Washington, London, and Moscow thought that it was happening to someone else, a strange people who were not winning medals for popularity in their own countries. They never understood that the chimneys of the crematoria and the chimneys of the factories, which allowed them to enjoy the highest living standard in the world, were part of the same industrial process. Only the death factories built by the SS were producing so many units of death, tolled by managers of the production line, fed by Europe's extensive railroad grid which brought the human raw material to the death machine. They failed to recognize a familiar industrial process. Their civilization had gone awry and was consuming its own children. They were mostly Jews but they were European too. The leaders in the Oval Office, Downing Street, and the Kremlin never remotely understood that it was their world that was burning.

Endnotes

1. The most recent work on the witness role of the Roosevelt administration almost completely discounts the part of antisemitism as an element in its indifference to rescue. See Richard Breitman and Alan M. Kraut, *American Refugee Policy and European Jewry, 1933–1945* (Bloomington: Indiana University Press, 1987). Anti-Bolshevism takes precedence over "judeophobia," to which it is linked, in Arno J. Mayer, *Why did the Heavens Not Darken? The "Final Solution" in History* (New York: Pantheon Books, 1989).

2. See Sarah Gordon, *Hitler, Germans, and the "Jewish Question"* (Princeton: Princeton University Press, 1984); Lucy S. Dawidowicz, "Towards A History of the Holocaust," *Commentary*, 47 (April 1969): 51–56; for an explanation of the new biological antisemitism see J.L. Talmon, "European History—Seedbed of the Holocaust," *Midstream* 19 (May 1973): 7.

3. Morris D. Waldman, *Nor By Power* (New York: International Universities Press, 1953), 79.

4. Karl Schleunes, *The Twisted Road to Auschwitz: Nazi Policies Towards the Jews, 1933–1939* (Urbana: University of Illinois Press, 1970).

5. *Louis Marshall, Champion of Liberty, Selected Papers and Addresses*, ed. Charles Reznikoff (Philadelphia, Jewish Publication Society, 1957), L. Marshall to Charles E. Hughes, April 27, 1921, 1:174–175.

6. *Hearings Before the House Committee on Immigration and Naturalization*, "Restriction of Immigration," 68th Congress, 1st Session, January 3, 1924.

7. See for example *The War Diary of Breckinridge Long*, ed. Fred L. Israel (Lincoln: University of Nebraska Press, 1966).

8. Richard D. Breitman and Alan M. Kraut, "Anti-Semitism in the State Department, 1933–44: Four Case Studies," in *Anti-Semitism in American History*, ed. David A. Gerber (Urbana: University of Illinois Press, 1986), 167–197.

9. David Engel, *In The Shadow of Auschwitz: The Polish Government-in-Exile and the Jews, 1939–1942* (Chapel Hill: University of North Carolina Press, 1987); Martin Gilbert, *Auschwitz and The Allies* (New York: Holt, Rinehart & Winston, 1981), 106.

10. Michael J. Cohen, *Churchill and the Jews* (London: Frank Cass, 1984).

11. Gilbert (n. 9), 76–77.

12. Gilbert (n. 9), 107.

13. Raul Hilberg, *The Destruction of the European Jews* (New York: Franklin Watts, 1973), 207–208.

14. Dov Levin, "The Attitude of the Soviet Union Toward Rescue Attempts During the Holocaust," *Proceedings of the Second Yad Vashem International Historical Conference*, April 9–17, 1974, pp. 230–235.

15. Owen Chadwick, *Britain and the Vatican During the Second World War* (Cambridge: Cambridge University Press, 1986); Michael R. Marrus, *The Holocaust In History* (Hanover, NH: University Press of New England, 1987), 179–183; John Morley, *Vatican Diplomacy and the Jews During the Holocaust, 1939–1943* (New York: Ktav, 1980).

Suggestions For Further Reading

Breitman, Richard and Alan Kraut. *American Refugee Policy and European Jewry, 1933–1945.* Bloomington: Indiana University Press, 1987. A recent work that plays down the significance of antisemitism in the American posture of indifference to the fate of European Jews, pointing up functional, ad hoc, non-ideological factors.

Engel, David. *In the Shadow of Auschwitz: The Polish Government-in-Exile and the Jews, 1939–1942.* Chapel Hill: University of North Carolina Press, 1987. Examines this crucial agency's policy towards the "final solution," much of which took place on Polish soil. Goes far to correct the impression of Polish indifference to the fate of the Jews.

Feingold, Henry L. *The Politics of Rescue, The Roosevelt Administration and the Holocaust, 1938–1945.* New York: Holocaust Library, 1980. A pioneer study, notable for its understanding of the inner workings of the Roosevelt government, especially of the roles of figures such as Secretary of State Cordell Hull, Breckinridge Long, and John J. McCloy.

Gilbert, Martin. *Auschwitz and the Allies.* New York: Holt, Rinehart, Winston, 1981. Perhaps the most judicious work in evaluating the various "deals" offered by Himmler and other Nazis for the release and rescue of Jews.

____. *The Second World War: A Complete History.* New York: Henry Holt, 1989. A large-scale work that sets the Holocaust and rescue diplomacy in the context of the war's day-to-day exigencies of policy-making and implementation.

Hilberg, Raul. *The Destruction of the European Jews.* 1961. Reprint. New York: Franklin Watts, 1973. The monumental work, concentrating on the perpetrators, that remains indispensable for students of the Holocaust; it is also available in a revised and expanded edition. 3 vols. New York: Holmes & Meier, 1985.

Morley, John. *Vatican Diplomacy and the Jews during the Holocaust, 1939–1943.* New York: Ktav, 1980. A balanced and reasoned defense of the Vatican, noting that the papacy did much but could have and should have done much more to assist Jews; Morley emphasizes Pius XII's timidity in not urging the nuncios to be forceful in aiding Jews and in condemnation of oppression and deportation. A much less satisfactory work for the latter and more critical part of the war is Robert A. Graham. *Pius XII's Defense of Jews and Others, 1944–45.* Milwaukee: Catholic League for Religious and Civil Rights, 1982.

Wasserstein, Bernard. *Britain and the Jews of Europe, 1939–1945.* London: Clarendon Press, 1979. A sober and sobering account, heavily based on archival research, of the British government's wartime policies barring Jews from finding refuge in Britain and from Palestine under the Mandate, giving leads which were often followed by the American government.

Wyman, David S. *The Abandonment of the Jews: America and the Holocaust, 1941–1945.* New York: Pantheon Books, 1985. A Protestant historian's work notable for its superb archival research and its searing indictment of American failures, of omission and commission, from President Roosevelt and State Department on down: "The Nazis were the murderers, but we were the all too passive accomplices" is his conclusion; ten summary judgments are conveniently stated on pages x–xi. A sequel to Wyman's valuable and insightful *Paper Walls: America and the Refugee Crisis, 1938–1941*. New York: Pantheon, 1968.

MARTIN NIEMÖLLER, ACTIVIST AS BYSTANDER: THE OFT-QUOTED REFLECTION*

Ruth Zerner

One of the great lessons of the Holocaust—drawn alike by scholars, journalists, the mass media, the person in the street, and the pupil in the classroom—is that the bystanders failed in their human responsibility as witnesses. Everyone quotes, that is to say, misquotes, the celebrated statement by Pastor Martin Niemöller that is the subject of the following essay. Ruth Zerner inquires into the origin of that pivotal reflection, establishes the correct rendering of it, and conveys the toil and hardship entailed to its author before he could overcome the antipathy/indifference to Jews and Judaism with which he, as a German nationalist and Christian, was imbued. It is an odyssey which so many of us have to traverse if we are to enter into dialogue that will cleanse the theological tablets and set the historical record straight.

Introduction

Born 1892 in a Protestant parsonage of Lippstadt, Germany, and descended on his mother's side from French Huguenots, Martin Niemöller was brought up as a son of the Reformation. But his own path to the Protestant pulpit led through the deep waters of the Atlantic naval battles of World War One, where he served as a German U-boat commander. Enthusiastically Niemöller had chosen a naval career that had included officer training, culminating in his 1911 oath of loyalty to the German Emperor Wilhelm II.

Committed to German national and military glory, Niemöller was troubled by the armistice of 1918 and the subsequent destruction of the German navy.

---

* Readers who wish a more general account of Protestant reactions to the Nazi German attack on the Jews before, during, and after the Third Reich are referred to Ruth Zerner, "German Protestant Responses to Nazi Persecution of the Jews," in *Perspectives on the Holocaust*, ed. Randolph L. Braham (Boston: Kluwer-Nijhoff, 1983), 57–68.

Rather than participate in what he conceived to be the humiliation of the German navy, he returned to civilian life as a farmer. During that physically demanding farming interlude of the 1920s, Niemöller would later reflect [in a film interview] that he "grew content again." Encouraged by his father, he studied theology at the University of Münster. After graduation he became an administrator in the German Inner Mission (1924–1931), until he was invited to become a pastor in the fashionable Berlin suburb of Dahlem.

From the pulpit of the Dahlem church Niemöller preached sermons that made history during the early years of Nazi rule (1933–1937). He became the most forceful and outspoken leader of the German Protestant Church Struggle against Nazi attempts to control and to regulate church life. In 1934 the Confessing Church was formed, composed of the one-third of the German Protestant clergy who broke away from the Protestant Church that was heir to the Reformation, but was capitulating to the demands of the Nazi state. Berliners thronged to hear Niemöller's Dahlem sermons, because his strident words resisted Nazi attempts to warp God's Word and Christian institutions. Just as he fought for his nation and Emperor in World War One, so he fought for his church and his God during the 1930s. His was the most powerful and popular voice of the Confessing Church. Thomas Mann [in his preface to Niemöller's sermons] recognized and admired the symbolic forms of military virtues that had been carried over into Niemöller's pastorate. Mann also perceived extraordinary psychological radicalism in this feisty churchman.

After the Second World War this radicalism so intensified that at the age of 92, Niemöller recalled that he had started his life as a very conservative person, but over time he became first a progressive and then a revolutionary. The turning point was probably linked to his imprisonment from 1937 to 1945, when he was held as Hitler's personal prisoner. The concentration camps of Sachsenhausen and Dachau, he said in a film interview, "really destroyed any self-righteousness in me." Prussian virtues such as loyalty were transformed into wider, human commitments, making him into an internationalist after the Second World War. Pride and self-righteousness yielded to clear confessions of guilt and responsibility for the failure to act during the Nazi terror. Active in the peace movement, critical of postwar militarism and the nuclear arms race, Niemöller traveled the world, both as a goodwill ambassador for Germany and as a critic of irresponsible use of power. Although the Protestantism in which he was raised and trained had strains of anti-Catholicism and theological antisemitism, Niemöller evolved into an energetic ecumenist, elected in 1961 as one of the presidents of the World Council of Churches. When he died in 1984 at the age of 92, Niemöller was a pacifist and a citizen of the world with profound concerns for all humanity.

Since Martin Niemöller spoke publicly so frequently (both with and without written statements) in an era before audio and video recordings were the order of the day, we have to rely on oral history, including the memories of those who were present at his meetings. There is no accurate, conclusive written document in which Martin Niemöller penned at the time of conception the words which have become the most popular quote associated with his post-concentration camp life. This essay attempts to record the relevant reflections of those closest to him and to the events of his unforgettable life.

Martin Niemöller, Activist as Bystander: The oft-quoted Reflection

Writing from a Nazi prison cell on January 5, 1938, Pastor Martin Niemöller bluntly told his wife:

> ...Dibelius's writing you that people will read about me in all the textbooks of church history is of little comfort. First, they are boring anyway and secondly, as the Berliners say quite correctly: 'What will that get me?'...[1]

Ambitious and energetic, Martin Niemöller, as a preacher, church official and public figure, was far from boring. His life in Germany during the Nazi era inspired church historian John S. Conway to assert: "The courage and energy of Martin Niemöller in the face of political persecution have redeemed some of the vacillating compromises of weaker men."[2] Although a U-boat officer and hero of World War One, Martin Niemöller in 1919 decided to follow in his father's footsteps as a Protestant pastor. Defending the rights of Protestants against Nazi attempts to control their church life, Niemöller was incarcerated by the Nazis in 1937 and held as Adolf Hitler's "personal prisoner" from 1938 to 1945. As the most outspoken leader of the Pastors' Emergency League (1933) and then of the Confessing Church (from 1934), which had challenged Nazi penetration and regulation of the Protestant Church, Niemöller, along with Karl Barth, shaped the course of the German church struggle. In the words of Franklin H. Littell: "If Karl Barth was the most important theologian of the church resistance to Nazism, Martin Niemöller was until his imprisonment its primary strategist."[3]

In spite of his reputation as an activist, Niemöller's verbal self-portrait of himself as a bystander has been the most frequently quoted and misquoted of his statements, especially in the United States during the past two decades. Not in his published sermons, but through the memories of those who heard him or were close to him, can we attempt to reconstruct the original phrasing of Niemöller's personal confession of failure to care enough during the 1930s in Berlin. Franklin Littell recalls that Niemöller, during his post-World War Two travels through the United States,

> concluded many of his addresses with the now famous statement:
> 'First they came for the socialists,

and I did not speak out—
because I was not a socialist.
Then they came for the trade unionists,
and I did not speak out—
because I was not a trade unionist.
Then they came for the Jews,
and I did not speak out—
because I was not a Jew.
Then they came for me—
and there was no one left to speak for me."[4]

Franklin Littell has assured me that he verified his recollection of these words with an American church official who organized Niemöller's speaking engagements in the United States after the war.[5] In addition, Littell confirmed the progression of groups cited by Niemöller with his second wife, Sibylle A. Niemöller von Sell, who had discussed this declaration with her husband. Although she was not present at Niemöller's postwar lectures, before his 1984 death she spoke with him about his use of these phrases. She maintains that Niemöller did not include Roman Catholics in the statement and that he could not remember the exact date on which he first spoke these words; but Mrs. Sibylle Niemöller says that this statement originated verbally—in discussion accompanying his postwar speeches, certainly not in written form.[6] Therefore, like Biblical tales, this biographical confession has its genesis in oral tradition. According to Sibylle Niemöller, "the famous quotation" should read:

First they came for the communists,
but I was not a communist—
so I said nothing.
Then they came for the social democrats,
but I was not a social democrat—
so I did nothing.
Then came the trade unionists,
but I was not a trade unionist.
And then they came for the Jews,
but I was not a Jew—
so I did little.
Then when they came for me,
there was no one left who could stand up for me.[7]

The most obvious addition in this version of Niemöller's reflection is the inclusion of the communists at the start of the statement. Historically, they were the first to suffer persecution and imprisonment in Nazi Germany. James Bentley, Niemöller's British biographer, cites numerous examples of Niemöller's insistence "on sharing the guilt which many hoped to push to one side" after 1945; Niemöller "now identified the sufferings of communists as well as Jews with those of Jesus Christ himself. As he told his fellow-countrymen, in refusing to speak out for them, German Protestants had again betrayed their Lord."[8] Looking back on the Nazi years, Niemöller, after liberation from prison, reminded the German churches of their failure to identify with all victims:

> If we had then recognized that in the communists who were thrown into concentration camps, the Lord Jesus Christ himself lay imprisoned and looked for our love and help, if we had seen that at the beginning of the persecution of the Jews it was the Lord Christ in the person of the least of our human brethren who was being persecuted and beaten and killed, if we had stood by him and identified ourselves with him, I do not know whether God would not then have stood by us and whether the whole thing would not then have had to take a different course.[9]

This postwar pattern of identification with the most scorned of Hitler's victims makes it likely that Niemöller *did* include communists in his famous reflection, as Sibylle Niemöller indicates. Although Littell's 1986 published version of this statement starts with socialists, not mentioning communists, Littell, in a later conversation, told me that the correct order should be: communists, socialists, trade unionists, Jews.[10] Perhaps his initial, published reference to the first group as "socialists" could be interpreted as a generic term, including both communists and social democrats.

The differences between Littell's and Sibylle Niemöller's versions of this quotation reflect the difficulties of transcribing and verifying oral communications, particularly years after the events occurred. Even Martin Niemöller himself probably made slight variations in phrasing or verbs when he repeated this comment in the numerous speeches he delivered during his worldwide travels. For example, in Littell's version, repeating the same phrase "speak out" heightens the oratorical drama and provides grammatical parallelism. It is likely that Niemöller sometimes employed such rhetorical repetition. On the other hand, the phrase "stand up for" in Sibylle Niemöller's version is familiar to a scholar who has studied Niemöller's sermons. In the months preceding his own imprisonment (on July 1, 1937), many of Niemöller's Berlin-Dahlem pulpit messages stressed the need to "stand up for" or "stand by" the Christians in prison:

> ...the Savior undertook to do battle for our sakes. Dear brethren, it should comfort us to hear that, when we think during these days...of those who are forsaken because none of their friends stand by them and because God does not open the doors of their prison. (February 18, 1937)[11]

> Today we hear the cry of our captive and exiled Christian brethren: *Who* will rise up for me against the evil-doers? or *who* will stand up for me against the workers of iniquity? (April 7, 1937)[12]

> Today, when a messenger of Jesus Christ is imprisoned because of his creed, it is not the case, as it was two years ago, that others stand up in his place, but on the contrary, the rest receive the news with apprehension. (April 24, 1937)[13]

> But we ought not to think that by taking sides we should have the faith for which we stand up...(May 2, 1937)[14]

Thus, "stand up," a favorite phrase of Niemöller's, might well have been his choice to conclude "the famous" reflection.

Stylistically, the word order of Sibylle Niemöller's version would be more congenial to an orator who grew up speaking German. In English, word order is not as regularly used to convey emphasis as in German; for instance, often in German sentences the verb appears at the end of the clause. Therefore, I think that Sibylle Niemöller's placement of the crucial utterances ("so I did nothing") at the end of the sentences, is closer to the way Martin Niemöller would have expressed himself, even when speaking English. In German the "weight" of the sentence is usually at the beginning or at the end.

Both Franklin Littell and Brigitte Johannesson, the only surviving daughter of Martin and Else Niemöller, claim that this oft-quoted remark was first used in English-speaking countries, probably spoken in English. According to Brigitte Johannesson, her father first used this statement in a speech in England, possibly in the early sixties, although it could have been any time between 1955 and 1969. Based on her conversations with her father in the 1970s, she thinks that dating the statement in the 1940s would be too early.[15] Littell, on the other hand, would date the first use of these words from the 1940s, during Niemöller's travels in the United States, immediately after the end of the Second World War.[16] Like Johannesson, Sibylle Niemöller thinks that the famed reflection originated in "a discussion after a lecture about 10–20 years after the war."[17] Mrs. Niemöller adds that "the origin of this quotation is no longer clear."[18] All three of these individuals agree that Martin Niemöller *never* included Catholics in the quote.

In fact, the most frequently repeated error in popular citations of this statement is the insertion of Catholics into Niemöller's catalogue of lost opportunities to identify with the victims of Nazi persecution. Those persons close to Niemöller, mentioned above, agree on this point. *Time* magazine and *Sojourners* magazine, along with many other publications, have all inaccurately added Catholics to Niemöller's quotation.[19] At least twice in the months before his imprisonment, Niemöller referred publicly to Roman Catholics. In an April 24, 1937 sermon he lamented:

> ...that God's word is bound...God's word is being put into chains and imprisoned.... And if we have read today and yesterday and the day before yesterday of law suits against Catholic ministers, that only goes to show that the Führer's decree of last August, according to which there were to be no major trials in ecclesiastical law-suits, has been liquidated, and that proceedings have again been instituted not only against Catholic but also against Evangelical ministers and laymen.[20]

Just two months before his imprisonment, Niemöller passionately preached about Christian men and women being "in the midst of a violent conflict about our faith.... In this struggle God desires us to stand and make a clear and courageous confession of our faith."[21] Calling on the power of the Word of God in "our fight for the Christian faith," Niemöller quoted at length the encouraging message he had received from the lips of a Catholic Bishop.[22] James Bentley, Niemöller's biographer, points out that in 1937 Niemöller publicly acknowledged "his solidarity with Roman Catholics in the struggle for the gospel."[23] Bentley refers to Niemöller's admiration for the public criticism of the new paganism in Nazi Germany leveled by Clemens August von Galen, Roman Catholic Bishop of Münster, whom Niemöller visited in April 1937.[24] Clearly Niemöller was in contact with and supportive of Catholics during this time of common struggle against the Nazi state. It would have made no sense for him to have declared after the war that he had said nothing regarding the persecution of Catholics.

Although Niemöller was spiritually nourished in Dachau by his conversations with three Catholic priests, who were fellow prisoners, he sometimes disagreed with papal statements in the postwar period.[25] Moreover, Niemöller "was born into a tradition of seeing Protestantism as in a sense part of the secular opposition to the government," in a region which had come under the jurisdiction of the Archbishops of Cologne, who for centuries had "rarely appointed Protestants to positions of governmental or departmental superiority." Hence, concludes his British biographer, "inevitably, Martin Niemöller's faith was Protestant, with more than a hint of anti-Catholicism."[26]

Conclusion

Although Niemöller's famous reflection will probably continue to appear in varied phrasings on organizational appeals for funds and on bumper stickers in the United States, at least two guidelines should be followed for the sake of historical accuracy:

- The category of Roman Catholics should not be included in Niemöller's listing;

- the progression should follow the historical chronology of intensified Nazi persecution strategies during the 1930s: communists, social democrats, trade unionists, Jews.

Based on my interviews with those closest to Niemöller, these points are essential in attempting to conform to Niemöller's original thought pattern. The precise wording, in terms of verbs and grammatical structure will probably never be retrieved. There will always be various versions. I have tried to preserve the two models which probably come closest to the original.

The contemporary popularity of Niemöller's quotation reflects not only concern for the lessons to be learned from the totalitarian era of Nazi persecutions, but also current interest in the behavior necessary to protect human rights in local communities and worldwide. In the words of M. Scott Peck: "Ultimately we are called out of national narcissism and away from purely local identities toward a primary identity with humanity and a state of global community."[27] That was the road Niemöller took. In his eighties, Martin Niemöller called himself "a revolutionary for freedom of the spirit and of the faith, for peace and justice."[28]

Paradoxically, a citizen in our complex twentieth-century nation states can become an ardent activist for group and individual rights in one group or community, while remaining a passive bystander regarding the violations of rights among other communities in the same society. Even moral leaders may don such blinders, focusing energy on their own group's suffering, to the exclusion of the neighboring "outsiders" in need. That is how Martin Niemöller responded in the Third Reich. He spoke out and acted vigorously to preserve the integrity and rights of his church, protesting the harassment and incarceration of his Christian brothers and sisters. But only after his eight years of imprisonment and the 1945 revelations of Nazi concentration camp horrors did he begin to grasp the consequences of his failure to stand up for the "outsiders."

Niemöller's spiritual journey from a particularist position to universal concerns foreshadowed the road traveled by many Christians and other persons of conscience during the second half of the twentieth century. In our time the path to spiritual and psychological recovery from this age of violence leads from fragmentation to integration, from partial insights to holistic understandings. Admitting that he had been a bystander to the suffering of communists and Jews from 1933 up to the time of his imprisonment in 1937, Niemöller candidly probed his antisemitic presuppositions and refused to formulate an alibi for his failure to act for those outside his church whom the Nazis had targeted. In 1956 he responded to a Jewish query about his prior antisemitism with honesty: "I have never concealed the fact and said it before the court in 1938 that I came from an 'anti-Semitic' past and tradition.... I believe that from 1933 I truly represented the Lutheran-Christian outlook on the Jewish question...but that I returned home after eight years' imprisonment as a completely different person."[29]

In 1962, the year after Amnesty International was formed in England by Peter Benenson, Niemöller participated in a BBC broadcast on behalf of prisoners of conscience. The spirit of his "confession" in the BBC script is similar to that of the more famous, shorter reflection analyzed in this essay. Based on scrutiny of the handwritten manuscript, James Bentley's biography masterfully records this significant moment in Niemöller's private and public odyssey:

> There was, said Niemöller, no way out. 'In 1933 I had been a free man, in 1933 when Göring proudly proclaimed that the danger of Communism had been eradicated because now every Communist, not previously in prison, had been thrown behind the barbed wires of the new concentration-camps.' God's question, put to him by the figures on the notice board in Dachau, was 'Martin Niemöller, what were you doing then?'... Through all those who had been suffering in Germany in 1933, Niemöller now believed, God in Jesus Christ had been saying to him: 'Are you prepared to save me?' 'I turned that service down!' Niemöller confessed.... This new understanding of the solidarity of all suffering people with the crucified Jesus forced Niemöller to jettison much that had been traditionally taught in Christendom about the Jews.[30]

Echoing his earlier prediction to Mrs. Else Niemöller, Bishop Otto Dibelius asserted in his postwar autobiography that "Niemöller's name will still be spoken long after all our names are forgotten."[31] Ironically, this prophecy is being fulfilled, not just because of Niemöller's challenge to Hitler and eight years of imprisonment, but because of his postwar reflection on his own human rights failures in the years *before* his imprisonment. After the contours of the German church struggle of the 1930s will have blurred and disappeared for many, Niemöller's famous statement will probably be repeated, revised, and pondered for generations to come. When Martin Niemöller launched his capsule self-appraisal of the years 1933–1937, it is unlikely that he could have plotted its wide trajectory or anticipated its glow.

Endnotes

1. Hubert G. Locke, ed., *Exile in the Fatherland: Martin Niemöller's Letters from Moabit Prison* (Grand Rapids, MI: William B. Eerdmans Publishing Co., 1986), 139. The comment that triggered Niemöller's response in this letter was sent to Mrs. Else Niemöller by Superintendent Otto Dibelius, who later became Bishop of the German Evangelical (Protestant) Church.

2. John S. Conway, *The Nazi Persecution of the Churches 1933–1945* (New York: Basic Books, 1968), 338.

3. Franklin H. Littell, "Foreword" in Locke, ed. (n. 1), viii.

4. Locke (n. 1), vii–viii.

5. Conversation of Ruth Zerner with Franklin Littell, July 17, 1990 (telephone). Professor Littell confirmed Niemöller's use of this statement with Ms. Marlene Maertens, who heard Niemöller speak these words in his North American travels after the war; she was working for Church World Service at that time and, therefore, was traveling with Niemöller. Ms. Maertens' first husband had been Niemöller's classmate in the German Naval Academy at the beginning of the twentieth century.

6. Letter of Sibylle A. Niemöller to Ingeborg Godenschweger, March 14, 1986 (Wiesbaden). Ms. Godenschweger, who is on the staff of the German Information Center in New York City, graciously allowed me to see this letter; previously, I had asked Ms. Godenschweger, if she would be able to secure a written version of Martin Niemöller's famous reflection from his widow.

7. Letter of Sibylle Niemöller (n. 6); I am responsible for the translation from the original German of the statement as it appears in Sibylle Niemöller's letter: "Erst holten sie die Kommunisten, aber ich war ja kein Kommunist, darum schwieg ich. Dann holten sie die Sozialdemokraten, aber ich war kein Sozialdemokrat, so tat ich nichts. Dann kamen die Gewerkschafter dran, aber ich war kein Gewerkschafter. Und dann holten sie die Juden, aber ich war kein Jude, so tat ich wenig. Als sie dann kamen und mich holten, da war niemand mehr da, der fuer mich haette einstehen koennen."

8. James Bentley, *Martin Niemöller 1892–1984* (New York: Macmillan, 1984), 164.

9. Quoted in Bentley (n. 8), 165.

10. Conversation of Ruth Zerner with Franklin Littell, July 17, 1990 (telephone).

11. Martin Niemöller, *The Gestapo Defied*, trans. from the German by Jane Lymburn (London: William Hodge and Company, 1942), 130.

12. Niemöller (n. 11), 166.

13. Niemöller (n. 11), 179. On June 27, 1937, Niemöller announced from the pulpit that forty-eight men and women (of the Confessing Church) were in prison; ibid., 250.

14. Niemöller (n. 11), 190.

15. Conversation of Ruth Zerner with Brigitte Johannesson, July 30, 1991 (telephone).

16. Conversation of Ruth Zerner with Franklin Littell, July 17, 1990 (telephone).

17. Letter of Sibylle Niemöller to Ingeborg Godenschweger, March 14, 1986 (Wiesbaden).

18. Letter of Sibylle Niemöller (n. 17).

19. In an article titled "Writing about the Unspeakable," Stefan Kanfer ended with this inaccurate rendering of Niemöller's quote:
"First the Nazis went after the Jews, but I was not a Jew, so I did not object. Then they went after the Catholics, but I was not a Catholic, so I did not object. Then they went after the Trade-Unionists, but I was not a Trade-Unionist, so I did not object. Then they came after me, and there was no one left to object." *Time*, March 2, 1981, p. 91. Not only is the addition of Catholics erroneous, but also the progression is faulty. According to his family, Niemöller followed the historical chronology of major acts of persecution: affecting first the political arch enemies of Hitler—the communists; then came the Social Democrats, then the trade unionists, and finally the Jews.

Nancy Lukens also quoted Niemöller inaccurately in a 1981 article titled "A Confessional Courage": "When the Nazis came to get the Communists, I was silent. When they came to get the Socialists, I was silent. When they came to get the Catholics, I was silent. When they came to get the Jews, I was silent. When they came to get me, there was no one left to speak." *Sojourners*, August 1981, p. 11. Lukens includes Catholics, a group which Mrs. Sibylle Niemöller emphatically claims should not be included: "NEVER were the Catholics named by him." Sibylle Niemöller adds: "Just yesterday, I received a newspaper clipping: Ann Landers quotes him, of course—as usual—incorrectly." (The reference here is to the "famous quotation.") Letter of Sibylle Niemöller (n. 17).

Charles Patterson concludes his informative popular account of *Anti-Semitism* (New York: Walker, 1982), 139, with this faulty rendering of the reflection: "First the Nazis went after the Jews, but I wasn't a Jew, so I did not react. Then they went after the Catholics, but I wasn't a Catholic, so I didn't object. Then they went after the worker[s], but I wasn't a worker, so I didn't stand up. Then they went after the Protestant clergy, but by then it was too late for anybody to stand up."

20. Martin Niemöller (n.11), 177.

21. Niemöller (n. 11), 190.

22. Niemöller (n. 11), 192.

23. Bentley (n. 8), 126.

24. Bentley (n. 8), 125. Bentley quotes from a June 18, 1937 sermon delivered in Bielefeld: "I truly believe I could join in common prayer with a man like the Bishop of Münster, whereas I find it inconceivable that I could ever go to the Lord's Supper with a 'German Christian' bishop," ibid., 126. ("German Christians" were the pro-Nazi members of the German Protestant Church.)

25. Bentley (n. 8), 149, 201.

26. Bentley (n. 8), 2.

27. M. Scott Peck, *The Different Drum: Community-making and Peace* (New York: Simon & Schuster, 1987), 288.

28. Erik Emig, "Das Porträt: Martin Niemöller," *Wiesbaden International* (1976), p. 36.

29. Bentley (n. 8), 166.

30. Bentley (n. 8), 165.

31. Otto Dibelius, *In the Service of the Lord: The Autobiography of Bishop Otto Dibelius*, trans. from the German by Mary Ilford (New York: Holt, Rinehart and Winston, 1964), 225.

Suggestions For Further Reading

Bentley, James. *Martin Niemöller 1892–1984*. New York: Macmillan, 1984. A concise, graceful biography, including valuable insights and comments from the author's numerous interviews and conversations with Niemöller in his later years.

Conway, John S. *The Nazi Persecution of the Churches 1933–1945*. New York: Basic Books. 1968. A thoughtful interpretation, based on careful documentary research and still useful for providing the background of Nazi religious policies.

Helmreich, Ernst. *The German Churches under Hitler: Background, Struggle, and Epilogue*. Detroit: Wayne State University Press, 1979. Informative and comprehensive, this survey shows that, however belated, the Christian churches offered sustained institutional challenge to Nazism. But, both Catholic and Protestant churches failed to resist effectively the State's antisemitic measures.

Niemöller, Martin. *Dahlmer Predigten 1936–1937*. Munich: Kaiser Verlag, 1981. Niemöller's 1936–37 sermons to his Dahlem congregation, reissued with the preface Thomas Mann wrote for the 1941 publication of the sermons: *God is my Fuehrer*.

____. *Exile in the Fatherland: Martin Niemöller's Letters from Moabit Prison*. Trans. from the German by Ernst Kaemke, Kathy Elias, Jacklyn Wilferd, ed. Hubert G. Locke. Grand Rapids, MI: William B. Eerdmans Publishing Company, 1986. Moving documents of family solidarity, personal courage, and continuing faith.

____. *First Commandment*. Trans. Jane Lymburn, with a foreword by James Moffatt. London: William Hodge and Company, 1937. 1933–1934 sermons preached by Niemöller.

____. *From U-Boat to Pulpit*. Trans. from the German by D. Hastie Smith. London: W. Hodge, 1936. Niemöller's autobiographical account of his youth, with vivid recollections of his naval career in the First World War. During the twenties he farmed and studied to become a Protestant pastor, while raising a family.

____. *"God is my Fuehrer," Being the last twenty-eight sermons by Martin Niemöller*. Trans. Jane Lymburn, with a preface by Thomas Mann. New York: Philosophical Library and Alliance Book Corp., 1941. Glorifying God and clinging to the Word of God, Niemöller challenged his Berlin-Dahlem parishioners to stand firm in their Christian faith (sermons from 25 October 1936 to 27 June 1937).

____. *Of Guilt and Hope*. Trans. Renee Spodheim. New York: Philosophical Library, 1947. Important post-World War II reflections and confessions of Niemöller, the ex-concentration camp inmate, transformed by his experiences during the Nazi years.

Scholder, Klaus. *The Churches and the Third Reich*. 2 vols. Trans. from the German by John Bowden. Philadelphia: Fortress Press, 1988. Thorough documentation and probing analysis characterize this monumental study, with vol. 2 ending in October 1934. Essential for re-creating the political/ideological/institutional setting in which the Confessing Church emerged.

Film

Martin Niemöller: What Would Jesus Say to That? (1985). Written and directed by Hannes Karnick, Wolfgang Richter. Camera: Wolfgang Richter. Sound: Hannes Karnick. Editor: Wolfgang Richter. Produced by Docfilm, Karnick & Richter OHG, SFB Berlin. Enlivened by conversations with the passionate pastor in his nineties. Compelling and essential for understanding Niemöller's complex odyssey from nationalism to internationalism, from militarism to pacifism. This film, when citing the "oft-quoted reflection" which is the subject of my paper, uses the same sequence which Sibylle Niemöller, the pastor's second wife, suggests is accurate: communists, social democrats, trade unionists, and then Jews (with no reference to a category of Roman Catholics).

THE HOLOCAUST AND CHRISTIAN THOUGHT

Alan Davies

Shaken by the mass destruction of European Jewry, Christian theologians, including Paul Tillich, Reinhold Niebuhr, Jürgen Moltmann, Paul van Buren, and Rosemary Radford Ruether, have investigated the Christian roots of antisemitism and rethought and redefined the Jewish-Christian relationship. Alan Davies examines the impact of the Holocaust on Christian thought.

Introduction

The mass destruction of the European Jews at the hands of Nazi Germany has had many consequences in post-war thought, not the least of which has been a new investigation of the history of antisemitism, including its Christian roots. Antisemitism (*Antisemitismus*), a term probably coined by Wilhelm Marr, an anti-Jewish pamphleteer of the Second Reich,[1] was not a Christian invention; rather, it arose out of the vague and fashionable race ideas of the late nineteenth century, and found favour because of its 'scientific' aura. In France, the new scientific form of anti-Judaism was popularized by Ernest Renan in his best-selling *Vie de Jésus*. While, in this sense, antisemitism was the product of modernity, few would deny that its concoction depended on older, pre-scientific ingredients as well, on myths, legends and dogmas embedded in the folkloric and religious memory of the West. Not only the modern era, but also the Middle Ages and the Graeco-Roman era (both pagan and Christian), contributed to the fate of the Jews in the twentieth century. Gradually, Christian scholars began to see that Christian theology was implicated in the evolution of anti-Jewish ideas, and that even the Christian Scriptures (the New Testament) were contaminated.

A complex anti-Jewish ideology, comprised of both biblical and extra-biblical elements, had emerged in the early church, leaving its legacy for future generations.

This classic negative myth, which the French Jewish historian Jules Isaac designated as Christendom's "teaching of contempt", consisted (as analyzed by Isaac himself) of seven interlocking themes: (1) the degenerate character of Judaism, (2) the carnal nature of the Jews, (3) the blindness of the Jews, (4) the reprobation of the Jews, (5) the deicidal crime of the Jews, (6) the dispersion and punishment of the Jews, (7) the diabolical character of the synagogue.[2] To these dark images, other anti-Jewish motifs were added in later eras, notably the vilification of the Talmud and the charge that the Jews, in league with the devil, were perpetual and incorrigible plotters against Christendom.

Isaac, however, remained convinced that Christianity in its essence excluded antisemitism. Christians were obligated to purge their faith of the teaching of contempt in order not to fuel the fires of another Holocaust. Then, presumably, all would be well. Today, no responsible Christian would defend the *adversus Judaeos* tradition; it is simply indefensible, and must be repudiated in the strongest possible terms. Some Christians, however, as well as some Jews, are less certain that Christianity in its essence—as the latter has been defined by classical theology and accepted by most of the church—excludes antisemitism. In their opinion, to excise only the obvious aberrations that comprise the teaching of contempt is insufficient; a more radical deconstruction and reconstruction of the religious and theological foundations of Christian belief is also necessary. Isaac's catalogue of anti-Jewish allegations can be disposed of in a relatively painless fashion. Its ugliness (to post-Holocaust eyes) is transparent, as well as its lack of empirical credibility. But the essence of Christianity—if, indeed, Christianity has an essence—is another matter.[3] If antisemitism is located at the core rather than the periphery, how much deconstruction is possible without eating into the substance of the faith itself?

The deeper surgery began with an attempt to reformulate the doctrine of the church. Since the second century, Christian writers have described the Christian community as the "new Israel" (or "true Israel") a term that implied the displacement of the Jews as the "old" (or "false") Israel, i.e. as the elect people. Recent scholarship has shown that the roots of Christian displacement theology (or supersessionism) lie in the gospels, e.g., in the parable of the wicked tenants in the vineyard (Mk 12:1–9: Mt 21:33–42).[4] However, the loss of its Jewish milieu rendered the new religion more susceptible to such ideas. Prompted by gentile pride and jealousy, as well as by an apologetic need to establish the antiquity of Christianity, the ex-pagans who composed Christian theology after the first century greatly intensified this and other modes of separating Christians from Jews. "The Sun of Righteousness", John Chrysostom (345?–407) declared, "rose early upon (the Jews), but they spurned its rays and sat in darkness; whereas we (Gentiles) who were brought up in darkness, welcomed the light...and were delivered from the darkness of our error...."[5] Not only the church and the synagogue, but also the Gentiles and Jews exchanged places, according to the Church Fathers: those outside stepped inside the circle of election, and those inside were pushed outside. In spite of its Jewish origins, Christianity became mainly a gentile religion, leaving the old Jewish churches to perish slowly as time wore on. Already ostracized in the second century, these lost congregations were the last remnants of the Jewish past; their disappearance left the so-called New Israel spiritually impoverished and ripe for the intrusion of alien anti-Jewish notions and sentiments. It was the long delayed discovery of a void in Christian life and faith that drove certain European Catholics to question classical doctrines following the Second World War. The Holocaust was the catalyst of their concern.

The Catholic Schism Theologians

Following Karl Barth's precedent,[6] these early Christian reconstructionists—Paul Démann, Karl Thieme, Heinrich Spaemann, Dom Oehmen—drew much of their initial inspiration from a new understanding of Pauline theology based on a radical interpretation of Romans 9-11.[7] In their eyes, the church had misread Paul for centuries, overlooking his dictum that the gifts and calling of God are irrevocable (Rom 11:29). This meant that the ancient covenant was still intact, and that Paul's own "kinsmen by race" had never been displaced as the people of God. In his exposition of Romans, Augustine had described the gentile Christians as healthy new branches grafted on a weakened old tree,[8] but this view was warped; the Gentiles were really appendages to a still vigorous trunk: the house of Israel. Taking the next step, the Catholic reconstructionists posited a "schism" in the people of God; i.e. the Jewish people and the Christian church. From this claim, a number of conclusions were drawn: (l) the relationship between Jews and Christians has a unique character, and cannot be compared to that between Christianity and any other religion or religious community; (2) this unique relationship is both structural and spiritual, placing the 'Jewish question' at the heart of Christian ecumenical concerns—indeed, the Jews are the ecumenical issue *par excellence*; (3) neither people is complete without the other, either structurally or spiritually; (4) the gentilization of Christianity has resulted in anti-Judaism and antisemitism; (5) the birth of the Jewish state of Israel in 1948 should be seen providentially by Christians as well as Jews; (6) Jews and Christians, now estranged brothers, are destined eventually to reunite; (7) Christians should abandon all attempts to convert Jews, since Israel has its own mission; (8) together, in spite of their mutual alienation and divided state, Israel and the church constitute a light to the world.

This early schism theology was not widely accepted, and probably created as many problems as it solved. For example, its Pauline logic seems to require a final *en masse* conversion of the Jews to Christianity, in spite of its accent on

Israel's continuing election; otherwise the schism remains unhealed and the notion of ecumenicity loses its force. If the Jewish-Christian relationship is structural as well as spiritual, only organic unity—the "church of Jews and gentiles"—can overcome the division. But the church of Jews and Gentiles implies the annihilation of Judaism, which in itself is a form of antisemitism. The schism theologians did not see this paradox. The trouble arose from a narrow preoccupation with Romans 9–11, endowing these short chapters in Paul's greatest letter with *ex cathedra* status. Although the schism theologians, unlike many fundamentalists and Christian Zionists, did not regard Romans 9-11 as a blueprint for the return of Christ, making the Jews and their conversion the hinge of history, they exaggerated the theological importance of these chapters for Jewish-Christian relations today. Paul's reflections on providence are too *ad hoc* and timebound to be used as a court of final appeal. Moreover, a dogmatic appeal to Paul's speculations about Jewish disbelief never allows Judaism to speak for itself; instead, the Jews (and Israel) are always subsumed under Christian categories as a theological "mystery" of some description—a designation that contains its own dangers, and to which most Jews object. The schism theologians were dominated by pre-Holocaust Christian assumptions; after all, dialogue was still in its infancy, and the serious study of Judaism was still a rarity among Christian scholars.

However, certain significant gains were achieved: (l) a recognition that the gentilization of Christianity had gone too far, and that the church must recover its Jewish roots, both historically and religiously; (2) a recognition that the continuing existence of the Jews as Jews has a positive rather than a negative significance for Christians; (3) a recognition that the church must see itself as unfinished and incomplete, awaiting its final fulfillment in the divine plan. As a result, an unfamiliar note of humility was introduced into Christian language.

This last point is especially important. There was nothing novel in the statement that Judaism is a fragmented religion, but the statement that Christianity is likewise fragmented was certainly novel, particularly when uttered by Catholic theologians steeped in ages of triumphalism. The Holocaust, as another Catholic, Johann Baptist Metz, later declared,[9] has made it impossible for post-Holocaust Christians to write theology as if nothing had happened. Augustinian language describing the church as the "Kingdom of God" on earth, or, as the German Catholic theologian Karl Adam wrote in 1929, a "new supernatural reality...arrayed in the garment of the transitory...the divine attesting itself under earthly veils",[10] cannot be used after Auschwitz. Such theologies of glory have been refuted by history, especially by the dismal record of most of the churches and most of their adherents during the Nazi era, and have a hollow ring today. Only more modest claims are morally defensible in the post-Auschwitz world. The church is better regarded as an anticipatory sign of a kingdom that has not yet transpired, or, to borrow the words of a Jewish prayer, "the beginning of the dawn of redemption" rather than its day.[11] It cannot be more. Christianity is still a distinctive religion, with distinctive gifts and a distinctive role in salvation-history, but it does not possess a monopoly on salvation, least of all with respect to the Jews.

With these ideas, Christian thought was ready for a new beginning. If, in fact, Jews and Christians are really members of the same family who have suffered a long and painful estrangement, reconciliation should be possible. Instead of competing with each other as rivals, they should follow their separate paths of obedience to the same biblical God with mutual forbearance. This much was clear. What are their separate paths? That was the problem to be solved. Some of the suggested solutions will be examined briefly.

Paul Tillich

The German Protestant theologian Paul Tillich (1886–1965), who, like his friend Martin Buber, was influenced by the pre-Holocaust Jewish Hegelian philosopher Franz Rosenzweig, held pronounced views on Jewish-Christian relations. Popular Christianity, Tillich declared, is forever tempted by the pagan gods of space—"will to power, imperialism, injustice, demonic enthusiasm and tragic self-destruction" (obviously he was thinking of Nazi Germany)—and hence requires a constant reminder of its Hebraic origins and the biblical/prophetic demand for justice.[12] It is not sufficient for the church to possess the Old Testament, as the pro-Hitler "German Christians" (*Glaubensbewegung deutscher Christen*) of his day also possessed the Old Testament, and were antisemitic and supernationalistic nonetheless.[13] A Christian society must interact with flesh-and-blood Jews, who, in their religious life, bear witness to the Abrahamic Lord of time; otherwise it will succumb to paganism. "Synagogue and Church should be united in our age, in the struggle for the God of time against the gods of space. This is a period in which more than ever...the gods of space show their power over souls and nations. If this would happen, if all those who struggle for the Lord of history, for his justice and truth, are united even under persecution and martyrdom, the eternal victory in the struggle between time and space will become visible once more as the victory of time and the one God who is the Lord of history".[14] Such a view was congenial to a theologian who, all his life, found "spiritual and physical emigration" more meaningful than rootedness and political allegiance.[15]

This vision of the Jewish-Christian relationship has not lost its relevance today. Not only was the Third Reich infested with idolatrous expressions of Christianity, notably the racist doctrine of the Aryan Christ, in which Jesus was metamorphosed from a Jew into an Aryan (i.e., German), but post-war society, despite de-nazification, may turn as easily to quasi-religious demonic enthusiasm in the form of nationalism and superpatriotism—witness the contemporary resurgence of neo-Nazism—and not in Germany alone. The figure of Christ, according to a more recent German Protestant theologian, Eberhard Bethge, always trembles on the verge of pagan idol worship in modern culture: once severed from his "Jewish biblico-historical roots", the "divinized Jesus" is quickly "transformed into a Greco-Roman, mythical, imperialist, Germanic or American god-figure fitted to our socio-cultural needs".[16] There are many examples of this phenomenon. Jews, however, remind Christians that Jesus was a Jew, not a German or American, and that Christians forget this historical fact at their peril. Tillich was one of the first post-war theologians to stress the continuing spiritual significance of the Jewishness of Jesus, and hence of the prophetic tradition of Israel, for the church. He did not think that Christianity was inferior to Judaism. When purified of false meanings, the central Christian symbols address the inner dilemmas of human life more directly than Jewish symbols. In spite of their historical and natural affinity the two religions are not identical. Their encounter is both reciprocal and dialectical; reciprocal, because each corrects a weakness in the other, and dialectical, because each in part contradicts the other, reflecting a "conflict which is rooted in human existence itself, in the deepest levels of man's nature".[17] This conflict is between two perceptions of reality—one which sees the world as unredeemed and the other which sees redemption as having occurred. Judaism dwells on future hope, whereas Christianity dwells on present realization. This difference in focus causes Jewish faith to emphasize the ethical side of religion, and Christian faith to emphasize the sacramental side. Both elements are necessary aspects of life itself. The dialectic, moreover, has tragic overtones, for each must finally reject the other.

In formulating these ideas, Tillich, like the Catholic schism theologians, was influenced by Romans 9–11 ("Judaism has a continuing function in the new eon")[18] and by Paul in general, whom he interpreted sympathetically, i.e., *not* as anti-Jewish. To Tillich, Paul's break with Judaism (his polemic against the law) had nothing to do with antisemitism; instead, Paul and Pauline thought represent the antithesis of antisemitism. Tillich's admiration was reserved for the prophetic rather than the legal elements in Judaism; indeed, he seemed to regard Reform Judaism as he regarded Protestant Christianity—a prophetic protest against religious legalism in the form of Orthodox Judaism analogous to the Reformation protest against the religious legalism of Catholic Christianity. Since Reform Judaism was born on German soil, this comparison is not surprising. Despite his reservations about Jewish ritualistic commandments, his high opinion of both Jews and Judaism was sincere, and strongly coloured by the Holocaust. "As an emigre in the catastrophic year of 1933, I sided with those who opposed everything which happened that year in Germany, especially everything which Germany inflicted on European Jewry".[19] Antisemitism filled him with horror, as did National Socialism and the mass psychosis that had descended on Germany in his own lifetime. From the beginning, he sensed its dangers, and attempted to protect Jewish students from Nazi mobs (at the University of Frankfort). Instead of seeking to restore German 'honour' by either denying or qualifying German guilt, Tillich believed that the past could be purified only if the nation assumed full responsibility for its crimes; otherwise, the "Jewish question as a German problem" could not be solved.[20]

Reinhold Niebuhr

No less than Tillich, the American Protestant theologian Reinhold Niebuhr (1892–1972) had a profound appreciation of the prophetic elements in Judaism, and their importance for Christianity. As a social prophet himself in modern America, he depended too much for his own ideas on the great prophets of ancient Israel not to recognize the vitality of their religious legacy in their spiritual descendants, the twentieth-century Jews. Moreover, Niebuhr had certain Jewish mentors, notably Justice Louis D. Brandeis, a man who personified the "Hebraic-prophetic passion for social justice".[21] Throughout his entire career, he spoke in admiring tones of the Jewish people as suffused with a passion for a just social order—"The glory of their religion is that they are really not thinking so much of 'salvation' as a saved society".[22] Protestantism, by contrast, was often weak in this respect, suffering from an excessive individualism in its theology and piety. However, the social gospel movement also stimulated Niebuhr's appreciation of the "Jewish capacity for civic virtue" because of its own affinity with the Old Testament prophets.[23] Like Tillich, he was an admirer of both Rosenzweig and Buber, and borrowed insights from these eminent Jewish thinkers. Like Tillich also, he detested German National Socialism and its deadly strain of antisemitism. His feelings on this subject were almost certainly intensified by his own German roots, and by personal encounters with antisemites during family visits to Germany. The Holocaust and its attendant irrationality merely confirmed and deepened convictions that Niebuhr already held, both regarding the nature of Nazism itself, as a pathological flight into primitivism, and the indispensable gifts of the Jews and Judaism to civilization. In his eyes, a healthy democracy is scarcely conceivable without a strong Jewish contribution, although the social creativity of the Jews is partly the product of their perennial minority status in Western society.

If Judaism is superior to Christianity with respect to civic virtue, Christianity, according to Niebuhr, is superior to Judaism with respect to personal virtue—the morality of the "nth degree" and the dynamics of individual faith (or grace).[24] Neither religion is *really* superior to the other, and neither must claim moral or spiritual superiority, since their differences are only relative, and since such claims immediately refute themselves. Each contains what the other has developed more fully, and, in that sense, they are reciprocal: variations on a theme, as Buber had declared,[25] as well as corrective influences on each other. "The Christian must not claim that redemption is unknown in Judaism, or that there is not a fully elaborated doctrine of the divine mercy in its relation to divine justice, even if he believes that this relation, explicated in the Old Testament, is fully defined in the New Testament doctrine of the atonement".[25] From this flows Niebuhr's much publicized assertion that Christians must not seek to convert Jews; they can be 'saved' within Judaism. Moreover, the symbol of Christ is too tainted by ages of Christian persecution to be accepted by most Jews as a symbol of redemption.[26] If this was true before the Holocaust, it is certainly and perhaps irrevocably true after the Holocaust. (Incidentally, according to Reinhold, his younger brother Richard was the first Protestant theologian to oppose Christian missions to the Jews on these grounds.[27])

In spite of his admiration for Jewish civil virtue, Niebuhr was as realistic in his assessment of the possibilities of the abuse of power in Jewish hands as he was in his assessment of the same abuse in Christian hands. Although pro-Zionist, he was never a 'Christian Zionist', i.e., a believer in the special biblical and religious status of the state of Israel. Instead, he spoke of Israel's "thrilling emergence as a kind of penance of the world for the awful atrocities committed against the Jews" by Nazi Germany, and described its foundation as a "glorious moral and political achievement".[28] Yet Israel is subject to the same temptations and ambiguities that power always bestows on national and political collectivities. A "sympathetic Christian cannot but observe that the Jewish ethic and faith, so impressively universal in the diaspora, so fruitful in leavening Western civilization, is not morally safe when it becomes embodied in a nation like other nations, and when in fighting for the survival of the nation, it comes in conflict with Arab forces".[29] His concern has not been invalidated by the history of the Middle East since his death in 1972, and by the tragic situation in which contemporary Israel finds itself as its leaders struggle with intractable geopolitical issues and the Palestinian question. These dilemmas, however, are neither peculiarly Jewish nor peculiarly Christian, but universal.

James Parkes

An original attempt to redefine the Jewish-Christian relationship that has attracted interest since the Holocaust, although its origins are pre-Holocaust, is associated with the English Anglican scholar-theologian James Parkes (1896–1981). One of the few Christians to discern the true depths of the Christian entanglement in antisemitism prior to the Nazi era, Parkes devoted much of his life to the quest for a solution to this entanglement, without compromising the integrity of either faith. Having rejected classical Christian displacement theology, he argued that Judaism and Christianity represent neither two different covenants, nor a schism in the same covenant (significantly, Romans 9–11 was not his point of departure—he did not like Paul), but rather two different aspects of the same general revelation symbolized by two different moments in historic time: Sinai and Calvary. Sinai is a revelation of the true meaning of human social existence; Calvary is a revelation of the true meaning of human personal existence. While later in time, Calvary does not displace Sinai, which remains eternally valid. The two revelations exist in creative tension, reflecting a dialectic in life itself between its collective and individual (or personal) poles. Each, as a result, completes and complements the other, the Torah standing for social and corporate righteousness and the Incarnation and Atonement for fulfilled human individuality. In historical terms, Judaism is of necessity the older religion, since social or corporate consciousness arose earlier than individual consciousness in the evolution of the human species; hence, the meaning of social identity had to be revealed first. However, the dawn of a sense of the personal self in subsequent time made necessary the birth of Christianity, or the revelation of God "in terms of a human life".[30] Christ, to Parkes, is an archetypal figure, a new Adam in whom human nature is recast. Each religion—the "elect nation" (Judaism) and the "elect from every nation" (Christianity)[31]—has its separate divine imperative, and, through their mutual interaction, each plays an indispensable role in the inauguration of the true messianic age of human redemption.

Anthropology undergirds this rationalistic schema. Nevertheless, Parkes' conclusions are not entirely dissimilar to Tillichian and Niebuhrian ideas. The prophetic demand for justice (or civic virtue) implies social righteousness, and the morality of the nth degree implies personal righteousness. Parkes, however, had a higher regard for the legal (Pharisaic) expressions of Judaism than Tillich or Niebuhr, as well as a more accurate grasp of rabbinic thought: "I realized how meaningless...was the conventional Christian criticism which contrasted the magnificence of the prophets with the pedestrian ordinariness of the Rabbis".[32] As an Anglican, moreover, he drew his inspiration from modernist rather than Reformation theology, emphasizing the rational aspects of religion, and even casting his reformulation of the Jewish-Christian relationship in a trinitarian mould. Thus humanism, or the search after truth associated with the main intellectual currents of the modern age, becomes a third, somewhat ill-defined, channel of the divine revelation along with Judaism and Christianity. "If to man as person God is Love, to man as social being God is Righteousness or Justice,... to man as seeker, God is Truth.... So I believe it is with the three expressions of the experience of man in Judaism, Christianity and Humanism. They are as related to each other as are the three circles of the trinity...."[33] Neither Niebuhr nor Tillich, both harsh critics of modern humanism and secularism, endorsed this elevation of the spirit of modernity to revelatory status; they were too sensitive to its demonic and nihilistic aspects. Parkes, on the other hand, was less critical of the fruits of intellectual freedom, although he was certainly aware of the anti-religious and other dangers embedded in the scientific and technological *Zeitgeist* of the twentieth century. Despite these dangers, however, he remained committed to what has been described as a modernist viewpoint,[34] and greatly disliked the stress on sin found in continental neo-orthodoxy. Indeed, his entire theology has an evolutionary cast, as its historical framework makes clear. The differences between Judaism and Christianity are reconciled in the gradual unfolding of a great revelatory drama throughout the ages. Divine providence finds a place for both religions, and for their humanistic offspring as well. However, even Parkes' admirers usually reject his peculiar trinitarianism, which seems to glorify Western civilization.

John Pawlikowski

Some of Parkes' ideas have been expanded by the American Catholic theologian John Pawlikowski. The two religions, Pawlikowski argues, are afflicted with opposite difficulties. "By starting with a solemn commitment to peoplehood, Judaism has had to struggle with the problem of the outsider; by beginning with the individual, Christianity has had to struggle with how it can maximize its communitarian ideal".[35] Hence, they stand, so to speak, back to back on the historic stage. From common origins—Second Temple Judaism "seeded" Christianity as well as rabbinic Judaism—the church and the synagogue developed in different directions in the course of time.[36] In the case of Christianity, the seed of Jewish spirituality ripened into a mature doctrine of the uniqueness and dignity of the individual self as the object of God's love, which became incarnate in human form. Thus the Incarnation was one fruit of the Pharisaic "internal revolution" (a term coined by the Jewish historian Ellis Rivkin)[37] and the final expression of its personalistic and introspective aspects. In the case of Judaism, the seed ripened into a more communal form of love, although one with an incarnational strain of its own. To Pawlikowski, the Incarnation, or the "Word made flesh", is also an initial sign of a still unrealized Kingdom of God that in its ultimate realization will embody perfect individuality and perfect community at once, or a fulfilled Christianity and a fulfilled Judaism.

This futuristic vision seems to owe its genesis to the evolutionary cosmology of the Jesuit palaeontologist and theologian Pierre Teilhard de Chardin, who wrote of the "personalizing universe" and the "Omega point".[38] Pawlikowski, however, unlike the originator of these concepts, is essentially a Holocaust theologian, a fact that serves to temper Teilhardian cosmic optimism. Radical evil frustrates every attempt to describe the universe as an evolutionary ascent to higher and more spiritual levels of existence. This creates a problem that Pawlikowski resolves by interpreting the Holocaust as a rational rather than irrational event—rational in the sense of explicable. It arose out of a distorted Nietzschean obsession with freedom, or the modern seizure of virtually unrestricted human powers in which, having abolished God, the ex-creature is free to remake himself as his own deity. "Under the impact of the new science and technology, mankind was beginning to undergo the Prometheus Unbound experience on a mass scale".[39] Prometheus Unbound can do anything he chooses; who is to restrain him? Such a loss of transcendence liberates not merely the creative but also the destructive tendencies in human nature, and the latter soon gain the upper hand.

Consequently, Christian theology must remind the world of the transcendent again, for only thus can the dignity and worth of human personhood be rediscovered, and the destructive impulses nullified. The church must reactivate its cosmic visions, pointing to norms and goals that stretch "beyond the narrow dimensions of this earth" in order to change the mental horizons of the potential Hitlers and Mengeles who, as the children of Prometheus, still populate the globe.[40] A "mere repetition of biblical precepts" will not suffice, for biblical language is no longer modern language, and, in any case, the human situation is significantly different from former ages.[41] For this reason, moral appeals that ignore the power of the demonic will fail. Transcendence in the form of divine love must be mediated with greater passion after Auschwitz, or it will lack conviction. In Pawlikowski's opinion, Christians must appeal to the same vitalistic instincts that the National Socialists enlisted with their Dionysian rites and myths, only for opposite ends. "I am convinced that the moral honing of this vitalistic dimension of humanity can effectively take place only in the context of liturgical celebration".[42]

A new liturgy is required—a liturgy that will awaken the human spirit from its moral slumbers by evoking symbols of eternity expressive of divine and human co-responsibility for the fate of the planet and its inhabitants is brought to the fore. Christianity, a religion rich in liturgical symbols, should be equal to this challenge. Judaism, another religion rich in liturgical symbols, has already immortalized the murdered in a beautiful and compelling religious rite on *Yom HaShoah* (Holocaust Memorial Day).

Pawlikowski's incarnational theology does not appeal to everyone. To Rosemary Ruether, it represents a "Platonic" flight from history into mysticism.[43] To Roy Eckardt, it has supersessionist overtones because Christianity is portrayed as a more highly evolved and therefore higher religion than Judaism.[44] But mysticism need not mean a flight from history. To deepen the personal and spiritual dimensions of life serves to enhance our humanity, and the humaneness that undergirds the whole of civilized existence.[45] Nor does Pawlikowski regard Christian personalism as a higher value than Jewish communalism. Hence, the problem of supersessionism does not arise. A more effective criticism might claim that the underlying model simplifies unduly the true nature of the two religions.

Rosemary Radford Ruether

The moral issues posed by supersessionist and triumphalistic dogmas lie at the heart of Rosemary Radford Ruether's post-Holocaust dissection of classical Christian theology. In her major book, *Faith and Fratricide*, and in subsequent writings, she has expounded the thesis that anti-Judaism constitutes the "left-hand" of christology, i.e., its dark and repressive side. Christian supersessionism arose when the church transformed scripture into a series of black-and-white contrasts in which the Jews were assigned the inferior or negative principle. The judgments pronounced by the prophets on ancient Israel, for example, were assigned to the post-biblical Jews, while the blessings and promises were assigned to the gentile church. Similarly, the tension between the particular and the universal in prophetic faith was translated into a contrast between Jewish tribalism and Christian pluralism. Similarly the distinction between the letter and the spirit of the laws and rites of biblical religion became a distinction between Jewish materialism and Christian spirituality. Thus, deprived of promise, a negated particularism transcended by Christian universalism, and "mere outwardness and moral turpitude" compared to Christian inwardness and perfection, Judaism was cast on the rubbish heap of history as inferior to Christianity in every sense—temporal, moral and religious.[46]

Ruether's solution is a new covenantal theology in which these polar contrasts are abolished, and in which the church accepts the fact that each of the negative poles is actually a mark of its own existence that has been denied. The key mistake made by the patristic theologians was to confuse the "eschatological" with the "historical", thereby injecting a note of finality and absoluteness into time and space where it does not belong. Jesus, however, both was and was not the messiah, and it is as important to say the latter as to say the former. In other words, the "messianic meaning of (his) life...is paradigmatic and proleptic in nature, not final and fulfilled".[47] Even Easter cannot be absolutized. Like Jews, Christians await a still unrealized future, albeit with their own distinctive symbols of crucifixion and resurrection. Following the earlier Catholic schism theologians, only in a more contextual vein, Ruether advocates an ecumenical perspective in which Judaism stands in a special relationship to Christianity in the "same household of faith".[48] Within this household, despite past errors, Christians continue to interject a note of messianic urgency into human affairs, making "history itself dynamic".[49] This is the peculiar genius of Christianity. Moreover, within the same broad context, she leaves theological space for other non-Christian religions with different paradigms.

Although a Roman Catholic, Ruether has employed what Tillich once called the 'Protestant principle' (the principle of prophetic self-criticism) in her critique of traditional theology.[50] In Roy Eckardt's judgment, she has not gone far enough. An element of triumphalism lurks in her christology, regardless of her insistence that the 'Great Refusal' of the Jews to recognize Jesus must be respected by Christians because it is founded on fidelity, not blindness and hardness-of-heart.[51] In John Oesterreicher's view, she has gone too far. Her biblical exegesis is ridden with errors, her interpretation of the Church Fathers is one-sided, she underestimates the pre-Christian pagan animosity, she misunderstands rabbinic thought, and she champions a "new, crippled theology"![52] Unquestionably, *Faith and Fratricide* provoked a not inconsiderable controversy in the Christian world.

Despite her concern with the lessons of the Holocaust, Ruether, in another controversial book, *The Wrath of Jonah*, has written critically of both Jewish and Christian 'Holocaust theology'. The latter, in her view, has erred by elevating Jewish suffering to unique status, thereby distorting historical reality and moral judgment in the Middle East.[53] Other 'holocausts' and genocides are minimized: a perception that works against Jewish interests, since antisemitism is often dismissed by Israel's critics as special pleading. Too narrow a preoccupation with the Holocaust (and with Israel as a 'Holocaust state') is thus as questionable as the more common attempt to write theology as if the Holocaust had never occurred. This judgment has caused a wave of anger in both Jewish and Christian circles, and cost her the goodwill of some members of both religious communities. Whatever the merits of her case, it is surely fallacious to declare, as Jacob Neusner has done, that she "is nothing more than an apologist and a propagandist for the enemies of the State of Israel"[54]—Neusner is unfair.

Jürgen Moltmann

The emergence of a 'theology of hope' in post-war Christian thought is most closely associated with Jürgen Moltmann, for whom, as a German Protestant and an ex-Luftwaffe auxiliary officer, the Holocaust is a paramount issue, although he also cannot be classified as a Holocaust theologian. Like Barth and the Catholic schism theologians, Moltmann is convinced of the continuing election of the Jews—the "Israel which rightfully exists alongside the church and which...cannot be abolished".[55] Like Tillich, he fears that Christians who ignore the Jewish people, Christianity's "original, enduring and final partner in history", will sink back swiftly into idolatry. "If the church loses sight of its orientation to Israel, then its religious, political and earthly relationships will also be turned into pagan ones, indeed into post-Christian and anti-Christian ones".[56] Anti-Judaism, in fact, more than anything else, has vitiated the power of hope contained in the Christian message as a redemptive force in the world. "After Auschwitz, the Christian church, which gives the name Christ to Jesus, the Jew, is bound to revolutionize its thinking.... The more the church frees itself from this abuse of itself, the more clearly it will recognize Israel as...its brother in hope".[57] True alienation, according to Moltmann, following the neo-Marxist philosopher Ernst Bloch, lies between what we are and what we have not yet become. Hence history should be seen as a dialectic between God's future and the human past and present.

To Moltmann, the unredeemed state of the world, of which the Holocaust is the most terrible testimony, is not an argument against belief in Jesus as the messiah (as Jews usually argue), but that which compels Christians to concentrate on the world's transformation in the image of the messiah. The gospel is the "light which salvation throws ahead of itself...the daybreak" of God's future.[58]

Even the resurrection is charged with messianic meaning, and stands "at the beginning of the new creation of the world".[59] While christology divides Jews and Christians, it need not degenerate into a Christian anti-Jewish ideology (e.g., Ruether's 'left hand'): "It is not in the christologies for Jesus'sake that we find anti-Judaism.... It is in the chiliastic christologies of empire and domination".[60] Jesus both is and is not the messiah: "He is not yet the Christ of the parousia".[61] Hence, the Christian 'yes' to Jesus as the messiah must accept the Jewish 'no' as part of the dialectic of faith: "We shall only put antisemitism behind us when we succeed theologically in making something positive out of the Jewish no to Jesus Christ".[62] The Christian yes is a provisional yes; it can never be an "excluding and excommunicating" yes.[63]

As the church's partner in history, it is Israel's special vocation to "hallow the divine name" as a "blessing for all nations"—in other words, to pursue social righteousness.[64] "Obedience to the Torah cannot be deprived of its legitimacy, for the Torah is the prefiguration and beginning of the divine rule on earth".[65] Judaism, therefore, is affirmed as an independent and autonomous religion. However, Moltmann refuses to abandon the classical structures of Christian thought, or to drain them of their traditional meanings. His God is a trinitarian God who participates in human suffering in such a way that it becomes divine suffering as well. Not only was God, so to speak, on the cross, but the cross, and all that it entails as an emblem of evil, was also in God, which means that Auschwitz—the "murdered and the gassed"—is also in God: "...even Auschwitz is taken up into the grief of the Father, the surrender of the Son and the power of the Spirit".[66] For God, who is all in all, absorbs and thereby negates the negative elements of existence. "God in Auschwitz and Auschwitz in the crucified God—that is the basis for a real hope which both embraces and overcomes the world, the ground for a love which is stronger than death and can sustain death. It is the ground for living with the terror of history and...nevertheless remaining in love and meeting what comes in openness for God's future".[67] The Holocaust and the other nightmares in the annals of murder are transcended by faith, although their horror remains. Christians can still be Christians if they pass through repentance and rebirth.

The spectacle of a German struggling with the collapse of German civilization and his own 'dark night of the soul' is impressive in itself, especially amid the neo-nationalism and historical revisionism of the post-war era. Moreover, as a Jewish critic has noted, he has demonstrated a willingness unusual among Christians to listen to Jewish voices.[68] But three objections have been raised: (1) his views of law and grace are replete with anti-Jewish patristic dualisms; (2) his dialectical method distorts reality; (3) his theology of the cross has a restricted focus.[69] Perhaps in response to the first objection, Moltmann has been careful in his later writings to distinguish Torah in its rich rabbinic sense from law in its narrow legalistic sense. The second objection is worth reflection, since reality is certainly falsified if it is seen as consisting only of light and darkness. All evil is not radical evil, and Auschwitz is not the only face of the twentieth century. The third objection argues that an "overemphasis on the cross" leads to an inadequate understanding of sin and grace because it misconstrues the social dimensions of sin.[70] In Catholic theology, according to John Pawlikowski, the atonement is interpreted in a less individualistic manner than in Protestantism. However, in his more recent books, Moltmann has turned increasingly to social and even cosmic themes, borrowing from Jewish and Catholic ideas.[71]

A. Roy Eckardt

The acknowledged dean of American Christian Holocaust theologians is A. Roy Eckardt, who has devoted his life to a consideration of these issues and their implications for Christian faith and ethics. No one has taken more seriously the dictum of the Jewish theologian Irving Greenberg that "no statement, theological or otherwise, should be made (after 1945) that would not be credible in the presence of the burning children".[72] No one has undertaken a more painstaking investigation of the traces of anti-Judaism in the religious soil of Christianity, leaving no stone unturned and no waters untested. No one has arrived at more controversial conclusions. To Eckardt, the Holocaust, because of its extraordinary irrationality and incomprehensible cruelty, as well as the special identity of its victims, possesses a "transcending uniqueness" that distinguishes it from the other genocides of history.[73]

To this thesis is added the claim that "totally unique evil" can only be explained by the existence of a "totally unique power" of evil, *to wit*, the devil, who is the ultimate author of both antisemitism and its supreme manifestation in the Nazi explosion against the Jews.[74] The devil, however, requires human agents, which Christendom readily supplied in its apostate children, but those apostate children only enacted what ages of religious Jew-hatred (the devil's preparatory work) had fostered and plotted. It is Christianity, therefore, not merely Christendom, that is indicted, or, to be more exact, Christian supersessionism, which is linked intrinsically to the allegedly triumphalistic doctrine of the resurrection. "The teaching of the past resurrection of Jesus cannot be separated from...the 'teaching of contempt'. For the dogma of the resurrection is the relentless force behind every other derogation of Jewry. It is the ideological cancer that helped...to create one Holocaust and will perhaps help to create new ones".[75] In his latest (christological) study, Eckardt reiterates this theme: "I think that the potentially chief moral anguish for Christians today is not so much the church's traditional 'teaching of contempt'.... I suggest that the really world-determining problem for the contemporary church is not the Friday before Easter, but Easter itself, with the church's repeated proclamation of a resurrectionist triumphalism and supersessionism—a proclamation that appears, on the surface, ever so innocent".[76]

This startling assertion is a distinguishing mark of Eckardt's thought. Being a Christian, however, he does not disavow the resurrection of Christ, but recasts it in order to purge it of its moral offense. If Jesus, a Jewish martyr, rose from the dead, as the church proclaims, he rose in order to affirm Israel in its unbroken covenant with God. The risen Jesus stands in the midst of the Jewish community as a Jew for other Jews. His true identity is that of a revolutionary (anti-Roman) Jewish patriot and proto-Zionist,[77] or as a "champion of Israel".[78] As soon as Christians repent of their crimes and commit themselves "to live and die in historical-moral solidarity with the Jewish people to whom the resurrection in the first instance belongs", they are free to embrace their ancient belief with a good conscience.[79] Its anti-Jewish sting has been drawn.

Behind this analysis lies Eckardt's devotion to the modern Jewish state as a "liberating, divine-historical event"—in a sense, the true resurrection—which at all costs, must be supported by Jews and Christians alike, indeed, with "guns and bombs" if necessary.[80] Jesus, the Jew for other Jews, was also a "second Abraham, the Abraham of the gentiles, patriarch to the pagans", who, by virtue of his failed messiahship, made available the blessings of Israel's covenant to the world outside its bounds.[81] In Eckardt's view, history holds sway over theology—"history transforming faith"—in such a fashion that certain historical events have a transcending uniqueness; they possess the moral authority to alter or even obviate traditional paradigms and symbols. Hence, the incarnation/crucifixion/resurrection matrix of classical Christian faith is placed under the jurisdiction of the Holocaust (or *Shoah*) and its sequel, "the return of the Jewish people from political powerlessness" in the foundation of Israel, and judged accordingly.[82] Following the Jewish philosopher Emil Fackenheim's call for a "Jewish return into history", he calls for a similar "Christian return into history".[83] Such a return constitutes the essence of his 'post-modernist', 'post-neo-orthodox', 'post-patriarchal', and 'post-Holocaust' theology.

In Eckardt's earlier writings, the Jewish-Christian relationship is described in dialectical language, with opposite strengths and weaknesses: "...relative to Christianity, Jewish thought paradoxically qualifies the unredeemedness of the world by a testimony to the goodness of man and creation, an emphasis conducive to a certain combination of social responsibility with social utopianism; while, relative to Judaism, Christian thought paradoxically counters the redeemedness of the world by a concentration upon human sin in a fallen creation, an emphasis conducive to a certain combination of social irresponsibility with social realism".[84] These paradoxes cast light on the theological configurations of the two religions as variations on a larger covenantal theme. In his later writings, however, Eckardt seems less dialectical, tending increasingly to interpret Christianity as a special derivative religion for prodigal sons and daughters—essentially a 'Judaism for the gentiles'[85]—with nothing really original to contribute to the religious understanding. While the prodigal possesses (through the father's grace) an equal dignity in the father's house, he remains the prodigal until the end of his days. What can Christians tell Jews in dialogue that Jews do not know already, and know better?

Also undialectical is Eckardt's almost Hegelian affirmation of the modern state of Israel. Has a profound concern for Jewish survival in an antisemitic world rendered the theologian too much of a partisan of Israeli political interests? Has dogma once again, the dogma of Israel as a divine-historical event, been superimposed on history, with problematic consequences for the stateless Palestinians? Is there a blind spot in Eckardt's vision? To Ruether at least, this is certainly the case.[86]

Paul van Buren

The theme of solidarity with Israel—biblical Israel, modern Israel, political Israel—is also the central emphasis in the thought of Paul van Buren, author of the first true systematic theology written in relation to the Holocaust. Three of four projected volumes have now been published.[87] The theologian asserts that two historic events—the Holocaust and the birth of the state of Israel—have virtual revelatory status for Christians as well as Jews in the modern world, requiring contemporary theology to revolve around them. The Holocaust reveals that God commands humanity in general, and Christians in particular, to accept unqualified responsibility for the creation in general, and for the human future in particular, so that no similar catastrophe can occur again. The birth of the state of Israel reveals that the Jews still exist as God's elect in the biblical and covenantal sense, and their existence itself is a sign of God's continuing concern both with them and with all humanity through them.

Although founded by human hands, therefore, the Jewish state has supernatural as well as natural connotations.[88] As the elect nation, Israel (in all its senses) is the channel of divine grace in the world, and the fountainhead of light and truth for pagan Gentiles. There are two spiritual ways, the way of the Jews and the way of the Gentiles, which run side by side in history as parallel paths headed in the same general direction. Israel's path is the original way; the gentile way is the newer subsidiary way, opened up by a single Jew, Jesus of Nazareth, through a strange series of occurrences that made available the blessings of the household of faith to non-Jews. "Jesus is not the LORD, but our Lord, the one Jew who has given us access to the God of the Jews".[89] "A dead Jew hanging from a Gentile gallows is where it has been given to countless Gentiles...to see the heart of the God of Israel".[90] However, since not all Gentiles are Christians, or ever likely to be Christians, other modes of revelation must also be recognized.

Under no circumstances can the Christ of faith be torn from the Jesus of history, and under no circumstances can one be close to Jesus without being close to the people of Jesus, "the people with whom he showed a solidarity unto death at the hands of a Gentile occupying power".[91] This solidarity is the heart of christology and its only true setting. Since, moreover, twentieth-century Jews constitute the people Israel as much as first-century Jews, and since the state of Israel is the state of the people Israel, that state "in all its ambiguity becomes an unavoidable part of the present context for the Church's confession of and reflection upon the things concerning Jesus of Nazareth".[92] Modern history and geopolitics, as a consequence, supply the stuff of theology for Christians as well as Jews.

This is not an overstatement. To van Buren, a geopolitical event such as Israel's transfer of its capital city to Jerusalem is fraught with (to employ Hegelian language) world-historical significance; it represents nothing less than a "third stage" in the history of Christianity—"the Church with Israel".[93] (The second stage—"the Church against Israel"—was inaugurated by the Roman, i.e., pagan gentile, destruction of Jewish independence in the first and second centuries.) Clearly, this is 'Christian Zionism'. Jerusalem, the capital of Israel, is, in effect, the Christian as well as the Jewish capital, to which, through Jesus, the Christian masses are bound, although always in a dependent and subordinate sense, serving the welfare of Jews by serving the welfare of the Jewish state. "As God's anointed...Jesus binds the nations of the world to the nation of Jesus—the nation of the covenant, the Jewish people".[94] The whole of Christian theology, moreover, including its central concepts, must be reconsidered and, if necessary, reinterpreted accordingly. As the gentile church is overshadowed by elect Israel, Golgotha, or the crucifixion of a single Jew, is overshadowed by Auschwitz, the mass murder of six million elect Jews, and Easter, the resurrection of a single Jew, is overshadowed by the rebirth of the people Israel—surely a more amazing victory over the power of evil and death, and one no doubt with greater spiritual significance in the long course of history. Golgotha and Easter are still authentic revelatory moments, but only in a relative sense; they do not belong at the centre of time either chronologically or symbolically. They are for Christians alone, whereas Auschwitz and Israel are definitive (in negative and positive terms) for both Christians and Jews.

To be sure, van Buren finds some novel elements in Christianity that are not merely derivative from Judaism, or, for that matter, classical humanism. However, they must not be exaggerated, or anti-Judaism will result. It is Jesus of Nazareth, Jesus the Jew, "the one called rabbi who spoke Aramaic and thought as a first century Galilean", who is paramount, not the Chalcedonian God-man.[95] Such a Christ loses his Jewish particularity, and can easily be transformed into a pagan or neo-classical idol. However, as Albert Schweitzer noted long ago, the racial Christs of the modern age had more to do with the rise of historical criticism than with ancient christological formulations.[96] As long as Christians were content with the Chalcedonian 'God-man', they were less likely to recast the Jesus of history in their own image. The Holocaust theologian forgets this point.

According to Ruether, van Buren has transferred Barth's "monistic concept of historical revelation" from an exclusively christological focus to an exclusively covenantal one—"the covenant of God with the Jewish people".[97] Hence, Christianity can never be more than an auxiliary to Judaism and to Jewish goals, both secular and religious, but especially religious. Since, moreover, Israel's elect status is the cornerstone of his thought, he is committed to a traditionalist view of "Israel's mission" that, in turn, forces him to decide on behalf of Jews the difference between authentic and inauthentic Jewish existence. The authentic Jew is the 'Torah-true' Jew; the inauthentic Jew disregards the covenant and the Torah.[98] Not only is the notion of a Christian making intra-Jewish value judgments for Jews anomalous, but, as Eckardt points out, so also is the very attempt to write a 'Christian theology of the people Israel'. Such enterprises are "pre-*Shoah*" in spirit, and reflect, in spite of van Buren's obvious intentions to the contrary, a "lingering triumphalism".[99] A more serious weakness lies in Christian Zionism itself. Does not Christian Zionist theology, even in its non-fundamentalist forms, verge on the sacralization of a modern nation-state—Israel is a state like other states and a state not like other states—and is not such sacralization always dangerous? Power is morally ambiguous, and nations are the creatures of history, here today and gone tomorrow. But there is nothing ambiguous about van Buren's position. To his critics, his theology has a curiously inverted character, representing, at least in part, as Ruether claims, a "self-abnegating philo-Semitism".[100] In his own defense, van Buren claims that such criticisms constitute a parody of his views, rendered especially pernicious in light of the volatile situation in the Middle East.[101]

Conclusion

This survey of post-Holocaust Christian thought is far from complete. Important figures as Dorothee Sölle, Franz Müssner, Clemens Thoma, Edward Schillebeeckx, Hans Küng, etc., have not been mentioned, nor their ideas examined.[102] Those theologians whose ideas have been summarized in the preceding pages have been dealt with in such a cursory fashion that the possibility of caricature cannot be discounted. However, certain general observations are in order: (1) Christian thought has not remained static following the mass destruction of the European Jews, but has moved in unprecedented directions; (2) no consensus exists among Christians concerning the theological issues posed by this monumental evil, although all believe that the crisis is serious; (3) the debate has embraced many topics: the church, election, eschatology, salvation, social justice, theological ethics, transcendence, spirituality, christology, divine suffering, radical evil, resurrection, providence, and the meaning of history; (4) post-Holocaust Christians agree that Judaism (or Israel) should be seen as a religious partner rather than religious rival of Christianity, but disagree about the nature of the partnership; (5) post-Holocaust Christians agree that Jesus must be understood in a Jewish context, but disagree as to the historical and theological implications of this assertion; (6) the survival of the Jewish people is a matter of paramount concern for Christian ethics; (7) in one way or another, Christian theology must come to terms with the existence of the state of Israel and its significance for Jewish-Christian relations; (8) the scope of the enterprise, as well as its complexity, suggests that a long time will pass before its lessons are finally exhausted.

Endnotes

1. See Moshe Zimmermann, *Wilhelm Marr: The Patriarch of Antisemitism* (New York: Oxford University Press, 1986). However, Paul Rose argues that the term 'antisemitic' was actually coined by the Jewish writer Moritz Steinschneider in 1860. See Paul Lawrence Rose, *Revolutionary Antisemitism in Germany: From Kant to Wagner* (Princeton: Princeton University Press, 1990), 288, n. 23.

2. Jules Isaac, *Has Anti-Semitism Roots in Christianity?* trans., (New York: Conference of Christians and Jews, 1962), 58–60.

3. Cf. Ludwig Feuerbach, *Das Wesen des Christentums*, (1841).

4. Cf. Samuel Sandmel, *Anti-Semitism in the New Testament?* (Philadelphia: Fortress Press, 1978).

5. John Chrysostom, "Dangers Ahead" (Sermon I), trans. C. Mervyn Maxwell.

6. Karl Barth, *Church Dogmatics*, "The Doctrine of God", trans., (Edinburgh: T. & T. Clark, 1957), 2:195–259.

7. See Alan Davies, *Anti-Semitism and the Christian Mind: The Crisis of Conscience After Auschwitz* (New York: Herder & Herder, 1969), ch. 5.

8. Augustine, "In Answer to the Jews" (homily).

9. Johann Baptist Metz, *The Emergent Church: The Future of Christianity in a Postbourgeois World*, trans., (New York: Crossroad, 1981), ch. 2.

10. Karl Adam, *The Spirit of Catholicism*, trans., (London: Sheed & Ward, 1929), 14.

11. Cf. Emil Fackenheim, "The Holocaust and the State of Israel: Their Relation" in Eva Fleischner, ed., *Auschwitz: Beginning of a New Era?* (New York: Ktav, 1977), 205.

12. Paul Tillich, "The Struggle Between Time and Space", *Theology of Culture* (New York: Oxford University Press, 1959), 38–39.

13. A movement in the German Protestant churches in 1932 that adopted Nationalist Socialist principles. Its leaders called for "positive Christianity" in the "German spirit of Luther", and denounced Jews, Marxists and Freemasons. The German Christians also affirmed "race, folk and nation" as divinely ordained orders and demanded that Germany be protected against the "unfit and inferior". The movement was strongly opposed by the (much smaller) anti-Nazi "confessing church".

14. Tillich (n. 12), 38–39.

15. Cf. A. James Reimar, *The Emanuel Hirsch and Paul Tillich Debate: A Study in the Political Ramifications of Theology* (Lewiston: Edwin Mellen Press, 1989), 110–111.

16. Eberhard Bethge, "Christology and the First Commandment", *Remembering for the Future: Jews and Christians During and After the Holocaust*, Papers presented at an International Scholars' Conference, Oxford, July 10–13, 1988 (Oxford: Pergamon Press, 1988), 691.

17. Paul Tillich, "Jewish Influences on Contemporary Christian Theology", *Cross Currents*, 2, no. 3 (Spring 1952): 35

18. Paul Tillich, "The Jewish Question: Christian and German Problem", *Jewish Social Studies*, 33, no. 4 (1971): 257.

19. Tillich (n. 18), 254.

20. Tillich (n. 18), 268.

21. Reinhold Niebuhr, "Jews After the War", *Love and Justice*, ed. D.B. Robertson (Philadelphia: Westminster Press, 1958), 138.

22. Reinhold Niebuhr, *Leaves from the Notebooks of a Tamed Cynic* (New York: Meridian Books, 1957), 215.

23. Reinhold Niebuhr, *Man's Nature and His Communities: Essays on the Dynamics and Enigmas of Man's Personal and Social Existence* (New York: Charles Scribner's Sons, 1965), 17.

24. Reinhold Niebuhr, "The Relations of Christians and Jews in Western Civilization", *Pious and Secular America* (New York: Charles Scribner's Sons, 1958), 103.

25. "Now to the Christian, the Jew is the incomprehensibly obdurate man, who declines to see what has happened; and to the Jew, the Christian is the incomprehensibly daring man, who affirms in an unredeemed world that its redemption has been accomplished." (Martin Buber, "The Two Foci of the Jewish Soul" in Will Herberg, ed., *The Writings of Martin Buber* (New York: Meridian Books, 1956), 276. These words were cited by Niebuhr many times, for example, in his tribute to Buber following the latter's death: "Martin Buber: 1878–1965", *Christianity and Crisis*, 25, no.12 (July 12, 1965): 146.

26. Niebuhr (n. 24), 105.

27. Reinhold Niebuhr, "The Unsolved Religious Problem in Christian-Jewish Relations", *Christianity and Crisis*, 26, no.21 (December 12, 1966): 282.

28. Niebuhr (n. 24), 109.

29. Niebuhr (n. 24), 110.

30. James Parkes, *God at Work, In Science, Politics and Human Life* (London: Putnam, 1952), 51.

31. James Parkes, *Prelude to Dialogue: Jewish-Christian Relationships* (London: Vallentine, Mitchell, 1969), 196.

32. Parkes (n. 31), 194.

33. Parkes (n. 31), 216.

34. Modernism was an important movement in twentieth-century English Anglicanism. See Robert Everett, *Christianity Without Antisemitism: James Parkes and the Jewish Christian Encounter* (Oxford, UK: Pergamon Press, 1992).

35. John T. Pawlikowski, *Christ in the Light of the Christian-Jewish Dialogue* (New York: Paulist Press, 1982), 126.

36. Pawlikowski, (n. 35), 111. At this point Pawlikowski is following the Jewish historian Ellis Rivkin.

37. "An internal city, a *politeuma*, engraved on the soul of the individual, this was the crucial achievement of Pharisaism", Ellis Rivkin, "The Internal City: Judaism and Urbanization", *Journal for the Scientific Study of Religion*, 5, no. 2 (Spring, 1966): 235. See also Rivkin's major study, *A Hidden Revolution: The Pharisee's Search for the Kingdom Within* (Nashville: Abingdon, 1978).

38. Pierre Teilhard de Chardin, *The Phenomenon of Man*, trans., (New York: Harper & Row, 1961), bk. 4, ch. 2. By "personalizing universe", Teilhard means the deepening of consciousness as the evolutionary process ascends to higher and more complex levels; by "Omega point," he means the attainment of a higher synthesis or state of being in which perfect individuality and perfect community are achieved at once. For a good critique of Teilhard, see Jürgen Moltmann, *The Way of Jesus Christ: Christology in Messianic Dimensions*, trans., (London: SCM Press, 1990), 292–297.

39. John T. Pawlikowski, *The Challenge of the Holocaust for Christian Theology*, The Center for Studies on the Holocaust (New York: Anti-Defamation League, 1978), 8.

40. Pawlikowski (n. 39), 13.

41. John T. Pawlikowski, "Christian Ethics and the Holocaust: A Dialogue with Post-Auschwitz Judaism", *Theological Studies*, 49, no. 4 (December 1988): 653.

42. Pawlikowski (n. 41), 663.

43. Cf. Rosemary Radford Ruether, "The *Faith and Fratricide* Discussion: Old Problems and New Dimensions" in Alan Davies, ed., *Antisemitism and the Foundations of Christianity*, (New York: Paulist Press, 1979), 243–246.

44. Cf. A. Roy Eckardt, *Jews and Christians: The Contemporary Meeting* (Bloomington: Indiana University Press, 1986), 144–145.

45. Pawlikowski (n. 39), 18.

46. Rosemary Radford Ruether, *Faith and Fratricide: The Theological Roots of Anti-Semitism* (New York: Seabury, 1974), 249.

47. Ruether (n. 46), 249.

48. Ruether (n. 46), 254.

49. Ruether (n. 46), 255.

50. Paul Tillich, *The Protestant Era*, trans., (Chicago: University of Chicago Press, 1948), ch. 11.

51. A. Roy Eckardt, *For Righteousness' Sake: Contemporary Moral Philosophies* (Bloomington: Indiana University Press, 1987), 308–310.

52. John M. Oesterreicher, *Anatomy of Contempt: A Critique of R.R. Ruether's 'Faith and Fratricide'*, Institute of Judaeo-Christian Studies (South Orange, NJ: Seton Hall University, n.d. [1975]), 31. For a more temperate assessment, together with a reply by Ruether, see Alan Davies (n. 43).

53. Rosemary Radford Ruether & Herman J. Ruether, *The Wrath of Jonah: The Crisis of Religious Nationalism in the Israeli-Palestine Conflict* (San Francisco: Harper & Row, 1989), 217. See also the symposium in the journal *Continuum* 1, no. 1 (Autumn 1990) and the Ruethers' reply, ibid., 1, no. 2 (Winter-Spring 1991).

54. See *Crosscurrents* 42, no. 3 (Fall 1992), 427.

55. Jürgen Moltmann, *The Crucified God: The Cross of Christ as the Foundation and Criticism of Christian Theology*, trans., (London: SCM Press, 1973), 134.

56. Jürgen Moltmann, *The Church in the Power of the Spirit: A Contribution to Messianic Ecclesiology*, trans., (London: SCM Press, 1977), 135.

57. Moltmann (n. 56), 136.

58. Moltmann (n. 38), 95.

59. Moltmann (n. 38), 214.

60. Moltmann (n. 38), 31–32.

61. Moltmann (n. 38), 32.

62. Moltmann (n. 38), 34, citing F.W. Marquardt.

63. Moltmann (n. 38), 33.

64. Moltmann (n. 56), 147.

65. Moltmann (n. 56), 147.

66. Moltmann (n. 55), 278.

67. Moltmann (n. 55), 278.

68. Eugene B. Borowitz, *Contemporary Christologies: A Jewish Response* (New York: Paulist Press, 1980), 87.

69. A. Roy Eckardt, with Alice L. Eckardt, *Long Night's Journey into Day: Life and Faith After the Holocaust* (Detroit: Wayne State University Press, 1982), 87–110; Eugene Borowitz (n. 68), 92–95; John T. Pawlikowski (n. 35), 143–145.

70. Pawlikowski (n. 35), 144.

71. Cf. Jürgen Moltmann, *The Trinity and the Kingdom of God: The Doctrine of God*, trans., (London: SCM Press, 1981); *God in Creation: An Ecological Doctrine of Creation*, The Gifford Lectures, 1984–1985, trans., (London: SCM Press, 1985); *The Way of Jesus Christ* (n. 38).

72. Irving Greenberg, "Cloud of Smoke, Pillar of Fire: Judaism, Christianity and Modernity After the Holocaust" in Eva Fleischner (n. 11), 23.

73. Alice L. Eckardt and A. Roy Eckardt, "The Holocaust and the Enigma of Uniqueness: A Philosophical Effort at Practical Clarification", *The Annals of the American Academy of Political and Social Science*, 450 (July 1980): 165–178.

74. The Eckardts, *Long Night's Journey into Day* (n. 69), 52–53.

75. A. Roy Eckardt, "Covenant-Resurrection-Holocaust" in *Humanizing America: A Post-Holocaust Imperative*, Second Philadelphia Conference on the Holocaust, February 16–18, 1977, p. 44.

76. A. Roy Eckardt, *Reclaiming the Jesus of History: Christology Today* (Minneapolis: Fortress Press, 1992), 172.

77. "We can envision a twentieth-century Jesus of Nazareth, somehow spared of the hell of Belzec or Sobibor, as a faithful citizen of the State of Israel, committed to justice for its people and resistance to its enemies", *For Righteousness' Sake* (n. 51), 284.

78. Eckardt, *Reclaiming the Jesus of History* (n. 76), 220.

79. Eckardt (n. 76), 216–217.

80. Eckardt, *Jews and Christians* (n. 44), 156; *For Righteousness' Sake* (n. 51), 294.

81. The Eckardts, *Long Night's Journey into Day* (n. 69), 126.

82. Eckardt, *For Righteousness' Sake* (n. 51), 241.

83. Emil L. Fackenheim, *The Jewish Return into History: Reflections in the Age of Auschwitz and a New Jerusalem* (New York: Schocken Books, 1978); Eckardt, *For Righteousness' Sake* (n. 51), 265.

84. A. Roy Eckardt, *Elder and Younger Brothers: The Encounter of Jews and Christians* (New York: Charles Scribner's Sons, 1967), 89.

85. Pawlikowski, *Christ in the Light of the Christian-Jewish Dialogue* (n. 35), 17.

86. The Ruethers, *The Wrath of Jonah* (n. 53), 208. The Eckardts (Roy and his wife Alice) have replied, *Contiuum* 1, no. 1 (Autumn 1990): 129, that they strongly affirm the equal rights of the Palestinians.

87. Paul van Buren, *Discerning the Way: A Theology of the Jewish-Christian Reality* (New York: Seabury, 1980); *A Christian Theology of the People Israel* (New York: Seabury, 1983); *A Theology of the Jewish-Christian Reality: Christ in Context* (New York: Harper & Row, 1988).

88. Van Buren, *Discerning the Way* (n. 87), 180–181.

89. Van Buren, *Discerning the Way* (n. 87), 85.

90. Van Buren, *Discerning the Way* (n. 87), 86.

91. Paul van Buren, *Jesus Christ Between Jews and Christiians*, (Cincinnati: Forward Movement Publications, 1985), 8.

92. Van Buren, *A Theology of the Jewish-Christian Reality* (n. 87), 65.

93. Van Buren, *A Theology of the Jewish-Christian Reality* (n. 87), 104.

94. Van Buren, *A Theology of the Jewish-Christian Reality* (n. 87), 137.

95. Van Buren, *A Theology of the Jewish-Christian Reality* (n. 87), 236.

96. "For historical criticism had become...a secret struggle to reconcile the German religious spirit with the Spirit of Jesus of Nazareth." Albert Schweitzer, *The Quest of the Historical Jesus: A Critical Study of Its Progress from Reimarus to Wrede*, trans., (London: Adam & Charles Black, 1952), 310.

97. The Ruethers, *The Wrath of Jonah* (n. 53), 211.

98. "A Jew without faith and disdainful of Torah is not a good Jew, but he or she remains a Jew", van Buren, *A Christian Theology of the People Israel* (n. 87), 227.

99. Eckardt, *For Righteousness' Sake* (n. 51), 268.

100. The Ruethers (n. 53), 215.

101. *Continuum* 1, no. 1 (Autumn 1990): 136.

102. Dorothee Sölle, "God's Pain and Our Pain: How Theology has to change after Auschwitz", *Remembering for the Future: The Impact of the Holocaust and Genocide on Jews and Christians*, Papers presented at an International Scholars' Conference, Oxford, July 10-13, 1988, suppl. vol., (Oxford: Pergamon, 1988), 448–464; Franz Müssner, *Tractate on the Jews: The Signifance of Judaism for Christian Faith*, trans., (Philadelphia: Fortress Press, 1984); Clemens Thoma, *A Christian Theology of Judaism*, trans., (New York: Paulist Press, 1980); Edward Schillebeeckx, *Jesus: An Experiment in Christology*, trans., (New York: Seabury Press, 1979); Hans Küng, *On Being a Christian*, trans., (Garden City, NY: Doubleday, 1976).

Suggestions For Further Reading

Buren, Paul van. *A Theology of the Jewish Christian Reality*. 3 vols. *Discerning the Way*. New York: Seabury, 1980. *A Christian Theology of the People Israel*. New York: Seabury, 1983. *Christ in Context*. New York: Harper & Row, 1988. The first Christian systematic theology on this subject.

Davies, Alan. *Anti-Semitism and the Christian Mind: The Crisis of Conscience After Auschwitz*. New York: Herder & Herder, 1969. A survey of early post-war theological materials.

____, ed. *Antisemitism and the Foundations of Christianity*. New York: Paulist Press, 1979. Twelve Christian scholars reply to Rosemary Radford Ruether.

Eckardt, A. Roy. *Elder and Younger Brothers: The Encounter of Jews and Christians*. New York: Charles Scribner's Sons, 1967. An early exploratory volume that raises most of the critical theological issues.

Eckardt, A. Roy, with Alice L. Eckardt. *Long Night's Journey Into Day: Life and Faith After the Holocaust*. Detroit: Wayne State University Press, 1982. The most provocative of Roy Eckardt's books, and the most radical; they have reissued it in a new edition as *Long Night's Journey Into Day: A Revised Retrospective on the Holocaust*. Oxford, UK: Pergamon Press, 1988.

Pawlikowski, John T. *Christ in the Light of the Christian-Jewish Dialogue*. New York: Paulist Press, 1982. Pawlikowski summarizes recent developments in Christian theology and states his own views.

Ruether, Rosemary Radford. *Faith and Fratricide: The Theological Roots of Anti-Judaism*. New York: Seabury, 1974. A modern classic that has captured widespread attention. James Parkes described it as "epoch-making".

Thoma, Clemens. *A Christian Theology of Judaism*. Trans. Helga Croner. New York: Paulist Press, 1980. A scholarly study of historical sources.

Willebrands, Johannes Cardinal. *Church and Jewish People: New Considerations*. New York: Paulist Press, 1992. A Catholic analysis, by the president of the Vatican's Commission for Religious Relations with the Jews.

World Council of Churches. *The Theology of the Churches and the Jewish People: Statements by the World Council of Churches and its Member Churches*. Geneva: World Council of Churches Publications, 1988. A comprehensive compilation.

ISRAEL REBORN:

SOME THEOLOGICAL PERSPECTIVES

Edward H. Flannery

What are the implications of Israel reborn for Christian theology? To some Christians it remains a matter of "scandal." And although Christian thinkers generally have been reluctant to submit the creation of Israel to theological analysis, some pioneering attempts have been made. It is to be hoped that the new direction taken by the Mid-East peace talks in the fall of 1993 will inaugurate a new departure in Christian theological analysis and dialogue. Edward H. Flannery characterizes and analyzes the efforts made to date.

The epochal return of the Jews to sovereignty in their ancient homeland in our time has been greeted with scant Christian theological reflection. This inattention is understandable for more than one reason. Firstly, no Christian theology of the State of Israel is conceivable prior to a thorough revision of the traditional theology of Judaism, a revision yet to be completed or widely agreed upon. On another level, pressures emanating from the Arab-Israeli conflict have tended to inhibit free and open discussion, theological or other, of the status or significance of the new State—pressures still with us today. The burden of this essay is to assist in remedying the inattention mainly by presenting a cursory survey of efforts that have already been made and an outline of a possible systematic approach to the construction of a positive Christian theology of the State of Israel.

It must be made clear at the outset that none of the reflections that follow are intended as support for either party to the Middle East conflict. Theological reflections, regardless of content, possess an autonomy of their own which renders them superordinate to political or other secular interests with which they may or may not coincide.

Is a Theology of Israel Possible?

The question has been raised: Should there be a Christian theology of Israel at all? Professor A. Roy Eckardt, who for many years has deeply probed the origin, character, and meaning of Israel as people, land, and State, has answered in the negative. He warns against Christian attempts to "assimilate Jewish historical fortune to the Christian imperium,"[1] and against failures to respect Israel's secular character. There are also those who see Israel exclusively as a political entity and deny it any theological significance.

On the other hand, the rights and requirements of theology must be fully respected. Christian theology has always reserved a section of its considerations for the course of natural, historical, and political events. In principle no subject worth serious consideration is exempt from study in the light of divine Revelation or Providence. Certainly, Israel, seen as a faith-tradition, peoplehood, or land—within which Christianity finds its origin and much of its meaning—hardly falls outside the reach of this criterion. Christian theologizing about Judaism need not be presumed to be an attempt as in times past to define or interpret Judaism for Jews, but rather as a means of providing Christians with an understanding of the Jewish-Christian relationship. A Christian theology of Judaism, in short, is not, or at any rate should not be, an apologia; rather is it by its very nature a venture in self-understanding. Robert Everett states this point with precision: "Zionism and the State of Israel have profound ramifications for Christians and Christian theology that, if understood correctly, have important implications for our theological self-identity."[2] Paul van Buren sees such a theology as a necessity: "If this God, the church's God, has set Israel in the world as his witness, then a Christian theology of Israel is no more optional for the church than its Christology."[3] Rabbi Jacob Petuchowski helps to lay the problem to rest with admirable simplicity: "We need a Jewish theology of Christianity and a Christian theology of Judaism."[4]

A Theology of the State?

There are theologians who question submitting a modern secular state to theological analysis. The problem here is mostly verbal. True, statehood and statecraft *as such* add nothing substantive, and certainly nothing religious, to the people, nation, or land it may encompass. The modern state, however, can and often does, as in the case of Israel, include these components. Orthodox philosopher Yeshayahu Leibowitz, who otherwise sees Israel in a profoundly religious perspective, puts it bluntly: "The State of Israel is a governmental and administrative apparatus that is devoid of all [religious] content."[5] For all that, to refer to Israel exclusively in terms of land or people does not adequately describe its full and present reality and, given the highly charged atmosphere affecting the

Arab-Israeli situation today, to denude it of its statehood, if only verbally, unavoidably gives off overtones of political partisanship. Moreover, any suggestion that the Jewish people could live today in peace and security without statehood betrays a woeful ignorance of the history of the Jewish people and of contemporary antisemitism. The terms "state," "land," and "nation" then will be used interchangeably, it being understood that in no instance will the term "state" refer to the purely political.

Jewish Perspectives

In an era in which Jewish and Christian theologians and scholars have been intimately and fruitfully engaged in dialogue and cooperation, the Christian theologian, embarking on his or her investigations on the rebirth of the Israeli State, is drawn naturally enough to look at Jewish religious thinking on the subject, always in the hope of finding insights helpful for a Christian understanding of the event.[6] What is known about the land of Israel as a Jewish homeland is found for the greater part in the Hebrew Scriptures, which though altered in content and differently interpreted form a part of the canon of the Christian Scriptures. This fact alone invites the Christian scholar to acquire a thoroughgoing familiarity with Jewish thought and theology on Zionism and the land or State of Israel. Regrettably, only a passing glance at this fascinating aspect of the subject is possible here.

A majority of Israelis and probably also of Diaspora Jews adopt, at least on the conscious level, a secularized outlook on the rebirth of the new State and accord it little or no religious significance. The "believing" minority meanwhile presents a striking array of diverging positions. A few examples will provide a notion of their breadth. In the birth-year of the fledgling state, Martin Buber issued a warning: "Israel must perish if it intends to exist as a political structure. It can persist...if it insists on its vocation of uniqueness, if it translates into reality the divine words spoken during the making of the covenant."[7] Abraham Heschel saw the event as a "miracle in disguise." "Things," he wrote, "look natural and conceal what is a radical surprise."[8] David Hartman finds that most of those who give a religious response to the rebirth "see in it God's providential hand."[9] He demurs at interpreting current developments as direct expressions of God's will or design, but celebrates them as "an opportunity...to renew the full scope of the covenantal spirit of Judaism."[10] Emil Fackenheim holds that whatever there is of the miraculous in the event resides in the heroic efforts of the Jewish people, efforts he considers to be "in touch with the Absolute."[11] David Novak, discussing Zionism, comments: "It is Judaically justifiable when it roots itself in God's promise of the Land of Israel to the elect people of Israel and when it enhances the unique opportunity Jews have to serve God most fully in the Land of Israel."[12] Orthodox communities in Israel include *Gush Emunim*, which sees the State of Israel as the beginning of messianic redemption, and *Oz Ve-Shalom*, a religious group which evaluates it entirely according to its contribution to Judaism and the worship of God. Yeshayahu Leibowitz, its founder, asserts: "In this it has failed. It has contributed nothing to Judaism."[13] There are also *Natore Kartha* and the American Council for Judaism, which reject the State as a violation of the traditional belief that it will be brought about by a divine messianic initiative.

Behind these contrasting interpretations, it must be emphasized, there exists a solidarity with the State that, excepting a few anti-Zionist Orthodox, is virtually unanimous in the world of unassimilated Jewry. Hartman expresses it this way: "For many Jews Israel has become the new substitute for traditional Judaism."[14] Theological opinion or the lack thereof apparently wields little influence on the communal attachment to Israel. How are we to explain this imperishable attraction? As a refuge from an unending antisemitism? A source of a renewed sense of self-identity? A sense of belonging long lost? Yes, all of these, but finally it must be understood historically as heir to an age-old yearning of the people of Israel for the land promised from the beginning, a land known as an integral part of the Covenant made with their fathers. This is a story that whoever will understand the Jewish people or undertake a theological study of the State of Israel cannot ignore.

The Development of a Positive Theology of Israel: A Survey

Despite the general hesitancy of Christian theologians to submit the return of Jews to the land and the establishment of the State to theological analysis several attempts have been made. The results to date, while in most cases inchoate, have been promising. Though not easily classifiable, they can be categorized according to their methodology as: 1) Evangelical, 2) biblical-critical, 3) secular-ethical, and 4) systematic-theological.

Biblical Fundamentalism: The Evangelicals

Historically, the earliest contribution to a Christian theology of Israel must be accredited to Evangelicalism, specifically, to pietistic Protestants and Puritans of sixteenth- and seventeenth-century England and to the Restorationist movement that followed.[15] The former, fundamentalist in hermeneutics and of eschatological bent in theology, placed a heavy emphasis on the Second Coming of Christ and its dependence on the return of the Jews to Zion. Restorationism was less a movement than a conglomerate of preachers, theologians, and public figures who in various ways fostered the idea of an actual restoration of the Jewish people in Palestine. These groups provide the first traces of practical Zionism long before

Jews could dare to contemplate the possibility of an actual return *en masse*. Little did these Christian dreamers realize how much their theologies would ready the political atmosphere in England over the years in such wise that in the early twentieth century acceptance of the Balfour principle, so vital to the eventual establishment of the Israeli State, became possible.[16]

In recent years Evangelical sects have continued along the main lines of traditional teaching: God rules in history; He has promised the land of Israel to the Jewish people as an everlasting possession. When the new State was established it was not seen as a human achievement. Some Evangelical theologians accepted it purely and simply as a fulfillment of the prophecies; others, acknowledging its secular nature, considered the fulfillment incomplete.[17] More recently, Malcolm Hedding, an Israeli, terms it the "herald of a soon-coming age."[18] Clarence Wagner assures us: "Prophecy is being unfolded before our eyes."[19] It should not go without notice, on the other hand, that there are Evangelical groups that are not only anti-Zionist but anti-Judaic, even antisemitic. Prominent among these are groups called Dominion, Neo-Kingdom, and Dominion-Reconstruction, which excoriate Israel and Jews betimes in insulting terms.

One of the most comprehensive Evangelical interpretations of the Israel of today comes from the pen of Professor Marvin Wilson. Focusing on the State in a "historical-existential perspective," with attention to "contemporary existential needs," he holds firm to the biblical-prophetic frame of reference. The biblical connection, he insists, must not be reduced to mere "proof-testing" or a "real estate" theology limited to extracting predictions from the Scriptures. Given the secular character of the State, he is not prepared "at this time" to accept it as a fulfillment of prophecy, but rather, as an "unfinished drama." His most original contribution to Evangelical thinking is his requirement that in virtue of its biblical commitment a Christian theology of Israel must include justice for both the Israeli and Palestinian peoples.[20]

Biblical-Critical Studies on the Land

The foremost question facing Christian scholars in the wake of the creation of the new State revolves on whether the land promise of the Hebrew Scriptures is affirmed, rejected, or transcended in the Christian Testament. The traditional answer has been one of rejection. Two Christian scholars have taken up the question and come to conclusions that give the lie to that tradition: W.D. Davies in his *The Gospel and the Land*,[21] an exhaustive exegesis of the land concept in the Christian Testament and in deutero-canonical and other Jewish writings, and Walter Brueggemann in *The Land*,[22] a study of the land tradition in the Hebrew and Christian Testaments. Both are in full agreement that the ancient promises are not rejected in the Christian Testament. Beyond this their interpretations diverge as to the degree of relevance the land concept holds in Christian thought and practice. Taking it in its broadest embrace as "storied place," "rootage," or place "for belonging," Brueggemann extols it as of great importance for both Judaism and Christianity. "For all its spiritualizing," he writes, "the New Testament does not escape this rootage. The Christian tradition has been very clear in locating the story in Bethlehem, Nazareth, Jerusalem, and Galilee."[23] On his part, Davies considers the Christian Scriptures ambivalent on the significance of the land of Israel. Some of the words of Jesus, he finds, give a tacit affirmation of the tradition, but his concern is more for Israel as a people of salvation. He states, "For holiness of place, Christianity has fundamentally, though not consistently, substituted the holiness of the person: it has Christified holy space...to be 'in Christ' is to be 'in the land'."[24] These two scholars present an option of two theologies of the land promise, one of continuity, the other of partial discontinuity. The all-important finding for our purpose consists in their agreement that the validity of the promise is not repudiated in the Christian Scriptures.

A Secular-Ethical Critique

With A. Roy Eckardt we reach another pole of the discussion.[25] As Evangelicals stressed Israel's biblical connection, so he takes the part of its secularity. In a penetrating article of 1979 he proposed a "secular theology" of Israel, yet in a more recent work he speaks rather of a "secular Christian ethic," apparently placing the subject beyond the reach of theology.[26] His critique of theologies stemming both from the left and the right renders a welcome service as a caution against the marked one-sidedness that mars so many of them. The Evangelical approach—in Eckardt's vocabulary "Christian Zionism"—he finds flawed by its scriptural literalism, which, he avers, strives to lay bare the designs of the Almighty in history. His criticism here is extended to all hermeneutics that would relate scriptural texts of a predictive genre to posterior historical happenings. Such attempts he discards as "biblicist," "historicizing God's judgment," and "misappropriating the events of history."[27] Nonetheless, he values Christian Zionists as friends of Israel and compliments them for "refusing to exclude God's active will from the common life."[28] At the same time he contrasts their "historicizing God's judgment" with what he believes to be the "more acceptable biblical teaching that the Sovereign of history assigns her own final meanings to the exigencies of time and place."[29] How and why God conceals his purpose and workings in history from his creatures desirous of knowing them is not explained.

Eckardt's critique of liberalist disfavor toward Zionism and Israel is of considerable interest.[30] He posits the root of this brand of anti-Zionism in the universalism-versus-particularism opposition. Liberal opinion prizes universality and accordingly favors social and political inclusiveness. The universal is favored as an ideal and as more spiritual than the particular, which conversely is seen as limiting and exclusive. He traces this penchant to the Enlightenment period when nationalism and ethnicity took on a pejorative meaning. One appreciates how a faith-tradition laying claim to a special national destiny and a predestined land stands forth in such an outlook. Probing for the theological implication of this ideology he concludes: "National identity and loyalty are identified as barriers to ideal human relationships and goals. A truly enlightened people of God will transcend all such barriers."[31] The liberalist disfavor, in short, manifests itself as an exaggerated universalism.

Eckardt's singular perspective on Israel remains a challenging one that serves well as a counterbalance to simplistic uses of scriptural sources and to theologies that would impose a Christian purpose on their readings of Israel.

Systematic-Theological Approaches

A goodly number of mainstream theologians have taken up the question of Israel's theological provenance but in a cursory manner. Most limit their attention to essentials they consider requisite to the subject, and almost all distance themselves from fundamentalist and secular approaches. All in all their contributions run a gamut of tentativeness and caution to forthright affirmation of a biblical derivation of the new State.

Charlotte Klein exemplifies the cautious approach.[32] Allowing that one may speak "with great caution" of a "certain theological dimension" respecting the State, she warns against the "impudence of imposing a theological dimension on Israel."[33] At the same time she concludes that the State's existence today gives evidence that "Israel is meant to survive.... and seems to be the necessary sign value that state may possess for the Christian today."[34] John Oesterreicher, less cautious, declares that he is unable to see "how the reborn State could be anything but a sign of God's concern for His people."[35] He continues: "I cannot see how the renewal of the land could be anything for the theologian but a wonder of love and fidelity," and concludes, "Today's Israel is new proof that God stands by his Covenant."[36]

Eva Fleischner, although maintaining that God is faithful to his promises, demurs at accepting the rebirth of the State as a prophetic fulfillment. It is seen rather as "one link in the chain of God's saving acts."[37] Implicit in this statement is a reference to the problem of Israel's secularity and the conditional nature of the promises. In Jewish biblical theology, she reminds us, the Jewish people, as a people of election, are called by God to holiness, to be a "light to the nations." Failure to live up to this calling is threatened with exile, *Galut*, from the land, *Eretz Yisrael*. Recognizing that Israel's secular character can to some extent be regarded as a lapse from Israel's calling, Fleischner concedes nonetheless that this does not render it unfit as a possible stage or link in God's redemptive plan.

Walter Harrelson takes another step along this path. Rejecting the possibility that the present State is the "literal fulfillment of the promises," he comments: "God keeps bringing Israel back to this place, for here is to be the scene of a new and glorious transfiguration of life on earth, with the holy land and Zion at the center of the transfiguration."[38] Here Harrelson introduces the eschatological component of the promises, an aspect apparently considered premature by most of the others surveyed.

Professor Hendrik Berkhof of the University of Leiden has written briefly on the Israeli State and with poignancy. Noting the frequent references to the State as a "sign" without specifying what Israel is a sign of, he asserts:

> Remarkably few theologians in the circles to which I refer venture an explicit answer to this question. They want to stop thinking in this direction after having uttered the word 'sign.' It is clear that a certain tentativeness, even uncertainty, hovers over the subject.[39]

For all that, in the end he concludes that a "sign value" is the most that can as yet be conceded to the State. His contribution can be summarized as follows:

Despite terrifying odds Israel as a people has escaped extinction and maintained its identity down the centuries. We already have here a "sign" of God's faithfulness and promise. With the coming of Christ and the universalization of God's plan, the Israelitic form of God's work, which in part is geographical, was not destroyed. Not all of the promises and prophecies of the Hebrew Scriptures were fulfilled. Moreover, we are not held merely to repeat biblical insights. The way is open to new reflections on the connection between God's promised future for all humankind and the promise land. This does not mean that we can draw a direct line between such convictions and the State of Israel. The eschatological *shalom* promised embraces the human heart, family, economy, social life, state, and even soil. No single feature, such as the land, can constitute the fulfillment. The land, then, cannot be more than a sign. Israel's vocation is not complete so long as it remains just a state among many others. God's promise will be fulfilled when it reflects his will for human fellowship as a whole and becomes a "blessing in the midst of the earth." Thus Professor Berkhof.

With Robert Everett, disciple of James Parkes, a theological leap is taken. Not only is the State an actual fulfillment of the promise but of the Zionist movement that brought it about as well. In his words:

> Theologically interpreted, Zionism is the fulfillment of God's promise to His people that they would have a land in which to live as a people, and that land is Israel.... The State of Israel can be interpreted as a holy reality for Jews as it is the most visible and concrete symbol of God's unending grace and love for His people. The State of Israel may well be of sacramental significance for Christians as

> well. It is, to be sure, a very mundane and historical sacrament, but a symbol of redemption nonetheless.[40]

Everett is joined, if not surpassed, in his unqualified affirmation of the theological relevance of Zionism and Israel by Paul van Buren.[41] He is undeterred by Israel's secular character and gives his reason: it will not last. We read:

> Given Israel's election...there seems no likelihood at all that the state of Israel could become a nation 'like all the nations,' however some of its Zionist citizens might wish it. No, the state of Israel is different.... I do not refer to social, racial, or historical differences.... A Jew cannot be adequately delineated by such considerations or criteria, for all of them omit the one essential reality that distinguishes this people: God's election of Israel and Israel's acceptance of God's Torah. The state of Israel is nothing other than the vital expression of the destiny of this people.[42]

Van Buren draws definite theological and practical conclusions concerning Christianity's role in Israel's vocation. Since Israel's election and mission are "in the vanguard in creation's struggle for completion," he writes, "the mission of the church to serve Israel as Israel is grounded in the election of Israel and the church's derivative election.... The church has no choice but to affirm the promise of the land if it believes God to be faithful."[43] The church has been called "to serve the world alongside Israel in the service of the world," to become a "servant of Israel,"[44] and "undertake its own mission of being its Anti-Defamation League," a function of which is "to protect the Jewish state."[45]

This brief extract from van Buren's extensive thought on Judaism and Israel gives but a sparse idea of its fullness, but may give an intimation of the richness and forcefulness of this remarkable new theology.

A Recapitulation and an Assessment

Before proceeding, a glance back and an evaluation may the better prepare us for the path ahead. Valuable insights and cautions can, assuredly, be gained from all contributions to our survey. Most of those situated more or less in mainstream thought provide a solid middle from which basic elements may be drawn, but regrettably have on the whole remained insufficiently developed for a comprehensive view of the subject. Evangelicals, burdened with a literalist exegesis, serve as a counterbalance to the more skeptical positions, but do not offer a sufficiently critical approach to obtain a wide hearing. The work of Marvin Wilson is exceptional here in virtue of its breadth and nuanced criticism. Berkhof's all to brief contribution, remarkable in its eloquent simplicity, provides an example of harmonious integration of the major components of the subject. The contributions of Eckardt and van Buren, the most highly developed, call for further comment.

Eckardt's insistence on full respect for the secular character of Zionism and the Israeli State is well taken. One may question, however, the change of entitlement of his discussion of Israel from that of "secular theology" to "secular Christian ethic." While the change may be construed merely as a refinement of definition, it betokens a gerrymandering of Israel beyond the reach of Christian theology, which may be viewed as a breach of its integrity. It is an unnecessary mutation. As one of the proper attributes of human existence, secularity lays claim to its place in the deliberations of systematic theology. Full respect for Israel and Zionism's secularity fits well within the confines of Christian theology adequately conceived.

His refusal to consider the new State as a possible legatee of the biblical promises tends to narrow the concept and scope of Christian theology, and by the same token places in doubt the Hebrew Scriptures themselves to which the advent of Christianity is so intimately tied. His philosophy of history and his syncretizing of the sacral and secular, of truth and action, and to some extent theology and ethics apparently forbid his endowing the prophecies or promise with a historical linkage.

In sum, his analysis of Israel's spiritual significance contributes to a better appreciation of the secularity of Israel and Zionism, and to a greater reserve in theologizing about them in a Christian idiom. His refusal to view them in the context of a possible biblical/prophetical bonding, on the other hand, falls short of what is generally looked for in a Christian theology that takes all pertinent data into account.

Van Buren's imposing synthesis proffers many important components of a positive theology of Israel and from a new standpoint. More than anyone else he has contributed a comprehensive systematic theology of Judaism and Israel as faith-tradition, people, and state. And yet despite his principle of covenantal pluralism, he subsumes Christianity's covenancy into Israel's Covenant by, *inter alia*, displacing its redemptive core, reducing its Scriptures to Apostolic writings, and assigning it a largely auxiliary *raison d'etre*, and thus fails to concede to both faith-traditions their age-old essential identities.[46] This theological transformation has clearly had a bearing and influence on his theology of the State of Israel. The question to be posed is whether his highly acceptable views on Israel are well founded on the basis of a Christian theology that is widely considered to be a radically revised one. The imbalance of the past is not best resolved by its reversal in the future. That the anti-Judaic aberration ("cancer" in van Buren's designation) of the traditional theology must be eliminated and that a certain de-Hellenization and re-Judaization of Christian thought and theology are necessary—these are hardly in serious contention in theological circles today. The problem before us now is that of effecting a new positive relationship of the church and the synagogue, of Jews and Christians, as covenanted peoples of election, without aggrandizing or reducing any of the essential truths and attributes to which both have perennially laid claim and have always considered inviolate. It is questionable whether van Buren's new synthesis satisfies this criterion. It is important that a theology of Israel that would serve as a guiding model be founded on a widely acceptable Christian theology of Judaism. Failing this, the ultimate goal, the reconciliation of the Jewish and Christian peoples—still far from realization—will not be achieved. Inherent in all efforts to revise past and present theologies is an inescapable pastoral-theological connection that should not be lost from sight. It is not a matter of subordinating the truth to the good or theological freedom to ecclesiastical authority but of proper means to the proper end. Van Buren's excellent theology of Israel, in sum, can be replicated on the foundation of Christian theologies of Judaism that should gain a wide hearing in churches and synagogues of most affiliations. It is only these latter that have access to the Jewish and Christian peoples in their reachable totality.

A Prolegomenon to Future Theologies of Israel

The remaining reflections of this essay are designed to examine further some of the basic issues that most of those surveyed have considered integral to a comprehensive Christian theology of Israel. Seen as a whole the reflections are to be viewed as suggestive and as preparatory, a prolegomenon for further endeavors. The consensus of theologians we have seen shows substantial agreement upon three things: the need of building on an adequate revision of erstwhile anti-Judaic theologies, the question of Israel's rootage in the biblical prophecies and promises, and the problem of the secular character of the present State of Israel.

Required Revisions

Throughout the centuries little need was felt among the Church Fathers and theologians to construct a comprehensive and affirmative theology of Judaism. The people Israel was seen, Apostle Paul to the contrary notwithstanding, as little more than a *praeparatio evangelica* and truant to the Christian faith. A Hellenizing influence that pervaded early Christianity set the stage for a de-Judaization of church theology and liturgy. The result was a theological anti-Judaism characterized by the deicidal myth and Augustine's "witness people" theory, which together held Jews to be rejected by God, bereft of their covenant, superseded by the church—"the true Israel"—and dispersed in perpetuity to serve as witnesses of the truth of the church and of their own iniquity, *testes iniquitatis sui et veritatis nostrae*. This theological complexus saw no significant change until our own time. It was a state of affairs, it goes without saying, that precluded all possibility of a theology of Israel as land or nation. Such a theology was realizable solely on the basis of a major revision of the established theology.

Fortunately, this first essential of the task is well under way today. All major churches and theologians have repudiated the above anti-Judaic strictures and gone on variously to acknowledge Christianity's Jewish heritage. The original Pauline teaching has to a large extent been reinstated: The people Israel, beloved of God, retains its covenants and promises, its glory and the law, and in some mysterious way will at the End-time become reconciled with the Israel that went to the Gentiles—possibly as a Judaeo-Christianity such as existed in the first moments of the church.[47] In virtue of this renewed theological groundwork the land and State of Israel could no longer be denied positive consideration as possible heir to the covenants and promises in Christian theology. It is something of an irony that it was the present return of Jews to their ancient homeland—following an exile therefrom always considered to be a divine and perpetual chastisement—that has not only demythologized that theology, but has effectively opened new theological vistas for the Christian theologian as well.

The Problem of Secularity

The reconstruction of the theology of Judaism confronts the Christian theologian with two obvious problems: the applicability of biblical prophecies and promises to post-biblical Israel and Israel's secularity. Of the two the problem of secularity, while not the more important theologically, claims first attention. If Israel's present secular status rules it out as a possible legatee of the promises the problem of the continuing applicability of the prophecies and promises is no longer at issue.

The secular character of both the Zionist movement which brought the present turn about and of the Israeli State itself has been fully acknowledged by Jewish as well as Christian observers of the scene. Does this secular condition deprive Israel of identification with the Israel of biblical times? The theologians consulted, we have seen, have, with the exception of Eckardt and Everett, deemed it to be a problem and recognized the need to resolve or neutralize it. Doubtless it is this secular status of the State which lies at the root of the general reluctance to confer more than a role of "sign" or "possible first stage of fulfillment" upon it. It helps also to explain why others again are unwilling to lend it any theological significance at all.

It is a deceptive problem. Secularity is not an attribute of existence that lies outside the compass of theology, nor is it one that necessarily robs an existent of redeemability. It would be a mistake, then, *prima facie* to banish a secular Israel beyond the bounds of a biblical or theological embrace. More than once in times past the people of Israel has strayed from the sacral path, from their calling. The temptation "to be like all the nations" (1 Sm 8:20) remains an ever recurring one. Prostrate before the golden calf, on the high places of the Baalim, or before the altars of modern secularism, Israel remains Israel, for their is but one Israel. Sometimes punished, Israel was never rejected for her infidelities. This truth is not to be understood to mean that a truant or secularized Israel and the religiously faithful one are spiritually equivalent and equally heir to the promise of the land. On the other hand, contemporary Israel's secularity is not to be exaggerated. A spiritual core has always been there, and even in her most secular moments one can discern a resonance of the messianic impulse.

From the Secular to the Sacral

The central problem confronting the theologian is not Israel's secularity but rather its historical and spiritual rootage in the biblical prophecies and promises. The ultimate question is: Do the biblical prophecies and promises from which Israel derived its theological provenance apply to present-day Israel or any other Israel of post-biblical times? It is a question that entails a story of history and scripture ceaselessly intermingled. The story begins and develops in the pages of the Hebrew Scriptures and continues through history to our own time. And few are its happenings that are comprehensible without their light. In the pages of scripture we read that the people of Abraham, the Hebrew people, are a people elected by God and that their land is His gift to them and their descendants. Their possession of the land, exile from it, and return to it have been an enduring preoccupation of the canonical, liturgical, and Talmudic writings and have remained a prominent concern of Jewish prose and poetry throughout the centuries. The biblical tradition concerned with possession of or return to the land of promise has engendered in the Jewish people an indestructible hope and conviction that there will always be a return, an ingathering, after every dispersion. It is a belief that has deeply marked Jewish history. It is possible to discern in that history, despite its traumas, a sense of inchoateness and an indeterminate yearning for a future liberation and ingathering that can only be understood as a resonance of the messianic aspiration, however muted or secularized. For many if not most Jews of today the age-old Zionist hope remains an enduring commitment. The present State, belated and secular as it may be, can hardly escape the embrace of the millennial tradition. It is an embrace that can be interpreted in historical or religious terms, but completely only in both.[48]

The Biblical Base

For the Christian theologian this is a story that finds affirmation in the Christian as well as the Hebrew Scriptures, but it is not one without difficulties. The biblical matrices upon which the land promises rest are clear: Israel's Election,

Covenant, and Tanakh, the foundation stones of the entire edifice of Judaism. It is from these fonts that Israel as a people, a faith-tradition, and a land of promise draw their existence as a people and their religious tradition. The "everlasting Covenant" (Gn 17:19) God initiated with the people of Israel included the gift of the Land as an "everlasting possession" (Gn 7:9). The Christian Scriptures corroborate this. In Romans 9:4 Paul is explicit. Two decades after the death and resurrection of Christ he reminds Christians that the Jews "*have* the adoption as sons and the glory and the *covenants* and the law and the worship and the *promises*." But they are not promises without conditions. The people Israel are held to covenantal obligations: to become a "holy nation" (Ex 19:6) and a "light to the nations" (Is 51:4). The penalty for serious infraction could be severe, to be "plucked off the land" (2 Chr 7:20)—exile. But always a return (Tanakh, passim).

The biblical promises and prophecies of possession and return present themselves in a prophetic mode, which when read today are often shrouded in obscurity and marked with uncertainty as to whether they speak of a historical return, the Eschaton in time or eternity or an admixture of these. How is this amorphous body of texts to be approached? Many methodologies beckon, which run from a literalist rendering that applies indefinite texts to definite historical times and events to a rationalist skepticism that consigns all or most of them to the realm of the mythical. There are, however, other approaches that account for the data better. One in particular seems appropriate to the problem before us. It has been proposed by Norbert Lohfink, *inter alia*, a German exegete, who enunciates the principle that in the case of biblical texts that resist definite interpretation they are not to be interpreted in isolation from other cognate texts, confirmatory or contradictory, or from the Bible as a whole, but rather in the light of all of these.[49] This collective approach to the prophetic texts provides a possible nexus between the promises of the past and possible fulfillments in the present, shedding light as it does on the enduring Zionist aspirations of Jewry we have touched upon—and providing an interesting example of parts creating a whole that is greater then their sum. It was the ensemble of all the texts that engendered in the Jewish people the belief and hope that culminated in the return that eventuated in the establishment of the present State in 1948. The problem of the prophecies, to be sure, calls for further study in Jewish and Christian scholarship. Its importance for a complete and authentic Christian theology of Israel cannot be overestimated.

Some Final Questions

As the process of change from the negative traditional theology of Judaism to an affirmative one goes forward, not only responses change but questions as well. Another question, inconceivable in earlier times, emerges now quite naturally.

Though not of equal import with those already discussed, it is not without its significance for the catechetical, pastoral, and ecumenical functions of the churches. The question: If the prophecies and promises pertaining to the land of Israel are affirmed in both the Hebrew and Christian Scriptures and found acceptable in a renewed Christian theology of Judaism, ought not Israel as their possible heir to be explicitly accorded the status of a *Christian* article of faith? Would not such a creedal affirmation simply make explicit what is clearly implicit in the Christian affirmation of Judaism's irrevocable Covenant, of which the land promise is an integral part? As a Christian tenet, should it not take its rightful place in the Christian doctrinal corpus? Israel's hereditary claim to her Election and Covenant in any epoch (conditioned as it is) cannot be negated in the context of a renewed Christian theology of Judaism. Such a Christian belief, moreover, stands wholly independent of a like affirmation on the part of Judaism. Should, Jewish adherence to her own tradition, hypothetically, dwindle or disappear, the Christian affirmation would remain unaffected.

Such a Christian creedal affirmation, furthermore, is not to be tied or necessarily motivated by eschatological interests. Rather is it to be connected to the earliest Christian theology of Judaism of Paul the Apostle, who affirmed the irrevocability of Israel's covenants and promises. The fact that this earliest teaching was circumvented and ignored over the centuries carries with it a warning for today. If this important given of Paul's theology fell prey to the anti-Judaic influences that overtook Christian theology, is it not expectable that a similar fate also attends a reaffirmation of Paul's teaching in the present? Or again, if Christian theology and biblical hermeneutics have been held throughout the centuries in the grip of an unrecognized semi-Marcionist strain, which relegates the Hebrew portion of our Christian Scriptures to a status of reduced authority and trustworthiness, is there not a possibility, indeed a probability, that the same unrecognized influence lives on in a more sophisticated but no less effectual guise?[50]

All of the above questions may not be esteemed as of critical importance in the process of constructing the new theology; they are nevertheless weighty in significance and consequences. Our very attempts to answer them may well open new and fruitful perspectives along the entire range of the theology of Israel and of Christian theology itself. The road from the theology of deicide to that of full appreciation of our Judaic heritage is a long one. Commendable gains have been made, but they too, as theologians of old used to say, are "ever perfectible" (*semper perfectibile*).

Endnotes

1. A. Roy Eckardt, "Toward a Secular Theology of Israel," *Religion in Life* 48, no. 4 (Winter): 465.

2. Robert A. Everett, "Zionism, Israel, and Christian Hope," in *Reflections* (New Haven: Yale Divinity School, 1985), 38.

3. Paul Van Buren, *A Theology of the Jewish-Christian Reality: Part II, A Christian Theology of the People Israel* (New York: Seabury, 1983), 21.

4. Jacob J. Petuchowski, "Toward a Jewish Theology of Christianity" in *Renewing the Judeo-Christian Wellsprings*, ed. Val Ambrose McInnes, O.P. (New York: Crossroad, 1987), 41.

5. Yeshayahu Leibowitz, "Jewish Identity and Christian Silence" in *Unease in Zion*, ed. Ehud Ben Ezer (New York: Quadrangle Books, 1974), 179.

6. See *The Land of Israel: Jewish Perspectives*, ed. Lawrence A. Hoffman (South Bend: Notre Dame University Press, 1986); also *Evangelicals and Jews in Conversation* (Grand Rapids: Baker Book House, 1978) ed. Marc Tanenbaum, Marvin Wilson and A. James Rudin; Abraham J. Heschel, *An Echo of Eternity* (New York: Farrar, Straus, & Giroux, 1967); and Jacob Petuchowski *Zionism Reconsidered* (New York: Twayne Publ., 1966).

7. Martin Buber, *Israel and the World: Essays in Time of Crisis* (New York: Schocken Books, 1948), 48.

8. Heschel (n.6), 61.

9. David Hartman, *A Living Covenant: The Innovative Spirit in Traditional Judaism* (New York: Macmillan, 1985), 287.

10. Hartman (n. 9), 287.

11. Emil L. Fackenheim, "The Holocaust and the State of Israel: Their Relation" in *Auschwitz: Beginning of a New Era? Reflections on the Holocaust*, ed. Eva Fleischner (New York: Ktav, 1977), 205.

12. David Novak, "Judaism, Zionism, and Messianism: Telling them Apart" in *First Things* 1, no. 10 (Feb. 1991): 25.

13. Leibowitz (n. 5), 188.

14. Hartman (n. 9), 287.

15. This early theological interpretation of Judaism is to be understood more as a fundamentalist application of Christian eschatology than as a revision of the traditional Christian theology of Judaism.

16. For a competent history of Christian interest in the return of Jews to Israel see Michael J. Pragai, *Faith and Fulfillment* (London: Vallentine and Mitchell, 1985); also Yona Malachy, "Christian Zionism" in *Encyclopaedia Judaica* (Jerusalem, 1971).

17. For contemporaneous Evangelical positions on Israel, see eds. Tanenbaum, Wilson, and Rudin, *Evangelicals and Jews in Conversation*; and eds. Rudin and Wilson, *A Time to Speak: The Evangelical-Jewish Encounter* (Grand Rapids: Eerdmans, 1987).

18. *Jerusalem Courier* 7, no. 2 (1988): 5.

19. *Dispatch from Jerusalem*, 3rd Quarter (1988): 1.

20. See Marvin Wilson, *Our Father Abraham: Jewish Roots of the Christian Faith* (Grand Rapids: Eerdmans, 1989); also his "Zionism as Theology: An Evangelical Approach" in *Journal of Evangelical Society* (March, 1979).

21. W.D. Davies, *The Gospel and the Land* (Berkeley: University of California Press, 1974).

22. Walter Brueggemann, *The Land*, (Philadelphia: Fortress, 1977).

23. Brueggemann (n. 22), 185.

24. W.D. Davies (n. 21), 28.

25. See A. Roy Eckardt, *For Righteousness' Sake: Contemporary Moral Philosophies* (Bloomington: Indiana University Press, 1987); also his "A Christian Perspective on Israel," *Midstream* 28, no. 8 (1972); *Your People and My People* (New York: Quadrangle, 1964); and Alice and A. Roy Eckardt, *Encounter with Israel* (New York: Association Press, 1970).

26. Eckardt, *For Righteousness' Sake* (n. 25), 284.

27. See "Towards a Secular Theology of Israel" (n. 1) and "A Christian Perspective on Israel" (n. 25), passim.

28. *For Righteousness' Sake* (n.25), 286–287.

29. *For Righteousness' Sake* (n. 25), 287.

30. *For Righteousness' Sake* (n. 25), 284–286.

31. *For Righteousness' Sake* (n. 25), 284; also "Towards a Secular Theology of Israel" (n. 1), pp. 462–464.

32. Charlotte Klein, "The Theological Dimensions of the State of Israel," *The Journal of Ecumenical Studies* 10, no. 4 (1973): 700–715.

33. Eckardt, *For Righteousness' Sake* (n. 25), 284.

34. Klein (n. 32), 714.

35. John M. Oesterreicher, *The Bridge: Brothers in Hope* (New York: Herder and Herder, 1970), 5:242.

36. Oesterreicher (n. 35), 5:242.

37. Eva Fleischner, "The Religious Significance of Israel: A Christian Perspective" in *Jewish-Christian Relations*, ed. Robert Heyer (New York and Paramus: Paulist Press, 1974), 32.

38. Walter Harrelson, "The Land in the Tanakh" (unpublished paper for the National Council of Christians and Jews, 1985), 9.

39. Hendrik Berkhof in *Face to Face: An Interreligious Bulletin* 1 (Fall 1975): 11.

40. Robert Everett (n. 2), 38–39.

41. See Paul van Buren (n. 3), especially ch. 6.

42. Van Buren (n. 41), 202.

43. Van Buren (n. 41), 334.

44. Van Buren (n. 41), 205.

45. Van Buren (n. 41), 334–336.

46. It is questionable whether van Buren's interpretation of Christian origins and bond to Judaism will appeal to adherents of Orthodox or of Reform, Conservative or Reconstructionist Judaism, and not for very different reasons. Such an origination and bond Orthodox will find too syncretist. Temples of the modern Reform tradition view this same hermeneutic as undercutting the direction they have taken.

47. Both Judaism and Christianity have laid claim to the final times of humankind. Most theologians in dialogue today prefer to leave Paul's hope in God's hands and, not without a touch of humor, to defer to the Almighty to manifest whether the Coming of the Messiah in the End-time will be the First or the Second.

48. For Jewish perspectives on the land see Lawrence A. Hoffman, ed., *The Land of Israel: Jewish Perspectives* (South Bend: University of Notre Dame Press, 1986); for a Christian perspective, see W.D. Davies, "Jewish Territorial Doctrine and the Christian Response" in *Renewing Judeo-Christian Wellsprings* (New York: Crossroad, 1987), ch. 1.

49. See Norbert Lohfink, "The Inerrancy of Scripture" in *The Christian Meaning of the Old Testament* (Milwaukee: Bruce Publishing, 1968).

50. Semi-Marcionism denotes an attenuated survival of the second-century heresy of Marcion, who denied the relevance of the Hebrew Scriptures for the church, attributing them to a "Demiurge." It may also refer to a present-day tendency, more or less conscious, to reduce the value or importance of the Old Testament for the Christian.

Suggestions For Further Reading

Berkoff, Hendrik. "Israel as a Theological Problem in the Christian Church." *Journal of Ecumenical Studies*. Vol. 6, no. 4. A succinct and comprehensive model of a positive Christian theology of Israel.

Brueggemann, Walter. *The Land.* Philadelphia: Fortress Press, 1977. A thorough-going study of the land concept and its importance in the Hebrew and Christian Scriptures.

Buren, Paul van. *A Theology of the Jewish-Christian Reality*. Part II, *A Christian Theology of the People Israel*. New York: Seabury, 1983. Ch. 6. A comprehensive systematic theology of Judaism that features the land tradition and its centrality to Judaism and its place in a Christian theology.

Davies, W.D. *The Gospel and the Land.* Berkeley: University of California Press, 1974. An exhaustive analysis of the land concept in the gospels and in deutero-canonical and Jewish writings.

Eckardt, A. Roy. "Toward a Secular Theology of Israel." *Religion in Life*. 38, no. 4, (1979). A challenging advance toward the construction of a "secularizing theology" of Israel.

Heschel, Abraham J. *Israel: An Echo of Eternity.* New York: Farrar, Straus & Giroux, 1967. A deeply spiritual, theological, and lyrical insight into what Israel means to Jews and what it should mean to Christians.

Hoffman, Lawrence A., ed. *The Land of Israel*. South Bend: University of Notre Dame Press, 1986. An excellent compendium of first-rate scholars who trace the Jewish link to the land from the beginning to the present.

Oesterreicher, John M. "The Theologian and the Land of Israel." *The Bridge: Brothers in Hope*. New York: Herder and Herder, 1970. Vol. 5. A pioneering essay by a Catholic theologian on the significance of Israel in Christian theology.

Pragai, Michael J. *Faith and Fulfillment*. London: Vallentine and Mitchell, 1985. A well-documented study of Christian involvement in Zionism, the Return, and contemporary Israel.

NOSTRA AETATE:

THE CHURCH'S BOND TO THE JEWISH PEOPLE: CONTEXT, CONTENT, PROMISE

Michael B. McGarry

The Second Vatican Council, 1962–1965, one of twenty ecumenical councils in the long history of the Roman Catholic Church, was momentous in the transformations it initiated, perhaps none more so than in its treatment of the relationship of the Roman Catholic Church to Judaism and the Jewish people. For the first time in nearly two millennia, the Church promulgated a statement, doctrinally binding on Catholics, that speaks affirmatively of Judaism and the Jewish people. Michael B. McGarry addresses the many controversies raised by the conciliar document that is so significant for the whole field of Christian-Jewish relations: its origins, contents, significance, and potential for long-term development. It was promulgated by Pope Paul VI on 28 October 1965.

1. Introduction

To understand and appreciate *Nostra Aetate* #4, the Second Vatican Council's treatment of the Church's relation to Judaism and the Jewish people, requires that the reader approach it within the context of the history of Catholic-Jewish relations in general, and the other writings of the Council in particular. In this short essay, I wish merely to highlight some of the salient parts of the general and specific context of *Nostra Aetate*. I wish to note, also briefly, the *subsequent* "paper trail" of Roman Catholic documents on Catholic-Jewish relations since they provide a prism of appreciation for the achievement of *Nostra Aetate*. One point I hope is clear by the end of this essay is that this conciliar document marks more of directional trajectory than a fully worked out content of the church's contemporary relation with Judaism and the Jewish people. So while we review the story of the conciliar decree, we will also discover how subsequent church documents have begun to fulfill *Nostra Aetate*'s promise.[1]

2. Background

Rabbi A. James Rudin, in an essay marking the twentieth anniversary of *Nostra Aetate*, suggested that the only way to understand the striking significance of the Vatican II document was first to imagine, however difficult, what it was like to be an ordinary Catholic in the early 1960s.

> We need to recall what ordinary Catholics and Jews (if there be such persons!) were thinking throughout history, what a Catholic or Jew would have said about 'the other' if he or she had been rudely awakened at 3:00 A.M. [in 1962].[2]

What might such a Catholic blurt out about the Jewish people? Depending on, but adding to, Rabbi Rudin's suggestions, our imaginary—even educated Catholic—might recite some of the following:

- the Jews are a spiritual people whose religious usefulness ceased with the death of Christ;
- the Old Testament should be honored mostly for its prophecies about the Messiah, all of which were clearly fulfilled in Jesus;
- the Jews, through hardheartedness, missed their chance for salvation when they did not recognize the Messiah, and they have been cursed to wander the world ever since;
- the Judaism of Jesus' time was mired in legalism and slavery to a wrathful God; Jesus, in his gentleness and compassion, repudiated this fossil religion and founded a religion based on Love and revealed a God who forgives[3];
- the Jews were, sad to say, "Christ-killers," as shown by "solid" biblical evidence ("His blood be upon us and our children," etc.);
- the Jews are a foreign people whose religious practices are curious but anachronistic in the contemporary world;
- the Jews are clannish and highly suspect in business dealings;
- it was sad what pagan Nazism did to them in Germany, but that has nothing to do with Christianity or Christian history.

Against the backdrop of such attitudes *Nostra Aetate* #4 stands as a profound ecclesial re-direction. While the Council document scarcely addressed all the problems of popular Catholic culture's view of the Jews, the church did begin a change of course which would bear much fruit in subsequent ecclesial documents.

In addition to popular religious attitudes, another context which provides some illumination on *Nostra Aetate*'s genesis was the *life experience* of *Pope John XXIII*; his openness to the world and his passion for new understanding surely were the proximate and effective cause of the conciliar document.[4]

During World War II, Angelo Roncalli (later Pope John) was the apostolic delegate to Turkey and Bulgaria. There he came to know firsthand the terrible sufferings of the Jewish people at the hands of the Nazis. During that difficult time, he personally worked to save hundreds if not thousands of Jews by helping them escape, forging baptismal certificates, and hiding them in monasteries and other church buildings. Apparently these experiences dramatically moved him to work for improved Catholic-Jewish relations even if they did not move him to look favorably on the Jewish return to Palestine.[5]

In addition to Roncalli's World War II experiences, one must cite a most important encounter between the later Pope John and the French historian Jules Isaac.[6] During their 13 June 1960 meeting, Isaac gave to the Pope a three-part dossier which included:

> [1] A brief for the correction of false and, indeed, unjust statements about the people of Israel in Christian instruction. [2] An example of such statements: the theological myth that the scattering of Israel was a punishment inflicted by God on the people for the crucifixion of Jesus. [3] An extract from the..."Catechism of Trent" which, in its treatment of the Passion, emphasized the guilt of all sinners [and not of the Jewish people in the infamous 'deicide charge'].[7]

At the end of this meeting, Jules Isaac inquired whether he, with the rest of the Jewish people, might hope for better relations with the Catholic people. Prophetically Pope John XXIII replied, "You have reason for more than a little hope."[8]

The third historical context, critical for understanding *Nostra Aetate*'s genesis, was the emerging importance of the *Shoah* in Christian self-understanding. In 1962, Western Christians, not unlike their Jewish counterparts, were beginning to allow the Holocaust's enormity to penetrate their consciousness. Disconcerting questions began to seep into their discussion: How could it have happened? How could it have happened in the heart of Western, civilized, *Christian* Europe? Some thoughtful Christians began to intuit that there was more to the *Shoah*'s preparation and execution than lack of Christian courage; that is, not only bad Christian behavior, but bad Christian theology needed to be investigated.[9]

The final general historical context within which *Nostra Aetate* must be recognized were two peculiarly American contributions to the Second Vatican Council: first, the positive American experience of religious freedom and the studies of how religious textbooks portrayed "the other"—especially Jews—and what effect these had on prejudice. As a land of European, Latin American, African, and Asian immigrants, the United States had survived the gathering of many ethnic groups and religious expressions. Hardly without fault or mistakes, the American experiment of religious freedom and living together neighborhood by neighborhood impressed on American bishops that Catholicism not only can survive such freedom; indeed, religious freedom provides a most healthy atmosphere for Catholicism. This experience stood in sharp contrast to Roman suspicion of religious freedom most notably expressed in Pius IX's *Syllabus of Errors*, 1864. Indeed, many of America's most celebrated church leaders—Francis Cardinal Spellman and Richard Cardinal Cushing among others—frequently turned to their Protestant and Jewish fellow Americans in friendship and common endeavors. This almost unique experience proved significant in their contribution to the Second Vatican Council, not least of which was their concern for a new relationship with the Jewish people.

At the same time, the early 1950s witnessed a series of studies and comparative analyses of religious textbooks, examining their fostering or muting ethnic and religious stereotypes. The results of these studies suggested to thoughtful educators that textbooks needed close scrutiny even as they sought faithfully to transmit a unique religious tradition. One of the concerns of Jules Isaac, then—how Christians teach about Jews—was anticipated by the American Catholic experience of looking at religious textbooks.[10]

3. Foreground

The church's relation to Judaism and the Jewish people is a concern reserved not only for its relation to the "outside world"; the church must contend also with the meaning of Israel even as it reflects on its own mystery and the meaning of the New Testament's in light of the Old. It is no surprise, then, to find that other conciliar documents spoke of the church's relation to Judaism and the Jewish people. These other documents, written for the most part by churchmen other than those who composed *Nostra Aetate*, preceded it both in time and importance.

First in importance was the "Dogmatic Constitution on the Church." This Constitution referred to biblical Israel as a model of God's choosing a people *as* a people. The church is described a few times therein as "the new Israel," Christ as the "founder of the new people of God"; "On account of their fathers, this people [Israel] remains most dear to God for God does not repent of the gifts He makes nor of the calls He issues (cf. Rom 11:28-29)" (Art. 16).[11]

A second very important document from the Second Vatican Council was the "Dogmatic Constitution on Divine Revelation." Although it did not speak about the Jewish people specifically, the Constitution addressed the Old Testament, the Bible of the Jewish People. There it showed a decidedly traditional, preparatory understanding of the Old Testament:

> The principal purpose to which the plan of the Old Covenant was directed was to prepare for the coming both of Christ, the universal

> Redeemer, and of the messianic kingdom, to announce this coming by prophecy...and to indicate its meaning through various types.[12]

Risking oversimplifying, one can say that the "Constitution on Divine Revelation" understood the Hebrew Scriptures almost exclusively as a prologue to the full revelation granted through Christ. Acknowledgment that there was more to the Hebrew Scriptures than this preparatory understanding is difficult to find in the document. Hence one looks hopefully for—and finds—development on the fuller meaning of the Hebrew Scriptures in later church documents.

Thirdly, one finds that the most lengthy and probably most influential of the Vatican II documents scarcely refers to Judaism and the Jewish people. "The Pastoral Constitution on the Church and the Modern World" speaks little of the Jewish people, but interestingly it does assert in Article 32 that the Hebrew Scriptures reveal that, from the beginning, God has chosen people "not just as individuals but as members of a certain community."[13] It would be pushing the document too far to claim that the Hebrew Scriptures reveal mostly the communitarian dimension of God's call and that the New Testament reveals mostly the individual dimension—as Franz Rozenzweig and Martin Buber have suggested[14]—but it is striking to see such a complementary notion hinted at here.

In summary, references to the church's relation to Judaism and the Jewish people in Vatican II documents other than *Nostra Aetate*, for the most part, reflect little that is new, and more that is traditional in describing this relationship. For a new understanding of the church's relationship, one looks to the document itself.

4. The Content of Nostra Aetate

To consider the content of *Nostra Aetate* requires two preliminary observations.

First, one must recognize that, once the Council Fathers decided to write a document on the church's relation to the Jewish people, there ensued up-front and behind-the-scenes battles as to just where such a document might rightly fit within the overall schema of the Council. Some argued that it should be placed in the "Constitution on the Church"; others lobbied that it be put in the "Decree on Ecumenism" or in the "Declaration on Religious Freedom." It found its final resting place, not altogether satisfactorily, in the "Declaration on the Relation of the Church to Non-Christian Religions."[15] While it is true that Judaism is another of the world's great religions, Christianity's relation to Judaism is unique. Only of Judaism can it be said that Christianity's own identity depends on another religion. Furthermore, Judaism and Christianity share a common scripture (although understanding its truth and interpretation quite differently) and both (along with Islam) claim the same God. Thus *Nostra Aetate*'s final placement in a document which dealt with world religions in general was less than satisfactory;

subsequent development of documents and theology has begun to underscore Judaism's unique relation to Christianity in contradistinction to that of other religions.

Second, one must remember that *Nostra Aetate* was not written in dialogue *with* Jews for Jews, but rather by Catholic Bishops and their staffs for Catholics. It was addressed to Roman Catholics concerning *their* attitude towards, and understanding of, the Jewish people. Nonetheless, Cardinal Bea, the primary author of the final document and the energy behind its final passage, received considerable input from members of the Jewish community, including the late Rabbi Abraham Heschel, Ms. Judith Banki, and the late Rabbi Marc Tanenbaum, all of the United States.[16] And the documents which later built on and developed *Nostra Aetate* benefited from Jewish input and criticism.

With regard to the content of the "Declaration on the Relationship of the Church to Non-Christian Religions," Paragraph #4 of which addresses the church's relation with the Jewish people, the following points are most important.

First, one notes that the conciliar declaration is positive about the Jewish people in almost every way: Christians, with Jews, find a common father in Abraham; Christians must look for their beginnings to the Jewish election; the church "continues" (note the *present* tense) to draw sustenance from the "root of that good olive tree" and Christ should be the cause of *unity*, not of division; "the Jews still remain most dear to God" (however, with the unfortunate qualification "because of their fathers").

Second, the church commits itself to a posture of *dialogue* vis-a-vis the Jewish people. Heretofore the church claimed that its mission was simply to proclaim the Good News; little did the Catholic community have to learn. A posture of dialogue changes all that. Now the church must listen as well as speak; the teacher must also become a student. This extraordinary turnabout in the church's history is largely lost on us in the United States today owing to our experience of pluralism, and because, since the Council, dialogue has become the *de facto* method of the Church and the Synagogue in relating to each other; as of 1974 the dialogue was instutionalized. But we must remember that 1960s Catholic so rudely wakened from his sleep—he or she could not have even imagined dialogue as the official way of the church's relation to the Jewish people.[17]

Third, the Council Fathers asserted that historical facts surrounding the crucifixion of Christ had to be clarified, most notably that no guilt for that action can be transferred to the Jews of today. The Jews should never be presented as repudiated or cursed by God—this simply is not in the Christian Scriptures. Rather Christians must grapple with God's abiding love for, and choice of, the Jews; they must ponder more profoundly the core of St. Paul's argument in Romans 9–11. The New Testament writers, for all their problems with regard to first-century anti-Jewish polemic, did not call the Jews accursed. It is primarily Christian theologians after the first century who depicted the Jews as wandering the earth, abandoned by their God.[18] With regard to the crucifixion, then, it is theologically more accurate for Christians to affirm that Jesus freely and lovingly embraced his death, which death was the consequence of all people's sins. (Remember Jules Isaac's reminder to Pope John XXIII from the Catechism of the Council of Trent.)

Fourth, in one (perhaps too) short sentence, the Council succinctly dealt with the tradition of antisemitism in the church and Western civilization: the church "deplores the hatred, persecutions, and displays of anti-Semitism directed against the Jews at any time and from any source." Many were disappointed by the Council's use of "deplore" rather than "condemn." This choice of words, however, was explicitly requested by Pope John XXIII so that the Second Vatican Council be free of the ancient conciliar habit of "anathematizing" people.[19]

5. Evaluation of Nostra Aetate

Candidly, one must admit that *Nostra Aetate* is rather superficial in terms of a full-blown understanding of "the Church's Bond to the Jewish People." Nonetheless, it is my conviction that any *revolutionary* character of the document is to be found not primarily in new content (although new content is present), but in fresh, tentative directions; not in a full-fledged theology of the church and the Jewish people, but in a not-to-be-reversed change of the tools for the renovated theology's construction. As Eugene Fisher has pointed out, Paragraph #4 of *Nostra Aetate* is probably the most original contribution of the Council Fathers to contemporary Roman Catholic theology. In vain does one search for footnotes in *Nostra Aetate* citing either the early Church Fathers or the tradition of the church on this topic. Something new, the Council Fathers say in effect, needs to be built; old building blocks are inadequate to the task.

Secondly, one notes that, after the "Declaration on Religious Freedom," *Nostra Aetate* was the conciliar document most influenced by Americans. This reflects the singular, graced American experience of religious pluralism, without denying its historic problems of religious prejudice.

Thirdly, I believe that early estimates of *Nostra Aetate* as an "abortion" or as "superficial" miss the point.[20] *Nostra Aetate's* usefulness and significant value lay precisely in its programmatic, not definitive, character. It is the starting place, not the ending place. If the bishops at Vatican II had been much more profound and elaborate thirty years ago, Catholics today would be less free to explore and construct *with their Jewish brothers and sisters* an emerging theology of mutual esteem.

The following simile captures *Nostra Aetate*'s significance: *Nostra Aetate* was much like an exploratory ship whose weighing anchor from a familiar port took much time and was met with all sorts of resistance. That resistance included the vigorous and heartfelt pleading from the Eastern Churches and Arab Catholic Church leaders that nothing be said at all.[21] Seasoned sailors knew that some rotting cargo had to be thrown overboard or the ship would have been unable even to make it out of the port. Here one must cite the deicide charge and any pretense that antisemitism could find tolerable theological or social foundation. And certain provisions had to be loaded on as absolutely indispensable. These included the affirmations that God has never abandoned the Jewish people, that the Jews have continued to be beloved by God, and that the Jewish faith has continued to grow in spiritual values from the time of Jesus to the present. While the ship was set in a direction of exploration (almost presuming the extraordinary claim that revelation lay ahead as well as behind it), it has been rocked by a few incidents of confusion and disheartenment. But the wisdom of the course it set can best be assessed in terms of the ports it has visited (and caused to be built) along the way since Vatican II. These would have to include the 1975 "Guidelines and Suggestions for Implementing the Conciliar Declaration *Nostra Aetate* (n. 4)" (amplified by the important "Statement on Catholic-Jewish Relations by the United States National Conference of Catholics Bishops")[22] and the 1985 "Notes on the Correct Way to Present the Jews and Judaism in Preaching and Catechesis in the Roman Catholic Church."[23]

At the same time, *Nostra Aetate*'s deficiencies cannot be said to be simply omissions to be filled in by later documents. Unfortunate and striking are some lacunae. One has to underscore at least three. First, sadly, the 1965 document did not mention the *Shoah*; however, it was, if inadequately, referred to in the 1985 "Notes" (para. 25) cited above and a joint commission is now working on a future document about the church and the years of the *Shoah*. Also, in *Nostra Aetate* there is little positive reference to postbiblical Judaism; this omission was partially addressed in the 1975 Guidelines and expounded upon by the United States National Conference of Catholic Bishops' statement of the same year. But just *how* the church "continues" to draw sustenance from Israel needs to be explored. Lastly, no mention is made in *Nostra Aetate* of a concept by which Jews profoundly understand themselves: attachment to the Land (more on this below).

What can one say, then, about the achievement of *Nostra Aetate*? *Nostra Aetate* (and its progeny) has moved Catholics from a position of ignorance to interest, from contempt to appreciation, and from proselytism to dialogue.[24] It repudiated antisemitism no matter what its form or source. Because of it, no church document on Catholic-Jewish relations has been attempted without spirited and eager Jewish input. Furthermore, recent papal statements underscore and develop the direction charted by *Nostra Aetate*.[25] And we look forward to the document from the Holy See on antisemitism and the *Shoah* which Pope John Paul II promised in his 1987 address to Jewish leaders in Miami. Currently, meetings between Catholic and Jewish scholars are taking place in preparation for this long—perhaps ten-year—project.[26]

Allow me here to digress to a not-strictly-related topic. There may well be some skepticism regarding the place and influence of *documents* in the Catholic

Church's life. Well may one wonder, Does anyone read (and, more telling, Is anyone affected by) *Nostra Aetate* and these other documents? On this point one must refer to the extraordinarily important research of Sister Rose Thering, O.P. Funded by the Anti-Defamation League, the American Jewish Committee, and Seton Hall University, Sr. Thering explored the influence of the important documents of the Council on Catholic textbooks and schools. This longitudinal study reveals an extraordinary turnabout in Catholic teaching about Judaism and the Jewish people, as well as the beginnings of Holocaust curricula in Catholic schools.[27] We have already alluded to the reform of the liturgy, particularly that of Holy Week, since Vatican II. Furthermore, one sees an explosion of Catholic theology books and popular articles about the portrayal of the Pharisees in the Gospels, the Jewishness of Jesus, the spiritual maturity of post-apostolic Judaism, and the importance of the Holocaust for Christian self-understanding. Accordingly, while few Roman Catholics actually read these documents, they have significant influence where Catholics in the pews are touched: through liturgy, catechetics, differently-trained clergy, and renewed biblical studies.

6. The Church's Bond to the Jewish People: The Continuing Fruitful Catholic Self-Understanding from Nostra Aetate.

Nostra Aetate spoke of the "spiritual bonds" between Jews and Christians. This has been a theme to which the pope and subsequent international and national documents have repeatedly returned. To illustrate, recently Pope John Paul II affirmed:

> The first [dimension of *Nostra Aetate* to be noted] is that the Church of Christ discovers her 'bond' with Judaism by 'searching into her own mystery'.... The Jewish religion is not 'extrinsic' to us, but in a certain way is 'intrinsic' to our own religion. With Judaism therefore we have a relationship which we do not have with any other religion. You are our dearly beloved brothers and, in a certain way, it could be said that you are our elder brothers.[28]

Remember the mythic Catholic, awakened at 3 A.M. in 1962....could he have imagined saying this, let alone hearing it from the pope? If the legacy of *Nostra Aetate* is heartening, there are still "ports of call" to be visited and (more) thoroughly explored. First and foremost, the *Shoah* needs to be explored further. In the 1985 document cited above, the Commission for Religious Relations with the Jews noted that: "Catechesis should...help in understanding the meaning for the Jews of the extermination during the years 1939–1945, and its consequences."[29]

This brief recommendation needs to be greatly filled out. The promise has already been made (see note 26), but fulfilling this promise must include 1) historical studies on the role of the church during the Nazi era, 2) theological discussions on theodicy, and 3) spiritualities which give solace to the bystander. Here by "spiritualities," I mean the prayer-styles and self-understandings which comprise a Christian's worldview. As David Tracy has noted,

> Insofar as one kind of Catholic spirituality is spiritualizing (or unworldly) and privatizing (or nonpublic) and insofar as that spirituality aided individual Christians to avoid their historical responsibilities in the situation of the Holocaust, contemporary Catholic theological reflection on salvation and spirituality needs to become yet more suspicious of all nonworldly, nonpolitical forms of spirituality.[30]

Secondly, we must explore together the sacredness of the Land and the State of Israel in Jewish self-understanding—a glaring omission in *Nostra Aetate* already noted. Catholics, who might draw on their own sense of the "sacredness of space" and holy places, need to engage the Jewish understanding of Land and their attachment to the *Eretz Israel* in particular. This direction has already been hinted at in the 1985 "Notes" where the Commission recommended that "Christians are invited to understand this religious attachment [to the Land] which finds its roots in biblical tradition."[31]

In recent years, however, the absence of full diplomatic relations between the Holy See and the State of Israel has left doubts in many minds about the Catholic Church's seriousness to rid itself of certain anti-Judaic theological affirmations about the post–70 C.E. meaning of Jewish survival. Was the church withholding diplomatic ties because of some of the theological affirmations which our mythic 1960s Catholic held? (Even good Pope John, when he worked in Turkey during World War II, voiced doubts about the Jewish return to their ancient homeland.) However, in 1987, after meeting with Pope John Paul II at Castel Gandolfo, Catholic and Jewish leaders issued a joint communique which read, in part:

> Representatives of the Holy See declared that here exist no theological reasons in Catholic doctrine that would inhibit such [diplomatic] relations, but noted that there do exist some serious and unresolved problems in the area.[32]

And as recently as the summer of 1992, a joint Vatican-Israeli commission was set up to look at certain "bilateral" issues, as well as beginning a process toward full diplomatic relations.[33] Nonetheless, as important as these relations may be in the short run, Catholics will still need to explore the meaning of the Land for Jewish self-understanding.

Thirdly, Catholics need to work more assiduously to root out supersessionism in its theology and preaching.[34]

Lastly, there needs to be further exploration of liturgical reform, especially assembling and deploying a new lectionary which presents the Hebrew Scriptures on their own terms and not just in terms of preparation for the messiah.[35]

7. A Final Thought

It seems to me that *the* most significant breakthrough of *Nostra Aetate* was its call to the church to become a *community of dialogue* with their Jewish brothers and sisters. And by dialogue the Council Fathers did not mean simply listening to one another, but rather being open to change; in the posture of dialogue, we have something to learn as well as something to say. In its simplicity their call to relate as dialogical partners (too infrequently lived up to) has considerable practical consequences. What happens to a community which heretofore had been committed to understand Jews only as religious dinosaurs or potential converts? We are only beginning to find out. The sad fact may remain, however, that it took the *Shoah* to shock us—tragically and belatedly—into listening to the Jews rather than "monologuing" at them. And *Nostra Aetate* is the church's initial commitment to listen, to learn...and to change.

Endnotes

1. For another presentation of the content of *Nostra Aetate* in the context of subsequent Roman Catholic Church documents, see Eugene J. Fisher, "Official Roman Catholic Teaching on Jews and Judaism: Commentary and Context" and "Appendix: The Development of a Tradition," in *In Our Time: The Flowering of Jewish-Catholic Dialogue*, ed. Eugene J. Fisher and Leon Klenicki (Mahwah, NJ: Paulist Press, 1990), 1–26; and Reinhard Neudecker, S.J., "The Catholic Church and the Jewish People," in Rene Latourelle, ed., *Vatican II: Assessment and Perspectives: Twenty-Five Years After (1962–1987)* (New York: Paulist Press, 1989), 3:282–383.

2. Rabbi A. James Rudin, "The Dramatic Impact of *Nostra Aetate*," in *Twenty Years of Jewish-Catholic Relations*, ed. Eugene J. Fisher, A. James Rudin, and Marc H. Tanenbaum (New York: Paulist Press, 1986), 9.

3. Sadly, one does not have to go back as far as the 1960s to hear such a gross comparison. A Catholic priest on the *Today* show said to a rabbi on the same program (after Pope John Paul's visit with Austrian President Kurt Waldheim), "Well, you just have to understand that Christianity is a religion of forgiveness and Judaism is a religion of vengeance."

4. Most of my material on Pope John XXIII comes from John M. Oesterreicher, *The New Encounter Between Christians and Jews* (New York: Philosophical Library, 1986), 103–298. Monsignor Oesterreicher himself had more than a little to do with the passage of the conciliar document, and one might read with much profit his essay cited here.

5. See Peter Hebblethwaite, *John XXIII: Pope of the Council* (London: Geoffrey Chapman, 1984), 192.

6. Jules Isaac, the late French Jewish historian, wrote *Jesus and Israel, Has Anti-Semitism Roots in Christianity?* and *The Teaching of Contempt*.

7. Oesterreicher (n. 4), 105. In response to the challenge of the Reformation in general and Martin Luther's catechism in particular, the Council of Trent (1545–1563) issued its own, which came to be known as the "Catechism of Trent."

8. Oesterreicher (n. 4), 108.

9. The literature on this is really quite extensive. See, among others, my *Christology After Auschwitz* (New York: Paulist Press, 1977); Abraham J. Peck, ed., *Jews and Christians After the Holocaust* (Philadelphia: Fortress Press, 1982); and Fisher and Klenicki, *In Our Time* (n. 1), 107–158.

10. See Bernard Olson, *Faith and Prejudice* (New Haven: Yale University Press, 1963); John T. Pawlikowski, *Catechetics and Prejudice* (New York: Paulist Press, 1973); and Eugene Fisher, *Faith without Prejudice* (New York: Paulist Press, 1977), 124–140, among others.

11. See "The Dogmatic Constitution on the Church," in *The Documents of Vatican II*, ed. Walter M. Abbott, S.J. (New York: The America Press, 1966), 14–101. For further analysis of the church and the Jewish people in the documents of Vatican II, see my *Christology After Auschwitz* (New York: Paulist Press, 1977).

12. See Abbott, *Documents* (n. 11), "Dogmatic Constitution on Divine Revelation" (Art. 15), 111–128, 122.

13. Abbott, *Documents* (n. 11), "The Pastoral Constitution on the Church and the Modern World" (Art. 32), 230.

14. See Franz Rozenzweig, *The Star of Redemption* (New York: Holt, Rinehart and Winston, 1970) and Martin Buber, *Two Types of Faith* (London: Routledge and Kegan Paul, 1951).

15. For the story of the rocky road of *Nostra Aetate*'s placement in the schema of the Council, see Oesterreicher (n. 4), 158ff.

16. See Oesterreicher (n. 4), 126–128, 160–162, and "The AJC [American Jewish Committee] and Vatican Council II: A Chronology of the Agency's Involvement," from the "Resource Kit on Vatican Council II and Catholic-Jewish Relations 1965–1985" (Mimeograph).

17. Pope Paul VI institutionalized the dialogue by setting up the Commission for Religious Relations with the Jews in 1974.

18. See Edward Flannery, *The Anguish of the Jews: Twenty-Three Centuries of Antisemitism* (1964; rev. and updated, New York: Paulist Press, 1985), 47–65; and Malcolm Hay, *The Roots of Christian Anti-Semitism* (1950; reprint, New York: Anti-Defamation League of B'nai B'rith, 1981), 68–110.

19. See "Declaration on the Relationship of the Church to Non-Christian Religions," Paragraph #4, in Abbott, *Documents* (n. 11), 666 n. 27. The word "condemn" is used, however, in the 1975 "Guidelines."

20. A. Roy Eckardt, *Your People, My People: The Meeting of Jews and Christians* (New York: Quadrangle Books, 1974), 74; Paul van Buren, "Twenty Years of Christian-Jewish Dialogue: A Protestant Perspective," in the *Proceedings of the Center for Jewish-Christian Learning: Inaugural Lecture Series* (St. Paul, MN: College of St. Thomas, 1985), 9–14, 9.

21. See Oesterreicher (n. 4), 130–131, 169ff.

22. See Helga Croner, comp., *Stepping Stones to Further Jewish-Christian Relations: An Unabridged Collection of Christian Documents* (New York: Stimulus Books, 1977), 11–15, 29–34.

23. See Helga Croner, comp., *More Stepping Stones to Jewish-Christian Relations: An Unabridged Collection of Christian Documents 1975–1983* (New York: Paulist Press/Stimulus Books, 1985), 220–232. See also Fisher et al., *Twenty Years* (n. 2); International Catholic-Jewish Liaison Committee, *Fifteen Years of Catholic-Jewish Dialogue 1970–1985, 23 Selected Papers* (Rome: Libreria Editrice Vaticana, 1988); and Fisher & Klenicki (n. 1), 18–24.

24. So, for example, the following: "Proselytism, which does not respect human freedom, is carefully to be avoided. While the Christian, through the faith life of word and deed, will always witness to Jesus as the risen Christ, the dialogue is concerned with the permanent vocation of the Jews as God's people, the enduring values that Judaism shared with Christianity and that together, the church and the Jewish people are called upon to witness to the

world." *Guidelines for Catholic-Jewish Relations*, Secretariat for Catholic-Jewish Relations, N.C.C.B., #4 of "General Principles," 4.

25. See Eugene Fisher & Leon Klenicki, eds., *Pope John Paul II on Jews and Judaism 1979–1986* (Washington: United States Catholic Conference, 1987) and Eugene Fisher's essay in this volume, pp. 405–423.

26. Pope John Paul II affirmed at Miami, September, 1987, the decision arrived at a month earlier at Castel Gandolfo that "a Catholic document on the *Shoah* and anti-Semitism will be forthcoming, resulting from...serious [joint Catholic-Jewish] studies." *Origins* 17 (24 September 1987): 243.

27. Rose Thering, O.P., Ph.D., *Jews, Judaism, & Catholic Education* (New York: Anti-Defamation League of B'nai B'rith, 1986). See also *Within Context: Guidelines for the Catechetical Presentation of Jews and Judaism in the New Testament* (Morristown, NJ: Silver Burdett & Ginn, 1987).

28. Pope John Paul II, 13 April 1986 address to the Roman Jewish Community, in Fisher & Klenicki (n. 25), 82.

29. "Notes on the Correct Way," Para. 25. See also Pope John Paul II's letter to Archbishop May: "With our hearts filled with this unyielding hope, we Christians approach with immense respect the terrifying experience of the extermination, the *Shoah*, suffered by the Jews during World War II, and we seek to grasp its most authentic, specific and universal meaning.... It is not permissible for anyone to pass by [the *Shoah*] with indifference." In *Origins* 17 (3 September 1987): 183.

30. David Tracy, "Religious Values After the Holocaust: A Catholic View," in Abraham Peck, ed., *Jews and Christians After the Holocaust* (Philadelphia: Fortress Press, 1982), 87–108, 96.

31. "Notes on the Correct Way," Para. 25.

32. *Origins* 17 (10 September 1987): 199. For a short exposition of the church's attitude toward the State of Israel, see Eugene J. Fisher, "The Holy See and the State of Israel: The Evolution of Attitudes and Policies," in *Journal of Ecumenical Studies* 2 (Spring 1987) 2:191–211; see also George E. Irani, *The Papacy and the Middle East: The Role of the Holy See in the Arab-Israeli Conflict, 1962–1964* (Notre Dame, IN: University of Notre Dame Press, 1986), and Andrej Kreutz, *Vatican Policy on the Palestinian-Israeli Conflict: The Struggle for the Holy Land* (New York: Greenwood Press, 1990); with regard to Jewish reaction to references to Israel in church documents, see Neudecker, "The Catholic Church," 300–301.

33. John Thavis, "Vatican-Israeli Commission: Bridge Over River of Problems," in *The Boston Pilot* (7 August 1992), 3; see also Lisa Palmieri-Billig, "Radical Change in the Vatican," *The Jerusalem Post* (International Edition), 15 August 1992, 8.

34. See here Bishops' Committee on the Liturgy, *God's Mercy Endures Forever: Guidelines on the Presentation of Jews and Judaism in Catholic Preaching* (Washington, DC: United States Catholic Conference, 1988), and John T. Pawlikowski and James A. Wilde, *When Catholics Speak about Jews* (Chicago: Liturgy Training Publications, 1987).

35. See Clark M. Williamson, *When Jews and Christians Meet: A Guide for Christian Preaching and Teaching* (St. Louis, CBP Press, 1989). But cf. Joseph Jensen, O.S.B., "Prediction—Fulfillment in the Bible and Liturgy," *Catholic Biblical Quarterly* 50 (1988): 646–662.

Suggestions For Further Reading

Croner, Helga, comp. *More Stepping Stones to Jewish-Christian Relations: An Unabridged Collection of Christian Documents 1975–1983*. New York: Paulist/Stimulus Books, 1985. An anthology of documents that includes the pivotal "Notes on the Correct Way to Present the Jews and Judaism in Preaching and Catechesis in the Roman Catholic Church."

____, comp. *Stepping Stones to Further Jewish-Christian Relations: An Unabridged Collection of Christian Documents*. New York: Stimulus Books, 1977. This anthology includes Vatican II's *Nostra Aetate* #4.

Fisher, Eugene and Leon Klenicki, eds. *Pope John Paul II on Jews and Judaism 1979–1986*. Washington, DC: United States Catholic Conference, 1987. An important resource on papal statements on the church's relation to the Jewish people.

Fisher, Eugene J. *Seminary Education and Christian-Jewish Relations: A Curriculum and Resource Handbook*. 2d ed. Washington, DC: The National Catholic Educational Association, 1988. A very good resource in its own right, this small booklet is a shining example of the church's effort to change the way it teaches about Jews and Judaism.

International Catholic-Jewish Liaison Committee. *Fifteen Years of Catholic-Jewish Dialogue 1970–1985, Selected Papers*. Rome: Libreria Editrice Vaticana, 1988. A fine collection of scholarly, yet accessible papers charting the theological course of the dialogue since 1970.

McGarry, Michael B. *Christology After Auschwitz*. New York: Paulist Press, 1977. This short book presents an analysis of the documents of Vatican II and other Christian bodies as they impact Jewish-Christian relations.

Neudecker, Reinhard. "The Catholic Church and the Jewish People." In *Vatican II: Assessment and Perspectives: Twenty-five Years After (1962-1987)*, ed. Rene Latourelle, 3: 282–383. New York: Paulist Press, 1989. This is an insightful and accessible history, analysis, and critique of *Nostra Aetate*.

Oesterreicher, John M. *The New Encounter Between Christians and Jews*. New York: Philosophical Library, 1986. This contains a long interesting essay on the story by one of *Nostra Aetate*'s architects about how the conciliar declaration on the Jewish people came to see the light of day.

Pawlikowski, John T. *What Are They Saying About Christian-Jewish Relations?* New York: Paulist Press, 1980. Although much has happened since this was published, it remains the most accessible explanation of the various critical areas in the Jewish-Christian dialogue.

Rudin, A. James, "The Dramatic Impact of Nostra Aetate." In Eugene J. Fisher, et al., eds., *Twenty Years of Jewish-Catholic Relations*. New York: Paulist Press, 1986. An insightful Jewish commentary on the content and influence of *Nostra Aetate* by a respected Jewish veteran in Jewish-Christian relations.

POPE JOHN PAUL II'S PILGRIMAGE OF RECONCILIATION: A COMMENTARY ON THE TEXTS

Eugene J. Fisher

Born in 1920 in Wadowice, near Cracow, Poland, John Paul II's life before becoming pope in 1978 spanned a grim period in Poland's history: the rebirth of the nation after World War I and its travail first as a faltering democracy and then a military despotism in the interwar period; the tortured years of the German conquest and occupation which cost the lives of six million Poles including three million Polish Jews during World War II; the cruel totalitarian regime of communism in the Soviet shadow after 1945. During the war Karol Wojtyla worked as a laborer in a stone quarry and chemical plant, decided to become a priest (a sentence of death under Nazi rule), and (equally dangerous) participated in an underground unit that secreted Jews out of ghettos, forged identity papers, and found hiding places for them. He was ordained a priest in 1946, earned a doctorate in divinity at the Pontifical University in Rome, traveled extensively in Western Europe, wrote poetry, and, on returning to Poland, entered on pastoral duties, became professor at the Catholic Lublin University, bishop in 1958, and archbishop of Cracow in 1963. He participated actively in Vatican Council II, 1962–65. He was a university professor of ethics and philosophy (deeply versed in Thomism and phenomenology), prolific scholar and master of many languages, the author of several books and numerous articles. His pontificate has been notable for his numerous journeys to countries round the world, where he characteristically addresses burning issues that demand redress—poverty, injustice, tyranny, the environment, civil war, peace and reconciliation. His momentous visits to Poland were prime movers in bringing down communism in his homeland and throughout the erstwhile communist bloc. With regard to Catholic teaching and practice, he is a strong traditionalist. He is tireless in his quest for the just reward of labor, the well-being of the human family, and ecumenicalism, both in the sense of Christian unity and the unity of all humankind as children of God. In word and deed, one of the most important themes of his pontificate is Catholic-Jewish relations. In the following essay Eugene J. Fisher analyzes John Paul II's actions in pursuing the goals set by John XXIII and continuing the process launched by Paul VI.

Introduction

Through the choice of the name that would mark his pontificate, Pope John Paul II paid homage and made a commitment to all three of his immediate predecessors: John XXIII, who called the Second Vatican Council and who mandated that it address the ancient, long-neglected question of the church's spiritual debt to Judaism; Paul VI, who implemented that mandate and who institutionalized it through the creation of the Holy See's Commission for Religious Relations with the Jews; and John Paul I, the "smiling pope," whose all too brief reign was marked by an appreciation for the "divine humor" of creation and a sense of abiding hope in humanity.

The declaration on the Jews, *Nostra Aetate*, 4, distilled in fifteen tightly worded Latin sentences the essence of the Second Vatican Council's major themes of biblical reappraisal, liturgical renewal, and openness to the Spirit working in the world beyond the visible boundaries of the church. Implementation of *Nostra Aetate*, then, can properly be seen as a "litmus test" for the success or failure of the Council's vision as a whole. How has Pope John Paul II fulfilled his commitment to his predecessors in the area of Catholic-Jewish relations, the area of the church's ministry that embodies the most ancient and, some would say, potentially divisive issues posed to the church by its own history?

Addresses and remarks by the pope on Judaism have been given on numerous occasions and in a remarkably wide range of locations throughout the world. Virtually wherever the pope has travelled, it can be said, there exists a Jewish community, whether large, as in the United States, or tragically small, as in the tiny remnant of the once-flourishing Jewish community of Poland. And, wherever the pope goes, he seeks out those communities to reach out to them in reconciliation and affirmation of the infinite worth of Judaism's continuing proclamation of the name of the One God in the world.

The papal talks discussed here represent those that have been officially printed. They provide a record of a profound spiritual pilgrimage for the pope and the church, almost two millennia after the church's birth as a Jewish movement in the land and among the people of Israel. In the thematic analysis that follows, I will argue that one can discern in the pope's addresses a growth and development in the pope's understanding of and appreciation for how "the Jews define themselves in the light of their own religious experience" (Prologue, 1974 *Guidelines* cited by the pope in his first address to representatives of Jewish organizations, 3/12/79).*

---

* The papal addresses cited in this commentary are referred to by the dates on which they were delivered. For complete texts through 1986, see E. Fisher and L. Klenicki, editors, *John Paul II on Jews and Judaism 1979–1986* (Washington, DC: U.S. Catholic Conference, 1987), from which this paper has been excerpted with permission. Later texts will be referenced as they arise.

Perhaps more important, this development teaches us much about how the church must reinterpret today its own understanding of its relationship to the Jewish people as "people of God."

The ongoing papal reconsideration and redefinition of ancient theological categories represent the fruits of a painstaking effort, supported by the efforts of thousands of Catholics and Jews in dialogue throughout the world, as the pope has acknowledged (Historic Visit to the Synagogue of Rome, 4/13/86, no. 4), to articulate anew the mystery of the church in the light of a positive articulation of the abiding mystery of Israel. The results, as the patient reader will discern, are as breathtaking as they have been painstaking.

Progress, in one sense, has been painfully slow since the Second Vatican Council. It is measured in small steps, a word here uttered to clarify an awkward phrase there; a slightly less ambiguous wording to replace a more ambiguous, potentially misleading theological formula; and so forth. But, the direction is clear, we believe, and the basic message starkly unambiguous: the church is not alone in the world as "people of God." The church is joined by the Jewish people in its proclamation of the oneness of God and the true nature of human history, which Jews and Christians alike pray daily and, through their prayers, proclaim universally (cf. 1985 Vatican "Notes," II, 9–11). The following thematic categories serve to organize just some of these small steps and interventions by which the pope has sought to frame and to move forward the church's side of historic dialogue between Catholics and Jews.

In assessing the major events of the year 1986 in the Diocese of Rome, the pope singled out his visit to "our elder brothers in the faith of Abraham in their Rome Synagogue" as his most significant action of the year. It will be remembered, he predicted, "for centuries and millenniums in the history of this city and this church. I thank Divine Providence because the task was given to me" (*National Catholic News Service*, 12/31/86).

1. The Spiritual Bond between the Church and the Jewish People: The Special Relationship

The notion of a "spiritual bond" linking the church and the Jewish people ("Abraham's stock") was central to *Nostra Aetate*. It has become a major theme of Pope John Paul II's own reflections on the subject over the years, one which he has consistently tried to probe and refine. In his first address to Jewish representatives, for example, he interpreted the conciliar phrase as meaning "that our two religious communities are connected and closely related at the very level of their respective identities" (3/12/79) and spoke of "fraternal dialogue" between the two.

Terms such as *fraternal* and addressing one another as *brothers* and *sisters*, of course, reflect ancient usage within the Christian community. They imply an acknowledgement of a commonality of faith, with liturgical implications. It was an ecumenical breakthrough, for example, when the Second Vatican Council and Pope Paul VI began the practice of addressing Orthodox and Protestant Christians in such terms. Pope John Paul II's extension of this terminology to Jews, therefore, is by no means accidental.

The relationship, he is saying, is not marginal to the church. Rather, it reaches to the very essence of the nature of Christian faith itself, so that to deny it is to deny something essential to the teaching of the church (cf. Vatican "Notes," 1, 2). The spiritual bond with Jews, for the pope, is properly understood as a "sacred one, stemming as it does from the mysterious will of God" (10/28/85).

In bringing this lesson home, the pope has used startling and powerful language. In his important allocution to the Jewish community of Mainz, West Germany (11/17/80), for example, the pope likened the relationship to that between "the first and second part" of the Christian Bible (i.e., between the Hebrew Scriptures and the New Testament).

The dialogue between Catholics and Jews, therefore, is not a dialogue between past (Judaism) and present (Christianity) realities, as if the former had been "superseded" or "replaced" by the latter, as certain Christian polemicists would have it. "On the contrary," the pope made clear in Mainz, "it is a question rather of reciprocal enlightenment and explanation, just as is the relationship between the Scriptures themselves" (cf. *Dei Verbum*, 11).

In this vein, the pope has also moved to assist Catholics to formulate more sensitive biblical terminology. Instead of the traditional *Old Testament* and *New Testament*, which might be understood to imply that the "old" has been abrogated in favor of the "new" (a false conclusion known from history as the Marcionite heresy), the pope, in his address to the Jews of Australia (11/26/86), has suggested the use of the terms, the *Hebrew Scriptures* and the *Christian Scriptures* as appropriate alternatives. Again, small changes can have major consequences in theological and sociological perception.

In the pope's view, so close is the spiritual bond between our two peoples of God that the dialogue is properly considered—unlike any other relationship between the church and a world religion—to be "a dialogue within our Church" (Mainz, 11/17/80). Interpreting *Nostra Aetate* during his visit to the Rome Synagogue, the pope brought these themes to a dramatic culmination:

> The Church of Christ discovers her 'bond' with Judaism by 'searching into her own mystery' (*Nostra Aetate*, 4). The Jewish religion is not 'extrinsic' to us, but in a certain way is 'intrinsic' to our own religion. With Judaism, therefore, we have a relationship which we do not have with any other religion. You are dearly beloved brothers and, in a certain way, it could be said that you are our elder brothers (Rome, 4/13/86).

2. A Living Heritage

The phrase, "elder brothers," used here with caution, raises the question of how the pope has dealt with the sometimes awkward (for Christians) question of the church's spiritual debt to Judaism. Traditionally, this debt has been acknowledged—as in medieval canon law's exception allowing Jews freedom of worship (within certain limitations)—a right granted to no other religious group outside Christianity.

Yet the acknowledgment often came negatively. For many Christians over the ages, for example, the use of the term *elder brother* applied to the Jews would have conjured images of apologetic interpretations of the younger/elder brother stories of Genesis in which the younger brother takes over the heritage or *patrimony* of the elder (e.g., Esau and Jacob). The powerful imagery of the gothic cathedrals of Europe is another example of this. Juxtaposed on either side of the portals of many medieval cathedrals is a statue of the Synagogue (portrayed in the physical form of a woman), her head bowed, holding a broken staff of the law, with the tablets of the Ten Commandments slipping from her fingers, on the one side, and the Church, resplendently erect and triumphant on the other. The pairings symbolized for the medieval artists the passage of the Covenant from Judaism to Christianity.

Here, as in so many other ways, however, the pope has sought to reinterpret ancient apologetics and to replace negative images with positive affirmations. In his address to the Jewish community in Mainz, the pope cited a passage from a declaration of the bishops of the Federal Republic of Germany, issued earlier that year, calling attention to "the spiritual heritage of Israel for the Church." He added to the citation, however, a single word that removed any possible ambiguity and opened up a new area of theological reflection, calling it "a *living* heritage, which must be understood and preserved in its depth and richness by us Catholic Christians" (11/17/80).

Speaking to delegates from episcopal conferences, gathered in Rome in March 1982, from around the world to discuss ways to foster improved Catholic-Jewish relations, the pope confirmed and advanced this direction of his thought:

> Christians have taken the right path, that of justice and brotherhood, in seeking to come together with their Semitic brethren, respectfully and perseveringly, in the common heritage, a heritage that all value so highly.... To assess it carefully in itself and with due awareness of the faith and religious life of the Jewish people *as they are professed and practiced still today*, can greatly help us to understand better certain aspects of the life of the Church ([3/6/82], italics added).

The "common spiritual patrimony" of Jews and Christians, then, is not something of the past but of the present. Just as the church, through the writings of its doctors and saints and the statements of its councils, has developed a rich tradition interpreting and clarifying its spiritual heritage over the centuries, so has Judaism developed, through rabbinic literature and the Talmud, through Jewish philosophers and mystics, what was given to its in its founding by God, as the 1985 Vatican "Notes" explicitly state (Section VI). Today, then, the pope calls us to understand the "common spiritual patrimony" not only positively but assertively as a joint witness of God's truth to the world: "Jews and Christians are the trustees and witnesses of an ethic marked by the Ten Commandments in the observance of which man finds his truth and freedom" (Rome Synagogue, 4/13/86). In the perspective of this renewed papal vision, one can imagine a new statue of the Synagogue on cathedrals, head held high in faithful observance of God's permanent covenant; and a new statue of the Church, with a look of saving humility mitigating the triumphal expression of the past. The two, while remaining distinct, would stand together to proclaim the divine truth that both share and, yet, interpret in unique ways.

3. Permanent Validity of God's Covenant with the Jewish People

Underlying the above considerations is a central message that Pope John Paul II has made his own wherever he has travelled. This message grows out of the Second Vatican Council, and what the pope has done is to make explicit what was implicit in the Council's teaching. Not only *Nostra Aetate* but the Dogmatic Constitution on the Church, *Lume Gentium*, drew upon the strong affirmation of St. Paul in Romans 11:28–29 when seeking to define the role of the Jewish people in God's plan of salvation, even after the time of Christ: "On account of their fathers, this people [the Jews] remains most dear to God, for God does not repent of the gifts He makes nor of the calls He issues" (*Lumen Gentium*, 16).

Logically, the conciliar affirmation means that the Jews remain God's chosen people in the fullest sense ("most dear"). This affirmation, the pope teaches, is unequivocal and in no way diminishes the church's own affirmation of its own standing as "people of God." In Mainz, the pope addressed the Jewish community with full respect as "the people of God of the Old Covenant, which has never been revoked by God," referring to Romans 11:29, and emphasized the "permanent value" of both the Hebrew Scriptures and the Jewish community that witnesses to those Scriptures as sacred texts (11/17/80).

In meeting with representatives of episcopal conferences, the pope stressed the present tense of Romans 9:4–5 concerning the Jewish people, "who have the adoption as sons, and the glory and the covenants and the legislation and the worship and the promises" (3/6/82), while also affirming "the universal salvific significance of the death and resurrection of Jesus of Nazareth" (ibid.). The pope does not seek a superficial reconciling of these two great truths but affirms them both together, commenting: "this means that the links between the Church and the Jewish people are founded on the design of the God of the Covenant" (ibid.). Or, as the pope put it in addressing the Anti-Defamation League of B'nai B'rith, "the respect we speak of is based on the mysterious spiritual link which brings us close together, in Abraham and, through Abraham, in God who chose Israel and brought forth the Church from Israel" (3/22/84).

Here, there is not the slightest hint of supersessionism or of that subtler form of triumphalism that would envision Israel as having exhausted its salvific role in "giving birth" to Christianity. The mystery, in the pope's profound vision, lies much deeper than any such "either/or" theological dichotomies can reach. It is precisely such a "both/and" approach that the pope is calling Catholic scholars and educators to develop today. In the words of the "Ecumenical Aids" for the Diocese of Rome, the mystery (a term reserved for the sacraments and the deepest truths of the Catholic faith) encompasses "the people of God, Jews and Christians."

The pope's remarkable formulation in Australia distills years of theological development: "The Catholic faith is rooted in the eternal truths of the Hebrew Scriptures and in the irrevocable covenant made with Abraham. We, too, gratefully hold these same truths of our Jewish heritage and look upon you as our brothers and sisters in the Lord" (11/26/86).

4. Catechetics and Liturgy

For the pope, it is not enough to rework the framework of Christianity's traditional understanding of Jews and Judaism. The renewed vision of the relationship needs to permeate every area of church life. In his address to representatives of bishops conferences, for example, the pope stressed especially, "the case of [Catholic] liturgy, whose Jewish roots remain still to be examined in depth, and in any case should be known and appreciated by our faithful" (3/6/82). Regarding catechesis, he encouraged a major effort: "We should aim, in this field, that Catholic teaching at its different levels, in catechesis to children and young people, presents Jews and Judaism, not only in an honest and objective manner, free from prejudices and without any offenses, but also with full awareness of the heritage sketched above" (ibid.).

In his response to the International Conference of Christians and Jews, the pope noted that the "great common spiritual patrimony" shared by Jews and Christians rests on a "solid" foundation of "faith in a God...as a loving father...; in a common basic liturgical pattern, and in a common commitment, grounded in faith, to all men and women in need, who are our 'neighbors' (cf. Lv 19:18, Mk 12:32 and parallels)" (7/6/84). Catechesis and the liturgy itself, in other words, have as a primary goal making clear the "spiritual bond" that links the church to the people Israel (cf. Vatican "Notes," II, VI).

Also needing to be made clear to Catholic youth is the often tragic history of Christian-Jewish relations over the centuries: "The proper teaching of history is also a concern of yours [the International Conference of Christians and Jews's]. Such a concern is very understandable, given the sad and entangled common history of Jews and Christians—a history that is not always taught or transmitted correctly" (7/6/84). As Fr. Edward Flannery commented in his classic study of that history, *The Anguish of the Jews* (New York: Paulist Press, 1985), "those pages of history that Jews have committed to memory are the very ones that have been torn from Christian history books" (p. 1).

Finally, in his visit to Rome Synagogue, the pope added a note of urgency and even impatience to his encouragement to Catholic educators and homilists "to present always and everywhere, to ourselves and others, the true face of the Jews and of Judaism...at every level of outlook, teaching, and communication" (4/13/86), reminding "my brothers and sisters of the Catholic Church" that guidelines "are already available to everyone." In the 1974 *Guidelines for the Implementation of "Nostra Aetate" (no. 4)*, and in the 1985 "Notes" issued by the Holy See's Commission for Religious Relations with Judaism, the pope concluded that "it is only a question of studying them carefully, of immersing oneself in their teachings, and of putting them into practice" (4/13/86).

5. Condemnations of Antisemitism and Remembrances of the *Shoah*

A major theme that runs through the following addresses is the pope's deep abhorrence of antisemitism. This abhorrence is not simply theoretical. The pope lived under Nazism in Poland and experienced personally the malignancy of the ancient evil of Jew-hatred.

In his very first audience with Jewish representatives, the pope reaffirmed the Second Vatican Council's repudiation of antisemitism "as opposed to the very spirit of Christianity," and "which in any case the dignity of the human person alone would suffice to condemn" (3/12/79). The pope has repeated this message in country after country throughout the world.

And, in country after country, especially in Europe, the pope has called on Catholics to remember, "in particular, the memory of the people whose sons and daughters were intended for total extermination" (Homily at Auschwitz, 6/7/79). From the intensity of his own experience, the pope is able to articulate both the *uniqueness* of the Jewish experience of the *Shoah* while, at the same time, revering the memory of all of Nazism's millions of non-Jewish victims. He would, it may be appropriate to say, agree unreservedly with the formulation of Elie Wiesel: "Not every victim of the Holocaust was a Jew, but every Jew was a victim."

Meeting with Jews in Paris (5/31/80), the pope made a point of mentioning the great suffering of the Jewish community of France "during the dark years of the occupation," paying homage to them as victims "whose sacrifice, we know, has not been fruitless." The pope went on to acknowledge that from the French Jewish survivors came the courage of "pioneers, including Jules Isaac" to engage in the dialogue with Catholics that led to *Nostra Aetate*. In Germany (11/17/80), the pope addressed the subject at some length. And, in his controversial homily at Otranto, he linked, for the first time, the Holocaust and the rebirth of a Jewish State in the land of Israel: "the Jewish People, after tragic experiences connected with the extermination of so many sons and daughters, driven by the desire for security set up the State of Israel" ([10/5/80], also see below).

Speaking as a Pole and as a Catholic on the fortieth anniversary of the uprising and destruction of the Warsaw Ghetto, the pope termed "that horrible and tragic event" a "desperate cry for the right to life, for liberty, and for the salvation of human dignity" (4/25/83). On the twentieth anniversary of *Nostra Aetate*, the pope stated that "anti-Semitism, in its ugly and sometimes violent manifestations, should be completely eradicated." He called the attention of the whole church to the mandate given in the 1985 Vatican "Notes" to develop Holocaust curricula in Catholic schools and catechetical programs: "For Catholics, as the 'Notes' (no. 25) have asked them to do, to fathom the depths of the extermination of many millions of Jews during World War II and the wounds thereby inflicted on the consciousness of the Jewish people, theological reflection is also needed" (10/28/85).

In Australia, the pope recalled that "this is still the century of the *Shoah*" and intensified the Council's condemnation of antisemitism by declaring that "no theological justification could ever be found for acts of discrimination or persecution against Jews. In fact, such acts must be held to be sinful" (11/26/86).

In his 1987 address to the Jews of Warsaw, the Pope probed the mystery even deeper, acknowledging the *priority* as well as uniqueness of Jewish suffering in the *Shoah*: "It was you who suffered this terrible sacrifice of extermination: one might say that you suffered it also on behalf of those who were likewise to be exterminated." From this, he derives the very significant theological insight that the Jewish witness to the *Shoah* is, for the church as well as for all of humanity, a "saving warning," indeed a continuation "in the contemporary world" of the prophetic mission itself. The church, in turn, is therefore called to listen to this uniquely Jewish proclamation and to unite its voice to that of the Jewish people in their continuing "particular vocation," one may say, to be a light to the nations.

The order of the pope's theological reflection on the *Shoah* is important. As he stated in his letter to Archbishop John L. May (8/8/87), an "authentic" approach first grapples with the "specific," and therefore specifically Jewish reality of the event. Only then, and with this continually in mind, he seems to be saying to us, can one begin to seek out its more "universal meaning."

In Miami, the pope spoke of the "mystery of the suffering of Israel's children," and called on Christians to learn from the "acute insights" of "Jewish thinkers" on the human condition and to develop in dialogue with Jews "common educational programs which...will teach future generations about the Holocaust so that never again will such a horror be possible. Never again!" (9/11/87). From "the suffering and martyrdom of the Jewish people," understood within the context of their "constant progression in faith and obedience to the loving call of God" over the centuries, then, our remembrance of the *Shoah* may lead to "even deeper hope, a warning call to all of humanity that may serve to save us all" (6/24/88, Vienna), a prophetic "prick of conscience" that may tell us "what message our century [can] convey to the next" (Mauthausen, 6/24/88).

The challenge to Christian complacency and to Christian teaching in these statements, taken together, I believe, is both very clear and very strong. Over the years the pope has issued strong statements of condemnation of acts of terrorism against synagogues and Jewish communities, sending messages of sympathy for their victims. For example, he condemned the August 29, 1981, bomb-throwing attack on a synagogue in Vienna, Austria as a "bloody and absurd act, which assails the Jewish community in Austria and the entire world," and warned against a "new wave of that same anti-Semitism that has provoked so much mourning through the centuries" (NC News 9/1/81).

During the October 7, 1985, seizure by Palestinian terrorists of the Italian cruise ship Achille Lauro, the pope condemned what he called "this grave act of violence against innocent and defenseless persons," calling on the hijackers to "put an end to their deed": "It is not through recourse to violence that one finds a just solution to problems. I wish that the perpetrators of this rash act would understand this."

After the September 1986 attack on the Istanbul Synagogue, the pope expressed his "firm and vigorous condemnation" of the act and his "heartfelt thought to the victims...brothers gathered together in a place of prayer" (*L'Osservatore Romano*, 9/22/86).

In his general audience of July 11, 1988, the pope summarized what to him was the essence of his trip to Austria in June of that year (see section no. 7, "Controversies and Dialogue," below). The pope stressed that 1988 marked the fiftieth anniversary of the "Anschluss," the annexation of Austria by Nazi Germany, "a traumatic event which left a tragic imprint on the history of Europe.... The dreadful years of Nazi terror caused millions of victims of many nations. A special measure of extermination was reserved, unfortunately, for the Jewish nation. This fact came to the fore in the meeting with the representatives of the Jewish community living in Austria" (*L'Osservatore Romano*, 7/11/88, n. 28, p. 3).

Similarly, in his June 5, 1990 discourse to those preparing the 1991 European Synod of Bishops, the pope commented that: "The Second World War... with its immense cruelty, a cruelty that reached its most brutal expression in the organized extermination of the Jews...revealed to the European the other side of a civilization that he was inclined to consider superior to all others.... Perhaps in no other war in history has man been so thoroughly trampled on in his dignity and fundamental rights. An echo of the humiliation and even desperation caused by such an experience could be heard in the question often repeated after the war: How can we go on living after Auschwitz?" (Washington, DC: *Origins*, Catholic News Service Documentary Service 20, no. 6 [1990], 92).

On September 26, 1990, in his annual Jasna Gora meditation celebrating the feast of Our Lady of Chestochowa, the pope spoke as a Pole to his fellow Poles, reminding them: "There is yet another nation, a particular people, the people of the Patriarchs, of Moses and the Prophets, the heirs of the faith of Abraham.... This people lived arm and arm with us for generations on that same land which became a kind of new homeland during the diaspora. This people was afflicted by the terrible deaths of millions of its sons and daughters. First they were marked with special signs, then they were shoved into ghettos, isolated quarters. Then they were carried off to the gas chambers, put to death simply because they were the sons and daughters of this people. The assassins did all this in our land, perhaps to cloak it in infamy. However one cannot cloak a land in infamy by the death of innocent victims. By such deaths the land becomes a sacred relic. The people who lived with us for many generations has remained with us after the terrible death of millions of its sons and daughters. Together we await the Day of Judgement and Resurrection" (Vatican City: Pontifical Council on Christian Unity: *Information Service*, n. 75, 4:172).

Indeed, in this period it appeared that the pope seldom missed a chance to remind Europeans of the *Shoah*. On November 8, 1990, when he received the first ambassador of re-united Germany, he stated for the permanent record: "It was really the Second World War which came to an end on October 3 [with the unification] and made many people aware of what fate and guilt mean to all peoples and individuals. We think of the millions of people, most of them totally innocent, who died in that war.... For Christians the heavy burden of guilt for the murder of the Jewish people must be an enduring call to repentance; thereby we can overcome every form of antisemitism and establish a new relationship with our kindred nation of the Old Covenant.... Guilt should not oppress and lead to departure for conversion" (ibid.).

Several times that fall and winter, the pope cited the statement of the 13th International Catholic-Jewish Liaison Committee meeting held in Prague with its call for Christian "*teshuvah* (repentance)" for antisemitism over the centuries and its statement that antisemitism is "a sin against God and humanity" (cited in ibid., 4:172–178), in order to place that joint statement firmly within Catholic teaching.

In the late summer of 1991, John Paul II took another trip through the now free countries of Eastern Europe. In informal remarks during his visit to his childhood home in Wadowice, Poland, he reminisced about his childhood friends, many of them Jewish. "In the school of Wadowice there were Jewish believers who are no longer with us. There is no longer a synagogue near the school....

Let us remember that we are near Auschwitz" (*Catholic News Service*, 8/15/91).

On August 16, 1991 in Hungary, he met with representatives of that country's 80,000 member Jewish community. He struck the themes of *teshuvah*, repentance and reconciliation: "Thousands of the Jewish community [of Hungary] were imprisoned in concentration camps and progressively exterminated. In those terrible days the words of the prophet Jeremiah once more became a reality: 'In Ramah is heard the sound of moaning, of bitter weeping! Rachel mourns her children, she refuses to be consoled because her children are no more' (Jer 31:15). My thoughts go with deep respect to the great believers who even in those days of devastation—*yom shoah* in the words of Zephaniah (cf. 1:15).... We are here now to adore the God of Israel, who this time too has stretched out his protecting hand over a blessed remnant of his people. How often this mysterious ransom has been repeated in your history! Sustained by its faith in the Lord, the Jewish people have preserved, even in their millenary dispersion, their identity, their rites, their tradition.... In the face of the risk of a resurgence and spread of anti-Semitic feelings, attitudes and initiatives, of which certain disquieting signs are to be seen today and of which we have experienced the most frightful results in the past, we must teach consciences to consider anti-Semitism and all forms of racism as sins against God and humanity" (*Origins* 21, no. 13 [9/5/91], 203).

6. Land and State of Israel

Because of the great complexities of the Middle East situation, which it is not within the purview of this essay to address, much less unravel, it must be acknowledged that papal teaching on this subject of such central concern to the Jewish community is more nuanced and, at times, ambiguous than that to be found in the other categories included in this analysis. Still, from the perspective of Catholic-Jewish dialogue, which is to say, from the perspective of how well Catholics, through dialogue, have come to understand "by what essential traits the Jews define themselves in the light of their own religious experience" (1974 *Guidelines*, Prologue), one can discern a measure of progress in understanding as reflected in the papal statements.

Clearly, there still exist differences of view between the Holy See and the State of Israel, such that the hope for an exchange of ambassadors between the two expressed by many Jewish and Catholic leaders has not yet been realized. The reasons, as stated by the Holy See, include the unsettled nature of the boundary between Israel and some of its neighbors, the disposition of the city of Jerusalem, and the security of Christian communities in Arab countries.

There are, however, certain diplomatic relations between the Holy See and Jerusalem. The Israeli Embassy in Rome includes an officer who relates to the Vatican Secretariat of State. The Apostolic Delegate in Jerusalem communicates with the Israeli Ministry of Foreign Affairs. When Israeli leaders meet with the pope, the protocol is that accorded to a state visit. Given the symbolic as well as practical nature of diplomatic relations, a full exchange of ambassadors would deepen greatly the relationship between Catholics and Jews.

The papal addresses included here represent something of the pope's own generally positive attitudes toward the State of Israel as well as toward the Palestinians and, above all, his very deep hopes that the holy city of Jerusalem can become "a crossroads of reconciliation and peace," a "meeting point" between Christians, Jews, and Muslims (Homily at Otranto, 10/5/80).

The pope's attitude toward the State of Israel is most completely revealed in his Apostolic Letter of April 20, 1984, *Redemptionis Anno*:

> For the Jewish people who live in the State of Israel and who preserve in that land such precious testimonies of their history and their faith, we must ask for the desired security and the due tranquility that is the prerogative of every nation and condition of life and of progress for every society.

This is an unambiguous affirmation of the right of the Jewish State to existence and security.

The Holy See's 1985 "Notes" distinguish between the people, land, and State of Israel. They affirm the validity of the Jewish people's attachment to the land and the existence of the State under international law, but caution against a biblical-fundamentalist interpretation of the religious implications of modern events. While not a statement by the pope personally, the reference in the "Notes" deserves to be cited here in full for the overall perspective it gives on the issue as it is raised in Catholic teaching today:

> The history of Israel did not end in A.D. 70 (cf. *Guidelines*, II). It continued, especially in a numerous Diaspora which allowed Israel to carry to the whole world a witness—often heroic—of its fidelity to the one God and to 'exalt him in the presence of all the living' (Tb 13:4), while preserving the memory of the land of their forefathers at the heart of their hope (Passover *Seder*).
>
> Christians are invited to understand this religious attachment, which finds its roots in biblical tradition, without, however, making their own any particular religious interpretation of this relationship (cf. *Statement on Catholic-Jewish Relations*, National Conference of Catholic Bishops, 11/20/75).
>
> The existence of the State of Israel and its political options should be envisaged not in a perspective which is in itself religious, but in their reference to the common principles of international law (*Notes on the Correct Way to Present Jews and Judaism in the*

Preaching and Catechizes of the Roman Catholic Church, Vatican Commission for Religious Relations with the Jews, May 1985).

On July 29, 1992, the Holy See announced that it had established with the State of Israel a "bilateral permanent working commission" as a first step toward the goal of an exchange of ambassadors, thus "normalizing" the diplomatic relationship between Israel and the Vatican. While much work remains for this committee, of course, its very existence by definition ends all prior speculation that the church still harbors any official theological positions which would make it doctrinally difficult to acknowledge without reservation the existence and validity of a Jewish State in *Eretz Israel* as recognized by international law.

7. Controversies and Dialogue

While the pontificate of John Paul II has been marked by the most solid and extensive advances in Catholic-Jewish relations, perhaps, in the history of the church, it has also seen some of the most vocal controversies between Catholics and Jews since the Second Vatican Council. These revolve, in retrospect not surprisingly, around the two key events of Jewish history in this century—and for many centuries: The Holocaust and the State of Israel. The substantive position of the pope on both of these issues has been stated above. But the continuing lack of full diplomatic relations with the State of Israel, on the one hand, and a series of incidents with regard to the *Shoah* on the other, have greatly increased our awareness of the fragility of the contemporary dialogue between our two communities.

The incidents to which I refer include the pope's meetings with Yasir Arafat and Kurt Waldheim, the beatification of Edith Stein, and, though the Holy See had nothing to do with the problem but only with its resolution, the Carmelite convent in the Auschwitz-Birkenau death camp complex. Each of these controversies has its specifics and, especially on the symbolic level for the Jewish perspective, commonalities with the others. Indeed, some Jewish commentators have perceived a rather ominous sort of pattern in these incidents: a continuing rejection of the people Israel by a denial of the State of Israel, on the one hand, and an attempt not so much to deny as to appropriate the Holocaust for the church on the other. Obviously, there is not space in this essay to go into a full exposition of why I believe such a pattern does not exist (always a tough case to prove in any event). With regard to the latter point, Rabbi Daniel Polish has published an excellent extended editorial in *Ecumenical Trends* (16:9 [Oct. 1987], 153–155; cf., my response in the Feb. 1988 issue, 24–28), for which he won an award from the Catholic Press Association. I have also gone into some detail on these matters in a feature article for the Vatican journal *SIDIC* (22, 1–2, [1989], 10–15). Here let it suffice for me to make just a few points to frame the situation, as it were, and to present what can be discerned of the pope's reaction to it all.

First, it needs to be said that in each of these events there has been, if one takes the time to look, a papal response. The Holy See's responses, it should be noted, tend to address the substance of Jewish concerns, and do not always have an eye to what we in this country would call "media relations." In the meeting with Arafat, for example, the Vatican Secretariat of State on the day of the meeting issued a tersely worded statement defining the meeting as not intending to give any credence whatsoever to PLO claims, and that the pope was meeting with Arafat to express humanitarian concerns for the Palestinian people and to exhort him to eschew violence against Jews. The Catholic press picked this up; but neither the Jewish nor the secular media did much with it. The result was that to this day many Jews will speak of the pope "embracing" Arafat. He did not, the photo shows only a rather distant handshake, nothing like an "embrace" at all. Catholics, on the other hand, felt rather satisfied that the pope, while meeting with Arafat took the occasion to lambast him about PLO terrorism.

Likewise, those Catholics who read carefully the text of the pope's homily in beatifying Edith Stein know that far from seeking to foster conversionism, as some have charged, the pope took the occasion to acknowledge the uniqueness of the *Shoah* for the Jews and to urge Catholics to greater sensitivity to the trauma suffered by the Jewish people. Again, the Catholic press tended to emphasize these healing elements of the pope's talks while the Jewish press expressed concern over what they saw as the possibility of a new wave of proselytism.

So, too, with the pope's visit to Austria in 1988. What the pope actually did and said during his meeting with the Jewish representatives in Vienna and later that same day in Mauthausen was reported very differently by and for our two communities. The point being made here is not to adjudicate between the two versions of John Paul II's pontificate that are emerging in the Jewish and Catholic communities, but simply to note the fact that they are two. Understood on their own, which is to say Catholic terms, the pope's actions in these very authentically sensitive areas for Jews do not carry the symbolic weight or intent that the Jewish community appears to derive from them. For Catholics, the pope's meetings with Arafat and Waldheim did not in any way give credence to either figure as such; in the course of his pastoral work, the pope, like any priest, meets all sorts of unsavory characters, one may say, and like any head of state has meetings with numerous people of whom he may or may not personally approve.

But this said and (for the sake of the discussion) at least provisionally accepted by the reader of this paper, it needs also to be said that this is exactly the problem. Catholics do not understand, I believe sufficiently, the suffering and trauma that lie behind these largely symbolic (for Jews more so than for Catholics) actions on the part of the pope. The symbolism is very different on the two sides. And while this pope, perhaps more than any other, is sensitive and open to Jews and Judaism, he acts, as in a very real sense he must act, as a Catholic. We need, then, both understanding of each other's symbolic referents (to Catholics, of course, much of what Jews have said about our Holy Father during these controversies is all but indistinguishable from the anti-Catholic bigotries of the old Protestant nativist movements in this country of the pre-ecumenical era) and a very real measure of mercy on and with each other's words and gestures. Too often, both sides tend to presume a negative intent when only a positive is meant.

One needs to recall also the extraordinary gestures of this pope not only in visiting and praying in the Great Synagogue of Rome in 1986, but equally remarkably during the summer of 1987 in inviting a group of Jewish leaders to visit with him at his summer residence in Rome. What will history say of the record of this pope on Catholic-Jewish relations? Only history and the historians can say, of course. But I would urge historians to check all sides of all these issues. The question, in terms of the judgment of history, is not just what a particular incident meant to Jews, however valid were Jewish concerns, but what it meant for Catholics (the latter factor being the more relevant when it comes to determining papal intent). More basically, Catholics and Jews need to develop the habit of listening to each other tell their version of such events to their own respective communities. It can be surprising and illuminating to discover that in many cases they will sound as if two different events involving entirely different people have occurred. But, I would submit, the days when we had the luxury, if we ever did, to attempt to tell each our own versions of our common history in isolation from the other are, or should be, over. Nothing in the long run is more dangerous or more likely to lead us into problems than that. The stakes are too high today.

With this sense of the future-orientation of the enterprise of dialogue, I would like to conclude with some reflections on what the pope in his many reflections on the matter sees as the future, which is to say the goal of the relationship between the church and the Jewish people.

8. A Vision for the Future: The Call to Joint Witness and Action in History

Central to the pope's vision of the Christian-Jewish relationship is the hope that it offers for joint social action and witness to the One God and the reality of the Kingdom of God as the defining-point of human history. In his address in Mainz, the pope calls this "third dimension" of the dialogue a "sacred duty": "Jews and Christians, as children of Abraham, are called to be a blessing for the world (cf. Gn 12:2ff) by committing themselves to work together for peace and justice among all peoples" (11/17/80).

Such joint action, for the pope, is far more than simple "good neighborliness." It is a fulfillment of what is essential to the mission of both Judaism and

Christianity for, "certainly, the great task of promoting justice and peace (cf. Ps 85:4), the sign of the messianic age in both the Jewish and Christian tradition, is grounded in its turn in the great prophetic heritage" (3/22/84). The possibility of a joint proclamation by word and deed in the world, which yet avoids "any syncretism and any ambiguous appropriation" (4/13/86), is seen by the pope as no less than a divine call: "The existence and providence of the Lord, our Creator and Saviour, are thus made present in the witness of our daily conduct and belief. This is one of the responses that those who believe in God and are prepared to 'sanctify his name' [*Kiddush ha-Shem*] (cf. Mt 6:9) can and should give to the secularistic climate of the present day" (4/19/85).

This way of collaboration "in service of humanity" as a means of preparing for God's Kingdom unites Jews and Christians on a level that, in a sense, can be said to be deeper than the doctrinal distinctions that divide us historically. "Through different but finally convergent ways we will be able to reach, with the help of the Lord, who has never ceased to love his people (Rom 11:1), true brotherhood in reconciliation and respect and to contribute to a full implementation of God's plan in history" (3/6/82). That "full implementation" the pope defines in religious terms. It is a "society...where justice reigns and where ...throughout the world it is peace that rules, the *shalom* hoped for by the lawmakers, prophets, and wise men of Israel" (4/13/86). To use the words of the 1985 Vatican "Notes" to summarize Pope John Paul II's thoughts on Christian-Jewish relations, one can say that it is his vision that through dialogue:

> We shall reach a greater awareness that the people of God of the Ancient [Hebrew] Scriptures and the New Testament are tending toward a like end in the future: the coming or return of the Messiah—even if they start from two different points of view. Attentive to the same God who has spoken, hanging on the same word, we have to witness to one same memory and one common hope in Him who is the master of history. We must also accept our responsibility to prepare the world for the coming of the Messiah by working together for social justice, respect for the rights of persons and nations, and for social and international reconciliation. To this we are driven, Jews and Christians, by the command to love our neighbor, by a common hope for the Kingdom of God, and by the great heritage of the Prophets.

Suggestions For Further Reading

Bartoszewski, Wladyslaw T. *The Convent of Auschwitz.* New York: George Braziller, 1991. Popular level historical description of the events making up the Auschwitz convent controversy from the point of view of a Polish Catholic deeply sensitive to Jewish concerns.

Croner, Helga, comp. *More Stepping Stones to Jewish-Christian Relations: An Unabridged Collection of Christian Documents 1975–1983.* Mahwah, NJ: Paulist Press/Stimulus Books, 1985. Includes Protestant as well as Catholic documents from around the world with insightful introductions and a Jewish response by Rabbi Mordecai Waxman.

Fisher, Eugene and Leon Klenicki, eds. *In our Time: The Flowering of Jewish-Catholic Dialogue.* Mahwah, NJ: Paulist Press, 1990. Contains official church documents on Catholic-Jewish relations, extensive commentary by a rabbi and a Catholic scholar, and a fifty-page annotated bibliography of the dialogue.

Fisher, Eugene and James Rudin, eds. *Twenty Years of Jewish-Catholic Relations.* Mahwah, NJ: Paulist Press, 1986. Essays by key American Jewish and Catholic participants in the dialogue, nationally and locally, covering questions of theology, scripture, religious education, liturgy, and the State of Israel.

Fisher, Eugene, ed. *Interwoven Destinies: Jews and Christians through the Ages.* Mahwah, NJ: Paulist Press, 1993. Historical Studies by leading Jewish and Christian scholars on the major periods of the relationship: Second Temple Judaism, the Parting of the Ways, Medieval Developments, the Reformation, and the Enlightenment.

International Catholic-Jewish Liaison Committee. *Fifteen Years of Catholic-Jewish Dialogue.* Rome: Pontifical Lateran University and Vatican Library, 1988. Contains the papers from the official consultations between the Holy See and the International Jewish Committee for Interreligious Consultations, and selected papal and Vatican Commission texts.

Kenny, Anthony John. *Catholic-Jewish Dialogue and the State of Israel.* Mahwah, NJ: Paulist Press, 1993. An indispensable and up-to-date work on what is still a burning issue, enabling one to grasp the theological and political dimensions of Israel reborn for Christians and Jews as well as the prospects for diplomatic recognition of Israel and the exchange of ambassadors.

Rittner, Carol and John K. Roth, eds. *Memory Offended: The Auschwitz Convent Controversy.* New York: Praeger, 1991. Selected Jewish and Catholic essays and documents on the controversy and its implications for Jewish-Christian relations.

Rhodes, Anthony. *The Vatican in the Age of the Dictators, 1922–1945.* New York: Holt, Rinehart, Winston, 1973. This book, centering on the papacy, will serve as a history of the church in a critical period and enable the reader to gain a keener appreciation of the period of Vatican Council II and the pontificate of John Paul II.

Willebrands, Johannes Cardinal. *Church and Jewish People: New Considerations.* Mahwah, NJ: Paulist Press, 1992. Addresses and essays by the Cardinal-President of the Holy See's Commission for Religious Relations with the Jews, with selected documents appended.

Williams, George H. *The Mind of John Paul II: Origins of his Thought and Action.* New York: Seabury, 1981. A substantial work, a kind of intellectual biography, valuable though out of date; among several biographies, none of them entirely satisfactory, are Paul Johnson. *Pope John Paul II and the Catholic Restoration.* New York: St. Martin's, 1981; Frank Pakenham, Earl of Longford. *Pope John Paul II: An Authorized Biography.* New York: William Morrow, 1982; Timothy Walch. *Pope John Paul II.* New York: Chelsea House, 1989; Wilton Wynn. *Keepers of the Keys: John XXIII, Paul VI, John Paul II, Three Popes Who Changed the Church.* New York: Random House, 1988.

GLOSSARY

Aggadah: The Rabbinic corpus that deals with legends and commentary on the historical and non-legal parts of the Bible. It seeks to instill values and theological beliefs through the telling of stories about biblical or post-biblical figures or the collection of pithy aphorisms.

Amoraim: The Rabbinic masters of the Babylonian and Galilean Jewries in the centuries following publication of the Mishnah, c. 200 C.E., on which they commented and presented lectures; their teachings are preserved in the Babylonian and Jerusalem Talmuds.

Antichrist: This term was used by Christian theologians to apply to the false Jewish messiah whom God will allow Satan to send to the Jews specifically because they had refused to believe in the true messiah, Jesus Christ (2 Thes 2). By the Middle Ages, Christian folklore had it that the antichrist was the offspring of the devil and a Jewish whore; his first followers were to be the Jews. After a climactic battle between the forces of "Christian good" and "Jewish evil," Christ would win out. For other biblical allusions to the day of the Lord, preceded by a "desolating sacrilege" or, in Christian terms, by the antichrist, see Dn 9:27, 11:31, 12:11; Mt 24:15; Mk 13:14; Lk 21:5–36; Rv 13.

Antinomian, Antinomianism: An attitude that attacks the presence of laws governing a society, and one of the chief ingredients of the hostile Christian assessment of Judaism as a religion of law in contrast to Christianity as one of the spirit.

Antisemitism: The term is today applied to all negative ideas about, feelings, and behavior toward Jews; it can be expressed as avoidance, anti-locution, discrimination, assault, expropriation, expulsion, physical attack, torture, murder, and mass murder.

Apocalyptic: Apocalyptic literature, found in both the Jewish and Christian traditions, contains what are purported to be revelations from on high granted to a seer, typically in the form of visions, for the benefit of the religious community. Such revelations provide insight into heavenly mysteries and especially end-time events that are expected to bring the divine purposes to completion, usually by means of an ultimate terrifying conflict between good and evil.

Bar Kochba revolt: The third (after the first 66–73 and second c.115–117) great Jewish rebellion and messianic upheaval against Roman rule of Judaea. Led by Simon bar Kosiba, or Kochba, or Kokhba, 132–135 C.E., for a time it was successful. The Jews regained Jerusalem and all of Judaea, and issued coins proclaiming "the redemption of Israel." Rome recovered and crushed Simon's forces; Christians interpreted the outcome as proof that God had deserted Israel.

Boethusians: An offshoot of the Sadducees or a related priestly group.

Chalcedon, Chalcedonian: The Council of Chalcedon, 451 C.E., where the decisive action was taken in defining the nature of Jesus Christ as human and divine.

Christology, Christological: *Christos* is a Greek word meaning *anointed one* and is equivalent to the Hebrew term *messiah.* Christology is that branch of Christian theology which devotes itself to reflection on the person and work of Jesus of Nazareth as the Christ and the Son of God.

Church Fathers: The term applies to the outstanding Christian thinkers and theologians writing before the eighth century; the study of their work is known as patristics.

Conversos and/or **New Christians:** The names given in Spain to those who converted from Judaism to Christianity; the term applied to all converts, regardless of whether their conversions were forced (i.e., feigned) or real. The term *converso* is preferable to *marrano* (which refers solely to Jews who outwardly converted to Christianity but continued to practice Judaism in hiding and to retain a secret Jewish identity), because it is very difficult to assess the true religious affiliation of most *conversos*.

Covenant: A treaty or agreement of God and the people of Israel initiated by Him, which contains the rules and obligations binding them to Him.

Docetism: A view of Jesus which so emphasizes his heavenly or divine status that it effectively undermines his humanity. According to docetic positions, which had already appeared by the second century C.E. and perhaps even earlier,

Jesus only seemed to be human, but in reality was not human like ourselves.

Doxology: The Greek term *doxa* was chosen to render the Hebrew word that is translated *glory*. Doxology is a prayer of praise and glorification of God.

Ecumenical: The word means *universal.* The ecumenical councils of Christian history were formal and official meetings of the bishops of the universal church, usually in the midst of controversy, to make policy decisions with regard to matters of doctrine and church discipline. Today the term is typically used to refer to the ecumenical movement which is characterized by dialogue between the divided Christian churches and by a desire for more amicable relations. It also refers to the emerging dialogue among the world religions and therefore includes a reference to the developing Jewish-Christian dialogue.

Eschatology: This is the area of religious reflection which concerns itself with the last things, the end of days or the messianic era, the ultimate destiny of individuals, communities, and even the cosmos. Eschatology focuses attention on the hopes of the religious community.

Eschaton: The final times ushering in the messianic era, the end of the world, and the afterlife.

Essenes: An ascetic group described by a number of sources as one of the major Jewish sects in the Hasmonean and Herodian periods, 162 B.C.E.–100 C.E.; they were casualties of the great Jewish revolt against Rome, 66–73 C.E. Many scholars identify the sect of the Dead Sea Scrolls as Essene.

Eucharist: The Greek term *thanksgiving* is used as a translation of the Hebrew word that is translated *blessing*. It comes to mean the Christian commemoration of the Last Supper of Jesus with his disciples.

Genizah, Cairo: The storehouse of the Ben Ezra Synagogue in Fustat, Old Cairo, Egypt, where Hebrew manuscripts were collected over a period of more than a thousand years, from the Middle Ages to modern times.

Golgotha: Literally *place of a skull*; the site of the crucifixion (Mk 15:23).

Haggadah: See Aggadah.

Halakhah: The Rabbinic corpus that deals with the legal matters of the Pentateuch and the legislation that evolved from it.

Hasid: A pious or holy man, a man of prayer, good deeds, and even in some cases of wonderworking.

Hasidim: *Pietists*, a loose definition for various groups of pious Jews in the Greco-Roman period, Middle Ages, and modern times. The various groups known by this name in different periods are not related to one other historically.

Hasmonean age: The historical period of Jewish independence in the land of Israel during Maccabean rule, from 162–37 B.C.E., but subject to Roman encroachment from 64 B.C.E. on when Pompey occupied Jerusalem; Hasmonean and Maccabean are interchangeable names for the ruling dynasty.

Hasmonean revolt: The revolt of the Maccabean family against extreme Hellenizing Jews and their Seleucid supporters, from 168–164 B.C.E. The Maccabean victory is celebrated in the festival of Hanukkah.

Hellenistic Diaspora: The Jewish communities scattered throughout the Hellenistic world, primarily in the Mediterranean basin.

Hermeneutic(s): The science or practice of interpretation, especially of the Scriptures.

Herodians: The dynasty founded by the infamous Herod; kings of Judaea or neighboring areas 37 B.C.E.–100 C.E.; Judaea was annexed as a province of Rome in 6 C.E

Hillel and Shammai: Noted and very influential rabbinical masters of the late first century B.C.E. and the early first century C.E. Comparisons are sometimes drawn between Rabbi Hillel and Rabbi Jesus of Nazareth.

Intertestamental: The period (second and first centuries B.C.E., and the first century C.E.) between the two testaments, i.e. the Old and the New Testaments, but especially the Jewish literature produced during that period, but never canonized, i.e. incorporated into the Scriptures.

Judaizing: The accusation referred to any association with or practice of the Jewish religion by Christians, converts (especially *conversos* in Spain), heretics, etc., and included proselytizing, fraternizing with Jews, or practicing any form of Jewish ritual or custom—in short, betraying any sort of Jewish affiliation or behavior.

Kabbala[h] or Cabala: The great medieval corpus of Jewish esoteric doctrine and mystical teaching for interpretation of Scripture, dating from as early as the sixth or seventh century, though its central text, *The Zohar* by Moses de Leon, dates from the thirteenth century. Kabbalah emphasizes the reception of wisdom through the emanations or manifestations of the Godhead in the forms of the *sefiroth* (the sum of all the aspects of creation), and the return of humanity to God through repentance.

Karaites, Karaism: A secessionist movement from Judaism that began in the eighth century. Representing a return to the "pure word" of Scripture and denouncing the Talmud, Karaism was one of the great crises in Jewish history.

Kerygma, Kerygmatic: *Proclamation, proclamatory.* A New Testament word used to signify the preaching of the gospel.

Maccabean revolt: The successful revolution 165 B.C.E.– led by the Maccabee family against the extreme Hellenizing policies of the Selucid ruler of Syria, Antiochus IV, who was defeated and expelled; an independent Jewish state under the Maccabean (also known as Hasmonean) dynasty endured until Roman encroachments began about a century later. The Maccabean victory and renewal of Jewish observance are celebrated in the festival of Hanukkah.

Marcion, Marcionism: Marcion was a second-century heretic who denied any relevance of the Hebrew Scriptures for Christianity. Marcionism, the opposite tendency to Judaizing, is the attitude or ideology that supports that view and seeks to "de-Judaize" Christianity.

Marrano: See *Conversos.*

Messianism: The belief that a messiah, an eschatological redeemer, will come to usher in the end of days, an era of ultimate perfection.

Midrash: Interpretation of the Bible by the Rabbis to derive either aggadic or halakhic lessons. Usually, in midrash, one biblical verse is interpreted in light of another.

Mishnah: The Rabbinic code of Jewish law that was edited by Rabbi Yehudah the Patriarch (Judah the Prince) at the turn of the third century C.E.; it preserved the legal Oral-Tradition of the Mishnaic period, i.e. the age of the Tannaim of the first two centuries C.E. The Mishnah is interpreted in the Talmud.

Monophysite: Literally, the term means *one nature* and refers to a christological position of the fifth century C.E., usually associated with the name of Eutyches, which spoke of the Christ as uniting the divine and human in one nature. This view was rejected by the Christian bishops at the fourth ecumenical council at Chalcedon (451 C.E.)

Noahide Laws: Those laws that are promulgated in the early chapters of Genesis, that are pre-Mosaic and therefore binding on all people who accept the biblical God as their author; according to the Tannaitic tradition these are seven: 1) belief in one God, 2) no murder, 3) no adultery, 4) no blasphemy, 5) no violence, 6) a system of justice, 7) no eating of raw flesh of animals.

Parousia: A Greek work meaning *presence*, used by Christian theologians to refer to the Second Coming of Christ.

Pharisees, Pharisaism: One of the several Jewish parties or "sects" and the only one to survive the cataclysm of the revolt against Rome, 66–73 C.E. Democratic and pluralistic as it was, there seems to have been varieties of Pharisaism and several groupings, to one of which—many scholars have concluded—Jesus himself adhered; another adherent was Rabbi Johann ben Zakkai, leader of the Javneh academy where Judaism was reconstituted following the Roman destruction of temple, city, and state. Traditionally interpreted as the forbear of the normative Judaism that has prevailed in the common era, Pharisaism also had a profound but notoriously maligned influence on Christianity; anti-Pharisaism, which has often been virtually synonymous with antisemitism, has vitiated Christian perception of Judaism. One great obstacle remains the paucity of sources, since apart from brief references by the Jewish historian Josephus, mention in rabbinic literature of "separatists" (*perushim*), and the animadversions in the New Testament, scholars have little to go on. In sum, a religio-political group that was careful about ritual purity, tithing, and enjoyed (Josephus says) popular support.

Pietists, Pietistic: Believers in experiential or emotional forms of religion.

Proleptic: *Anticipatory, prefiguration;* in Christian interpretation the Old Testament prefigures or is proleptic to the New Testament.

Prometheus, Promethean: Greek demigod who stole fire from Olympus and was chained to a rock by Zeus as punishment; symbolic of defiance and daring, creativity and life-giving.

Rabbinic Judaism: The Pharisaic-Rabbinic approach to Judaism which was developed during the first six centuries C.E. in Palestine and Babylonia, and is embodied in the Mishnah, both Talmuds, and the Midrashim.

Sadducees: Traditionally, the great rivals of the Pharisees, the conservative aristocracy and ruling group that served as priests of the Temple; the sect—as it is usually designated—was destroyed in the course of the revolt against Rome, 66–73 C.E.

Samaritans: A sect that probably dates from the fifth century B.C.E.; they adhere only to the five Mosaic books of the Bible; animosity between Samaritans and Jews is apparently utilized in the New Testament in such a figure as the Good Samaritan to vilify Jews and Judaism.

Second Temple Period: The years between the rebuilding of the Jewish Temple in 520 B.C.E. and its destruction by the Romans in 70 C.E.

Shoah: A Hebrew words which simply means *destruction*. It is preferred by some writers to *Holocaust*, a biblical word meaning *burnt offering* or *hecatomb* to God and thus has a religious connotation that many object to as entailing a Christian bias and inappropriate for mass murder.

Sitz im Leben: A German expression meaning *setting in life*. It is usually employed in biblical studies to refer to the concrete historical circumstances of religious communities in which religious traditions developed and by which the traditioning process itself was influenced.

Supersession: The concept that one religion completely replaces another and makes the other religion no longer necessary nor valid.

Talmud: The comments and discussion of the Rabbis of Babylonia and Palestine c.200–500 C.E. on the Mishnah, the compilation of earlier Jewish legal tradition.

Tanakh: The Hebrew Scriptures including the Torah, the prophetical, sapiential, and historical books; usually called the Old Testament by Christians.

Tannaim: The Rabbinic masters of the Judaean and Galilean schools of the first two centuries C.E.; their opinions are recorded in the Mishnah.

Tosaphists: The Franco-German schools of Rabbinic masters who represented the families of Rashi (Rabbi Shlomo ben Isaac of Troyes, 1040–1105 C.E.) and their disciples, until the fifteenth century; *Tosaphot* means *supplements* to Rashi's commentary on the Talmud.

Zeitgeist: *Spirit of the times*, reference to the climate of ideas, opinions, attitudes, values, and so forth prevailing at a given time and distinctive of it.

CONTRIBUTORS

NORMAN A. BECK is Professor of Biblical Studies and Chairperson of the Department of Modern and Classical Languages at Texas Lutheran College in Seguin, Texas. A former parish pastor, he is the author of *Mature Christianity: The Recognition and Repudiation of the Anti-Jewish Polemic of the New Testament*. Active in the quest for Christian-Jewish understanding, he is engaged in the translation and redaction of the entire New Testament in order to eliminate anti-Jewish biases in its interpretation.

ALAN DAVIES is Professor of Religion at Victoria College, University of Toronto. He is the author of *Antisemitism and the Christian Mind* and *Infected Christianity: A Study of Modern Racism*, and the editor of *Antisemitism and the Foundations of Christianity* and *Antisemitism in Canada: History and Interpretation*.

HENRY L. FEINGOLD is Professor of American Jewish and American Diplomatic History at Baruch College and the Graduate Center of CUNY. He is the General Editor of the five-volume series *The Jewish People in America* and the author of the fourth volume in that series, *A Time for Searching: Entering the Main Stream, 1920–1945*.

ASHER FINKEL is currently chairperson of the graduate Department of Jewish-Christian Studies at Seton Hall University. He specializes in Rabbinic writings and Early Christianity, and has published in both areas, including *The Pharisees and the Teacher of Nazareth*.

EUGENE J. FISHER has been Associate Director of the Secretariat for Ecumenical and Interreligious Affairs of the National Conference of Catholic Bishops since 1977, Consultor to the Holy See's Commission for Religious Relations with the Jewish People since 1981, and is the author or editor of over two hundred articles and a dozen books on Christian-Jewish relations.

REV. EDWARD H. FLANNERY is Director of Catholic-Jewish Relations of the Diocese of Providence, Rhode Island, and former Executive Secretary of the Secretariat of Catholic-Jewish Relations of the National Conference of Catholic Bishops, consultor to the Vatican Secretariat of Catholic-Jewish Relations, and Associate Director of the Institute of Judaeo-Christian Studies at Seton Hall University. He is the author of *The Anguish of the Jews*, a classic study of antisemitism that was reissued in a revised and expanded form in 1985.

SCARLETT FREUND is a doctoral candidate in the department of English, Princeton University. Her area of research is late nineteenth-century British literature.

REV. LAWRENCE E. FRIZZELL, a priest of the Roman Catholic Archdiocese of Edmonton, Canada, has been associated with the Institute of Judaeo-Christian Studies at Seton Hall University, South Orange, New Jersey. He is Associate Professor in its Department of Jewish-Christian Studies, specializing in the literature of the Second Temple period.

DONALD F. GRAY is Professor of Religious Studies at Manhattan College. He is the author of *The One and the Many. Teilhard de Chardin's Vision of Unity* and *Jesus: The Way to Freedom*. He has also published extensively in theological journals such as *Theological Studies*, *Cross Currents*, *Horizons*, and *The Teilhard Review*.

ERIC W. GRITSCH is Maryland Synod Professor of Church History and Director of the Institute for Luther Studies at the Gettysburg Lutheran Seminary in Gettysburg, Pennsylvania. He is the author of *Martin—God's Court Jester*, *Lutheranism* (with R.W. Jenson), *Born Againism*, and *Thomas Müntzer—A Tragedy of Errors*.

CELIA S. HELLER is Professor Emeritus of Sociology at Hunter College and the Graduate Center of CUNY. She is the author of many articles on Jewish life and of the prize-winning book on the Jews of Poland between the world wars, *On the Edge of Destruction*, as well as studies of Mexican-Americans; her forthcoming book will deal with the Jewish question in post-war Poland—under communism and democratization.

SUSANNAH HESCHEL holds the Abba Hillel Silver Chair in Jewish Studies in the Department of Religion, Case Western Reserve University, in Cleveland, Ohio. She has written in the area of women's studies and on Jewish-Christian relations in Germany. During the winter of 1992–93, she held the Martin Buber Visiting Professorship in Jewish Religious Philosophy at the University of Frankfurt, Germany.

REV. MICHAEL MCGARRY, C.S.P., is a Paulist priest and the author of *Christology after Auschwitz*. He recently completed seven years as rector of St. Paul's College, Washington, D.C., the major seminary of the Paulist Fathers; currently he serves as pastor of Holy Spirit Parish at the University of California, Berkeley, and as a member of the Advisory Committee to the Secretariat for Ecumenical and Interreligious Relations (Catholic-Jewish Relations) for the National Conference of Catholic Bishops.

ROBERT MICHAEL is professor of European History at the University of Massachusetts, Dartmouth. He is the author of *The French Radicals and Nazi Germany* and the forthcoming *Fatal Image: A History of American Antisemitism*; *Holy Hatred: A History of the First Fifteen Centuries of Christian Antisemitism*; and *Fatal Vision: A History of Christian Antisemitism from Luther through the Holocaust.*

JOHN T. PAWLIKOWSKI, O.S.M., is Professor of Social Ethics at the Catholic Theological Union, the University of Chicago. The author of many books and articles on the Holocaust and Jewish-Christian relations, including *The Challenge of the Holocaust for Christian Theology*, he has been active in promoting Jewish-Christian understanding, most recently as a participant in Polish-Jewish dialogue.

MARVIN PERRY, co-editor, is Associate Professor of History at Baruch College, CUNY. He is the author of *An Intellectual History of Modern Europe* and *Arnold Toynbee and the Crisis of the West,* and co-editor of *Arnold Toynbee: Reappraisals*.

TEOFILO F. RUIZ is Professor of History at Brooklyn College and of Spanish Literature at CUNY Graduate Center. His area of research is late medieval Castile. He is the author of *Burgos in the Middle Ages* and *Society and Royal Authority in Castile* (both in Spanish) and co-editor of *Order and Innovation in the Middle Ages*, a book of essays in honor of his mentor Joseph R. Strayer.

LAWRENCE H. SCHIFFMAN is Professor of Hebrew and Judaic Studies at New York University's Skirball Department of Hebrew and Judaic Studies and is the author of many books and articles on the Dead Sea Scrolls, and on Judaism in the Second Temple and Rabbinic periods. He has been active in editorial preparation of the remaining scrolls for publication, has been appointed an editor-in-chief of the *Oxford Encyclopedia of the Dead Sea Scrolls*, and was featured in the PBS Nova series documentary on "The Secrets of the Dead Sea Scrolls." Recently, he joined the team publishing the scrolls in the Oxford series, *Discoveries in the Judean Desert*, and will serve as Executive Editor of the new journal, *Dead Sea Discoveries*.

FREDERICK M. SCHWEITZER, co-editor, is Professor of History at Manhattan College. He is the author of *A History of the Jews since the First Century A.D.* (being updated and expanded) and is active in Jewish-Christian dialogue.

RUTH ZERNER is Associate Professor of History at Lehman College, CUNY. She has written about Otto von Bismarck, the Holocaust, and the German Church Struggle, including the commentary for Dietrich Bonhoeffer's *Fiction from Prison.* Very active in Jewish-Christian dialogue, she is currently completing a book on Bonhoeffer.

ACKNOWLEDGEMENTS

The editors wish to acknowledge the many persons who made the 1989 conference and now the book possible. Most of the articles in this book derive from the memorable conference held at Baruch College on the first three days of March 1989. The following persons also participated in the conference either as panelists, moderators, or keynote speakers: Dina Abramowicz, Walter G. Emge, Clara Feldman, Thomas Frazier, Thomas S. Ferguson, FSC, Tzipora Weiss Halivini, Stephen Kaplan, John W. Keber, Michael R. Marrus, John McGarraghy, Judith Herschlag Muffs, Pearl M. Oliner, Samuel P. Oliner, Joseph Peden, Jay Rock, John Barry Ryan, H. Kenneth Snipes, Fritz R. Stern, and Michael Wyschograd.

We wish to thank the following administrators, Walter Emge of Manhattan College and Lois S. Cronholm and Norman Fainstein of Baruch College, for helping to defray publication costs.

For collegial assistance in solving intellectual, research, linguistic, and word processing conundrums our special thanks go to Thomas S. Ferguson, FSC, John W. Keber, Robert Michael, Mary Ann O'Donnell, Claudia J. Setzer, and Andrea Zalaznick.

The librarians and libraries of Manhattan College, Fordham University, the Jewish Theological Seminary of America, Columbia University, The Public Library at 42nd Street have all been courteously helpful and highly professional.

To our wives Phyllis and Jacqueline we owe the proverbial debt of gratitude, proverbially immense and proverbially beyond payment.

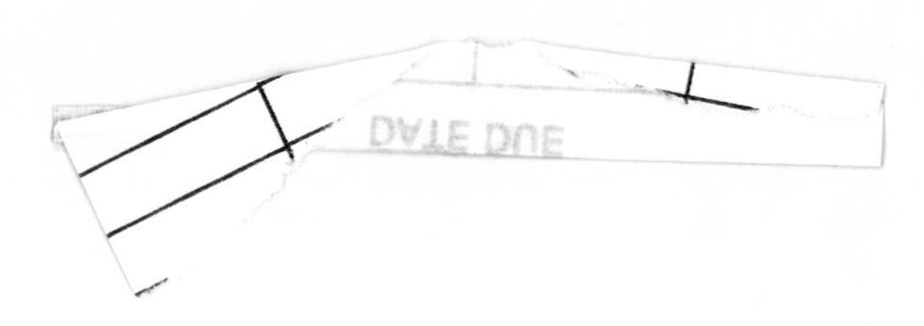